Frommer's

Costa Rica
day BY day

1st Edition

by Eliot Greenspan

WILEY

John Wiley and Sons, Inc.

> The red-eyed tree frog, one of
Costa Rica's native amphibians.

Contents

PAGE 5

PAGE 39

PAGE 62

PAGE 195

PAGE 197

PAGE 300

PAGE 346

PAGE 378

PAGE 386

PUBLISHED BY

Wiley Publishing, Inc.

111 River St., Hoboken, NJ 07030-5774

ISBN 978-0-470-49770-8

Frommer's®

Editorial by Frommer's

EDITOR Linda Barth	**PHOTO EDITOR** Cherie Cincilla
CARTOGRAPHER Andrew Murphy	**CAPTIONS** Amy K. Hughes
COVER PHOTO EDITOR Richard Fox	**COVER DESIGN** Paul Dinovo

Produced by Sideshow Media

PUBLISHER Dan Tucker	**MANAGING EDITOR** Megan McFarland
PROJECT EDITOR Amy K. Hughes	**PHOTO RESEARCHER** John Martin
DESIGN Kevin Smith, And Smith LLC	**SPOTLIGHT FEATURE DESIGN** Em Dash Design LLC

For information on our other products and services or to obtain technical support, please contact our Customer Care Department within the U.S. at 800/762-2974, outside the U.S. at 317/572-3993 or fax 317/572-4002.

Wiley also publishes its books in a variety of electronic formats. Some content that appears in print may not be available in electronic formats.

MANUFACTURED IN CHINA

5 4 3 2 1

How to Use This Guide

The Day by Day guides present a series of itineraries that take you from place to place. The itineraries are organized by time (The Best of the Northern Zone in 1 Week), by region (Dominical and the Coastline Southward), by town (Tamarindo), and by special interest (The Southern Zone's Best Bird-Watching). You can follow these itineraries to the letter, or customize your own based on the information we provide. Within the tours, we suggest cafes, bars, or restaurants where you can take a break. Each of these stops is marked with a coffee-cup icon ☕. In each chapter, we provide detailed hotel and restaurant reviews so you can select the places that are right for you.

The hotels, restaurants, and attractions listed in this guide have been ranked for quality, value, service, amenities, and special features using a **star-rating system.** Hotels, restaurants, attractions, shopping, and nightlife are rated on a scale of zero stars (recommended) to three stars (exceptional). In addition to the star-rating system, we also use a kids icon to point out the best bets for families.

The following **abbreviations** are used for credit cards:

AE American Express
V Visa
MC MasterCard
DISC Discover
DC Diners Club

A Note on Prices

In this guide, Frommer's lists prices in U.S. dollars. Before departing consult a currency exchange website such as **www.oanda.com/convert/classic** to check up-to-the-minute conversion rates.

In the "Take a Break" and "Best Bets" sections of this book, we have used a system of dollar signs to show a range of costs for 1 night in a hotel (the price of a double-occupancy room) or the cost of an entree at a restaurant. Use the following table to decipher the dollar signs:

COST	HOTELS	RESTAURANTS
$	under $50	under $10
$$	$50–$100	$10–$20
$$$	$100–$200	$20–$30
$$$$	$201–$350	$30–$40
$$$$$	over $350	over $40

How to Contact Us

In researching this book, we discovered many wonderful places—hotels, restaurants, shops, and more. We're sure you'll find others. Please tell us about them, so we can share the information with your fellow travelers in upcoming editions. If you were disappointed with a recommendation, we'd love to know that, too. Please email us at frommersfeedback@wiley.com or write to:

Frommer's Costa Rica Day by Day, 1st Edition
Wiley Publishing, Inc.
111 River Street
Hoboken, NJ 07030-5774
frommersfeedback@wiley.com

Travel Resources at Frommers.com

Frommer's travel resources don't end with this guide. **Frommers.com** has travel information on more than 4,000 destinations. We update features regularly, giving you access to the most current trip-planning information and the best air-fare, lodging, and car-rental bargains. You can also listen to podcasts, connect with other Frommers.com members through our active reader forums, share your travel photos, read blogs from guidebook editors and fellow travelers, and much more.

An Additional Note

Please be advised that travel information is subject to change at any time—and this is especially true of prices. We suggest that you write or call ahead for confirmation when making your travel plans. The authors, editors, and publisher cannot be held responsible for the experiences of readers while traveling. Your safety is important to us, so we encourage you to stay alert and be aware of your surroundings.

About the Author

Eliot Greenspan is a poet, journalist, musician, and travel writer who took his backpack and typewriter the length of Mesoamerica before settling in Costa Rica in 1992. Since then, he has worked steadily as a travel writer, food critic, freelance journalist, and translator, and continued his travels in the region. He is the author of *Frommer's Belize, Frommer's Costa Rica, Frommer's Ecuador, Frommer's Guatemala, Costa Rica for Dummies,* and *The Tico Times Restaurant Guide to Costa Rica,* as well as the chapter on Venezuela in *Frommer's South America.*

Acknowledgments

I'd like to thank Linda Barth for her patience, keen eye, and editorial diligence.

About the Photographers

Central American–based British photographer **Thornton Cohen** (www.thorntoncohen.com) has photographed more than 40 countries and regularly contributes to international travel publications and regional media outlets.

Adrian Hepworth, twice a winner in the BBC Wildlife Photographer of the Year competition, leads photo tours around Costa Rica and is the author of two coffee-table books.

Ken Cedeno is a Washington, D.C., photojournalist who has covered politics and breaking news in Congress and the White House for more than 20 years. His clients include major wire services such as Agence France Presse, Reuters, and Bloomberg, as well as news outlets *Time, Newsweek,* the *New York Times,* the London *Sunday Times,* and other publications worldwide. He has traveled to many countries on assignment, including Costa Rica, Cuba, Croatia, Iceland, Italy, Spain, and Turkey

Photographer **Jason Kremkau** (www.jasonkremkauphotography.com) has spent the last four years traveling throughout Costa Rica. He is currently working on a book that captures the heart and spirit of the Ticos and their incredible land.

1

The Best of Costa Rica

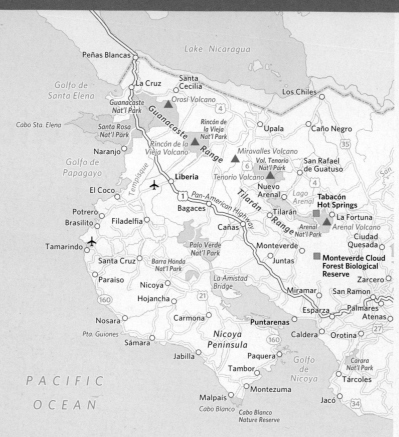

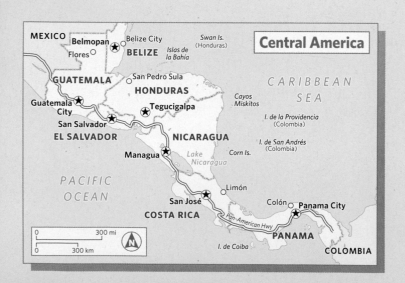

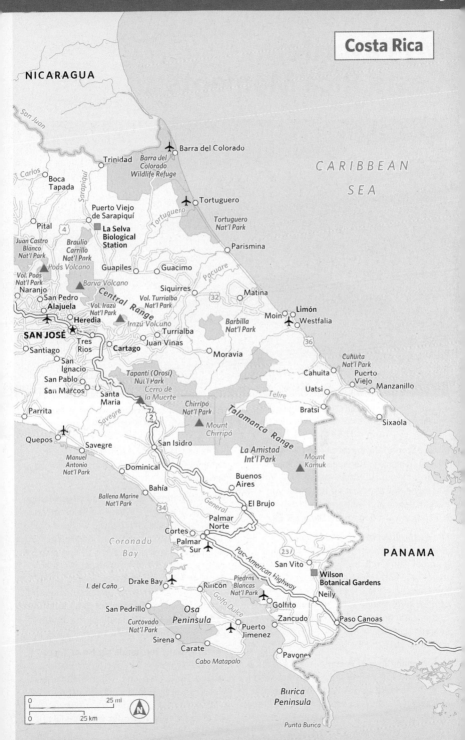

Costa Rica

NICARAGUA

CARIBBEAN SEA

San Juan

Barra del Colorado

Trinidad

Barra del Colorado Wildlife Refuge

Carlos

Boca Tapada

Sarapiquí

Puerto Viejo de Sarapiquí

Tortuguero

Tortuguero Nat'l Park

Pital

4

La Selva Biological Station

Parismina

Juan Castro Blanco Nat'l Park

Braulio Carrillo Nat'l Park

Poás Volcano

Guapiles

Guacimo

Pacuare

Vol. Poás Nat'l Park

Barva Volcano

Siquirres

Vol. Turrialba Nat'l Park

32

Matina

Naranjo

Central Range

San Pedro

Vol. Irazú Nat'l Park

Moin

Limón

Alajuela

Heredia

Irazú Volcano

Turrialba

Barbilla Nat'l Park

Westfalia

SAN JOSÉ

Tres Rios

Cartago

Juan Vinas

36

Santiago

Moravia

San Ignacio

Tapanti (Orosi) Nat'l Park

Cahuita Nat'l Park

San Pablo

Telire

Cahuita

Puerto Viejo

San Marcos

Cerro de la Muerte

Uatsi

Manzanillo

Santa Maria

Chirripó Nat'l Park

Talamanca Range

Bratsi

Parrita

Savegre

2

Mount Chirripó

Sixaola

Quepos

San Isidro

La Amistad Int'l Park

Mount Kamuk

Savegre

Manuel Antonio Nat'l Park

Dominical

Buenos Aires

Ballena Marine Nat'l Park

Bahía

General

El Brujo

34

Palmar Norte

Cortes

23

PANAMA

Palmar Sur

Pan-American highway

San Vito

Coronado Bay

Wilson Botanical Gardens

Drake Bay

Rincón

Piedras Blancas Nat'l Park

Neily

I. del Caño

Golfito

Paso Canoas

San Pedrillo

Osa Peninsula

Golfo Dulce

Zancudo

Curcovado Nat'l Park

Sirena

Puerto Jimenez

Carate

Pavones

Cabo Matapalo

Burica Peninsula

Punta Burica

0   25 mi

0   25 km

N

My Favorite Costa Rica Moments

> PAGE 1 *Blue Lake and La Cangreja Falls in Rincón de la Vieja National Park, Guanacaste, one of Costa Rica's hidden gems.* THIS PAGE *From land or sea, the sunset over the Pacific is not to be missed.*

Hiking around the crater at Poás Volcano. With a massive crater spewing smoke and sulfur fumes, the Central Valley's Poás Volcano is a stunning sight. Just off the crater you'll find several gentle and well-groomed trails through a lush tropical cloud forest. See p. 58, **❻**.

Dining barefoot in the sand at Lola's. The word is out on this restaurant, located just south of Tamarindo in Guanacaste. You'll need to get here early most days to snag a table or hammock, but there's no finer beachfront restaurant in the country. You'll have a great view of the water and waves as you savor some seared fresh tuna in the shade of a canvas umbrella. See p. 151.

Experiencing Arenal Volcano. You'll hear the rumble and roar of this surprisingly active volcano in the Northern Zone, as fresh lava and Volkswagen-size rocks tumble down its steep slopes. On a clear night the lava glows red and

lights up the sky. By day, the smoke plume rising out of the crater is an impressive sight. See p. 230, **❺**.

Basking in jungle luxury at a plush ecolodge. Just because you're in the middle of the rain forest, surrounded by the wild world, it doesn't mean you have to give up on luxury. You'll find top-notch ecolodges all across Costa Rica, particularly in the Osa Peninsula, Northern Zone, and Tortuguero areas. There's plenty of competition, and worthy runners-up abound, but my favorite is **Bosque del Cabo Rainforest Lodge,** on the Osa Peninsula in the Southern Zone. See p. 364.

Floating along the jungle canals of Tortuguero. Likened to the Amazon basin, the area around Tortuguero, on the Caribbean coast, features a staggeringly complex network of rain-forest rivers, lagoons, and natural canals. All of the lodges here offer wildlife-viewing trips on small flat-bottomed boats that wind their way through this lush tropical maze. See p. 417, ❹.

Taking a sunset cruise. I love watching the sun set, whether from a high hillside perch or from the soft sands of a near-deserted beach. But nothing quite beats the experience of watching the spectacle from the deck of a sailboat, when the horizon appears as if it's just beyond your reach. Sunset cruises are offered up and down the Pacific coast, from Guanacaste to Manuel Antonio—they're well worth your time.

Exploring Corcovado National Park. There are rain forests, and then there are rain forests. Corcovado National Park, on the Osa Peninsula, is the single largest expanse of lowland tropical rainforest in Central America, and has been described by National Geographic magazine as "the most biologically intense place on earth." Whether you visit on a day trip offered by a nearby ecolodge, or challenge yourself with a multiday camping trek, you're bound to be thrilled by what you see. See p. 348.

Surfing Costa Rica's famed breaks. Costa Rica has become a surf mecca, and with good reason: The waves are outstanding year-round. For first-timers, there are plenty of patient instructors and plenty of beginner-friendly beaches, including those at **Tamarindo.** And for those who have already embraced the joys of surfing? The possibilities are endless, up and down both coasts. See p. 302.

Walking miles of deserted beach. With coastlines running the entire length of the country, Costa Rica is blessed with a bounty of long, broad, empty stretches of beach. If I really want to get away from it all, I head to either the beaches of the Nicoya Peninsula, especially those just north of **Santa Teresa,** or those along the Caribbean coast, just south of **Puerto Viejo.** See p. 188 and p. 399.

Spotting a resplendent quetzal. Even if you're not a bird-watcher—indeed, even if you think bird-watching is, well, for the birds—you won't soon forget the sight of one of these remarkable creatures. The resplendent quetzal was sacred to the indigenous people of Mesoamerica (see "The Resplendent Quetzal: Mesoamerica's Holiest Bird," p. 10). It's easy

> Don't let the kids have all the fun—take a surf lesson and try out Costa Rica's famous waves.

to see why: The iridescent green feathers, brilliant blood-red vest, and bright yellow beak are nothing compared to the male's tail feathers, which can reach nearly 64cm (2 ft.) in length. The best place to see one is **Monteverde Cloud Forest Biological Reserve,** in the Northern Zone. See p. 218, ❶.

Soaking in a hot spring. Vacations should be relaxing, and in my opinion, there are few things more soothing than a good soak in a natural hot spring. The volcanoes running down Costa Rica's spine have blessed the country with an abundance of thermal springs, which can be found, among other places, on and around the flanks of both Arenal and Rincón de la Vieja Volcanoes. My favorite? **Tabacón Hot Springs,** at the foot of Arenal, where you can get a massage and a volcanic mud mask after your soak. See p. 224, ❿.

The Best of Natural Costa Rica

> *Corcovado National Park, on the Southern Zone's Osa Peninsula, protects a large tract of tropical jungle that is home to jaguars, tapirs, scarlet macaws, squirrel monkeys, and other rare wild creatures.*

Rincón de la Vieja National Park, Guanacaste. This is an area of rugged beauty and high volcanic activity. Rincón de la Vieja Volcano rises to 1,916m (6,286 ft.), with a seemingly endless series of geysers, vents, and fumaroles scattered along its flanks, just waiting to be explored. There are also waterfalls, mud baths, hot springs, and cool jungle swimming holes. See p. 111, ❽.

Arenal Volcano and nearby natural hot springs, Northern Zone. When the skies are clear and the lava is flowing, Arenal Volcano offers a thrilling light show accompanied by an earthshaking rumble that defies description. At the foot of this massive molten mountain you will find a host of naturally heated hot springs, many of which offer fabulous volcano views. Let Mother Nature wow you while you soak. See p. 230, ❺.

Monteverde Cloud Forest Biological Reserve, Northern Zone. There's something both eerie and awe-inspiring about walking through the forest mist surrounded by towering trees hung heavily with broad bromeliads, flowering orchids, mosses, and vines. The reserve has a well-maintained network of trails that makes it easy to experience all this forest has to offer. See p. 218, ❶.

Osa Peninsula, Southern Zone. This is Costa Rica's most remote and biologically rich region. Corcovado National Park, the largest remaining patch of virgin lowland tropical rain forest in Central America, takes up most of the Osa Peninsula, and jaguars, crocodiles, and scarlet macaws all call this place home. Whether you stay in a luxury ecolodge or camp in the park itself, you will be surrounded by some of the most lush and intense jungle this country has to offer. See p. 362.

Tortuguero, Caribbean Coast. Tortuguero is a tiny village, surrounded by a national park of the same name, set on a narrow spit of land between the Caribbean and a dense maze of jungle canals. The canals alone are worth a visit—they're rugged, isolated, and filled with birds and wildlife. But if you visit between June and October, you may get to see the truly moving spectacle of a green turtle nesting—the small stretch of beach here is the last remaining major nesting site of this endangered animal. See p. 416.

My Favorite Hikes

> The beach trail in Corcovado National Park, one of the most biologically diverse places on earth, runs 37km (23 miles) along the Osa Peninsula, with Pacific waters on one side and rain forest on the other.

Blue Lake & La Cangreja Falls, Rincón de la Vieja National Park. This hike inside Rincón de la Vieja National Park takes you to a pristine turquoise lake at the foot of a rushing forest waterfall. The hike is long and vigorous, but it passes through several different ecosystems, and you are rewarded all along with stunning views and excellent wildlife viewing. Be on the lookout for spider monkeys, blue morpho butterflies, and collared peccaries. See p. 144, **B**.

Sendero Cantarrana, La Selva Biological Station. This combination research facility and nature lodge in the Northern Zone has an extensive and well-marked network of trails that weave through a mix of primary lowland tropical rain forest and swampland. The Sendero Cantarrana begins with a series of bridges and raised walkways over wetlands before connecting to a couple of other loop trails deep in the rain forest. Sign up to go with one of the station's highly informed naturalists. See p. 251.

La Sirena, Corcovado National Park. Most folks come to Corcovado National Park as part of a day trip from one of the nearby ecolodges. But if you really want to say you've conquered this wild and remote park, take a few days to hike through dense rain forest to La Sirena ranger station. Spend at least one night there, basking in the almost surreal sights and sounds of the abundant jungle life around you. See p. 350, **S**.

Sendero Coladas, Arenal National Park. There's great hiking all around this area, but my favorite hike is Sendero Coladas (Lava Flow Trail), which brings you to a massive cooled lava flow. As you scramble over the hardened lava, you will have a pristine (and very close-up) view of the volcano in front of you and Lake Arenal behind it. See p. 232, **A**.

Sendero El Río, Monteverde Cloud Forest Biological Reserve. This misty cloud forest is a lush and biologically rich world, with hiking trails leading through a dense mass of trees, epiphytes, vines, and mosses. The signature trail here is Sendero El Río (River Trail), which leads to a pretty little jungle pool fed by a small waterfall. See p. 220, **A**.

Rain-forest & beach loop, Cahuita National Park. With both a beach and rain-forest trail, this national park offers gorgeous scenery and a great chance for seeing wildlife. I like to start off in the rain forest, looking for birds and monkeys, and finish with a walk back along the soft white sands, with the Caribbean at my feet. See p. 382.

The Best Beaches

> *Playa Espadilla Sur, in Manuel Antonio National Park, affords a sweeping, sandside view of densely forested Cathedral Point.*

Playa Avellanas, Guanacaste. This white-sand beach has long been a favorite haunt of surfers, locals, and those in-the-know. Why? Because Playa Avellanas stretches on for miles, backed largely by protected mangrove forests. The beach is on the verge of being discovered, but as yet there's still very little going on here. See p. 134.

Playa Flamingo, Guanacaste. One of the most picturesque beaches in the country, this short, straight stretch of soft white sand is bound on either end by rocky headlands. Rarely crowded, this is a great place to lay out a beach mat and enjoy the solitude. Just be careful, as the surf can sometimes be a bit rough for casual swimming. See p. 135.

Beaches around Playa Sámara, Nicoya Peninsula. Playa Sámara itself is nice enough, but if you venture just slightly farther afield, you'll find some of the best beaches on the Nicoya Peninsula. **Playa Carrillo** is an almost always deserted crescent of palm-backed white sand located just south of Playa Sámara, while **Playa Barrigona** is a hidden gem tucked down a dirt road to the north. See p. 202.

Malpaís, Nicoya Peninsula. While the secret is certainly out, there's still time to visit Costa Rica's newest hot spot before the throngs and large resorts arrive. This is the place to come if you're looking for miles of deserted beaches and great surf. Don't miss out. See p. 174, ⑥.

Playa Espadilla Sur, Manuel Antonio, Central Pacific Coast. The first beach you reach upon entering Manuel Antonio National Park, this broad expanse of white sand is backed by thick forest and bordered by the stunning Punta Catedral (Cathedral Point). Even better, it doesn't get the crowds that tend to flock to neighboring Playa Manuel Antonio—which is also pretty darn nice. See p. 291, ①.

Punta Uva & Manzanillo, Caribbean Coast. Located south of Puerto Viejo, these beaches offer up some true Caribbean splendor, with turquoise waters, coral reefs, and soft white sand. Tall coconut palms line the shore, providing a shady respite for those who need a break from the sun. You can also cool off with a refreshing dip—the water is usually quite calm and good for swimming. See p. 398 and p. 399.

The Best Bird-Watching

> Birders flock to Carara National Park, on the Pacific coast, to see the endangered scarlet macaw.

La Selva Biological Station, Northern Zone. With an excellent trail system through a variety of habitats, from dense primary rain forest to open pasturelands and cacao plantations, this is one of the finest places for bird-watching in Costa Rica. Because of the variety of habitats, the number of species spotted here runs to well over 300. See p. 253.

Caño Negro National Wildlife Refuge, Northern Zone. Caño Negro Lake and the Río Frío that feeds it are incredibly rich in wildlife and a major nesting and gathering site for a wide range of aquatic bird species. This is also a prime place to spot a jabiru. See p. 253.

Carara National Park, Central Pacific Coast. Home to Costa Rica's largest population of scarlet macaws, Carara is a special place for both devoted bird-watchers and recent converts. The macaws spend their days in the park but roost near the coast. They arrive like clockwork every morning and head for the coastal mangroves around dusk. The daily migrations virtually guarantee that vistors will have a chance to see these magnificent birds in flight. See p. 308.

Monteverde Cloud Forest Biological Reserve, Northern Zone. Hundreds of bird species call this cloud forest reserve home. Perhaps the most famous is the resplendent quetzal (p. 10). Bird-watchers won't want to leave Costa Rica without crossing this bird off their list. And neophytes might be hooked for life after seeing one of these iridescent green wonders fly overhead, flashing its brilliant red breast and trailing 64cm-long (2-ft.) tail feathers. See p. 252.

Wilson Botanical Gardens, Southern Zone. With more than 7,000 species of tropical plants and flowers, the well-tended trails and grounds of this beautiful research facility are both lovely and alluring to all sorts of avian beings. Hummingbirds and tanagers are particularly plentiful, but the bounty doesn't end there. See p. 357.

Aviarios Sloth Sanctuary of Costa Rica. Situated on an oceanfront estuary with a network of canals and lagoons, Aviarios Sloth Sanctuary is the prime bird-watching destination on the Caribbean. If it flies along this coast, chances are very good that you'll spot it here; more than 330 species of birds have been recorded so far. See p. 402.

THE RESPLENDENT QUETZAL
Mesoamerica's Holiest Bird

BY LINDA BARTH

WITH IRIDESCENT EMERALD feathers, a ruby red breast, and tail feathers that can stretch an astonishing 64cm (2 ft.), nearly twice the length of its body, the endangered resplendent quetzal is one of the most spectacular birds on earth. At one time, the bird's tail feathers were traded as far north as what is now New Mexico and as far south as the Andes. Its range extends from southern Mexico to northern Panama, and Costa Rica is one of the best places to spot one, thanks to the country's dedication to preserving the bird's cloud-forest habitat. Quetzals can be found foraging for fruit (avocado is a favorite), frogs, and insects in the canopies of Costa Rica's cloud forests. Keep your binoculars trained on the branches above you, and you might get lucky.

God in Bird Form

The Aztecs believed the quetzal was the incarnation of Quetzalcoatl, their creator god. Indeed, the Aztec word *quetzalli* means "precious," and the bird's tail feathers, which were used in religious ceremonies, were considered more valuable than gold. In fact, they could be worn only by kings and priests. The bird was also considered divine by the Maya, and killing a quetzal was punishable by death. Many legends surround the bird—according to one, the quetzal sang a beautiful and melodic song until the Spanish arrived, when its call became simple and plain, and it won't sing that way again until the region is truly free.

Another says that the quetzal's breast was once green. But in 1524, when conquistador Pedro de Alvarado struck down Mayan king Tecún Umán, a quetzal descended and draped itself over the fallen warrior's body. It kept a vigil, and when the great leader died, the bird ascended to the sky, its breast now stained red with the king's blood.

What You Need to Know

The forest-dwelling quetzal is 37cm (15 in.) long and a member of the trogon family. It is a solitary bird, except during breeding season, when it is found in pairs or small flocks. The females are rather

plain—they aren't the reason people come from around the world to see one. And they do have to come to Central America to see one—with few exceptions, these birds can't be kept in captivity. According to local lore, quetzals commit suicide if they are caged. As a result, the quetzal has become a symbol of freedom throughout Central America.

When and Where to See Them

If you're hoping to see a quetzal, plan to get an early start—they are most active in the morning. March to May is mating season, when the males venture lower in the canopy in search of partners—making it prime quetzal-spotting time. The birds establish their nests in rotting trees, so keep an eye out. The **Monteverde Cloud Forest Biological Reserve** (p. 218, ❶) is *the* place to see quetzals, although the throngs of people traipsing the reserve's trails now make the pursuit a little more difficult. Other good options include **Poás Volcano National Park** (p.58, ❻), **Santa Elena Cloud Forest Reserve** (p. 249), and **Chirripó National Park** (p. 294).

The Best Adventures in & on the Water

> *Thrill-seekers find plenty of white-water rapids on Costa Rica's many rivers.*

Rafting the Río Pacuare, Caribbean Coast. This class III and IV white-water river offers rafters a long, bumpy, and thrilling ride. As an added bonus, the Pacuare winds through emerald green primary and secondary forests and a steep gorge. If you have the time in your schedule, the best way to enjoy this river is on a 2-day trip. See p. 73 and p. 397.

Kayaking on the Golfo Dulce, Southern Zone. Slipping through the waters of the Golfo Dulce in a kayak brings you intimately in touch with the raw beauty of this wild region. Kayaking opportunities range from poking around in the veritable maze of coastal mangrove swamps to fishing in estuaries and watching dolphins frolic out in the bay. See p. 354.

Taking a sunset cruise, Guanacaste. I certainly love watching the sun set from a nice hillside perch or while sitting in the sand, but given my druthers, I'd choose to watch the spectacle from the deck of a sailboat. Sunset cruises are offered up and down the Pacific coast, from Guanacaste all the way south to Manuel Antonio and beyond. Try the *Blue Dolphin* out of Tamarindo, a long-running and excellent operator. See p. 132.

Scuba diving or snorkeling off Isla del Caño, Southern Zone. Located off the coast of the Osa Peninsula, this uninhabited island is believed to have been used as a ceremonial burial site by pre-Columbians. Today, the underwater rocks and coral formations just off its shores offer up arguably the best scuba diving and snorkeling opportunities in the country. See p. 343, **12**.

Surfing Pavones, Southern Zone. Just 13km (8 miles) from the Panamanian border, at the southern reaches of Costa Rica's Pacific coast, lies Pavones, which has what is reputed to be one of the longest rideable waves in the world. When this left-point break is working, surfers enjoy rides that go on for almost a mile. See p. 354.

Battling a billfish, Southern Zone. Billfish are plentiful all along Costa Rica's Pacific coast, and boats operate from Playa del Coco to Playa Zancudo. Costa Rican anglers hold world records for both blue marlin and Pacific sailfish. For my money, you can't beat the **Zancudo Lodge** as a base for some fantastic fishing fun—they'll make all the arrangements for you. See p. 355.

The Best Adventures on Land

> Quiet back roads and stunning scenery make the area around Lake Arenal and Arenal Volcano great for biking.

Sky Walk canopy tour, Northern Zone. Canopy tours have become ubiquitous in Costa Rica, but my favorite remains the **Sky Walk** near the Santa Elena Cloud Forest Reserve. You'll wander through the treetops on suspended bridges that reach heights of up to 39m (128 ft.), spotting monkeys, birds, and lots of flora along the way. See p. 249.

Mountain biking around Lake Arenal, Northern Zone. The lack of infrastructure and paved roads that many folks bemoan in Costa Rica is a huge boon for mountain bikers. There are endless back roads and cattle paths to explore, and tours of differing lengths and difficulty levels are available. But for my money, the area around Lake Arenal is your best spot for mountain biking, and the local operator **Bike Arenal** will happily hook you up. See p. 242.

Canyoning around La Fortuna, Northern Zone. Canyoning involves hiking along and through the rivers and creeks of steep mountain canyons, with periodic breaks to rappel down the face of a waterfall, jump off a rock into a jungle pool, or float down a small rapid, and it's as fun as it sounds. **Pure Trek Canyoning** and **Desafío Adventure Company** are the prime operators in La Fortuna. **Psycho Tours**, near Puerto Jiménez is a kid-friendly operator in the Southern Zone. See pp. 245–246 and p. 341, **7**.

Hiking Mount Chirripó, Central Pacific Coast. This is the highest mountain in Costa Rica. The hike to Chirripó's 3,820m (12,530-ft.) summit is vigorous but not technically challenging; it takes you through a number of distinct bioregions, ranging from lowland pastures to a cloud forest to a high-altitude paramo—a tundralike landscape with stunted trees and morning frosts. See p. 294.

The Best Views

> *The secret is out: Villa Caletas, on a bluff above Jacó, showcases the best sunsets on the central Pacific coast.*

Summit of Irazú Volcano, near San José. On a very clear day, you can see both the Pacific Ocean and the Caribbean Sea from this vantage point just outside the capital. On days when visibility is low and this experience eludes you, you can still view the volcano's spectacular landscape and the Central and Orosí Valleys. See p. 64, **1**.

El Mirador, Arenal National Park. Arenal Volcano seems so close, you'll swear you can reach out and touch it. Unlike Irazú Volcano (see above), when *this* volcano rumbles and spews, you may feel the urge to seek cover. See p. 232, **C**.

Villa Caletas, near Playa Hermosa de Jacó. Thanks to its hillside perch over the Golfo de Nicoya, with the Pacific Ocean sprawling beyond, sunsets at this hotel's outdoor amphitheater are legendary. It's beautiful here during the day as well. See p. 276, **4**.

Agua Azul, Manuel Antonio. This roadside restaurant has one of the finest views in Manuel Antonio. You'll have to arrive early to snag a prime seat for the sunset, but trust me, it's well worth it. And happily, the food and views here are really very good any time of day or night. See p. 281, **10**.

Summit of Mount Chirripó, Central Pacific Coast. At 3,819m (12,530 ft.), this is the highest spot in Costa Rica. What more can one say? When the skies are clear the views are soaring and seem to go on forever. Even if it isn't clear, you will still catch some pretty amazing views of the spectacular glacier-carved, lake-dotted landscape. See p. 296, **3**.

The Best Luxury Hotels & Resorts

> The spa at the Four Seasons Resort on the Papagayo Peninsula in Guanacaste, the most luxurious lodging in Costa Rica.

Peace Lodge, near Poás Volcano. The bathrooms (yes, bathrooms) of the deluxe units in this unique lodge are the most luxurious in the country, and everything else is done in grand style as well. Each room comes with at least one custom-tiled Jacuzzi tucked neatly on a private balcony. See p. 92.

Four Seasons Resort Costa Rica, Papagayo Peninsula. A beautiful setting, sumptuous rooms, a world-class golf course, and stellar service continue to make this the current king of the hill in the upscale resort market. See p. 158.

JW Marriott Guanacaste Resort & Spa, Hacienda Pinilla. Set on the picturesque and rocky Playa Mansita, this massive resort boasts plush rooms, extensive facilities, and the largest pool in Central America. Better still, fabulous Playa Avellanas is just a mellow meander away. See p. 149.

Hotel Punta Islita, Nicoya Peninsula. Location, location, location: This place sits on a high, flat bluff overlooking the Pacific. The rooms are large and comfortable, the food is excellent, and the setting is stunning. If you venture away from your room and the hotel's inviting hillside pool, there's a long, almost always deserted beach to explore. See p. 205.

Tabacón Grand Spa Thermal Resort, near Arenal Volcano. An outgrowth of the fabulous Tabacón hot springs, this hotel offers up a great restaurant, volcano views, and the sort of rooms you won't want to leave. On top of all that, you'll have nearly unfettered access to the aforementioned hot springs, which are not to be missed. See p. 262.

Villa Caletas, north of Jacó. Spread out over a steep hillside high above the Pacific, the opulent individual villas here have a Mediterranean feel. The hotel's infinity pool was one of the first in Costa Rica and is still my favorite. Relaxing in a lounge chair at the pool's edge, you'll swear that it joins the sea beyond. See p. 315.

Arenas del Mar, Manuel Antonio. This one is simple: With ample and spotless rooms, excellent service and amenities, a high-end spa, and the best beach access and location in Manuel Antonio, this hotel is hard to resist. See p. 321.

My Favorite Boutique Hotels & Small Inns

> *Finca Rosa Blanca Coffee Plantation & Inn is set in the lush green hills of a working organic coffee farm.*

Hotel Grano de Oro, San José. San José boasts dozens of old homes that have been converted into hotels, but few offer the cozy yet chic accommodations or professional service found at the Grano de Oro. All the guest rooms have attractive hardwood furniture, and some come with a private patio garden. See p. 91.

Finca Rosa Blanca Coffee Plantation & Inn, Santa Bárbara de Heredia. If the cookie-cutter rooms of most resorts and hotels leave you cold, then try one of the inventive rooms at this charming inn. Square corners seem to have been prohibited here in favor of arched windows, turrets, and curving walls. The service is excellent, too. See p. 89.

Sueño del Mar, Playa Langosta. Rooms at this hotel just south of Tamarindo feature African dolls on the windowsills, Kokopelli candleholders, and open-air showers with hand-painted tiles and lush tropical plants. Add in the hammocks under shade trees right on the beach and a small pool, and you really have someplace special. See p. 149.

Arco Iris Lodge, Santa Elena. The rooms at this homey lodge are cozy and well kept, but the private cabins are even better. Ask for the "honeymoon cabin," which has a Jacuzzi tub and a private balcony (as do several of the others). The forest views are memorable, and you'll get plenty of bird-watching done right from your room. Set right in Santa Elena, the lodge is the best deal in the Monteverde area. See p. 258.

Florblanca Resort, Santa Teresa. The individual villas at this intimate resort are some of the largest and most decadent in the country. The service and food are outstanding, and the location—spread over a lushly planted hillside steps away from Playa Santa Teresa—is breathtaking. See p. 200.

Tree House Lodge, Punta Uva. The private houses at this small beachfront resort make up the most creative, spoil-you-rotten accommodations to be found on the Caribbean coast. My favorite is the namesake Tree House, although the Beach Suite is spectacular as well. See p. 409.

The Best Ecolodges

> *Individual cabins on a private jungle cove offer a truly private getaway at Playa Nicuesa Rainforest Lodge..*

Arenal Observatory Lodge, near La Fortuna. Originally a research station, this place now has a wide variety of rooms and excellent facilities, along with impressive views of Arenal Volcano. There are trails to nearby lava flows, toucans frequent the trees near the lodge, and howler monkeys provide the wake-up calls. See p. 262.

Monteverde Lodge & Gardens, Santa Elena. One of the first ecolodges to open in the Monteverde area, this place has only improved over the years, with great guides, frequently updated rooms, and lush gardens. The operation is run by the very dependable and experienced Costa Rica Expeditions. See p. 258.

La Paloma Lodge, Drake Bay. The gorgeous individual bungalows here are set on the edge of a steep hillside, with views of the Pacific Ocean and Isla del Caño in the distance. If you decide to leave the comfort of your room, the Osa Peninsula's lowland rain forests are just outside your door. See p. 361.

Bosque del Cabo Rainforest Lodge, near Puerto Jiménez. The large, plush private bungalows perched on the edge of a cliff overlooking the Pacific Ocean and surrounded by lush rain forest make this lodge one of my favorite spots in the country. There's plenty to do, the food's terrific, and there are always great guides here. See p. 364.

Playa Nicuesa Rainforest Lodge, Golfo Dulce. This lodge is by far the best option on the isolated Golfo Dulce. Set in deep primary rain forest, the individual bungalows strike a perfect blend between rusticity and luxury. See p. 369.

Tortuga Lodge, Tortuguero. Set right on the jungle side of the main canal of Tortuguero, this is one of the most comfortable options in the area, and another of the excellent ecolodges run by Costa Rica Expeditions. See p. 419.

Selva Bananito Lodge, near Cahuita. This is one of the few lodges providing direct access to the southern Caribbean lowland rain forests. Hike along a riverbed, ride horses through the rain forest, climb 30m (100 ft.) up a ceiba tree, or rappel down a jungle waterfall. There's fabulous bird-watching in the area, and Caribbean beaches are nearby. See p. 403.

2

Strategies
for Seeing
Costa Rica

Strategies for Seeing Costa Rica

Costa Rica has become such a popular (and dare I say it, trendy) tourist destination that you may think it's old hat. You'd be wrong—the reason Costa Rica is so popular is that there is so much to discover here. Whether you are a first-time visitor or honorary Tico (as the locals are known), the following tips and suggestions will help you maximize your time, increase your enjoyment, and zero in on the best ways to discover what Costa Rica has to offer.

> *PREVIOUS PAGE Small planes are a great way to reach more remote destinations.* **THIS PAGE** *Costa Rica's rich biodiversity means lots of insects and spiders and other creeping, crawling creatures.*

Tip #1: Learn to love the rain. Costa Rica's rainy season, called the "green season," is long, extending from May through mid-November, and you can expect at least a little rain to fall every day during this time. However, this can be a good time to visit Costa Rica because there are fewer tourists and better deals, and the countryside, forests, and coastal hills are incredibly verdant. Much of the rainy season is characterized by clear, sunny mornings and early afternoons, followed by incoming cloud cover and an afternoon thunderstorm; if you like to indulge in an afternoon siesta, the timing of the weather is perfect.

During the months of August, September, and October, there are substantially longer and heavier periods of rain, although late September through mid-October tends to be clear and relatively rain-free on the Caribbean coast. For the rest of the country, I especially recommend traveling during the "shoulder period," which runs from May through mid-July, when the rains tend to be lighter. In general, Guanacaste is the driest region of the country, even during the rainy season, while the Southern and Northern Zones and the Caribbean coast get the highest levels of precipitation.

Tip #2: Make peace with the notion of bugs. Many people have a serious and somewhat understandable aversion to insects. That's a shame, since insects are fascinating, abundant, varied, and probably destined to outlast most mammals. Happily, there are very few biting bugs to worry about in Costa Rica, and so they are far less of a problem than most people assume. Sure, you should bring along some good repellent and some lightweight, long-sleeved shirts and long pants, but leave the fear and the *ick* factor behind and try embracing the insect world. Many remote ecolodges have naturalist guides on hand to explain the intricacies and intimacies of the lives of bugs. In fact, one of my favorite tours in the whole country is offered by Tracie Stice, affectionately known as the "Bug Lady" (p. 358, ❷), down in Drake Bay, at the northern tip of the Osa Peninsula.

Tip #3: Consider flying direct to Liberia.

San José is still home to the country's principal airport, with far more flight options, and it is a much more convenient gateway if you are planning to head to Manuel Antonio or another town on the central Pacific coast, the Caribbean coast, or the Southern Zone. However, more and more international flights are arriving at and departing from Liberia's Daniel Oduber International Airport. Liberia is the principal gateway to the beaches of the Guanacaste region and the Nicoya Peninsula. If you are planning to spend all or most of your vacation time in the Guanacaste or Nicoya region, you'll definitely want to fly in and out of Liberia. Doing so will eliminate the need for a separate commuter flight in a small aircraft or roughly 5 hours in a car or on a bus. Liberia also provides easy access to such inland destinations as Monteverde and the La Fortuna and Arenal Volcano region, in the Northern Zone.

Tip #4: Negotiate directly with hotels.

One of the world's best-kept travel secrets is that just about everyone is willing to negotiate, and that's certainly true in Costa Rica. Most hotels here are small to mid-size operations. Most pay hefty commissions to travel agencies and wholesalers—as much as 25%. In many cases, if you book directly and ask politely but insistently, a hotel will pass along the equivalent of at least part, or even all, of this commission. Even the smallest and most remote hotels have their own websites and email addresses these days. Just bear in mind that in many cases, the smaller and more remote hotels may be slow to respond, and some may have few staff members with reasonable English-language skills. Be patient and diplomatic, but also be wary if communications seem unusually erratic or unclear.

> Come prepared to get wet, especially if you're planning to visit Costa Rica's rain and cloud forests.

Tip #5: Don't leave anything of value unattended, ever. It's an unfortunate fact that petty crime and theft are big problems in Costa Rica. Minimize your risk by taking simple commonsense precautions and keeping a close eye on your belongings. I repeat, never leave anything

> *You'll see a lot more wildlife in Costa Rica if you bring your own binoculars rather than share a communal pair.*

of value unattended . . . ever. That means you should use the hotel safe and secure parking lots whenever possible. Rental cars and the contents of their trunks are particularly popular targets, so don't leave anything you care about in the car while you're off exploring.

Again, it's unfortunate, but you also need to be wary of "good Samaritans" who come to your aid, especially if you've unexpectedly acquired a big mustard stain on your clothing while walking downtown, or find that your tire is suddenly flat—two common scams. You should even keep an eye on your sunglasses and sandals when you go to play in the surf.

Tip #6: If you want to see wildlife, bring your own binoculars. Even though most ecolodges and naturalist guides will provide a pair of binoculars for their guests to share, if you really want to see wildlife while in Costa Rica, bring your own pair. Even more important, perhaps, practice with them a little bit beforehand. It would be a shame to miss a clear sighting of a resplendent quetzal or blue-crowned motmot because you are too busy futzing with the focus knob on a pair of borrowed binos.

Tip #7: Try the *gallo pinto*, but be careful about what you eat and drink. Costa Rica is a developing country. While public water supplies are generally safe, with good treatment facilities in most cities and major tourist destinations, visitors should still be careful about what they eat and drink. Personally, I think you can eat and drink as you please in most major tourist destinations and restaurants that cater to the tourist trade. I certainly don't want to scare you away from trying local fare, like *gallo pinto*—a mixture of white rice and black beans that is the unofficial national dish. In fact, I think it's safe to try a few of the more humble local restaurants, as long as they seem clean and respectable. Still, you don't want stomach troubles to cramp your style. Easy, if conservative, precautions include drinking soft drinks and beer directly from the bottle or can (after wiping the lid or rim), never

> *Costa Rican restaurants serve the rice and bean dish known as* gallo pinto *at breakfast, lunch, and dinner.*

asking for ice in a drink, and eating only fruits that you can peel and vegetables that have been cooked. Except in the most established and hygienic of restaurants, it's also advisable to avoid raw seafood dishes, such as ceviche; raw seafood, especially shellfish, can be home to any number of bacterial critters.

Some travelers, even those who have taken all precautions, will encounter intestinal difficulties. Most of these are due to tender northern stomachs coming into contact with slightly more aggressive Latin American intestinal flora; sadly, there's not much to be done about that. If you're unlucky enough to develop what's aptly known as traveler's diarrhea, make sure you stay hydrated by drinking lots of clear fluids. Generally this nuisance will resolve itself within a day or two, but in severe cases, you may need to see a doctor. He or she will likely prescribe an antibiotic or antimicrobial treatment.

Tip #8: This is Latin America—slow down.
Things go slower in Costa Rica. Buses and tours don't always leave precisely at their appointed hour, nor do they run as smoothly as a Swiss watch. Meals may take longer and restaurant service can seem sluggish and inattentive. Costa Ricans regularly show up 15 to 20 minutes late for an appointment—it's called "Tico time." Don't try to fight it. Relax. You're on vacation. Get into the flow and rhythm of things, and everything will be *pura vida*.

Tip #9: Use this book as a reference, not a concrete blueprint. My suggestions throughout the book are geared to help you maximize your time and experience the best sights, attractions, and activities in a variety of destinations around the country. However, if followed to the letter, many of the tours and itineraries in this guide will result in long, tiring days and a sense of rushing about the country. Pick and choose the destinations and activities most important to you, and focus on those. Feel free to extend your time at any particular destination.

3

The Best Costa Rica Itineraries

Costa Rica Highlights

You can pack a lot of Costa Rica goodness into a week. You'll manage to squeeze in a quick visit to the capital before hitting the trifecta of the country's primary tourist attractions: Arenal Volcano, Monteverde, and Manuel Antonio. By the time you're through, you'll have experienced a bit of the tropics, spent some quality time on the beach, and enjoyed a few high-adrenaline adventures to boot. You'll need to rent a car to get around once you leave San José—traffic there is a problem, so stick to using taxis while in the city. To save much needed time, you'll leave the car in Manuel Antonio and fly back to the capital for your journey home.

> *PREVIOUS PAGE Costa Rica is known for its miles of unspoiled Pacific shoreline backed by lowland rain forest. THIS PAGE Hot springs at Tabacón Grand Spa Thermal Resort, near Arenal Volcano.*

START San José, Plaza de la Cultura, between Avenidas Central and 2 and Calles 3 and 5. **TOUR LENGTH** 638km (396 miles).

1 San José. Start your first day in Costa Rica in the heart of the capital city, at the **Plaza de la Cultura** (p. 48, **1**). Visit the **Museos del Banco Central de Costa Rica** (p. 48, **2**). The sparkling Gold Museum is the prime attraction at this museum complex. Once you've had your gold

fix, cross the plaza and take a tour of the spectacular neo-baroque **Teatro Nacional** (National Theater; p. 50, **3**) and, if you're interested, pick up tickets for the evening's show.

Next, pay a visit to the **Museo de Jade Marco Fidel Tristán Castro** (p. 50, **5**), the Jade Museum, which houses the largest collection of pre-Columbian jade in the Americas. You'll see ceremonial and decorative pieces dating from 500 B.C. to A.D. 800, among many

NICARAGUA

Lake Nicaragua

La Cruz
Santa Cecilia
Guanacaste Nat'l Park
Los Chiles
San Juan
Barra del Colorado
Santa Rosa Nat'l Park
Rincón de la Vieja Nat'l Park
Upala
San Rafael de Guatuso
Trinidad
Barra del Colorado Wildlife Refuge
CARIBBEAN SEA
Naranjo
Liberia
Nuevo Arenal
Lago Arenal
Puerto Viejo de Sarapiquí
Tortuguero
El Coco
Bagaces
Cañas
2 La Fortuna
Arenal Volcano
Pital
Tortuguero Nat'l Park
Potrero
Filadelfia
Palo Verde Nat'l Park
Arenal Nat'l Park
Juan Castro Blanco Nat'l Park
Parismina
Tamarindo
Barra Honda Nat'l Park
Monteverde
3 Ciudad Quesada
Vol. Poás Nat'l Park
Braulio Carrillo Nat'l Park
Guacimo
Paraiso
Nicoya
Zarcero
San Ramon
Alajuela
Heredia
Siquirres
Vol. Turrialba Nat'l Park
Matina
Limón
Nosara
Nicoya Peninsula
Esparza
Atenas
Santa Ana
★ SAN JOSÉ
Vol. Irazú Nat'l Park
Turrialba
Barbilla Nat'l Park
Sámara
Puntarenas
Caldera
Orotina
1
Cartago
Moravia
Jabilla
Golfo de Nicoya
Carara Nat'l Park
San Ignacio
San Pablo
Santa Maria
Tapanti (Orosi) Nat'l Park
Chirripó Nat'l Park
Cahuita
Puerto Viejo
Tambor
Montezuma
Jacó
Parrita
Savegre
Mt. Chirripó
La Amistad Int'l Park
Malpaís
Cabo Blanco
Cabo Blanco Nature Res.
Quepos
4 Savegre
San Isidro
Buenos Aires
PACIFIC OCEAN
Manuel Antonio Nat'l Park
Dominical
Bahía
Ballena Marine Nat'l Park
Cortes
Palmar Norte
Loronodo Bay
Palmar Sur
Piedras Blancas Nat'l Park
San Vito
Drake Bay
Rincón
Neily
I. del Caño
San Pedrillo
Corcovado Nat'l Park
Osa Peninsula
Golfo Dulce
Golfito
Paso Canoas
Sirena
Carate
Pto. Jimenez
PANAMA
Burica Peninsula
Punta Burica

1 San José
2 La Fortuna & Arenal Volcano
3 Monteverde
4 Manuel Antonio

other things. As an added bonus, the museum's lobby is on the 11th floor and offers panoramic views of the city and its surroundings. Spend some time marveling, and then make your way to the **Plaza de la Democracia** (p. 52, **0**) for shopping at the **open-air street market** (p. 79) along its western edge.

As you make your way around town, be sure to stop at one of the roadside stands or kiosks selling small bags of precut and prepared fruit. Depending on the season, you might find mango, pineapple, or papaya on offer. If you're lucky, they'll have *mamon chino,* an odd-looking but tasty golf ball–size fruit also known as rambutan or litchi nut.

> *Printed textiles color the market in San José's Plaza de la Democracia.*

> *The Teatro Nacional, erected in San José in 1897, celebrated the nation's success as a coffee exporter.*

After you've stocked up on souvenirs, take a taxi to the **Parque La Sabana** (La Sabana Park; p. 56, ❷). You can spend the rest of the afternoon walking around the park, sign up for the **Urban Canopy Tour** (p. 56, ❸), or visit the **Museo de Arte Costarricense** (Costa Rican Art Museum; p. 54, ❶). ⏱ 1 day.

Start off early on Day 2 and take the Pan-American Hwy. (CR1) north to San Ramón. Follow signs for the road to La Fortuna; the drive will take about 3½ hours.

❷ **La Fortuna and Arenal Volcano.** You'll arrive in La Fortuna in time for lunch. I recommend **El Novillo del Arenal** (p. 263), which is on the way to Arenal National Park and has a great view of the volcano. After lunch, head into **Arenal National Park** (p. 230, ❺) and hike the **Sendero Coladas** (Lava Flow Trail). After your scramble over the cooled-off lava, head to the *mirador* (lookout) inside the park. If you've timed things right, it will be near dusk, and you'll be able to see the glow of lava as it cascades down the volcano's flank.

Spend your evening soaking in the hot springs at the **Tabacón Grand Spa Thermal Resort** (p. 224, ❿).

On the morning of Day 3, head out on a **canyoning tour** with **Desafío Adventure Company** (p. 246) or **Pure Trek Canyoning** (p. 245). You'll want to sign up for the earliest trip, because after lunch, which is provided by your tour company, you will be driving around Lake Arenal en route to Monteverde. ⏱ 2 days.

On the afternoon of Day 3, take CR142 west out of La Fortuna. You'll circle Lake Arenal, and just before the town of Tilarán take the turnoff for Monteverde. This road soon becomes a rough but well-traveled dirt road. While the total distance is 108km (67 miles), you should give yourself 3½ hours for the drive.

❸ **Monteverde.** You'll get into Monteverde in time for a sunset cocktail at the **Hotel El Sapo Dorado** (p. 258). After dinner, pay a visit to the **Frog Pond of Monteverde** (p. 219, ❺). While many of the most interesting amphibians here are nocturnal, some are diurnal (active during

> *Manuel Antonio National Park is brimming with wildlife, from sea turtles in its waters to monkeys in its trees.*

the day). Since your entrance ticket is good for the following day, make sure you allow time to return at some point to see those critters you missed.

Get yourself up and out early on Day 4, and take a guided tour of the **Monteverde Cloud Forest Biological Reserve** (p. 218, ❶). When you're done, stop in at the **Hummingbird Gallery** (p. 219, ❷), which is at the entrance to the reserve. There's great shopping and scores of brilliant hummingbirds buzzing around—watch your head. Spend the afternoon visiting some of the area's other attractions, which might include any combination of the following: the **Butterfly Garden** (p. 254, ❸), **Orchid Garden** (p. 219, ❹), **Serpentario Monteverde** (p. 237, ❽), **Bat Jungle** (p. 235, ❷), and **Mundo Insectos** (p. 237, ❼). And, of course, don't forget your return visit to the Frog Pond of Monteverde (above).

On Day 5, take a **zip-line canopy tour**—I recommend **Selvatura Park** (p. 222, ❼), which has a wonderful canopy tour as well as other exhibits. Be sure to schedule the tour early enough so that you can hit the road by noon for your drive to Manuel Antonio National Park. ◷ 2 days.

On the afternoon of Day 5, take the Pan-American Hwy. south to Barranca, and pick up CR27 south. Just before Orotina, CR27 hooks up with CR34, the Costanera, or Coastal Hwy., which leads south into Quepos and Manuel Antonio. The trip is 187km (116 miles) and will take about 4½ hours.

❹ **Manuel Antonio.** Once you arrive in Manuel Antonio, you can drop off your rental car and rely on taxis and tours for the rest of your trip. After settling in at your hotel, head for a sunset drink at **Agua Azul** (p. 281, ❿). Next, pay a visit to the rough-and-tumble little port city of Quepos. Enjoy an evening stroll before having dinner at **El Patio Bistro Latino** (p. 324).

On the morning of Day 6, take a boat tour of the **Damas Island Estuary** (p. 276, ❻). In the afternoon, reward yourself for all the hard touring by lazing on one of the beautiful beaches inside **Manuel Antonio National Park** (p. 290) or hiking the loop trail through the rain forest here and around **Punta Catedral.**

On Day 7, you'll likely have some extra time before your flight to San José, so head back into Manuel Antonio National Park, do some souvenir shopping, or simply lounge by your hotel pool, soaking in a bit of *pura vida*. ◷ 2 days.

The Best of Costa Rica in 2 Weeks

Several of Costa Rica's greatest attractions and destinations are farther afield than those covered in "Costa Rica Highlights" (p. 26), and require several days to fully explore and enjoy. After you've completed the week-long highlights tour, I highly recommend you head south to the wild and remote Osa Peninsula, and then east to the mellow and mellifluous Caribbean coast. You'll travel by boat, airplane, and taxi, so leave your rental car behind.

> On the beach trail in Corcovado National Park, Costa Rica's wildest tract of tropical rain forest.

START Puerto Jiménez. **TOUR LENGTH** 627km (390 miles). To get to Puerto Jiménez, fly from San José (flight time: 1 hour).

❶ Osa Peninsula. Puerto Jiménez is the main gateway to the Osa Peninsula and **Corcovado National Park** (p. 348), and you'll be basing all your activities out of one of the isolated ecolodges in this area. There are many excellent options, but **Bosque del Cabo Rainforest Lodge** (p. 364), **Lapa Ríos** (p. 365), and **El Remanso** (p. 365) are my top choices. All offer day hikes inside Corcovado National Park, as well as a host of other active vacation options. I highly recommend the full-day adventure-oriented **Psycho Tours** (p. 341, ❼), which combines a host of activities (hiking, rappelling—you get the idea). You might also try a **kayak** (p. 344, ❶) or **dolphin-watching sunset tour** (p. 347,

❻) with **Escondido Trex**, and a tour of **Herrera Botanical Gardens** (p. 345, ❷). Be sure to save a little time before or after your flight (in or out) to shop at the unique **Jagua Arts & Craft Store** (p. 363, ❹). ⏱ 3 days.

On the morning of Day 11, fly from Puerto Jiménez to San José, with an onward connection to Tortuguero. Your total travel time will be about 4 hours, including the layover.

❷ Tortuguero. Often compared to South America's Amazon basin, Tortuguero (p. 416) is a pristine and remote area accessible only by boat or small aircraft. In fact, there are no cars in the tiny village of Tortuguero. In addition to outstanding bird and wildlife viewing, the area is a prime nesting site for four different types of **sea turtles.** Witnessing the amazing spectacle

1 Osa Peninsula
2 Tortuguero
3 Puerto Viejo

of female sea turtles digging nests and laying eggs is often the highlight of a trip here (p. 417, **6**)—be sure to book a tour.

Don't miss taking a quiet **boat tour** (p. 417, **4**) into the network of canals that wind through the thick rain forest. You'll also get a chance to wander around the tiny Caribbean coastal town, with its stilt-raised houses, unique Afro-Caribbean culture, and small turtle museum, the **Caribbean Conservation Corporation visitor center and museum** (p. 416, **2**). ⏱ 2 days.

On the morning of Day 13, take a boat transfer to Moín (travel time: 2 hours), and from there a taxi south along the Caribbean coast to the village of Puerto Viejo (travel time: 1 hour).

3 Puerto Viejo. This tiny surfer town (p. 404) is nearly the end of the line—the border with Panama is just a few miles down the coast. In between Puerto Viejo and the border are some of Costa Rica's finest beaches, including **Playa Cocles**, **Punta Uva**, and **Manzanillo**.

Spend Day 14 hiking in the **Gandoca-Manzanillo Wildlife Refuge** (p. 407, **7**) or at nearby **Cahuita National Park** (p. 381, **2**). At both sites, you can combine your hike with snorkeling on a couple of Costa Rica's only surviving coral reefs. While in Puerto Viejo, be sure to have dinner at **La Pecora Nera** (p. 411), one of the finest restaurants in the country. ⏱ 2 days.

Undiscovered Costa Rica

One of the most amazing things about Costa Rica is that in spite of its booming tourism industry, there are still plenty of places to go that are relatively easy to access and yet off the beaten track. And believe me you'll be richly rewarded for venturing down the road less traveled. This 10-day tour offers a chance to truly get away from it all—you'll see spectacular natural beauty, discover lovely isolated beaches, and have lots of face time with the local wildlife, all while avoiding the masses (or most of them, at least). Because many of these locations are remote, you'll travel by airplane, boat, and rental car.

> It's no mystery how Blue Lake in Rincón de la Vieja National Park got its name.

START **Playa Zancudo.** TOUR LENGTH 1,135km (705 miles). To get to Playa Zancudo, fly from San José to Golfito (flight time: 1 hour), and take a boat transfer from there to Playa Zancudo (travel time: 30 minutes).

❶ **Playa Zancudo.** Playa Zancudo is a sleepy, isolated beach town on a narrow strip of land set between the Golfo Dulce and a saltwater mangrove lagoon. If you've ever pondered throwing it all away, downsizing, and moving to the beach, the kitchen-equipped cabins at **Cabinas**

0   30 mi
0   30 km

NICARAGUA

Lake Nicaragua

CARIBBEAN SEA

PACIFIC OCEAN

PANAMA

1 Playa Zancudo
2 Rincón de la Vieja National Park
3 Barra Honda National Park
4 Playa Sámara
5 Montezuma
6 Malpaís & Santa Teresa

Los Cocos (p. 373) are a good choice for a trial run. While you're here, you can go **sportfishing** (p. 370, **2**), visit nearby **Pavones** (p. 370, **3**) for a surf session, or take an organized tour with **Zancudo Boat Tours** (p. 373, **1**).

One of the better day trips will take you southward to **Tiskita Jungle Lodge** (p. 373, **5**), which has a wonderful network of trails through the rain forests and fruit orchards of its private reserve. Any wannabe botanist will also want to allot enough time for a visit to the **Wilson Botanical Gardens** (p. 367, **4**), the most impressive botanical gardens in all of Costa Rica (which is saying something). Because of timing issues, you won't be able to visit both these sites in 1 day, so plan accordingly. ⏲ **2 days.**

> With 7,000 species of tropical plants, Wilson Botanical Gardens are a must for flora lovers.

On Day 3, take a morning flight from Golfito to San José, with an onward connection to Liberia (travel time: about 3½ hours, including layover). Make arrangements to have your lodge pick you up on arrival.

❷ Rincón de la Vieja National Park. Because it's not nearly as popular as the Arenal Volcano, the **Rincón de la Vieja Volcano,** along with its namesake **national park,** is an underexplored gem. The park features challenging and rewarding hikes, sulfur hot springs, volcanic mud deposits, and the ubiquitous (but stunning nonetheless) jungle waterfalls. I suggest you spend the afternoon of Day 3 doing the most popular hike here, the relatively short and gentle **Las Pailas loop,** which showcases the park's famed volcanic fumaroles (holes in the earth from which smoke and volcanic gases escape) and mud pots (spots where the heat from below causes the topsoil to boil).

On Day 4, try the hike to **Blue Lake and La Cangreja Falls,** a vigorous 2-hour trek that pays off with a beautiful forest waterfall emptying into a postcard-perfect turquoise lake. This is a great spot for a picnic lunch and a cool dip. ⏱ 1½ days. See p. 111, ❽.

Get an early start on Day 5, taking a taxi to Liberia (a 45-minute ride), where you'll pick up a four-wheel-drive rental car. Take CR21 south from Liberia, following signs to San José and La Amistad Bridge. The entrance to Barra Honda National Park is on your left, a few miles before the bridge. The trip length is about 75km (47 miles) and it will take 1½ hours.

❸ Barra Honda National Park. Encompassing a seemingly endless network of caves, this fascinating (and often ignored) national park (p. 179, ❽) is ideal for an afternoon of exploring. You'll be treated to an enormous variety of rock formations (not just stalactites and stalagmites) as you make your way through these mysterious limestone caverns. The park is also home to one of Costa Rica's last dry forests— one of the rarest habitats on earth. Cacti and capuchin monkeys may seem like a strange mix, but you'll find them both here. ⏱ 4 hr.

On the afternoon of Day 5, take CR21 north to the small city of Nicoya. Turn left into the city, and follow signs to the beach town of Playa Sámara (62km/39 miles total).

❹ Playa Sámara. Although popular with Costa Ricans as a weekend and holiday destination, Playa Sámara (p. 202) is often overlooked by tourists. That may be because the town and its beach themselves are nothing special. But nearby you will find several of this coastline's most stunning stretches of sand. Take the time

> *Costa Rica is home to four kinds of monkeys, including the white-faced capuchin, shown here.*

> Take an ultralight flight with Flying Crocodile to get a bird's-eye view of the Pacific coastline near Playa Sámara.

to explore and enjoy such hidden gems as **Playa Barrigona** (p. 188) and **Playa Carrillo** (p. 188). And don't miss a chance to take to the skies on an ultralight flight with the folks at **Flying Crocodile** (p. 178, ❺). ⏱ 2 days.

On the morning of Day 7, drive back to Nicoya and take CR21 south to Paquera. The final section of this drive is on a dirt road, which gets rough during the rainy season—your four-wheel-drive will come in handy. From Paquera, the road is paved all the way to Cóbano, and it's just a few kilometers on another dirt road south to Montezuma. You'll need 4 hours to cover the 160km (99 miles).

❺ **Montezuma.** The Nicoya Peninsula has many of the same charms and nearly as many miles of beach as Guanacaste, but far sparser crowds. Montezuma (p. 192) is the original beach destination out this way, and it remains a great place to get in some sun and sand time, while also visiting a couple of spectacular waterfalls. You can hike to the foot of the **Montezuma Waterfall** (p. 192, ❶), but I prefer visiting it as part of the **Montezuma Waterfall Canopy Tour** (p. 172, ❶). After this, take a horseback tour to **Cataratas El Chorro** (El Chorro Falls) (p. 173, ❷). If you time it right, you can be riding home along the beach as the sun sets.

Spend Day 7 at the **Cabo Blanco Nature Reserve** (p. 173, ❹), the country's first officially protected area. The main trail inside this park, Sendero Sueco, leads to the gorgeous and almost always deserted Playa Balsita. A trip to Cabo Blanco Nature Reserve can easily be combined with a **kayak and snorkel tour** (p. 173, ❸) to the little cemetery island located just off the village of Cabuya. Finally, don't miss out on eating at **Playa de los Artistas** (p. 197), a rustic yet enchanting beachfront restaurant. ⏱ 2 days.

Make the short (19km/12-mile) drive on the morning of Day 8 back to Cóbano and then south on the well-marked dirt road to Malpaís and Santa Teresa.

❻ **Malpaís and Santa Teresa.** Although the argument can be made that this area is no longer the country's best-kept secret, this outpost on the southern tip of the Nicoya Peninsula is remote, romantic, and still crowd-free. Very few visitors to Costa Rica make an effort to reach this remote beach destination. It's their loss. Spoil yourself with a splurge at **Florblanca Resort** (p. 200), settle in for some simpler rustic luxury at **Milarepa** (p. 201), or bunk with the surfers and backpackers at the **Malpaís Surf Camp & Resort** (p. 201). Spend your remaining days beachcombing, sunbathing, and surfing—this is what relaxation is all about. ⏱ 3 days.

The Best Costa Rica Adventures

If you're looking for thrills, you've picked the right destination. Costa Rica is all about adventure travel, and the following itinerary packs a lot of excitement into a single week. Adrenaline junkies, this is your dream trip: white-water rafting, mountain biking, zip-lining, canyoning—take your pick. And the best part? All of these adventures are set against a backdrop of some of Costa Rica's most stunning scenery. Along the way, there will be great wildlife viewing, plenty of camaraderie and sore muscles, and a steady stream of wow-inducing moments.

> *The Río Pacuare has plenty of challenging rapids along its run down Costa Rica's eastern slope to the Caribbean Sea.*

START Río Pacuare, just outside of Turrialba, 60km (37 miles) east of San José.
TOUR LENGTH 480km (298 miles).

1 Río Pacuare. Start things off wet and wild with a white-water rafting expedition on the Río Pacuare with **Exploradores Outdoors** (p. 73 and p. 397). Covering nearly 50 distinct rapids that run some 36km (22 miles), this trip will take almost 2 full days, allowing you plenty of time for playing in the water and taking hikes to nearby jungle waterfalls. You'll spend the night in a rustic, yet cozy, cabin camp on the river's edge. When you finish running the Pacuare, Exploradores will bring you to your hotel in the La Fortuna and Arenal Volcano area. ⏱ **2 days.**

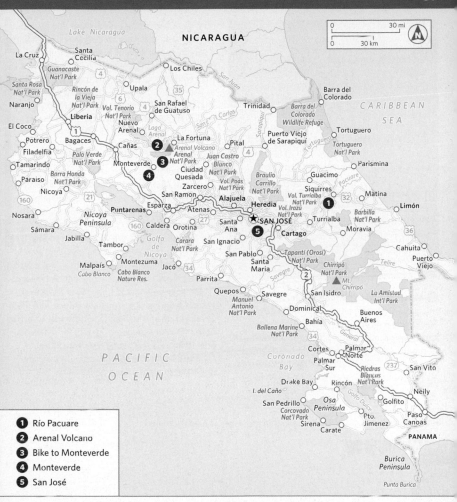

1. Río Pacuare
2. Arenal Volcano
3. Bike to Monteverde
4. Monteverde
5. San José

2 Arenal Volcano. After checking in at your hotel, you can either head for a volcano lookout to watch the nighttime light show or hit the hot springs at **Eco Termales** (p. 247). For Day 3, sign on for **Desafío Adventure Company's** (p. 246) "6x1" adventure package. This very full day tour—for which you'll be picked up and dropped off at your hotel—includes their signature "Lost Canyon" adventure: a mix of hiking, wading, and swimming—with periodic rappels down the faces of waterfalls—as you make your way down a narrow box canyon in the rain forest. You will hike along the cooled lava flows at the foot of Arenal Volcano, visit a private reserve and animal shelter, and wrap up with a soak in the hot mineral pools at **The Springs Resort & Spa** (p. 262). There's a great view of the volcano from this resort and its hot springs, and you'll be treated to a feast here as well. You'll want to carbo-load, because you'll definitely be working hard on this trip. ⏱ 1 day

Day 4 of your trip will begin early, with a pickup at your hotel. Have your bags packed, as you'll be dropped off at your hotel of choice in Monteverde that evening.

Alternative Adventures

This itinerary is an excellent outline for a well-rounded, all-purpose adventure trip, but there is an abundance of other opportunities for true adventure hounds. If you want to do more mountain biking or kayaking, I recommend you schedule additional time in the **La Fortuna** area (p. 260). If you're into serious windsurfing or kiteboarding (p. 240), you'll want to visit **Lake Arenal** between December and March, when the winds are howling. And hard-core hikers should think about trekking into and around **Corcovado National Park** (p. 348). You'll find more information on a whole host of adventure options in the various regional destination chapters, as well as in "The Best Special Interest Trips" (p. 444).

3 **Mountain bike to Monteverde.** Actually, this day will involve a taxi–boat–mountain bike–taxi trip from La Fortuna. If that sounds complicated, not to worry: **Desafío Adventure Company** will make all the travel arrangements for you; see "Going by Boat & Taxi," p. 225. After an early-morning pickup, you'll be taken to a boat dock beside the Arenal Dam and ferried across the lake to your waiting bikes. From here it's 3 hours and 40km (25 miles) of rugged off-track riding. Then you'll be picked up by a four-wheel-drive taxi for the final 1½-hour ride to Monteverde. After checking into your hotel, chill out for a little while, but be sure to sign on for a night hike in **Monteverde Cloud Forest Biological Reserve** (p. 233, **15**). ⏱ 1 day.

Day 5 starts with a pickup from your hotel.

4 **Monteverde.** Get an early start with a guided tour of **Monteverde Cloud Forest Biological Reserve** (p. 218, **1**)—your hotel will help you make arrangements. After your hike, linger to explore some of the trails here on your own. In the afternoon, catch the shuttle bus to **Sky Trek** (p. 245) for their combination package, which includes both a zip-line canopy tour and a walk on their system of trails and suspended bridges.

On your second and final day in Monteverde, I recommend mixing some adventure with a bit of relaxation and healing. The best way to work both into your schedule? Sign up for a half-day horseback ride and sauna tour with **El Sol** (p. 246), located about a 10-minute taxi ride down the mountain from Santa Elena, the

> At dusk, the glowing lava starts to show on the slopes of Arenal Volcano.

> A zip-line canopy tour high among the jungle treetops is a not-to-be-missed Costa Rica experience.

gateway village to Monteverde. Their guides will take you by horseback to an isolated little waterfall with an excellent swimming hole. After the ride back, you'll find the wood-burning traditional Swedish sauna all fired up, with a refreshing and beautiful little pool beside it. ⊕ 2 days.

At the end of Day 6, take an evening bus or private transfer back to San José—your hotel can help you make arrangements. While it may be tempting to spend one more day in Monteverde, I urge you not to wait until the morning of your flight to try to get back to San José, as it may take longer than you anticipate.

⑤ San José. Unless you have a very early flight home, you'll have a bit of time left in which to squeeze in some final adventures in the capital city—take full advantage. Your best bet is **Parque La Sabana** (La Sabana Park; p. 56, **②**). If you're up for it, join one of the many pick-up *fútbol* (soccer) games held on the fields scattered throughout the park. Ticos take their soccer seriously—if you do, too, consider packing a pair of cleats. If you don't feel like playing,

the games are still a lot of fun to watch. And if you're still craving one last adventure, you can always sign up for the **Urban Canopy Tour** (p. 56, **③**). ⊕ 1 day.

La Ruta de los Conquistadores

Each year, Costa Rica hosts what many consider to be the most challenging mountain-bike race on the planet. **La Ruta de los Conquistadores** (The Route of the Conquerors) retraces the path of the 16th-century Spanish conquistadores from the Pacific coast to the Caribbean Sea—all in 4 days. It's a grueling course that takes its toll on both bike and rider. The race is usually held in mid-November, near the end of the rainy season, and thick mud is often a major obstacle. Nevertheless, it draws hundreds of top-flight competitors from around the world. For more information, check out www.adventurerace.com.

Costa Rica with Kids

Costa Rica may not seem all that kid-friendly, but don't be fooled—this is a terrific family destination. If you've got very small children, stick close to the beaches—you won't want to take a toddler zip-lining. But for slightly older kids and teens, particularly those with an adventurous streak, Costa Rica is a lot of fun. Plan to spend about 9 days; you'll get some serious family bonding done over a range of activities and terrains, from sailing to scrambling over cooled lava tubes.

> Even young kids can safely swing through the trees in the Monteverde Cloud Forest.

START San José. TOUR LENGTH 405km (252 miles).

1 **San José.** On your first morning in the capital city take a taxi to **La Paz Waterfall Gardens** (p. 58, **7**). From the serpentarium, butterfly garden, and massive aviary to the trout pond, waterfall trails, and hummingbird feeders, there's something of interest and wonder at nearly every turn. In the afternoon, take a taxi to the **Museo de los Niños** (Children's Museum; p. 62. **3**).

On Day 2, get an early start, as you'll be visiting both **Zoo Ave** (p. 63, **4**), and **INBio Park** (p. 59, **8**), two top-notch attractions that blend education and entertainment. ⏱ 2 days.

On Day 3, take a morning flight from San José to La Fortuna (flight time: 30 minutes).

2 **La Fortuna and Arenal Volcano.** Kids (and grown-ups) will marvel at the sights and sounds of active Arenal Volcano, and the surrounding area has much to offer as well. Spend the afternoon on a tour with **Pure Trek Canyoning** (p. 245). They run a thrilling canyoning excursion suitable for children as young as 8. In the evening, take in the stunning sight of lava spewing forth from Arenal's peak.

On Day 4, book a **Fourtrax Adventure** (p. 242) all-terrain-vehicle tour—kids will love the bumpy ride. Drivers must be 16 or older, but youngsters can share a vehicle with their parents. In the afternoon, hit **Arenal National Park** (p. 230, **5**) for an up-close look at cooled lava tubes—and keep an eye out for wildlife. ⏱ 2 days.

Take the organized jeep-boat-jeep transfer on the morning of Day 5 (travel time: 3 hours; see p. 225) from your Arenal-area hotel to your Monteverde hotel. Once in Monteverde, you'll rely on taxis and organized tours.

3 **Monteverde.** On the afternoon of Day 5, hike the gentle, kid-friendly trails at the **Monteverde Cloud Forest Biological Reserve** (p. 218, **1**), and then get your fill of cool creatures with visits to the **Bat Jungle** (p. 235, **2**) and the **Frog Pond of Monteverde** (p. 219, **5**).

On Day 6, you'll start off with a ride on **The Original Canopy Tour** (p. 244), which offers the perfect way for even very small fry to see the rain-forest canopy. Then spend some time with the creepy crawlies at **Mundo Insectos** (p. 237, **7**) and **Serpentario Monteverde**

NICARAGUA

Lake Nicaragua

La Cruz
Santa Cecilia
Guanacaste Nat'l Park
Los Chiles
Santa Rosa Nat'l Park
Naranjo
Rincón de la Vieja Nat'l Park
Upala
San Juan
Barra del Colorado
CARIBBEAN SEA
El Coco ❹
Liberia
Vol. Tenorio Nat'l Park
Nuevo Arenal
San Rafael de Guatuso
Trinidad
Barra del Colorado Wildlife Refuge
Tortuguero
Potrero
Filadelfia
Bagaces
Cañas
Lago Arenal
La Fortuna ❷
Arenal Volcano
Pital
Puerto Viejo de Sarapiquí
Tortuguero Nat'l Park
Tamarindo
Palo Verde Nat'l Park
Arenal Nat'l Park ❸
Juan Castro Blanco Nat'l Park
Parismina
Paraiso
Barra Honda Nat'l Park
Monteverde
Ciudad Quesada
Vol. Poás Nat'l Park
Guacimo
Nicoya
Zarcero
Braulio Carrillo Nat'l Park
Siquirres
Matina
Nosara
Esparza
San Ramon
Alajuela
Vol. Turrialba Nat'l Park
Barbilla Nat'l Park
Limón
Nicoya Peninsula
Puntarenas
Atenas
Santa Ana
Heredia
Vol. Irazú Nat'l Park
Turrialba
Moravia
Sámara
Caldera
Orotina
★ SAN JOSÉ ❶
Cartago
Jabilla
Golfo de Nicoya
San Ignacio
San Pablo
Tapanti (Orosi) Nat'l Park
Cahuita
Tambor
San Ignacio
Santa Maria
Chirripó Nat'l Park
Puerto Viejo
Malpaís
Cabo Blanco
Montezuma
Cabo Blanco Nature Res.
Jacó
Carara Nat'l Park
Parrita
Savegre
Mt. Chirripó
La Amistad Int'l Park
PACIFIC OCEAN
Quepos
Manuel Antonio Nat'l Park
Savegre
San Isidro
Buenos Aires
Dominical
Ballena Marine Nat'l Park
Bahía
Coronado Bay
Cortes
Palmar Norte
Palmar Sur
Piedras Blancas Nat'l Park
San Vito
Drake Bay
Rincón
Neily
I. del Caño
Golfito
San Pedrillo
Osa Peninsula
Golfo Dulce
Paso Canoas
Corcovado Nat'l Park
Pto. Jimenez
PANAMA
Sirena
Carate
Burica Peninsula
Punta Burica

❶ San José
❷ La Fortuna & Arenal Volcano
❸ Monteverde
❹ Guanacaste

(p. 237, ❽)—always a hit with young ones. You'll finish everything off *ooh*-ing and *aah*-ing at the creatures you encounter on a night tour back at the **Monteverde Cloud Forest Biological Reserve** (p. 233, ⓯). ⏱ 2 days.

Early on Day 7, take a taxi north to Liberia, where you'll pick up a rental car. Then take CR21 west, following signs to the Papagayo Peninsula. Give yourself 3 hours for the 153km (95-mile) drive.

❹ **Guanacaste.** With miles of beaches, loads of activities and attractions, and a host of full-service resorts, Guanacaste is prime family-friendly territory. I suggest staying at a place with an on-site children's program, such as the Hilton Papagayo Resort or the Four Seasons. Should you choose to take a break from the resort's offerings, you might want to try a gentle rafting trip on the **Río Corobicí** (p. 107, ❺), a safari-style trip to **África Mía** (p. 119, ❸), or a snorkel-and-sail outing on the **Blue Dolphin** (p. 132). I also recommend driving to **Tamarindo** (p. 146), where the waves can be gentle, for a morning or more of **surf lessons** (p. 130). Finally, if it's nesting season, be sure to sign the family up for a **turtle tour** (p. 120, ❼) to Playa Grande to watch the leatherbacks lay their eggs. ⏱ 3 days.

My Favorite San José Moments

San José, founded in 1737, was a forgotten backwater of the Spanish empire until the late 19th century, when it boomed thanks to the coffee-export business. Today the city has issues: traffic, poorly maintained sidewalks, and street crime. Still, there is much to see and do here. At 1,125m (3,690 ft.) above sea level, San José enjoys springlike temperatures year-round. Its location in the Central Valley—the lush green Talamanca Mountains rise to the south, the Poás, Barva, and Irazú Volcanoes to the north—is both beautiful and convenient as a base of exploration. And San José is home to dynamic dining and nightlife scenes, several excellent museums, and, of course, the lingering scent of roasting coffee.

> PREVIOUS PAGE *Las Ruinas, in the Central Valley city of Cartago, are the remains of a church destroyed in a devastating earthquake in 1910.* THIS PAGE *A* mirador *is a view—and in Costa Rica often refers to a hillside restaurant, such as this one looking over the night lights of San José.*

❶ Catching a show at the Teatro Nacional.
The lavish, neo-baroque National Theater opened in 1897, and it's still going strong. Even if you don't attend a performance here, it's worth stopping by to check out the building's elaborate design and decor. Look for the series of murals depicting life in San José—the coffee mural in particular—gleaming marble statues, and the outrageously gilded foyer. See p. 97.

❷ Taking the kids to the Museo de los Niños.
Built on the site of a former prison barracks, the Children's Museum has a wealth of interactive exhibits aimed at young minds, including a simulated earthquake that's sure to please. Besides, if the kids misbehave, you can always send them to spend some time in the reconstructed prison cell on-site. See p. 62, ❸.

> *Poás and the other volcanoes of Costa Rica's Central Valley are part of the Pacific Ring of Fire, a chain of tectonically active spots around the Pacific basin.*

❸ **Dining at a mirador.** San José is surrounded by steep volcanic mountains—take advantage. With the lights of the city and the entire Central Valley at your feet, you can't beat the vista from a typical Costa Rican *mirador* (mountainside restaurant with a view). The food, while generally simple, tends to be quite good, too—my favorite is **Mirador Tiquicia.** See "Dining with a View," p. 83.

❹ **Exploring La Paz Waterfall Gardens.** This multifaceted place is the best one-stop attraction in the Central Valley. It is home to a series of tall rain-forest waterfalls, butterfly and hummingbird gardens, a massive aviary, a serpentarium, and a trout-fishing pond. Basically, a little something for everyone. See p. 58, ❼.

❺ **Mingling with the local boho crowd at Café Mundo.** This popular downtown restaurant occupies the interior main-floor rooms and various open-air patios and gardens of a restored old mansion. It's usually hopping both day and night. See p. 82.

❻ **Hiking to the crater at Poás Volcano.** A cloud forest rings the mile-wide crater, which is said to be the second largest in the world, so take your time and enjoy the walk to the top. If you're lucky, you'll get to see the crater spew steam and muddy water—the geysers can reach heights of 180m (590ft.). See p. 58, ❻.

❼ **Taking a coffee tour.** San José was built on the riches of the coffee industry—it went rapidly from small town to boomtown as the drink grew more popular in the late 1800s. The hillsides that surround the city still produce some of the world's best beans. A coffee tour (Café Britt's is the best) will teach you everything you ever wanted to know about the planting, growing, harvesting, and processing of this black gold. You'll also learn how to sip and spit like a professional coffee taster. See "Get Your Coffee Fix," p. 57.

❽ **Seeing a wealth of Costa Rican fauna at Zoo Ave.** The aptly named Zoo Ave (roughly, "bird zoo") began its life as a bird sanctuary, but the current menagerie is far broader. There are excellent monkey and reptile exhibits, in addition to a host of other Costa Rican wildlife. But bird lovers shouldn't fret—their feathered friends are still the main focus, and the sheer variety of species housed here is impressive. See p. 63, ❹.

My Favorite San José Moments

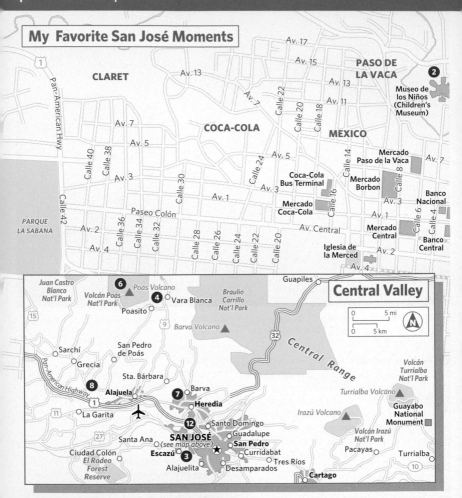

CLARET

PASO DE LA VACA

② Museo de los Niños (Children's Museum)

COCA-COLA

MEXICO

Mercado Paso de la Vaca

Coca-Cola Bus Terminal

Mercado Borbon

Banco Nacional

Paseo Colón

Mercado Coca-Cola

PARQUE LA SABANA

Mercado Central

Banco Central

Iglesia de la Merced

Av. Central

Central Valley

Juan Castro Blanco Nat'l Park

Volcán Poás Nat'l Park

⑥ *Poás Volcano*

④ Vara Blanca

Poasito

Guapiles

Braulio Carrillo Nat'l Park

0   5 mi
0   5 km

Barva Volcano

Central Range

Sarchí

San Pedro de Poás

Volcán Turrialba Nat'l Park

Grecia

Sta. Bárbara

Turrialba Volcano

⑧ Alajuela

Barva

⑦

Irazú Volcano

Guayabo National Monument

La Garita

Heredia

Santo Domingo

⑫

SAN JOSÉ
(see map above)

Guadalupe

Escazú

San Pedro

Curridabat

Volcán Irazú Nat'l Park

Santa Ana

Ciudad Colón
El Rodeo Forest Reserve

③

Alajuelita

Desamparados

Tres Ríos

Pacayas

Turrialba

Cartago

---

⑨ Checking out the bling at the Museo de Oro. The glittering Gold Museum has a collection of pre-Columbian gold (what else?) that weighs in at a whopping 20,000 troy ounces. Happily, this unique subterranean museum (it's beneath the Plaza de la Cultura) shows off its bling to great effect—the design of the place is almost as big a draw as the gold. See p. 48, **②**.

⑩ Salsa dancing at El Tobogán. The dance floor at this classic club is massive, and the locals who come here know their moves. Thankfully, the vibe is relaxed enough that you won't feel even slightly intimidated should you decide to strut your stuff. See p. 96.

> *Ticos—as Costa Ricans are known—tear up the floor at El Tobogán dance club.*

Map labels:

32
10
EL PUEBLO
109
108
Río Torres
Calle Central
Calle 1
Av. 11
CARMEN
OTOYA
Parque Zoológico Simón Bolívar
AMÓN
Av. 15
Av. 9
Calle 13
Calle 15
Av. 11
Av. 15
5
Calle 17
Av. 19
Calle 21
Av. 13
Av. 5
Calle 3
Edificio Metálico
Parque España
CENAC
Av. 7
Calle 19
Calle 9
Calle 33
Calle 35
Correos Central
Calle 5
Parque Morazán
Biblioteca Nacional
Calle 23
Calle 25
Calle 31
ESCALANTE
Teatro Melico Salazar
pedestrians only
Tribunal Supremo de Elecciones
Calle 15
Parque Nacional
Av. 3
11
9
Plaza de la Cultura
Av. Central
Asamblea Legislativa
CALIFORNIA
Parque Central
1
Catedral Metropolitana
Plaza de la Democracia
Museo Nacional
Av. 1
Av. 3
Av. 2
pedestrians only
Av. 6
Iglesia de la Soledad
Calle 17
Calle 19
LOS YOSES
Ave. Central
Calle Central
Calle 1
Calle 7
Calle 9
Calle 11
Av. 8
Calle 21
BELLA-VISTA
Calle 29
SOLEDAD

Map legend:

1. Teatro Nacional
2. Museo de los Niños
3. Mirador Tiquicia
4. La Paz Waterfall Gardens
5. Café Mundo
6. Poás Volcano
7. Taking a coffee tour at Café Britt Farm
8. Zoo Ave
9. Museo de Oro
10. El Tobogán
11. Cafeteria 1930
12. INBio Park

11 People-watching at Cafeteria 1930. With verandah seating facing the bustling Plaza de la Cultura, this is one of the most atmospheric spots in San José. The food isn't the best in town (it's certainly not the worst, either), but you probably won't notice. You'll be too busy enjoying the old-world feel and the view. See p. 83.

12 Visiting INBio Park. Run by the National Biodiversity Institute, this place is part museum, part educational center, and part nature park. It's also one of the best places in the country to learn about Costa Rica's biodiversity and natural wonders. See p. 59, 8.

> Get up close and personal with a green-and-black poison-dart frog at INBio park.

The Best of San José in 1 Day

It's very easy to see the best that San José has to offer in 1 day, assuming you get an early start and are prepared to spend lots of time on your feet. With a population of nearly 1 million, the city itself is sprawling and crowded, but the sites I suggest you visit are all grouped around the city's center, which makes touring convenient. You'll find the people here very friendly, but I do suggest you keep an eye or a firm grip on your wallet, camera, and bag at all times, as pickpockets are a big problem.

> There's usually plenty of action on the Plaza de la Cultura, home to the National Theater, Gold Museum, and the Gran Hotel Costa Rica.

START Take a taxi to the Plaza de la Cultura, between Avenidas Central and 2 and Calles 3 and 5.

1 ★ **Plaza de la Cultura.** This breezy, multi-level, open-air plaza is a good spot to get a feel for the city. There are usually a few performers working the crowd, plenty of fresh fruit stands, and you can buy a handful of popcorn to feed the pigeons. ⏱ 20 min. Btw. Avenidas Central and 2 and Calles 3 and 5.

2 ★★ **Museos del Banco Central de Costa Rica.** This underground museum complex, tucked beneath the Plaza de la Cultura, houses a number of museums worthy of a look. The best is the **Museo de Oro** (Gold Museum). The ancient indigenous peoples of Mesoamerica were very serious about their gold, and the quantity of jewelry, ornaments, and religious idols on display here is surprising. You may also want to check out Costa Rica's principal numismatic and

1 Plaza de la Cultura
2 Museos del Banco Central de Costa Rica
3 Teatro Nacional
4 Cafetería 1930
5 Museo de Jade Marco Fidel Tristán Castro
6 Café Mundo
7 Centro Nacional de Arte y Cultura
8 Plaza de la Democracia
9 Museo Nacional de Costa Rica

EL PUEBLO

PASO DE LA VACA

Museo de los Niños (Children's Museum)

MEXICO

Mercado Borbón

COCA-COLA

Coca-Cola Bus Terminal

Mercado Coca-Cola

Parque de la Merced

MERCED

Iglesia de la Merced

Mercado Central

Banco Central

Banco Nacional

Correos Central

Teatro Melico Salazar

Parque Central

Catedral Metropolitana

Iglesia de la Soledad

SOLEDAD

Mercado Paso de la Vaca

CARMEN

Castillo del Moro

Plaza de la Cultura

Teatro Nacional (National Theatre)

Parque Morazán

Edificio Metálico

Parque España

Parque Zoológico Simón Bolívar

Río Torres

AMÓN

CENAC

Tribunal Supremo de Elecciones

Asamblea Legislativa

Plaza de la Democracia

Parque Nacional

Biblioteca Nacional

Museo Nacional de Costa Rica

SAN JOSÉ

CARIBBEAN SEA

NICARAGUA
PANAMA

PACIFIC OCEAN

Calle Central
Calle 1
Calle 3
Calle 5
Calle 7
Calle 9
Calle 11
Calle 13
Calle 15
Calle 17
Calle 19

Calle 2
Calle 4
Calle 6
Calle 8
Calle 10
Calle 12
Calle 14
Calle 16

Av. 13
Av. 11
Av. 9
Av. 7
Av. 5
Av. 3
Av. 1
Av. Central
Av. 2
Av. 4
Av. 6

Av. Central

32
108

Pedestrian only

200 yc.
200 m

0
0

> *The Museo de Oro—or Gold Museum—houses a vast collection of pre-Columbian gold objects, many in the shapes of animals.*

philatelic museums, and there is a large exhibition space reserved for traveling exhibits. ⏱ 2 hr. Calle 5 btw. Avenidas Central and 2, beneath the eastern end of Plaza de la Cultura. ☎ 2243-4202. www.museosdelbancocentral.org. Admission $9 adults, $4 students, 80¢ children 11 and under. Daily 9:30am–5pm.

❸ ★★ **Teatro Nacional.** While you're on the plaza, take a guided tour of the lavishly decorated 100-year-old National Theater. Be sure to see if there's a concert or show on during your stay; if there is, buy your tickets now. ⏱ 1 hr. Plaza de la Cultura. See p. 97.

❹ 🍽 **Cafeteria 1930.** You can charge up with some coffee or order a fresh fruit drink at this 24-hour spot right on the plaza. Grab an outdoor table and you'll be treated to a great view of the crowds passing by. If you're lucky, there'll be a marimba band playing on the plaza—street musicians are a common and welcome sight. Avenida 2 btw. Calles 1 and 3. ☎ 2221-4011. $$$. See p. 83.

❺ ★★ **Museo de Jade Marco Fidel Tristán Castro.** Jade was the most valuable commodity among the pre-Columbian cultures of Mexico and Central America, worth more even than gold. The popular Jade Museum houses a huge collection of artifacts dating from 500 B.C. to A.D. 800. Most are large pendants, primarily of human and animal figures, that were parts of presumably massive necklaces. A fascinating display illustrates how the primitive peoples of the region carved this extremely hard stone.

The museum also has a large and surprisingly varied collection of pre-Columbian polychrome terra-cotta vases, bowls, and figurines. Some of these pieces are surprising in their modern design and advanced technique. Particularly fascinating are a vase that incorporates real human teeth and a display that shows how jade was embedded in human teeth for decorative reasons. ⏱ 40 min. Avenida 7 btw. Calles 9 and 9B, INS building. ☎ 2287-6034. Admission $7 adults; children 11 and under free. Mon–Fri 8:30am–3:30pm; Sat 9am–1pm.

❻ 🍽 ★ **Café Mundo.** For lunch, try to nab one of the open-air patio tables at this lively place. Artistic whimsy is perfectly combined with age-old charm in the restored old mansion. Choose from a range of salads, pastas, pizzas, and daily specials. I particularly like the sandwich of roasted vegetables on thick bread. Calle 15 and Avenida 9, 200m (2 blocks) east and 100m (1 block) north of the INS building. ☎ 2222-6190. $$–$$$. See p. 82.

> *If you follow the travel prescriptive to eat where the locals eat, you won't want to miss Café Mundo.*

The Civil War

Costa Rica's Civil War, in 1948, lasted a mere 44 days, but it was costly—some 2,000 soldiers and civilians died in the fighting. And while the war itself was terrible, the end result was a progressive new constitution, which is still in place today.

For many years, Rafael Angel Calderón had dominated Costa Rican politics. He served as president from 1940 to 1944, and though he was no longer in office, his successor, Teodoro Picado, was widely viewed as his puppet. Their National Republican Party had grown unpopular, and there were frequent protests and strikes. In the spring of 1948, Calderón again ran for president, this time against the opposition party candidate Otilio Ulate. But despite Calderón's power, he lost the closely contested election—not that he let it stop him. Instead, he had his followers in the legislature void the election results and ordered the arrest of Ulate on March 12. And that's when all hell broke loose.

A group of rebels calling themselves the National Liberation Army declared war and quickly began to win. The government simply couldn't hold this ragtag band of freedom fighters at bay. After the rebels laid claim to Cartago—the country's second biggest city—Picado finally signed a treaty ending the war, on April 19.

On May 8, 1948, a group of rebels, led by the recently exiled activist José "Pepe" Figueres, instituted a military junta, which lasted for the next 18 months. During that period a new National Assembly was elected and a new constitution was drafted. It abolished the army, and gave both women and blacks the right to vote. As the constitution was put into effect, Ulate was finally seated as the country's rightful president.

> *Jewelry-makers are among the artisans selling their creations in the market stalls on the Plaza de la Democracia.*

7 Centro Nacional de Arte y Cultura. The large, contemporary National Center of Art and Culture has a steady stream of major traveling exhibitions, often highlighting prominent Latin American artists or architects. If you arrive early, grab a light bite and glass of wine or coffee at the elegant little **Café del Teatro Nacional** (☎ 2221-1329; entrees $5–$12), just off the lobby. ⏲ 40 min to view the exhibits. Calle 13 btw. Avenidas 3 and 5. ☎ 2257-7202 or 2257-9370. Admission $1 adults, 60¢ students with valid ID; seniors and children 11 and under free; free admission Mon. Mon–Sat 9:30am–4:45pm.

8 ★★ Plaza de la Democracia. This lovely plaza takes up a full square city block. Take a seat, and watch the city's bustle pass you by. If you'd like some Latin American souvenirs, this is a good place to pick up items like leather bracelets and wool sweaters. ⏲ 1 hr. Btw. Avenidas Central and 2 and Calles 13 and 15.

9 ★ Museo Nacional de Costa Rica. The National Museum, Costa Rica's most important historical museum, is housed in a former army barracks that was the scene of fighting during the civil war of 1948 (see "The Civil War," p. 51). As you approach the building, you'll see bullet holes on the turrets at its corners. Inside are displays on Costa Rican history and culture from pre-Columbian times to the present. The standout attraction in the pre-Columbian rooms is a 2,500-year-old jade carving shaped like a seashell and etched with an image of a hand holding a small animal.

Among the most fascinating objects unearthed at Costa Rica's numerous archaeological sites are the many *metates* (grinding stones); some of them are the size of a small bed and are believed to have been used in funeral rites. One large section of the museum houses the museum's collections of pre-Columbian gold and jade jewelry and figurines, neither of which is anywhere near as elaborate as those found in the individual Gold **2** and Jade **5** Museums. In the courtyard you'll be treated to a wonderful view of the city and see some of Costa Rica's mysterious stone spheres. ⏲ 2 hr. Calle 17 btw. Avenidas Central and 2, at the Plaza de la Democracia. ☎ 2257-1433. www.museocostarica.go.cr. Admission $6 adults, $3 students and children 11 and under. Tues–Sat 8:30am–4:30pm; Sun 9am–4:30pm. Closed Jan 1, May 1, Dec 25, and Holy Thursday, Good Friday, and Easter Sunday.

> *Visitors to the Museo Nacional ponder the origins and purpose of Costa Rica's mysterious granite spheres (for more on these see "Mysterious Spheres," p. 429).*

The Arcane Art of Finding an Address in San José

The lack of regular addresses is one of the most confusing aspects of visiting Costa Rica in general and San José in particular. Although there are often street addresses and building numbers for locations in downtown San José, they are almost never used. Addresses are instead given as a set of coordinates, such as "Calle 3 between Avenidas Central and 1." It's then up to you to locate the building within that block, keeping in mind that the building could be on either side of the street. Many addresses include additional information, such as the number of meters from a specified intersection or some other well-known landmark. (These "meter measurements" are not precise but are a good way to give directions to a taxi driver. In basic terms, 100m = 1 block, 200m = 2 blocks, and so on.) Unfortunately, these landmarks become truly confusing for visitors to the city because they are often restaurants, bars, or shops familiar only to locals.

Things get even more confusing when the landmark in question no longer exists. The classic example of this is "the Coca-Cola," one of the most common landmarks used in addresses in the blocks surrounding San José's main market, the Mercado Central. The trouble is, the Coca-Cola bottling plant that it refers to is no longer there; the edifice is long gone, and one of the principal downtown bus depots stands in its place. Old habits die hard, though, and the address description remains. In outlying neighborhoods, addresses can become long directions, such as "50m (½ block) south of the old church, then 100m (1 block) east, then 20m (2 buildings) south." Luckily for the visitor, most downtown addresses are more straightforward.

Oh, and if you're wondering how letter carriers manage, well, welcome to the club. Some folks actually do have their mail delivered this way, but most individuals and businesses in San José use a post office box; this is called an *apartado*, abbreviated "Apdo." or "A.P." in mailing addresses.

San José & the Central Valley in 3 Days

On Days 2 and 3 you'll explore some of the parks and natural wonders that surround San José. You'll rely heavily on taxis to get around, but believe me, it's much better than having to deal with a rental car (see "Go Car-Free," p. 56). This tour includes a mix of museums, parks, and cultural sites.

> *Sulfurous clouds often conceal the lake in the center of Poás Volcano's mile-wide main crater.*

START For Day 1, follow the itinerary given in the tour starting on p. 48. Begin Day 2 by taking a taxi to the Museo de Arte Costarricense, at Calle 42 and Paseo Colón, Parque La Sabana Este.

1 ★★ **Museo de Arte Costarricense.** Start your day at the Costa Rican Art Museum, which is housed in an old airport terminal. This is the country's top art venue, with a fabulous and varied collection of the best Costa Rican art in a wide range of media. The works date from the colonial era to contemporary times, and show how Costa Rican artists have interpreted and imitated major European movements over the years. Of particular interest is the beautiful and ever-evolving sculpture garden. ⏱ 1 hr. Calle 42 and Paseo Colón, Parque La Sabana Este. ☎ 2222-7155. www.musarco.go.cr. Admission $5 adults, $3 students with valid ID; seniors and children 5 and under free; free admission Sun. Tues–Fri 9am–5pm; Sat–Sun 10am–4pm.

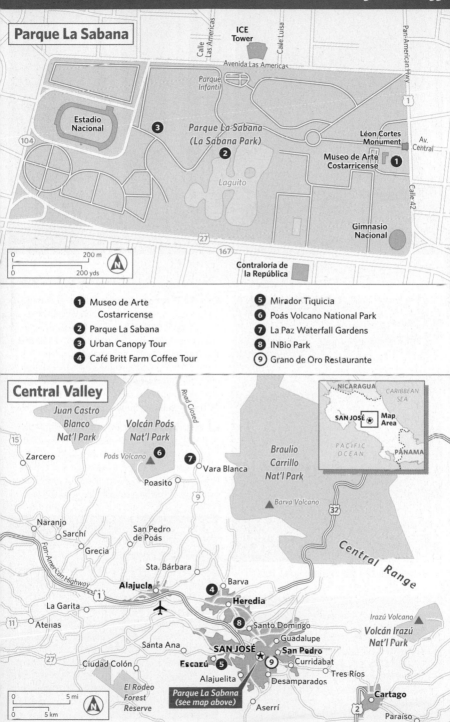

Parque La Sabana

Calle Las Americas
ICE Tower
Calle Luisa
Pan-American Hwy
Avenida Las Americas
Parque Infantil
Estadio Nacional
③
Parque La Sabana (La Sabana Park)
②
Léon Cortes Monument
Av. Central
Museo de Arte Costarricense
①
Laguito
104
Calle 42
27
167
Gimnasio Nacional
Contraloría de la República

0 — 200 m
0 — 200 yds
N

① Museo de Arte Costarricense
② Parque La Sabana
③ Urban Canopy Tour
④ Café Britt Farm Coffee Tour
⑤ Mirador Tiquicia
⑥ Poás Volcano National Park
⑦ La Paz Waterfall Gardens
⑧ INBio Park
⑨ Grano de Oro Restaurante

Central Valley

Juan Castro Blanco Nat'l Park
Volcán Poás Nat'l Park
Road Closed
NICARAGUA
CARIBBEAN SEA
SAN JOSÉ ★ Map Area
PACIFIC OCEAN
PANAMA

15
Zarcero
Poás Volcano **⑥**
⑦
Vara Blanca
Braulio Carrillo Nat'l Park
Poasito
9
Barva Volcano
32
Naranjo
Sarchí
Grecia
San Pedro de Poás
Sta. Bárbara
Central Range
Pan-American Highway
1
Alajuela
Barva
④
Heredia
La Garita
11
Atenas
⑧ Santo Domingo
Guadalupe
Irazú Volcano
Volcán Irazú Nat'l Park
Santa Ana
SAN JOSÉ
⑨ San Pedro
Curridabat
Tres Ríos
Ciudad Colón
Escazú **⑤**
Alajuelita
Desamparados
Parque La Sabana (see map above)
Aserrí
Cartago
2
Paraíso
El Rodeo Forest Reserve

0 — 5 mi
0 — 5 km
N

> *A quiet moment in San José's Parque La Sabana.*

> *The Urban Canopy Tour zips through La Sabana.*

2 ★ kids **Parque La Sabana**. Take a stroll through San Jose's principal park—it's an urban oasis. In addition to the Museo de Arte Costarricense (**1**), there are also a couple of small lakes, some forested areas, and a network of concrete paths through the complex. At the park's far western edge, the new National Stadium is under construction, expected to be completed sometime in 2011. ⏱ 40 min. At the western end of Paseo Colón.

3 kids **Urban Canopy Tour.** If you're chomping at the bit to experience the adrenaline rush of a zip-line canopy tour, this downtown option is worth a try. The tour has eight zip-line cables; the longest is some 200m (655 ft.) and crosses over one of the lakes inside the park. ⏱ 1 hr.

Go Car-Free

It may seem easiest to rent a car and drive to these destinations, but it's not a great idea. In fact, it's a bad idea. Roads around the capital city are not well marked, and driving in San José itself is a real nightmare. Gridlocked traffic is the norm—not to mention the all-too-real threat of having your car stolen. My advice is to take taxis: They're pretty cheap—having a rental car will cost more—and easy to pick up at all the places mentioned in this tour. Even better, I suggest you ask your hotel to help you arrange for a car and driver.

Adventure, Anyone?

You may want to substitute 1 day of this itinerary for a full-day adventure tour. Options include white-water rafting on the Río Pacuare, a trip to the Rain Forest Aerial Tram, or a cruise to Isla Tortuga. For a full listing of such options, see "San José's Best Adventures" (p. 68).

> *Poás Volcano National Park is one of the remaining refuges of the resplendent quetzal.*

Parque La Sabana. ☎ 2215-2544. Admission $25. Daily 9am–5pm.

Return to your hotel to be picked up for the following tour.

④ ★★ **Café Britt Farm Coffee Tour.** Café Britt is one of the country's largest coffee exporters, and their facilities and coffee tour are top-notch. Spend your afternoon in the hills on this informative and entertaining tour of Café Britt's plantations and processing plant. The excursion even features a fun little theater production. I suggest you sign up for a package that includes lunch and round-trip transportation to and from your hotel. ⏲ 3–4 hr. North of Heredia on the road to Barva. ☎ 2277-1600. www.coffeetour.com. Admission $20 adults, $16 children 6–11; children 5 and under free. Tour from downtown San José $37 adults, $33 children 11 and under; fee includes a coffee drink. Full buffet lunch additional $15 per person. Store and restaurant daily 8:00am–5pm. Reservations required.

You'll be dropped off at your hotel after the coffee tour. For dinner, take a taxi to Escazú.

⑤ ★ **Mirador Tiquicia.** You can't beat the view from this hillside lookout restaurant, and it serves up some pretty darn good local Costa Rican cuisine as well. Be sure to order some *chicharrones* (fried pork rinds), one of the country's most emblematic snack foods. Most nights you'll be treated to a brief show of local folkloric dancing. See "Dining with a View," p. 83.

Get Your Coffee Fix

The hills surrounding San José are famous for their coffee crop, and justifiably so. Costa Rican coffees are some of the finest in the world. Many of the nearby plantations offer informative (and tasty) tours that get you into the science and art of coffee growing, harvesting, roasting, and tasting. These tours make for an excellent half-day outing, and you could easily combine one with another nearby attraction.

If a visit to Café Britt (④), which is the country's most popular brand, only whets your appetite, or if you'd rather try a spot that's a little less visited, consider these two options.

★ **Doka Estate.** This large and long-standing coffee estate in Alajuela offers up a tour that takes you from "seed to cup." Along the way, you'll get a full rundown of the processes involved in the growing, harvesting, curing, packing, and brewing of their award-winning coffee. ⏲ 2½ hr. Sabanilla de Alajuela. ☎ 2449-5152. www. dokaestate.com. Admission $18 adults, $12 students with valid ID, $10 children 6–11; children 5 and under free. Packages including transportation and breakfast or lunch available. Daily 9, 10, and 11am; 1:30 and 2:30pm. Reservations required.

★★ **Finca Rosa Blanca Coffee Plantation & Inn.** This gorgeous boutique hotel (p. 89) in Heredia also has its own organic coffee plantation, with some 40 acres of shade-grown Arabica under cultivation. The hotel offers up daily coffee tours led by a very knowledgeable guide. I recommend combining the coffee tour with lunch at the open-air restaurant here; sitting under the shady gazebos, you'll enjoy a wonderful view of the Central Valley along with some fine, healthful dining. There is also a good in-house spa, with several of the treatments featuring homemade, coffee-based products; if you want to get really decadent, combine your visit with a massage or facial. ⏲ 2 hr. Santa Bárbara de Heredia. ☎ 2269-9392. www.fincarosablanca.com. Admission $25 adults; children 11 and under free. Reservations required.

> *It's best to hit the road into Poás Volcano National Park early, before clouds envelop the crater.*

Get an early start on Day 3 and take a taxi for the hour-long ride to:

6 ★★★ kids **Poás Volcano National Park.** It may seem a little scary that an active volcano is so close to the city, but don't worry. Poás, which stands at 2,640m (8,661 ft.), will likely groan and belch, but you won't see any lava. Poás's crater, said to be the second largest in the world, is more than a mile across, and geysers there sometimes spew steam and muddy water 180m (590 ft.) into the air, making them the world's highest. From the entrance to the park, the main crater is an easy 1km (½-mile) hike through dense stands of virgin forest, where you may see resplendent quetzals.

There are also a couple of well-groomed and -marked hiking trails through the cloud forest that rings the crater. My favorite is a short hike through dense cloud forest to an overlook onto beautiful Botos Lake, which formed in one of the volcano's extinct craters. Near the entrance and parking area you'll find a modern information center with several informative exhibits about the volcano. Be prepared when you come to Poás: This volcano is often enveloped in dense clouds. If you want to see the crater, it's best to come early and during the dry season. Moreover, it can get cool up there, especially when the sun isn't shining, so dress appropriately. ⏱ 2 hr. Poás de Alajuela. ☎ 2482-2424. Admission $10. Daily 8:30am–3:30pm.

Take a taxi from the national park entrance to the next spot, just 15 minutes away.

7 ★★ kids **La Paz Waterfall Gardens.** The main attraction here is the series of trails through primary and secondary forests alongside the Río La Paz, which has lookouts over a series of powerful falls, including the namesake La Paz Waterfall. But there is much more to see and do here. Check out the orchid garden, hummingbird garden, and huge butterfly garden, easily the largest in Costa Rica. A neighboring massive enclosure has a mix of dramatic-looking birds, including scarlet macaws, chestnut-mandibled toucans, and blue-crowned motmots. A small serpentarium features venomous and nonvenomous native snakes, and terrariums contain various frogs and lizards. ⏱ Minimum 2 hr. 6km (3¾ miles) north of Vara Blanca on the road to

> *Visitors encounter some of Costa Rica's most graceful flutterers in the butterfly enclosure at La Paz Waterfall Gardens.*

San Miguel. ☎ 2225-0643. www.waterfallgardens. com. Admission $32 adults, $20 children and students with valid ID. A buffet lunch at the large cafeteria-style restaurant costs an extra $12 for adults, $6 for kids. Daily 8:30am–5:30pm.

A taxi ride from La Paz to INBio Park will take about 30 minutes.

❽ ★★ kids **INBio Park.** Wrap up your day at this top-notch natural history museum, which is a living monument to the biological diversity that has made Costa Rica famous. Paved trails lead through re-creations of several distinct eco-systems found around the country, and there are numerous attractions and play areas for children. Throughout the park, you can enjoy an extensive collection of the somewhat abstract animal sculptures by famed Costa Rican artist José Sancho. ⊕ 2 hr. Santo Domingo de Heredia. ☎ 2507-8107. www.inbio.ac.cr. Admission $23 adults, $13 children 12 and under. Daily 8am–6pm (doors close at 4pm). INBio Park can arrange round-trip transportation from downtown San José for $18 per person.

> *Cross-species interaction at INBio Park.*

⑨   🍴 ★★★ **Grano de Oro Restaurant.** Treat yourself to an elegant and refined dinner at this boutique hotel's courtyard restaurant. Be sure to save room for a piece of the signature Grano de Oro pie. Calle 30, no. 251, btw. Avenidas 2 and 4, 150m (1½ blocks) south of Paseo Colón, San José. ☎ 2255-3322. $$$$. See p. 83.

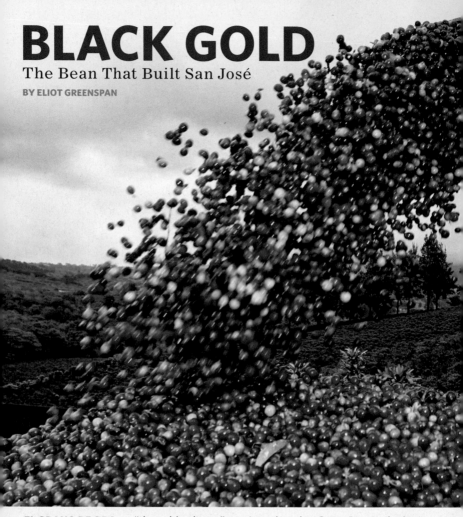

BLACK GOLD
The Bean That Built San José
BY ELIOT GREENSPAN

EL GRANO DE ORO, or "the golden bean," was introduced to Costa Rica in the late 1700s, when Father Félix Velarde, a Catholic priest, founded the first coffee plantation in downtown San José. Growing conditions were ideal, and by the early 1800s, beans were being shipped to Chile to be packaged and sold in Europe. In 1843, a group of growers shipped beans directly to London—and profoundly changed the face of Costa Rica. A poor, sleepy backwater became a booming, progressive nation. Fortunes were made, young Costa Ricans began to study abroad, learning about developments in medicines and engineering, and the Teatro Nacional was built, bringing culture to San José. And coffee became an integral part of Costa Rican life.

A Better Bean?

Costa Rica is blessed with near-perfect coffee-growing conditions: rich volcanic soil, near-constant subtropical temperatures, and plenty of shade, which the plants prefer. More than 1,100 sq. km (425 sq. miles), primarily in the Central Valley and surrounding highlands, are devoted to coffee. There is a wide variety of Costa Rican coffees, and a distinction is made between those grown in the mountains and those grown in valleys. If a bean comes from volcanic slopes, expect it to be more full-bodied and acidic. Lighter, slightly more aromatic brews generally come from valleys.

From Crop to Cup

GROWING: Coffee plantations take 8- to 12-month-old seedlings and plant them in rows that stretch across the hillsides (to prevent erosion). It takes a bush about 4 years to mature, but once it begins producing, it will do so for 40 years. The higher the elevation, the better the coffee, as the soil tends to be more acidic. Costa Rica's best beans are grown between 1,200 and 1,800m (3,900–6,000 ft.).

HARVESTING: In Costa Rica, the bright red beans, or "cherries," are harvested by hand when they are firm and glossy. The time of year depends on the type of bean, but the prime season is from December to March. Approximately 5 to 10kg (10–20 lb.) of export coffee are garnered for every 50kg (100 lb.) of raw beans harvested.

PROCESSING: The beans are shipped to a *beneficio*, where they are cleaned and sorted in water baths. Then the outer pulp and hull are removed from the true bean (or seed), generally by hand. Traditionally, seeds are then sun-dried on large, outdoor patios, though some plantations now use hot-air driers. The final steps are the removal of the bean's skin and the roasting.

PREPARATION: Much of Costa Rica's coffee production is considered "gourmet" or "quality." Once ground, the brew can be prepared in any number of ways, but typically Costa Ricans simply pour boiling water through a cloth bag, or "sock," suspended over a pot or cup (see p. 80).

TIMELINE: Coffee in Costa Rica

1779
The first coffee is cultivated

1820
100 pounds are exported to Panama—the first recorded foreign export of coffee

1821
Municipality of San José gives away free coffee saplings to encourage farming

1830s
Coffee becomes Costa Rica's biggest export

1860
Costa Rican coffee is exported to the United States

1890s
Money from coffee exports funds the construction of schools, hospitals, the Teatro Nacional,

and a railway to the Caribbean coast

1989
Executive order bans the production of any coffee variety except Arabica

1992
True to its environmental consciousness, Costa Rica passes ecofriendly laws regarding coffee cultivation

1990s
The worldwide coffee market crashes, and many plantations go out of business

San José with Kids

While Costa Rica's capital may seem family-unfriendly at first glance, it is actually a good place to visit with kids. San José is home to several excellent attractions geared specifically toward children and young adults, all of them engaging for the whole family. Most include a hefty dose of hands-on experiences, ranging from feeding hummingbirds out of your hand to powering a light bulb by pedaling a stationary bike. Over the course of 2 days you'll see so many birds, snakes, monkeys, and frogs, that you just might forget you're staying in the country's largest city. Again, you'll be relying on taxis, or a private car and driver, to get around (see "Go Car-Free," p. 56).

> Zoo Ave's parrots come in a rainbow of colors.

START Take a taxi to La Paz Waterfall Gardens, 37km (23 miles) north of San José.

❶ ★★ **La Paz Waterfall Gardens.** This place seems to have a little bit of everything. While you might have to carry very young children on the namesake waterfall trail, which runs alongside the Río La Paz, kids of all ages will be impressed by the series of rain-forest waterfalls you pass along the way. If you decide to skip the trail, there's still plenty for little ones to see and do. Kids will love the bright, fluttering energy of the butterfly and hummingbird gardens, and the snake, reptile, and amphibian enclosures will enthrall those with a love for the creepy and crawly. You and your crew can even all take a shot at landing a trophy trout at their man-made two-tiered trout pond. ⏱ Minimum 2 hr. See p. 58, ❼.

Give yourself about 30 minutes for a taxi ride from La Paz to the next stop.

❷ ★★ **INBio Park.** Learning is fun at this rambling nature park—many of the exhibits feature hands-on displays that illustrate and explain the ecological, scientific, and geological makeup of Costa Rica. You'll learn quite a bit, and your kids will get to climb on, play with, and generally interact with a variety of the natural and biological wonders Costa Rica has to offer. There's also plenty of room for little ones (and their parents) to stretch their legs: A network of paved trails winds through a series of re-creations of distinct Costa Rican ecosystems. ⏱ Minimum 2 hr. See p. 59, ❽.

❸ ★★★ **Museo de los Niños.** Start Day 2 at the Children's Museum. The only downside of this place is that it's so huge that you can't really let your kids run wild because they could easily get lost. No big deal, though, as you'll enjoy walking through the rambling old grounds of this converted prison. Throughout you'll find a wide range of hands-on and participatory exhibits

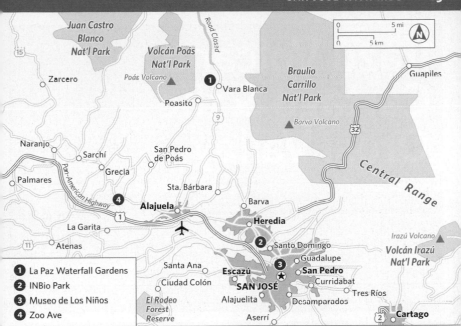

- **1** La Paz Waterfall Gardens
- **2** INBio Park
- **3** Museo de Los Niños
- **4** Zoo Ave

and games. ⏱ Minimum 2 hr. Calle 4 and Avenida 9, San José. ☎ 2258-4929. www.museocr.com. Admission $2 adults, $1.20 students and children 17 and under. Tues–Fri 8am–4:30pm; Sat–Sun 10am–5pm.

The trip to Zoo Ave will take about 45 minutes by taxi.

4 ★★★ **Zoo Ave.** Unlike many such places, this zoo houses only injured, donated, or confiscated birds and animals, so you can visit guilt-free. Scarlet macaws, reclusive owls, majestic raptors, several different species of toucans, and a host of brilliantly colored birds from Costa Rica and around the world make this one exciting place. Indeed, it's one of only two places in the world where you'll see the resplendent quetzal in captivity. There are also large exhibits of iguanas, deer, tapirs, ocelots, pumas, and monkeys—and keep an eye out for the 3.6m-long (12-ft.) crocodile. Zoo Ave is completely kid-friendly, with gentle trails, enormous enclosures for easy viewing, and lots of fun displays that will keep you as engaged as your young ones. ⏱ Minimum 2 hr. La Garita, Alajuela. ☎ 2433-8989. www.zooave.com. Admission $15 adults, $13 students with valid ID, $3 children 2–9; free for children under 2. Daily 9am–5pm.

> Just a few of the katydid specimens at INBio, the National Institute of Biodiversity.

Irazú Volcano, Cartago & the Orosí Valley

Southeast of San José, the city of Cartago and its environs are brimming with history. Founded in 1563, Cartago was Costa Rica's first capital—indeed, it was the country's first city. It was home to glorious colonial-era mansions, and was the site of a decisive battle during the 1948 Civil War (p. 51). Unfortunately, its location at the foot of Irazú Volcano has made it vulnerable to earthquakes, so much of the old architecture has been destroyed. I suggest you ask your hotel to arrange for a car and driver for this busy day-longtrip (see "Go Car-Free," p. 56).

> *Minerals washing down from the sides color the lake in Irazú's main crater a vivid green.*

START Take a taxi to Irazú Volcano, 52km (32 miles) east of San José. **TOUR LENGTH** 155km (96 miles).

❶ ★★ Irazú Volcano. Start your day at the peak of the 3,378m-tall (11,083-ft.) Irazú Volcano, which has historically been one of Costa Rica's most active volcanoes. Don't worry, it has been relatively quiet of late—it last erupted with force on March 19, 1963, the day President John F. Kennedy arrived in Costa Rica for a visit.

I encourage you to get here as early in the day as possible, as clouds usually descend by noon. There's a good paved road all the way to

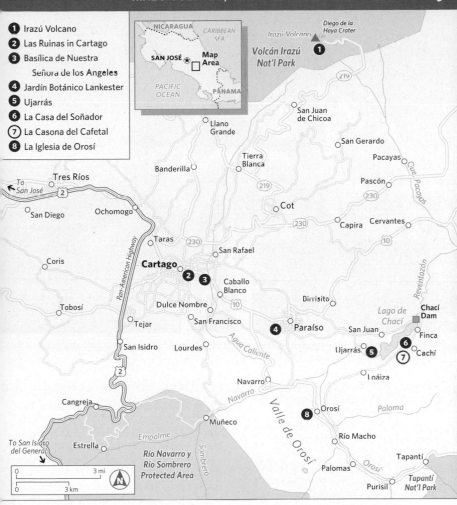

1 Irazú Volcano

2 Las Ruinas in Cartago

3 Basílica de Nuestra
    Señora de los Angeles

4 Jardín Botánico Lankester

5 Ujarrás

6 La Casa del Soñador

7 La Casona del Cafetal

8 La Iglesia de Orosí

the top, where a desolate expanse of gray sand nurtures few plants and the air smells of sulfur. The landscape here is often compared to that of the moon. If you're lucky and the day is very clear, you might be able to see both the Pacific Ocean and the Caribbean Sea. A short trail leads to the rim of the volcano's two craters, their walls a maze of eroded gullies feeding into the lake on the floor far below. A 2km (1.25-mile) trail loops around the rim of the Playa Hermosa Crater.

There's a visitor center with information on the volcano and the natural history of the area that's worth a look, as well as a restaurant. ⏱ 2 hr. Irazú de Cartago. ☎ 2551-9398. Admission $10. Daily 8:30am–3:30pm.

From the volcano, it's a quick taxi ride to downtown Cartago and the city's central park.

2 **Las Ruinas in Cartago.** In the center of the city of Cartago, you'll find Las Ruinas (The Ruins), the remains of a large church that was destroyed by an earthquake in 1910. Today the ruins sit at the heart of the pretty and peaceful park (known locally as Parque Central), which also features quiet paths, well-tended gardens, and plenty of benches. ⏱ 45 min. Btw. Avenidas 1 and 2 and Calles 1 and 4. Cartago.

3 ★ **Basílica de Nuestra Señora de los Angeles.** Dedicated to the patron saint of Costa Rica, the impressive Basilica of Our Lady of the Angels anchors the east side of the city. Within the walls of this Byzantine-style church is a shrine contain-

> *Cartago's Basílica de Nuestra Señora de los Angeles houses a shrine to La Negrita, a diminutive figure of the Virgin ascribed healing powers.*

ing the tiny carved figure of **La Negrita,** the Black Virgin (see "The Legend of La Negrita," p. 67), which is nearly lost amid its ornate altar.

The walls of the shrine are covered with a fascinating array of tiny silver objects left in thanks for cures credited to La Negrita by believers. Amid a plethora of diminutive silver arms and legs, there are also hearts, lungs, kidneys, eyes, torsos, breasts, and—oddly—guns, trucks, beds, and planes. Outside the church, vendors sell a selection of these trinkets, as well as little candle replicas of La Negrita. ⏲ 45 min. Calle 16 btw. Avenidas 2 and 4, Cartago. ☎ 2551-0465. Free admission. Daily 6:30am–5pm.

Give yourself 15 minutes to get from Cartago by taxi to Lankester Botanical Gardens.

❹ ★★ **Jardín Botánico Lankester.** This extensive botanical garden is best known for its collection of some 800 different orchid species. In case that's not enough of a draw, you'll also see a wealth of other local and regional flora as you wander the well-marked trails. The newest addition is a Japanese garden and pavilion, donated by the government of Japan. ⏲ Minimum 1 hr. Paraíso de Cartago. ☎ 2552-3247. www.jardin botanicolankester.org. Admission $5 adults, $3.50 children 6–16; children 5 and under free. Daily 8:30am–5:30pm.

The drive by taxi to Ujarrás should take 25 minutes.

❺ **Ujarrás.** This tiny village houses the ruins of Costa Rica's oldest church, built in 1693. Little remains beyond the worn brick and adobe facade, but the surrounding gardens are a lovely retreat and feature excellent views. ⏲ 30 min. Orosí Valley.

You're about 15 minutes by taxi from the next site.

Spending the Night in the Orosí Valley

If you'd prefer to stay outside San José for a night, check out the charming **Orosí Lodge** (☎ 2533-3578; www.orosilodge.com; $53–$85 double), which is located on the south side of the tiny town of Orosí, right next to some simple hot-spring pools.

> *Orchids at the Lankester Botanical Gardens.*

6 ★ **La Casa del Soñador.** "The House of the Dreamer" is the home and gallery of the late sculptor Macedonio Quesada. Quesada earned fame with his primitive sculptures of La Negrita (see "The Legend of La Negrita," right) and other religious and secular characters carved from coffee tree roots and trunks. You can see some of Macedonio's original work here, including his version of *The Last Supper* carved onto one of the walls of the main building. Today, his sons carry on the family tradition and there is a shop where you can choose from among their collection of small sculptures, carved religious icons, and ornate walking sticks. ⏱ 30 min. 1km (½ mile) south of Cachí. ☎ 2577-1186. Daily 9am–6pm.

⑦   🍽 ★ **La Casona del Cafetal.** Though geared toward tourists, this popular restaurant is an excellent option for lunch. The food is typical Tico fare, done very, very well. In addition to the long list of menu items, there's a massive buffet and several daily specials. When the weather's nice, grab a patio table with a view of Lake Cachí. Cachí. ☎ 2577-1414. www.lacasonadelcafetal.com. $$. Open 11am–6pm daily. AE, MC, V.

You'll need 15 minutes for the ride to Orosí.

8 **La Iglesia de Orosí.** The town of Orosí is home to yet another colonial church and convent worth a visit. Built in 1743, this is, in fact, the oldest functioning church in the country. The small **Museo de Arte Religioso** (Religious Art Museum) is located on the south side of the church and features a modest collection of religious artworks and relics. On display are 18th-century paintings, Bibles, and religious icons, as well as period pieces of clothing and furniture. It's worth a look, since such displays are relatively rare in Costa Rica. Along the main road near the town of Orosí, there are several scenic overlooks that offer a sense of this lush valleyscape; take the time to pull over and admire the views and snap a photo or two. ⏱ 30 min. The church and museum are on the west side of the soccer field in Orosí. ☎ 2533-3051. Museum admission $1. Tues–Sun 8:30am–5pm.

The Legend of La Negrita

The story goes that in 1635, an indigenous girl named Juana Pereira stumbled upon the statue of La Negrita, sitting atop a rock, while she was out gathering wood. Juana took the statue home, but the next morning it was missing. She went back to the rock, and there it was, just as it had been the day before. Juana brought the statue home three times, only to find it back on its rock the next morning. Finally, she took her find to a local priest, who put it in his church for safekeeping. The next morning the statue was again gone, only to be found sitting upon the same rock later that day. The priest decided that the strange occurrences were a sign that the Virgin wanted a temple or shrine to her built upon the spot. And so work was begun on what would eventually become today's impressive basilica.

Miraculous healing powers have been attributed to La Negrita, and over the years, a parade of pilgrims has come to the shrine seeking cures for their illnesses and difficulties. Each year on August 2, La Negrita's saint's day, tens of thousands of Costa Ricans and foreigners walk to Cartago from San José and elsewhere in the country in devotion to this powerful statue.

San José's Best Adventures

San José makes a great base for travelers looking for an adrenaline rush, offering a host of guided adventure tours within easy access of the city. These range from white-water rafting on class IV rapids to riding a mountain bike down the side of an active volcano. Most of these tours and activities take a full day and require some travel outside the city center. All are best undertaken as part of an organized tour.

> A rafting trip on the Río Pacuare, which runs from Costa Rica's mountainous interior down to the Caribbean, is within easy reach of Central Valley hotels.

Bungee Jumping

If you have always had the urge to jump off a bridge, this place is custom-made for you. **Tropical Bungee** (☎ 2248-2212; www.bungee.co.cr) has a bungee setup on a rickety old bridge over the wild Río Colorado. A leap off this 80m (262-ft.) bridge will run you $65, including transportation to and from your hotel in San José and a video of your jump. A second jump will cost you another $30.

Canopy Tours

The quickest and easiest way to experience a zip-line canopy tour while based in San José is to visit Parque La Sabana for the kids **Urban Canopy Tour** (p. 56, ❸).

If you've got some time, ★★ **Original Canopy Tours** (☎ 2291-4465; www.canopytour.com) have an operation about 1½ hours outside of San José. The tour here features 11 platforms, and at the end you have the choice of taking a

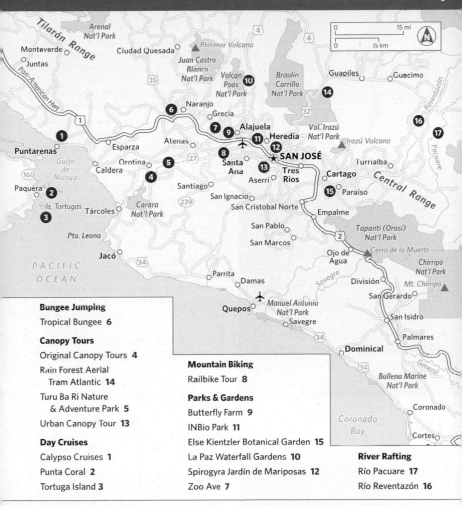

Bungee Jumping

Tropical Bungee 6

Canopy Tours

Original Canopy Tours 4

Rain Forest Aerial
   Tram Atlantic 14

Turu Ba Ri Nature
   & Adventure Park 5

Urban Canopy Tour 13

Day Cruises

Calypso Cruises 1

Punta Coral 2

Tortuga Island 3

Mountain Biking

Railbike Tour 8

Parks & Gardens

Butterfly Farm 9

INBio Park 11

Else Kientzler Botanical Garden 15

La Paz Waterfall Gardens 10

Spirogyra Jardín de Mariposas 12

Zoo Ave 7

River Rafting

Río Pacuare 17

Río Reventazón 16

cable to a ground station or doing an 18m (60-ft.) rappel down to finish off. The actual canopy tour takes around 2 hours. However, they also offer a full-day tour, including pickup and drop-off at any San José hotel, for $80 to $100 per person, depending upon group size.

Another option is the ★★ kids **Rain Forest Aerial Tram Atlantic.** Located on the Guápiles Highway (CR32) 40km (25 miles) northeast of San José, this property sits on a private reserve bordering **Braulio Carrillo National Park**. The modern, gondola-style tram takes visitors on a 90-minute ride through the treetops for a glimpse of the complex web of life that makes these rain forests unique. Additional attractions

include a butterfly garden, serpentarium, frog collection, zip-line canopy tour, well-groomed trails through the rain forest, and a restaurant. Admission, which includes the tram ride, a short guided hike, and unlimited access to the trail system, butterfly garden, and other attractions, is $55 for adults, $27.50 for children 2–11 and students with valid ID, and free for children 1 and under. It's an extra $15 for the zip-line canopy tour.

Finally, ★ kids **Turu Ba Ri Nature & Adventure Park** (☎ 2250-0705 or 2428-6070; www.turubari.com) aims to cover as many bases as possible. Located about 1½ hours outside San José, this park features a series of gardens,

> *The Urban Canopy Tour affords visitors a zip-line view of La Sabana Park in San José.*

All-Purpose Adventure Tour Operators

In addition to the specific operators recommended in this section, a number of local tour agencies offer a wide variety of active, adventure- or nature-related day tours out of San José. These include guided hikes and bird-watching tours as well as full-day outings offering one or more active pursuits. The most reputable of these operators include ★★ **Costa Rica Expeditions** (☎ 2257-0766; www.costaricaexpeditions.com), **Costa Rica Sun Tours** (☎ 2296-7757; www.crsuntours.com), and ★★ **Horizontes Nature Tours** (☎ 2222-2022; www.horizontes.com). For more information on active and adventure opportunities, see Chapter 12, "The Best Special Interest Trips," starting on p. 444.

trails, and exhibits set in a deep valley that you can reach by means of a gondola-style lift, by cable and zip-line canopy tour, or on horseback. Once in the valley, you can wander around the botanical gardens, orchid gardens, and butterfly gardens or grab a bite at the restaurant, which serves typical Costa Rican fare. You might want to take a turn on the massive climbing wall. The gondola ride here features enclosed cabin cars (with windows that open) and doesn't provide nearly the sense of intimacy or contact with the forest that the Rain Forest Aerial Tram does.

Basic admission is $60 for adults, $55 for students, and $40 for children; the various adventure and activity options cost extra; several combination package tours, with or without transportation and meals, are available.

Day Cruises

San José may be landlocked, but it's still possible to spend a day on the high seas while you're here. ★ **Calypso Cruises** (☎ 2256-2727; www.calypsocruises.com) offers two different full-day cruises on the beautiful Gulf of Nicoya. Both require an early departure from San José for the 2½-hour chartered bus ride to Puntarenas, where you board your vessel. A basic continental breakfast is served on the bus. The ★★ **Tortuga Island** cruise takes you to the white-sand beaches of Tortuga Island; you will have several hours to explore and enjoy this uninhabited island, during which you can swim or snorkel, lie on the beach, play volleyball, or try the small canopy tour.

The cruise to ★ **Punta Coral** and a private nature reserve is a more intimate journey, although the beach here is far less appealing. Still, you can hike the forest trails or take a kayak out to explore the gentle waters offshore. Calypso Tours will get you to either destination on a large motorized catamaran that has plenty of deck space. Rates are $119 per person, including round-trip transportation from San José, breakfast and lunch, and soft drinks.

Mountain Biking

The best mountain biking is found outside San José's city limits—on dirt roads, where you're not likely to be run off the highway by a semi or to run head-on into someone coming around a blind curve in the wrong lane. ★★ **Costa Rica Biking Adventure** (☎ 2225-6591; www.bikingincostarica.com) offers a variety of moun-

> *A day cruise in the Gulf of Nicoya can include snorkeling off Tortuga Island.*

tain-biking tours using high-end bikes and gear. Don't worry if you're not in great shape—several of their tours are entirely or primarily descents. Rates run between $95 and $150 per person for a full-day outing.

A unique option is a ★ **Railbike Tour** (☎ 8303-3300; www.railbike.com), which involves a mountain bike rigged to a contraption that fits over abandoned railroad tracks running through the countryside outside San José. The 1-day tour costs $75 and includes all equipment, plus a light breakfast and a full lunch.

Parks & Gardens

San José and the surrounding area are home to a wide variety of parks and gardens (both botanical and butterfly). In addition to those I've already mentioned—★★ kids **INBio Park** (p. 59, **8**), ★★ kids **La Paz Waterfall Gardens** (p. 58, **7**), and ★★★ kids **Zoo Ave** (p. 63, **4**)—there are a few others worthy of mention.

At any given time you're likely to see hundreds of Costa Rica's 1,000 butterfly species flying about at the ★★ kids **Butterfly Farm** (☎ 2438-0400; www.butterflyfarm.co.cr) in La Guácima de Alajuela. Keep a lookout for both the glittering blue morpho and a large butterfly that mimics the eyes of an owl. You'll see butterfly eggs, caterpillars, and pupae—there are

Finding a Good Group Tour

Before signing on for a tour of any sort, find out how many fellow travelers will be accompanying you, how much time you'll spend in transit and eating lunch, and how much time you'll have for the primary activity itself. I've heard complaints about tours that were rushed, that spent too much time on a bus or on secondary activities, or that had a cattle-car, assembly-line feel to them.

> *Outside the San José city limits, bikers can find quiet back roads to explore.*

cocoons trimmed in a shimmering gold color and others that mimic a snake's head to frighten away predators.

Admission includes a 2-hour guided tour, which teaches you everything you need to know about these fascinating creatures. The last guided tour of the day begins at 3pm. The farm also offers three daily bus tours that run from more than 20 different hotels in the San José area at a cost of $35 for adults, $30 for students, $20 for children 5 to 12, and free for kids 4 and under. General admission is $15 for adults, $10 for students, $7 for children 5 to 11, and free for children 4 and under. Whether you

come as part of a tour or on your own, reservations are recommended. The park is open daily from 8:45am to 3pm.

The ★ kids **Spirogyra Jardín de Mariposas** (☎ 2222-2937; www.infocostarica.com/butterfly) is much smaller than the Butterfly Farm, but it provides a good introduction to the life cycle of butterflies. This butterfly garden is a calm and quiet oasis quite close to the noise and bustle of downtown San José—it's 100m (1 block) east and 150m (1½ blocks) south of El Pueblo shopping center. You'll be given a self-guided-tour booklet when you arrive, and an 18-minute video show runs continuously throughout the

> At Else Kientzler Botanical Garden trails cut through plantings of 2,000 different kinds of flora.

day. In addition to the butterfly exhibit, there's a coffee shop, a simple restaurant, a gift store, and a small art gallery. Admission is $6 for adults, $3 for children 3 to 12 and students with a valid ID, and free for children 2 and under. It's open daily from 8am to 4pm (the cafe opens at 7:30am).

Kids and botanical gardens may not seem like such a great mix, but the amazing topiary labyrinth at the ★★ kids **Else Kientzler Botanical Garden** (☎ 2454-2070; www. elsekientzlergarden.com) is sure to grab their attention (and yours). Located on the grounds of an ornamental flower farm on the outskirts of the tourist town Sarchí, these are extensive, impressive, and lovingly laid out botanical gardens. Over 2.5km (1.5 miles) of trails run through a collection of more than 2,000 flora species. All of the plants are labeled with their Latin names, and there are further explanations around the grounds, given in both English and Spanish. There are plenty of scenic lookouts, gazebos, and shady benches. A children's play area features water games, jungle-gym setups, and a little, child-friendly zip-line canopy tour.

More than 40 percent of the gardens, which are open daily from 8am to 4pm, are wheelchair-accessible. Be advised that reservations are a must here. Admission is $14 for adults, $6 for students with valid ID and children 5 to 12; children 4 and under free. Guided tours, for groups of up to 15, cost an extra $15 per guide per hour.

River Rafting

If I had to choose just one day trip out of San José, it would be a white-water rafting excursion. Trips are run on both the ★★ **Pacuare** and **Reventazón** rivers. The Pacuare is a wild ride of class III and IV rapids that finishes up with a slow float through a stunning narrow canyon. The Reventazón trip is quite a bit mellower—class II and III rapids—and better suited for the timid and families. Both pass through a beautiful mix of rain forest and farmland. Some of the most reliable rafting companies are ★ **Nature Adventures** (p. 450), ★ **Exploradores Outdoors** (p. 450), and ★ **Ríos Tropicales** (p. 450). Rates run between $75 and $120 for a full-day trip; multiday trips are also available. For more information, see p. 397.

San José Shopping A to Z

Art Galleries

Arte Latino DOWNTOWN

This gallery carries original artwork in a variety of media, featuring predominantly Central American themes. Some of it is pretty gaudy in my opinion, but this is generally a good place to find Nicaraguan and Costa Rican "primitive" paintings. The gallery also has storefronts in the Multiplaza Mall in Escazú and at the Mall Cariari, which is on the Pan-American Highway about halfway between the airport and downtown, across from the Hotel Herradura. **Calle 5 and Avenida 1, San José. ☎ 2258-7083. AE, MC, V. Map p. 76.**

★★★ Galería 11–12 ESCAZÚ

This outstanding gallery deals mainly in high-end Costa Rican art, from neoclassical painters such as Teodorico Quirós to modern masters such as Francisco Amighetti and Paco Zúñiga to current stars Rafa Fernández, Rodolfo Stanley, Fernando Carballo, and Fabio Herrera. **Plaza** Itzkatzu, off Prospero Fernández Hwy., Escazú. **☎ 2288-1975. www.galeria11-12.com. AE, MC, V. Map p. 76.**

★★ Galería Jacobo Karpio DOWNTOWN

Here you'll find some of the more adventurous modern art for sale in Costa Rica—stop in to take a look even if you're not in the market to buy. Karpio represents a steady stable of prominent Mexican, Cuban, and Argentine artists, as well as some local talent. **Avenida 1, no. 1352, btw. Calles 13 and 15, San José. ☎ 2257-7963. MC, V. Map p. 76.**

★ Galería Kandinsky SAN PEDRO

Owned by the daughter of one of Costa Rica's most prominent modern painters, Rafa Fernández, this small space usually has a good selection of high-end contemporary Costa Rican paintings, be it from the house collection or a temporary exhibit. **Centro Comercial Calle Real, San Pedro. ☎ 2234-0478. AE, MC, V. Map p. 76.**

> *The market stalls at Plaza de la Democracia provide a good overview of the shopping scene in San José.*

> *The works of local artists and craftspeople form colorful displays at Boutique Annemarle.*

★★ TEOR/éTica DOWNTOWN

This tiny downtown spot is run by one of the more adventurous and internationally respected collectors in Costa Rica, Virginia Pérez-Ratton. You'll often find cutting-edge exhibits here. Calle 7 btw. Avenidas 9 and 11, San José. ☎ 2233-4881. www.teoretica.org. AE, MC, V. Map p. 76.

Bookstores

Librería Internacional DOWNTOWN

This is the closest thing Costa Rica has to a ubiquitous bookstore chain. Most of what you'll find here is in Spanish, but there is a reasonable selection of English-language contemporary fiction, nonfiction, and natural history texts to be found as well. Librería Internacional has several outlets around San José, including storefronts in most of the major modern malls. Avenida Central, ¾ block west of the Plaza de la Cultura, San José. ☎ 2257-2563. www.libreriainternacional.com. AE, MC, V. Map p. 76.

★★ Seventh Street Books DOWNTOWN

For English-language fiction, field guides, coffee-table books, general guidebooks, and natural history books, there's no better spot in San José. Calle 7 btw. Avenidas 1 and Central, San José. ☎ 2256-8251. AE, MC, V. Map p. 76.

Handicrafts

★★ Biesanz Woodworks ESCAZÚ

Barry Biesanz makes a wide range of high-quality items, including bowls, jewelry boxes, humidors, and some wonderful sets of wooden chopsticks. And you can feel good about buying here—Biesanz Woodworks is actively involved in local reforestation. Bello Horizonte, Escazú. ☎ 2289-4337. www.biesanz.com. AE, MC, V. Call for directions and off-hour appointments. Map p. 76.

Insider Art

Art lovers should check out Molly Keeler's excellent 1-day **Art Tour** (☎ 8359-5571 or 2288-0896; www.costaricaarttour.com), which includes scheduled visits to the studios and personal shops of prominent local artists working in a wide range of media.

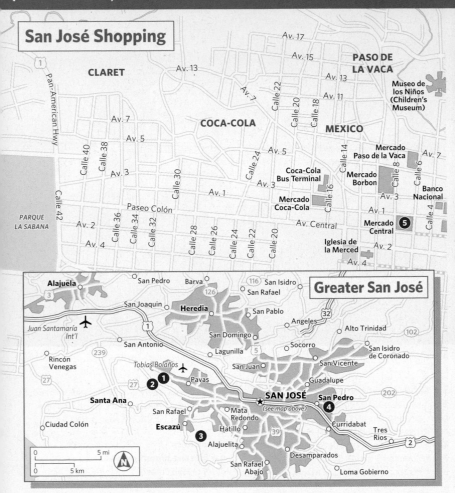

San José Shopping

Av. 17
Av. 15
PASO DE
LA VACA
CLARET
Av. 13
Av. 13
Pan-American Hwy
Av. 7
Museo de
los Niños
(Children's
Museum)
COCA-COLA
Av. 7
Av. 11
MEXICO
Av. 5
Av. 5
Calle 40
Calle 38
Calle 22
Calle 20
Calle 18
Mercado
Paso de la Vaca
Av. 7
Av. 3
Calle 30
Calle 24
Coca-Cola
Bus Terminal
Calle 14
Mercado
Borbon
Calle 8
Calle 6
Banco
Nacional
Paseo Colón
Av. 1
Av. 3
Av. 3
Calle 16
Mercado
Coca-Cola
PARQUE
LA SABANA
Calle 42
Av. 2
Calle 36
Calle 34
Calle 32
Calle 28
Calle 26
Calle 24
Calle 22
Calle 20
Av. Central
Mercado
Central   5
Calle 4
Av. 4
Av. 1
Av. 2
Iglesia de
la Merced
Av. 4

Greater San José

Alajuela
San Pedro
Barva
116   San Isidro
San Rafael
3
126
San Joaquin
San Rafael
Heredia
San Pablo
32
Juan Santamaría
Int'l
1
San Domingo
Angeles
Alto Trinidad
102
239
San Antonio
Lagunilla
5
Socorro
San Isidro
de Coronado
Rincón
Venegas
Tobias Bolaños
San Juan
San Vicente
27
2   1
Pavas
Guadalupe
202
Santa Ana
SAN JOSÉ
(see map above)
San Pedro
4
Ciudad Colón
San Rafael
Mata
Redondo
Curridabat
Escazú
3
Hatillo
39
Tres
Ríos
2
Alajuelita
Desamparados
5 mi
San Rafael
Abajo
Loma Gobierno
5 km

★★★ **Boutique Annemarie** BARRIO AMÓN
Occupying two floors at the Hotel Don Carlos
(p. 90), this shop has an amazing array of
wood products, leather goods, papier-mâché
figurines, paintings, books, cards, posters, and
jewelry. You'll see most of this stuff at the other
shops, but not in such quantities or in such a
relaxed and pressure-free environment. At the
Hotel Don Carlos, Calle 9 btw. Avenidas 7 and 9,
Barrio Amón, San José. ☎ 2221-6063. AE, MC, V.
Map p. 76.

★★★ **Boutique Kiosco** BARRIO AMÓN
This store features a range of original and one-
of-a-kind functional, wearable, and practical
items made by contemporary Costa Rican and

regional artists and designers. The offerings
change regularly, but you'll usually find a mix
of jewelry, handbags, shoes, clothing, dolls,
furniture, and knick-knacks, often made with
recycled or sustainable materials. Calle 7 and
Avenida 11, Barrio Amón, San José. ☎ 2258-1829.
AE, MC, V. Map p. 76.

★★ **Galería Namu** BARRIO AMÓN
Galería Namu offers some very high-quality arts
and crafts, specializing in truly high-end indigenous works, including excellent Boruca and
Huetar carved masks and "primitive" paintings.
It also carries a good selection of more modern
arts and crafts pieces, including the ceramic
work of Cecilia "Pefi" Figueres. The gallery orga-

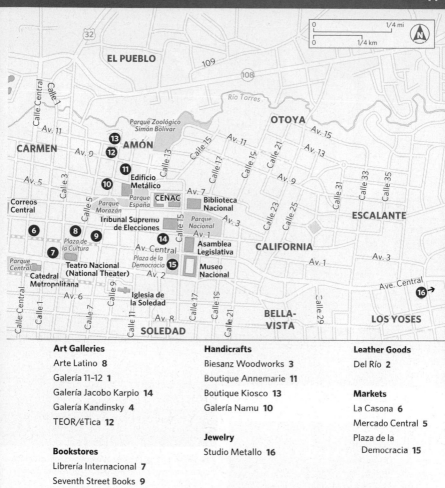

Art Galleries

Arte Latino **8**

Galería 11–12 **1**

Galería Jacobo Karpio **14**

Galería Kandinsky **4**

TEOR/éTica **12**

Bookstores

Librería Internacional **7**

Seventh Street Books **9**

Handicrafts

Biesanz Woodworks **3**

Boutique Annemarie **11**

Boutique Kiosco **13**

Galería Namu **10**

Jewelry

Studio Metallo **16**

Leather Goods

Del Río **2**

Markets

La Casona **6**

Mercado Central **5**

Plaza de la
Democracia **15**

nizes tours to the locales of various indigenous tribes and artisans. Avenida 7 btw. Calles 5 and 7, Barrio Amón, San José. ☎ 2256-3412. www.galeria namu.com. AE, MC, V. Map p. 76.

Jewelry

★★ Studio Metallo BARRIO ESCALANTE
The outgrowth of a jewelry-making school and studio, this shop has excellent handcrafted jewelry in a range of styles made from materials ranging from 18-karat white and yellow gold and pure silver to less exotic and expensive alloys. Some pieces incorporate gemstones, others focus on metalwork. 6½ blocks east of Iglesia Santa Teresita, Barrio Escalante, San José.

☎ 2281-3207. www.studiometallo.com. AE, MC, V. Map p. 76.

Leather Goods
Del Río ESCAZÚ
In general, Costa Rican leather products are not of the highest grade or quality, and prices are not particularly low. I'm happy to report that Del Río is an exception, producing its own line of functional and wearable leather goods. It has outlets in virtually every major shopping mall in the city. Multiplaza Mall, on CR27 just west of downtown. ☎ 2262-1415. www.delrioleathers.com. AE, MC, V. Map p. 76.

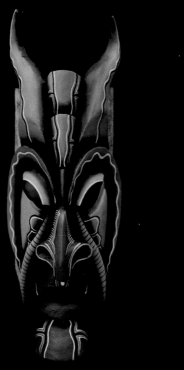

> *A Boruca mask at Galería Namu.*

The Inside Scoop

Serious shoppers should be prepared for disappointment. Aside from coffee and hand-made oxcarts, there isn't much that's distinctly Costa Rican. To compensate for its own relative lack of goods, Costa Rican souvenir shops do a brisk business selling crafts and clothes imported from Guatemala, Panama, and Ecuador.

While you're shopping, be mindful of what you're purchasing. International laws prohibit trade in endangered wildlife, so don't buy plants or animals, even if they're readily for sale. Also on the "do not buy" list: sea-turtle products (including jewelry); wild birds; lizard, snake, or cat skins; corals; or orchids (except those grown commercially). No matter how unique, beautiful, insignificant, or inexpensive such a product might seem, your purchase will directly contribute to the further destruction of these species.

> *Barry Biesanz, of Biesanz Woodworks, uncovers the shape inherent in the wood when he carves a bowl.*

Markets

★ **La Casona** DOWNTOWN

Just off Avenida Central, in the heart of downtown, La Casona is a 3-story warren of stalls. There's a lot of repetition among the offerings, and many of the goods for sale are imported from Guatemala, Ecuador, Panama, and even China. Still, it's a good place to find souvenirs. On a rainy day, this is a great alternative to the outdoor market on the Plaza de la Democracia (p. 79). Calle Central btw. Avenidas Central and 1, San José. ☎ 2222-7999. AE, MC, V. Map p. 76.

★★ **Mercado Central** DOWNTOWN

Although this tight maze of stalls is primarily a food market, inside you'll find all manner of vendors selling souvenirs, leather goods, musical

> *The works of some of Costa Rica's best fine artists make up the sophisticated display at Galería 11–12.*

instruments, and many other items. Be especially careful with your wallet, purse, and prominent jewelry, as skilled pickpockets frequent the area. All the streets surrounding the Mercado Central are jammed with produce vendors selling from small carts or loading and unloading trucks. It's always a hive of activity, with crowds of people jostling for space on the streets. Your best bet is to visit on Sunday or a weekday; Saturday is particularly busy. **Btw. Avenidas Central and 1 and Calles 6 and 8, San José. No phone. Map p. 76.**

★ Plaza de la Democracia DOWNTOWN

On the western edge of the Plaza de la Democracia, you'll find two long rows of outdoor stalls selling T-shirts, Guatemalan and Ecuadorian handicrafts and clothing, ceramic *ocarinas* (small musical wind instruments), and handmade jewelry. The atmosphere is more open than that of Mercado Central (above), which I find a bit claustrophobic. You might be able to bargain prices down a little, but bargaining is not a traditional part of the vendor culture here, and you'll have to work hard to save a few dollars. **Calle 13 btw. Avenidas Central and 2, San José. No phone. No credit cards. Map p. 76.**

> *Central American handiworks, including colorful and sturdy string hammocks, are in abundance at the stalls along the Plaza de la Democracia.*

Coffee: Stock Up

Coffee is the best shopping deal in Costa Rica. It is a truly local product that makes a great gift, and a kilo (about 2 lb.) sells for only about $6 to $12. Just be sure to buy whole beans, as Costa Rican grinds are often too fine for standard coffee filters. If you buy prepackaged coffee, it will be marked either *grano* (grain) or *grano entero* (whole bean). If you opt for ground varieties (*molido*), be sure the package is marked *puro;* otherwise, it will likely be mixed with a good amount of sugar, the way Ticos like it.

As for brands, **Café Britt** (p. 57, ④) is the big name in Costa Rican coffee. This operation has the largest export business in the country, and its blends, although high-priced, are very dependable. The brand is widely available at gift shops around the country and at souvenir concessions in both international airports. My favorite coffee beans, however, are those roasted and packaged in Manuel Antonio and Monteverde by local brands **Café Milagro** and **Café Monteverde,** respectively. If you visit either of these places, definitely pick some up.

In general, the best place to buy coffee is in a supermarket. Why pay more at a gift or specialty shop? You can also try **Café Trébol,** on Calle 8 between Avenidas Central and 1 (on the western side of the Mercado Central; ☎ 2221-8363), open Monday through Saturday from 7am to 6:30pm and Sunday from 8:30am to 12:30pm.

One good coffee-related gift is a coffee sock and stand. This is the most common mechanism for brewing coffee in Costa Rica. It consists of a simple circular stand made of wood or wire, which holds a sock. Put the ground beans in the sock, place a pot or cup below it, and pour boiling water through. You can find a basic coffee sock and stand at most supermarkets or the Mercado Central (p. 78); fancier crafts shops sell ones made of ceramic. Depending on its construction, a stand will cost you between $1.50 and $15; socks run around 30¢, so buy a few spares.

San José Restaurant Best Bets

Best Local Cuisine
Restaurante Nuestra Tierra $$ Avenida 2 and
Calle 15 (p. 86)

Best Fusion Fare
Park Café $$$$ 1 block north of Rostipollos,
Parque La Sabana Norte (p. 85)

Best Italian
Bacchus $$$$ Downtown Santa Ana, west of San
José (p. 82)

Best Fine Dining
Grano de Oro Restaurant $$$$ Calle 30, no.
251, btw. Avenidas 2 and 4 (p. 83)

Best for Vegetarians
Tin Jo $$$–$$$$ Calle 11 btw. Avenidas 6
and 8 (p. 86)

Best Costa Rican Caribbean Cuisine
Whappin' $$$ Barrio Escalante, 200m
(2 blocks) east of El Farolito (p. 86)

Most Romantic
La Cava Grill $$$ 1.5km (1 mile) south of Centro
Comercial Paco (p. 84)

Best View
Mirador Ram Luna $$$$ Aserri (p. 83)

Best Place for an Inexpensive Meal a la Tica
Soda Tapia $ Calle 42 and Avenida 2, across from
the Museo de Arte Costarricense (p. 86)

Best People-Watching
Cafeteria 1930 $$$ Gran Hotel Costa Rica
(p. 83)

> *Delicious food and creative presentation are the hallmarks of a meal at Bacchus.*

San José Restaurants A to Z

★★★ Bacchus SANTA ANA *ITALIAN*

My favorite Italian restaurant in San José (located in a western suburb), Bacchus is housed in a historic home that dates back more than a century. Nevertheless, it somehow seamlessly blends the old with the new in an elegant yet understated atmosphere. The best tables are on the covered back patio, where you can observe the open kitchen and wood-burning pizza oven in action—be sure to ask for one. The regularly changing menu features a range of antipasti, pastas, pizzas, and main dishes. Everything is perfectly prepared and beautifully presented. The desserts are also excellent, and the wine list is extensive and fairly priced. Downtown Santa Ana, west of San José. ☎ 2282-5441. Entrees $8–$24. AE, MC, V. Lunch and dinner Tues–Sun. Map p. 84.

> Café Mundo has patio, garden-side, and indoor seating, some amid stunningly colorful murals by a Costa Rican artist.

★ Café Mundo BARRIO AMÓN *INTERNATIONAL*

Almost always filled with a broad mix of San José's gay, bohemian, theater, arts, and university crowds, Café Mundo combines contemporary cuisine with an ambience of casual elegance. Wood tables and Art Deco wrought-iron chairs are spread spaciously around several rooms and open-air patios in this former colonial mansion. One room boasts colorful wall murals by Costa Rican artist Miguel Casafont. Appetizers include vegetable tempura and chicken satay alongside more traditional Tico standards such as *patacones* (fried plantain chips) and fried yucca. There's a long list of pastas and pizzas, as well as more substantial main courses, nightly specials, and delicious desserts. Calle 15 and Avenida 9, 200m (2 blocks) east and 100m (1 block) north of the INS building, San José. ☎ 2222-6190. Entrees $6–$14. AE, MC, V. Lunch and dinner Mon–Fri; dinner Sat. Map p. 84.

Dining with a View

There are myriad unique experiences to be had in Costa Rica, and one of my favorites is dining on the side of a volcano with the lights of San José shimmering below. These mountainside restaurants, called *miradores,* are a resourceful response to the city's topography. San José is set in a broad valley surrounded on all sides by volcanic mountains, and the people who live in these mountainous areas have no place to go but up—so they do, building roadside cafes vertically up the sides of the volcanoes.

The food at most of these establishments, while not bad, is not spectacular, but the views often are, particularly at night, when the wide valley sparkles in a wash of lights. The town of **Aserri,** 10km (6¼ miles) south of downtown San José, is the king of *miradores,* and ★★★ **Mirador Ram Luna** (☎ 2230-3060; $$$; AE, MC, V; Tues–Fri dinner, Sat–Sun lunch and dinner) is the king of Aserri. Grab a window seat and, if you've got the fortitude, order a plate of *chicharrones* (fried pork rinds). There's often live music. You can hire a cab for around $12 or take the Aserri bus at Avenida 6 between Calles Central and 2. Just ask the driver where to get off.

There are also *miradores* in the hills above Escazú and in San Ramón de Tres Ríos and Heredia. The most popular of these is ★★ **Le Monestère** (☎ 2289-4404; $$$$; AE, MV, V; Mon–Sat dinner), an elegant converted church serving somewhat overrated French and Belgian cuisine in a spectacular setting above the hills of Escazú. I recommend coming to Escazú for the less formal ★ **La Cava Grill** (☎ 2228-8515; $$$; AE, MV, V; Mon–Sat dinner), which features live music, mostly folk-pop but sometimes jazz, or, perhaps the better bet, ★ **Mirador Tiquicia** (☎ 2289-5839; $$$; AE, MC, V; Tues–Fri dinner, Sat–Sun lunch and dinner), which occupies several rooms in an old Costa Rican home and has live folkloric dance shows on Thursday.

> *A setting on the Plaza de la Cultura keeps things lively at Cafeteria 1930.*

★ **Cafeteria 1930** DOWNTOWN *INTERNATIONAL* With veranda and patio seating directly fronting the Plaza de la Cultura, this is one of the most atmospheric spots for a casual bite and some good people-watching. A wrought-iron railing, white columns, and arches create an old-world atmosphere. Stop by for breakfast and watch the plaza vendors set up shop. The menu covers a lot of ground, and the food is respectable, if unspectacular; but there isn't a better place downtown to bask in the tropical sunshine while you sip a beer or have a light lunch, and it's a great stop before or after a show at the ★★ **Teatro Nacional.** At the Gran Hotel Costa Rica, Avenida 2 btw. Calles 1 and 3, San José. ☎ 2221-4011. Sandwiches $6.50–$12, entrees $7–$32. AE, DC, MC, V. Daily 24 hr. Map p. 84.

★★★ **Grano de Oro Restaurant** PASEO COLÓN *INTERNATIONAL* At this restaurant set around the lovely interior courtyard of the superb Hotel Grano de Oro (p. 91), the atmosphere is intimate, relaxed, and refined all at the same time. Try the *lomito piemontes* (two medallions of filet mignon stuffed with Gorgonzola cheese in a sherry sauce) or the *pernil de conejo* (a rabbit thigh stuffed with mushroom pâté and served with a Dijon mustard sauce). Be sure to save room for the "Grano de Oro pie," a decadent dessert with layers of chocolate and coffee mousses and creams. Calle 30, no. 251, btw. Avenidas 2 and 4, 150m (1½ blocks) south of

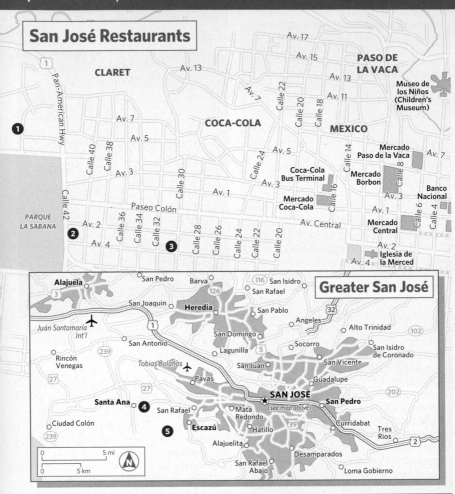

San José Restaurants

Paseo Colón, San José. ☎ 2255-3322. www.
hotelgranodeoro.com. Entrees $12–$44. AE, MC,
V. Breakfast, lunch, and dinner daily. Map p. 84.

★ **La Cava Grill** ESCAZÚ *COSTA RICAN/STEAK*
This is a cozy and warm spot located beneath
the popular yet overpriced and overrated Le
Monestère Restaurant. While the decor is much
less ornate, the service much less formal, and
the menu much less French, the view is just
as spectacular. Grab a window seat on a clear
night and enjoy the sparkle of the lights below.
More adventurous diners can try the *tepezquintle* (a large rodent, also called a *paca*), which
is actually quite tasty. There's live music and a
festive party going on most weekend nights in

the attached bar. 1.5km (1 mile) south of Centro
Comercial Paco, Escazú; follow signs to Le Mon-
estère. ☎ 2289-4404. Entrees $6–$22. AE, MC, V.
Dinner Mon–Sat. Map p. 84.

★★ **La Esquina de Buenos Aires** DOWNTOWN
ARGENTINE/STEAKHOUSE This restaurant
stands out for its jovial and authentic *porteño*
vibe and cuisine. The front doors were actually
brought in from Buenos Aires; the antique cash
register dates back to 1918. A host of different
cuts of meat are cooked simply on the grill or
served with a variety of sauces and presentations, and there's a selection of homemade
pastas, as well. Calle 11 and Avenida 4, San José.
☎ 2223-1909. www.laesquinadebuenosaires.com.

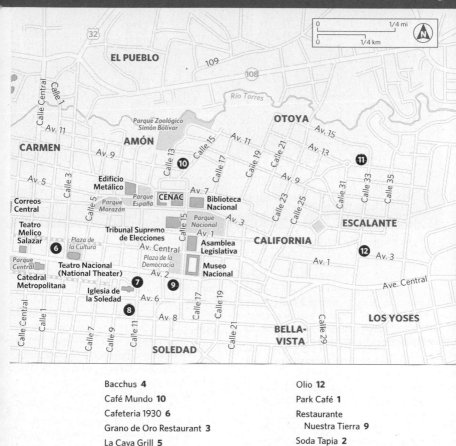

CARMEN

EL PUEBLO

AMÓN

Parque Zoológico
Simón Bolívar

Río Torres

OTOYA

ESCALANTE

CALIFORNIA

LOS YOSES

BELLA-
VISTA

SOLEDAD

Edificio
Metálico

Correos
Central

Teatro
Melico
Salazar

Parque
Central

Catedral
Metropolitana

Parque
España

Parque
Morazán

CENAC

Plaza de
la Cultura

Teatro Nacional
(National Theater)

Iglesia de
la Soledad

Tribunal Supremo
de Elecciones

Plaza de la
Democracia

Biblioteca
Nacional

Parque
Nacional

Asamblea
Legislativa

Museo
Nacional

Bacchus **4**

Café Mundo **10**

Cafeteria 1930 **6**

Grano de Oro Restaurant **3**

La Cava Grill **5**

La Esquina de
Buenos Aires **7**

Olio **12**

Park Café **1**

Restaurante
Nuestra Tierra **9**

Soda Tapia **2**

Tin Jo **8**

Whappin' **11**

Entrees $8–$22. AE, MC, V. Lunch and dinner daily. Map p. 84.

★ **Olio** BARRIO CALIFORNIA *MEDITERRANEAN*
Exposed brick walls, dark wood wainscoting, and stained-glass lamps imbue this place with character and romance. The extensive tapas menu features traditional Spanish fare, as well as bruschetta, antipasti, and a Greek meze plate. For a main dish, I recommend the chicken Vesuvio, which is marinated first in a balsamic vinegar reduction and finished with a creamy herb sauce; or the *arrollado siciliano,* a thin filet of steak rolled around spinach, sun-dried tomatoes, and mozzarella cheese and topped with a tomato sauce. The midsize wine

list features reasonably priced wines from Italy, France, Spain, Germany, Chile, Greece, and even Bulgaria. Barrio California, 200m (2 blocks) north of Bagelman's. ☎ 2281-0541. Entrees $5–$12. AE, DC, MC, V. Lunch and dinner Mon–Fri, dinner Sat. Map p. 84.

★★★ **Park Café** LA SABANA *FUSION*
Having opened and run a Michelin two-star restaurant in London and another one-star joint in Cannes, Richard Neat is now turning out his fusion cuisine in an intimate space spread around the interior patio courtyard of a stately old downtown mansion, which also doubles as an antiques and imported furniture store. Presentations are artfully done and often served

> *La Esquina de Buenos Aires truly is a "corner" (esquina) of Argentina in San José, serving up the country's famous beefsteaks.*

in such a way as to encourage sharing. The well-thought-out and fairly priced wine list is a perfect complement to the cuisine. 100m (1 block) north of Rostipollos, Parque La Sabana Norte, San José. ☎ 2290-6324. Entrees $13–$22. V. Lunch and dinner Tues–Sat. Map p. 84.

kids Restaurante Nuestra Tierra DOWNTOWN *COSTA RICAN* Sure it's touristy, but if you want a *casado* (a sort of blue-plate special) or some *gallo pinto* (a mix of rice and beans), this is the place to come any time of day or night. The decor seeks to replicate a humble country ranch, with heavy wooden tables, chairs and paneling, and strings of fresh onions and bunches of bananas hanging from the rafters and columns. Service is friendly and efficient; the waitstaff are in typical *campesino* dress and periodically break out into traditional folkloric dances. Avenida 2 and Calle 15, San José. ☎ 2258-6500. Entrees $4–$8. MC, V. Daily 24 hrs. Map p. 84.

kids Soda Tapia PASEO COLÓN *COSTA RICAN* The food is dependable and inexpensive at this very popular local joint. There's seating both inside the brightly lit dining room and on the sidewalk patio fronting the parking area. Dour but efficient waitstaff take the order you mark down on your combination menu/bill. There is another site in a small strip mall in Santa Ana (☎ 2203-7174). Calle 42 and Avenida 2, across from the Museo de Arte Costarricense, San José. ☎ 2222-6734. Sandwiches $2–$4, entrees $4.50–$9. MC, V. Breakfast, lunch, and dinner daily. Map p. 84.

★★★ **kids Tin Jo** DOWNTOWN *CHINESE/PAN-ASIAN* This downtown standout features a wide and varied menu, with an assortment of Cantonese and Szechuan staples, as well as a range of Thai, Japanese, and Malaysian dishes, and even some Indian food. Dishes not to miss include the salt-and-pepper shrimp, beef teriyaki, and Thai curries. For dessert, try the sticky rice with mango, or the passion-fruit tart. The decor features artwork and textiles from across Asia, and there are real tablecloths and cloth napkins. Tin Jo is also a great option for vegetarians and vegans. Calle 11 btw. Avenidas 6 and 8, San José. ☎ 2221-7605 or 2257-3622. www.tinjo.com. Entrees $6–$15. AE, MC, V. Lunch and dinner daily. Map p. 84.

★★ **Whappin'** BARRIO ESCALANTE *COSTA RICAN/CARIBBEAN* You don't have to go to Limón or Cahuita to get good home-cooked Caribbean food. In addition to *rondon,* a coconut milk–based stew or soup, you can also get the classic rice and beans cooked in coconut milk, as well as a range of fish and chicken dishes from the coastal region. I like the whole red snapper covered in a spicy sauce of sautéed onions. Everything is very simple, and prices are quite reasonable. Barrio Escalante, 200m (2 blocks) east of El Farolito, San José. ☎ 2283-1480. Entrees $6.50–$14. AE, MC, V. Lunch and dinner Mon–Sat. Map p. 84.

San José Hotel Best Bets

Best Restored Colonial-Era Mansion
Hotel Britannia $$$ Calle 3 and Avenida 11
(p. 90)

Best Art & Architectural Touches
Finca Rosa Blanca Coffee Plantation & Inn
$$$$$ Santa Bárbara de Heredia (p. 89)

Best Former President's Mansion
Hotel Don Carlos $$ 779 Calle 9 btw. Avenidas
7 and 9 (p. 90)

Best Budget Choice
Hotel Aranjuez $ Calle 19 btw. Avenidas 11
and 13 (p. 89)

Best for Families
Peace Lodge $$$$$ Heredia (p. 92)

Best In-House Restaurant
Hotel Grano de Oro $$$ Calle 30, no. 251,
btw. Avenidas 2 and 4 (p. 91)

Best In-House Spa
Xandari Resort & Spa $$$$ Alajuela (p. 92)

**Best Option for Those Driving to
Guanacaste, Monteverde, or Arenal**
Vista del Valle Plantation Inn $$$ Alajuela
(p. 92)

> *The whimsical architecture of the charmingly turreted main building at Finca Rosa Blanca Coffee Plantation
  & Inn extends to the accommodations inside.*

San José Hotels A to Z

★★★ Alta Hotel SANTA ANA
This boutique hotel is infused with old-world charm. Curves and high arches abound. I especially like the winding interior alleyway that snakes down through the hotel from the reception area. Most rooms have a private balcony with wonderful views of the Central Valley; others have pleasant garden patios. Alto de las Palomas, old road to Santa Ana. ☎ 888/388-2582 in U.S. and Canada, or 2282-4160 in Costa Rica. www.thealtahotel.com. 23 units. $149 double; $820 penthouse. Rates include continental breakfast and round-trip airport transfers. AE, DC, MC, V. Map p. 89.

★★ Casa de las Tías ESCAZÚ
This old Victorian–style home is brimming with local character. The rooms are homey and simply decorated in a sort of Costa Rican country motif. The hotel has a wonderful covered veranda for sitting and admiring the well-tended gardens, as well as a TV room and common areas inside the house. The owners live on-site and are extremely helpful and friendly—you really get the sense of staying in someone's home here. 100m (1 block) south and 150m (1½ blocks) east of El Cruce de San Rafael de Escazú. ☎ 2289-5517. www.hotels.co.cr/casatias.html. 5 units. $82–$92 double. Rates include breakfast. AE, MC, V. Map p. 89.

★ kids Clarion Amón Plaza Hotel BARRIO AMÓN
There's nothing distinctive about the property or rooms here; however, in terms of service, location, and price, this hotel gets my nod as the best downtown business-class hotel. The rooms are good-size, well kept, and come with plenty of amenities, and you are close to all the downtown action. Avenida 11 and Calle 3 , Barrio Amón, San José. ☎ 877/424-6423 in U.S. and Canada, or 2523-4600 in Costa Rica. www.hotelamonplaza.com. 87 units. $130–$160 double; $220 suite. AE, DC, MC, V. Map p. 90.

> Set in the hills north of San José, Xandari has wonderful views of the surrounding countryside.

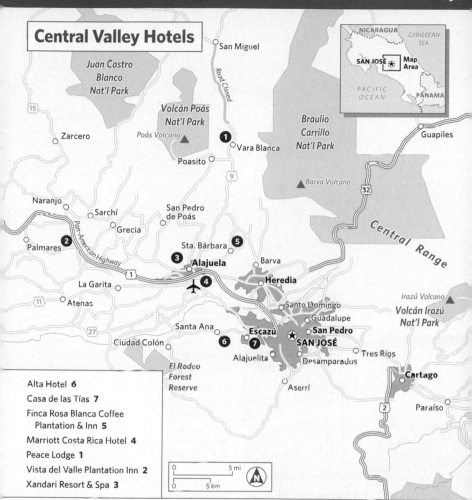

Central Valley Hotels

Alta Hotel **6**

Casa de las Tías **7**

Finca Rosa Blanca Coffee
    Plantation & Inn **5**

Marriott Costa Rica Hotel **4**

Peace Lodge **1**

Vista del Valle Plantation Inn **2**

Xandari Resort & Spa **3**

★★★ **Finca Rosa Blanca Coffee Plantation & Inn** HEREDIA Finca Rosa Blanca is an eclectic architectural gem set amid the lush, green hillsides of a coffee plantation. Throughout, the glow of polished hardwood blends with white stucco walls and brightly painted murals. The restaurant and spa here are top-notch, and the owners have a real and noticeable dedication to sustainable practices. Santa Bárbara de Heredia. ☎ 2269-9392. www.fincarosablanca.com. 13 units. $290–$450 double. Rates include breakfast. AE, MC, V. Map p. 89.

Gran Hotel Costa Rica DOWNTOWN

The Gran Hotel Costa Rica has arguably the best location of any downtown hotel (bordering the Teatro Nacional and the Plaza de la Cultura), and recent remodeling has brought the rooms and amenities almost up to snuff. But the rooms still feel a bit Spartan, and some will find the street noise a problem. Avenida 2 btw. Calles 1 and 3, San José. ☎ 800/949-0592 in U.S. and Canada, or 2221-4000 in Costa Rica. www.grand hotelcostarica.com. 104 units. $85–$107 double; $149–$185 suite. Rates include breakfast buffet. AE, DC, MC, V. Map p. 90.

★★ **kids Hotel Aranjuez** BARRIO OTOYA

This is the best and most popular budget option close to downtown. The rooms are simple and clean; they vary greatly in size, and some are a little dark, so ask when reserving, or try to see a

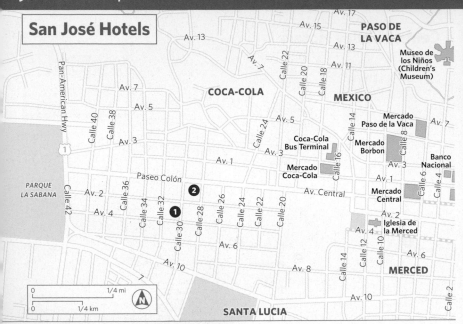

San José Hotels

units, 6 with shared bathroom. $26 double with shared bath; $40–$47 double with private bath. Rates include breakfast buffet. V. Map p. 90.

★★ Hotel Britannia BARRIO AMÓN

Built in 1910, this large, converted mansion with a wraparound veranda is one of the most attractive buildings in the core of downtown San José. Tile floors, stained-glass windows, and reproduction Victorian decor all help set a tone of tropical opulence. Although the street-side rooms have double glass, light sleepers will still want to avoid them; the quietest rooms are toward the back of the addition. **Calle 3 and Avenida 11, Barrio Amón, San José.** ☎ 800/263-2618 in U.S. and Canada, or 2223-6667 in Costa Rica. Fax 2223-6411. www. hotelbritanniacostarica.com. 24 units. $89–$105 double; $117 junior suite. AE, MC, V. Map p. 90.

★★ Hotel Don Carlos BARRIO AMÓN

Located in an old residential neighborhood only blocks from the business district, the Don Carlos was a former president's mansion. Inside you'll find a slew of arts and crafts works and archaeological reproductions, as well as orchids, ferns, palms, and parrots. The rooms vary greatly in size, so be specific when you reserve, or ask if it's possible to see a few when you check in. **779 Calle 9 btw. Avenidas 7 and 9, Barrio Amón, San José.** ☎ 2221-6707. www.doncarlos

> The Gran Hotel Costa Rica is a bastion of elegance on the Plaza de la Cultura, steps from some of San José's top attractions.

few when you arrive. In addition to the convivial hostel-like vibe, you'll appreciate the lush, shady gardens; the hanging orchids, bromeliads, and ferns decorating the hallways and nooks; and the numerous open lounge areas. **Calle 19 btw. Avenidas 11 and 13, Barrio Otoya, San José.** ☎ 877/898-8663 in U.S. and Canada, or 2256-1825 in Costa Rica. www.hotelaranjuez.com. 36

hotel.com. 33 units. $80–$90 double. Rates include continental breakfast. AE, MC, V. Map p. 90.

★★ Hotel Grano de Oro PASEO COLÓN

On a quiet side street off Paseo Colón, the Grano de Oro offers a range of room types to fit a range of budgets and tastes. I favor the patio rooms, which have French doors opening onto private patios. Even if you don't grab one of the suites, which come with a private Jacuzzi, you still have access to the hotel's two rooftop Jacuzzis. The hotel owners support a noble shelter for young, unwed mothers, Casa Luz. Feel free to inquire as to how you can help. Calle 30, no. 251, btw. Avenidas 2 and 4, 150m (1½ blocks) south of Paseo Colón, San José. ☎ 2255-3322. www.hotelgranodeoro.com. 40 units. $115–$165 double; $210–$305 suite. AE, MC, V. Map p. 90.

★★★ Hôtel Le Bergerac LOS YOSES

The charming and sophisticated Hôtel Le Bergerac has ingratiated itself over the years with business travelers and members of various diplomatic missions. Almost all the rooms are fairly large, and each is a little different. I prefer those with private patio gardens. In the evenings candlelight and classical music set a relaxing and romantic mood. The hotel's long-standing Ile de France restaurant serves gourmet French and continental dinners for guests and the public

by reservation only. Calle 35, no. 50, Los Yoses. ☎ 2234-7850. www.bergerachotel.com. 26 units. $90–$145 double. Rates include full breakfast. AE, DC, MC, V. Map p. 90.

★ Hotel Rosa del Paseo PASEO COLÓN

This hotel is housed in a beautiful stucco home right on busy Paseo Colón. However, the rooms are all located away from the street and are pretty well insulated against the noise. Try to grab one of the rooms on the second floor, which feature wooden floors and front doors that open onto the open-air courtyard. The master suite comes with its own balcony and Jacuzzi. Beautiful details are spread throughout the hotel, including transoms, stucco door frames, and hardwood floors. 2862 Paseo Colón btw. Calles 28 and 30, San José. ☎ 2257-3225. www.rosadelpaseo.com. 19 units. $85 double; $100–$140 suite. Rates include continental breakfast. AE, DC, MC, V. Map p. 90.

★ Hotel Santo Tomás DOWNTOWN

Built more than 100 years ago by a coffee baron, the house has been lovingly restored. Throughout the hotel you'll enjoy the deep, dark tones of well-aged and well-worked wood. The rooms vary in size, but most are fairly spacious and have a small table and chairs. There's a small outdoor pool with a Jacuzzi above it; the two are solar-heated and connected by a tiny water slide. This

> *The intimate Alta Hotel has an appealing old-world gentility.*

neighborhood is a little bit sketchy after dark, so you'd be advised to take a taxi to and from the hotel for any evening excursions. **Avenida 7 btw. Calles 3 and 5, San José. ☎ 877/446-0658 in U.S. and Canada, or 2255-0448 in Costa Rica. www. hotelsantotomas.com. 20 units. $80–$110 double. Rates include breakfast buffet. MC, V. Map p. 90.**

★★★ Marriott Costa Rica Hotel AIRPORT

For my money, the Marriott is the best large luxury resort hotel in the San José metro area. The hotel is designed in a mixed colonial style, with hand-painted Mexican tiles, antique red-clay roof tiles, weathered columns, and heavy wooden doors, lintels, and trim. All rooms are plush and well appointed; the bathrooms are up to par, although they seem slightly small for the price. **San Antonio de Belén. ☎ 888/236-2427 in U.S. and Canada, or 2298-0844 in Costa Rica. www.marriott.com. 299 units. $260 double; $310 executive level; $450 master suite; $1,000 presidential suite. AE, DC, MC, V. Map p. 89.**

★★★ Peace Lodge VARA BLANCA DE HEREDIA

Peace Lodge is part of the popular La Paz Wa-

terfall Gardens. The rooms are impressive, all of them featuring sparkling wood floors, handcrafted four-poster beds, beautiful stone fireplaces, intricately sculpted steel light fixtures, and a host of other creative details—along with a private balcony fitted with a mosaic-tiled Jacuzzi. The deluxe bathrooms come with a second oversize Jacuzzi set under a skylight in the middle of an immense room that features a full interior wall planted with ferns, orchids, and bromeliads and fed by a functioning waterfall system. **6km (3¾ miles) north of Vara Blanca on the road to San Miguel. ☎ 954/727-3997 in U.S., or 2482-2720 or 2225-0643 in Costa Rica. www.waterfallgardens. com. 17 units. $245–$305 double; $395 villa. Rates include breakfast and admission to La Paz Waterfall Gardens. AE, MC, V. Map p. 89.**

★★ Vista del Valle Plantation Inn ROSARIO DE NARANJO

Individual and duplex villas are spread around this wonderfully landscaped property. The architecture, from the open and airy villas to the comfortable wraparound decks, has a strong Japanese influence. My favorite rooms are the Mona Lisa and Ilan-Ilan suites, octagonal affairs set on the edge of the bluff with great views and private outdoor showers. The hotel is 20 minutes north of the Juan Santamaría International Airport; staying here can cut as much as an hour off your travel time if you're heading out to the Pacific coast beaches, Arenal Volcano, or the Monteverde Cloud Forest. **Rosario de Naranjo, Alajuela. ☎ 2450-0800 or 2451-1165. www.vistadelvalle.com. 11 units. $100 double; $150–$175 villa. Rates include full breakfast. AE, MC, V. Map p. 89.**

★★ kids Xandari Resort & Spa ALAJUELA

Set on a hilltop above Alajuela, Xandari commands wonderful views of the surrounding coffee farms and the Central Valley below. The owners are artists, and their original works and innovative design touches abound. The villas are huge private affairs with high curved ceilings, stained-glass windows, living rooms with rattan sofas and chairs, and small kitchenettes. The hotel grounds contain several miles of trails that pass by at least five jungle waterfalls, as well as lush gardens and fruit orchards. **Alajuela. ☎ 866/363-3212 in U.S. and Canada, or 2443-2020 in Costa Rica. www. xandari.com. 22 villas. $230–$315 double. Rates include continental breakfast. AE, DC, MC, V. Map p. 89.**

San José Nightlife & Entertainment A to Z

Bars, Clubs & Lounges
★ Café Expresivo BARRIO ESCALANTE
Laid-back and funky, this cafe, restaurant, and gallery often features DJs spinning dance beats. When there's no act, it's a mellow place to have a drink and good conversation. **4 blocks east of the Santa Teresita church, Barrio Escalante, San José. ☎ 2224-1202. Map p. 94.**

Chelles DOWNTOWN
This downtown bar and restaurant makes up for its lack of ambience with plenty of tradition and a diverse and colorful clientele. The lights are bright, the chairs surround simple Formica-topped card tables, and mirrors adorn most of the walls. Simple sandwiches and meals are served, and pretty good *bocas* (bar snacks) come with the drinks. **Avenida Central and Calle 9, San José. ☎ 2221-1369. Map p. 94.**

> *Teatro Nacional hosts the National Symphony Orchestra as well as international performances.*

★★ El Cuartel de la Boca del Monte BARRIO CALIFORNIA
This place began life as an artist-and-bohemian hangout. Today it attracts foreign exchange students, visitors, and a broad cross section of San José's youth, so there's always a diverse mix. One corner has been separated into a more bohemian-style bar or pub called La Esquina, or "The Corner." **Avenida 1 btw. Calles 21 and 23 (50m/½ block west of the Cine Magaly), San José. ☎ 2221-0327. Map p. 94.**

Snack Time

The best part of the bar scene in San José is the *boca*, the equivalent of a *tapa* in Spain, a dish of snacks that arrives at your table when you order a drink. Although this is a dying tradition, you will still find *bocas* served in the older, more traditional drinking establishments. In most, the *bocas* are free, but in some, where the dishes are more sophisticated, you'll have to pay for these treats.

San José Nightlife & Entertainment

Greater San José

★★ Gaira ESCAZÚ

Chic and contemporary, this enormous club has an open dance space, two floors of seating, impressive lighting and design effects, and a creative drink and food menu. Next to the Ferreteria EPA, Escazú. ☎ 2288-2367. www.clubgaira.com. Wed–Sat. Map p. 94.

★ Key Largo DOWNTOWN

Prostitution is legal in Costa Rica, and this meticulously restored downtown mansion is one of San José's top pickup spots. But don't let that put you off—the scene here isn't sleazy. Housed in a beautiful old building just off Parque Morazán in the heart of downtown, Key Largo is worth a visit to take in the mansion, even if you

don't want to linger. Calle 7 btw. Avenidas 1 and 3, San José. ☎ 2221-0277. Map p. 94.

★ Mosaikos SAN PEDRO

The entrance to this happening spot is a long, narrow corridor/bar that is generally packed solid. A larger room in the back has another bar, some tables, and some funky art. The crowd here is young and can get quite rowdy. They often have live DJs playing a mix of house, techno, and trance-style dance music, although you're also just as likely to hear reggae, ska, or hip-hop tunes blasting. 200m (2 blocks) east and 150m (1½ blocks) north of the church in San Pedro. ☎ 2280-9541. Map p. 94.

Bars, Clubs & Lounges

Café Expresivo **11**

Chelles **7**

El Cuartel de la Boca del Monte **8**

Gaira **15**

Key Largo **6**

Mosaikos **16**

Terra U **17**

Utopia **13**

Vértigo **1**

Gay & Lesbian Clubs

Club Oh **3**

La Avispa **4**

Latin Dance Clubs & Discos

Castro's **2**

El Tobogán **12**

Live Music Clubs

El Observatorio **9**

Jazz Café **18**

Jazz Café Escazú **14**

Latino Rock Café **10**

Theaters & Performing Arts

Teatro Nacional **5**

★ Terra U SAN PEDRO

Set on a busy corner in the heart of the university district, this joint is one of the most popular bars in the area. Part of this is due to the inviting open-air patio and mezzanine areas, which provide a nice alternative to the all-too-common smoke-filled rooms found at most other trendy spots. 200m (2 blocks) east and 150m (1½ blocks) north of the church in San Pedro. ☎ 2225-4261. www.terrau.com. Map p. 94.

★ Utopia SANTA ANA/BELÉN

In a strip mall on the road between the western suburbs of Santa Ana and San Antonio de Belén, this club is one of the hippest places to see and be seen. In fact, bouncers out front often screen the incoming clientele, admitting only the prettiest and best connected. Music is loud and modern, and the decor is minimal. Radial San Antonio de Belén–Santa Ana. ☎ 2221-6655. Map p. 94.

Vértigo PASEO COLÓN

Tucked inside a nondescript office building and commercial center on Paseo Colón, this club remains one of the more popular places for rave-style late-night dancing and partying. The dance floor is huge, the ceilings are high, and electronic music rules the roost. If you want quiet conversation, this is not the place for it. Edificio Colón, Paseo Colón, San José. ☎ 2257-8424. www.vertigocr.com. Map p. 94.

> *The many bars and restaurants in the university district in San Pedro cater to a lively young crowd.*

Gay & Lesbian Clubs

★★ Club Oh DOWNTOWN

This place is gay-, lesbian-, and straight-friendly, with two large dance floors and loud dance music pumping. The music tends toward techno and electronic mixes, and the club features midnight drag shows. It's one of the best dance clubs in town. Calle 2 btw. Avenidas 14 and 16, San José. ☎ 2248-1500. Map p. 94.

★ La Avispa DOWNTOWN

This is San José's longest-running gay and lesbian bar and club, and it's still going strong. The music here is a mix of contemporary dance tracks and more traditional Latin rhythms. Calle 1 btw. Avenidas 8 and 10, San José. ☎ 2223-5343. www.laavispa.co.cr. Map p. 94.

Latin Dance Clubs & Discos

★★ Castro's BARRIO MEXICO

This is a classic Costa Rican dance club. The music varies throughout the night, from salsa and merengue to reggaeton and occasionally electronic trance. There are several rooms and various environments, including some intimate and quiet corners, spread over a couple of floors. Avenida 13 and Calle 22, Barrio Mexico, San José. ☎ 2256-8789. Map p. 94.

★★★ El Tobogán NORTH OF DOWNTOWN

The dance floor in this place is about the size of a football field, yet it still fills up. This is a place where Ticos come with their loved ones and dance partners. The music is a mix of classic Latin dance rhythms—salsa, cumbia, and merengue. It's open only on the weekends, but there's always a live band here, and sometimes it's very good. 200m (2 blocks) north and 100m (1 block) east of La República main office, off Guápiles Hwy., San José. ☎ 2257-3396. Map p. 94.

What's Goin' On?

To find out what's going on in San José while you're in town, pick up a copy of the *Tico Times* (English) or *La Nación* (Spanish). The former is a good place to find out where local expatriates are hanging out; the latter's "Viva" and "Tiempo Libre" sections have extensive listings of discos, movie theaters, and live music.

> *Despite the modern signage, Key Largo is housed in a beautifully restored old mansion, worth a look even if you aren't into the bar scene.*

Live Music Clubs

★★ El Observatorio BARRIO CALIFORNIA

Owned by a local filmmaker, this club has a decor that includes a heavy dose of cinema motifs. The space is large, with high ceilings and one of the best (perhaps the only) smoke-extraction systems of any popular bar. That means the air is bearable, even though most of the clientele is chain-smoking. There's often live music or movie screenings and a decent menu of appetizers and main dishes drawn from various world cuisines. Calle 23 btw. Avenidas Central and 1, San José. ☎ 2223-0725. Map p. 94.

★★★ Jazz Café SAN PEDRO

The Jazz Café is consistently the best place to find live music and one of the more happening bars in San Pedro. Wrought-iron chairs, sculpted busts of famous jazz artists, and creative lighting give the place ambience. There's live music here most nights. The café has opened a sister **★★ Jazz Café Escazú** (☎ 2288-4740), located just off the Prospero Fernández Hwy., which leads between Escazú and Santa Ana, on the western end of town. The original Jazz Café is next to the Banco Popular on Avenida Central, San Pedro. ☎ 2253-8933. www.jazzcafecostarica.com. Map p. 94.

★ Latino Rock Café BARRIO CALIFORNIA

This place has a large stage, good sight lines, and a steady line-up of bands—it is *the* place to come for rock. The music ranges from original pop-rock, to head-banging metal. Avenida Central, Barrio California, San José. ☎ 2222-4719. www.latinorockcafe.com. Map p. 94.

Theaters & Performing Arts Venues

★★ Teatro Nacional DOWNTOWN

Built in the 1890s, thanks to the largesse of local coffee barons, this architectural jewel features Art Nouveau chandeliers, wall and ceiling murals, and marble floors throughout the lobby. In addition to being the home of the National Symphony Orchestra, the National Theater hosts a range of concerts, dance performances, and theater pieces throughout the year. Call or check the website to see what's playing— prices range from $5 to $50, depending on the performance. Avenida 2 btw. Calles 3 and 5, San José. ☎ 2221-5341. www. teatronacional.go.cr. Map p. 94.

San José Fast Facts

American Express

American Express Travel Services is represented in Costa Rica by **ASV Olympia,** Oficentro La Sabana, Sabana Sur, San José (☎ 2242-8585; www.asvolympia.com), which can issue traveler's checks and replacement cards and provide other standard services. To report lost or stolen Amex traveler's checks within Costa Rica, call the number above or ☎ 2295-9000, or call collect to ☎ 336/393-1111 in the United States.

ATMs

Automated-teller (*cajero automatico*) machines are all over San José at banks, modern malls, most large supermarkets, and many gas stations, convenience shops, and other strategic spots. To find a bank, look for signs saying *banco*.

Dentists & Doctors

Clínica Bíblica, Avenida 14 between Calles Central and 1 (☎ 2522-1000; www.clinicabiblica. com), is conveniently located close to downtown and has several English-speaking doctors. **Hospital CIMA** (☎ 2208-1000; www.hospitalsanjose. net) is located in Escazú on the Próspero Fernández Hwy., which connects San José and the western suburb of Santa Ana; this hospital has the most modern facilities in the country.

If you have a mild medical issue or dental problem while traveling in Costa Rica, call your embassy for a list of recommended doctors and dentists. Alternatively, most hotels will be able to refer you to a local English-speaking doctor (*medico*) or dentist (*dentista*).

Many bilingual dentists advertise in the *Tico Times*. Because treatments are so inexpensive in Costa Rica, dental tourism has become a popular option for foreigners needing extensive work.

Emergencies

In case of emergency, call ☎ 911 (there should be an English-speaking operator); if 911 doesn't work, contact the police at ☎ 2222-1365 or 2221-5337, and ask them find someone who speaks English to translate. For an ambulance, call ☎ 128; to report a fire, call ☎ 118.

For a medical emergency that doesn't require an ambulance, see "Dentists & Doctors," above. To report lost or stolen items, see "Police," p. 99.

Getting There & Getting Around

BY PLANE Most visitors arrive at the **Juan Santamaría International Airport** (☎ 2437-2626 for 24-hr. airport information; airport code SJO), located about 20 minutes from downtown San José. A taxi into town costs between $18 and $22. In terms of taxis, you should stick with the official airport taxi service, **Taxis Unidos Aeropuerto** (☎ 2221-6865; www.taxiaeropuerto. com), which operates a fleet of orange vans and sedans charging fixed prices according to your destination. Head to their kiosk, in the no-man's land just outside the exit door for arriving passengers, but keep a very watchful eye on your bags. Thieves have historically preyed on newly arrived passengers and their luggage. You should tip porters about 50¢ per bag.

BY CAR I can't put this strongly enough: do *not* rent a car for your time in San José. Traffic can be unbearable, roads are largely lacking in signage, directions are confusing, and urban drivers are fairly aggressive. Moreover, taxis are readily available and relatively inexpensive, and just about every hotel tour desk can arrange transportation for you.

Although taxis in San José have meters (*marías*), the drivers sometimes refuse to use them, particularly with foreigners, so you'll occasionally have to negotiate a price. Always try for the meter first (say, "*Ponga la maría, por favor*"). The official rate at press time is around 80¢ for the first kilometer (½ mile) and around 60¢ for each additional kilometer. If you have a rough idea of how far it is to your destination, you can estimate how much it should cost from these figures. After 10pm taxis are legally allowed to add a 20% surcharge.

Depending on your location and the time of day, it's relatively easy to hail a cab downtown. You'll always find taxis in front of the Teatro Nacional and around the Parque Central at Avenida Central and Calle Central. You can also get a cab by calling **Cinco Estrellas Taxi** (☎ 2228-3159), which claims to always have an English-speaking operator on call.

Internet Access

Internet cafes are all over San José. Rates run between 50¢ and $2 per hour. Many hotels have their own Internet cafe or allow guests to send and receive e-mail. Many also have wireless access, either for free or a small charge. You can also try **Racsa,** Avenida 5 and Calle 1 (☎ 2287-0087; www.racsa.co.cr), the state Internet monopoly, which sells prepaid cards in 5-, 10-, and 15-hour denominations for connecting your laptop to the Web via a local phone call.

Pharmacies

Pharmacies, which are called *farmacias*, are easy to find in San José. Most will fill foreign prescriptions with little or no hassle. Farmacias are the place to buy over-the-counter medicines like ibuprofen or cough syrup, feminine hygiene products, and even sunblock; these articles are often also available at supermarkets.

Police

To report a lost or stolen article, such as a wallet or passport, visit the local police. Depending upon your location, that may be either the OIJ (judicial police), *guardia rural* (rural guard), or *policía metropolitana* (metro police). The number for the *policía de tránsito* (transit police) is ☎ 800/8726-7486, toll-free nationwide, or ☎ 2222-9330. See also "Emergencies," p. 98.

Post Offices

The main post office (*correo*) is on Calle 2 between Avenidas 1 and 3 (☎ 800/900-2000 toll-free in Costa Rica, or 2202-2900; www.correos.go.cr).

Many international courier and express-mail services have offices in San José, including **FedEx,** which is based in Heredia but will arrange for pickup anywhere in the metropolitan area (☎ 800/463-3339; www.fedex.com); and **United Parcel Service,** in Pavas (☎ 2290-2828; www.ups.com).

Safety

Pickpockets and purse slashers are rife in San José, especially on public buses, in the markets, on crowded sidewalks, near hospitals, and lurking outside bank offices and ATMs. Leave most valuables in your hotel safe, and carry only as much money as you need when you go out. If you do carry anything valuable with you, keep it in a money belt or around your neck in a special passport bag. Day packs are a prime target of brazen pickpockets. One common scam involves someone dousing you or your pack with mustard or ice cream. Those who rush to your aid are usually much more interested in cleaning you out than cleaning you up.

Stay away from the red-light district northwest of the Mercado Central, and be advised that the Parque Nacional is not a safe place for a late-night stroll. Take care to walk around corner vendors, rather than between them and a building. The tight space between a vendor and a building is a favorite spot for pickpockets.

If you rent a car to get to outlying attractions or because you're leaving town, never park it on the street, and never leave anything of value in it, even if it's in a guarded parking lot. Don't even leave your car unattended by the curb in front of a hotel while you check in.

With these precautions in mind, you should have a safe visit to San José.

Toilets

These are known as *sanitarios* or *servicios sanitarios*. You might also hear them called *baños*. They are marked *damas* (women) and *hombres* or *caballeros* (men). Public restrooms are rare, but most hotels and restaurants will let you use their restrooms. Downtown, you can find one at the entrance to the Museos del Banco Central de Costa Rica (p. 48, ❷).

Visitor Information

There's an **Instituto Costarricense de Turismo (ICT)** (☎ 2443-1535; www.visitcostarica.com) desk at the Juan Santamaría International Airport, located in the baggage claims area, just before Customs. You can pick up maps and browse brochures, and they might even lend you a phone to make or confirm a reservation. It's open daily from 9am to 10pm. If you're looking for the **main ICT visitor information center** in San José, it's located below the Plaza de la Cultura, at the entrance to the Gold Museum (p. 48, ❷), on Calle 5 between Avenidas Central and 2 (☎ 2222-1090). The people here are helpful, although they have rather limited information. This office is open Monday through Saturday from 9am to 5pm.

Water

The water in San José is perfectly fine to drink though some travelers experience stomach discomfort during their first few days in Costa Rica. If you want to be cautious, drink bottled water or *frescos* made with milk instead of water. *Sin hielo* means "no ice"—even when it's frozen, it's still water.

5
Guanacaste

My Favorite Guanacaste Moments

Guanacaste, in the northwestern corner of the country, is known as the "Gold Coast," both because of its plethora of beautiful beaches and because it's the country's prime tourist destination. And no wonder—the beaches range from miles-long white-sand swaths to tiny pocket coves. While some of the region has been rapidly developed, it's still possible to find a near-deserted spot or two along the coast. Inland Guanacaste is Costa Rica's "Wild West," home to dry, flat plains, cattle ranches, and cowboys. But perhaps most important, Guanacaste is where you'll find incredible natural wonders, from the massive sea turtle nestings at Santa Rosa National Park, to the looming (and active) Rincón de la Vieja Volcano.

> *PREVIOUS PAGE Witch's Rock looms above a beach in Santa Rosa National Park. THIS PAGE La Cangreja waterfall pours its azure waters into Blue Lake.*

❶ Getting a mud treatment and hot soak at Hotel Borinquen Mountain Resort. The nearby Rincón de la Vieja Volcano heats up the soaking pools, set on the edge of a forest. Before you take the plunge, grab a handful (or more) of the hot volcanic mud that the staff gathers and stores in large wooden drums, and smear it all over yourself. The mud is supposed to have healing properties. I can't vouch for that, but it will make you feel relaxed. See p. 110, ❼.

❷ Hiking to Blue Lake and Catarata La Cangreja. This 2-hour hike in Rincón de la Vieja National Park can be arduous at times, but the beauty of La Cangreja waterfall and the Blue Lake—and the refreshing dip that awaits you

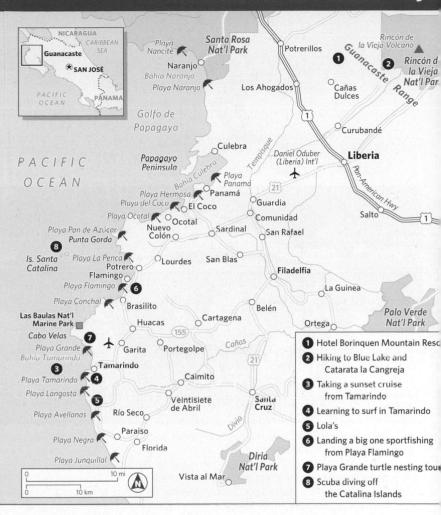

1. Hotel Borinquen Mountain Reso...
2. Hiking to Blue Lake and
   Catarata la Cangreja
3. Taking a sunset cruise
   from Tamarindo
4. Learning to surf in Tamarindo
5. Lola's
6. Landing a big one sportfishing
   from Playa Flamingo
7. Playa Grande turtle nesting tou...
8. Scuba diving off
   the Catalina Islands

when you reach it—make it all worthwhile. The clear turquoise water is mesmerizing, so don't resist the urge to take a swim. See p. 114, **B**.

3 Taking a sunset cruise. Up and down the Guanacaste coast, an itinerant fleet of sailboats offers sunset cruises that depart daily. Most leave early enough to allow time for a snorkel stop or at least a swim. I recommend setting sail on a catamaran like the **Blue Dolphin,** working out of Tamarindo. Vessels like this usually offer the most deck space and cruising comfort. See p. 132.

4 Learning to surf. Take a chance and surprise yourself. You may not be ripping radical bottom turns off double overhead barrels, but most folks in decent physical condition will at least manage to stand up on their boards after a couple of hours of lessons. Most of the major surf breaks up and down the coast have shops offering equipment rentals and lessons, but Tamarindo is the place. It features a variety of beach breaks to suit most skill levels. See p. 130.

5 Dining barefoot at Lola's. Although this charming restaurant recently mourned the

> *TOP* A visit to Guanacaste isn't complete without a surf lesson. *BOTTOM* It's not fancy, but Lola's is one of the region's best places to chow down.

passing of its namesake pet pig, Lola's continues to serve up some of the coast's finest fresh fish, salads, and fruit smoothies in its delightful open-air setting, just steps from the sea on Playa Avellanas. See p. 151.

6 Landing a big one. The offshore waters of the Pacific Ocean here are prime sportfishing grounds. Black and blue marlins, sailfish, dorado, tuna, and roosterfish are all prime game. Playa Flamingo has the best harbor and biggest fleet of charter boats to choose from. See p. 131.

7 Watching leatherbacks lay their eggs on Playa Grande. The leatherback is the largest of the world's sea turtles. Each year between late September and late February, these massive reptiles come ashore at night on Playa Grande

to lay their eggs. Patience is required, but the payoff is the chance to witness a truly remarkable natural phenomenon. See p. 120, **7**.

8 Scuba diving off the Catalina Islands. Located a short boat ride from most of Guanacaste's beach towns, this outcropping of small mid-ocean islands provides some of the best diving in Costa Rica. You're likely to see an abundance of pelagic (open-ocean) species; whitetip reef sharks and spotted eagle rays are common sightings. See p. 133.

> *OPPOSITE PAGE* The leatherback, shown here on a Guanacaste beach, spends its life at sea, except when it hatches from its egg and when it returns to land to lay its own clutch of eggs. The giant sea turtle's flipperlike limbs are better for swimming than for getting around on land.

Best of Guanacaste in 3 Days

You could easily spend a week or two exploring Guanacaste, but 3 days will give you a sense of the best the region has to offer. The beaches here are legendary, with good reason. I recommend using Tamarindo as a base—this beach town is lively, charming, and within easy distance of everything you'll want to see. Since you have limited time, don't bother with a rental car. Instead, take taxis or organized tours (book in advance) to the suggested places.

> Surf's always up in Tamarindo, one of Guanacaste's liveliest towns.

START Tamarindo, 73km (45 miles) southwest of Liberia; 295km (183 miles) northwest of San José. To get to Tamarindo, take an early morning flight from San José (flight time: 1 hour). **TOUR LENGTH** 470km (292 miles).

1 ★★ **Playa Tamarindo.** Hit the beach early in the day, before the sun gets too strong, and stake out a spot in the sand at the far southern end of Playa Tamarindo, near the Hotel Capitán Suizo. The surf is calmer, and the crowds are thinner. If you'd prefer to play in the waves, stick closer to the center of town, or sign up for a surf lesson at ★★ **Witch's Rock Surf Camp** (p. 130). ⊕ Minimum 2 hr. for surf lesson. See p. 137.

Grab a taxi (your hotel can help) for the quick, 19km (12-mile) drive to Playa Avellanas.

2 🍽 ★★★ **Lola's.** Grab a table at this seafood place, set right on the sands of Playa Avellanas. After lunch, if you're lucky you'll be able to snag one of the hammocks thoughtfully strung from the surrounding coconut palms. Playa Avellanas. ☎ 2652-9097. $$–$$$. See p. 151.

More Information

For detailed information on sights and recommended hotels and restaurants in Tamarindo, see the section starting on p. 146; for sights near Rincón de la Vieja, see p. 111.

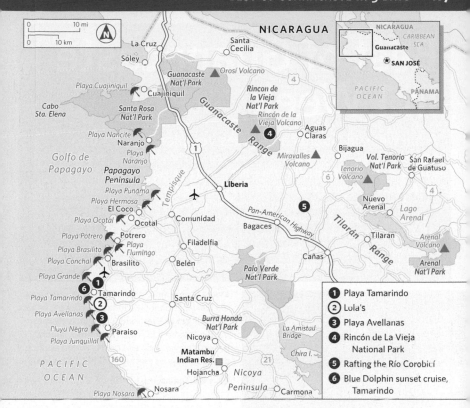

Legend:

1. Playa Tamarindo
2. Lola's
3. Playa Avellanas
4. Rincón de La Vieja National Park
5. Rafting the Río Corobicí
6. Blue Dolphin sunset cruise, Tamarindo

3 ★★★ **Playa Avellanas.** Spend the afternoon on one of the prettiest beaches on the entire Guanacaste coastline. Playa Avellanas is a mostly undeveloped stretch of white sand. You can choose whether to select a patch of sand where you can relax and contemplate the waves rolling in, or grab the opportunity to practice what you learned at your surf lesson along the miles of beach break. See p. 134.

Arrange with your hotel for a trip to Rincón de la Vieja National Park on Day 2. Plan to get a very early start, as the round-trip travel time is 4 hours, not including your time in the park.

4 ★★★ **Rincón de la Vieja National Park.** There are several excellent hikes inside this national park—you could spend days exploring it. But since you have just one, I suggest you take the short Las Pailas loop and the Blue Lake and La Cangreja Falls trail. ⏱ **1 day. See p. 111, 8 .**

On Day 3, you'll be picked up at your hotel—and again, aim for an early start. It will take about 2 hours to get to the put-in for your rafting trip.

5 ★★ kids **Rafting the Río Corobicí.** Just south of Liberia, the gentle Río Corobicí offers you the opportunity to float downstream while enjoying the region's fabulous scenery and some stellar bird-watching. **Safaris Corobicí** runs several different trips—I recommend the 3-hour version. ⏱ 2-3 hr. Off the Pan-American Hwy., 45km (28 miles) south of Liberia. ☎/fax 2669-6191. www.nicoya.com. Rates $38 for a 2-hr. tour, $46 for a 3-hr. tour, $62 half-day tour; children 12 and under half-price.

You'll be returned to your hotel in Tamarindo in plenty of time to walk or take a taxi to the waterfront.

6 ★★ kids **Blue Dolphin sunset cruise.** In keeping with the water/boat theme of the day, be sure to get back to Tamarindo in time for a sunset cruise aboard the *Blue Dolphin*. It's a trip you definitely won't want to miss. ⏱ 4 hr. See p. 132.

Best of Guanacaste in 1 Week

A full week in Guanacaste gives you plenty of time to explore and play. The extra time will allow you the chance to soak up some rays on several of the better beaches here. But it's not all about the sand and sun. You'll also take several adventure tours and excursions, check in on the local arts and crafts scene, and pamper yourself with a soak in hot springs, a mud bath, and a massage. I recommend starting off in Tamarindo, then spending a couple of nights in the hills bordering Rincón de la Vieja National Park. Divide the remainder of your time between two distinct beach destinations. You'll want to pick up a rental car in Tamarindo on your second day.

> *Playa Tamarindo at twilight.*

START Tamarindo, 73km (45 miles) southwest of Liberia; 295km (183 miles) northwest of San José. To get to Tamarindo, take an early morning flight from San José (flight time: 1 hour). Everything you'll do on Day 1 is within walking distance. TOUR LENGTH 324km (201 miles).

1 ★ kids **Tamarindo.** On your first morning, get to know this bustling little beach town. Browse the line of souvenir shops along the main road, and stroll the length of Playa Tamarindo, from the estuary's river mouth out to the southern rocky headlands. It's only about 30 minutes walking, each way. ⊕ Minimum 3 hr. See p. 146.

2 🍴 kids **Hotel Capitán Suizo.** Stop in for a cool drink at the beachfront restaurant in this hotel, located just before Playa Tamarindo's rocky southern headlands. $$. For information on the hotel, see p. 149.

3 ★★ kids **Blue Dolphin Sailing.** Spend the afternoon aboard the *Blue Dolphin*. The half-day cruise typically leaves around 1:30pm and stays out for the sunset. You'll be treated to several snorkel stops, as well as a paddle aboard a sea kayak. ⊕ Minimum 4 hr. See p. 132.

4 🍴 ★★ **La Laguna del Cocodrilo Bistro.** This is the most elegant and upscale restaurant in Tamarindo, and the chef's nightly tasting menu is always a good choice. On the beach, north end of Tamarindo. ☎ 2653-3897. $$–$$$. See p. 150.

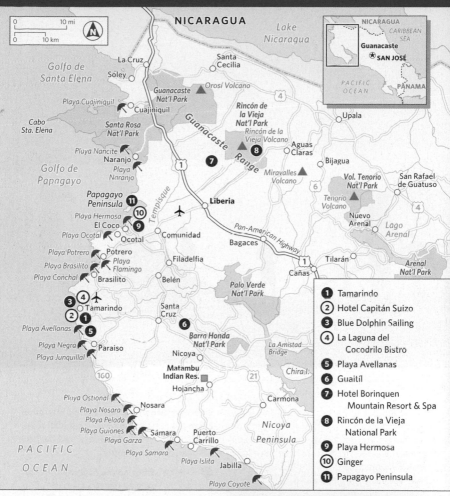

NICARAGUA

Lake Nicaragua

NICARAGUA

CARIBBEAN SEA

Guanacaste

★ SAN JOSÉ

PACIFIC OCEAN

PANAMA

Golfo de Santa Elena

La Cruz

Soley

Playa Cuajiniquil

Cuajiniquil

Cabo Sta. Elena

Guanacaste Nat'l Park

Santa Rosa Nat'l Park

Playa Nancite

Naranjo

Playa Naranjo

Golfo de Papagayo

Papagayo Peninsula

⓫

Playa Hermosa

⑩

El Coco

⑨

Playa Ocotal

Ocotal

Playa Potrero

Potrero

Playa Brasilito

Playa Flamingo

Playa Conchal

Brasilito

③ ④

② ①

Tamarindo

⑤

Playa Avellanas

Playa Negra

Paraiso

Playa Junquillal

Orosí Volcano

Santa Cecilia

Rincón de la Vieja Nat'l Park

Rincón de la Vieja Volcano

⑧

⑦

Aguas Claras

Upala

Bijagua

Miravalles Volcano

Guanacaste Range

Tempisque

Liberia

Comunidad

Pan-American Highway

Bagaces

Filadelfia

Belén

Santa Cruz

⑥

Barra Honda Nat'l Park

Palo Verde Nat'l Park

Nicoya

Matambu Indian Res.

Hojancha

La Amistad Bridge

Vol. Tenorio Nat'l Park

Tenorio Volcano

San Rafael de Guatuso

Nuevo Arenal

Lago Arenal

Tilarán

Cañas

Arenal Nat'l Park

Chira I.

Playa Ostional

Nosara

Playa Nosara

Playa Pelada

Playa Guiones

Sámara

Playa Garza

Playa Samara

PACIFIC OCEAN

Carmona

Puerto Carrillo

Jabilla

Nicoya Peninsula

Playa Islita

Playa Coyote

❶ Tamarindo
❷ Hotel Capitán Suizo
❸ Blue Dolphin Sailing
❹ La Laguna del Cocodrilo Bistro
❺ Playa Avellanas
❻ Guaitíl
❼ Hotel Borinquen Mountain Resort & Spa
❽ Rincón de la Vieja National Park
❾ Playa Hermosa
❿ Ginger
⓫ Papagayo Peninsula

On the morning of Day 2, pick up a rental car and drive out of Tamarindo past the airstrip to the intersection at Santa Rosa. There you'll turn right (the road soon becomes gravel), following signs to Hacienda Pinilla and Playa Avellanas. The total distance is 19km (12 miles), and the drive will take 30 minutes.

❺ ★★★ **Playa Avellanas.** Bring boogie boards and play in the surf, or just lounge and soak up the rays. For lunch, walk a few steps over to Lola's (p. 151).

Retrace your steps out of Playa Avellanas and turn right toward Santa Cruz at the main dirt road. Just north of Santa Cruz, take CR21 west for 12km (7½ miles) to the turnoff for Guaitíl.

> *La Laguna del Cocodrilo Bistro is one of the coast's dining hot spots.*

The entire drive is 49km (30 miles). You should allow yourself 75 minutes.

> *Don't miss a sunset cruise on the Pacific Ocean.*

6 ★ **Guaitíl.** Before you head back to Tamarindo, do some shopping in this artisan town, which offers some of the country's best ceramics. Guaitíl is one of the few towns in Costa Rica with a longstanding indigenous arts and crafts tradition. ⏱ 2 hr. See "Local Low-Fire Ceramics," p. 111.

On Day 3, follow signs to Liberia, where you'll pick up the Pan-American Hwy. Go north 12km (7½ miles) to the well-marked turnoff to Cañas Dulces. Follow signs to the Hotel

Borinquen Mountain Resort & Spa, another 22km (14 miles) along a rough gravel road. You'll cover 107km (66 miles), and the drive will take close to 2 hours.

7 ★★★ **Hotel Borinquen Mountain Resort & Spa.** This beautiful resort sits on the edge of Rincón de la Vieja National Park (**8**). Start things off with one of the resort's adventure tours—options include all-terrain-vehicle or horseback rides through the neighboring forests and farmlands and an in-house zip-line canopy tour. After your adventure, head to the hot-spring pools and mud baths at the resort's ★★★ **Anáhuac Spa**; if you really want to pamper yourself, book a massage treatment in advance. ⏱ Varies, depending on tours and spa treatments. Cañas Dulces, 34km (21 miles) northeast of Liberia. ☎ 2690-1900. www.borinquen resort.com. Admission $25 adults, $15 children 11 and under. Adventure tours and activities range from $55 to $80; children 12 and under are half-price. Massage and spa treatments (range from 30 to 60 min.) $40–$70. Daily 8am–8pm.

Spending the Night near Rincón de la Vieja

It's possible to visit the Rincón de la Vieja area as a day trip from any of the Guanacaste beach destinations, but if you stay nearby you'll have more time. I recommend the ★★★ **Hotel Borinquen Mountain Resort & Spa** (p. 165) or ★★ kids **Hacienda Guachipelin** (p. 165), both excellent options.

> *Hotel Borinquen's hot springs.*

Local Low-Fire Ceramics

The lack of any long-standing local arts and crafts tradition across Costa Rica is often lamented. One of the notable exceptions to this is the small village of Guaitil, located on the outskirts of the provincial capital of Santa Cruz. The small central plaza—actually a soccer field—of this village is ringed with craft shops and artisan stands selling a wide range of ceramic wares. Most are low-fired, relatively soft clay pieces, with traditional Chorotega indigenous design motifs. You'll find a large selection of decorative and functional pieces, including plates, bowls, and pots. I especially like the pieces adorned with 3-dimensional lizards or frogs, although these are more modern designs. Some of the plates and pots are quite large, making them a little hard to transport home. Also keep in mind that the low-fire technique used to make the pieces renders them more fragile than other types of ceramic wares. Hotels and tour agencies in all of the towns listed in this chapter can arrange trips to Guaitil.

After spending the night nearby, arrange for your hotel to bring you (or direct you) to the park on the morning of Day 4.

SITE GUIDE
PAGE 114

8 ★★★ **Rincón de la Vieja National Park.** The name means "the old woman's corner" and refers to a local fable about a young woman whose father threw her lover into the namesake volcano's crater. Despondent, she became a recluse, refusing to the leave the mountain where her true love died. As you'll see, it's no wonder this place is linked to a legend—blasted craters loom above cloud forests, and in places, the ground literally boils.

You'll need more than 1 day to tackle all the hikes in this magical place, so you'll have to choose: Spend an extra day here, and only 1 day enjoying the beaches of the Papagayo Peninsula (**11**), or tackle the shorter hikes, which are doable in 1 day.

All the trails I recommend start at the ranger station, where you can (and should, if you're aiming to reach the summit) hire a guide. 25km (16 miles) northeast of Liberia, much of it down a rutted dirt road. ☎ 2661-8139. Admission $10. Daily 7:30am–4:30pm.

> *The elevated deck is a superb spot for sampling the wide variety of tapas plates at Ginger.*

In the late afternoon, take the Pan-American Hwy. south. In Liberia, turn east on CR21 and follow signs to Playa Hermosa, where you'll spend the night. The total distance is 63km (39 miles), and the drive will take an hour.

9 ★★ **kids Playa Hermosa.** After your mountain adventures, spend Day 5 soaking up some sun. Playa Hermosa is a delightful little town, with several excellent boutique hotels. The broad, crowd-free beach is well protected from

Be Prepared

It might be hot and sunny down by Rincón de la Vieja's ranger station but chilly, cloudy, and maybe even wet as you reach the summit. Come prepared with layers of clothes—and rain gear in the rainy season. Bring lots of water and take breaks, particularly if the weather is hot and humid. Finally, be aware that some trails may be closed because of bad weather or volcanic activity.

most swells, making it excellent for swimming. There's also great snorkeling and scuba diving nearby—see "Dive Time" (p. 113) for more information. An added bonus: The sunsets are stunning here, whether enjoyed from the beach or a bar stool. See p. 136.

10 🍴 ★★ **Ginger.** For dinner, make a reservation at this hip spot in Playa Hermosa, which serves up a wide range of eclectic dishes from around the world in tapas-size portions. Inland, near the center of Playa Hermosa. ☎ 2672-0041. $. See p. 158

On Day 6, take CR151 to CR21, heading toward Liberia. Take a left at the large Do It Center store and follow signs to the Papagayo Peninsula. The total drive is 38km (24 miles) and will take an hour.

11 ★★ **kids Papagayo Peninsula.** Finish off your time in Guanacaste with some chilling at a full-service beach resort on the Papagayo Peninsula—there are several excellent options

> *The beach anchored by Witch's Rock is as famous for its beauty as it is for its surfing.*

(see p. 158). The beaches here are arguably the best in the region, especially if you're looking for calm waters and quiet sun-worshipping time.

Lounging around on the beach or beside the pool may be your priority, but if not, all the resorts around here feature full-service tour and activity desks. Options range from free salsa and aerobics classes to watersports to an organized tour or adventure. My personal favorite is the ★★★ **Witch's Rock Canopy Tour** (p. 142), which offers both thrills and views. And be absolutely sure to take a ★★★ **kids** **turtle-nesting tour to Playa Grande** (p. 120, **7**).

Dive Time

★★★ **kids** **Diving Safaris de Costa Rica** (p. 156, **1**) in Playa Hermosa is one of the country's top scuba and snorkeling operators. Sign up for a snorkeling or scuba diving tour to the nearby offshore rocky outcroppings and reefs. Most trips include a lunch stop on a beautiful and deserted white-sand beach. Snorkelers will see schools of colorful grunts and solitary angelfish and parrotfish, while scuba divers will enjoy an even greater bounty, including whitetip reef sharks, eagle rays, moray eels, sea turtles, and, if you get really lucky, whale sharks.

SITE GUIDE

⑧ Rincón de la Vieja National Park

You'll see bubbling mud pots (pictured at right) and fumaroles formed by ongoing volcanic activity along Ⓐ ★★ kids **Las Pailas loop.** Don't get too close, or you could get scalded. Happily, the strong sulfur smell given off by these formations works well as a natural deterrent. This is a gentle 3.2km (2-mile) trail, with very little climbing involved. Be prepared: The trail crosses a river, so you'll have to either take off your shoes or let them get wet. The whole loop takes about an hour.

My favorite hike here is the one that goes to Ⓑ ★★★ **Blue Lake and Catarata La Cangreja** (pictured above). The trailhead begins at the ranger station, and the total trip takes about 5 hours. Along this well-marked 9.6km (6-mile) round-trip trail you will pass through several different ecosystems, including tropical dry forest (think cactus), transitional moist forest, and open savanna. The diversity of terrain means you may spot, in addition to the flora, toucans, tapirs, and a host of other birds and animals. If nothing else, odds are good that you'll encounter a group of coatimundis—a raccoon-

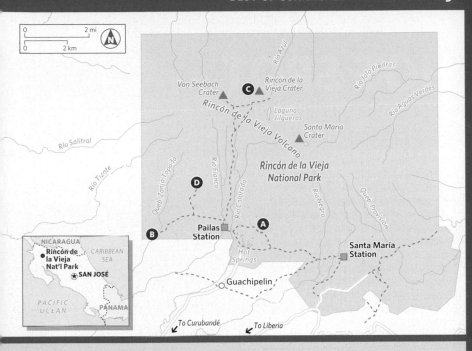

like local. They may beg for food, but don't be tempted to share, as it's bad for them.

While this hike doesn't involve steep climbs or dramatic descents, it is arduous nonetheless. It ends at the Blue Lake, which is fed by the rushing 30m (100-ft.) La Cangreja waterfall—you've earned a swim in the turquoise waters, so don't hesitate to take the plunge.

The best hike in the park is also the most adventurous: the trail to the Ⓒ ★★★ **summit of Rincón de la Vieja Volcano.** A word of warning: This climb can be dangerous—the way is dotted with hot springs and geysers, and hikers have been seriously burned. I suggest you hire a guide at the ranger station or through your hotel rather than trying this on your own. If you do go without a guide, check in with the rangers before you begin.

That said, don't let my warning put you off. This is an incredible experience—you'll pass through lush tropical cloud forests en route to the cratered moonscape at the summit. On a clear day you'll have views of the plains of Guanacaste and the Pacific Ocean.

The trail itself is 16.6km (10.3 miles) round-trip and should take about 7 hours. It heads pretty much straight up the volcano—you'll be climbing some 1,000m (3,280 ft.) in altitude—and is steep in places.

About 6km (3.7 miles) into the hike, the trail splits. Take the right-hand fork to the Crater Activo (Active Crater). Filled with rainwater, this crater is some 700m (2,300 ft.) in diameter and still active. If visibility is poor because of fog (and it often is), stay well back from the jagged edge of the crater. Off to the side is the massive Laguna Jilgueros (Goldfinch Lake). Because this crater lake emits large amounts of sulfur and acidic gases, it's not recommended that you linger here long.

If you're spending additional time at the park, you can also opt to try the Ⓓ **Cataratas Escondidas** (Hidden Waterfalls) trail. This 6.5km (4-mile) round-trip trail should take 3½ hours. It breaks off from the Blue Lake and La Cangreja Falls trail and leads to a narrow, rocky canyon and a series of waterfalls, the tallest of which is some 70m (230 ft.). The final section is steep in places. ⏱ **Minimum 3 hr.**

HOT SPOT
Costa Rica's Volcanoes

BY ELIOT GREENSPAN

COSTA RICA SITS ATOP the famed Pacific Ring of Fire—an area of shifting tectonic plates that stretches from Asia to Central America and is home to 75% of the world's volcanoes. So it's little wonder that Costa Rica has more than 100 volcanoes identified as currently active. Beginning over 65 million years ago, the same plate tectonics that created these volcanoes also created the land bridge that joins North and South America. Since then, these portals to the earth's center have brought death and tremendous destruction. Ironically, they've also brought prosperity—they're responsible for the rich and fertile soil used to grow coffee, pineapples, and bananas, and for the abundance of flora that in turn supports the country's biodiversity. And these days, they're major tourist attractions: You can hike or horseback ride to their summits, fly down their flanks on a zip-line canopy tour, and soak in natural hot springs at their bases.

BIG, BELCHING BLOWHARDS: The Most Active Volcanoes

IRAZÚ
Location: 52km (32 miles) east of San José
Elevation: 3,378m (11,083 ft.)
Last major blow: 1963
Good to know: Costa Rica's highest volcano: On a clear day you can see both the Caribbean Sea and Pacific Ocean from its

summit. Its name is said to mean "thunder" in the local indigenous dialect. Irazú's 1963 eruption killed more than 20 people and coated downtown San José in ash. See p. 64 for more.

POÁS
Location: 37km (23 miles) northwest of San José
Elevation: 2,640m (8,661 ft.)
Last major blow: 2008
Good to know: Poás

features the world's second widest crater, at more than a mile in diameter. The main crater is filled with a boiling blue-

green lake, and the volcano's ongoing eruptions sometimes cause geyserlike blasts of water and

steam. "Acid rain" from these eruptions has damaged crops and led to localized evacuations. See p. 58 for more.

RINCÓN DE LA VIEJA
Location: 25km (16 miles) northeast of Liberia
Elevation: 1,916m (6,286 ft.)
Last major blow: 1998
Good to know: The local Guatuso people believed a heartbroken woman grew old in this crater where her lover

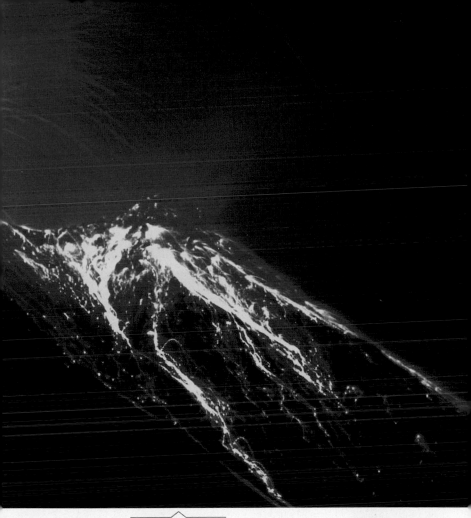

died, and its name translates as "the old woman's corner." Encompassing a large and broad complex of

volcanic activity, it has nine identified craters and many more vents. You'll find therapeutic hot springs and mud baths on its lower flanks. See p. 111 for more.

ARENAL

Location: 129km (80 miles) northwest of San José
Elevation: 1,670m (5,479 ft.)
Last major blow: August 24, 2000
Good to know: Costa Rica's most active volcano. You can watch lava stream down its sides at night. It is a geological baby (about 3,000 years old), and it's an *enfant terrible*. A 1968 eruption—its most destructive— wiped out several towns and villages and killed some 80 people. See p. 230 for more.

TURRIALBA

Location: 36km (22 miles) northeast of San José
Elevation: 3,340m (10,958 ft.)
Last major blow: 1866, but recent rumblings and releases of gases have caused authorities to shut down the

adjacent national park (that is why it is not covered in this book) and put volcanologists on alert.

Good to know: This is the second highest volcano in Costa Rica. Steady, tall plumes of smoke and ash led colonial-era residents to dub it Torre Alba or "White Tower."

Guanacaste with Kids

With calm beaches, loads of tour and activity options, and full-service beach resorts, the Papagayo Peninsula will seem custom-made for easy-going family-friendly travel. Resorts here (and there are more to come over the next few years) have excellent on-site children's programs and extensive in-house tour operations. Book your hotel, and they'll handle arranging all of your tours. See? I told you it was easy. You'll want to pick up a rental a car in Liberia.

> Guanacaste's dry uplands provide the setting for Africa Mía's wildlife safari.

START Papagayo Peninsula, 258km (160 miles) northwest of San José; 38km (24 miles) west of Liberia. To get to Papagayo Peninsula, fly from San José to Liberia (flight time: 1 hour), rent a car, and drive west on CR21 until you reach the peninsula road; follow that to your hotel (the ride will take about 25 minutes). **TOUR LENGTH** 5 days; 597km (370 miles).

Your resort. You've just arrived at your resort, and you're probably feeling pretty wowed by

it, so spend the day exploring all it has to offer. For recommended hotels and resorts on the Papagayo Peninsula, see p. 158.

On Day 2, take the peninsula road back to Liberia and go south 45km (28 miles) on the Pan-American Hwy. Safaris Corobicí is just off the highway. Give yourself 1½ hours for the drive.

❶ ★★ Rafting the Río Corobicí. Safaris Corobicí offers leisurely river trips on the Río Corobicí that are appropriate for all ages (well,

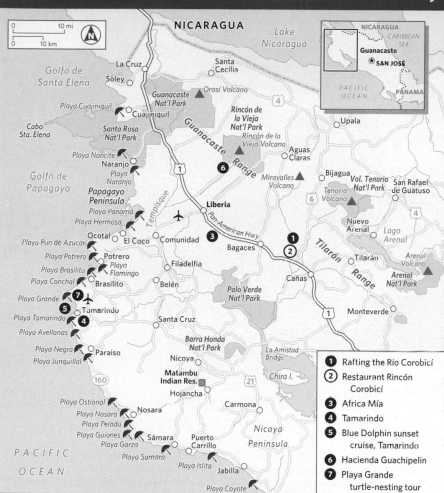

1 Rafting the Río Corobicí
2 Restaurant Rincón Corobicí
3 Africa Mía
4 Tamarindo
5 Blue Dolphin sunset cruise, Tamarindo
6 Hacienda Guachipelin
7 Playa Grande turtle-nesting tour

nearly all ages—they're not for infants). In addition to the slow float and occasional mellow rapids, there'll be chances to cool off in the water and to spot wildlife along the way. ⊕ Minimum 2 hr. See p. 107, ➎.

② 🍽 ★★ Restaurant Rincón Corobicí.

Not only does this riverside joint serve up good food, there are expansive grounds and a small playground down by the river where kids can run around and let off some steam. Pan-American Hwy., 5km (3 miles) north of Cañas. ☎ 2669-6262. $$. Breakfast, lunch, and dinner daily. AE, MC, V.

After lunch, take the Pan-American Hwy. 39km (24 miles) north to Africa Mía.

③ ★★ Africa Mía.

The dry, flat savannas of Guanacaste are surprisingly similar to those in Africa. Africa Mía (My Africa) offers safari-style open-jeep tours through its 100-hectare (245-acre) private reserve, which is populated with a wide range of predominantly non-native species. Your kids will love animal-spotting, and all the residents are herbivores, so there's nothing too scary. You'll see giraffes, zebras, gemsboks, warthogs, and elands. Basic admission includes a 90-minute guided tour; more extensive tours, which get you much closer to the animals, are also offered.

> *A Hacienda Guachipelin river-tubing excursion gets wet and wild.*

🕐 Minimum 2 hr. Just off the Pan-American Hwy. ☎ 2666-1111. www.africamia.net. Admission $16 adults, $11 children 11 and under. Daily 8am–6pm.

On the morning of Day 3, take the peninsula road to CR21 south. When you reach Belén, pick up CR155 south to Tamarindo. You'll need an hour for the 40km (25-mile) drive.

❹ ★★ **Tamarindo.** Start with a family-friendly surf lesson at ★★ **Witch's Rock Surf Camp** (p. 130). Try not to feel too bad if your kids are better than you are.

You'll have worked up an appetite, so have lunch overlooking the waves at **Nogui's Café** (p. 151)—there's enough action on the beach to keep little ones from getting bored. Then stock up on souvenirs on Tamarindo's main street. 🕐 1 day. See p. 146.

❺ ★★ **Blue Dolphin sunset cruise.** 🕐 2 hr. See p. 132.

On the morning of Day 4, take the peninsula road to CR21 to Liberia. In Liberia, take the Pan-American Hwy. north about 3km (1¾ miles) to the well-marked turnoff for the dirt and gravel access road to Hacienda Guachipelin. Give yourself an hour for the 57km (35-mile) drive.

❻ ★★★ **Hacienda Guachipelin.** Book a full-day outing to Hacienda Guachipelin—there is plenty to do on this working farm and cattle ranch for kids of all ages. Options include horseback riding, hiking, white-water river inner-tubing, a waterfall canyoning and rappel tour, and a zip-line canopy tour—all of which are kid-friendly. 🕐 1 day. See "One-Stop Adventure Shop," p. 141.

Return to your hotel to be picked up for your evening trip to Playa Grande.

❼ ★★★ **Playa Grande turtle-nesting tour.** If you're here between late September and late February, take an evening turtle tour to Playa

Parents' Day Off

Check your guilt with the concierge and drop the kids off at your resort's children's program. In the morning, treat yourself to a spa treatment at the in-house spa. After you've achieved a sufficiently mellow mood, head to ★★★ **Playa Avellanas** for lunch at ★★★ **Lola's** (p. 151). Even by day, this is one of the most romantic restaurants in the country. After lunch, drive to the artisan town of Guaitíl (p. 110, ⑥) to check out the local ceramics.

Grande to witness the amazing spectacle of giant leatherback turtles digging their nests and laying their eggs. Be forewarned: These tours are entirely dependent upon the turtles' schedule. That may mean long walks and long waits in the still of the night, with a premium on remaining quiet. Older kids will be enthralled—it's the sort of experience they'll never forget. But very young or especially fidgety children might be better left with a babysitter. ***Note:*** Make reservations in advance, as spots are limited. ☺ Minimum 2 hr. Book through your hotel or call the National Park Service directly (☎ 2653-0470). Admission $25 per person.

> *ABOVE A leatherback sea turtle. BELOW A day cruise on the Pacific Ocean.*

Guanacaste's History & Culture

You won't find an abundance of museums, art galleries, or historical sites around Guanacaste, but that doesn't mean there isn't any history here. The local Chorotega culture was well established by the time the Spanish arrived, and the two cultures quickly merged. Today, the inland culture revolves around the *sabaneros*, or cowboys, whose traditions date to colonial times, when this region was home to haciendas built by cattle barons. Along the coast, residents still rely on fishing—just as their pre-Columbian ancestors did.

> *La Casona, in Santa Rosa National Park, played an important role in Costa Rica's history (see p. 126).*

START **Plaza Central, Liberia. Liberia is 217km (135 miles) northwest of San José (flight time: 1 hour). TOUR LENGTH 1 day; 84km (52 miles).**

❶ Plaza Central, Liberia. The heart of the great colonial city of Liberia, this plaza features well-tended gardens, small stone fountains, and an abundance of concrete benches. This is the city's social, and physical, center. Take a seat, relax, and people-watch. Or, if you're feel-ing adventurous, strike up a conversation with a passerby—Liberians are quite friendly. ⊙ 30 min. Downtown Liberia.

Fun Fact

Guanacaste is the only region of Costa Rica that has its own provincial flag. You can see it flying above Liberia's town hall, next door to the Iglesia de la Inmaculada Concepción.

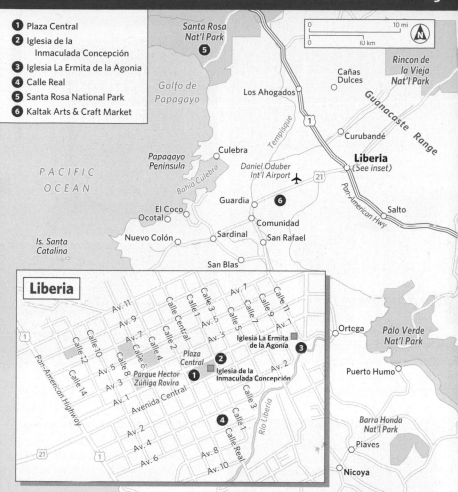

1 Plaza Central
2 Iglesia de la Inmaculada Concepción
3 Iglesia La Ermita de la Agonía
4 Calle Real
5 Santa Rosa National Park
6 Kaltak Arts & Craft Market

2 Iglesia de la Inmaculada Concepción.
Located on the edge of the Plaza Central, the Church of the Immaculate Conception is Liberia's main house of worship. The church was built in 1972 and features a tall A-frame–style central nave and a separate clock tower that rises up sharply—a contemporary concrete obelisk. ⊕ 20 min. Plaza Central, Liberia.

3 ★ Iglesia La Ermita de la Agonía. Built in 1865, this whitewashed stone church is in surprisingly good shape. Inside it is plain and bare, but it is the only remaining colonial-era church to be found in Guanacaste. The visiting hours are seriously limited (2:30–3:30pm daily), but not to worry: Local tour agencies can some-times arrange visits during off hours. Even if you can't enter, you'll still get a good feel for the place by checking out its stuccoed exterior.

Shady Business

This province gets its name from the abundant Guanacaste (*Enterolobium cyclocarpum*), Costa Rica's national tree. This tree is known for its broad, full crown, which provides welcome shade on the hot plains and savannas of Guanacaste. The Guanacaste is also called the elephant-ear tree for its large, distinctively shaped seedpods. Its fragrant white flowers bloom between February and April.

> *The Iglesia de la Inmaculada Concepción rises above Plaza Central, Liberia.*

> *Spanish colonial architecture lines Liberia's Calle Real.*

Learning the Language

Language-study programs abound throughout Costa Rica, and you might as well combine your studying with some beach time and interesting exploration. The **Centro Panamericano de Idiomas** (CPI; ☎ 2654-5002; www.cpi-edu.com) has schools in San José and Monteverde, as well as a branch in Playa Flamingo (p. 160), across from the Flamingo Marina facing Potrero Bay. Rates run $315 per week for 4 hours of classes per day. Many lodging options are offered, including area hotels and resorts or a home stay with a local family. In Tamarindo, check out the **Wayra Instituto de Español** (☎/fax 2653-0359; www.spanish-wayra.co.cr). A weeklong course, including 4 hours of classes per day and a home stay, costs $300 to $350. Longer courses are available, and you can combine your language studies with surf lessons.

🕐 20 min. Northeast end of Avenida Central, Liberia. See p. 164, ❷.

❹ ★ **Calle Real.** Calle Real is home to Liberia's greatest concentration of colonial-era homes and mansions, many of them immaculately restored. You'll see fine examples of classic Spanish colonial architecture—adobe buildings with ornate wooden doors, heavy beams, central courtyards, and faded, sagging red-tile roofs. The adobe facades are the source of Liberia's nickname, the White City. Massive windows facing the street are often left wide open, without so much as a screen—a sign of the city's safe and subdued vibe.

The best way to enjoy Calle Real is to simply stroll along, soaking in the charm. Remember, you're in Costa Rica, so no need to rush. On your way, keep an eye out for the Casa de Vico (Newspaper House), where Liberia's residents post news stories—you'll find it two blocks south of Plaza Central. 🕐 20 min. South of Plaza Central, Liberia.

Give yourself an hour to drive north from Liberia on the Pan-American Hwy. to the well-marked entrance for Santa Rosa National Park; the total distance is 42km (26 miles).

SITE GUIDE
PAGE 126

5 ★★ Santa Rosa National Park. Occupying a large tract of land that encompasses most of the Santa Elena Peninsula, this national park contains one of the country's principal historical sites, La Casona, where Costa Ricans battled and defeated the infamous William Walker (see "William Walker's War," below).

The 49,515-hectare (122,354-acre) park also contains and protects an important tract of endangered tropical dry forest, one of the most unique habitats on earth. Expect to find cacti here.

The park's pristine beaches, especially **Playa Nancite,** are a prime nesting site for several species of sea turtle. And two of the country's most coveted surf breaks, Witch's Rock and Ollie's Point (p. 132), are found here. ☎ 2666-5051. Admission $10; includes park and La Casona. Daily 7:30am–4:30pm.

Retrace your route to Liberia on the Pan-American Hwy. At the main intersection in Liberia, turn right onto CR21. Kaltak is just beyond the airport. The total distance is 55km (34 miles), and the drive will take an hour.

6 Kaltak Arts & Craft Market. Decidedly a tourist trap, albeit a charming one, this large retail space spreads out over several rooms in several buildings. Don't hesitate to explore them all. You'll find a large selection of traditional craft works ranging from functional and decorative ceramic wares to wood carvings to jewelry and beyond. Shop here for the typical Guanacaste leather and wood rocking chair, which you can have shipped home. ⊙ 30 min. ☎ 2667-0696. Mon–Sat 8am–6pm, Sun 9:30am–5pm. AE, DC, MC, V.

William Walker's War

The story of William Walker is one of the stranger chapters in Central American history. Born in 1824 in Nashville, Tennessee, Walker studied to be a doctor, but his medical training soon fell by the wayside, as his real ambitions lay elsewhere: His dream was to extend slavery throughout the Americas. And he set about making that dream a reality.

That he was pro-slavery was not unusual—so were many whites in the American South at the time. Walker took things quite a bit further. In 1855 he raised a small army of mercenaries and invaded Nicaragua. The ever-ambitious Walker had the de facto blessing of America's president James Buchanan, who hoped Walker would install a pro-U.S. government there. But Buchanan failed to take into consideration just what kind of man would raise an army and attack a sovereign power. Walker promptly named himself president of Nicaragua.

Costa Rican president Juan Rafael Mora predicted that Walker planned to expand his power south into Costa Rica. He was right—and when Walker invaded in 1856, Mora was ready. Costa Rica had no standing army, so Mora rallied farmers and merchants, armed primarily with machetes and farm tools.

Rather miraculously, the ragtag band of fighters managed to defeat Walker's well-armed forces at what became known as the Battle of Santa Rosa, on March 20, 1856. The filibusters were holed up in La Casona (p. 126, **Ⓐ**), the main building of an old hacienda, and Mora's men surrounded them. The fighting lasted a mere 14 minutes, thanks in part to the heroic efforts of 19-year-old Juan Santamaría, the "Little Drummer Boy" (p. 427). Santamaría volunteered for what was essentially a suicide mission—he set fire to La Casona in an effort to drive the filibusters out. Walker survived, Santamaría did not.

It was the beginning of the end for Walker. The U.S. government was embarrassed by his behavior. They were more than happy to have friendly leaders in Central America to help boost American businesses investing in the area, but a power-mad, pro-slavery zealot wasn't really what they had in mind. Without America's silent support, Walker lost his grip on Nicaragua and spent 3 years in jail. Undaunted, Walker continued to fight after he was freed, and in 1860 he attempted to raise a coup in Honduras. He failed, and was executed by firing squad.

SITE GUIDE

⑤ Santa Rosa National Park

A humble old ranch house, ⓐ ★ **La Casona,** played an important role in Costa Rican history. It was here, on March 20, 1856, that Costa Rican forces fought the decisive Battle of Santa Rosa, forcing the U.S.-backed soldier of fortune William Walker and his men to flee into Nicaragua (see "William Walker's War," p. 125). Sadly, La Casona was completely destroyed by arson in 2001. The current structure, an impressively accurate re-creation of the original building, houses a small museum. There's a monument to those who lost their lives at the famous battle, and nearby are some colonial-era horse corrals built of stone.

Exit La Casona and walk around the north side of the building to the trailhead for ⓑ ★ **Indio Desnudo** (Naked Indian). This 2.6-km (1.6-mile) loop trail should take you about 45 minutes. It leads through a small patch of tropical dry forest (expect to see cacti) and into an overgrown former pastureland. If you're lucky, you might spot a white-tailed deer, coatimundi, or mantled howler monkey (above, right) along the way.

Your next stop, ⓒ ★★ **Playa Naranjo,** is reached via a very rough 11km (6¾-mile) dirt road starting from in front of La Casona. A high-clearance vehicle is necessary to make the drive,

and if you've got one, it's well worth the trek to this isolated and pristine white-sand beach, which stretches on for some 2km (1¼ miles). At the northern end you'll find a wide estuary and, just offshore, the singular behemoth known as ⓓ **Roca Bruja** (Witch's Rock, opposite). In addition to its striking appearance, Witch's Rock marks one of Costa Rica's greatest surf breaks (p. 132), making it an important part of the country's recent cultural history. There's a well-maintained trail through the thick mangrove forests that back the beach; the trail is flat and gentle but 4km (2.5 miles) long, and will take you almost an hour each way. Bring your binoculars, as birdwatching along the trail is fabulous. ⏱1 day.

Palo Verde National Park

Most of this national park's 19,800 hectares (48,900 acres) are wetlands—this is where the Río Tempisque meets the Golfo de Nicoya. The park is home to more than 300 species of resident and migratory birds, particularly waterfowl like egrets, storks, and herons. You'll find other wildlife here as well, including a very healthy population of crocodiles. During the height of the dry season (from January to March), it's easy to spot coatimundi, monkeys, and other animals around watering holes. You'll also find a bit of rare dry tropical forest—home to cactus and other desert-dwellers. A popular way to visit the park is by tour boat, but there is also a series of hiking trails and elevated lookout points.

START The park entrance is 20km (12 miles) southwest of the town of Bagaces, which is 25km (16 miles) south of Liberia.

Entering the park. From the entrance, it's another 8km (5 miles) to the OTS biological research station (see "An Insider's View of the Park," p. 129) and the start of the trail system, and another 1.5km (1 mile) to the main ranger station. If you're a serious bird-watcher or just love hiking, plan to spend a few days in the park; either camp or nab one of the bunk beds at the main Palo Verde ranger station. The best time to visit is between December and March. This is the driest season, and it's also when the park hosts its greatest abundance of migratory bird species. ☎ 2200-0125 or 2695-5108. www.acarenaltempisque.org. Admission $10. Camping $2 per person per night. Daily 7am–5pm.

❶ La Roca. This short, simple trail (.5km/.3 mile) leads to a lovely lookout point over the Río Tempisque and Gulf of Nicoya beyond. The trail will take you only around 10 minutes each way, but allow a little time to linger and take in the view.

❷ El Guayacán. El Guayacán, which means "the botanist," is a good trail for those wanting a longer and more challenging hike—and for those interested in seeing great flora. It basically connects the OTS biological station with the Palo Verde ranger station, taking you through tropical dry forest on the way. There are two main lookout points, El Guayacán and

> The boat-billed heron is one of 300-plus birds recorded in the park.

El Cactus. El Cactus is reached via a short spur trail and requires a little scrambling over a rock outcropping. The lookouts afford great elevated views of the bird-filled Palo Verde lagoon and Río Tempisque basin. The 1.5km (1-mile) hike should take a little less than an hour, one way.

❸ La Martilla. This is another trail that more or less connects the Palo Verde and OTS stations. Keep an eye out for white-tailed deer and coatimundis. When combined with El Guayacán, the

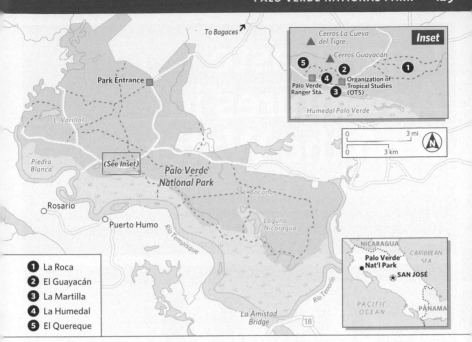

1 La Roca
2 El Guayacán
3 La Martilla
4 La Humedal
5 El Quereque

two trails form a loop. However, this mostly flat trail follows a lower line, bordering the park's marshland and principal lagoon. It is an excellent hike for spotting waterfowl, including the black-crowned night-heron. As with El Guayacán, the trail (2km/1.25 miles) should take just around an hour, one way.

An Insider's View of the Park

The **Organization for Tropical Studies (OTS)** runs a biological research station inside Palo Verde National Park. Aside from hosting scientists, researchers, and students, OTS also rents out rooms, which are slightly plusher than those at the ranger station, and offers guided hikes and boat trips through the park. If you plan to take a guided tour of Palo Verde, I recommend you book one with OTS, which has top-notch naturalist guides. ☎ 2524-0607. www.three-paths.co.cr. Rooms: $83 per person double occupancy, including 3 meals, 1 guided hike, and taxes. Tours: 3-hr. guided hike $18 adults, $12 children under 12; 4-hr. boat tour $35 adults, $25 children under 12. Advance reservations necessary for tours and overnight stays.

4 La Humedal. Located just off the main Palo Verde ranger station, this is a short (100m/330 ft.) elevated boardwalk-type trail that takes you over and through a thick marsh (the name of the trail means "wetlands"). If you're lucky, you'll see a crocodile.

5 El Quereque. If you want a change of pace, this is it. You'll head inland from the Palo Verde ranger station into a section of dense forest. Here you'll be able to walk through tall Guanacaste, pochote, cocobolo, and cedro trees; all of these species are common hardwoods used throughout Costa Rica, but they are protected here. Keep an eye out for monkeys and coatimundis. The .65km (.4 mile) trail should take around 40 minutes round-trip.

Spending the Night in the Park

You have a couple of options for staying at or near the park: camp out or stay at the ranger station (see "Entering the park," p. 128); rent a room at the OTS biological research station (see "An Insider's View of the Park," left); or come here as part of a guided day trip and base yourself in nearby Liberia (see p. 164).

Guanacaste Adventures in & on the Water

Guanacaste's roughly 250km (155 miles) of varied Pacific coastline create a playground of almost unlimited potential. Whether you want to catch some waves, scuba dive under the waters, or stalk a sailfish (note that it's all catch-and-release for sailfish and marlin), you will have your fill of options.

> Guanacaste has several fine surfing beaches.

Body Boarding & Surfing

There are amazing surf breaks up and down the Guanacaste coast. The prime surfing season is between December and late March, when the winds are strong and predominantly off-shore, though swells can be found year-round. For most surfers, the beaches of ★★ **Playa Tamarindo** (p. 137), ★★★ **Playa Grande** (p. 136), and ★★★ **Playa Avellanas** (p. 134) are the prime destinations. Hard-core surfers will want to head for more remote breaks like ★★ **Ollie's Point** and ★★★ **Witch's Rock** (see "Charlie Don't Surf, but Ollie Does," p. 132),

both of which are primarily accessed only by sea. Most of these breaks are beach breaks.

To rent equipment or take a lesson, head to Tamarindo and check in with ★ **kids** **Tamarindo Surf School** (☎ 2653-0923; www.tamarindo surfschool.com), ★ **Banana Surf Club** (☎ 2653-1270; www.bananasurfschool.com), or ★★ **kids** **Witch's Rock Surf Camp** (☎ 2653-1262; www.witchsrocksurfcamp.com).

Surf lessons run between $30 and $50 per person for a 2-hour session, including equipment. Board rentals range from $10 to $25 per day.

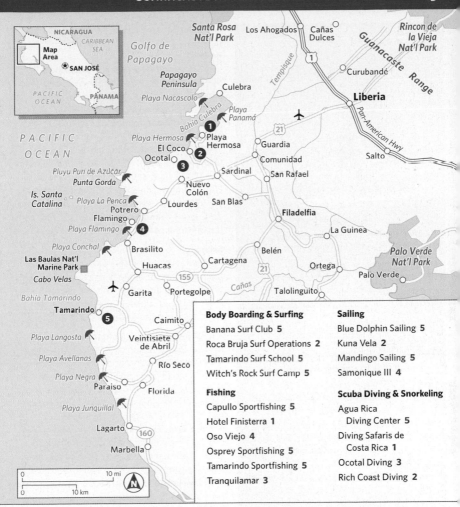

Body Boarding & Surfing

Banana Surf Club **5**
Roca Bruja Surf Operations **2**
Tamarindo Surf School **5**
Witch's Rock Surf Camp **5**

Fishing

Capullo Sportfishing **5**
Hotel Finisterra **1**
Oso Viejo **4**
Osprey Sportfishing **5**
Tamarindo Sportfishing **5**
Tranquilamar **3**

Sailing

Blue Dolphin Sailing **5**
Kuna Vela **2**
Mandingo Sailing **5**
Samonique III **4**

Scuba Diving & Snorkeling

Agua Rica
   Diving Center **5**
Diving Safaris de
   Costa Rica **1**
Ocotal Diving **3**
Rich Coast Diving **2**

Bodysurfing

The best places for bodysurfing are at the southern end of ★★ **Playa Tamarindo** (p. 137), ★★★ **Playa Avellanas** (p. 134), and ★★★ **Playa Grande** (p. 136). However, experienced and intrepid bodysurfers can try their luck at any of the major surf breaks on the coast.

Fishing

The waters off Guanacaste's coast are prime sportfishing grounds for a range of game fish, from large marlin and sailfish to feisty roosterfish to delectable dorado (mahimahi) and tuna. Although fishing is good year-round, the peak season for billfish is between mid-April and August. A number of captains offer anglers a chance to go after the "big ones" that abound in the offshore waters. The main destinations for fishing charter fleets are Playa Flamingo, Playa Hermosa, and Playa Tamarindo. Rates run between $700 and $2,500 per person per day,

Empty Sails?

Winds along the Guanacaste coast are inconsistent and fickle. They can range from dead calm to blustery with radically strong gusts. Sailing tours and charters often rely on motor power, with the sails providing little more than atmosphere and charm.

Charlie Don't Surf, but Ollie Does

★★ **Ollie's Point** is named after Oliver North, the infamous former lieutenant colonel at the center of the Iran-Contra scandal. During the 1980s, the beaches and ports of northern Guanacaste were a staging ground for supplying the Nicaraguan Contra rebels. Legend has it that during a news broadcast of an interview with North, some surfers noticed a fabulous point break going off in the background, hence the discovery and naming of Ollie's Point. Nearby, ★★★ **Witch's Rock** (locally known as **Roca Bruja**) is a legendary beach break, with a stunning offshore rock just behind it. For all intents and purposes, these two isolated surf breaks are reached only by boat. Tour operators at all the major beach towns along the coast offer day trips to them. Or you can contact ★★ **Roca Bruja Surf Operations** (☎ 2670-1020 or 8387-2359), which specializes in such trips. A boat carrying six surfers should run around $300 for a full day, including lunch and beer.

Tip: Both Witch's Rock and Ollie's Point are technically within Santa Rosa National Park, and permits are sometimes required to get to them. While enforcement is sporadic, boats without permits are sometimes turned away, so be sure your boat captain is licensed and has cleared access to the park.

depending upon the size of the boat, number of anglers, and distance traveled to the fishing grounds.

In Tamarindo, contact ★★ **Tamarindo Sportfishing** (☎ 2653-0090; www.tamarindo sportfishing.com), **Capullo Sportfishing** (☎ 2653-0048; www.capullo.com), or ★★ **Osprey Sportfishing** (☎ 2653-0162; www. osprey-sportfishing.com). They're all good, knowledgeable operators. In Playa Flamingo, **Oso Viejo** (☎ 8827-5533; www.flamingbeachcr. com) has a fleet of fishing charter vessels. In Playa Hermosa, check out ★ **Hotel Finisterra** (☎ 2672-0227; www.lafinisterra.com). In Playa del Coco, ★ **Tranquilamar** (☎ 8814-0994; www. tranquilamar.com) runs the best operation.

Sailing

Well-established cruisers offer a range of sailing tours out of most of the beach towns and destinations in Guanacaste. Offerings range from short sails and sunset cruises to full-day outings with lunch and snorkeling stops.

★★ 🔲 **Blue Dolphin Sailing.** The 12m (40-ft.) *Blue Dolphin* catamaran is run by the most established operator out of Tamarindo. The vessel's broad deck provides ample opportunity for sunbathing. Tamarindo. ☎ 2653-0446. www. sailbluedolphin.com. Rates $50–$75 per person half-day; $90–$140 per person full day.

★ **Kuna Vela.** The *Kuna Vela* is a spacious 14m (46-ft.) ketch plying the waters off Playa del Coco. A full-day cruise includes a couple of snorkeling stops and lunch, snacks, and an open bar. Playa del Coco. ☎ 8301-3030. www.kunavela. com. Rates $70 per person.

★★ **Mandingo Sailing.** If you want a classic sailing experience, climb aboard the *Lemuria,* a 15m (50-ft.) gaff-rigged schooner. The decks are of weathered teak, and the ship has a seaworthy feel. Tamarindo. ☎ 8831-8875. www.tamarindo sailing.com. Rates start at $55 per person.

★ **Samonique III.** Sailing out of Playa Flamingo (p. 135), the *Samonique III,* a 15.5m (51-ft.) ketch, has a variety of different tour options. Playa Flamingo. ☎ 8388-7870. www.costarica-sailing. com. Rates $50–$110 per person.

Scuba Diving & Snorkeling

Guanacaste's underwater wonders are better revealed to scuba divers than snorkelers. While visibility can be great for divers 12 to 27m (40–90 ft.) beneath the waves, snorkelers close

> *The Pacific waters off Guanacaste are prime sportfishing grounds for marlins and other billfish.*

to the surface often have only moderate visibility. That said, all of the scuba diving operators also offer snorkeling trips, and depending upon sea conditions, these can be quite rewarding. You can get scuba-certified (you'll be instructed on land and in a pool before you dive) with virtually all of these operators. Rates run from $70 to $140 per person for a two-tank dive, including equipment; and $50 to $75 person for snorkelers. The range in rates is mostly related to the distance traveled to the dive sites.

The **Catalina Islands** are the most popular destination, easily reached from Playa del Coco, Playa Ocotal, Playa Hermosa, and the Papagayo Peninsula. You can usually see whitetip reef sharks and other interesting marine life in these waters. A little farther afield, the **Bat Islands** are considered the region's top dive site. Bull sharks, whale sharks and mantas may be seen.

Top dive operations in the area include ★★ **Ocotal Diving** (☎ 2670-0321; www. ocotaldiving.com) in Playa Ocotal; ★★ **Rich Coast Diving** (☎ 800/434-8464 in U.S. and Canada, or 2670-0176 in Costa Rica; www. richcoastdiving.com) in Playa del Coco; ★ **Agua Rica Diving Center** (☎ 2653-0094; www. aguarica.net) in Tamarindo; and ★★★ **Diving Safaris de Costa Rica** (p. 156, **1**) in Playa Hermosa.

Capturing It on Film

No longer are underwater photography and video the exclusive realm of professionals with expensive equipment. Generic and custom waterproof housings can be purchased for most modern digital still and video cameras. If you don't own your own underwater camera or casing, you might want to bring cheap, disposable waterproof or underwater cameras. Alternatively, most dive shops rent professional or semiprofessional underwater still and video cameras for about $20 to $40 per day.

Guanacaste Beaches A to Z

★★★ **Playa Avellanas.** This white-sand beach stretches for miles and miles. There is very little development, aside from the legendary restaurant Lola's (p. 151); the gated resort community of Hacienda Pinilla, with its new JW Marriott resort (p. 149); and a handful of simple restaurants, rustic hotels, and envy-inducing homes. Good surf breaks can be found up and down Playa Avellanas; "Little Hawaii," just north of Lola's, is the best. 19km (12 miles) south of Tamarindo via a marked turnoff on the dirt road btw. Santa Rosa and Santa Cruz.

★★ **Playa Conchal.** *Conchal* is Spanish for "shell," and this beach was once made up almost entirely of soft crushed shells. Nearly every inch was a shell-collectors' paradise. Sadly, recent exploitation has had a noticeable effect on the beach, but it's still a beauty: broad and curving, overlooking a jaw-droppingly blue

sea, and still with thousands upon thousands of shells to marvel over. The beach is backed by shade trees and the ★★ **Paradisus Playa Conchal** (p. 162). *Warning:* The shoreline drops off steeply, and the surf and undertow can be pretty powerful, so be careful. 67km (42 miles) southwest of Liberia. Take CR21 west to Belén and then CR155 toward Playas Flamingo and Conchal; public access is via a coastal beach road from Playa Brasilito.

Playa del Coco. This was one of the first developed beach destinations in Guanacaste, and it's still very popular with local weekenders and

Beach Access

All of Costa Rica's beaches are public property, even those in front of exclusive resorts. However, this doesn't mean you can just traipse through the resort grounds and facilities. Ask nicely, and you will be shown the way to the waves.

> *The long curve of Playa Tamarindo encompasses popular surfing spots as well as quiet areas for swimmers.*

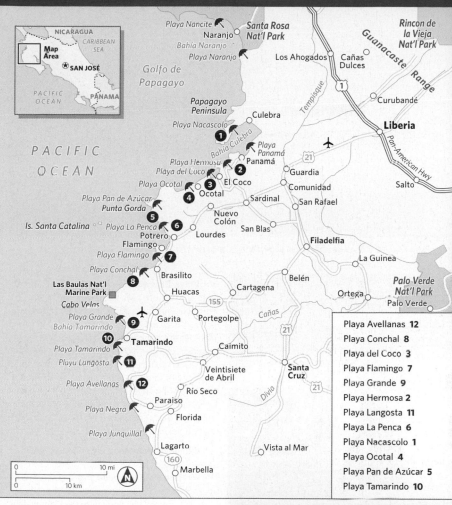

Playa Avellanas **12**
Playa Conchal **8**
Playa del Coco **3**
Playa Flamingo **7**
Playa Grande **9**
Playa Hermosa **2**
Playa Langosta **11**
Playa La Penca **6**
Playa Nacascolo **1**
Playa Ocotal **4**
Playa Pan de Azúcar **5**
Playa Tamarindo **10**

San José Ticos on holiday. The dark-sand beach is relatively calm for swimming, although not particularly attractive. Artisanal fishing boats and traveling cruisers bob at anchor just off the main pier at the center of the beach and at the spot where the main road into town dead-ends. All along the road leading toward the beach, you'll find a tight jumble of souvenir shops and stands, restaurants, and bars. 35km (22 miles) west of Liberia via a well-marked turnoff from CR21.

★★★ **Playa Flamingo.** This short, straight beach is one of the prettiest in the country. Locals say the soft, white sand's pink tinge gave foreign developers the idea to dub it Flamingo. A rocky

> *Lola's restaurant sits under the palms right on Playa Avellanas.*

> *Playa Conchal ("Shell Beach") is, not surprisingly, a good spot for shell seekers.*

> *In Guanacaste, where there are waves there are surfers.*

headland on the northern end of the beach rises high above the action and is home to a handful of hotels, restaurants, and private homes. The waves here are generally not big enough for surfing; nevertheless, it can be a bit rough for casual swimming at times. **71km (44 miles) southwest of Liberia. Take CR21 west to Belén, then CR155 toward Playas Flamingo and Conchal.**

★★ **Playa Grande.** The consistent beach break here is a favorite with surfers in the know. However, this long, straight, white-sand beach is also Costa Rica's prime nesting ground for giant leatherback turtles, the largest marine reptile in the world (see "The Spectacular Sea Turtle," p. 180). Because much of the marine and coastal territory is protected (to shield the turtle-nesting sites), you'll find only a handful of hotels, restaurants, and private homes here. **74km (46 miles) southwest of Liberia. Take CR21 west to Belén, then CR155.**

★★ kids **Playa Hermosa.** Surrounded by steep, forested hills, this curving gray-sand beach is backed by a swath of trees that stays surprisingly green even during the dry season. The shade they provide, along with the calm waters offshore, is a big part of the beach's appeal. The surf is generally small and safe for swimming, making this a popular spot for families. A range of hotels, restaurants, and shops line the beachfront, and operators renting watersports equipment often set up shop right on the sand. **39km (24 miles) southwest of Liberia via a well-marked turnoff on CR21.**

★ **Playa Langosta.** Much of the ocean fronting this uncrowded white-sand beach is very rocky. At lowest tide, there are several protected and calm pools. These are great to explore—you'll see all sorts of sea life in them—and a few are big enough to swim in. When the tide is high, you can swim only at the far southern end of the

> *There's often a volleyball game going on Playa Langosta near the Barceló resort.*

beach, near the Barceló Playa Langosta Resort (p. 151) and the mouth of the little estuary. You can cross the estuary and hike out toward Playa Avellanas to the south, but be careful, as the crossing can be tricky around high tide. A couple of small bed-and-breakfasts and several impressive luxury vacation homes line the beach. Just south of Tamarindo via the dirt road from the center of Tamarindo toward the Hotel Capitán Suizo.

★★★ **Playa La Penca.** This is one of the most beautiful and isolated beaches you will find along the Guanacaste coast. There are no hotels, restaurants, or facilities on the short, straight, white-sand beach. A few lucky folks have vacation homes on Playa La Penca, but overall, this spot is almost always uncrowded, if not downright deserted. 5km (3 miles) north of Playa Flamingo via a well-marked dirt road btw. Playas Flamingo and Pan de Azúcar.

★★★ kids **Playa Nacascolo.** Located on a calm bay and backed by the exclusive ★★★ **Four Seasons Resort** (p. 158), this broad strip of soft white sand is the prime stretch of beach on the Papagayo Peninsula. Set on the protected side of the peninsula, the beach drops off very gradually, and the waters are almost always perfect for swimming. A public parking lot and regular free shuttle service provides access for non-guests of the hotel. 40km (25 miles) southwest of Liberia. Take CR21 west to the well-marked turnoff for Papagayo Peninsula and the Four Seasons Resort, near the Do It Center store.

★ **Playa Ocotal.** A tiny, salt-and-pepper beach, Playa Ocotal provides a quiet alternative to the party vibe found at neighboring Playa del Coco. The protected waters are good for swimming, and a couple of small offshore islands and rocky outcroppings add to the charm. 38km (24 miles) southwest of Liberia via a well-marked turnoff from CR21; after Playa del Coco, look for the turnoff.

★ **Playa Pan de Azúcar.** This pretty salt-and-pepper beach, which translates as Sugar Beach, is backed by the Hotel Sugar Beach (p. 162) and almost never used by anyone other than the hotel guests. 78km (48 miles) southwest of Liberia; 7km (4⅓ miles) north of Playa Flamingo via a well-marked dirt road.

★★ kids **Playa Tamarindo.** Tamarindo's beach is long, wide, and gently curved, with some sections calm enough for swimmers and others just right for surfers. The best surf can be found toward the southern end of town and around the Tamarindo estuary. Swimmers looking for calmer waters should head to the far southern end, where a sandy islet makes a great destination if you're a strong swimmer. Playa Tamarindo is one of the few beaches around with ample restaurants and bars, which are set just off the sand and have a view of the water and waves. Itinerant sellers walk the beach hawking jewelry, cool drinks, and ice cream. 73km (45 miles) southwest of Liberia at the end of CR155.

Guanacaste Adventures on Land

Although Guanacaste is best known and most often visited for its incredible beaches, there are plenty of things to do on land, from riding along back roads and through dry forests on an all-terrain vehicle to bird-watching to taking a zip-line canopy tour through the treetops. In addition, the inland rivers provide opportunities for riding downstream on rafts and inner tubes.

> *A Fourtrax Adventure ATV tour involves wildlife-watching in addition to some rough riding.*

All-Terrain-Vehicle (ATV) Tours

★★ kids **Fourtrax Adventure.** The folks that run this operation have a fleet of late-model Hondas and offer a range of daily tours. Most stop at a couple of nearby beaches and small towns and villages, and end up with lunch and refreshments at the company's private farm. Along the way, you'll have the chance to spot mantled howler monkeys, coatimundi, and other wildlife. A typical tour is a 2½-hour affair, although longer ones are available, including some that combine an ATV excursion with a zip-line canopy tour or horseback ride. Kids can ride with their parents. Tamarindo. ☎ 2653-4040. www.four

traxadventure.com. Rates $75–$110 per person.

★★ **Hightide Adventures.** You'll find a variety of tours offered here, but my favorites are the 1-hour ride to watch the sunset from high above the ocean and the full-day surf excursion to isolated beaches and breaks along the coast. On that trip, picnic lunches, cool drinks, and surfboards are all strapped aboard the ATVs—you're good to go for a full day's adventure. As with Fourtrax, there are tours that include a zip-line canopy tour or some horseback riding. Tamarindo. ☎ 2653-0108; www.tamarindo adventures.net. Rates $55–$125 per person.

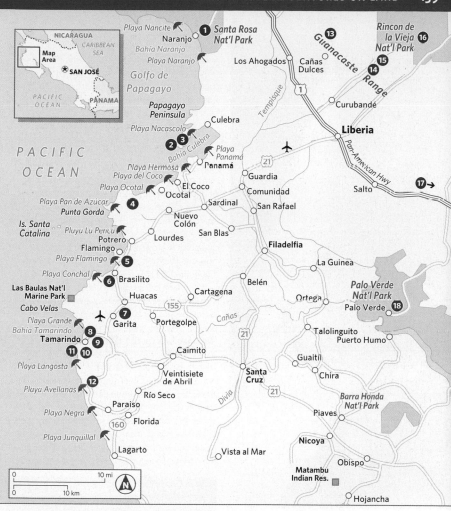

ATV Tours
Fourtrax Adventure **11**
Hightide Adventures **10**

Bicycling
Blue Trax Bike Shop **9**

Bird-Watching
Palo Verde National Park **18**
Rincón de la Vieja
    National Park **16**
Santa Rosa National Park **1**

Canopy Tours
Hacienda Guachipelin **15**
Cartagena Canopy Tour **7**
Congo Trail Canopy Tour **4**
Witch's Rock
    Canopy Tour **2**

Horseback Riding
Brasilito Excursions **6**
Casagua Horses **8**
Flamingo Equestrian
    Center **5**

River Rafting & Tubing
Hacienda
    Guachipelin **10**
Safaris Corobicí **17**

Spas
Anáhuac Spa **13**
Four Seasons Resort
    Costa Rica **3**
JW Marriott Guanacaste
    Resort & Spa **12**
Simbiosis Spa **14**

> *Among the many adventure offerings at Hacienda Guachipelin is a visit to a jungle waterfall.*

Bicycling

If you can handle the heat and dust, or schedule around it, there are some great back roads and trails to explore on mountain bikes. Most of the large resorts and hotels in the region have mountain bikes for guest use or rental. So far, **Blue Trax Bike Shop** (☎ 2653-1705) in Tamarindo is the only dedicated operator specifically focused on high-end mountain bike rentals. Late-model Trek and Specialized mountain bikes are available for around $20 per day. There is also a wide range of guided mountain-bike tours and excursions.

Bird-Watching

The coastlines and mangrove forests of Guanacaste provide excellent habitat for spotting all manner of shore and water birds, while the sparse, dry forests inland are great terrain for finding any number of local and migrant species.

★★★ **Rincón de la Vieja National Park** (p. 111, ❽) is one of the prime destinations for bird-watchers. This 14,100-hectare (35,000-acre) park ranges in elevation from 1,000 to almost 2,000m (3,300–6,500 ft.), with a mix of deciduous forests and savannas. Common species sighted here include rock wren, Botteri's sparrow, white-throated thrush, laughing falcon, Hoffmann's woodpecker, ruddy woodcreeper, and golden-crowned warbler. For more information, see the Rincón de la Vieja National Park site guide (p. 114).

With gentle trails and a variety of ecosystems, including tropical dry forest, savanna, mangrove forest, deciduous and evergreen forests, and coastal beaches and estuaries, ★★ **Santa Rosa National Park** (p. 125, ❺) is another excellent choice for bird-watching. More than 300 bird species have been recorded here. Some of the more prominent forest species you are likely to see include crested guan, great curassow, elegant trogon, and long-tailed manakin. Near the coast and in the mangroves you'll be treated to a plethora of waterfowl, including both the boat-billed heron and bare-throated tiger-heron. Throughout the park you'll hear the cries and see the bright

Extreme Weather Alert: Dust Storms & High Heat Ahead

Throughout the dry season (mid-November–mid-May), nary a drop of rain falls on the Guanacaste plains, mountains, and towns. The dirt roads and cattle paths used for ATV, mountain-bike, and horseback excursions get mighty dusty. For some this adds to the thrill and adventure, while for others it's quite a bummer. Be sure your operator offers goggles and dust masks when necessary. It can also get hot in Guanacaste, especially on a tour that ventures away from the ocean and pools. During the dry season, I recommend taking these tours either early in the morning or late in the afternoon, avoiding the hottest parts of the day.

> *Mealy parrots act like a couple of lovebirds at Santa Rosa National Park.*

flashes of yellow-naped and mealy parrots. For more information, see the Santa Rosa National Park site guide (p. 126).

On the southern edge of Guanacaste province, ★★★ **Palo Verde National Park** (p. 128) is prized by bird-watchers for its extensive network of marshes and wetlands. Including large portions of the Río Tempisque River basin, this habitat is home to gallinules, jacanas, limpkins, grebes, rails, and the least bittern.

Canopy Tours
★★★ kids **Hacienda Guachipelin.** This is one of the most extensive and varied canopy tours in the country. In addition to the traditional tree platform to tree platform zip-lines, this tour includes some bits of rappelling, rock climbing, "Tarzan swings," and hanging bridges. You even take a short horseback ride to get to the starting point of the adventure. Just before the entrance to Rincón de la Vieja National Park, 23km (14 miles) northeast of Liberia. ☎ 2665-3303 (reservations) or 2666-8075 (lodge). www.guachipelin. com. Rates $50 adults, $30 ages 4–12. Daily 8am–5pm.

kids **Cartagena Canopy Tour.** This canopy tour is convenient for folks staying at all of the beach destinations between Tamarindo and Playa

Flamingo. Set in a dense patch of tropical dry forest, the zip lines here don't provide the speed or thrills of some of the other options, but the surroundings are beautiful. On CR155, 56km (35 miles) southwest of Liberia. ☎ 2675-0801. Admission $45. Daily 8am–5pm.

One-Stop Adventure Shop

★★★ kids **Hacienda Guachipelin** (p. 165) offers many adventure tour options, including horseback riding, hiking, white-water river tubing, waterfall canyoning and rappelling, and the more traditional zip-line canopy tour. The hacienda's popular ★★ **1-Day Adventure Pass** allows you to choose as many of the hotel's different tour options as you want and fit them into 1 adventure-packed day. The price for this is $80, including a buffet lunch. Almost all the beach hotels and resorts of Guanacaste offer day trips here, or you can book directly with the lodge, which includes transportation in their fee. Be forewarned: During the high season, there's a bit of a cattle-car feel to the whole operation, with busloads of day-trippers coming in from the beach.

> Be sure to sign up for horseback riding with a reputable operator (such as those listed below) who takes good care of the horses and is conscientious of environmental concerns.

★ kids **Congo Trail Canopy Tour.** Located in a patch of thick forest on the outskirts of Playa del Coco and Playa Hermosa, Congo Trail features 11 treetop platforms and a small butterfly enclosure. The forest here is thick and rich, and it's quite common to see the attraction's namesake, *mono congo,* the howler monkey. 11km (7¾ miles) outside Playa del Coco, on the "Monkey Trail" dirt road to Playa Pan de Azúcar. ☎ 2200-2176. Admission $50. Daily 8am–5pm.

★★★ **Witch's Rock Canopy Tour.** With more than 3km (1¾ miles) of cables touching down on 23 platforms, this is one of the area's prime adventure tours. Its high perch over the Pacific and the Papagayo Peninsula makes it a worthy destination for the views alone. **On the loop road around the Papagayo Peninsula, just before the entrance to the Four Seasons Costa Rica Resort.** ☎ 2667-0661. Rate $65. Daily 8am–5pm.

Golf
See "Guanacaste's Best Golf Courses," p. 144.

Horseback Riding
Before the tourists arrived, Guanacaste was Costa Rica's "Wild West," with extensive cattle ranches and open dry savannas. Much of inland Guanacaste remains this way. You can rent horses at just about every beach destination and all of the inland adventure tour hot spots. I recommend not riding on the beach; few operators clean up after their horses, making for an ecological and aesthetic nightmare.

In addition to the numerous freelancers you'll find roaming the beaches, there are a few good specialized operators I recommend. **Flamingo Equestrian Center** (☎ 2654-4089) in Playa Flamingo; **Casagua Horses** (☎ 2653-8041) in Tamarindo; and **Brasilito Excursions** (☎ 2654-4237) in Playa Brasilito are all excellent operators with well-cared-for horses. All offer options that range from a quick ride at sunset to a longer trek through the savannas and dry forests of Guanacaste.

Rates run between $15 and $30 per hour. For an inland tour and excursion, I recommend Hacienda Guachipelin (see under "Canopy Tours," p. 141).

River Rafting & Tubing
★★★ kids **Hacienda Guachipelin.** One of the most unique river adventures in Costa Rica is this trip down the Río Negro aboard a large, specially designed inner tube. The trip is wet and wild and even includes a bit of horseback riding to the put-in point. Be forewarned: When the rains

> *A quiet float down the Río Corobicí is a good choice for those who want to look for wildlife—creatures of the water, the air, the trees, and the shoreline.*

are heavy, this river swells and the trip can be somewhat harrowing. **For directions and contact information, see under "Canopy Tours," p. 141. Rates $50 adults, $40 children 11–17, $30 children 4–10; not appropriate for children 3 and under.**

★★ kids **Safaris Corobicí.** These folks specialize in mellow river-rafting trips (with little white water) on their namesake Río Corobicí. They offer a range of tours, including 2-hour, 3-hour, and half-day outings that are great for families and bird-watchers. See p. 107, ⑤

Spas

If you're looking for a modern, high-end spa treatment, your best bets by far are at the ★★★ **Four Seasons Resort Costa Rica** (p. 158) and ★★★ **JW Marriott Guanacaste Resort & Spa** (p. 149). Both of these luxurious, large-scale resorts have extensive spa facilities and services. If you want a little local flavor, try one of the following.

★★ **Simbiosis Spa.** For something a bit simpler and more rustic than the traditional hotel spas mentioned above, head to Simbiosis, run by the neighboring Hacienda Guachipelín. This small

complex features several naturally fed sulfur hot springs, as well as a natural steam shower. My favorite thing about the spa is the freshly harvested warm volcanic mud, served up for a self-applied mud bath. The pools themselves don't get quite hot enough for my tastes, but they are warm and soothing. A wide range of massages, mud wraps, facials, and other treatments are available at reasonable prices. **For directions and contact information, see Hacienda Guachipelín under "Canopy Tours," p. 141. Admission $25 adults, $20 children 4–10; children 3 and under free. Massage and spa treatments (ranging from 30 to 150 min.) $35–$180.**

★★★ **Anáhuac Spa.** With a beautiful outdoor setting on the edge of a thick forest and with bubbling volcanic mud just steps away, this spa at the Hotel Borinquen Mountain Resort gets my vote as the best place for a local spa experience. While nowhere near as fancy or professional as the spas at the major resorts, this place does offer an extensive array of treatments. You could easily spend an entire day here. See p. 110, ⑦.

Guanacaste's Best Golf Courses

Costa Rica hasn't become a major golf destination, and it will probably be decades before that changes. That's not necessarily a bad thing—it doesn't mean there isn't golfing to be had, it just means it's often easier to get a tee time. Indeed, the country's greatest concentration of courses is found in Guanacaste and at least a few of these are world-class resort courses, with stunning ocean views and rich forest surroundings.

> The course at the Four Seasons Resort Costa Rica makes good use of its stunning Papagayo Peninsula location and sweeping Pacific Ocean views.

★★★ **Four Seasons Resort Costa Rica.** You have to stay here to play here, but for serious golfers (with serious cash to spend) it will be well worth it. This Arnold Palmer–designed course is Costa Rica's most spectacular. The course runs the length of a narrow peninsula, and there are ocean views from 15 of the 18 holes. The course itself plays relatively easy, which is a good thing, because the impressive scenery tends to take your mind off the game. The pro shop is top-notch and rents out high-end gear. End of the loop road on Papagayo Peninsula. ☎ 800/819-5053 in U.S. and Canada, or 2696-0000 in Costa Rica. www.fourseasons.com/costarica. Greens fees $195, including cart; twilight rate (after 2pm) $130. Four Seasons guests only; see p. 158.

★ **Garra de León at Paradisus Playa Conchal.** This gentle Robert Trent Jones–designed resort course—which translates as "the Lion's Paw"—features several holes with wonderful ocean vistas. Fairways are broad and open, and natural obstacles are at a minimum. In addition to the golfing, there's great bird and wildlife viewing on this course; I've even heard of a crocodile or two hanging out in the larger water hazards. Greens fees include unlimited use of the driving range and putting greens, and as many rounds as you can squeeze in. Paradisus Playa Conchal (p. 162), on Playa Conchal ☎ 888/741-5600 in U.S. and Canada, or 2654-4123 in Costa Rica. www.paradisus-playa-conchal.com. Greens fees $200, including cart.

★★ **Hacienda Pinilla.** South of Tamarindo, this Mike Young–designed 18-hole links-style course is the most challenging in Guanacaste. Many of the greens are protected by strategically placed

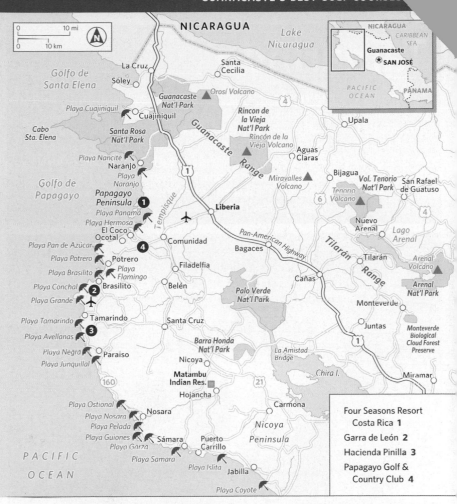

Four Seasons Resort
Costa Rica **1**

Garra de León **2**

Hacienda Pinilla **3**

Papagayo Golf &
Country Club **4**

pot bunkers. Clubhouse and pro-shop facilities are very well done. The nearby JW Marriott resort (p. 149) makes a good base for those seeking a plush golfing experience. Hacienda Pinilla, near Playa Avellanas. ☎ 2680-7000 www.hacienda pinilla.com. Greens fees $185, including cart.

Papagayo Golf & Country Club. This humble course has the feel of a public course in the United States; it is the most economical option in Guanacaste. Greens fees here are about half of what you'll pay at other courses in the area. Fittingly, the dress code and overall vibe are also more relaxed. The course is inland, so you won't have any ocean views, but you are welcome to enjoy the club's pool, restaurant, and bar facilities after your round. Just off CR151, 10km (6¼ miles) from Playa del Coco. ☎ 2697-1313. www.papagayo-golf.com. Greens fees $95, including cart.

Watch Those Winds

From mid-November through mid-May strong winds are very common in Guanacaste, and all the courses are affected. Many find this is a good opportunity to work on their bump and run game. Personally, I prefer to play during the early part of the rainy season, from mid-May through July, when the winds have died and the foliage and forests are at their most lush.

Tamarindo

Tamarindo is the hottest, hippest, and most booming beach town in Guanacaste. While that means you'll often find it more crowded here, you'll also find the greatest variety of hotels, restaurants, bars, nightclubs, casinos, and tour operators. That's because Tamarindo, in addition to having a gorgeous beach, makes an excellent base from which to explore the region. Just north of Tamarindo lies Playa Grande, a beach popular with both surfers and nesting sea turtles. To the south, you'll find the beach destinations and surf breaks of Playa Langosta, Playa Avellanas, and Playa Negra.

> Right in front of town, Tamarindo beach really gets hopping.

START Tamarindo is 73km (45 miles) southwest of Liberia; 295km (183 miles) northwest of San José.

1 ★★ kids **Playa Tamarindo.** I've mentioned this before in this chapter, but I can't stress it enough: Hit the sand before the sun gets too high. The beaches here can be scorching by the early afternoon.

The odds are good that if the waves are up you'll find scores of surfers doing their thing. If you'd like to join them, or if you just like to watch, the biggest swells can be found close to the cen-

ter of town or slightly south near the Tamarindo estuary. Beginners can sign up for a surf lesson at ★★ **Witch's Rock Surf Camp** (p. 130).

Refreshment on the Beach

Itinerant vendors are a big part of the beach scene in Tamarindo—take advantage and try the juice of a freshly cut green coconut. The sweet, watery juice is extremely refreshing and allegedly very good for you. The better vendors keep theirs on ice and charge about a dollar apiece.

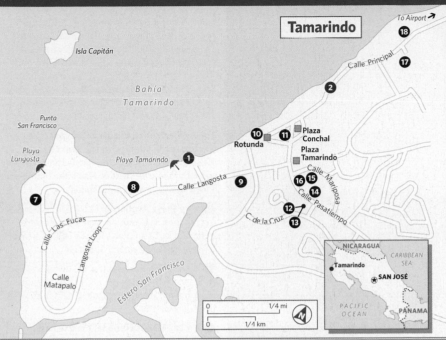

Tamarindo

To Airport ↗

Calle Principal

Isla Capitán

Bahía Tamarindo

Plaza Conchal

Plaza Tamarindo

Rotunda

Punta San Francisco

Playa Langosta

Playa Tamarindo

Calle Langosta

Calle Mariposa

Calle Pasatiempo

C. de la Cruz

Calle Las Fucas

Langosta Loop

Calle Matapalo

Estero San Francisco

0   1/4 mi
0   1/4 km

NICARAGUA

CARIBBEAN SEA

Tamarindo

⭐ SAN JOSÉ

PACIFIC OCEAN

PANAMA

1 Playa Tamarindo
2 Main Street
3 Playa Avellanas
4 Lola's
5 Las Baulas National Marine Park
6 Playa Grande turtle-nesting tour

Where to Stay

Best Western Tamarindo
  Vista Villas **17**
Cabinas Zullymar **11**
Hotel Arco Iris **12**
Hotel Capitán Suizo **8**
Hotel Pasatiempo **16**
JW Marriott Guanacaste
  Resort & Spa **19**
Sueño del Mar **7**

Where to Dine

Carolina's Restaurant & Grill **9**
Dragonfly Bar & Grill **14**
La Baula **15**
La Laguna del Cocodrilo Bistro **18**
Lola's **20**
Nogui's Café **10**
Seasons By Shlomy **13**

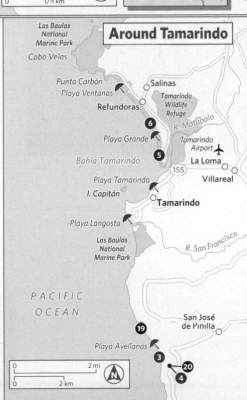

Around Tamarindo

Las Baulas National Marine Park

Cabo Velas

Punta Carbón
Playa Ventanas

Salinas

Tamarindo Wildlife Refuge

Refundoras

R. Matapalo

Playa Grande

Tamarindo Airport ✈

Bahía Tamarindo

La Loma

(155)

Villareal

Playa Tamarindo

I. Capitán

Tamarindo

Playa Langosta

Las Baulas National Marine Park

R. San Francisco

PACIFIC OCEAN

San José de Pinilla

Playa Avellanas

0   2 mi
0   2 km

> *A newly hatched leatherback turtle heads for the open sea on Playa Grande.*

Those who prefer to bodysurf may be tempted to ride the same waves as the surfers, but be warned that you run the risk of getting run over or bonked by an errant board. I suggest heading south of the heavy board-surfing action and finding a quieter section.

Swimmers looking for calm waters should head to the far southern end of the beach. Strong swimmers may want to make for the sandy islet just offshore, but it's best to attempt this swim with diving flippers. See p. 137.

② **Main Street.** It's easy to overlook Tamarindo's main drag in the quest for more beach time, but it would be a shame not to take at least a brief stroll through this funky surf town. You'll find a dense string of souvenir shops along the main road through town. Most offer a mix of locally produced crafts and Indonesian imports. Those looking for higher-end beach fashions should stop in at **Diamante** (☎ 2653-1126; daily 9am–6pm), in the little strip mall across from the Hotel Diriá. ⏱ 1 hr. Main road through town.

Follow the main road out of town past the airstrip to the intersection at Santa Rosa. Head south on CR152 (the road soon becomes gravel), following signs to Hacienda Pinilla and Playa Avellanas (19km/12 miles).

③ ★★★ **Playa Avellanas.** Make sure you arrive in time for lunch—not only is the beach here delightful, but it's home to Lola's (**④**), my favorite beachside restaurant. See p. 134.

④ ★★★ **Lola's.** Named after the owner's now-deceased 800-pound pet pig, this beachside restaurant is a real treat. Stop in for a drink or lunch. See p. 151.

⑤ ★★ **Las Baulas National Marine Park.** Leatherback Turtle Marine National Park encompasses both 440 hectares (1,100 acres) of beach and 220 sq. km (85 sq. miles) of ocean—primarily with the goal of protecting leatherbacks. A visit to the park, which surrounds Tamarindo, is a must, whether it's to see turtle nestings on Playa Grande (p. 120, **⑦**), go scuba diving, or explore the park's fascinating mangroves by boat. Just keep in mind that aside from the turtle tours in season, this spot doesn't operate as a national park per se—there are no hiking trails or visitor's center, and the tiny office is open only during turtle-nesting season. But you can book scuba diving and other tours through your hotel.

⑥ ★★★ kids **Turtle-nesting tour at Playa Grande.** It bears repeating: Seeing the turtles come ashore to lay their eggs is a can't-miss activity. Minimum 2hr. See p. 120, **⑦**.

Alternative Ending

If you're not here at prime turtle-nesting season (late September to late February), then spend an evening aboard the *Blue Dolphin*, taking one of the excellent sunset cruises (p. 132).

Where to Stay

> *Comfortable digs at the Sueño del Mar.*

Best Western Tamarindo Vista Villas

TAMARINDO This converted condo development offers a range of accommodations, from simple garden-view rooms to the fully equipped Tropical and Corona suites. The former are basic budget affairs, while the latter have full kitchens, large living rooms, and either a private patio or a balcony with fabulous views of the Pacific Ocean. This hotel caters to surfers, and there is often a lively, beach-party-at-spring-break atmosphere around the pool and at the bar. On the road into town, Tamarindo. ☎ 800/536-3241 in U.S. and Canada, or 2653-0114 in Costa Rica. www.tamarindovistavillas.com. 33 units. $89–$119 double; $159–$229 suite. AE, DC, MC, V.

Cabinas Zullymar TAMARINDO

Located in the heart of Tamarindo, just across the street from the beach, this long-standing local favorite offers neat and contemporary rooms at a good price. Across from Playa Tamarindo. ☎ 2653-0140. www.zullymar.com. 25 units. $46–$79 double. AE, MC, V.

Hotel Arco Iris TAMARINDO

This is a great option in this price range. Rooms feature minimalist contemporary Asian decor. Deluxe rooms are more spacious than bungalows; I especially like the second-floor deluxe units. The hotel is set a few blocks inland from the beach, but there's a small rectangular pool and the restaurant here, Seasons by Shlomy (p. 151), is one of the best in town. About .5km (⅓ mile) from the turnoff for the road to Playa Langosta. ☎ 2653-0330. www.hotelarcoiris.com. 10 units. $89–$99 double. AE, MC, V.

★★ kids Hotel Capitán Suizo TAMARINDO

With a prime location on the calmer and quieter southern end of Playa Tamarindo (p. 137), this is a great choice for all, including families. The grounds are lush, vibrant, and shady, and the pool is one of the larger in the area. Rooms are relatively plain but spacious, cool, and cozy. On the beach, near the southern end of Playa Tamarindo. ☎ 2653-0353. www.hotelcapitansuizo.com. 30 units. $175–$360 double. Rates include breakfast buffet. AE, MC, V.

Hotel Pasatiempo TAMARINDO

Located several blocks inland from the beach, this popular place has a party vibe. Most rooms are housed in duplex buildings, but each room has its own private patio with a hammock or chairs. The suites are cushy and well equipped, with separate sitting rooms. A small and inviting pool sits in the center of the complex, and the bar and restaurant here rage most nights. Inland, Tamarindo. ☎ 2653-0096. www.hotelpasatiempo.com. 17 units. $109–$139 double. AE MC, V.

★★★ kids JW Marriott Guanacaste Resort & Spa HACIENDA PINILLA

Costa Rica's newest large-scale resort is extremely luxurious, with an extensive spa and the largest pool in Central America. The resort features several excellent restaurants, and the rooms, amenities, and service are all top-notch. Hacienda Pinilla. ☎ 888/236-2427 in U.S. and Canada, or 2681-2000 in Costa Rica. www.marriott.com. 310 units. $225–$1,770 double. AE, DC, MC, V.

★ Sueño del Mar PLAYA LANGOSTA

This small, intimate bed-and-breakfast features attractive rooms with outdoor showers and a fabulous beachfront location. The "honeymoon suite" is a second-floor unit with much room, plus ocean views. Playa Langosta. ☎ 2653-0284. www.sueno-del-mar.com. 6 units. $195–$295 double. Rates include breakfast. MC, V.

here to Dine

> *A great way to while away an afternoon Costa Rica–style is lunch on the beach at Lola's.*

★★ **Carolina's Restaurant & Grill** TAMARINDO *INTERNATIONAL/FUSION* This elegant restaurant is run by a Costa Rican–Swiss couple who met at culinary school. The red-clay tile ceiling is exposed through heavy wood beams, and tables feature white cloths and glass candle holders. Start things off with the hot ginger and papaya soup, and follow that up with some sesame–seared tuna. Or opt for one of the nightly four- or five-course tasting menus. Presentations are artful, service impeccable, and the wine list excellent. On the road to Playa Langosta. ☎ 2653-1946 or 8379-6834. Entrees $12–$24. AE, MC, V. Dinner daily.

★★ **Dragonfly Bar & Grill** TAMARINDO *INTERNATIONAL/FUSION* Tucked away on a back street, this restaurant has earned a loyal following with its excellent food, large portions, and cozy ambience. The menu mixes and matches several cuisines, with the southwestern United States and Pacific Rim fusion the strongest

influences. Calle Mariposa, near the Hotel Pasatiempo. ☎ 2653-1506. Entrees $10–$16. AE, MC, V. Dinner Mon–Sat.

★ kids **La Baula** TAMARINDO *PIZZA* This open-air place serves up excellent wood-fired thin-crust pizzas at excellent prices. The ambience is convivial, and there's even a playground out back to keep the kids entertained while parents linger over drinks or dessert. Tamarindo. ☎ 2653-1450. Pizzas $8–$14. AE, MC, V. Dinner daily.

★★ **La Laguna del Cocodrilo Bistro** TAMARINDO *FUSION* The open-air garden dining here is elegant and romantic. The menu changes regularly, but the chefs always focus on using only the freshest and best ingredients available. One of the best options is the nightly tasting menu, which will feature anywhere from 5 to 7 courses, including dessert. On the beach, north end of Tamarindo. ☎ 2653-3897. Entrees $12–$29. MC, V. Dinner Mon–Sat.

Tamarindo after Dark

Tamarindo has the most happening nightlife in Guanacaste. The most consistently hopping bars in town are ★★ **Bar 1** (☎ 2653-2586, pictured above), on the second floor of a mini-mall on the road to Playa Langosta, and ★ **Aqua** (☎ 2653-2782), on the main road into town. Other popular spots open throughout the week include the **Crazy Monkey Bar** (☎ 2653-0114), at the Best Western Tamarindo Villas on the main road into town,

and the bar at the **Hotel Pasatiempo** (p. 149). Both of these places have televisions for sporting events and sometimes feature live music.

For those looking for some gaming, there are two casinos in town: the **Jazz Casino** (☎ 2653-0406), across from El Diriá hotel, and the casino at the **Barceló Playa Langosta** resort (☎ 2653-0363), out in Playa Langosta.

★★★ **Lola's** PLAYA AVELLANAS INTERNATIONAL/ SEAFOOD Lola's is arguably the best beachfront restaurant in the country—that's why I mention it so often in this chapter. It's got tons of charm and a relaxed *pura vida* vibe, and the food is great, too. Favorites here include fresh seared tuna, large salads, and Belgian French fries. You can also get fresh fruit smoothies and delicious sandwiches on just-baked bread. You'll have to come early on weekends to get a seat. On Playa Avellanas. ☎ 2652-9097. Entrees $4.50–$12.50. No credit cards. Lunch and dinner daily.

kids **Nogui's Café** TAMARINDO COSTA RICAN/ SEAFOOD This simple open-air cafe serves hearty breakfasts and well-prepared salads,

sandwiches, burgers, and casual meals. It's perfect for a quick bite. Just off the beach on the small traffic circle, Tamarindo. ☎ 2653-0029. Entrees $6–$17. AE, MC, V. Breakfast, lunch, and dinner daily.

★★ **Seasons by Shlomy** TAMARINDO MEDITERRANEAN/SEAFOOD Israeli-born chef and owner Shlomy Koren serves up contemporary cuisine with a heavy Mediterranean influence. Fresh fish and seafood are usually at the center of the regularly changing menu. The pool-side open-air dining is casual. Hotel Arco Iris, about .5km (⅓ mile) from the turnoff for Playa Langosta. ☎ 8368-6983. Entrees $13–$15. No credit cards. Dinner Mon–Sat.

Playa del Coco & Playa Ocotal

One of the busiest and most developed beach towns in Costa Rica, Playa del Coco is not for everyone. The beach here is a bit of a scene—the crowds seem to like their music loud and constant. Neighboring Playa Ocotal, on the other hand, is a cute little patch of sand backed by steep hillsides. Both beach towns (the names of the beaches and the towns themselves are interchangeable—Playa del Coco is also known as El Coco) are excellent places to stay if you're looking to scuba dive, as they are within easy reach of some of Costa Rica's—and perhaps the world's—best dive sites.

> Ocotal beach sits on a quiet cove.

START **Playa del Coco is 35km (22 miles) southwest of Liberia. Playa Ocotal is an additional 3km (1¾ miles) south.**

1 Playa del Coco. Playa del Coco's gray-sand beach is the center of all action here. The main road into town basically dead-ends at the water. Fishing boats and charter sailboats bob at anchor just offshore. Head off in either direction and you're sure to find a perfect spot to plop down.

When you've had enough of the surf and sand, spend some time browsing the souvenir shops and stands that line the main road through town. Most are simple, open-air tables and kiosks piled high with trinkets, T-shirts, and Indonesian imports. Beach is at the end of the road into town.

2 ★ Café de Playa Beach Club. Even if you're not staying at the Suites at Café de Playa, you might consider taking advantage of its facilities. A day pass costs $15 per person and gives you access to the club's pool and Jacuzzi and on-site spa (spa massages and treatments are extra). Perhaps the biggest draw here, aside from the excellent restaurant, is the broad grassy area fronting the beach, with rows of teak lounge chairs spread out under the shade of tall coconut palms. See p. 155.

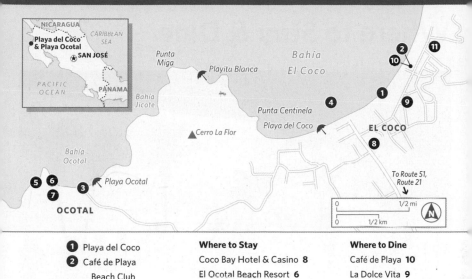

1. Playa del Coco
2. Café de Playa
   Beach Club
3. Playa Ocotal
4. Ocotal Diving

Where to Stay

Coco Bay Hotel & Casino **8**
El Ocotal Beach Resort **6**
Hotel Villa Casa Blanca **7**
The Suites at Café de Playa **10**
Villa del Sol B&B **11**

Where to Dine

Café de Playa **10**
La Dolce Vita **9**
Papagayo
   Pura Vida **5**

> Spend a day at the spa at Café de Playa.

Party Central

The most popular activities in Playa del Coco seem to involve hanging out—at the beach, at the *sodas*, at bars. If that's not your thing, plan to spend most of your days here on the water—charter boats for everything from diving to fishing and surfing are in abundance here. Ask your hotel for help booking trips.

3 ★ **Playa Ocotal.** This tiny pocket cove offers a nice change of pace. Plan to spend some time parked beneath one of the shade trees that come right down to the salt-and-pepper-colored sand. At the end of the road to Playa Ocotal.

4 ★★ kids **Ocotal Diving.** There's good snorkeling all around this area, but Playa Ocotal offers up arguably the closest and easiest access to the best sites. This is also a world-class dive destination—scuba divers take note and take advantage. Sign on for a scuba or snorkeling trip with Ocotal Diving (p. 133), which has an excellent operation. ⏱ 3 hr. Rates $50, including equipment and snack.

Where to Stay & Dine

> *The Suites at Café de Playa is a full-service resort with a spa and an open-air restaurant, all just steps from the beach.*

★ **Café de Playa** PLAYA DEL COCO *FUSION*
This is the most creative and eclectic restaurant in town, serving everything from fresh seared tuna and Mediterranean pastas to a cold Thai beef salad. There is a very tasty oriental rice salad with smoked tuna, caviar, and avocado. Lobster is served several ways, as is tenderloin filet. The open-air dining room and outdoor deck areas are set next to a well-tended grassy lawn that fronts the beach. On the beach, north end of town. ☎ 2670-1621. www.cafedeplaya.com. Entrees $12–$20. AE, DC, MC, V. Breakfast, lunch, and dinner daily.

kids **Coco Bay Hotel & Casino** PLAYA DEL COCO
This two-story hotel is the biggest thing in Playa del Coco and is an acceptable choice if you're looking for a cookie-cutter-style room close to the beach, restaurants, and action. The bland rooms are identical in size but have a variety of bedding options for singles, couples, and families. They share a common veranda, which gets blasted by the hot afternoon sun. You can't miss this large building on your right, on the main road into Playa del Coco—about 2 blocks before you hit the beach. Playa del Coco. ☎ 2670-0494. 33 units. $79–$107 double. V.

★ **El Ocotal Beach Resort** PLAYA OCOTAL
With a commanding hilltop perch and fabulous views, this place has the best rooms and facilities in the area. Guest rooms vary considerably in size and styling. Each of the six duplex bungalows shares a small ocean-view plunge pool. Bungalows at the top of the hill overlook a dramatic stretch of rocky coastline and have fabulous views, although if you want quick access to the beach, choose one of the lower units.

Note: It's a steep, vigorous hike from bottom to top at this resort. Playa Ocotal. ☎ 877/862-6825 in U.S. and Canada, or 2670-0321 in Costa Rica. www.ocotalresort.com. 42 units. $180–$340 double. Rates include breakfast. AE, DC, MC, V.

★ **Hotel Villa Casa Blanca** PLAYA OCOTAL
With friendly staff, beautiful gardens, and attractive rooms, this bed-and-breakfast located several blocks inland from the beach at Playa Ocotal is one of my favorite options in the area. All of the guest rooms feature fine furnishings and are well maintained. Some are a tad small, but others are quite roomy and even have kitchenettes. The suites are higher up and have ocean views. My favorite has a secluded patio with lush flowering plants all around. A little *rancho* (an open-air, thatch-roofed structure) serves as a bar and breakfast area; beside this is a pretty little lap pool with a bridge over it. Inland from the beach, Playa Ocotal. ☎ 2670-0518. www.hotelvillacasablanca.com. 10 units. $105–$125 double. Rates include breakfast. AE, MC, V.

La Dolce Vita PLAYA DEL COCO *ITALIAN*
The top Italian restaurant in Playa del Coco, this place features an extensive menu. Fresh pasta, risotto, and just-caught seafood are the highlights, but you can also get excellent thin-crust pizza. There's both indoor and patio seating. I prefer the latter when the weather permits. Inside the Centro Comercial El Pueblito. ☎ 2670-1384. www.ladolcevitacostarica.com. Entrees $8–$26. AE, DC, MC, V. Breakfast, lunch, and dinner daily.

Papagayo Pura Vida PLAYA OCOTAL
INTERNATIONAL The large, open-air dining room here is set poolside and overlooking the sea. The menu is heavy with fresh fish; daily specials might include a dorado (mahimahi) curry, or Cajun-style blackened grouper. At the Bahia Pez Vela resort, Playa Ocotal. ☎ 2670-0901. Entrees $9–$18. MC, V. Breakfast, lunch, and dinner daily.

★ **The Suites at Café de Playa** PLAYA DEL COCO
The five suites here are the best beachfront accommodations to be had right in Playa del Coco. The design and decor are minimalist, with contemporary fixtures, furnishings, and art. Rooms are arranged around a central pool area and come with either one or two queen-size beds. The best thing about the rooms is the fact that they are just a few steps from the sand. The on-site restaurant (p. 154) and beach club (p. 152, ❷) make this the top choice in town. On the beach toward the northern end, Playa del Coco. ☎ 2670-1621. www.cafedeplaya.com. 5 units. $160 double. AE, DC, MC, V.

Villa del Sol B&B PLAYA DEL COCO
This bed-and-breakfast is a friendly, family-run affair. The best rooms are the six studios, each with a small kitchenette, private bathroom, television, and telephone. Those on the second floor even have a bit of an ocean view from the shared veranda. There's a small pool with a covered barbecue area. Tasty dinners from a small menu of European-influenced dishes are prepared nightly for guests. Inland, toward the northern end, Playa del Coco. ☎ 866/793-9523 in U.S. and Canada, or 2670-0085 in Costa Rica. www.villadelsol.com. 13 units. $65–$75 double; $87 studio apt. Rates include taxes and breakfast (for rooms only, not studio apts.). AE, MC, V.

Playa del Coco after Dark

Playa del Coco is one of the liveliest beach towns on the Guanacaste coast. **Cocomar** (☎ 2670-0167) is the main dance club in town. Although it's getting a run for its money from the new, massive, open-air **Zi Lounge** (☎ 2760-1978). For a more sophisticated scene, head to **Zouk Santana** (☎ 2670-0191; www.zouksantana.com) a hip, Euro-style nightclub with local and visiting DJs spinning dance tunes most nights. For a mellower scene, try the **Lizard Lounge** (☎ 2760-0307), which has a pool table and a laid-back tropical vibe. All of these places are located within a few blocks of each other, along the main road into and through town. If you want to try your luck, the **casino** at the Coco Bay Hotel & Casino (p. 154) is the best in the area.

Playa Hermosa & the Papagayo Peninsula

Playa Hermosa (the name means "beautiful beach") is home to wide swaths of sand, tide pools, and calm, protected shores, which make it an excellent spot for families (though not so much for surfers). In spite of booming development that has brought big hotels and condos to the area, the place maintains its charm—as does neighboring Playa Panamá, which is relatively undeveloped. The Papagayo Peninsula is best known for its all-inclusive resorts, which are home to some of the best beaches around.

> *View of Playa Nacasolo from the Four Seasons Resort Costa Rica.*

START Playa Hermosa is 39km (24 miles) southwest of Liberia. The Papagayo Peninsula is 38km (24 miles) southwest of Liberia.

❶ ★★★ Diving off the Catalina and Bat Islands. The Catalina and Bat islands are easily accessible from this area and offer up some of the country's best and most reliable diving. Though many outfitters offer trips, I highly recommend **Diving Safaris de Costa Rica.** They're the top dive operator in Playa Hermosa, and they offer certification in addition to trips. Sign up for a morning of either snorkeling or scuba diving. ⏱ 3–4 hr. ☎ 2672-1260. www.costaricadiving.net. Rates including equipment $50–$75 per person snorkeling, $70–$140 per person two-tank dive.

❷ ★ kids Hotel Playa Hermosa Bosque del Mar. Whether or not you stay here, you must at least stop in for a drink or a meal at the open-air restaurant. It has the best setting (beachfront) and the best view (green forests cascading down to the ocean) of any place in this area. See p. 159.

Take CR21 north toward Liberia; at the Do It Center store, take the well-marked Papagayo Peninsula road, following signs toward the Four Seasons Resort. Witch's Rock Canopy Tour is on your right (total distance: 40km/25 miles).

❸ ★★★ Witch's Rock Canopy Tour. With fabulous views and more than 3km (1¾ miles) of cables touching down on 23 platforms, the Witch's Rock Canopy Tour is an excellent way to get your adrenaline pumping. ⏱ 2½ hr. See p. 142.

Take the peninsula road to the entrance of the Four Seasons Resort. If you are not a guest at the resort, you will be directed to a public parking area. A resort shuttle will take you to and from Playa Nacascolo.

❹ ★★★ kids Playa Nacascolo. You don't want to leave the area without spending at least some time on one of the most beautiful beaches in the area. The entire tip of the Papagayo Peninsula is taken up by the luxurious Four Seasons Resort. However, all beaches in Costa Rica are public property, and even people staying elsewhere can enjoy the sun, sand, and sea here. Near the southern tip of the Papagayo Peninsula. There's free public parking and a shuttle to the beach.

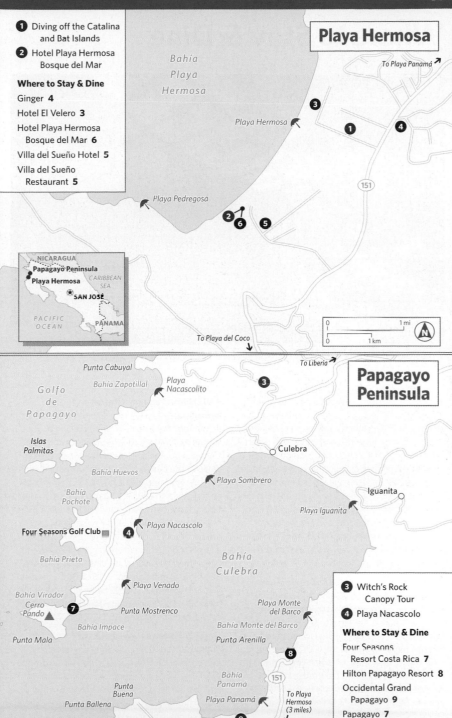

1 Diving off the Catalina and Bat Islands

2 Hotel Playa Hermosa Bosque del Mar

Where to Stay & Dine

Ginger **4**

Hotel El Velero **3**

Hotel Playa Hermosa Bosque del Mar **6**

Villa del Sueño Hotel **5**

Villa del Sueño Restaurant **5**

Playa Hermosa

To Playa Panamá ↗

Bahía Playa Hermosa

Playa Hermosa

Playa Pedregosa

3

1

4

151

To Playa del Coco ↓

NICARAGUA

Papagayo Peninsula

Playa Hermosa

CARIBBEAN SEA

★ SAN JOSÉ

PACIFIC OCEAN

PANAMA

0   1 mi
0   1 km

Papagayo Peninsula

Punta Cabuyal

Bahía Zapotillal

Playa Nacascolito

To Liberia ↗

3

Golfo de Papagayo

Islas Palmitas

Bahía Huevos

Culebra

Playa Sombrero

Iguanita

Playa Iguanita

Bahía Pochote

Four Seasons Golf Club

4   Playa Nacascolo

Bahía Prieta

Bahía Culebra

Playa Venado

Bahía Virador

Cerro Pando

7

Punta Mostrenco

Bahía Impace

Punta Mala

Playa Monte del Barco

Bahía Monte del Barco

Punta Arenilla

8

151

Punta Buena

Bahía Panamá

To Playa Hermosa (3 miles) ↓

Punta Ballena

Playa Panamá

9

3 Witch's Rock Canopy Tour

4 Playa Nacascolo

Where to Stay & Dine

Four Seasons Resort Costa Rica **7**

Hilton Papagayo Resort **8**

Occidental Grand Papagayo **9**

Papagayo **7**

Where to Stay & Dine

> The shady setting makes Hotel Playa Hermosa Bosque del Mar a great spot for a tropical drink on a hot afternoon.

★★★ Four Seasons Resort Costa Rica
PAPAGAYO PENINSULA Set on a narrow spit of land between two stunning white-sand beaches, this is the most luxurious and impressive resort in Costa Rica. The architecture is unique, with most buildings featuring flowing roof designs and other touches imitating the forms of turtles, armadillos, and butterflies. The rooms are large and plush, the service stellar, and the resort boasts the best golf course in the country. **Papagayo Peninsula.** ☎ 800/819-5053 in U.S. and Canada, or 2696-0000 in Costa Rica. www.fourseasons.com. 153 units. $815–$1,500 double. AE, DC, MC, V.

★★ Ginger PLAYA HERMOSA INTERNATIONAL/
TAPAS A range of creative dishes, with influences as wide-ranging as Asian and Italian, are served in tapas-size portions in a contemporary open-air space. Order the house special ginger-glazed chicken wings, along with some spring rolls and a plate of fresh dorado (mahimahi) marinated in vodka and Asian spices. **Inland near the center of Playa Hermosa.** ☎ 2672-0041. Entrees $4.50–$8. MC, V. Dinner Tues–Sun.

★ kids Hilton Papagayo Resort PAPAGAYO
PENINSULA This resort is quite spread out, so if you don't want to do a lot of walking or wait for the minivan shuttles, request a room near the main pool and restaurants—which are both close to the beach. Most of the duplex villas can be separated into two rooms or shared by a family or two couples. All rooms have marble floors, large bathrooms, and small private patios or balconies. If you want a view, ask for one on the hill overlooking the bay. The hotel has a large, modern, plush spa facility. **Just beyond Playa Panamá, Papagayo Peninsula.** ☎ 800/445-8667 in U.S. and Canada, or 2672-0000 in Costa Rica. www.hilton.com. 202 units. $229–$579 double; $530–$630 junior suite. Rates include meals, drinks, activities, taxes. AE, DC, DISC, MC, V.

Hotel El Velero PLAYA HERMOSA
Simple, airy, and bright rooms are offered up at a good price. The hotel is just steps from the sand and has a small pool, as well as an excellent restaurant. **On the beach near the center of Playa Hermosa.** ☎ 2672-1017. www.costaricahotel.net. 22 units. $89 double. AE, MC, V.

★ kids **Hotel Playa Hermosa Bosque del Mar**
PLAYA HERMOSA This place features cozy and
environmentally conscious accommodations
in a shady oceanfront setting. The grounds and
gardens are lush, and several rooms even have
large trees coming up through the outdoor deck
areas. On the beach at the southern end of Playa
Hermosa. ☎ 2672-0046. www.hotelplaya
hermosa.com. 32 units. $175–$275 double. AE,
MC, V.

★★ **Occidental Grand Papagayo** PAPAGAYO
PENINSULA Rooms here are spread over a
broad and contoured hillside above the ocean,
but not all come with an ocean view. The resort
is geared toward couples, and the vast majority of the rooms come with just one king-size
bed. The Royal Club rooms and suites are the
best; they include beefed-up concierge services.
The beach here is very protected and calm,
but it almost entirely disappears at peak high
tide. Between Playa Hermosa and Playa Panamá,
Papagayo Peninsula. ☎ 800/858-2258 in U.S.
and Canada, or 2672-0191 in Costa Rica. www.
occidentalhotels.com. 169 units. $426–$470
double; $747–$1,160 Royal Club room double.
Rates include meals, drinks, a range of activities,
and taxes. AE, DC, MC, V.

★ **Papagayo** PAPAGAYO PENINSULA *NUEVO
LATINO* This is my favorite restaurant inside
the Four Seasons Resort. Creative fusion meets
traditional local and Latin American fare and
offers it up in a relaxed, yet elegant ambience.
Inside the Four Seasons Resort, Papagayo Peninsula. ☎ 2696-0006. Entrees $25–$40. AE, DC,
MC, V. Dinner daily.

★ **Villa del Sueño Hotel** PLAYA HERMOSA
Villa del Sueño offers cozy rooms at a good
price. All the rooms have cool tile floors, high
hardwood ceilings, ceiling fans, and well-placed
windows for cross ventilation. The second-floor
superior rooms are larger, with larger windows.
Also under this hotel's management is the
neighboring "El Oasis" condominium development, which has additional apartment and
efficiency units available for nightly and weekly
rentals, as well as its own pool. Just inland, on
the southern end of Playa Hermosa. ☎ 800/378-

> *Dining at Ginger, a Playa Hermosa hot spot.*

8599 in U.S. and Canada, or 2672-0026 in Costa
Rica. www.villadelsueno.com. 45 units. $75–$105
double; $130–$255 condo unit. AE, MC, V.

★ **Villa del Sueño Restaurant** PLAYA HER-
MOSA *INTERNATIONAL* A mellow yet refined
atmosphere presides under slow-turning ceiling fans at this simple open-air restaurant. In
addition to lots of fresh fish, there are well-
prepared pasta dishes and meat and poultry
options. A small selection of specials is offered
nightly. During high season, there is live music most nights. At the Villa del Sueño Hotel.
☎ 2672-0026. Entrees $13.50–$25. AE, MC, V.
Breakfast, lunch, and dinner daily.

Getting Out of Town

If you're bored with beach time, no need to
worry. There are plenty of easy day trips from
this area. The friendly folks at ★ **Swiss Travel
Service** (☎ 2668-1020) will happily set you
up with tours of neighboring national parks,
rafting rides, and a range of other options.
Prices vary depending on the tour. If you'd
rather surf, ★★★ **Diving Safaris de Costa Rica**
(p. 156, ❶) can get you to Ollie's Point and
Witch's Rock for the day. Trips for up to six
surfers run $250 to $350 including lunch.

Playas Flamingo & Conchal & Nearby Beaches

At one time, this string of beaches (and the tiny towns that share their names) was the heart of Costa Rica's Gold Coast. They've been eclipsed by booms in Tamarindo and along the Papagayo Peninsula, but this is still a prime area for beach lovers. In addition to beach time, there are plenty of watersport opportunities, and horseback riding is a major pastime. If you're looking for action, these towns probably aren't for you—but if you'd like some quiet time to relax, this is the place to do it. One unnamed coastal road connects all of the beaches mentioned here.

> *Playa Flamingo is one of Guanacaste's prettiest beaches.*

START Playa Flamingo is 71km (44 miles) southwest of Liberia. Playa Conchal is 67km (42 miles) southwest of Liberia.

① ★ **Golfing at Paradisus Playa Conchal.** See p. 144.

kids ② **Horseback riding.** Explore the surrounding beaches on horseback, either on your own or as part of a tour. ☉ Minimum 1 hr. See p. 142.

③ ★★★ **Diving trip to the Catalina and Bat Islands.** It's an easy trip from here to these islands (p. 156, **①**), which feature excellent diving. The two dive shops in Playa Flamingo are the **Edge Adventure Company** (☎ 2654-4946)

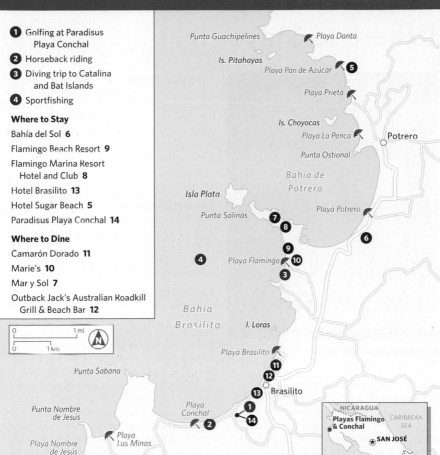

1 Golfing at Paradisus
   Playa Conchal
2 Horseback riding
3 Diving trip to Catalina
   and Bat Islands
4 Sportfishing

Where to Stay

Bahía del Sol **6**

Flamingo Beach Resort **9**

Flamingo Marina Resort
   Hotel and Club **8**

Hotel Brasilito **13**

Hotel Sugar Beach **5**

Paradisus Playa Conchal **14**

Where to Dine

Camarón Dorado **11**

Marie's **10**

Mar y Sol **7**

Outback Jack's Australian Roadkill
   Grill & Beach Bar **12**

Map labels:
Punta Guachipelines · Playa Danta · Is. Pitahayas · Playa Pan de Azúcar **5** · Playa Prieta · Is. Choyocas · Playa La Penca · Potrero · Punta Ostional · Bahía de Potrero · Isla Plata · Playa Potrero · Punta Salinas · **7** · **8** · **6** · **9** · **4** · Playa Flamingo · **10** · **3** · Bahía Brasilito · I. Loras · Playa Brasilito · **11** · **12** · **13** · Brasilito · Punta Sabana · Playa Conchal · **1** · **14** · **2** · Punta Nombre de Jesús · Playa Las Minas · Playa Nombre de Jesús · Playa Real · To Huacas, Tamarindo

Inset map: NICARAGUA · **Playas Flamingo & Conchal** · CARIBBEAN SEA · ★ SAN JOSÉ · PACIFIC OCEAN · PANAMA

and **Costa Rica Diving** (☎ 2654-4148). They both offer dive certification in addition to trips to the islands. Expect to pay $80 to $120 per person. ⏲ Minimum 4 hr.

4 **Sportfishing.** ⏲ Full day. See p. 131.

Beaches, Beaches, & More Beaches

This is prime beach territory, and most visitors come for the sand and sea. In addition to Playas Flamingo and Conchal, check out: ★★★ **Playa La Penca,** ★★ **Playa Pan de Azúcar, Playa Brasilito, and Playa Potrero.** See "Guanacaste Beaches A to Z," p. 134, for more on area beaches.

> *The course at Paradisus Playa Conchal was designed by Robert Trent Jones.*

Where to Stay

> *Hotel Sugar Beach is a secluded hideaway.*

Bahía del Sol PLAYA POTRERO
This small resort is the top place to stay on Playa Potrero. The hotel sits right on the water's edge, with direct access to the calm and quiet beach. Rooms are large and feature contemporary decor with bright primary colors at every turn, although the furnishings are sparse. All have either a private balcony or shared veranda, most of these strung with hammocks. On the beach, Playa Potrero. ☎ 866/223-2463 in U.S. and Canada, or 2654-4671 in Costa Rica. www.bahia delsolhotel.com. 28 units. $165–$375 double. Rates include full breakfast. AE, MC, V.

Flamingo Beach Resort PLAYA FLAMINGO
This large hotel boasts an enviable location fronting a gorgeous section of Playa Flamingo. The hotel is constructed in a horseshoe shape around a large pool and opens out onto the ocean. Half the rooms have clear views of the ocean across a narrow dirt road. The rest are deemed "mountain view" rooms and are not nearly as desirable. On the beach, toward the southern end, Playa Flamingo. ☎ 2654-4444. www.resortflamingobeach.com. 120 units. $119–$399 double. Rates include full breakfast. AE, MC, V.

★ **Flamingo Marina Resort Hotel and Club**
PLAYA FLAMINGO A wide range of rooms and furnished apartments are offered at this hillside hotel and beach club. All the rooms have patios or balconies, and most have pretty good bay views. Up the hill, north end of Playa Flamingo. ☎ 800/276-7501 in U.S. and Canada, or 2654-4141 in Costa Rica. www.flamingomarina.com. 89 units. $119–$280 double. AE, DC, MC, V.

Hotel Brasilito BRASILITO
This place offers up a great deal on clean and basic beachfront rooms. The best rooms have air-conditioning and small balconies with ocean views. On the beach, Brasilito. ☎ 2654-4237. www.brasilito.com. 15 units. $39–$56 double. V.

★ **Hotel Sugar Beach** PLAYA PAN DE AZÚCAR
Set on a beautiful, semiprivate salt-and-pepper-colored beach, this is the only hotel in the immediate area. It offers up oodles of seclusion and privacy. Nature lovers will be thrilled to find that howler monkeys and iguanas abound on the grounds. My favorite rooms are the oceanfront standard rooms, which have great views and easy access to the beach. However, the deluxe rooms and suites are larger and more luxurious, and some have excellent ocean views from a private balcony. On the beach, Playa Pan de Azúcar. ☎ 2654-4242. www.sugar-beach.com. 30 units. $125–$350 double. Rates include breakfast. AE, MC, V.

★★ **Paradisus Playa Conchal** PLAYA CONCHAL
This sprawling large-scale resort features plush rooms, a massive free-form pool, a regulation golf course, and a prime location fronting the all-shell beach, Playa Conchal (p. 134). All rooms are suites with a raised bedroom nook, marble bathroom, and garden patio or small balcony. While the rooms are almost identical, the Royal level suites come with butler service and access to a private, adults-only pool. Very few rooms have ocean views. On the beach, Playa Conchal. ☎ 888/336-3542 in U.S. and Canada, or 2654-4123 in Costa Rica. www.solmelia.com. 406 units. $319–$503 double. AE, DC, MC, V.

Where to Dine

> *You'll find it hard to tear your eyes away from the view at Mar y Sol.*

★★ Camarón Dorado BRASILITO *SEAFOOD*

Plastic tables set in the sand and fresh seafood well prepared make this one of my top choices in the area. More tables are available in the simple, open-air dining room for those who don't want to shake out their shoes after dinner. Service can be spotty at times, from lax to downright rude; however, when it's good, it's quite good. I once asked to see the wine list, and two waiters came over carrying about 12 different bottles between them, held precariously between the straining fingers of each hand. On the beach, Brasilito. ☎ 2654-4028. Entrees $6–$23. MC, V. Lunch and dinner daily.

★ Marie's PLAYA FLAMINGO *INTERNATIONAL/ SEAFOOD*

A Playa Flamingo institution, this place has large, new digs and continues to serve up excellent fresh fish, local specialties, and assorted Mexican fare, all at excellent prices. Check the daily blackboard specials, which usually highlight the freshest catch. In a small shopping center, center of town, Playa Flamingo. ☎ 2654-4136. Entrees $7.50–$25. V. Breakfast, lunch, and dinner daily.

★★★ Mar y Sol PLAYA FLAMINGO *INTERNA-TIONAL/SEAFOOD*

Set on a high hilltop this open-air restaurant serves up excellent and elegant meals. For starters, try the escargot in puff pastry. Lobster bisque and bouillabaisse are standout dishes, or for something different, try the duck served with a sauce made of passion fruit and cognac. Up the hill, north end of Playa Flamingo. ☎ 2654-4151. Entrees $17–$39. AE, DC, MC, V. Lunch and dinner daily Nov–Aug.

★ kids Outback Jack's Australian Roadkill Grill & Beach Bar BRASILITO *INTERNATIONAL*

This beachfront open-air joint has a menu almost as long, eclectic, and varied as its name. You can get nachos, quesadillas, and spicy wings, as well as fresh fish and seafood in a variety of preparations. There's even a full children's menu, which is hard to come by in these parts. There's a full, thatched Tiki style bar inside the large dining area, as well as tables set in the sand under shade trees and large, canvas umbrellas. Just across from the beach, Brasilito. ☎ 2654-5463. Entrees $6–$14. AE, MC, V. Lunch and dinner daily.

Liberia

Liberia, with a population of 37,000 is Guanacaste's provincial capital and the main transportation hub for the region. Founded in 1769, it's also the only spot left in the region that retains some of its colonial-era architecture— it's known as La Ciudad Blanca, or the White City, for its whitewashed adobe buildings. In fact, Liberia's narrow streets are lined with old homes, which feature ornate stonework, red tile roofs, and carved wood doors. Mango and palm trees shade the streets, and you may even see a horse-drawn cart making its way through the city. Still, Liberia is best appreciated as a day trip, or as a stop en route to Guanacaste's beaches—there's simply too much to see elsewhere.

> *Colonial architecture on Calle Real.*

START Liberia is 217km (135 miles) northwest of San José.

1 ★ **Calle Real.** This street was once the city's main boulevard, and it is lined with colonial-era homes and mansions. Some of these have been lovingly restored in recent years, and a stroll down this surprisingly quiet stretch will leave you feeling as though you've stepped back in time. Southeast of Plaza Central. See p. 124, **4**.

2 ★ **Iglesia La Ermita de la Agonía.** If you've timed it right, you will arrive at this old stone and stucco church during its very limited visiting hours. Built in 1865, the church is relatively plain inside, but a small collection of colonial-era religious relics is on display. ⏱ 20 min. Northeast end of Avenida Central. ☎ 2666-0107. Daily 2:30–3:30pm.

3 **Plaza Central.** Taking up an entire city block, Liberia's lovely central plaza is the heart and soul of the city. ⏱ 30 min. See p. 122, **1**.

Take the Pan-American Hwy. 8km (5 miles) south from Liberia to the well-marked entrance of Africa Mía.

4 ★★ **kids** **Africa Mía.** The non-native animals at this safari-style park range from gemsbok to giraffe. ⏱ Minimum 1½ hr. See p. 119, **3**.

Take the Pan-American Hwy. north 23km (14 miles) to the well-marked turnoff for the national park.

5 ★★★ **Rincón de la Vieja National Park.** ⏱ Minimum 3 hr. See p. 111, **8**.

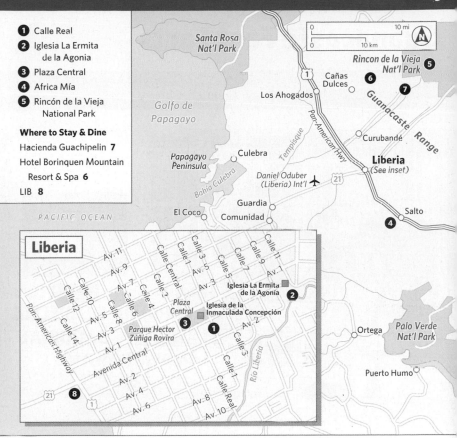

1. Calle Real
2. Iglesia La Ermita de la Agonia
3. Plaza Central
4. Africa Mía
5. Rincón de la Vieja National Park

Where to Stay & Dine
Hacienda Guachipelin **7**
Hotel Borinquen Mountain Resort & Spa **6**
LIB **8**

Where to Stay & Dine

★★ kids **Hacienda Guachipelin** RINCÓN DE LA VIEJA Set on the edge of Rincón de la Vieja National Park, this lodge is built around a still-operating 19th-century cattle-and-horse ranch. Rooms are simple, comfortable, and well kept. The best are in a series of long buildings enclosing a large lawn and garden. Rincón de la Vieja (23km/14 miles northeast of Liberia). ☎ 2665-3303 (reservations) or 2666-8075 (lodge). www.guachipelin.com. 52 units. $169–$180 double. Rates include 3 meals and taxes. AE, MC, V.

★★★ **Hotel Borinquen Mountain Resort & Spa** RINCÓN DE LA VIEJA This place offers the most luxurious accommodations and facilities close to Rincón de la Vieja National Park. The rooms,

spread along a verdant hillside, are large, plush, and well equipped. In the foot of the valley are several natural hot-spring pools of varying temperatures, a natural sauna, and the resort's ★★★ **Anáhuac Spa** (p. 110, **7**). Cañas Dulces, 34km (21 miles) northeast of Liberia. ☎ 2690-1900. www.borinquenresort.com. 33 units. $185–$323 double. AE, MC, V.

★ **LIB** LIBERIA SEAFOOD
Large and new, this place serves up good seafood and local cuisine and also has a very lively bar scene. There are live music and dancing most Friday and Saturday nights. Centro Comercial Santa Rosa, Liberia. ☎ 2665-7106. Entrees $8–$22. AE, DC, MC, V. Lunch and dinner daily.

Guanacaste Fast Facts

> *Local buses run from Liberia to the towns of Guanacaste.*

Accommodations Booking Services
In just about all instances, you are best off booking direct with the hotels and resorts listed in this guide. If you're looking for a longer stay or a condo rental, you might try some of the local real estate agencies, like Remax Tamarindo (☎ 2653-0073; www.remax-oceansurf-cr.com) or Century 21 (☎ 866/978-4492 in U.S. and Canada, or 2653-0030 in Costa Rica; www.costarica1realestate.com).

ATMs
Every major town and tourist destination in Guanacaste has at least one bank with a cash machine (*cajero automatico*). Check the main streets for signs saying *banco*.

Dentists & Doctors
The only major hospital in Guanacaste is the Liberia Hospital in Liberia (☎ 2666-0011). If you

have a mild medical issue or dental problem while traveling in Guanacaste, most hotels will be able to refer you to a local doctor (*medico*) or dentist (*dentista*) who speaks English.

Emergencies
In case of emergency, call ☎ 911 (there should be an English-speaking operator); if 911 doesn't work, contact the police at ☎ 2222-1365 or 2221-5337, and ask them to find someone who speaks English to translate. For an ambulance, call ☎ 128; to report a fire, call ☎ 118.

Getting There & Around
BY PLANE Liberia's **Daniel Oduber International Airport** is one of Costa Rica's two major airports and the most convenient gateway to Guanacaste. American, Continental, Delta, United, and U.S. Airways all have direct flights to Liberia. In addition, throughout the high sea-

son, numerous charter flights fly direct to Liberia from a number of cities in the United States, Canada, and Europe. If you fly into San José, you have several options for onward travel to Guanacaste. Two local commuter airlines—**Sansa** (☎ 877/767-2672 in U.S. and Canada, or 2290-4100 in Costa Rica; www.flysansa.com) and **Nature Air** (☎ 800/235-9272 in U.S. and Canada, or 2299-6000 in Costa Rica; www.natureair.com)—offer a host of daily flights from San José to both the airport in Liberia and the small airstrip in Tamarindo. Fares run between $115 and $130 one way. **BY CAR** If you're renting a car, take the Pan-American Hwy. north from San José to Liberia (217km/135 miles). At Liberia's principal intersection, a prominently marked road, CR21, heads west, with connecting, and similarly well-marked, spurs to all of the beach towns and destinations described in the guide. Once you're in Guanacaste, roads vary widely, from rough dirt and gravel tracks to recently paved two-lane thoroughfares. Rent a four-wheel-drive vehicle. **BY BUS OR SHUTTLE** Though a rental car gives you more freedom and flexibility, Guanacaste's main towns and beaches can be reached by local buses and private shuttles. **Gray Line** (☎ 2220-2126; www.graylinecostarica.com) and **Interbus** (☎ 2283-5573; www.interbusonline.com) are two private shuttle companies with daily scheduled departures to all the major tourist destinations in Guanacaste. Local buses are extremely economical, but you are at the mercy of their schedules and time-consuming stops along the way—unless you're staying for a few weeks, I don't suggest relying on them.

Internet Access

More and more hotels, resorts, and retailers around Costa Rica are offering high-speed Wi-Fi access, either free or for a small fee. You'll readily find Internet cafes in all major towns and tourist destinations around Guanacaste. Rates run between 50¢ and $3 per hour, and connection speeds are generally pretty good.

Pharmacies

Farmacias are easy to find in Guanacaste, particularly in beach towns like Tamarindo. If you can't find one, just ask your hotel for help.

Police

To report a lost or stolen article, such as a wallet or passport, visit the local police. Depending upon your location, that may be either the OIJ (judicial police), *guardia rural* (rural guard), or *policía metropolitana* (metro police). The number for the *policía de tránsito* (transit police) is ☎ 800/8726-7486, toll-free nationwide, or ☎ 2222-9330.

Post Offices

You'll find post offices in most of the beach towns, Liberia, and Tamarindo.

Safety

Most of the beach towns and tourist destinations of Guanacaste are relatively safe. That said, never leave items of value unattended in rental cars or hotel rooms (unless locked in a safe) or on the beach. Moreover, single women, couples, and small groups of tourists should probably avoid walking on desolate stretches of beach or back roads after dark.

Toilets

These are known as *sanitarios* or *servicios sanitarios* or sometimes *baños*. They are marked *damas* (women) and *hombres* or *caballeros* (men). Public restrooms are rare to nonexistent, but most hotels and restaurants catering to tourists will let you use their restrooms.

Visitor Information

There are no official information offices or bureaus in Guanacaste. Your best source of information—beyond this guide book—will be your hotel front desk and the local tour agencies.

Water

The water at most major resorts in Guanacaste is perfectly fine to drink. Most restaurants that cater to tourists use bottled or treated water. Nonetheless, some travelers experience stomach discomfort during their first few days in Costa Rica. If you want to be cautious, drink bottled water or *frescos* made with milk instead of water. *Sin hielo* means "no ice," and this is what you'll want to say if you're nervous about the water—even when frozen it's still water.

6
The Nicoya Peninsula

My Favorite Nicoya Peninsula Moments

For many visitors to Costa Rica, the Nicoya Peninsula is an afterthought. The beaches are not as famous as those in Guanacaste, and the rain forests, national parks, and ecotourism opportunities aren't nearly as well known as those in the Northern and Southern Zones. But in many ways, that's a plus—you won't find sprawling resorts or hordes of tourists here, but you will find lush jungles, quiet beaches, and plenty of adventure tours.

> PREVIOUS PAGE *As this bird's-eye view near Playa Sámara reveals, Nicoya has miles of unspoiled coastline.* THIS PAGE *The infinity pool at Hotel Punta Islita spills off into the horizon.*

❶ **Walking miles of deserted beach.** The Nicoya Peninsula is loaded with long, broad, and, best of all, empty stretches of beach. My favorite place to get away from it all is **Santa Teresa.** Not only is the beach gorgeous, but you can also walk along it all the way to Playa Hermosa and encounter virtually nothing but sand and sea. See p. 189.

❷ **Horseback riding from Montezuma to Cataratas El Chorro.** Given its isolation and natural wonders, this is one of the best places in the country to saddle up for a ride on the beach. The ride from Montezuma to El Chorro Falls (p. 173, ❷) is my favorite, but you'll have the chance to saddle up just about anywhere you go on the Nicoya Peninsula. See p. 191.

3 Taking a Flying Crocodile ultralight flight. One of the best ways to enjoy the stunning scenery of the Nicoya Peninsula is aboard an ultralight. You'll get a bird's-eye view of the coastline, treetops, and tiny towns of the region. You might even get to buzz low over one of the tour's namesake crocodiles. See p. 178, **5**.

4 Sunbathing on Playa Barrigona. Don't be surprised to find paparazzi lurking on this gorgeous beach—Mel Gibson owns quite a bit of the land around it. You may not end up on the cover of *People* magazine, but you'll definitely feel special lounging in the sun on this show-stopping stretch of sand. See p. 188.

5 Watching thousands of sea turtles come ashore at an *arribada*. The olive ridley sea turtles that come ashore on the Nicoya Peninsula's **Playa Ostional** do so en masse, hundreds at a time. Known locally as an *arribada,* this is an amazing spectacle, one not to be missed—and quite unlike the turtle-nesting tours in Tortuguero (p. 417, **6**) or on Guanacaste's Playa Grande (p. 120, **7**), which involve seeing small numbers of solitary turtles. See p. 209, **4**.

6 Taking a canopy tour over the Montezuma Waterfall. There are canopy tours all over Costa Rica, but this is one of my favorites: It sends you zigzagging over a rain forest canyon and the impressive Montezuma Waterfall. The tour even includes a swimming stop at the pool at the base of the falls. See p. 172, **1**.

7 Hiking inside Cabo Blanco Nature Reserve. Set on the very southernmost point—Cabo Blanco—of the Nicoya Peninsula, this is Costa Rica's oldest protected reserve. In addition to fabulous wildlife viewing, the park has post-card perfect beaches. My advice? Hike the longer, but more beautiful, Sendero Sueco trail to get to those beaches. See p. 173, **4**.

8 Lapping in the luxury at Hotel Punta Islita. This remote little resort is one of the premier boutique hotels in the country. With a fabulous hilltop location overlooking the ocean, over-the-top private villas, and stellar service, this is a romantic and luxurious getaway. See p. 205.

9 Watching the sunset while dining at Brisas del Mar. It's hard to say which is better, the fabulous food or the stunning setting overlooking the beach in Malpaís. The combination of the excellent Asian fusion cuisine and the oceanside views make this a not-to-be-missed dining experience. See p. 200.

The Best of the Nicoya Peninsula in 3 Days

With just 3 days to explore this peninsula, a finger of land running south from Guanacaste with the Pacific to the west and the Golfo de Nicoya to the east, you'll want to stick to the very southern tip. This will give you easy access to Montezuma and the Malpaís–Santa Teresa area, where you'll find the best beaches and the nicest hotels and restaurants. Since access to this region is primarily by ferry, it has a more isolated and undiscovered feel than most of Costa Rica's Pacific beach destinations. It also means that getting around is a bit more challenging. Plan to stay in Montezuma, which is a major departure point for many of the area's best tours. You'll want to rent a car to get around.

> *Santa Teresa's beach appeals to both tranquility-seekers and wave-riders.*

START **Montezuma, 145km (90 miles) west of San José. To get to Montezuma, take the Pan-American Hwy. from San José to Puntarenas, then catch the car ferry to Paquera; Montezuma is a 1-hour drive southwest on CR160.** TOUR LENGTH **80km (50 miles).**

❶ ★★★ Montezuma Waterfall Canopy Tour. One of the more interesting zip-line tours in the country, this one is built right alongside Montezuma's famous waterfall. The tour features 9 cables connecting 11 platforms and includes a swim at the foot of the falls. It is an excellent way to get in your visit to the waterfall without the hike. ⏱ 2½ hr. Downtown Montezuma. ☎ 8823-6111 or 2642-0808. www.montezuma traveladventures.com. Rates $40 per person. AE, MC, V. Tours depart 8:30am, 10am, 1pm, and 3pm.

0 ━━━ 2 mi
0 ━━━ 2 km

Río Ario
Bahía Ballena
Pánica
Tambor
Playa Tambor
Pta. Piedra Amarilla
Playa Manzanillo
Manzanillo
Cóbano
160
Río Negro
Playa Cocalito
2
Golfo de Nicoya
Playa Cocal del Peñón
Santa Teresa
San Isidro
Playa Montezuma
1
Playa Santa Teresa
8
Río Enmedia
5
Montezuma
PACIFIC OCEAN
Playa Carmen
Punta Barrigona
Playa Cabuya
Malpaís
6
7
3
Cabuya
Co. Buenos Aires
Isla Cabuya
NICARAGUA
Co. Altiliano
Cabo Blanco Nature Reserve
Pta. Mocha
CARIBBEAN SEA
Playa San Miguel
Pta. El Flor
SAN JOSÉ
4
Cabo Blanco
Playa Balsitas
Playa Cabo Blanco
PACIFIC OCEAN
PANAMA
Cabo Blanco
Isla Cabo Blanco

1 Montezuma Waterfall Canopy Tour
2 Cataratas El Chorro
3 Cabuya kayak & snorkel tour
4 Cabo Blanco Nature Reserve
5 Playa de los Artistas
6 Malpaís
7 Artemis Café
8 Santa Teresa

2 ★★ kids **Cataratas El Chorro.** After lunch, take a hike or a horseback ride from downtown Montezuma to this waterfall, which cascades into a tide pool at the edge of the ocean. The pool here is a refreshing mix of fresh and salt water, and you can bathe while gazing out over the sea and the rocky coastline. However, a massive landslide in 2004 filled in much of the pool and somewhat lessened the drama and beauty of the falls. More important to know, the pool is tidal—and disappears entirely at very high tide. Given that it will take you about 2 hours for the hike to El Chorro, it is wise to check the tide charts before you start off. The entirely flat hike is along the beach, so be sure to wear a hat and plenty of sunscreen. Alternatively, you can take a horseback tour to the falls with the folks at **Finca Los Caballos** (see p. 191). ⏱ Minimum 3 hr. The falls are 8km (5 miles) northeast of Montezuma. Finca Los Caballos: ☎ 2642-0124. www.naturelodge.net. Horseback ride $50 per person.

On the morning of Day 2, take the dirt road southwest out of Montezuma to Cabuya (6.5km/4 miles).

3 ★★ kids **Cabuya kayak & snorkel tour.** One of the most popular tours in the area is this kayaking trip through the generally calm and protected waters off the tiny village of Cabuya. The tour goes to a small island just offshore that serves as the town's cemetery. It includes an easy trek around the cemetery, as well as a snorkeling stop at some rocky outcroppings. ⏱ 3-4 hr. Cabuya is 6.5km (4 miles) southwest of Montezuma. Rates $40 per person, including picnic lunch.

Continue on the dirt road, heading southwest from Cabuya, to the Cabo Blanco reserve entrance (4.5km/2¾ miles).

4 ★★★ **Cabo Blanco Nature Reserve.** Occupying the entire southern tip of the Nicoya Peninsula, this was the first official protected area in Costa Rica. Spend the afternoon hiking through the preserve's lush forest right down to two deserted, pristine beaches 4km (2.5 miles) away. Or take a shorter, 2km (1.25-mile) loop trail through the primary forest here. The longer hike has several steep sections and is quite strenuous. But it's worth it: The beautiful, white-sand beaches here are backed by a lush tropical forest that is home to howler monkeys, which

More Information

For detailed information on sights and recommended hotels and restaurants in Montezuma, see p. 192. For information on booking tours, see "Book It!" (p. 194).

> *The Montezuma Waterfall Canopy Tour takes visitors swinging through the treetops around the famous cascade.*

you are pretty much guaranteed to hear, even if you don't see them. ⏲ Minimum 2 hr. 11km (6¾ miles) southwest of Montezuma. ☎ 2642-0093. Admission $10 adults, $1 children 6–12; children 5 and under free. Wed–Sun 8am–4pm.

Catching the Car Ferry

The quickest way to get to the Nicoya Peninsula is by taking the ferry from Puntarenas to Paquera. **Naviera Tambor** (☎ 2661-2084) runs car ferries roughly every 2 hours between 5am and 9pm. The trip takes 1½ hours and the fare is $12 per car, including the driver; $1.50 for each additional adult, and 80¢ for children. Get there early during the peak season and on weekends, because lines can be long, and if you don't make it aboard, you don't want to have to wait for the next one. Moreover, the ferry schedule changes frequently, with fewer ferries during the low season, and the occasional extra ferry added during the high season to meet demand. It's always best to check in advance.

⑤ 🦑 ★★★ **Playa de los Artistas.** You'll definitely want to have dinner at this open-air oceanfront joint in Montezuma. Why? Because the fresh grilled seafood is superb and there is always an array of delicious nightly specials to choose from. Across from the Hotel Los Mangos (p. 196). ☎ 2642-0920. $$. See p. 197.

On the morning of Day 3, head inland from Montezuma to the town of Cóbano; then follow the well-marked dirt road to Malpaís and Santa Teresa (12km/7½ miles).

❻ ★ ᴋⁱᵈˢ **Surfing lessons in Malpaís.** The neighboring beaches of Malpaís and Santa Teresa are two of Costa Rica's top surfing spots. Whether you're a rank beginner or a more experienced surfer looking to improve your style, check in at the **Malpaís Surf Shop** (☎ 2640-0173), on the beach in the center of town. A typical lesson lasts about 2 hours and costs $35 to $50 per person per hour, including the use of a board. Even beginners—including kids, who are often faster learners than adults—should be able to stand up on the board and ride a few

> *The setting sun silhouettes a rock formation off Santa Teresa, one of the peninsula's most beautiful beaches.*

waves after a single lesson. ⏱ Minimum 2 hr. See p. 198, ❶.

Head 4km (2½ miles) north along the beach to Playa Carmen, where you'll stop for lunch.

⑦ 🍵 ★★ **Artemis Café.** You'll need some energy after the morning's surf session, so bulk up on your proteins with a beer-battered fresh fish panini at this popular local joint. **Centro Comercial Playa Carmen.** ☎ 2640-0579; www.artemiscafe.com. $$. No credit cards. Breakfast, lunch, and dinner daily.

❽ ★★ **Beachcombing in Santa Teresa.** One of the most appealing aspects of this area is its tranquil, undeveloped coastline. You can satisfy your wanderlust by roaming along miles and miles of deserted beaches, scanning the sand for shells and other treasures washed ashore. I recommend starting around Playa Santa Teresa and walking as far north as you want. Be sure to take into consideration the time you'll need to walk back. ⏱ Minimum 2 hr. See p. 189.

> *Be sure to have a meal at Playa de los Artistas in Montezuma.*

The Best of the Nicoya Peninsula in 1 Week

Exploring the Nicoya Peninsula is truly going off the beaten path, at least by Costa Rican standards. Several of the area's most enchanting destinations are reached only by rough dirt roads (make sure you rent a four-wheel-drive!), so having a full week will come in handy. Plus, the beaches here are so inviting that you'll want plenty of time to lounge and enjoy.

> *Barra Honda National Park, in the peninsula's interior, protects a deep, underground cave system.*

START **Nosara, 266km (165 miles) west of San José.** To get to Nosara, take a 1-hour flight from San José; pick up a rental car in Nosara. TOUR LENGTH **295km (183 miles).**

❶ ★★★ **Playa Guiones.** Stretching for miles, the beach breaks here are a great place to learn how to surf. Even if you don't surf or want to learn, this beach, just outside Nosara town, is stunning, and there are a host of tours and adventure activities available. If you want a surfing lesson or

equipment, there are surf shops and surf schools nearby (p. 208, ❶). ☺ 2 hr. for a surf lesson.

Head to the main dirt road that leads from Playa Guiones to Nosara, and when you hit it (in about 1km/⅔ mile), turn right.

❷ **Nosara Yoga Institute.** You don't want your muscles to tighten up after surfing, so be sure to come here for the afternoon public yoga class. This is one of the top yoga centers in the country. The open classes focus on flow, relaxation,

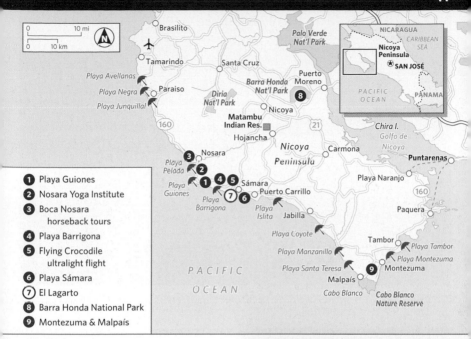

1. Playa Guiones
2. Nosara Yoga Institute
3. Boca Nosara horseback tours
4. Playa Barrigona
5. Flying Crocodile ultralight flight
6. Playa Sámara
7. El Lagarto
8. Barra Honda National Park
9. Montezuma & Malpaís

and stretching. Generally three are offered daily; reservations are recommended. ⏱ 1½ hr. Near the main access road to Playa Guiones. ☎ 2682-0360. www.nosarayoga.com. Open class $10 per person. Daily 8am, 10:30am, and 3pm.

On the morning of Day 2, take the main dirt road to the town of Nosara (5km/3 miles).

3 ★ **Boca Nosara horseback tours.** These folks have gentle, well-cared-for horses and excellent guides. Tours can be custom-tailored to your group's needs; I recommend mixing a bit of beach riding with a trip to a nearby jungle waterfall. Unless you're very comfortable in the saddle, the 2½-hour tour is probably plenty. ⏱ 2½ hr. Town of Nosara, near the airport. ☎ 2682-0280. www.bocanosaratours.com. Rates $85 single rider, $65 per person for 2 riders; price decreases with number. Daily 8am–4pm.

More Information

For detailed information on sights and recommended hotels and restaurants in and around Nosara (1–3), see p. 208; for Playa Sámara (4–8), p.202; for Montezuma (9), p. 192; and for Malpaís (9), p. 198.

> *Nosara Yoga Institute is the place to get out the kinks after your first surfing lesson.*

> *Playa Guiones and other beaches of the Nicoya Peninsula's Pacific coast offer miles of solitude.*

After your ride, take the coastal beach road south 9km (5½ miles) out of Nosara to Playa Barrigona.

④ ★★★ **Playa Barrigona.** Before you head for this fabulous and remote little beach, stop and pick up sandwiches and fixings for a picnic lunch from Café de Paris (p. 210), on the main road out of Nosara. You'll be all set for an afternoon of quiet lounging. See p. 188.

Continue another 9km (5½ miles) south on the coastal road to Playa Sámara, where you will spend the night. On Day 3, take the road north 2km (1¼ miles) from Playa Sámara to Playa Buena Vista.

⑤ ★★ **Flying Crocodile ultralight flight.** There's no better way to get a feel for the lay of the land and the big picture than aboard one of the Flying Crocodile's low-tech flying machines. I recommend taking a flight all the way to Cabo Blanco, on the southern end of the peninsula. ⊙ 2 hr. On Playa Buena Vista, north of Playa Sámara. ☎ 2656-8048 or 8827-8858; www. flying-crocodile.com. Rates $75 per person for a 20-min. introductory flight; $120 for 1-hr. flight. Daily 7am–5pm.

⑥ ★★ **Playa Sámara.** Spend the afternoon enjoying the calm waters and uncrowded sands of Playa Sámara. If you're looking for solitude,

head to either end, but if you want to be close to a cold drink or snack, stick to the center of the action. See p. 202.

⑦ 🍖 ★★ **El Lagarto.** You'll want to come to this open-air grill on the beach for dinner. The steaks are excellent, but I recommend asking what the catch of the day is and getting it grilled whole over hot coals. On the beach, north end of Playa Sámara. ☎ 2656-0750. $$$. See p. 207.

What's in a Name?

Nosara is an umbrella term used to refer to several neighboring beaches and tiny communities spread along this extremely isolated stretch of coast. In addition to the namesake town (a couple of kilometers inland) and beach, Playa Guiones, Playa Pelada, Playa Garza, and (sometimes) even Playa Ostional are also considered part of Nosara. Perhaps more confusingly, the term "playa" can sometimes refer to both a beach and a beach town.

Malpaís, likewise, refers to a string of neighboring beaches and tiny towns, including Malpaís, Playa Carmen, Santa Teresa, Playa Hermosa, and Playa Manzanillo.

On Day 4, take CR150 north out of Playa Sá-mara to Nicoya (37km/23 miles). Turn right onto CR21 and follow signs to San José and La Amistad Bridge. The entrance to Barra Honda is on your left, a few miles before the bridge. The whole trip is 62km (39 miles) and will take 2 hours.

8 ★★ kids **Barra Honda National Park.** Whether or not you're an experienced spe-lunker, you'll want to head to this unique na-tional park. Barra Honda features an extensive system of caves, some of which reach a depth of more than 200m (655 ft.). Human remains and indigenous relics have been found in some caves here, but those are not open to the pub-lic. **La Cueva Terciopelo** is the only one that is open to the public—but it's got enough thrills to satisfy most visitors. You begin your visit with a descent of 19m (62 ft.) straight down a wooden ladder with a safety rope attached. Once inside, you'll see plenty of impressive stalactites and stalagmites while visiting several chambers of varying sizes.

If you plan to visit Terciopelo Cave, you'll need to rent equipment and hire a local guide at the park entrance station. These guides are always available, and will provide harnesses, helmets, and flashlights. *Note:* The cave is open only during the dry season.

Even if you don't make the descent into Terciopelo, the trails around Barra Honda and its prominent limestone plateau are great for hiking and bird-watching. Be sure to stop at **La Cascada,** a gentle waterfall that fills a series of calcium and limestone pools, some of them large enough to bathe in. ⏱ Minimum 3 hr. 62km (39 miles) northeast of Playa Sámara on the road to La Amistad Bridge. ☎ 2685-5267 or 2659-1551. Daily 8am–4pm mid-Nov to Apr. Admission to park $10; guided tour $20–$35 per person.

In the afternoon, take CR21 south, following signs to Jicaral and Lepanto, to Paquera (the road is dirt and gravel for the final 10km/6¼ miles). From Paquera, take CR160 southwest to Cóbano and then Montezuma. Give yourself 3½ hours to make the 133km (83-mile) drive.

9 **Montezuma to Malpaís.** You'll spend the rest of your time on the peninsula's southern tip, between Montezuma and Malpaís. For Days 5, 6, and 7, follow the recommendations in the

Isla del Coco: World-Class Diving

A tiny speck of land some 480km (300 miles) off Costa Rica's Pacific coast, Isla del Coco is considered one of the world's greatest diving destinations. This is a prime place to see schools of scalloped hammerhead sharks. On a recent dive there, I spotted a ham-merhead just 4m (13 ft.) below me within 15 seconds of hitting the water. You're also likely to see silvertip reef sharks; marbled, manta, eagle, and mobula rays; octopi; hawksbill tur-tles; and the list goes on and on. While many dives around Costa Rica are fairly simple af-fairs, this one is not. There are often strong currents and choppy swells—not to mention all those sharks. This is not a trip for novice divers. And just getting there by boat takes nearly 36 hours. Still, if you're serious about diving, don't miss Isla del Coco.

To plan a trip, you should book with **Agressor Fleet Limited** (☎ 800/348-2628 in U.S. and Canada, or 2257-0191 in Costa Rica; www.aggressor.com) or with **Under-sea Hunter** (☎ 800/203-2120 in U.S. and Canada, or 2228-6613 in Costa Rica; www.underseahunter.com). Prices vary depend-ing on the length and time of the trip.

3-day tour (p. 172). Feel free to forgo the extra surf lesson, instead simply heading out on your own, chilling on the beach, or taking an alterna-tive tour or adventure. Hotel tour desks and independent operators in both Montezuma and Malpaís offer a wide range of opportunities.

THE SPECTACULAR SEA TURTLE

From Sand to Sea and Back **BY LINDA BARTH**

THE AMAZING SPECTACLE of sea turtles hauling themselves ashore to lay their eggs is a highlight of a trip to Costa Rica. Although these turtles can't breathe underwater—they surface for air—they spend nearly their entire lives in the water. The only time they're on land is when females lay eggs, and when new hatchlings make a mad dash from the sand to the surf. Sadly, every species of sea turtle is either threatened or endangered, and three of Costa Rica's five species—olive ridley, leatherback, and hawksbill—are considered critically endangered. These beautiful reptiles have fallen victim to poaching for eggs, meat, and their shells (do *not* buy turtle shell products, under any circumstances). Their numbers have also been battered by accidental catching in commercial fishing nets, pollution, development and habitat destruction on or near nesting sites, and global climate change.

Costa Rica's Sea Turtles

GREEN TURTLE
Good to know: Unlike most of its cousins, who are omnivorous or carnivorous, the green sea turtle is almost exclusively herbivorous, feeding on sea grasses and algae. **Nesting sites & seasons:** Caribbean coast around Tortuguero National Park, from July through mid-October, with a peak from August through September.

LEATHERBACK
Good to know: The world's largest sea turtle, the leatherback also has the greatest range, from as far north as Alaska and the edges of the Arctic Circle to as far south as Australia and the Cape of Good Hope. **Nesting sites & seasons:** Playa Grande (p. 120, **7**), near Tamarindo, from early October through mid-February; Tortuguero (in lesser numbers) from February through June, peaking during March and April.

OLIVE RIDLEY
Good to know: These turtles are famous for their massive group nestings, called *arribadas*, during which as many as 200 females per hour will come ashore at the same beach. **Nesting sites & seasons:** Playa Nancite in Santa Rosa National Park (p. 125, **5**) and Playa Ostional (p. 209, **4**), near Nosara; large *arribadas* occur from July through December, and smaller ones from January through June.

HAWKSBILL
Good to know: Named for its distinctive beak, this is one of the most hunted species in the world—in addition to its eggs and meat, its shell is highly coveted and used to produce jewelry, guitar picks, and eyeglass frames. **Nesting sites & seasons:** Caribbean coast, March through October, with a peak in September.

LOGGERHEAD
Good to know: This massive turtle, which can weigh up to 350kg (nearly 800 lb.), was once hunted for its fat, an ingredient in medicines and cosmetics. It is now endangered; shrimp and crab trawlers pose its biggest threats today. **Nesting sites & seasons:** Caribbean coast, May through August, with a peak in July.

Life Cycle of a Sea Turtle

BIRTH Gender is dependent upon the temperature of the sand during incubation, which lasts about 2 months. Most eggs in a single nest hatch more or less simultaneously, and the babies waste no time as they scramble for the water. But only a very small percentage make it, as gulls, frigatebirds, dogs, raccoons, sharks, and other predators lie in wait.

LIFE AT SEA Once they're in the water, sea turtles, which can live between 50 and 80 years, are solitary creatures. Most travel solo, except during mating season, when they will congregate to find partners. They feed on seaweed and plankton, and, particularly when they're young, they are prey for sharks, barracuda, and other large fish and invertebrates.

MATING While a hawksbill turtle can begin reproducing at only 3 years, it can take several decades for loggerhead and green turtles to reach mating age. Once sexually mature, these turtles mate at sea, usually in shallow water. Males have enlarged claws on their front flippers that help them hold on to females.

NESTING When it's time to lay eggs, the female turtle makes a laborious slog onto a beach (usually the same one where she was born), digs a massive hole, and deposits up to 200 soft-shelled eggs roughly the size of Ping-Pong balls. She then uses her flippers to cover the eggs with sand, and returns to the sea, her parental duties completed. Adult females nest every 2 to 3 years, although they come ashore and lay eggs several times per season.

The Nicoya Peninsula with Kids

The Nicoya Peninsula is best suited to adventurous families—you won't find much in the way of modern amenities here, and there are no resorts with a dedicated children's program. But if your family enjoys surfing, kayaking, wildlife viewing, and the like, the Nicoya Peninsula will make for a rewarding and memorable trip.

> *Howler monkeys, the loudmouths of the rain forest, are in residence at Curú National Wildlife Refuge.*

START Playa Sámara, 245km (152 miles) west of San José; 118km (73 miles) south of Liberia. TOUR LENGTH 4 days; 231km (144 miles). Fly from San José to Nosara (flight time: 1 hour), rent a car, and take the coastal road south 25km (16 miles) to Playa Sámara.

❶ ★★ Wingnuts Canopy Tours. Start your family adventure with a shared adrenaline rush on a high-wire adventure tour. Even very young children can strap on a harness and take a ride on this zip-line adventure attraction. ⊕ 2 hr. On the beach toward the southern end of Playa Sámara. ☎ 2656-0153. Rates $55 adults, $35 kids 17 and under. Tours daily at 7am, 10:30am, and 2pm.

Take the coastal road south out of Playa Sámara to Playa Carrillo (8km/5 miles).

❷ ★★ Playa Carrillo. Bring a picnic lunch to this gorgeous beach. The gentle waves are often perfect for kids and beginner body boarders to get some practice. If you don't have your own

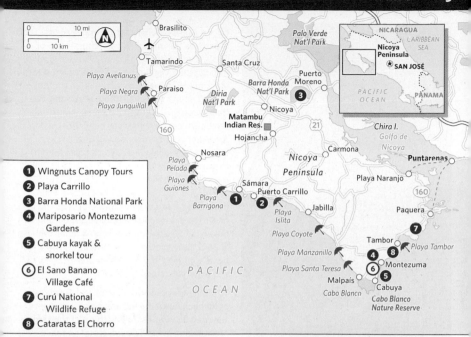

Map legend:

1. WIngnuts Canopy Tours
2. Playa Carrillo
3. Barra Honda National Park
4. Mariposario Montezuma Gardens
5. Cabuya kayak & snorkel tour
6. El Sano Banano Village Café
7. Curú National Wildlife Refuge
8. Cataratas El Chorro

More Information

I recommend that you use Playa Sámara as a base for ❶, ❷, and ❸; see p. 202 for information on additional sights and recommended hotels and restaurants. The sites in ❹–❽ are accessed from the center of Montezuma village (see p. 192). In most cases, you will be taking organized tours that provide transportation to and from your hotel.

boards, rent a few in Playa Sámara before setting out. See p. 202, ❷.

On Day 2, take CR150 north from Playa Sámara to Nicoya (37km/23 miles). Turn right onto CR21, and follow signs to San José and La Amistad Bridge. The entrance to Barra Honda is on your left, a few miles before the bridge. Total distance: 62km (39 miles).

❸ ★★ **Barra Honda National Park.** This large cave complex provides a perfect introduction to spelunking, with plenty of easy, kid-friendly options. Afterward, be sure to take a dip at **La Cascada,** a series of gentle waterfalls and limestone pools. ☺ Minimum 3 hr. See p. 179, ❽.

> Before you and your kids go swinging from the trees on a canopy tour, you'll be safely harnessed.

> The caves at Barra Honda National Park offer a good introduction to spelunking.

Take CR21 south, following signs to Jicaral and Lepanto, to Paquera (the road is dirt and gravel for the final 10km/6¼ miles). From Paquera, take CR160 southwest through Cóbano to Montezuma, where you will spend the night. Total distance: 133km (83 miles). On the morning of Day 3, take the road toward Cabuya and Cabo Blanco. After a few miles turn right onto the dirt road just past the entrance to the Montezuma Waterfall and the Amor de Mar hotel (p. 196).

④ ★★ **Mariposario Montezuma Gardens.** This is perhaps the most wild and natural of all of Costa Rica's butterfly gardens. Walkways wind through thick vegetation (which is covered with black mesh, to keep the butterflies in). If that doesn't sound appealing, there are additional trails through open forested areas—you'll still see butterflies, and you may see other wildlife, too. After a 45-minute tour (in English) led by knowledgeable guides, you'll be allowed to explore the trails at your leisure. Come in the morning, when the butterflies tend to be most active. Your kids will get a kick out of seeing how many different kinds they can spot. ⏲ 2 hr. On the dirt road heading uphill just beyond the entrance to the Montezuma Waterfall trail. ☎ 2642-1317. Admission $6.80 adults, $5.10 students with valid ID, $3.40 children 6–12; children 5 and under free. Daily 8am–4pm.

From the Mariposario Montezuma Gardens, head back down the hill and turn right where the road dead-ends; follow this dirt road from Montezuma out to Cabuya (total distance: 6.5km/4 miles).

⑤ ★★ **Cabuya kayak & snorkel tour.** This tour is a mix of mellow, kid-friendly paddling, snorkeling, and a short hike around a small island cemetery. All of the local tour agencies and hotel tour desks in Montezuma can help you book the tour, and honestly, none is better than the other. When necessary, be sure to rent two-person kayaks so that parents can paddle for the smaller kids. ⏲ 3–4 hr. See p. 173, ❸.

Retrace your route to downtown Montezuma.

⑥ 🎬 **Movie night at El Sano Banano Village Café.** Head to El Sano Banano for dinner and a movie—flicks are shown on a big screen while casual cuisine like burgers is served. Just check ahead to see what is playing. If it's too artsy for your kids or is otherwise age-inappropriate, you might want to save this for the next night. On the main road into Montezuma. ☎ 2642-0944. $$$. See p. 197.

On the morning of Day 4, take the main road from Montezuma northeast toward Paquera, and turn into the well-marked entrance to Curú (32km/20 miles).

> The whole family will enjoy a horseback ride to El Chorro, an oceanside waterfall.

7 ★★ **Curú National Wildlife Refuge.** This refuge has some prime wildlife viewing (hello, howler monkeys!) that will keep even the most easily bored kids enthralled. Add in a number of beautiful beaches, and you've got one of the nicest little refuges in the country. Rent horses to go exploring or just enjoy the beach and trails. Better yet, while you can easily explore Curú on your own, come as part of a guided tour. The naturalist guides will help you spot birds and beasts and fill you in on what you're seeing. ☺ Minimum 2 hr. See p. 194, **8**.

Retrace your drive to your hotel in Montezuma, where you'll be picked up for the following tour.

8 ★★ **Horseback ride to Cataratas El Chorro with Finca Los Caballos.** The horses are gentle, and the ride is short enough that kids won't get bored. The payoff is a seaside waterfall and a swim in its pool. ☺ 4 hr. See p. 173, **2**.

> Budding naturalists will take note of Nicoya's seaside denizens, including ubiquitous sand crabs.

Nicoya Peninsula Adventures in & on the Water

Although you'll find fewer hotels, towns, and tour operators here than you will in Guanacaste, you won't lack for adventure and activity options anywhere on the Nicoya Peninsula. Surfing and deep-sea fishing are both world-class here. You'll also find ample opportunities to get out onto the water on a sailboat, or paddle over the waves in a sea kayak.

> Billfish—including marlins and swordfish—are plentiful in the Pacific waters off the peninsula's western shore.

Bodysurfing, Body Boarding & Surfing

There are great waves to ride up and down the coastline. Almost across the board, these are caused by beach breaks, with plenty of peaks to go around. The most consistent and best-formed waves can be found at ★★★ **Playa Guiones** (p. 188), ★★ **Playa Carmen** (p. 188), and ★★★ **Santa Teresa** (p. 189). However, with the exception of Playa Montezuma, it's possible to find rideable waves most of the beaches here.

Beginners and bodysurfers might want to try ★★ **Playa Sámara** (p. 178, ❻) and ★ **Playa Pelada** (p. 189); when the swells are small, though, beginners will find excellent opportuni-ties for lessons at most of the beaches on this peninsula, even those known for their stalwart waves, such as Playa Guiones and Playa Carmen.

For lessons and board rentals see my recom-mendations in the individual beach town sec-tions (p. 198 ❶, p. 202 ❷, and p.208 ❶).

Sailing

The scarcity of good harbors makes it hard to find sailing tours out of most of the beach towns and destinations of the Nicoya Peninsula. Your best option is Playa Sámara, where ★ **Sámara Sailing** (☎ 2565-0235) offers a range of op-tions from short sails to sunset cruises to full-

Bodysurfing, Body Boarding & Surfing
Playa Carmen **8**
Playa Guiones **3**
Playa Pelada **2**
Playa Sámara **4**
Santa Teresa **7**

Sailing
CocoZuma Traveller **10**
Sámara Sailing **5**

Scuba Diving & Snorkeling
Cabuya **9**
Sámara Diving **5**

Sea Kayaking
Iguana Expeditions **1**

Sportfishing
Hotel Guanamar **6**
Kingfisher **5**
Sámara Sport Fishing **5**

day excursions. In Montezuma, check in with ★ **CocoZuma Traveller** (☎ 2642-0911; www. cocozuma.com), which can arrange a variety of sailing excursions.

Scuba Diving & Snorkeling

In general, the large swells, open seas, and dearth of calm harbors and offshore islands mean that snorkeling and scuba diving options are limited along the Nicoya Peninsula. One of the most popular tours out of Montezuma is a kayak and snorkel outing to a small island off the village of **Cabuya** (p. 173, **9**). The island's rocks and reefs are unusually rich in sea life, and the waters are generally very calm and protected. In Playa Sámara, check in with ★★ **kids Sámara Diving** (☎ 2656-0235), which is an excellent operation and the only game in town for scuba diving.

Sea Kayaking

Based out of the Gilded Iguana hotel in Nosara, ★★ **Iguana Expeditions** (☎ 2682-4089; www. iguanaexpeditions.com) is a well-established all-purpose tour operator with a wide range of full- and half-day tours around the area. They specialize in sea kayaking outings. Explore the inland coastal mangroves, or combine some

open-water paddling with a snorkeling break at San Juanillo. Half-day tours cost around $50; full-day tours run $100.

Sportfishing

As you'll find all along Costa Rica's Pacific coast, there's great offshore sportfishing but few good harbors. That said, all of the hotels in the area can arrange fishing charters. Fishing is good year-round; the peak season for billfish is between mid-April and August. Playa Carrillo, south of Playa Sámara, is the main center for sportfishing on the Nicoya Peninsula, with numerous top-end boats and captains. When deciding where to stay, keep in mind that ★★★ **Hotel Guanamar** (p. 206) is a particularly good base for sportfishing enthusiasts, as it has contacts with many of the area's best captains. If you're not staying at the Hotel Guanamar, contact ★ **Sámara Sport Fishing** (☎ 2656-0589) or ★★ **Kingfisher** (☎ 2656-0091; www. costaricabillfishing.com); both are located in Playa Sámara, although their boats actually operate out of Puerto Carrillo.

Rates for one to four people range from $200 to $500 for a half-day and $400 to $1,200 for a full day, depending on the size and accoutrements of the boat.

Nicoya Peninsula Beaches A to Z

★★★ **Playa Barrigona.** Many think this isolated and undeveloped white-sand beach is the prettiest one on the entire Nicoya Peninsula. The beach is backed by forested hillsides, and there's some good shade to be found where the forest meets the sand. Be careful of riptides when the surf is up. 9km (5½ miles) north of Playa Sámara (p. 202).

★★ kids **Playa Carrillo.** The long row of coconut palms lining the back of this white-sand beach only makes Playa Carrillo that much more striking. No building and development has been allowed anywhere close to the beach and water, giving it a remote and isolated feel, even though the beach itself can get crowded with locals and day-trippers from nearby Playa Sámara. The waves are usually pretty gentle here, making it the area's best beach for kids. 8km (5 miles) south of Playa Sámara (p. 202) on the coastal road.

★★ **Playa Carmen.** This stretch of sand begins right in front of the main crossroads entering Malpaís. There are excellent beach break peaks all along Playa Carmen. The beach is also often called, simply, Malpaís, although technically Malpaís runs south from here all the way to the rocky headlands of Cabo Blanco Nature Reserve. On the waterfront, north of the Malpaís crossroads.

★★★ **Playa Guiones.** This spot offers excellent surfing opportunities along its entire length and is the most popular beach in the Nosara area. As it is backed by sand dunes and grasses, there's very little in the way of trees or natural shade here, so come prepared with sunblock. South from the point shared with Playa Pelada.

★ **Playa Montezuma.** Thanks to its location, right on the edge of the town of Montezuma, this beach is quite popular. There are several

> *Playa Guiones offers plenty of waves and lots of room for settling on the sand.*

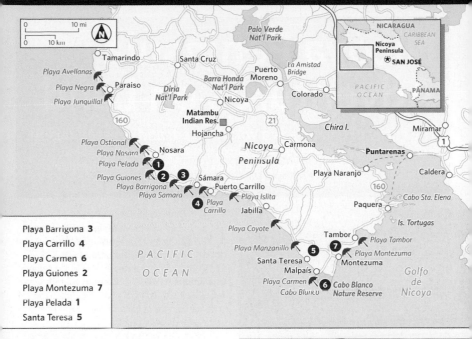

rocky patches that become exposed at low tide, so be careful when swimming. The best swimming spots are a few hundred yards north of town, in front of El Rincón de los Monos campground, or farther on just before the Ylang Ylang Beach Resort (p. 196). **Northeast edge of the town of Montezuma.**

★ **Playa Pelada.** Diminutive Playa Pelada is a white-sand beach with three deep scallops backed by mangroves. There isn't too much sand at high tide, so you'll want to come here when the tide's out. At either end of the beach, rocky outcroppings reveal tide pools at low tide. Surfers take note: On certain swells, there's a good point that breaks against an exposed offshore rock here. **Just north of Playa Guiones, near Nosara.**

★★★ **Santa Teresa.** More isolated and less crowded than Malpaís and Playa Carmen, this long, straight stretch of white sand features dozens of peaks to surf, body board, or bodysurf on. Near the northern end of Santa Teresa you'll find the plush boutique hotel Milarepa (p. 201) and Florblanca Resort (p. 200). **North of Playa Carmen, stretching several miles.**

> *Playa Carrillo and its swaying palms.*

Nicoya Peninsula Adventures on Land

The Nicoya Peninsula is a wild, rugged, and isolated region with plenty of opportunities for adventurous travelers. The hiking and bird-watching are top-notch, and you'll find plenty of other land-based adventure options in most of the main beach towns and destinations.

> Horseback riding is a popular activity in Nicoya.

All-Terrain-Vehicle (ATV) Tours

The rugged terrain, deserted beaches, and dirt back roads of the Nicoya Peninsula are perfect for exploring in an ATV. A guided tour is best if you are interested in seeing wildlife, learning about the region's natural history, or going to secret spots known only by locals. Venturing off on your own affords a sense of adventure and discovery and is quite safe. Just be sure you don't get lost.

In Montezuma, check in with ★ **CocoZuma Traveller** or **Sun Trails**, both of which offer guided and unguided options; see "Book It!,"

p. 194. In Malpaís and Santa Teresa, you can rent a quad vehicle from **Malpaís ATV Rentals** (p. 199, ❸). In Nosara, try **Monkey Quads** (☎ 2682-1001) or **Gunter's Quads** (☎ 2682-0300), or for an organized ATV tour, ★★ **Iguana Expeditions** (p. 209) or **Coconut Harry's Quad Tours** (☎ 2682-0574). All are located in the main tourist hub of Nosara, between Playa Guiones and town.

Rates for ATVs run around $35 to $50 for a half-day, and $60 to $80 for a full-day rental. Guided tours run from $45 to $110 per person, depending upon the size of the group and the length of the tour.

Bird-Watching

The mix of coastline, mangrove forest, lowland tropical forest, and farmland and pastures makes the Nicoya Peninsula an excellent spot for bird-watchers. Some of the area's more common and prominent species include the long-tailed manakin, crested caracara, elegant trogon, and sulphur-winged parakeet. My advice is to bring your own binoculars so you don't have to share—birds won't linger while you swap specs.

Bird-watchers will definitely want to visit ★★ kids **Curú National Wildlife Refuge** (p. 194, ❽) and ★★★ **Cabo Blanco Nature Reserve** (p. 173, ❹). Both areas offer a mix of forest and coastal birding opportunities. All of the local hotels and tour agencies can arrange for guided bird-watching tours to these reserves. Tours generally last around 2 hours and cost from $20 to $35 per person, depending upon group size. Ask at your hotel for suggestions for the best local bird guides.

ATV Tours

Coconut Harry's
Quad Tours 2

CocoZuma Traveller 6

Gunter's Quads 2

Iguana Expeditions 2

Malpaís ATV Rentals 4

Monkey Quads 2

Sun Trails 6

Bird-Watching

Cabo Blanco
Nature Reserve 5

Curú National
Wildlife Refuge 7

Canopy Tours

Canopy del Pacífico 4

Montezuma Waterfall
Canopy Tour 6

Wingnuts Canopy
Tours 3

Caving

Barra Honda
National Park 1

Hiking

Cabo Blanco
Nature Reserve 5

Horseback Riding

Boca Nosara Tours 2

Finca Los Caballos 6

Turtle-Nesting Tours

Iguana Expeditions 2

Tío Tigre Tours 3

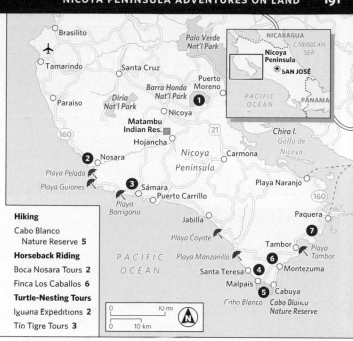

Canopy Tours

You'll find zip-line canopy tours in Playa Sámara, Montezuma, and Malpaís. My favorite is the ★★★ **Montezuma Waterfall Canopy Tour** (p. 172, ❶) in Montezuma. Two other excellent operations are ★★ kids **Wingnuts Canopy Tours** (p. 182, ❶) in Playa Sámara and ★ **Canopy del Pacífico** (p. 199, ❷) in Malpaís.

Caving

Costa Rica's best spelunking can be had smack dab in the middle of the Nicoya Peninsula, at ★★ kids **Barra Honda National Park** (p. 179, ❽). The Terciopelo Cave here provides an excellent experience for both first-time cave explorers and experienced hands. There are also some cool pools and hiking trails outside the cave.

Hiking

Aside from its miles of untouched and unexplored beaches, the Nicoya Peninsula's best hiking can be found inside the ★★★ **Cabo Blanco Nature Reserve** (p. 173, ❹). The main trail here, Sendero Sueco (Swiss Trail), is a rugged and sometimes steep hike through thick rain forest. The trail leads to the beautiful Playa Balsita and Playa Cabo Blanco, two white-sand stretches that straddle either side of the namesake Cabo Blanco point. The beaches are connected by a short trail.

Horseback Riding

The beaches and back roads of the Nicoya Peninsula provide excellent horseback-riding opportunities at every turn. You'll find offerings by both organized tour operators and simple local farmers and ranchers, or *campesinos*, at every town and destination in the area. The most dedicated and specialized operators are ★★ kids **Finca Los Caballos** (☎ 2642-0124; www.naturelodge.net), in Montezuma, which offers rides to Cataratas El Chorro (p. 173, ❷), and ★ **Boca Nosara Tours** (p. 177, ❸), in Nosara. Horseback-riding tours run from $20 to $30 per hour depending upon group size.

Turtle-Nesting Tours

The massive *arribadas* (p. 209, ❹) of olive ridley sea turtles on Playa Ostional, north of Nosara, are a real treat. The tours are at night and involve a drive to the beach at Ostional, where the turtles come ashore to lay their eggs. Nosara is your best base for trying to catch this amazing natural phenomenon, and ★★ **Iguana Expeditions** (p. 209) is an excellent local operator, charging just $25 per person. If you're in Playa Sámara, contact ★ **Tío Tigre Tours** (p. 203), which offers turtle-nesting tours in season for $35 per person.

Montezuma

Long the haunt of UFO seekers, hippie expatriates, and European budget travelers, Montezuma is starting to attract a wider range of visitors. However, the tiny town still maintains its alternative vibe. The natural beauty, miles of almost deserted coastline, and diversity of wildlife first made Montezuma famous, and they continue to make this one of my favorite beach towns in Costa Rica.

> After working up a sweat getting there, you'll want to take the plunge at Montezuma Waterfall.

START Montezuma is 201km (125 miles) south of Liberia; 145km (90 miles) west of San José; 36km (22 miles) southwest of Paquera.

1 ★★ Montezuma Waterfall. It requires a bit of a hike to reach this beautiful rain-forest waterfall, with its deep pool that is perfect for swimming. The well-marked trail entrance is just across from the Amor de Mar hotel (p. 196). At the first major outcropping of rocks, the trail disappears and you'll have to scramble amid rocks and riverbank for a bit. The trail occasionally reappears for short stretches—just stick close to the stream, and after about 20 minutes you'll come to the first of the three falls. Happily for those in the mood for a short hike, these first falls are by far the most spectacular. They're also the tallest and feature the largest and deepest swimming hole, making them the most popular and, at times, most crowded of the falls. Off the right side of the main waterfall, a steep trail leads to two higher falls, each with a swimming hole at its base, and each featuring a rope swing for launching yourself into the water.

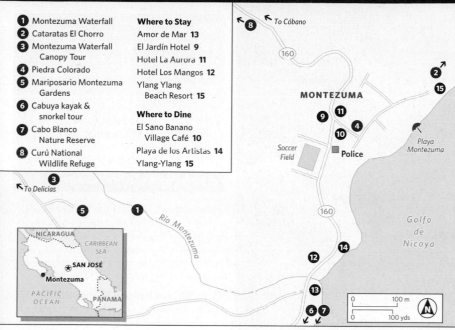

	Where to Stay
1 Montezuma Waterfall	Amor de Mar **13**
2 Cataratas El Chorro	El Jardín Hotel **9**
3 Montezuma Waterfall	Hotel La Aurora **11**
Canopy Tour	Hotel Los Mangos **12**
4 Piedra Colorado	Ylang Ylang
5 Mariposario Montezuma	Beach Resort **15**
Gardens	
6 Cabuya kayak &	**Where to Dine**
snorkel tour	El Sano Banano
7 Cabo Blanco	Village Café **10**
Nature Reserve	Playa de los Artistas **14**
8 Curú National	Ylang-Ylang **15**
Wildlife Refuge	

Warning: Be very careful when climbing close to the rushing water, and even more so if you plan on taking any dives into the pools below. Each year several people get scraped up, break bones, or otherwise manage to hurt themselves on the slippery rocks. ◷ Minimum 2 hr. Trailhead on the southwestern outskirts of town, across from the Amor de Mar hotel.

2 ★★ kids **Horseback ride to Cataratas El Chorro with Finca Los Caballos.** ◷ Minimum 3 hr. See p. 173, **2**.

3 ★★★ **Montezuma Waterfall Canopy Tour.** This is my favorite way to visit the Montezuma Waterfall. You get to combine a swim in the waterfall's main pool with a zip-line canopy tour that runs alongside the waterfall and through some beautiful rain forest. ◷ 3 hr. See p. 172, **1**.

4 ★ **Piedra Colorado.** There are plenty of simple souvenir stores and itinerant artisans selling their wares on the street and beach, but it's worth stopping in at this tiny downtown storefront. The owners produce impressive silver, stone, and polished-shell creations. Inside the tiny strip mall in the center of Montezuma. ☎ 2642-0612 or 8841-5855. Daily 9am–5pm. AE, MC, V.

> *A peaceful ride on the beach at Montezuma.*

> You'll get to really explore the falls on the Mont-
ezuma Waterfall Canopy Tour.

5 ★★ kids **Mariposario Montezuma Gardens.**
Come in the morning, when the butterflies tend
to be most active. ⊕ 2 hr. See p. 184, **4**.

6 ★★ kids **Cabuya kayak & snorkel tour.** Every
tour agency in Montezuma offers kayaking trips
to a small offshore island where the tiny village
of Cabuya maintains its town cemetery. You'll
also have the chance to snorkel among the
rocks and reefs here. ⊕ 3–4 hr. See p. 173, **3**.

7 ★★★ **Cabo Blanco Nature Reserve.** Spend
an afternoon hiking and exploring this beautiful and historic park. It's worth the effort to

Book It!

★ **CocoZuma Traveller** (☎ 2642-0911; www.
cocozuma.com) and **Sun Trails** (☎ 2642-
0808; www.montezumatraveladventures.
com) are the two main tour operators in
town. Both can arrange all of the tours mentioned here, as well as ATV outings, scuba
diving, rafting trips, car and motorcycle
rentals, and airport transfers. In addition,
all of the hotels in town have their own tour
desks or will help you book any of the tours
and activities available in Montezuma.

make the 4km (2.5-mile) hike to Playa Balsita,
a stretch of fine white sand backed by thick,
lush forest at the end of the Sendero Sueco trail.
Playa Balsita is almost always deserted, so enjoy
the solitude. ⊕ Minimum 2 hr. 11km (6¾ miles)
southwest of Montezuma. See p. 173, **4**.

8 ★★ kids **Curú National Wildlife Refuge.** This
is a private reserve, with several very pretty,
secluded beaches, as well as forests and mangrove swamps and a small system of trails. The
area is extremely rich in wildlife: Mantled howler and white-faced monkeys are often spotted
here, and there are quite a few species of birds.
You will usually see scarlet macaws, as the refuge is actively involved in a macaw protection
and repopulation effort.

Horses are available to rent in the refuge for
$10 per hour. Typically, the horse rentals work

Hitching a Ride to Cabo Blanco

If you don't feel like driving to the Cabo
Blanco Nature Reserve, there is an easy
alternative. Shuttle vans run from Montezuma roughly every 2 hours beginning at
8am (remember, you're on Tico time, so be
prepared to be flexible), and then immediately make the return trip. Keep in mind that
the last shuttle leaves Cabo Blanco around
5pm. The fare is $2 each way, and the ride
takes around 30 minutes. Be forewarned:
The shuttles often don't run at all during
the off-season. If the shuttle isn't running,
or you've managed to miss it, you can take
a taxi without seriously breaking the bank.
The fare is around $15 to $20 per taxi, which
can hold four or five passengers.

> *White-faced capuchins charm visitors to Curú National Wildlife Refuge.*

like this: You'll ride, with a guide, for about an hour to a lovely beach, hang out on the sand for about an hour, and then ride back. Happily, you only get charged for the time you're actually on horseback, so trips run about $20. If you'd like to take a longer ride, simply ask if they'll accommodate you. If you don't have a car, arrange transportation in advance with the folks who manage the refuge, or plan to come as part of an organized tour. ⏲ Minimum 2 hr. 32km (20 miles) northeast of Montezuma on the road to Paquera. ☎ 2641-0004. www.curuwildliferefuge. com. Admission $8. Daily 7am–3pm (last entry; the park closes at dusk).

Where to Stay

> The rooms at Amor de Mar have simple, tropical charm.

★ Amor de Mar

This hotel has simply appointed rooms in a two-story wooden building with an idyllic setting. The best feature is a tide pool big enough to swim in on a rocky coral outcropping fronting the hotel. There is also a large, fully equipped two-story, four-bedroom house for rent next to the hotel. **Just outside of Montezuma, along the road to Cabuya.** ☎ 2642-0262. www.amordemar. com. 11 units, 9 with private bathroom. $50–$60 double with shared bathroom; $70–$95 double with private bathroom; $200 house. V.

★ Hotel El Jardín

This is a good choice if you're looking for a well-equipped room close to the action. The rooms are located in a series of buildings spread across a steep hillside. Number 9 is my favorite, with pretty stonework in the bathroom, a greater sense of privacy than some of the others, and a good view from the private terrace. There's a two-level pool and Jacuzzi in a relaxing little garden area. **On the main road into Montezuma.** ☎ 2642-0074 or 2642-0548. www.hoteleljardin. com. 15 units. $65–$75 double. MC, V.

★ kids Hotel La Aurora

Rooms in this long-standing budget favorite are spread over three floors in two neighboring buildings fronting the town's small park and playground. The hotel features a couple of common sitting areas, a small lending library, some hammocks and comfortable chairs for chilling out, a communal kitchen, and flowering vines growing up the walls. **Montezuma.** ☎/fax 2642-0051. www.playamontezuma.net. 18 units. $45–$70 double. AE, MC, V.

Hotel Los Mangos

Built in the midst of a mini mango plantation, the shared-bathroom budget rooms here are basic and worn, but you do have access to the pool. The hardwood bungalows are the better accommodations, but even these are pretty Spartan. The former restaurant has been converted into a yoga studio, with daily classes offered. **Just outside of Montezuma, along the road to Cabuya.** ☎ 2642-0076. www.hotellosmangos.com. 19 units. $35 double with shared bathroom; $75 double with private bathroom; $95 bungalow. AE, DC, MC, V.

★★ Ylang Ylang Beach Resort

Set in a lush patch of forest just steps away from the sand, this hotel offers accommodations in a variety of shapes and sizes. There are a series of private bungalows and suites, as well as "jungalows"—large tents set on wooden platforms, featuring an indoor sink, small fridge, ceiling fan, private deck, and shared bathroom. **On the beach northeast of Montezuma.** ☎ 2642-0636. www.ylangylangresort.com. 26 units. Jungalow $160 double; beachfront room $195 double; bungalows and suites $235–$295. Rates include breakfast and dinner. AE, MC, V.

Where to Dine

★★ kids **El Sano Banano Village Café**
VEGETARIAN/INTERNATIONAL Delicious vegetarian meals, sandwiches, and salads are the specialty of this popular and casual spot. The café also offers a variety of fish and chicken dishes, as well as nightly specials. The natural yogurt fruit shakes are fabulous, but I like to get a little more decadent and have one of the mocha chill shakes. On the main road into the village. ☎ 2642-0944. Entrees $4–$21. AE, MC, V. Breakfast, lunch, and dinner daily.

★★★ **Playa de los Artistas** *ITALIAN/MEDITERRANEAN* This wonderful open-air restaurant has only a few tables, so arrive early, because it fills up fast. If you don't get a seat and you're feeling adventurous, try the low wooden table surrounded by tatami mats on the sand. The menu changes nightly but it always features a good selection of fresh seafood dishes—the outdoor brick oven and grill turn out consistently spectacular grilled fish and shellfish. In particular, the fresh grouper in a black-pepper sauce is phenomenal. Across from the Hotel Los Mangos (p. 196). ☎ 2642-0920. Entrees $13–$22. No credit cards. Lunch and dinner Thu–Sat, dinner only Mon–Wed.

★★ **Ylang-Ylang** *INTERNATIONAL*
A tropically elegant, open-air affair, Ylang-Ylang has both a covered dining area and outdoor tables, and a bar sculpted with indigenous and wildlife motifs. The menu is ample, with a

> *Playa de los Artistas offers the perfect blend of refined cuisine and beachside funkiness, serving fresh fire-grilled seafood in an open-air setting.*

prominent Asian influence, ranging from sushi to vegetarian teriyaki stir-fry. There are also pasta options and plenty of fresh seafood dishes. At the Ylang Ylang Beach Resort (p. 196). ☎ 2642-0402 or 8833-4106. Entrees $10–$25. AE, MC, V. Breakfast, lunch, and dinner daily.

Montezuma after Dark

The local action is centered on a couple of bars in downtown Montezuma. Head to either **Chico's Bar** (no phone) or the bar at the **Hotel Moctezuma** (☎ 2642-0058). Both are located on the main strip in town facing the water. If your evening tastes are mellower, **El Sano Banano Village Café** (☎ 2642-0944) doubles as the local movie house, with DVD releases projected nightly on a large screen; the selection ranges from first-run to quite artsy, and there's a constantly growing library of more than 800 movies. The movies begin at 7:30pm; there's a minimum charge of $5.50.

Malpaís & Santa Teresa

Malpaís translates as "badlands," a moniker that in no way currently describes this booming area, which includes the beaches at Malpaís, Playa Carmen, Santa Teresa, and Playa Hermosa. Most of these beaches are quite good for surfing. This is one of Costa Rica's hottest and fastest-growing destinations; nevertheless, it remains one of the most isolated and least crowded. It is a great place to get away from it all and spend some quality time beachcombing and lazing in the shade of a coconut palm.

> Malpaís is one of the Nicoya Peninsula's great surfing towns.

START Malpaís is 156km (97 miles) west of San José.

1 ★ kids **Malpaís Surf Shop.** Surfing is the main draw in Malpaís. The seemingly endless number of beach breaks here means there are enough peaks to go around, so it's rarely overcrowded, making this a great place to learn. The Malpaís Surf Shop is an excellent local operation. On Playa Carmen. ☎ 2640-0173. Lessons $35 for 1½ hr. private; $30 per person for 1½ hr. group; equipment included. Surfboard rentals $8 per day. Daily 8am–5pm.

The Road Less Taken

There are lots of lovely places to stay in and around Malpaís and Santa Teresa, but before you book, be aware that this is a remote and undeveloped area. That means there are very few attractions and organized activities in Malpaís and Santa Teresa proper. Accordingly, many folks who stay in the area head to Montezuma (p. 192) for the day to enjoy the tour and activity options offered there. For more information on booking such trips, or for booking tours of Cabo Blanco Nature Reserve (p. 173, **4**), see "Book It!" (p. 194).

If you want to stick close to Malpaís and Santa Teresa, it's possible (and advisable) to make reservations for the various locally based tours and activities, including ATV excursions, horseback riding, nature hikes, and bird-watching tours. Just ask at your hotel desk.

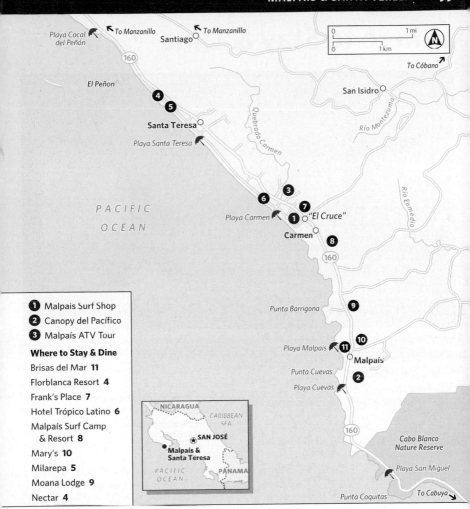

1 Malpais Surf Shop
2 Canopy del Pacífico
3 Malpaís ATV Tour

Where to Stay & Dine

Brisas del Mar 11

Florblanca Resort 4

Frank's Place 7

Hotel Trópico Latino 6

Malpaís Surf Camp
  & Resort 8

Mary's 10

Milarepa 5

Moana Lodge 9

Nectar 4

2 ★ **Canopy del Pacífico.** This zip-line canopy tour features nearly 1km (½ mile) of cables touching down on eight platforms. In case that's not enough excitement for you, you'll also do two rappels, and through it all you will be able to enjoy the added bonus of good views of both the surrounding forest and the Pacific Ocean. The tour includes transportation to and from your hotel, which will be arranged when you sign up. ⏱ 2 hr. Southern end of Malpaís. ☎ 2640-0091. Rate $35 per person. Daily 9am–4pm.

3 ★ **Malpaís ATV tour.** The rugged dirt roads and deserted beaches that run through this region are great to explore in an all-terrain vehicle. I recommend heading northwest along the main dirt road leading from Malpaís to Santa Teresa and continuing on to Playa Hermosa and beyond. Feel free to explore the various beach accesses, and spend some time cruising along in the sand as well. ⏱ Varies, depending on itinerary. Malpaís ATV Rentals: office in Pachamama Houses & Bungalows, just south of main Malpaís crossroads (El Cruce). ☎ 2640-0195. Rates $50 per ATV per day. Daily 7:30am–6pm.

Where to Stay & Dine

> At Milarepa in Santa Teresa the elegance is in the simplicity of the accommodations.

★★ Brisas del Mar MALPAÍS *FUSION*

With a large, open-air deck jutting out over a steep hillside, this place serves top-notch fusion fare from a chalkboard menu that changes weekly. Thai and Asian dishes are common, though the British-born chef and owner is also likely to make beer-battered fish and chips. Desserts are excellent, and the wine list is fine and fairly priced. This is a great place to come for a sunset cocktail, and then linger on for dinner and dessert. I recommend taking a taxi here, as the walk up is daunting. Heck, even the drive up is daunting—it's a very steep hill. On the hillside in Malpaís. ☎ 2640-0941. Entrees $10–$17. No credit cards. Dinner Tues–Sun.

★★★ Florblanca Resort SANTA TERESA

The lush and plush Florblanca Resort is the top option in this neck of the woods and one of the best boutique hotels in the country. Unfortunately for some, it's **adults only,** so if you're traveling with kids 13 and younger, you'll need to stay elsewhere. If you're not traveling with kids, you're in luck: The individual villas are huge, with a vast living area opening onto a spacious veranda and a large open-air bathroom with a garden shower and teardrop-shape tub set amid flowering tropi-

cal foliage. The beautiful free-form pool is on two levels connected by a sculpted waterfall. On the beach, northern end of Santa Teresa. ☎ 2640-0232. www.florblanca.com. 16 units. $475–$600 double. Rates include transfer to and from Tambor Airstrip. AE, DC, MC, V.

Frank's Place MALPAÍS

This spot offers a range of rooms in a variety of styles, price ranges, and configurations. Some are very basic and feature a shared bathroom. Some come with a kitchenette, and some have air-conditioning. The midrange rooms are a decent value and the hotel is well located, but I don't think the higher-priced rooms here are worth it. At the main crossroads (El Cruce) in Malpaís. ☎ 2640-0096. www.franksplacecr.com. 33 units. $40 double with shared bathroom; $75–$95 double with private bathroom. AE, MC, V.

★★ Hotel Trópico Latino SANTA TERESA

The best accommodations at this well-located, good-value spread are the beachfront bungalows. The older rooms are housed in four duplex units; these are huge, although none have an ocean view. The grounds are shaded by native pochote trees, which are known for their spiky trunks. On the beach, southern end of Santa Teresa. ☎ 2640-0062. www.hoteltropicolatino.com. 16 units. $103–$155 double. MC, V.

★★ Malpaís Surf Camp & Resort MALPAÍS

As the name implies, this place caters to surfers. The wide range of accommodations is reflected in the equally wide range of prices, and the overall vibe is loose and funky. There's a free-form tile pool in the center of the complex, and the large, open main lodge area serves as a combination restaurant, bar, lounge, and surfboard-storage area. Inland, south of the main crossroads (El Cruce), Malpaís. ☎ 2640-0031 or 2640-0061. www.malpaissurfcamp.com. 16 units. $70 double with shared bathroom; $95–$115 double with private bathroom. AE, MC, V.

★ Mary's MALPAÍS PIZZA/SEAFOOD

This humble, open-air restaurant is a local favorite. The thin-crust wood-oven pizzas are deservedly popular, but don't overlook the excellent fresh fish and other substantial main dishes. Southern end of Malpaís. ☎ 2640-0153. Entrees $5–$18. MC, V. Dinner daily.

★ Milarepa SANTA TERESA

Named after a Buddhist sage, this small collection of bungalows is spread around shady grounds fronting the beach. The bungalows are simple, roomy, and understated. All have wooden floors, a mix of teak and bamboo furniture, beds with mosquito netting, and a private porch. The more expensive units are closest to the beach and have ocean views. On the beach, northern end of Santa Teresa. ☎ 2640-0023. www.milarepahotel.com. 10 units. $194–$225 double. Rates include breakfast. AE, MC, V.

★ Moana Lodge MALPAÍS

The rooms here are all decorated in some variation on an African theme. The lodge is set on a steep hillside, and the higher-situated units have a bit of an ocean view. There's a pretty free-form pool, with a shady gazebo beside it, as well as some mattresses hung like swings under another shade structure. There's no restaurant here, but breakfasts are served and guests can use the communal kitchen and barbecue area. Inland, south of the main crossroads (El Cruce), Malpaís. ☎ 2640-0230. www.moanalodge.com.

> Fine dining on the beach at Nectar.

10 units. $115–$140 double; $195–$295 suite. Rates include breakfast and taxes. MC, V.

★★★ Nectar SANTA TERESA FUSION

With the waves crashing just steps away, the dimly lit open-air setting of this restaurant is elegant yet casual. There's a heavy Pacific Rim influence to the fusion cuisine. You can almost always start with some sushi or sashimi made with the daily catch. In addition to fresh seafood and several vegetarian entrees, you might also find lamb, rabbit, or duck on the regularly changing menu. At Florblanca Resort in Santa Teresa. ☎ 2640-0232. Entrees $18–$35. AE, MC, V. Breakfast, lunch, and dinner daily.

Malpaís & Santa Teresa after Dark

There's not much in the way of raging nightlife in this area. The most popular bar is **D&N** (☎ 2640-0353), which stands for Day & Night, located about 1 block north of the crossroads into town off the main road. Surfers and budget travelers also gather in the evenings at **Frank's Place** (☎ 2640-0096) and the **Malpaís Surf Camp & Resort** (☎ 2640-0031). Out in Santa Teresa, **La Lora** (☎ 2640-0132) is the most happening spot. This is definitely the place to come on Saturday night, to dance some salsa and merengue with the locals.

Playa Sámara

Playa Sámara has a broad beach that curves along a horseshoe-shape bay. In addition to drawing intrepid foreign travelers, this small town and its beach are popular with Tico families seeking a quick and inexpensive getaway, and with young Ticos looking to do some serious beach partying. On weekends, in particular, Playa Sámara can get crowded and rowdy. Still, the calm waters and steep cliffs on the far side of the bay make this a very attractive spot, and the beach is so long that the crowds are usually well dispersed.

> Down the coast from Playa Sámara, Playa Carrillo's graceful coconut palms beckon to beach lovers.

START Playa Sámara is 245km (152 miles) west of San José; 118km (73 miles) south of Liberia.

1 ★★ **kids Wingnuts Canopy Tours.** This family-run operation has a long-standing, local zip-line canopy tour operation. The tour features 10 separate cables touching down on 12 treetop platforms. ⏱ 2 hr. See p. 182, **1**.

2 ★ **C & C Surf Shop and School.** Because Playa Sámara's beach is somewhat protected by a large, offshore island, the waves are usually perfect for beginners. You'll find several surf schools around town. I recommend C & C, which sets up shop each day right on the beach

in the center of town. ⏱ Minimum 1 hr. Main office inside Tico Adventure Lodge, 2 blocks inland from the beach, Playa Sámara. ☎ 2656-0590. Rates $40 per hr. private lesson; $4 per hr. board rental. Daily 8am–5pm.

3 ★★ **kids Playa Carrillo.** This crescent of soft white sand is backed along its entire length by a neat row of coconut palms. There is no waterside development on Playa Carrillo, which means it tends to be quieter than other beaches in the area. It also means you should bring your own drinks and snacks. 8km (5 miles) south of Playa Sámara on the coast road. See p. 188.

Map legend / location map

NICARAGUA
CARIBBEAN SEA
★ SAN JOSÉ
Playa Sámara
PACIFIC OCEAN
PANAMA

Buenavista
To Nicoya
Taranta
To Garza, Nosara
Río Lagarto
Esterones
See "Sámara" map below
Cantarrana
Sámara
Mango
Playa Barrigona
Playa Buenavista
Cangrejal
Playa Sámara
Punta Buenavista
Bahía Sámara
Playa Carrillo
Bahía Carrillo
Puerto Carrillo
Punta Sámara
Isla Chora
Punta Indio
Punta Carrillo
Punta Islita
PACIFIC OCEAN

1 Wingnuts Canopy Tours
2 C & C Surf Shop and School
3 Playa Carrillo
4 Flying Crocodile ultralight flight
5 Playa Barrigona
6 Barra Honda National Park

Where to Stay
Fenix Hotel **13**
Hotel Belvedere **12**
Hotel Casa del Mar **9**
Hotel Guanamar **14**
Hotel Punta Islita **15**
Sámara Tree-House Inn **11**

Where to Dine
El Lagarto **7**
Las Brasas **8**
Shake Joe's **10**

Sámara
Main St.
160
Police
Playa Sámara

4 ★★ Flying Crocodile ultralight flight.

Although it might feel like little more than a modified tricycle with a nylon wing and lawnmower motor, the winged wonder featured

Traveler's Tip

All of the area hotels can help you arrange any number of tour options, including horseback rides, boat trips, sea kayaking, scuba diving, snorkeling outings, and trips to watch the turtles nest in Ostional (p. 209, 4). If your hotel's tour desk isn't up to the task, try ★ **Tío Tigre Tours** (☎ 2656-1060), a good all-around local tour operator.

> One of Flying Crocodiles' flying machines.

> *The stone formations at Barra Honda's Terciopelo cave have an eerie, organic quality.*

> *The blue-crowned motmot, a local resident.*

here is very safe. These folks also offer flights on a two-seat (one for you, one for the pilot) Gyrocopter, the ultralight equivalent of a helicopter. ⊕ 2 hr. Playa Buena Vista, 2km (1¼ miles) north of Playa Sámara. See p. 178, **⑤**.

⑤ ★★★ **Playa Barrigona.** A wide patch of soft white sand, this beach made international news, or at least tabloid fodder, after Mel Gibson bought a huge estate alongside it. Be careful when swimming, as riptides can be strong

Learning the Language

If you want to acquire or polish some language skills while here, check in with **Playa Sámara Language School** (☎ 866/978-6668 in U.S. and Canada, or 2656-0127 in Costa Rica; www.samaralanguageschool. com). The facility here even features classes with ocean views, although that might be a deterrent to your lessons. These folks offer a range of programs and private lessons and can arrange for a home stay with a local family.

Hotel Punta Islita

South of Playa Sámara and Playa Carrillo on an isolated beach, you will find one of the most exclusive and romantic luxury resorts in Costa Rica. There's not much else around for miles. If you're looking for fabulous rooms, great views, a semi-private beach, personalized service, and plenty of amenities and activities to choose from, this is a perfect spot.

★★ **Hotel Punta Islita** is set on a high bluff between two mountain ridges that meet the sea. The rooms, suites, and villas are done up in a Santa Fe style, with red Mexican floor tiles, neo-Navajo-print bedspreads, and adobe-colored walls offset by sky blue doors and trim. The suites come with a separate sitting room and a private two-person plunge pool or Jacuzzi; the villas have two or three bedrooms, their own private swimming pool, and a full kitchen. The beach below the hotel is a crescent of gray-white sand with a calm, pro-tected section at the northern end. It's about a 10-minute hike, but the hotel will shuttle you down and back if you don't feel like walking. You can take the hotel's small canopy tour, which leaves from just below the small gym and ends steps away from the beach. The hotel has an excellent little spa offering a full range of treatments and services, including regular classes and activities. Punta Islita even has a 9-hole executive golf course and driving range.

Although you can drive here from San José or Liberia, I highly recommend flying. Punta Islita is such a luxury resort that it has its own airstrip; they can book your travel and add it onto your bill. Rates run from $115 to $130 per person each way. Playa Islita. ☎ 866/446-4053 in U.S. and Canada, or 2231-6122 in Costa Rica. www.hotelpuntaislita.com. 20 units, 17 villas. $300 double; $420-$480 suite; $625-$920 villa. Rates include continental breakfast. AE, MC, V.

when the surf is up. And try not to spend all of your time gazing at the ocean—be sure to check out the thick tropical dry forest that backs the beach. It's not uncommon to spot howler monkeys, green iguanas, and the occasional blue-crowned motmot here. 9km (5½ miles) north of Playa Sámara. See p. 188.

Drive north to Nicoya and turn right onto CR21. Follow signs to San José and La Amistad Bridge. The entrance to Barra Honda is on your left, a few miles before the bridge (62km/39 miles).

❻ ★★ kids **Barra Honda National Park.** I know, I know, it's hard to tear yourself away from the beach. But trust me, it's worth heading inland and underground to explore this easily accessible cave complex. The wild rock formations you'll see and the unique caving experience you'll have deep underground inside La Cueva Terciopelo are well worth the sacrifice of some time in the sun. ⏱ Minimum 3 hr. See p. 179, ❽. Closed in the rainy season.

Where to Stay

> *Relaxation is at the top of the agenda at Sámara Tree-House Inn.*

★ kids Fenix Hotel PLAYA SÁMARA

Set right on the beach, all of the rooms here are really studio apartments, with a fully equipped kitchenette. They are simple but well maintained. There's a postage stamp–size pool and some hammocks hung in the shade of coconut trees. The ocean is just steps away. The owners are personable and accommodating, and the kitchens are a boon for families and those planning a longer stay. **On the beach, toward the southern end of Playa Sámara.** ☎ 2656-0158. www.fenixhotel.com. 6 units. $90 double. No credit cards.

Hotel Belvedere PLAYA SÁMARA

This German-run hotel is located a few blocks inland and uphill from the beach. Rooms are housed in two separate buildings. Those in the newer annex feature modern air-conditioners, a coffee maker, and a small fridge; those in the older section are more basic. Everything is well maintained and immaculate, and there's a pool at both buildings. **Inland, downtown Playa Sámara.** ☎ 2656-0213. www.belvederesamara. net. 21 units. $66–$105 double. Rates include breakfast. MC, V.

★★ Hotel Casa del Mar PLAYA SÁMARA

Casa del Mar is just across the street from the beach, on the inland side of the beach access road and 1 block south of downtown. The rooms are immaculate and most are quite spacious. Although the units with shared bathrooms are the best bargains here, I'd opt for a second-floor room with a private bathroom. The owners and staff are extremely friendly and helpful. **On the beach access road, downtown Playa Sámara.** ☎ 2656-0264. www.casadelmarsamara.com. 17 units, 11 with private bathroom. $30 double with shared bathroom; $75 double with private bathroom and A/C. Rates include full breakfast and taxes. AE, MC, V.

★★★ Hotel Guanamar PLAYA CARRILLO

Set on a high bluff overlooking Playa Carrillo, this place offers great views, large rooms, and access to one of the best beaches in the region. The pool is set on the best vantage point on the property, with large, broad wooden decks all around. The open-air restaurant and bar share the view from under soaring thatch roofs. **Playa Carrillo.** ☎ 2656-0054. www.guanamar.net. 41 units. $123–$158 double; $239 suite. Rates include continental breakfast. AE, DC, MC, V.

★★★ Sámara Tree-House Inn PLAYA SÁMARA

Set right on the beach, the four namesake rooms are built on stilts made from tree trunks. Inside, they are awash in varnished wood. There is also a ground-floor unit that is wheelchair-accessible and quite beautiful in its own right. You won't find air-conditioning here, but there are fans in each of the bedrooms. **On the beach, toward the center of Playa Sámara.** ☎ 2656-0733. www.samaratreehouse.com. 5 units. $80–$130 double. Rates include breakfast. AE, MC, V.

Where to Dine

> You can get almost anything you want, grilled to order, at El Lagarto, on the beach in Playa Sámara.

★★ kids **El Lagarto** PLAYA SÁMARA *STEAK-HOUSE/GRILL* The first things you notice as you enter this large, open-air restaurant are the massive grill stations gravity-fed with fresh glowing wood coals via metal troughs from a huge overhead fire. The menu is almost as massive and features every form of meat, poultry, or seafood you could imagine, all cooked to order over the coals. At night, atmospheric lighting gives the place a very romantic vibe. On the beach, north end of Playa Sámara. ☎ 2656-0750. Entrees $8.50–$29. AE, MC, V. Lunch and dinner daily. Closed Sept 16–Oct 31.

★ **Las Brasas** PLAYA SÁMARA *SPANISH/SEAFOOD* This place serves authentic Spanish cuisine and fresh seafood. The whole fish *a la catalana* is excellent, as is the paella. The gazpacho Andaluz is a refreshing lunch choice on a hot afternoon. There's also a good selection of Spanish wines, a rarity in Costa Rica. On the main road into Playa Sámara, about 90m (295 ft.) before the beach. ☎ 2656-0546. Entrees $5–$32. V. Dinner Sat–Thurs.

★★ **Shake Joe's** PLAYA SÁMARA *INTERNATIONAL* Set right on the beach, in the shade of coconut palms and sea grape trees, this place serves up delectable fresh fruit shakes and smoothies, as well as sandwiches, salads, burgers, pastas, and a few steak and fish dishes. They also have a breakfast menu, although they don't open till 11am. On the beach in the center of town. ☎ 2656-0252. Entrees $4–$12. V. Lunch and dinner daily.

Playa Sámara after Dark

After dark, the most happening place in town is **La Góndola Bar** (no phone), which has a pool table, dartboards, and board games. If you're looking for loud music and dancing, head to the beachfront **Tutti Frutti** (no phone). You might also try the mellow lounge scene at **Shake Joe's** (☎ 2656-0252) or **La Vela Latina** (☎ 2656-0418), both located on the main road fronting the ocean, right near the center of the action.

Nosara

Nosara is a remote beach destination primarily coveted by surfers, with plenty of nearby adventure activities and wildlife-viewing options. Several separate beaches actually make up the Nosara area, including Nosara, Guiones, Pelada, and Garza. Playa Guiones is one of Costa Rica's most dependable beach breaks, and surfers come here in good numbers throughout the year. However, the waves here are still much less crowded than those at the more popular surf spots in Guanacaste and along the central Pacific coast.

> *Olive ridley sea turtles come ashore en masse for egg-laying, an event called an* arribada.

START Nosara is 266km (165 miles) west of San José; 138km (86 miles) south of Liberia.

❶ ★ **Surfing lessons on Playa Guiones.** With miles of excellent beach breaks and relatively small crowds, this is a great place to learn how to surf. If you want to try to stand up for your first time, check in with the folks at **Safari Surf School** (☎ 866/433-3355 in U.S. and Canada, or 2682-0573 in Costa Rica; www.safarisurfschool.com), **Coconut Harry's Surf Shop** (☎ 2862-0574; www.coconutharrys.com), or **Corky Carroll's Surf School** (☎ 888/454-

7873 in U.S. and Canada, or 2682-0385 in Costa Rica; www.surfschool.net). All offer hourly solo or group lessons, multiday packages with accommodations and meals included, and board rentals. ⊙ Minimum 1 hr. All have offices around Playa Guiones. Rates $40–$50 per hr. private lesson; $20–$30 per hr. group lesson. Board rental may entail additional fee. Daily 7am–5pm.

❷ ★ **Boca Nosara horseback tours.** These folks have a large stable of well-cared-for horses and a range of beach, jungle, and waterfall rides

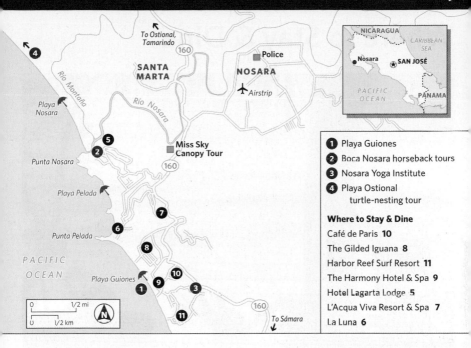

1 Playa Guiones
2 Boca Nosara horseback tours
3 Nosara Yoga Institute
4 Playa Ostional
    turtle-nesting tour

Where to Stay & Dine

Café de Paris **10**
The Gilded Iguana **8**
Harbor Reef Surf Resort **11**
The Harmony Hotel & Spa **9**
Hotel Lagarta Lodge **5**
L'Acqua Viva Resort & Spa **7**
La Luna **6**

to choose from. Most tours start off on the banks of the Río Nosara and take you through mangrove and lowland forests. The wildlife viewing is often wonderful, and the German owners are excellent, multilingual guides. ⏱ 2–3½ hr. Nosara; office near the airport. See p. 177, ❸.

❸ **Nosara Yoga Institute.** This is an internationally recognized and renowned retreat and training center offering intensive daily yoga classes, teacher training, and a host of custom-designed "retreat" options. There is a regular schedule of drop-in public classes, and mats are provided. ⏱ 1½ hr. Where the road from Nosara meets the entrance to Playa Guiones at Café de Paris. See p. 176, ❷.

❹ ★★★ **Playa Ostional turtle-nesting tour.** On this remote beach, olive ridley sea turtles come ashore by the thousands in a mass egg-laying phenomenon known as an *arribada*. These *arribadas* take place 4 to 10 times between July and December; each occurrence lasts between 3 and 10 days. Consider yourself very lucky if you happen to be around during one of these fascinating natural phenomena.

The *arribadas* are so difficult to predict that no one runs regularly scheduled turtle-viewing trips, but when the *arribada* is in full swing, several local guides and agencies offer tours. Tours are generally run at night, but because the turtles come ashore in such numbers, you can sometimes catch them in the early morning light as well. Your best bet is to ask the staff at your hotel or check in with Joe at ★★ **Iguana Expeditions** (☎ 2682-4089; www.iguanaexpeditions.com). ⏱ Minimum 3 hr. 8km (5 miles) north of Nosara. Rates $35–$55 per person.

Traveler's Tip

All of the hotels in Nosara can help you arrange any number of tour options, including horseback rides, rain-forest hikes, boat trips, fishing expeditions, sea kayaking, scuba diving, snorkeling outings, and trips to watch the turtles nest in Ostional (❹). If your hotel's tour desk isn't up to the task, contact ★★ **Iguana Expeditions** (☎ 2682-4089; www.iguanaexpeditions.com), an excellent all-around local tour operator.

Where to Stay & Dine

> *If the timing is right, you'll be able to dine under moonlight at La Luna on Playa Guiones.*

★★ **Café de Paris** PLAYA GUIONES *BAKERY/ BISTRO* This place is one of Nosara's social hubs. You can get excellent fresh-baked goods and a wide assortment of light bites and full-on meals. I enjoy stopping in for a cup of espresso and a fresh almond croissant; breakfasts are also excellent. Sporting events or movies are shown nightly, and there's a pool table and

Internet cafe. On the main road into Nosara at the crossroad for Playa Guiones. ☎ 2682-0087. Baked goods 75¢–$4; entrees $4–$18. AE, MC, V. Breakfast, lunch, and dinner daily.

The Gilded Iguana PLAYA GUIONES This long-standing hotel began as a very basic budget option. It now has some newer, more upscale rooms, as well as a swimming pool with a high waterfall emptying into it. The new rooms, set back from the pool among some shade trees, have high ceilings, lots of space, air-conditioning, and a minifridge. The older rooms are much more rustic, lack air-conditioning, and are located close to the road. About 90m (300 ft.) inland from the beach at Playa Guiones. ☎ 2682-0259. www.thegildediguana.com. 12 units. $45–$55 double, $65–$80 suite. AE, MC, V.

★ **The Gilded Iguana Restaurant** PLAYA GUIONES *SEAFOOD/GRILL* This simple restaurant serves fish so fresh that it's still wiggling: The owner's husband, Chiqui, is a local fisherman. There are also great burgers, *casados* (a Costa Rican blue-plate special), and a list of nightly specials. Sporting events are shown on a not-quite-big-enough television. Overall, the vibe is sociable and lively. Most of the tables and chairs here are low-lying affairs and, for some, a bit challenging to get in and out of. About 90m (300 ft.) inland from the beach at Playa Guiones. ☎ 2682-0259. Entrees $5–$17. V. Breakfast, lunch, and dinner daily.

★ **Harbor Reef Surf Resort** PLAYA GUIONES With spacious rooms, private homes, and villas about 2 blocks from the beach, this place caters to surfers, fishermen, and all-around vacationers. There's a cool, oasislike feel to the lush grounds. The best rooms are the Surf City rooms and suites, set around the hotel's second, and larger pool, which is reserved for hotel guests—the other pool, which is just off the restaurant, is open to diners and walk-ins. About 100m (330 ft.) inland from the beach at Playa Guiones. ☎ 2682-0059. www.harborreef.com. 22 units. $119–$129 double; $159–$239 suite. AE, MC, V.

★ **The Harmony Hotel** PLAYA GUIONES The Harmony Hotel is set right off the beach on Playa Guiones. The rooms are simple but attractive, with white-tile floors, contemporary furnishings, well-designed bathrooms, and king-size beds. All rooms have a patio or wooden deck. The hotel has a well-run and pretty spa, with various treatment options and regular yoga classes. The best perk here is the proximity to the beach—it's only about 90m (300 ft.) away, reached via a short path through some sea grass and dunes. On the beach at Playa Guiones. ☎ 2682-4113. www.harmonynosara.com. 26 units. $220–$280 double. Rates include breakfast buffet. AE, MC, V.

★ **Hotel Lagarta Lodge** NOSARA Located on a hillside high over the Nosara River, this small lodge is an excellent choice for bird-watchers and travelers who are more interested in flora and fauna than easy access to the beach. The lodge borders its own private reserve, which has trails along the riverbank and through the mangrove and tropical humid forests here. From the restaurant and most rooms, there are spectacular views over the river and surrounding forest, with the beaches of Nosara and Ostional in the distance. On the hill above Playa Nosara. ☎ 2682-0035. www.lagarta.com. 6 units. $70 double. AE, MC, V.

★★★ **La Luna** PLAYA PELADA *INTERNATIONAL* With its striking location overlooking the water and casually elegant ambience, this is my favorite restaurant in Nosara. I especially like grabbing one of the outdoor tables closest to the waves for breakfast or lunch. It's also quite beautiful at night, with candles spread around generously. The chalkboard menu changes regularly but usually includes a Thai or Indian curry as well as pasta dishes, hearty steaks, and fresh fish and seafood. Just below the Playa Pelada hotels. ☎ 2682-0122. Entrees $8–$36. MC, V. Breakfast, lunch, and dinner daily.

★★ **L'Acqua Viva Resort & Spa** PLAYA GUIONES This resort hotel has the most architecturally stunning and well-equipped facilities in the Nosara area. The name translates as "living water," and there are pools and water elements all around. The whole complex is beautifully done, with soaring thatch roofs and Balinese-inspired furnishings and decor. Rooms are large and beautifully appointed and feature loads of amenities. However, the beach is a 10-minute drive or shuttle away. Inland from Playa Guiones. ☎ 2682-1087. www.lacquaviva.com. 35 units. $205–$341 double; $525–$735 villa. Rates include breakfast. AE, MC, V.

Nicoya Peninsula Fast Facts

> If you're doing the driving in the Nicoya Peninsula, a four-wheel-drive is the way to go.

Accommodations Booking Services

On the Nicoya Peninsula, you are best off booking direct with the hotels and resorts that are listed in this guide.

ATMs

All of the towns and tourist destinations on the Nicoya Peninsula have at least one bank with a cash machine (*cajero automatico*). You'll find ATMs on the main streets in Montezuma, Malpaís, and Santa Teresa.

Dentists & Doctors

From Montezuma, Malpaís, or Santa Teresa, the closest hospital is Hospital Monseñor Sanabria in Puntarenas (☎ 2663-0033); there are also several doctors and a local clinic (☎ 2642-0208) in Cóbano. From Playa Sámara or Nosara, the closest hospital is Hospital La Anexión in Nicoya (☎ 2685-8400).

If you have a mild medical issue or dental problem while traveling on the Nicoya Peninsula, most hotels will be able to refer you to a local doctor (*medico*) or dentist (*dentista*) who speaks English.

Emergencies

In case of emergency, dial ☎ 911 (there should be an English-speaking operator); if 911 doesn't work, contact the police at ☎ 2222-1365 or 2221-5337, and ask them to find someone who speaks English to translate. For an ambulance, call ☎ 128; to report a fire, call ☎ 118.

Getting There & Around

BY PLANE Liberia's **Daniel Oduber International Airport** is one of Costa Rica's two major airports, and the closest gateway to the Nicoya Peninsula. American, Continental, Delta, United, and U.S. Airways all have direct flights to Liberia. In addition, throughout the high season, numerous charters fly direct to Liberia from a number of cities in the United States, Canada, and Europe.

If you fly into San José, you have several options for onward travel to the Nicoya Peninsula. Two local commuter airlines—**Sansa** (☎ 877/767-2672 in U.S. and Canada, or 2290-4100 in Costa Rica; www.flysansa.com) and **Nature Air** (☎ 800/235-9272 in U.S. and Canada, or 2299-6000 in Costa Rica; www.natureair.com)—have daily flights from San José to Liberia, as well as to small airstrips in Tambor, Carrillo, Nosara, and Punta Islita. Fares run between $115 and $130 each way.

BY CAR If you're driving to either Nosara or Playa Sámara, your main access will be via CR21, reached either from Liberia or via La Amistad Bridge over Río Tempisque.

If you're heading to either Malpaís or Montezuma from San José, take the Pan-American Highway to Puntarenas and catch the ferry to Paquera. See "Catching the Car Ferry" on p. 174 for more information. From Paquera, take CR160 south to the beach towns of Malpaís and Montezuma.

This is a very remote area, and many of the roads in and around the Nicoya Peninsula are dirt and gravel. You can definitely drive yourself around—just be sure to rent a four-wheel-drive vehicle. You can pick up a rental in San José, Liberia, Playa Sámara, Nosara, or Malpaís.

If you'd rather not worry about driving, you can fly to Nosara and take a taxi to your hotel. You'll also find taxis at all of the major tourist destinations.

Internet Access

More and more hotels, resorts, and retailers around Costa Rica are offering high-speed Wi-Fi access, either free or for a small fee. Moreover, you'll readily find Internet cafes in all major towns and tourist destinations around the Nicoya Peninsula. Rates run between 50¢ and $3 per hour, and connection speeds are generally pretty good.

Pharmacies

You'll find *farmacias* in Montezuma, Malpaís, Playa Sámara, and Nosara.

Police

To report a lost or stolen article, such as a wallet or passport, visit the local police. Depending upon your location, that may be either the OIJ (judicial police), *guardia rural* (rural guard), or *policía metropolitana* (metro police). I suggest you enlist the assistance of your hotel when contacting the police. The number for the *policía de tránsito* (transit police) is ☎ 800/8726-7486, toll-free nationwide, or ☎ 2222-9330. See also "Emergencies," p. 212.

Post Offices

There are post offices on the main streets of all the towns listed in this chapter.

Safety

Most of the beach towns and tourist destinations on the Nicoya Peninsula are relatively safe. That said, never leave items of value unattended in rental cars, hotel rooms (unless locked in a safe), or on the beach. Moreover, single women, couples, and small groups of tourists should probably avoid walking on desolate stretches of beach or back roads after dark.

Toilets

These are known as *sanitarios* or *servicios sanitarios*. You might also hear them called *baños*. They are marked *damas* (women) and *hombres* or *caballeros* (men). Public restrooms are rare to nonexistent on the Nicoya Peninsula, but most hotels and restaurants catering to tourists will let you use their restrooms if you ask.

Visitor Information

There are no official information offices or bureaus on the Nicoya Peninsula. Your best source of information—beyond this guide book—will be your hotel front desk and any of the local tour agencies.

Water

This is a very remote area, and most hotels advise you to drink bottled water. Most restaurants that cater to tourists use bottled or treated water. If you want to be cautious, drink bottled water or *frescos* made with milk instead of water. *Sin hielo* means "no ice," and this is what you'll want to say if you're nervous about the water—even when frozen it's still water.

The Northern Zone

My Favorite Northern Zone Moments

Costa Rica's Northern Zone offers a beguiling mix of natural wonders and adventure opportunities. It is the site of misty and mysterious Monteverde Cloud Forest Biological Reserve, the spectacularly active Arenal Volcano, and rain forests, jungle rivers, mountain lakes, and lowland marshes—all home to a wealth of birds and wildlife. It's also a must for adventure travelers, with excellent opportunities for mountain biking, hiking, canyoning, and river-rafting. And after you partake in any number of these activities, you can hop into a soothing natural hot spring to soak your tired muscles. An unofficial designation, to be sure, the Northern Zone, for our purposes, is the central inland region of the country extending from just north of San José to the Nicaraguan border.

> *PREVIOUS PAGE A suspension bridge in the forest at Selvatura Park. THIS PAGE Waterfall climbing is part of the fun on a canyoning tour.*

❶ Watching Arenal Volcano erupt. If you're lucky enough to be visiting on a clear evening when the volcano is active, you're in for a treat. From the massive volcano's glowing cone to the sights and sounds of blazing chunks of lava cascading down its slopes, this is an amazing show. See "Volcano Viewing," p. 238.

❷ Soaking in a hot spring. The same volcanic activity that provides the spectacle mentioned above also heats up several natural hot springs around the La Fortuna, Tabacón, and Arenal Volcano area. In addition to the soothing warm waters and beautiful rain-forest and garden settings of these hot springs, spa services and volcanic mud treatments are offered at most. See p. 247.

❸ Hiking in a cloud forest. Cloud forests are lush ecosystems created by an almost constant mist that hangs low over the trees. They support an amazing amount of biodiversity. Trees drip with mosses, bromeliads, and orchids—and that's just the flora. Bird-watchers, budding botanists, wildlife-seekers—anyone with an interest in the natural world will be enchanted by these unique spots, which dot the Monteverde area. See p. 218, ❶.

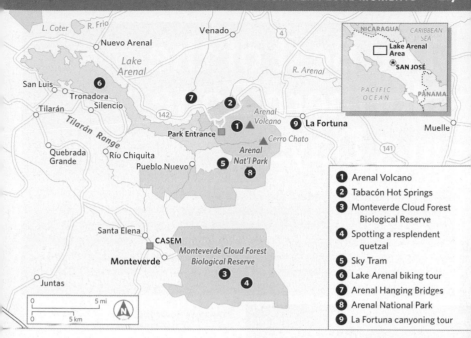

1. Arenal Volcano
2. Tabacón Hot Springs
3. Monteverde Cloud Forest Biological Reserve
4. Spotting a resplendent quetzal
5. Sky Tram
6. Lake Arenal biking tour
7. Arenal Hanging Bridges
8. Arenal National Park
9. La Fortuna canyoning tour

4 Spotting a resplendent quetzal. Revered by indigenous peoples throughout Mesoamerica, the resplendent quetzal (p. 10) is a remarkable bird, with iridescent green feathers, a brilliant blood-red vest, and a bright yellow beak. Males of the species have two rather astounding tail feathers that can reach nearly 64cm (24 in.) in length. The **Monteverde Cloud Forest Biological Reserve** is a prime place to catch a glimpse of one. See p. 252.

5 Taking a canopy tour. Zip-line canopy tours are a quintessential Costa Rica experience. The Northern Zone, with its forested mountains, has a mind-bogglingly complete selection of such tours. But for sheer speed, distance, and thrill, it's hard to beat the zip-lines at the **Sky Tram.** See p. 245.

6 Mountain biking on the shores of Lake Arenal. The scenery is stunning, the dirt roads are almost entirely devoid of cars, and the mild climbs and descents make the ride around Lake Arenal both unforgettable and relatively easy, even for inexperienced riders. **Bike Arenal** is the best operator in the field, with a collection of top-notch bikes and equipment and a wide range of tour possibilities. See p. 243.

7 Walking through the treetops. While decidedly less adrenaline-pumping than a zip-line tour, crossing suspended bridges through rain- and cloud-forest canopies is just as memorable. And the bird-watching, of course, is excellent. My favorite is **Arenal Hanging Bridges.** See p 250.

8 Scrambling over cooled lava in Arenal National Park. You'll have plenty of opportunities to hike in rain forests and along quiet beaches all across Costa Rica, but I like the adventure of exploring the sharp and porous surface of cooled, hardened lava flows. Arenal National Park is just the place to give it a try—trails here cross massive flows while offering first-class views of the volcano's looming dome. See p. 230, 5.

9 Rappelling down the face of a jungle waterfall. Canyoning tours involve walking and wading into a tight forest canyon, along with the tour's main thrill: a rappel down the face of a waterfall. Two excellent operators, **Pure Trek Canyoning** and **Desafío Adventure Company,** run canyoning tours out of La Fortuna. See p. 245 and p. 246.

The Best of the Northern Zone in 3 Days

If you've got only 3 days to give to the Northern Zone, not to worry—it's enough time to get a good taste of what the area has to offer. This is the rural heart of the country, and the small agricultural towns remain much as they were years ago. Slight changes in elevation create unique microclimates and ecosystems here, and the region teems with wildlife. On this trip you'll visit Monteverde's famed cloud forest before taking in Arenal Volcano and all that La Fortuna has to offer. You'll want to rent a four-wheel-drive vehicle to get around.

> Molten lava often lights up Arenal Volcano at night, and the show can be spectacular.

START Monteverde Cloud Forest Biological Reserve, 167km (104 miles) northwest of San José. To reach the reserve, take the Pan-American Hwy. (CR1) north to the turnoff for Sardinal, Guacimal, and Santa Elena (the road is paved as far as Guacimal). It's another 20km (12 miles) to Santa Elena; the Monteverde Cloud Forest Biological Reserve is just 6km (3¾ miles) beyond town. *Warning:* Parts of the road to the reserve are very rough dirt and mud. **TOUR LENGTH** 148km (92 miles).

SITE GUIDE
PAGE 220

1 ★★★ kids **Monteverde Cloud Forest Biological Reserve.** Get an early start and be sure to make a reservation in advance, since the number of visitors allowed in at any one time is strictly controlled. I highly recommend you take a guided tour—you're more likely to spot elusive wildlife (guides know where to look!) and you'll learn much more about your surroundings. Since the entrance ticket is good for the whole day, stick around after the tour and explore on your own. But be forewarned: The road to the reserve is paved only about halfway and then becomes rough dirt and mud. End of a well-marked road 6km (3¾ miles) from Santa Elena. ☎ 2645-5122. www.cct.or.cr. Admission $17 adults, $9 students, seniors, and children 6–12; children 5 and under free. Guided tour $17 per person. Daily 7am–4pm. ☉ Minimum 3 hr.

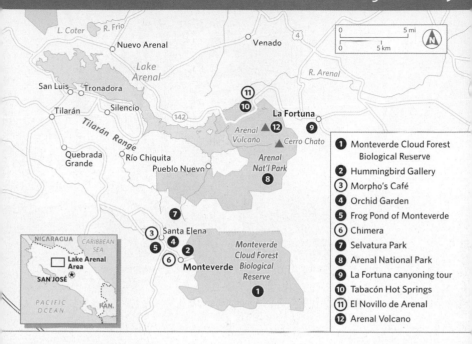

1 Monteverde Cloud Forest Biological Reserve
2 Hummingbird Gallery
3 Morpho's Café
4 Orchid Garden
5 Frog Pond of Monteverde
6 Chimera
7 Selvatura Park
8 Arenal National Park
9 La Fortuna canyoning tour
10 Tabacón Hot Springs
11 El Novillo de Arenal
12 Arenal Volcano

The Hummingbird Gallery is located off the main road, just beyond the reserve's parking area.

2 ★★ kids **Hummingbird Gallery.** As you leave the reserve, stop to do some shopping at the Hummingbird Gallery. This is the best gift shop in the area; it also features a collection of hummingbird feeders right outside the entrance, which is always abuzz with the sound of a dozen or more of these amazing birds sipping nectar and whirling about. ⏱ 30 min. At the entrance to the Monteverde Cloud Forest Biological Reserve. ☎ 2645-5030. Daily 7am–6pm.

Retrace your route to Santa Elena.

3 🍴 ★★ **Morpho's Café.** Have lunch at the most popular place in the town of Santa Elena. I recommend one of the hearty sandwiches on thick fresh bread, washed down with a fresh fruit smoothie. In Santa Elena center, across from the supermarket. ☎ 2645-5607. $$–$$$. See p. 259.

4 ★ **Orchid Garden.** A local labor of love, this garden contains an extensive collection of orchids. A visit here includes a fascinating tour that will fill you in on the life cycle and pollination peculiarities of orchids, while also providing you with tips on growing and

caring for orchids at home. I especially like the collection of miniature orchids. There's often good bird-watching right on the grounds here. ⏱ 30–50 min. Santa Elena center. ☎ 2645 5308. www.monteverdeorchidgarden.com. Admission $10; includes guided tour; discounts available for students and children. Daily 8am–5pm.

The Frog Pond is located on the outskirts of Santa Elena, on a well-marked side road near the Monteverde Lodge & Gardens.

5 ★★ kids **Frog Pond of Monteverde.** The Ranario Monteverde, as it's known in Spanish, is one of the more extensive and better-run captive creature exhibits in Monteverde. In addition to the wide range of frogs, lizards, and reptiles in glass enclosures, there's a butterfly garden. Several of the more interesting frog species, including the striking red-eyed tree frog and the glass-bellied tree frog—which as its

More Information

For stops **1**–**8** of this tour we recommend a base in or around Monteverde (p. 254); and for stops **9**–**12** in or around La Fortuna (p. 260), near the Arenal Volcano and Arenal National Park.

① Monteverde Cloud Forest Biological Reserve

Whether you're hiking on your own or as part of a guided tour, you'll probably want to start on the well-used and well-maintained ④ ★★★ **Sendero El Río** (River Trail), which heads north from the park information office. It puts you immediately in the midst of dense primary cloud forest, where heavy layers of mosses, bromeliads, and epiphytes cover every branch and trunk. This very first section of trail is a prime location for spotting a resplendent quetzal.

After 15 or 20 minutes, you'll come to a little marked spur leading down to a ⑬ *catarata* (waterfall). This diminutive waterfall fills a small, pristine pond and is quite picturesque, but if you fail in your attempts to capture its beauty, look for its image emblazoned on postcards at souvenir stores all around the area. The entire trek to the waterfall and back is 1.5km (1 mile) and should take you less than an hour.

You now have the option of continuing on the River Trail for another 1km (.6 mile) to connect to the Sendero Naturale (Nature Trail), which

leads to the Sendero Chomogo loop trail. The entire hike is 3.2km (2 miles) and should take you 3 to 4 hours. However, unless you plan 2 full days of hiking in the reserve, I recommend you take the alternative route I outline below.

From the *catarata,* turn around and retrace your steps along the River Trail until you come to a fork and the ⓒ **Sendero Tosi** (Tosi Trail). Follow this shortcut, which leads through varied terrain, back to the reserve entrance.

You've gotten the River Trail and waterfall under your belt, and now I recommend a slightly more strenuous hike to a lookout atop the Continental Divide. Take the ⓓ ★★★ **Sendero Bosque Nuboso** (Cloud Forest Trail) southeast from the reserve entrance. As its name implies, the trail leads through thick, virgin cloud forest. Keep your eyes open for any number of bird and mammal species, including toucans, trogons, honeycreepers, and howler monkeys. There are some massive specimens of strangler figs on the trail; these trees start as parasitic

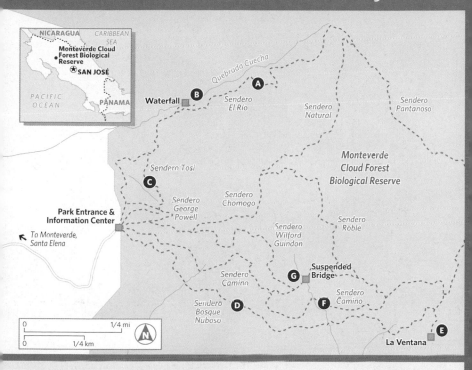

vines and eventually engulf their host tree. After 1.9km (1.2 miles), you will reach the Continental Divide. Despite the grand sounding name, there's only a modest elevation gain of around 65m (213 ft).

There are a couple of lookout points on the Divide through clearings in the forest, but the best is **E** ★★ **La Ventana** (The Window), located just beyond the end of the Cloud Forest Trail and reached via a short spur trail that you can walk in 5 minutes. Here you'll find a broad, elevated wooden deck with panoramic views. However, be forewarned: It's often misty and quite windy up here.

On the way back, return via the 2km (1.2-mile) **F** ★ **Sendero Camino** (Road Trail), which runs nearly parallel to the Sendero Bosque Nuboso. Much of this aptly named trail was once used as a rough, all-terrain-vehicle road. Since it is wide and open in many places, it's particularly good for bird-watching. About halfway along, you'll want to take a brief detour to a **G** ★★ **suspended bridge.** Some 100m (330-ft.) long, this midforest bridge gives you a bird's-eye view of the forest canopy. The entire loop should take around 3 hours. ⏱ Minimum 3 hr.

> *The Orchid Garden has about 450 species of Costa Rica's native orchids, plus the world's smallest orchid.*

name implies, has a see-through stomach—are nocturnal. Be sure to visit at least once in the daytime and once at night (the same ticket can be used for both visits). ⏱ 1–2 hr. Outskirts of Santa Elena, near the Monteverde Lodge & Gardens. ☎ 2645-6320. Admission $10 (good for 2 days); includes 45-min. guided tour. Daily 9am–8:30pm.

Drive back toward the Monteverde Cloud Forest Biological Reserve until you see a sign for Cerro Plano. Chimera is not far past the sign, 2.5km (1½ miles) from Santa Elena.

⑥ 🍴 ★★ **Chimera.** For dinner, try this hip tapas bar and restaurant. The menu features a range of contemporary dishes borrowing bits and pieces, and sometimes more, from world cuisines ranging from all around Latin America to Asia and Europe and beyond. Cerro Plano, on the road btw. Santa Elena and the Monteverde Cloud Forest Biological Reserve. ☎ 2645-6081. $. See p. 259.

On Day 2, get an early start and drive 6km (3¾ miles) north from Santa Elena on a dirt and gravel road to Selvatura Park, which is near the Santa Elena Cloud Forest Reserve.

⑦ ★★ kids **Selvatura Park.** There's a lot to do at this one-stop adventure park, but you only have the morning, so you'll either have to choose among the offerings, or hurry. I suggest starting off with the canopy tour and following that with self-guided visits to the hummingbird and butterfly gardens and the snake exhibit. If there's time, stop in at the insect museum, or better yet, take a hike on the park's network of trails and suspended bridges. ⏱ 3–4 hr. 6km (3¾ miles) from Santa Elena on the road to the Santa Elena Cloud Forest Reserve. ☎ 2645-5929. www.selvatura.com. Rates: Zip-line tour $45 adults, $35 children 12–18, $30 children 4–11; children 3 and under free. Walkways and bridges $25 adults, $20 children 12–18, $15 children 4–11; children 3 and under free. Combination packages available. AE, MC, V. Daily 7am–4:30pm.

> *Selvatura Park's walkways through the treetops bring you right into the cloud forest.*

From Selvatura Park take the dirt and gravel road to Tilarán (35km/22 miles). In Tilarán, pick up the paved CR142, which circles Lake Arenal, skirts Arenal Volcano, and leads into La Fortuna (73km/45 miles). The entire drive will take 4 hours. Alternatively, leave your rental car behind and take the quicker (2 hours) and easier taxi-boat-taxi transfer (see "Going by Boat & Taxi," p. 225).

8 ★ ★ **kids Arenal National Park.** Before you drive into the town of La Fortuna, if you've arrived in time, stop to take a hike over the cooled lava flows inside Arenal National Park. ⏱ Minimum 2 hr. See p. 230, **5**.

From Arenal National Park, continue on your route to your hotel in the La Fortuna area. You'll be picked up for a canyoning tour on the morning of Day 3.

9 ★ ★ **La Fortuna canyoning tour.** Either Pure Trek Canyoning or Desafío Adventure Company will take you into a tight box canyon in the midst of thick rain forest for hiking interspersed with rappels down the face of jungle waterfalls. Anyone in reasonably good shape can take part

Santa Elena: Gateway to Monteverde

Throughout this chapter, you'll see references to both Monteverde and Monteverde's "gateway," Santa Elena—it can be a bit confusing. Here's the deal: Monteverde is not a town or village in the traditional sense; it's more of an area, and it includes Santa Elena. There is no "Monteverde" town center, just dirt lanes leading off the main road to hotels, restaurants, farms, homes—you get the idea. This nameless main road has signs that will direct you to the hotels and restaurants mentioned here, and it dead-ends at the entrance to the Monteverde Cloud Forest Biological Reserve.

Follow that? Santa Elena *is* a town, albeit a tiny one, and as such it is considered, as I said earlier, the gateway to Monteverde and to the reserve, which is just 6km (3¾ miles) away. Santa Elena has a bus stop, a health clinic, a bank, a general store, a laundromat, and a few simple restaurants, budget hotels, souvenir shops, and tour offices. There's not much to see here, but you'll pass through it more than once as you explore the area.

in one of these tours, but Desafío's is a bit more challenging and adventurous. Pure Trek's is probably better suited to the not-so-nervy and to families with young children. Tours provide round-trip transportation from all area hotels. ⏱ 3–4 hr. See p. 245.

From La Fortuna, drive 12km (7½ miles) northwest along CR142.

🔟 ★★★ **Tabacón Hot Springs.** This is the most extensive, luxurious, and, it must be noted, expensive spot to soak your tired bones. It is part of ★★★ **Tabacón Grand Spa Thermal Resort** (p. 262), but visitors are welcome. Pools of varying sizes are spread among almost laughably lush gardens. Each of these pools is fed by warm natural springs. The centerpiece of this layout is a large, warm, spring-fed swimming pool with a waterslide, a swim-up bar, and a great view of Arenal Volcano. Indeed, the pools and springs closest to the volcano are some of the hottest—makes sense, doesn't it?

The gardens themselves are extensive and worth exploring. And that's not all: The resort also has an excellent spa offering professional massages, mud masks, and other treatments, as well as yoga classes (appointments required). A full-service restaurant, a garden grill, and a couple of bars are available for those seeking sustenance. The pools are busiest between 2 and 6pm, and management enforces a policy of limiting visitors, so reservations (made online or by phone) are recommended for those not staying at the resort. Spa treatments must be purchased separately, and reservations are required for these. **On the road to Arenal National Park (CR142), 12km (7½ miles) northwest of La Fortuna.** ☎ 2519-1900. www.tabacon.com. Admission $85 adults, $40 children 11 and under; includes buffet lunch or dinner. After 6pm $45 adults, $25 children; meal not included. AE, DC, MC, V. Daily noon–10pm; spa treatments daily 8am–10pm.

⑪ 🍴 ★ kids **El Novillo de Arenal.** This steakhouse packs quite a bit of charm into a simple setting. You'll be sitting on plastic chairs at a plastic lawn table, but the food is well prepared and hearty, and it's served up with a fabulous view of the volcano. **On the road btw. La Fortuna and the volcano.** ☎ 2479-1910. $$. See p. 263.

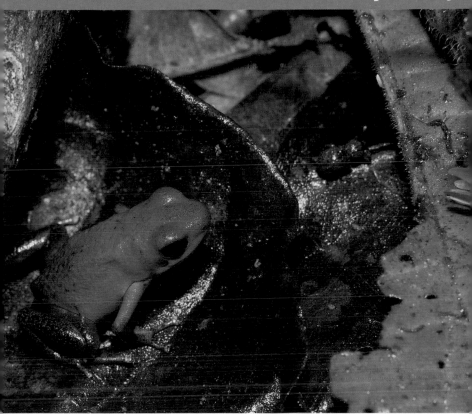

From La Fortuna, head 15km (9⅓ miles) northwest along CR142 to the well-marked turnoff for the entrance to Arenal National Park, another 3km (1¾ miles) farther.

⓬ ★★★ kids Night viewing Arenal Volcano. After dinner, sign on for a volcano-viewing tour, or take in the light show on your own. There's no need to enter Arenal National Park (**⑧**), as the views are just fine along the dirt road a bit beyond the entrance. ⊙ Minimum 1 hr. See "Volcano Viewing," p. 238.

> *OPPOSITE PAGE A canyoning tour through the jungle really gets the adrenaline pumping, as it leads you up and down waterfalls along its course. THIS PAGE Look for this little Costa Rica resident, the strawberry poison-dart frog, at the Frog Pond of Monteverde. It may be the color of strawberries, but it is definitely not edible—toxins in its skin keep predators from eating it.*

Going by Boat & Taxi

Instead of driving, you can travel between Santa Elena/Monteverde and La Fortuna/Arenal Volcano by boat and taxi. If you have a rental car, you can arrange to have it driven around for you (check with your rental car company first). It's about a 1½-hour four-wheel-drive taxi ride between Santa Elena and the Río Chiquito dock on Lake Arenal. From here it's a 20-minute ride across the lake, which cuts out hours of driving time. Once you're on the other side, La Fortuna is about a 25-minute taxi ride farther along. These trips can be arranged in either direction for $25 to $50 per person, all-inclusive. **Desafío Adventure Company** (☎ 2479-9474; www.desafio costarica.com) has two daily departures in each direction at 7am and 4pm, and can also arrange a leg by mountain bike (p. 38).

ANATOMY
OF A CLOUD
FOREST

Life at Every Layer, BY LINDA BARTH

CANOPY

MID LEVEL

GROUND LEVEL

TROPICAL CLOUD FORESTS are a unique and ecologically rich phenomenon, enveloped in a near-constant swirl of cloud, mist, and fog. It doesn't really rain, but moisture condenses on the foliage and then drips to the ground. While sunlight is at a minimum, the flora is extremely dense, thanks to rich soil and all that water—at times, you'll feel as though you're facing an impenetrable wall of ferns, mosses, orchids, and bromeliads. The end result is that the forest is really a series of microclimates—the forest floor can be much warmer than the canopy—that support a wildly diverse range of life forms. Monteverde Cloud Forest alone is home to 3,000 species of plants, tens of thousands of insects, 130 kinds of amphibians and reptiles, 120 different mammals, and 400 types of birds.

Canopy

EMERALD TOUCANET
(*Aulacrhynchus prasinus*)

This smaller member of the toucan family features a large yellow and black bill, green body, and blue throat, and is one of the more easily spotted toucans in the cloud forest.

VIOLET SABREWING
(*Campylopterus hemileucurus*)

The largest of Costa Rica's hummingbirds, this beauty is deep dark purple, with white-tipped tail feathers and a thick, curved beak.

GUARIA MORADA
(*Cattleya skinneri*)

This orchid is Costa Rica's national flower.

Mid Level

BLUE MORPHO BUTTERFLY
(*Morpho peleides*)

As you walk the cloud-forest trails, be on the lookout for a blue flash—it's most likely the reflection of sunlight splintering off the wings of one of these wonders.

FLEISCHMANN'S GLASS FROG
(*Hyalinobatrachium fleischmanni*)

This lime-green frog has a translucent belly through which you can see its internal organs.

JAGUAR
(*Panthera onca*)

The largest of the New World cats, the elusive jaguar is nocturnal, and seeing one in the wild is a rare treat.

KINKAJOU
(*Potos flavus*)

Known as a "night monkey," this big-eyed mammal is strictly nocturnal. You may just see those big eyes shining back at you, reflecting a spotlight, on a night tour.

Ground Level

ARBOREAL ARCHITECTURE
Aside from a thin, rich top layer, the soil is dense clay and rock. Consequently, many cloud-forest trees have adapted broad rather than deep root systems, known as buttress roots.

EYELASH VIPER
(*Bothriechis schlegelii*)
This strikingly beautiful pit viper comes in three distinct colorings:

bright yellow, deep olive green, and mottled green. The last closely mimics the pattern of moss on a rock.

TREE FERN
(Order Cyatheales)
This prehistoric forest plant is not a true tree. Its "leaves" are large fronds, and its "trunk"

is a nonwoody stem. A "pioneer species," tree ferns are among the first plants to sprout up after a landslide or tree fall.

Getting Misty

Costa Rica's cloud forests are formed when hot, humid air from the Caribbean coast rises over the mountain ranges that run like a spine down the middle of the country. Rain falls on the Caribbean slope, while warm, moist air continues up over the mountains, forming a semi-permanent cloud layer over the Pacific slope. Be prepared: The climatic conditions that make cloud forests a biological hot spot can leave you feeling chilled to the bone, especially from August through November.

The Best of the Northern Zone in 1 Week

The Northern Zone is one of Costa Rica's most-visited regions, and no wonder: Some of the country's best natural attractions are here, and despite development (and the presence of huge, clear-cut plantations), it still feels wild. A week will give you plenty of time to properly explore the Northern Zone, which has a character all its own. You'll get to explore the cloud forests of Monteverde, experience rumbling Arenal Volcano, and indulge in plenty of adventure tours. You'll want to rent a four-wheel-drive vehicle to get around.

> Volcano-heated water flows from pool to pool at the lushly planted Tabacón Hot Springs.

START Puerto Viejo de Sarapiquí, 82km (51 miles) northwest of San José. Take the Guápiles Hwy. (CR32) to the well-marked turnoff for Puerto Viejo de Sarapiquí. La Selva is 3km (1¾ miles) south. TOUR LENGTH 495km (308 miles).

❶ ★★★ **La Selva Biological Station.** Begin your tour at this rain-forest research facility and reserve. Take the half-day guided hike: You will see loads of wildlife, and the guides are real pros. ⏱ 4 hr. See p. 251.

In the afternoon, walk to the docks in downtown Puerto Viejo de Sarapiquí.

❷ ★★ **Río Sarapiquí boat ride.** Treat yourself to a great view of the local flora and fauna on a boat ride along the Sarapiquí River. If you're lucky, you may see a crocodile sunning on the banks. You'll definitely see loads of bird species. All the hotels and tour operators in the area can arrange this for you. Or simply head down to the docks and negotiate a ride with one of the boat captains. ⏱ 1–3 hr. Downtown

1 La Selva Biological Station
2 Río Sarapiquí
3 Parque Archeologico Alma Ata
4 Don Rufino
5 Arenal National Park
6 La Fortuna canyoning tour
7 Catarata Río Fortuna
8 Los Tucanes
9 Tabacón Hot Springs
10 Río Toro
11 El Novillo de Arenal
12 Caño Negro National Wildlife Refuge
13 Selvatura Park
14 Orchid Garden
15 Monteverde Cloud Forest Biological Reserve
16 Mata 'e Caña
17 Monteverde Cloud Forest Biological Reserve
18 Café Caburé
19 Sabine's Smiling Horses
20 Sofia

docks, Puerto Viejo de Sarapiquí. No phone. Rates $10–$20 per person per hr. Daily 7am–5pm.

On Day 2, take CR4 west 17km (11 miles) toward La Virgen. Parque Archeologico Alma Ata will be on your left before you reach La Virgen.

More Information

For stops **1**–**3** you'll want to stay in Puerto Viejo de Sarapiquí (see p. 264); for stops **4**–**12** in the La Fortuna/Arenal Volcano area (see p. 260); and finally, for stops **13**–**20**, in the Santa Elena/Monteverde region (see p. 254).

> A tour boat plies the Río Sarapiquí on a wildlife-viewing excursion.

> *Watch for spider monkeys in Caño Negro National Wildlife Refuge.*

3 ★ **Parque Archeologico Alma Ata.** Start off your busy day with a stop en route to La Fortuna at this very small but very important archaeological park. It is one of the few excavated pre-Columbian sites in Costa Rica that is open to the public. You'll see a series of graves and some petroglyphs and get to tour the small museum, which displays examples of the ceramics, tools, clothing, and carvings found here, as well as other natural history exhibits. There is also a self-guided tour of Chester Field Biological Gardens, which feature well-tended and nicely displayed examples of local medicinal and ornamental plants and food crops. ⊙ 2 hr. ☎ 2761-1004. www.sarapiquis.org. Museum admission $15 adults, $8 children 7–16. Museum and archaeological site, including guided tour, $24 adults, $12 children 7–16. Children 6 and under free. Daily 8am–5pm.

Get back on CR4 toward San Miguel and take the well-marked turnoff for Venecia and

Spending the night in Caño Negro

If you're serious about bird-watching, consider spending a night at the ★ **Caño Negro Natural Lodge** (☎ 2265-3302; www.canonegrolodge.com; doubles $95). The rooms are simple but clean, and the location is prime for exploring the refuge.

Aguas Zarcas. Continue through Aguas Zarcas to Ciudad Quesada, following signs for La Fortuna. The entire trip is 80km (50 miles); give yourself 1½ hours.

④ 🍽 ★ **Don Rufino.** By the time you pull into La Fortuna, you'll be ready for lunch. This downtown joint is right on the main road, and you can even see the volcano from the sidewalk out front. These folks specialize in grilled meats, with excellent cuts and a skilled touch. If that sounds too heavy for lunch, try some ceviche or a sandwich. Downtown La Fortuna. ☎ 2479-9997. $$$. See p. 263.

In the afternoon, drive 15km (9⅓ miles) northwest from La Fortuna along CR142 to the well-marked turnoff for Arenal National Park; the entrance is 3km (1¾ miles) farther.

SITE GUIDE
PAGE 232

5 ★★ 🧒 **Arenal National Park.** Spend the afternoon exploring Arenal Volcano, La Fortuna's main attraction. I recommend you get a good feel for the power and presence of this massive and constantly evolving mountain by hiking the trails inside its namesake national park. The park is situated on the lower flanks of the volcano. When the volcano is active you can hear and feel it rumble. Rocks and pyroclastic flows tumble down its side regularly. 12km (7½ miles) west of La Fortuna off the main road (CR142) to Tilarán. ☎ 2461-8499. Admission $10. Daily 8am–4pm.

You'll be picked up at your hotel early on Day 3 for a canyoning tour.

6 ★★ **La Fortuna canyoning tour.** Begin with a canyoning tour through the rain forests near the slopes of Arenal Volcano. I recommend the tour offered by Desafío Adventure Company for a wet and wild time. ⊙ 3–4 hr. See p. 246.

After you've returned to your hotel, take the well-marked CR142 south toward La Tigre/San Ramón. The entrance to the falls is on your right (5.5km/3½ miles).

7 ★ **Catarata Río Fortuna.** Located just on the outskirts of La Fortuna, this beautiful jungle waterfall plunges some 70m (230 ft.) into a perfectly round pool. Perhaps the best way to visit these falls is as part of a horseback-riding tour (p. 246). ⏱ 2–3 hr., including horseback ride. See p. 260, **5**.

Retrace your steps to La Fortuna and continue 12km (7½ miles) northwest along CR142 to the Tabacón Grand Spa Thermal Resort.

⑧ ♨ ★★ **Los Tucanes.** For dinner, treat yourself to the fine cuisine at this superb restaurant at the Tabacón Grand Spa Thermal Resort. ☎ 2460-2020. $$$. See p. 263.

9 ★★★ **Tabacón Hot Springs**. After dinner, walk across the street and down the hill to the natural hot springs at the ★★★ **Tabacón Grand Spa Thermal Resort** (p. 262)—the springs are open to the public. The main pool features a swim-up bar, waterslide, and view of the volcano, although I prefer the smaller, more isolated, and less crowded pools scattered around the grounds. ⏱ Minimum 2 hr. See p. 224, **10**.

You'll be picked up at your hotel early on the morning of Day 4 for a rafting trip.

10 ★★ **Rafting on the Río Toro.** Prepare to spend all of Day 4 on the class III and IV rapids of this wild river (for you nonrafters, that means big waves). The action is pretty continuous, and the scenery is stunning. ⏱ 1 day. See p. 241.

You'll be returned to your hotel in time for dinner in La Fortuna.

⑪ ♨ ★★ kids **El Novillo de Arenal.** Dinner here will give you the chance to combine typical Costa Rican cooking with some prime volcano viewing. The menu features a barebones selection of grilled meats and poultry, but everything offered is perfectly prepared, and the portions are hefty. On the road btw. La Fortuna and the volcano. ☎ 2479-1910. $$. See p. 263.

On the morning of Day 5, you will be picked up from your hotel for the following boat tour.

12 ★ **Caño Negro National Wildlife Refuge.** This vast network of marshes and rivers (notably the Río Frío) located on the Nicaraguan border is best known for its amazing abundance of bird life. Indeed, it's got some of the best bird-watching and wildlife viewing in the country—sloths, monkeys, caimans, and countless

> *Plenty of white water makes for an exciting day on the Río Toro.*

species of birds are found here. But the big draw is the chance to see a jabiru, one of the world's largest birds, standing as tall as 1.5m (5 ft.), with a wingspan of up to 2.4m (8 ft.). Almost all visitors come as part of an organized boat tour. ⏱ Full day. 100km (62 miles) north of La Fortuna. No phone. Admission to the refuge is free; tours cost $45 to $60 per person, and can be arranged with any tour agency in the La Fortuna area.

On Day 6, take CR142 west from La Fortuna, circling Lake Arenal, to the town of Tilarán (73km/45 miles). Watch for signs that will connect you to the dirt and gravel road to Santa Elena (35km/22miles). Selvatura Park is 6km (3¾ miles) north of the town center. Alternatively, take the quicker and easier taxi-boat-taxi (see "Going by Boat & Taxi," p. 225) to Santa Elena.

13 ★★ kids **Selvatura Park.** Spend the morning and have lunch at this extensive adventure park. There's a lot to do here, so pick one of the package tours that includes several of the attractions. ⏱ Minimum 3 hr. See p. 222, **7**.

Retrace your steps to Santa Elena.

14 ★ **Orchid Garden.** Spend your afternoon in the town of Santa Elena. Visit this fascinating collection of orchids, and then use the rest of the afternoon to shop at the series of downtown souvenir stores and gift shops. ⏱ 1½ hr. See p. 219, **4**.

In the early evening, you'll be picked up at your hotel for the following tour.

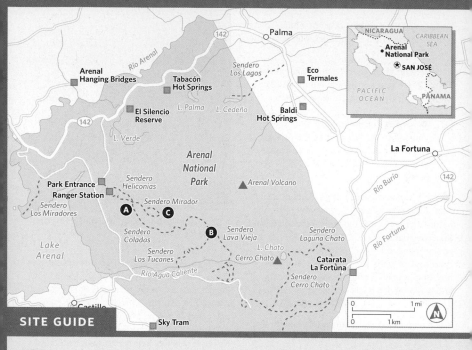

⑤ Arenal National Park

I recommend starting on the Ⓐ ★ **Sendero Coladas** (Lava Flow Trail), a gentle, broad trail that begins in a flat stretch of secondary forest and brush. (From the ranger station at the entrance, you can drive the .6km/⅓ mile to a parking lot near the trailhead for the Lava Flow Trail.) After about 30–40 minutes (1.8km/1.1 miles), you will reach a stand of lush forest, and a few minutes later a rocky landscape formed by a massive Ⓑ ★★ **1992 lava flow** (pictured at right). A short natural stairway here takes you to a broad, open lava field. Be careful, as the rocks are jagged and it's easy to lose your footing in places. You can climb and scramble to your heart's content, while enjoying fabulous views of the volcano in the foreground and Lake Arenal in the background. The walk should take you about 1½ to 2 hours round-trip.

From the Lava Flow trailhead parking lot, you have the option of hiking or driving the 1km (.6 miles) farther to Ⓒ ★ **El Mirador** (The Lookout), a small concrete platform with a high zinc roof and a few concrete benches. This lookout provides one of the closest and best views of the volcano to be had. It is a great place

to listen for the low grumbles and moans the massive volcano periodically emits. If it really lets out an eruption while you're here—hold on to your britches. ⏱ 2–4 hr.

> *A ride in the Northern Zone can encompass both open terrain and dense forest.*

⑮ ★ **Night tour of Monteverde Cloud Forest Biological Reserve.** Sign up for a night tour of the Monteverde Cloud Forest Biological Reserve to see loads of nocturnal wildlife. Spiders and insects are the prime attraction, but if you're lucky you'll see an owl, vine snake, kinkajou, or even a wildcat. Make reservations directly with the folks at the reserve, or have your hotel desk do it for you. ⏱ Minimum 2 hr. See p. 218, ❶.

⑯ ★★ **Mata 'e Caña.** After your tour, join the locals for a nightcap at this popular club. The crowd is always a lively mix of locals, tour guides, and tourists. The music is a broad mix of Latin and contemporary American pop and dance music. Some nights, you'll find plenty of people dancing. **Just north of Santa Elena. ☎ 2645-5883. $.**

On the morning of Day 7, take the well-marked road from Santa Elena to the Monteverde Cloud Forest Biological Reserve. The road is paved about halfway to the reserve, and rough dirt and mud the rest of the way (6km/3¾ miles).

⑰ ★★★ kids **Monteverde Cloud Forest Biological Reserve.** This is the area's main attraction, and with good reason. The well-maintained trails weave through a rich and varied cloud forest (see "Anatomy of a Cloud Forest," p. 226). Be sure to have an early reservation, and take a guided tour. After the tour, you can use your entrance ticket to further explore the network of trails here. ⏱ Minimum 3 hr. See p. 218, ❶.

Take the main road back to Santa Elena, stopping on the way for lunch.

⑱ ★★ **Café Caburé.** This second-floor open-air café is a great place to stop for lunch. Enjoy a couple of cheese and spinach empanadas, and be sure to save room for their homemade chocolates. **On the road btw. Santa Elena and the Monteverde Cloud Forest Biological Reserve. ☎ 2645-5020. $.** See p. 259.

After lunch return to your hotel, where you'll be picked up for a riding tour.

⑲ **Horseback riding.** Enjoy an afternoon horseback-riding tour (I recommend ★★ **Sabine's Smiling Horses,** though the local operators are all good). The mix of pastureland, back roads, and primary forest make for an excellent riding experience. ⏱ 2 hr. See p. 246.

You'll be returned to your hotel. When you're ready for dinner, take the road back toward the Monteverde Cloud Forest Biological Reserve and turn right onto the dirt road when you see signs for Cerro Plano.

⑳ ★★★ **Sofia.** On your last night in Monteverde, treat yourself to a fine meal of this restaurant's contemporary and creative takes on Latin American cuisine. **Cerro Plano, on the road btw. Santa Elena and Monteverde Cloud Forest Biological Reserve. ☎ 2645-7017. $$$–$$$$.** See p. 259.

The Northern Zone with Kids

Families will love the Northern Zone, as virtually all of the attractions and adventures here are kid-friendly. Children will be especially taken with the wildlife and bird action here. And while you may not want to ruin their time by pointing this out, they're bound to learn a lot while they're having a blast. Your time here will include a visit to cloud forests in Monteverde, a chance to check out the lava at Arenal Volcano, and lots of opportunities for both adventure tours and wildlife viewing. You'll want to rent a four-wheel-drive vehicle to get around.

> Suspended bridges provide good views and easy access in Monteverde Cloud Forest.

START Monteverde Cloud Forest Biological Reserve, 167km (104 miles) northwest of San José. To reach the reserve, take the Pan-American Hwy. (CR1) north to the turnoff for Sardinal, Guacimal, and Santa Elena (the road is paved as far as Guacimal). It's another 20km (12 miles) to Santa Elena; the Monteverde Cloud Forest Biological Reserve is just 6km (3¾ miles) beyond town. *Warning:* Parts of the road to the reserve are very rough dirt and mud. TOUR LENGTH 148km (92 miles).

❶ ★★★ **Monteverde Cloud Forest Biological Reserve.** They won't see any lions, tigers, or bears, but kids will get a real feel here for what it's like to walk in the jungle. The tropical flora and fauna are exuberant—take a guided tour so you don't miss anything. Your entrance ticket is good for the whole day, so you should definitely plan to linger and explore some of the trails on your own after the tour. ☺ Minimum 3 hr. See p. 218, ❶.

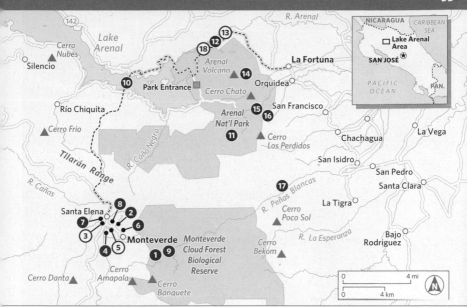

1. Monteverde Cloud Forest Biological Reserve
2. Bat Jungle
3. Morpho's Café
4. Frog Pond of Monteverde
5. Johnny's Pizzeria
6. The Original Canopy Tour
7. Mundo Insectos
8. Serpentario Monteverde
9. Monteverde Cloud Forest Biological Reserve
10. Jeep and boat trip to La Fortuna
11. Arenal National Park
12. Tabacón Hot Springs
13. Ave de Paraiso
14. Arenal Volcano
15. Pure Trek Canyoning
16. Fourtrax Adventure ATV Tour
17. Safari Float
18. El Novillo de Arenal

Take the main road back toward Santa Elena, stopping after 2.5km (1½ miles) at the following.

2 ★★ Bat Jungle. Bats may inspire fear or fascination, but everyone in the family will get a kick out of seeing and learning about these creatures of the night. Beyond the guided tour, educational exhibits, and video, the main thrill here is entering a darkened enclosure where several different species are in action. The bats have been tricked into thinking day is night, so you'll get to see them feed and fly around. Don't worry, they're behind glass; but still, you are up close and personal, even picking up their sounds and calls via microphones broadcast into the room. ⏱ 1½ hr. On the main road btw. Santa

Elena and the Monteverde Cloud Forest Biological Reserve. ☎ 2645-6566. Admission $10 adults, $8 children 18 and under. Daily 9am–8pm.

Continue 3.5km (2¼ miles) on the main road back to Santa Elena.

3 🍽 ★★ Morpho's Café. There's something for everyone at this joint. Be sure the kids try one of the fresh fruit smoothies. The sandwiches and burgers are great, and there's always a daily blue-plate special. For dessert, have a banana split made with locally produced ice cream. In Santa Elena center, across from the supermarket. ☎ 2645-5607. $$–$$$. See p. 259.

> *In Northern Zone forests keep your eyes open for blue-crowned motmots, with their colorful plumage and paddle-shaped tail feathers.*

The Frog Pond is located on the outskirts of Santa Elena, on a side road near the Monteverde Lodge & Gardens.

④ ★★ Frog Pond of Monteverde. This place (also called Ranario Monteverde) features a wide range of frogs and lizards in glass terrariums. If you're lucky, one of the glass tree frogs will be clinging to a wall of its terrarium. These frogs have transparent skin on their belly, which lets you see the internal workings of their organs and viscera. The attraction also has a butterfly garden with a couple of different enclosures. Save your entrance ticket, because you should make a return visit after dinner, when some of the more interesting amphibians are active—in particular, the red-eyed tree frog. ◷ 2 hr. See p. 219, ❺.

Johnny's is just outside of Santa Elena center on the road leading to Monteverde Cloud Forest Biological Reserve.

⑤ 🍽 **Johnny's Pizzeria.** The pizzas here are fresh and delicious, the dining room is large, and the atmosphere is lively. All in all, it's a great family spot. **Just outside of Santa Elena.** ☎ 2645-5066. $$$.

On Day 2, you'll be picked up early at your hotel for the following.

⑥ ★★ The Original Canopy Tour. There are loads of canopy tours—which let you explore the upper reaches of a rain forest—around the country and particularly here in Monteverde. This one is unique, beginning with an ascent up the inside of a strangler fig and finishing with a

More Information

For stops ❶–❾ of this tour we recommend a base in or around Monteverde (p. 254); and for stops ❿–⓲ in or around La Fortuna (p. 260), near the Arenal Volcano and Arenal National Park.

rappel down from a treetop platform. Children as young as 5 years old can actually do this tour. ⏱ 3 hr. See p. 244.

You'll be dropped off back at your hotel. In the afternoon, take the road from the supermarket in Santa Elena center 300m (1,000 ft.) west and downhill to Mundo Insectos.

❼ ★ Mundo Insectos. The World of Insects features more than 30 terrariums filled with a wide range of invertebrates. My favorites include the aptly named walking-stick insects and the giant horned beetles. ⏱ 1 hr. Outskirts of Santa Elena. ☎ 2645-6859. Admission $9 adults, $6 children 5–12; children 4 and under free. Daily 9am–7pm.

Serpentario Monteverde is just on the outskirts of Santa Elena on the road toward Monteverde Cloud Forest Biological Reserve.

❽ ★ Serpentario Monteverde. Round out your critter viewing with a stop at this place, which is filled with slithering snakes. You'll see a host of local specimens, including the beautiful eyelash viper and the feared fer-de-lance. Don't worry, they're all behind glass. In fact, they are in spacious, well-lit, and well-designed terrariums and enclosures. ⏱ 1 hr. Outskirts of Santa Elena, on the road to Monteverde Cloud Forest Biological Reserve. ☎ 2645-5238. www.snaketour.com. Admission $8; includes guided tour. Daily 8am–8pm.

Get back to your hotel in time to be picked up in the early evening for a night tour.

❾ ★ Night tour of Monteverde Cloud Forest Biological Reserve. If your kids have the stamina, be sure to take a night tour into the cloud forest. It's one thing seeing bugs, frogs, spiders, and snakes behind glass, but this tour will give you all a chance to see a fair number of these creatures in the wild. ⏱ 2–3 hr. See p. 233, ⑮.

On Day 3, Desafío Adventure Company will pick up you and your rental car in Santa Elena for your trip to La Fortuna.

❿ ★ Jeep and boat trip to La Fortuna. This (relatively) fast trip from Santa Elena to La Fortuna also happens to be a lot of fun. You'll be picked up at your hotel and taken by jeep to Lake Arenal, where you'll board a boat that

> *Morpho's Café has something for everyone.*

will bring you close to La Fortuna. Then it's into another jeep for the trek to your hotel. In the meantime, Desafío will drive your rental car around the lake for you. Kids will love the bouncing jeep rides and the boat, and parents will love cutting what would have been a 4-hour drive down to a 2-hour trip. ⏱ 2 hr. See "Going by Boat & Taxi," p. 225.

You'll be dropped off at your hotel, and your rental car should arrive within the next 2 hours. Once you have it, take CR142 15km (9⅓ miles) northwest to the well-marked turnoff for Arenal National Park. The entrance is 3km (1¾ miles) farther up the road.

⓫ ★★ Arenal National Park. The bird-watching is wonderful here, and your kids will enjoy scrambling over the tangled mass of cooled lava. Keep an eye on the little ones, as the rocks can be sharp. ⏱ Minimum 2 hr. See p. 230, ⑤.

From the park, take CR142 3km (1¾ miles) east toward La Fortuna; the hot springs will be on your right.

> *Whether you sign up for a tour or strike out on your own, you will be awed by Arenal's volcanic display lighting up the night.*

⑫ Tabacón Hot Springs. In the late afternoon and evening you'll have plenty of time to soak and play in the extensive natural hot springs at the **Tabacón Grand Spa Thermal Resort** (p. 262), which are open to the public. The kids will want to play on the waterslide that feeds the main pool; parents might want to treat themselves to a massage or mud treatment.

Volcano Viewing

Watching the lava flow from Arenal Volcano is one of the highlights of a trip to this region. All of the tour agencies and hotel desks offer night tours to view the glowing lava—the best combine volcano watching with a stop at one of the local hot springs. Prices range from $15 to $70 per person. But you don't need to take a tour—the dirt road near the park entrance offers great views, and so do a number of nearby hotels and resorts. Be forewarned, though, that this is an unpredictable natural phenomenon. While the light show is generally amazingly consistent, variations in volcanic activity or heavy cloud cover may impact your experience.

The whole family can meet under the broad artificial waterfall located between the main pool and the spa. ☺ Minimum 2 hr. See p. 224, ⑩.

⑬ 🍽 Ave de Paraiso. Have dinner at the resort's restaurant, where you can choose from the extensive buffet (there's something for even the pickiest eaters) or a host of a la carte dishes, including healthful "spa cuisine." At the Tabacón Grand Spa Thermal Resort. ☎ 2460-2020. $$$.

After dinner, you can either watch the volcano from the resort or, for a closer view, retrace your steps 3km (1¾ miles) to the entrance to Arenal National Park.

⑭ Night viewing of Arenal Volcano. Sign on for a volcano-viewing tour or head out yourself. Kids will get a real thrill watching the deep red glow of the lava flow—and so will you. If you go on your own, I recommend choosing a quiet spot along the dirt road a little bit beyond the entrance to **Arenal National Park** (⑪). The benefit of a tour is that you're likely to learn a bit about the volcano itself. ☺ Minimum 2 hr. See "Volcano Viewing," left.

> *Older teenagers can drive their own vehicle, but the little ones need to double up with an adult on a Fourtrax Adventure ATV tour.*

On Day 4, you'll be picked up at your hotel for the following.

15 ★★ **Pure Trek Canyoning.** I recommend Pure Trek's wonderful canyoning tour, which is suitable for children as young as 5 years old. This adventure features some light hiking interspersed with rappels down the face of jungle waterfalls; it includes lunch. ⊙ 3 hr. See p. 245.

Pure Trek will drop you back at your hotel in time for you to be picked up for your next adventure.

16 ★ **Fourtrax Adventure ATV tour.** In the afternoon, take this more mechanically enhanced adventure tour, a 3-hour excursion on all-terrain vehicles through both farmlands and virgin cloud forests, with a stop for a dip in a clear, natural jungle swimming hole. The tour also includes a visit to a local butterfly garden. The minimum age for a driver is 16. Younger children must share an ATV with a parent. ⊙ 3 hr. See p. 242.

On Day 5, you'll be picked up at your hotel for a rafting trip.

17 ★★ **Safari float with Desafío Adventure Company.** For your final day in the Northern Zone, take a white-water rafting trip. The scenery is spectacular, and there are a variety of rivers and rides to choose from, with something suitable for all ages and ability levels. For those with younger kids, I recommend Desafío's safari float (the local term for a gentle boat ride) on the Peñas Blancas; or, for a little more adventure, try their tour on the class II and III section of the Río Blasa. For those with teenagers seeking more thrills and chills, I suggest you give the class III and IV Río Toro outing a try. ⊙ 4–5 hr. See p. 241.

You'll be dropped off at your hotel in time for dinner: From La Fortuna, take CR142 12km (7½ miles) northwest.

18 🍽 ★★ **El Novillo de Arenal.** For your final dinner in La Fortuna, come to this simple, local joint for some fine Costa Rican cooking and great last-minute volcano viewing. On the road btw. La Fortuna and the volcano, 12km (7½ miles) northwest of La Fortuna. ☎ 2479-1910. $–$$. See p. 263.

Northern Zone Adventures in & on the Water

There may not be a beach in sight, but there's no reason you can't get busy in and on the water while you're visiting the Northern Zone. The white-water rivers cascading down from the mountains and volcanoes are perfect for rafting and kayaking, while Lake Arenal is a playground custom-made for watersports, offering opportunities for fishing, canoeing, windsurfing, and kiteboarding.

> Lake Arenal is a hot spot for windsurfers and kiteboarders in the landlocked Northern Zone.

Kiteboarding & Windsurfing

Lake Arenal is one of the world's top spots for both of these high-octane adventure sports. Many of the regulars from Washington's Columbia River Gorge take up residence around the shores of Lake Arenal during the winter months, when the wind here howls. Small boards, water starts, and fancy jibes are the norm. If you want to try windsurfing, check out either ★★ **Tilawa Windsurf Center** (☎ 2695-5050; www.windsurfcostarica.com) or ★★ **Tico Wind** (☎ 2692-2002; www.ticowind.com). Both of these operators rent equipment and give lessons. Rates run between $55 and $75 per day for equipment rentals.

River Rafting, Kayaking & Canoeing

If you enjoy having a paddle in your hand, the lakes and rivers of the Northern Zone have a lot to offer.

The Puerto Viejo de Sarapiquí area is a hotbed of paddling activities. Opportunities range from simple floats on class I and II sections of the Río Puerto Viejo to serious class IV rapids

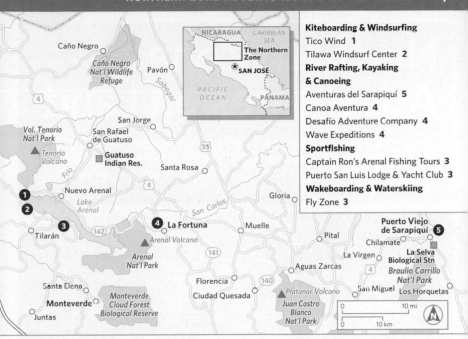

Kiteboarding & Windsurfing
Tico Wind **1**
Tilawa Windsurf Center **2**
River Rafting, Kayaking & Canoeing
Aventuras del Sarapiquí **5**
Canoa Aventura **4**
Desafío Adventure Company **4**
Wave Expeditions **4**
Sportfishing
Captain Ron's Arenal Fishing Tours **3**
Puerto San Luis Lodge & Yacht Club **3**
Wakeboarding & Waterskiing
Fly Zone **3**

in rafts or kayaks. ★ **Aventuras del Sarapiquí** (☎ 2766-6768; www.sarapiqui.com) is the best operator in the area, offering a full slate of daily rafting trips, as well as kayak rentals, classes, and organized tours.

In the La Fortuna and Lake Arenal area, check in with ★★ **Desafío Adventure Company** (☎ 2479-9464; www.desafiocostarica.com) or ★★ **Wave Expeditions** (☎ 2479-7262; www.waveexpeditions.com). Both companies offer daily raft rides on class I to II, III, and IV to V rapids on different sections of the **Ríos Toro, Peñas Blancas,** and **Sarapiquí.**

A more laid-back alternative is a canoe tour with ★ **Canoa Aventura** (☎ 2479-8200; www.canoa-aventura.com), which offers half-, full-, and multiday excursions on a variety of rivers in the region.

Rates range from around $45 to $65 per person for a half-day trip to $75 to $95 per person for a full-day excursion.

Sportfishing
Most anglers come to Costa Rica to tackle big game fish in the oceans and estuaries, but Lake Arenal is a major destination for freshwater fishing. The big action is *guapote,* a Central American species often referred to as rainbow bass. You can also book fishing trips to Caño Negro (see p. 231, **12**), where snook, tarpon, and other game fish can be stalked.

Most hotels and adventure-tour companies throughout the Northern Zone can arrange fishing excursions. Costs run around $150 to $250 per boat for a half-day, while a full day goes for $250 to $500. In the Arenal area, I recommend you check in with ★★ **Captain Ron's Arenal Fishing Tours** (☎ 2694-4678; www.arenalfishing.com) or the folks at ★ **Puerto San Luis Lodge & Yacht Club** (☎ 2695-5750; www.hotelpuertosanluiscr.com).

Wakeboarding & Waterskiing
Lake Arenal, the largest freshwater lake in Costa Rica, features plenty of calm quiet corners to practice wakeboarding. Whether you're a novice or an old hand, if you're interested in wakeboarding or waterskiing, call **Fly Zone** (☎ 8339-5876; www.flyzone-cr.com; daily 8am–5pm)). These folks offer lessons or will simply give you a pull behind their specialized *Ski Nautique* boat. Rates for lessons or a pull are $85 per hour, including equipment. An hour can be shared by up to four people.

Northern Zone Adventures on Land

The Northern Zone is a hot spot for adventure travelers.
The rugged terrain, thick cloud and rain forests, and active volcanoes make this a prime area to practice and enjoy a range of adventure activities and tours. For hiking see p. 248, and for bird-watching see p. 252.

> *Arenal Bungee's fixed tower allows for a jump of about 14 stories.*

All-Terrain-Vehicle (ATV) Tours

★ **kids Fourtrax Adventure.** Fourtrax has a fleet of late-model Hondas, and they offer a fun and varied 3-hour ATV tour. The tour passes through farmlands with great volcano views, as well as through patches of primary rain forest. Included in the tour are a swimming stop at a pristine natural pool in the middle of the forest and a visit to one of the local butterfly gardens. There are three fixed departures daily. La Fortuna. ☎ 2479-8455. www.fourtraxadventure.com. Rates $85 per person per ATV; $110 for 2 riders sharing an ATV. Departures at 7am, 11am, and 2:30pm.

Bicycling

I find the back roads and forest trails of the Northern Zone to be some of the best places to mountain bike in all of Costa Rica. Most of the hotels and tour agencies in the region can hook you up with bike rentals or a half-day tour. However, if you're serious about it you might want to check out a dedicated operator.

In the Puerto Viejo de Sarapiquí region, ★ **Hacienda Pozo Azul** (☎ 877/810-6903 in U.S. and Canada, or 2761-1360 in Costa Rica; www.pozoazul.com) is a multipurpose adventure tour company with a good mountain biking operation. Their mountain biking tour runs $45

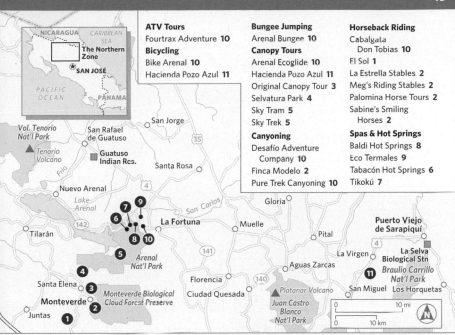

ATV Tours	Bungee Jumping	Horseback Riding
Fourtrax Adventure **10**	Arenal Bungee **10**	Cabalgata
Bicycling	**Canopy Tours**	Don Tobias **10**
Bike Arenal **10**	Arenal Ecoglide **10**	El Sol **1**
Hacienda Pozo Azul **11**	Hacienda Pozo Azul **11**	La Estrella Stables **2**
	Original Canopy Tour **3**	Meg's Riding Stables **2**
	Selvatura Park **4**	Palomina Horse Tours **2**
	Sky Tram **5**	Sabine's Smiling
	Sky Trek **5**	Horses **2**
	Canyoning	**Spas & Hot Springs**
	Desafío Adventure	Baldi Hot Springs **8**
	Company **10**	Eco Termales **9**
	Finca Modelo **2**	Tabacón Hot Springs **6**
	Pure Trek Canyoning **10**	Tikokú **7**

per person for a half day, $60 for a full day.

Perhaps the best mountain biking in the Northern Zone can be found around the Arenal Volcano, which offers everything from mellow beginner-level rides to some serious climbing and descents. Nearly all rides come with great volcano and lake views. ★★ **Bike Arenal** (☎ 866/465-4114 in U.S. and Canada, or 2479-7150 in Costa Rica; www.bikearenal.com) is the only dedicated operator in the area, with an excellent collection of top-notch bikes and equipment and a wide range of tour possibilities. Rates run around $67 to $96 for a day trip. Multiday trips and custom itineraries are also available—call for information and pricing.

Bungee Jumping

★ **Arenal Bungee.** This place is located in the heart of downtown La Fortuna. Its centerpiece is a 40m (130-ft.) steel tower. In addition to a straight bungee jump, you can try a water landing into a small pool on the ground; or sign up for a "rocket launch," which is kind of the equivalent of becoming a human slingshot. The long hours allow you to try your jump by day or by night. La Fortuna. ☎ 2479-7440. www.arenalbungee.com. Rates $50 for jump, fall, or rocket launch. Various packages available. Daily 9:30am–9:30pm.

> *Fourtrax Adventure's ATV tours include wildlife and volcano viewing and a stop for a swim.*

> *Bikers in the Arenal area are treated to stunning views of both the volcano and the lake.*

Canopy Tours

There's a glut of canopy tours in the Northern Zone, but I can only wholeheartedly recommend the ones mentioned below. Anybody in average physical condition is capable of doing any of the canopy tours, although they're not for the fainthearted or acrophobic.

★ **Arenal Ecoglide.** Located just outside the center of La Fortuna, this place features excellent volcano views and a journey over 15 different cables; its "Tarzan Swing" replaces the classic hero's jungle vine with a rope and harness setup. The entire tour lasts about 2½ hours. 3.5km (2¼ miles) from La Fortuna on the road to Tabacón. ☎ 2479-7120. www.arenalecoglide.com. Rates $45 adults; children 11 and under half-price. MC, V. Daily 8am–3pm.

★ **Hacienda Pozo Azul.** Hacienda Pozo Azul is both a working cattle farm and a one-stop shop for a wide range of adventure activities in the heart of the Puerto Viejo de Sarapiquí region. These folks have an extensive zip-line canopy tour operation, with 17 platforms connected by 12 different cable runs. The tour lasts 2½ to 3

hours, with the cables crisscrossing a beautiful rain-forest canyon several times. The tour can be combined with a rappel down a canyon wall. La Virgen de Sarapiquí, 18km (11 miles) west of Puerto Viejo de Sarapiquí. ☎ 877/810-6903 in U.S. and Canada, or 2761-1360 in Costa Rica. www.pozoazul.com. Zip-line tour $45 adults, $36 students and children. Zip-line/rappel combo $70 adults, $56 students and children. AE, MC, V. Daily 8am–5pm.

★★ kids **The Original Canopy Tour.** This is one of the oldest and more interesting canopy tours in Costa Rica. The initial ascent climbs up the hollowed-out interior of a giant strangler fig tree. The tour lasts 2½ hours and has 11 platforms and 2 rappels. You'll need to book in advance, and you'll be picked up and dropped off at your hotel. Monteverde. ☎ 2645-5243. www.canopytour.com. Rates $45 adults, $35 students, $25 children 11 and under. AE, MC, V. Daily 7:30am, 10:30am, and 2:30pm.

★★ kids **Selvatura Park.** The canopy operation here features an extensive zip-line tour, with 15 cables connecting 18 platforms, as well as a

> *The Sky Tram canopy tour includes a zip-line through the trees.*

network of trails and suspended bridges. Other on-site attractions include a huge butterfly garden, a hummingbird garden, a snake exhibit, and a wonderful insect display and museum. Prices vary, depending upon how much you want to see and do. See p. 222, ❼.

★★★ **Sky Tram.** This extensive and varied canopy operation begins with an open gondola-style ride that rises up from near the shores of Lake Arenal, providing excellent views of the lake and volcano. The tour continues over a series of trails and suspended bridges. At the end, you can hike, take the gondola, or strap on a harness and ride the zip-line canopy tour down to the bottom. The zip-line tour features several very long and very fast sections; the longest cable is some 750m (2,460 ft.) and achieves a speed of 75kph (47 mph). On the shores of Lake Arenal, on the dirt road btw. Arenal National Park and El Castillo. ☎ 2479-9944. www.skytrek.com. Rates for tram ride up and zip-line down $60 per person; for tram round-trip $50; discounts available for students with valid ID and children. AE, MC, V. Daily 7:30am–7pm.

★★ **Sky Trek.** This is one of the more extensive canopy tours in the country, with two very long cables to cross (the longer of these some 770m/2,525 ft.) high above the forest floor. The total distance is about 4km (2½ miles). There

> *Rapelling down the face of a waterfall is one of the highlights of a canyoning tour.*

are no rappel descents; you brake using the pulley system for friction. 3.5km (2¼ miles) outside Santa Elena on the road to the Santa Elena Cloud Forest Reserve. ☎ 2645-5238. www.sky adventures.travel. Rate $60 per person; includes zip-line tour and trails and bridges of the Sky Walk (p. 249). Round-trip transportation from Santa Elena $2 per person. AE, MC, V. Daily 7:30am–4pm.

Canyoning

If you'd like a bigger rush than that offered by the now-ubiquitous zip-line canopy tours, go "canyoning." This adventure sport is a mix of hiking through and alongside a jungle river, punctuated with periodic rappels through and alongside the faces of rushing waterfalls. Be forewarned: You will get wet on a canyoning tour.

If you're staying in or around La Fortuna and Arenal, try ★★ kids **Pure Trek Canyoning** (☎ 866/569-5723 in U.S. and Canada, or 2479-1313 in Costa Rica; www.puretrekcostarica.com)

> *A horseback tour is yet another way to see the La Fortuna area.*

or ★★ **Desafío Adventure Company** (☎ 2479-9464; www.desafiocostarica.com). Pure Trek's canyoning trip is better for first-timers and families with kids, because it's pretty easygoing. That said, you still get five thrilling rappels, four of which are either alongside or right through a rainforest waterfall. The $95 tour lasts about 4 hours, and includes lunch. Tours leave daily at 7am and noon. The tour offered by Desafío is a bit more rugged and adventurous, with a series of six waterfalls and more time spent hiking through and swimming in the river. This tour, which costs $90 per person, also takes around 4 hours and includes lunch. Tours leave daily at 7:30am, 10am, and 1pm.

Both of these companies also offer combination full-day excursions that mix canyoning with other adventure tours. Both provide round-trip transportation to and from your hotel.

If you're staying around Monteverde, try the ★ **Finca Modelo** (☎ 2645-5581; www.familia brenestours.com) canyoning tour, which involves a mix of hiking and rappelling down the faces of a series of forest waterfalls. The tallest of these waterfalls is around 40m (130 ft.). The cost is $60, and round-trip transportation to and from your hotel will be provided.

Horseback Riding

The back roads and forest trails that make for such good mountain bike riding are also ideal for horseback tours. The Monteverde and Arenal Volcano areas are the prime spots to saddle up.

In the Arenal Volcano area, a trip to the Río Fortuna Waterfall is the most popular ride, and all of the tour agencies and hotel tour desks in the area can arrange this for you. In the Monteverde area, **Meg's Riding Stables** (☎ 2645-5560), **La Estrella Stables** (☎ 2645-5075), **Palomina Horse Tours** (☎ 2645-5479), and ★★ **Sabine's Smiling Horses** (☎ 2645-6894; www.smilinghorses.com) are the most established operators, offering guided rides for around $15 to $20 per hour.

For a more extensive ride, check in with ★ **Cabalgata Don Tobias** (☎ 2479-1212; www.cabalgatadontobias.com). These folks run a 2½-hour tour on their private land, which is a mix of farmland and primary and secondary forests. Along the way you'll enjoy some great views of the Arenal Volcano. The tour costs $55 for adults and $45 for children, and leaves daily at 9am and 1:30pm.

Another option is to set up a day tour and sauna at ★ **El Sol** (☎ 2645-7214; www.elsol nuestro.com), located about a 10-minute car ride down the mountain from Santa Elena. These folks will take you on a roughly 3-hour ride either to San Luis or to an isolated little waterfall with an excellent swimming hole. After the ride back, you'll find the wood-burning traditional Swedish sauna all fired up, with a refreshing and beautiful little pool beside it. The half-day tour costs $60 per person, including lunch, and leaves daily at 8am.

> *In addition to smoke and lava, the plethora of hot springs is another sign of Arenal Volcano's active status.*

Spas & Hot Springs

In addition to the amazing natural spectacle that is Arenal Volcano, the Northern Zone is home to a host of naturally heated thermal hot springs. One of the best aspects of the pools and springs in this area is that the hot, soothing mineral waters lack the heavy sulfur smell commonly found at hot springs.

Baldi Hot Springs. These are the first hot springs you'll come to as you drive from La Fortuna toward Tabacón. The place has grown significantly over the years. There are now pools, slides, bars, and restaurants spread across the expansive grounds. While there are excellent volcano views from many of the pools and lookout spots, I find these hot springs to be a far less attractive option than the others mentioned here. There's more of a party vibe at Baldi, with loud music often blaring at some of the swim-up bars. Next to Volcano Look Disco (p. 263), on the road btw. La Fortuna and Arenal National Park. ☎ 2479-9651. Admission $34 adults, $17 children 12 and under. AE, MC, V. Daily 10am–10pm.

★★ Eco Termales. Eco Termales is smaller and more intimate than Tabacón Grand Spa and, with several pools set amid lush forest and gardens, almost as picturesque and luxurious. The place is a local family affair, run with love and care by Doña Mireya Hidalgo and the rest of the Hidalgo clan. There are poolside bars (run on an honor system) and a restaurant that serves good local cuisine. However, there are no spa services and no view of the volcano. Because admission is limited, it's never crowded, and reservations are absolutely necessary. On the road btw. La Fortuna and Arenal National Park, across from Baldi Hot Springs. ☎ 2479-8484. Admission $29 adults, $20 children 10 and under. MC, V. Daily 10am–10pm.

★★★ Tabacón Hot Springs. See p. 224, .

Tikokú. The newest entrant in the field, Tikokú features a row of eight descending, sculpted pools, some with good volcano views and some featuring Jacuzzi jets. The downside of this spa is its location, right beside Baldi, sometimes the loud music and partying there impinges on the quiet vibe many are seeking. On the road btw. La Fortuna and Arenal National Park, next to Baldi Hot Springs. ☎ 2479-1700. Admission $20 adults, $10 children 9 and under. AE, MC, V. Daily 10am–8pm.

The Northern Zone's Best Hikes

There's fabulous hiking in the Northern Zone. Choices are are plentiful throughout the region, with national parks and private reserves, lush cloud forests and rain forests, trails on the ground and through the treetops. Because much of the terrain is mountainous and volcanic, the hiking can be strenuous at times. However, most of the major reserves and parks have one or more gentle trails for day-trippers or the less adventurous.

> *You'll know you're in the tropics when you hike through lush, green Monteverde Cloud Forest.*

Monteverde

★ **Ecological Sanctuary.** This is a family-run wildlife refuge and private reserve. There are four main trails that lead through a variety of ecosystems, and wildlife viewing is often quite good. Things begin at the site of a former coffee and banana farm and proceed through habitats ranging from open pasture and farmland to secondary forest and primary cloud forest. There are a couple of pretty waterfalls along the trails. On the Cerro Plano road. ☎ 2645-5869. Admission $10 self-guided hiking; $25 2-hr. guided tour; $20 2-hr. guided night tour. Daily 7:30am–5pm; night tour 5:30pm.

★★★ kids **Monteverde Cloud Forest Biological Reserve.** This is one of the prime parks and reserves in the country. The extensive network of trails is clearly marked, regularly traveled, and generally gentle in terms of ascents and descents. The cloud forest is lush and largely untouched. Because most of the birds, such as the resplendent quetzal, and mammals are rare and elusive, and often nocturnal, I strongly recommend you go with a guide. If you have only one hike inside this park, take the **Sendero El Río** (River Trail), which leads to a picturesque small waterfall plunging into a pretty little pool. See p. 220, ⓐ.

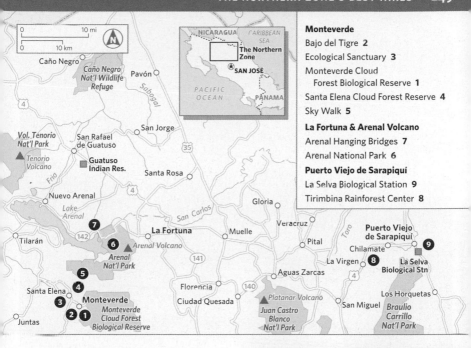

Monteverde
Bajo del Tigre **2**
Ecological Sanctuary **3**
Monteverde Cloud
    Forest Biological Reserve **1**
Santa Elena Cloud Forest Reserve **4**
Sky Walk **5**

La Fortuna & Arenal Volcano
Arenal Hanging Bridges **7**
Arenal National Park **6**
Puerto Viejo de Sarapiquí
La Selva Biological Station **9**
Tirimbina Rainforest Center **8**

★★ **Santa Elena Cloud Forest Reserve.** This 310-hectare (765-acre) reserve has 13km (8 miles) of hiking trails. Because it borders the Monteverde Cloud Forest Biological Reserve (p. 248), a similar richness of flora and fauna is found here, although quetzal sightings are not nearly as common. Still, with a maximum elevation of 1,680m (5,510 ft.), this is the highest cloud forest in the Monteverde area. The reserve is a community-based project, with proceeds going directly to local causes and improvements. 5km (3 miles) outside Santa Elena, at the end of the road to the Santa Elena Cloud Forest Reserve. ☎ 2645-5390. www.reservasanta elena.org. Admission $12 adults, $6 students and

> Some hikes in the Northern Zone include a canopy tour.

children 15 and under. Guided tour an additional $15 per person. Daily 7am–4pm.

children 15 and under. Guided tour an additional $15 per person. Daily 7am–4pm.

★★ **Sky Walk.** The web of forest paths and suspension bridges here provides visitors with a view previously reserved for birds, monkeys, and much more adventurous travelers. The bridges reach 39m (128 ft.) above the ground at their highest point, so those with a fear of heights should think carefully before heading out. There's an observation tower not far from the main entrance, as well as several other lookout points that provide views of Lake

Going Solo?

At all of the national parks, and most private reserves, you can hike the trails on your own or as part of a guided tour. In all cases, you will undoubtedly see and learn a lot more with an experienced local naturalist guide. That said, most trails are wide, well marked, and well maintained, and most pose no particularly great challenge to someone in reasonable shape.

> *Trails in Arenal National Park traverse lava and forest on the flanks of the active cone.*

Arenal and the Arenal Volcano. 3.5km (2¼ miles) outside Santa Elena, on the road to the Santa Elena Cloud Forest Reserve. ☎ 2645-5238. www.skyadventures.travel. Admission $30; discounts available for students and children. Round-trip transportation from Santa Elena $2 per person. Daily 7:30am–4pm.

kids **Bajo del Tigre.** Part of the Bosque Eterno de los Niños (Children's Eternal Forest), this 3.5km (2.2-mile) network of trails is administered by the Monteverde Conservation League. The trails are self-guided, relatively easy hiking, and good for families. Toward one end of the principal loop trail a steep canyon provides nice views over the Gulf of Nicoya—especially striking toward sunset. In fact, there is a guided twilight tour, leaving daily at 5:30pm. About midway along the road btw. Santa Elena and the Monteverde Cloud Forest Biological Reserve. ☎ 2645-5305. www.acmcr.org. Admission $8 adults, $5 children 12–18; children 11 and under free. Guided twilight tour $30 per person. Daily 8am–5pm; 5:30–7:30pm.

La Fortuna & Arenal Volcano

★★ **Arenal Hanging Bridges.** Located just over the Lake Arenal dam, this attraction is a complex of gentle trails and fixed and suspension bridges through a beautiful tract of primary forest. The entire loop trail covers a little more than 3km (1.9 miles). The daily 6am early-bird guided hike offers a great opportunity for bird-watching; this tour also includes one re-entry to the trails any time during the subsequent 3-day period. Off the main road (CR142) btw. La Fortuna and Tilarán, 4km (2½ miles) west of Tabacón. ☎ 2290-0469. www.hangingbridges.com. Admission $22 adults, $17 seniors, $12 children 12–18; children 11 and under free. Guided tours, bird-watching tours, and transportation available. Daily 7:30am–4:30pm.

★★ kids **Arenal National Park.** Located on the western flank of the Arenal Volcano, this park has several short trails. The principal trail, ★ **Sendero Coladas** (Lava Flow Trail), is just under 2km (1.25 miles) and passes through secondary forest and over cooled lava flows.

> *La Selva Biological Station's many miles of trails pass through lush, green, wildlife-rich rain forest.*

Scrambling over the cooled lava is a real treat, but be careful, as the rocks can be sharp in places. There are great views of the volcano from many spots throughout the park; for an up-close-and-personal view, take the ★ **Mirador** trail to a lookout point where you can not only see the volcano better, but really hear it rumble and roar. For more information, see p. 230, ❺.

Puerto Viejo de Sarapiquí

★★★ **La Selva Biological Station.** With some 56km (35 miles) of well-maintained trails, this area is my favorite hiking spot in the Puerto Viejo de Sarapiquí region (see the tour starting on p. 264). The protected land here is home to an amazing abundance of flora and fauna. My favorite hike starts off on the **Sendero Cantarrana** (Singing Frog Trail), which includes a section of low bridges over a rain-forest swamp. From here, you can join up with either the near or far circular loop trails—**CCC** and **CCL,** respectively. If you're not staying at La Selva, you'll have to take a guided hike, led by experienced and well-informed naturalists. Some of the trails

are equipped for disabled travelers. 3km (1¾ miles) south of Puerto Viejo de Sarapiquí. ☎ 2524-0607 for reservations or 2766-6565 to reach the reserve. www.threepaths.co.cr. Rates $30 half-day guided hike; $38 1-day guided hike; reservations necessary. Guided hikes daily 8am and 1:30pm. For staying at La Selva, see p. 266.

★ **Tirimbina Rainforest Center.** This private reserve offers 9km (5.6 miles) of hiking trails, including a 380m (.25-mile) trail suitable for people with disabilities. There are several impressive suspension bridges, both over the river and through the forest canopy. Most of the trails are actually on an island, between the Sarapiquí and Tirimbina Rivers. You might want to bring a bathing suit, as the trails pass by a couple of excellent swimming holes on the Sarapiquí River. 17km (11 miles) west of Puerto Viejo de Sarapiquí. ☎ 2761-1579. www.tirimbina.org. Admission $15; $22 for 2-hr. guided tour. Night tours and specialized bird-watching tours available.

The Northern Zone's Best Bird-Watching

The Northern Zone is one of Costa Rica's prime bird-watching regions, with a host of varied ecosystems and subregions. The Northern Zone contains low-, mid-, and high-elevation rain forests, as well as several extremely lush and biologically diverse cloud forests. The Continental Divide rises up and more or less bisects this region; bird-watching sites range from near sea level to some 1,650m (5,400 ft.) elevation, on both the Caribbean and Pacific slopes of the Divide.

> The cloud forests of Monteverde and Santa Elena are among the best places to see the resplendent quetzal.

Monteverde

Bird-watchers will definitely want to head to the Monteverde area. The misty cloud forests of the ★★★ **Monteverde Cloud Forest Biological Reserve** (p. 218, ❶) and ★★ **Santa Elena Cloud Forest Reserve** (p. 249) are justly revered by bird-watchers. The resplendent quetzal is the most sought-after sighting, but a range of other fascinating birds might be spotted here, including the three-wattled bellbird, emerald toucanet, black guan, slate-throated redstart, and numerous ovenbirds, tanagers, and hummingbirds. The cloud forests inside these reserves are quite dense and often dark. Bird-watchers should also check out the more open farmlands, pastures, and secondary forests outside of them. The ★ **Ecological Sanctuary** (p. 248) is an excellent local destination with both open clearings and dense forest habitats.

Lake Arenal

There's also great bird-watching all around the Lake Arenal area. Again, ecosystems are varied here, allowing bird-watchers to try their luck in everything from dense rain forest to open pastures and farmland to the shores and reeds of **Lake Arenal**.

Arenal Volcano & La Fortuna

Inside ★★ **Arenal National Park** (p. 230, ❺), the open areas around cooled lava flows on the flanks of Arenal Volcano provide some excellent bird-watching opportunities. Commonly sighted species in this region include violaceous and slaty-tailed trogons, keel-billed motmot, keel-billed and chestnut-mandibled toucans, mealy parrot, and spectacled owl.

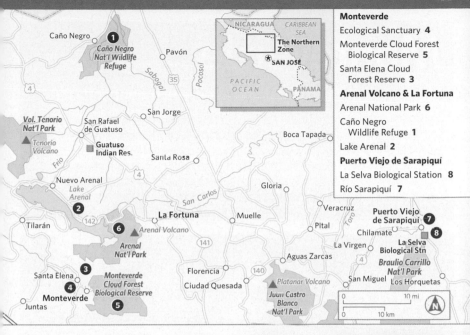

Monteverde

Ecological Sanctuary **4**

Monteverde Cloud Forest Biological Reserve **5**

Santa Elena Cloud Forest Reserve **3**

Arenal Volcano & La Fortuna

Arenal National Park **6**

Caño Negro Wildlife Refuge **1**

Lake Arenal **2**

Puerto Viejo de Sarapiquí

La Selva Biological Station **8**

Río Sarapiquí **7**

Bird-watchers staying in La Fortuna should consider a side trip to nearby ★ **Caño Negro National Wildlife Refuge** (p. 231, ⑫) for the chance to spot a wealth of water birds—both migrant and resident—that take advantage of the reserve's lakes, lagoons, rivers, and other assorted waterways. The jabiru, a species of stork, is this area's star attraction; other prominent and commonly sighted birds include glossy and white ibises, anhinga, wood stork, black-bellied whistling-duck, snail kite, and green heron.

Puerto Viejo de Sarapiquí

More than half of Costa Rica's bird species—that's more than 450 species—have been recorded in the **Puerto Viejo de Sarapiquí** area (p. 264). The lush understory of the lowland wet forests here is home to a broad selection of antbirds, manakins, hummingbirds, and honeycreepers, as well as the great tinamou. Overhead, a wide range of hawks and other raptors can be spotted, especially during the annual spring and fall migrations. Of the various reserves and localities that provide bird-watching opportunities in this area, perhaps the best spot is ★★★ **La Selva Biological Station** (p. 251), which offers daily guided tours. A boat ride on the area's namesake ★★ **Río Sarapiquí** (p. 228, ②) is another bird-watching must.

> The chestnut-mandibled is one of two toucan species found in Arenal National Park.

Traveler's Tip

All of the hotel tour desks and tour agencies throughout the Northern Zone can arrange for guided bird-watching tours or hook you up with a local bird guide. In Monteverde, many of the best local guides seem to work for the **Monteverde Cloud Forest Biological Reserve** (p. 218, ①). In the Puerto Viejo de Sarapiquí area, you will often find excellent bird-watching guides in residence at **La Selva** (p. 251).

Monteverde

Monteverde, which translates as "green mountain," is a remote region of coffee farms and cattle ranches. It is the gateway to and guardian of one of Costa Rica's most popular and important areas of protected high-elevation cloud forests. The popularity, rapid growth, and tourist traffic have led some—myself included—to dub the region "Monteverde Crowd Forest." That said, the extensive network of public and private reserves here is incredibly rich in biodiversity, and the abundance of tour options and attractions guarantees a rewarding experience for both first-time and experienced ecotravelers. Plan to spend at least 2 days here.

> *A suspension bridge in Monteverde Cloud Forest is a great spot for seeing the plant and animal life.*

START Monteverde is 167km (104 miles) northwest of San José.

1 ★★★ **kids** **Monteverde Cloud Forest Biological Reserve.** Get an early start at the Monteverde Cloud Forest Reserve. Be sure to have a reservation for a guided tour. Your entrance ticket is good for the whole day, so feel free to linger after the guided tour and explore some of the trails on your own. With the guided tour under your belt, perhaps you'll be able to spot a resplendent quetzal or a troop of mantled howler monkeys. ⏲ Minimum 3 hr. See p. 218, **1**.

2 ★★ **kids** **Hummingbird Gallery.** This is the best gift shop in the area, featuring a broad selection of locally produced arts and crafts products, as well as more typical tourist items like T-shirts and postcards. Be sure to check out the stunning wildlife photographs of Patricia and Michael Fogden. The shop is also known for the hummingbird feeders hanging outside the entrance. You'll see dozens of these frenetic and brightly colored birds feeding and buzzing about. ⏲ 30–45 min. See p. 219, **2**.

3 ★ **Butterfly Garden.** A visit here begins with an informative tour and an explanation of the stages in the life cycle of butterflies. Hundreds of well-preserved specimens are mounted and on display. One of the more interesting parts of the tour is the pupa or chrysalis collection. If you're lucky, you'll actually get to see a brand-new butterfly emerge from its cocoon. The tour ends with a trip through a large enclosure that

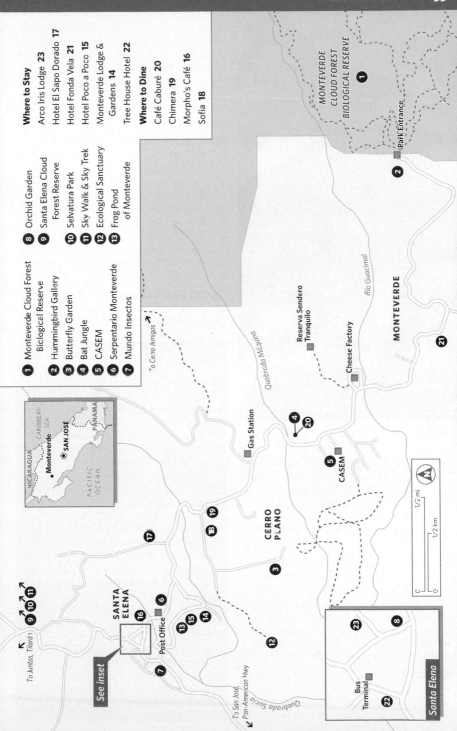

Where to Stay

Arco Iris Lodge 23
Hotel El Sapo Dorado 17
Hotel Fonda Vela 21
Hotel Poco a Poco 15
Monteverde Lodge & Gardens 14
Tree House Hotel 22

Where to Dine

Café Caburé 20
Chimera 19
Morpho's Café 16
Sofia 18

1 Monteverde Cloud Forest Biological Reserve
2 Hummingbird Gallery
3 Butterfly Garden
4 Bat Jungle
5 CASEM
6 Serpentario Monteverde
7 Mundo Insectos
8 Orchid Garden
9 Santa Elena Cloud Forest Reserve
10 Selvatura Park
11 Sky Walk & Sky Trek
12 Ecological Sanctuary
13 Frog Pond of Monteverde

MONTEVERDE CLOUD FOREST BIOLOGICAL RESERVE

Park Entrance

Río Guacimal

MONTEVERDE

Reserva Sendero Tranquilo

Cheese Factory

Quebrada Máquina

To Cerro Amigos

Gas Station

CERRO PLANO

CASEM

NICARAGUA
CARIBBEAN SEA
SAN JOSÉ
Monteverde
PANAMA
PACIFIC OCEAN

SANTA ELENA

Post Office

See inset

To Juntas, Tilarán

To San José, Pan-American Hwy

Quebrada Sucia

½ mi
½ km

N

Santa Elena

Bus Terminal

> *The blue morpho butterfly.*

coffee; and many other items to remind you of your visit to Monteverde. Overall, the quality of the goods isn't as high as that found at the Hummingbird Gallery (**②**), but some of them seem more authentic, or homemade. ⏲ 30 min. On the main road btw. Santa Elena and the reserve. ☎ 2645-5190. Mon–Sat 8am–5pm; Sun 10am–4pm. AE, MC, V.

⑥ ★★ kids Serpentario Monteverde. More than 40 species of snakes, venomous and nonvenomous, are on display in the large, well-lit terrariums here. Some of the more deadly snakes include the coral snake, bushmaster, eyelash viper, and fer-de-lance. There are also boa constrictors, false coral snakes, and a host of others. Rounding out the exhibit are terrariums housing poison-dart frogs, turtles, lizards, and other assorted critters. ⏲ 45 min. See p. 237, **⑧**.

⑦ ★ kids Mundo Insectos. Fans of invertebrates will want to visit World of Insects, which focuses on some of the area's most fascinating

features hundreds of butterflies flying about. The best time to visit is between 9:30am and 1pm, when the butterflies are most active. ⏲ Minimum 1½ hr. On the Cerro Plano road. ☎ 2645-5512. Admission $10 adults, $8 students and children. Rate includes guided tour. Daily 9:30am–4pm.

④ ★★ kids Bat Jungle. This is a good place to tackle your chiroptophobia (fear of bats). Scores of live fruit- and nectar-feeding bats are the stars of the show here. The bats are kept in a darkened enclosure, tricking their biological clocks so that they will be active when you visit. A visit here includes a guided educational, interactive, and fun tour. ⏲ 45 min. See p. 235, **②**.

⑤ CASEM. This local crafts cooperative sells embroidered clothing, T-shirts, posters, and postcards picturing local flora and fauna; Boruca weavings; locally grown and roasted

The Founding of Monteverde

Monteverde was settled in 1951 by Quakers from the United States. Quakers are a religious sect opposed to violence of any kind, and these settlers were seeking to leave behind both the Cold War and their obligation to support militarism in the form of U.S. taxes. They chose Costa Rica, a country that had abolished its army a few years earlier, in 1948.

Although Monteverde's founders came here primarily to farm the land, they wisely recognized the need to preserve the rare cloud forests that covered the mountain slopes above their fields. To that end, they dedicated the largest adjacent tract of cloud forest as the Monteverde Cloud Forest Biological Reserve.

If you want an in-depth look into the lives and history of the local Quaker community, try to pick up a copy of the *Monteverde Jubilee Family Album*. Published in 2001 by the Monteverde Association of Friends, this collection of oral histories and photographs is 260 pages of local lore and memoirs. It's very simply bound and printed but well worth the $20 price.

> The Orchid Garden displays the beauties and mysteries of orchids of all colors and sizes.

creepy-crawlies. More than 30 terrariums display a wide range of invertebrates. You'll see tarantulas, scorpions, and praying mantises, as well as a host of more benign bugs. ⏱ 45 min. See p. 237, ❼.

❽ ★ **Orchid Garden.** This pretty little exhibit is located right in the heart of Santa Elena. It features a collection of nearly 450 orchids. Many of the flowers are so small you'll need a magnifying glass, which is provided, to see them. ⏱ 1½ hr. See p. 219, ❹.

❾ ★★ **Santa Elena Cloud Forest Reserve.** Similar in many respects to its more famous neighbor, and often much less crowded and busy, this 310-hectare (765-acre) reserve features gentle hiking trails, lush forests, and several superb lookout points. The reserve is a community-based project; proceeds go toward local improvements. ⏱ Minimum 3 hr. See p. 249.

❿ ★★ kids **Selvatura Park.** The most comprehensive one-stop adventure and nature attraction in the area, this place has a zip-line canopy tour, trails and suspension bridges through the forest, hummingbird and butterfly gardens, a serpentarium, and an extensive insect exhibit. ⏱ 2½–4 hr. See p. 222, ❼.

⓫ ★★ **Sky Walk & Sky Trek.** These neighboring sister attractions are both geared toward giving tourists a bird's-eye view of the cloud forest canopy. Sky Walk features a network of forest paths and suspension bridges, while Sky Trek is a more typical zip-line canopy tour. A combination tour gives you the best of both worlds. ⏱ 2–4 hr. See p. 245 and p. 249.

⓬ ★ **Ecological Sanctuary.** There's great, gentle hiking here, and excellent wildlife-viewing and bird-watching opportunities. I especially recommend the 5:30pm twilight tour, which peaks at a wonderful lookout point providing views of the Gulf of Nicoya and a sunset display. ⏱ Minimum 2 hr. See p. 248.

⓭ ★★ kids **Frog Pond of Monteverde.** See p. 219, ❺.

Talk the Talk

Monteverde is a beautiful place in which to sign up for a Spanish language program. ★ **Centro Panamericano de Idiomas** (☎ 2645-5441; www.spanishlanguageschool. com) offers immersion language classes in a wonderful setting. A 1-week program costs $465 and includes 4 hours of classes per day and a home stay with a Costa Rican family.

Where to Stay

> Hillside cabins at Hotel El Sapo Dorado—which means "the golden toad."

★ Arco Iris Lodge SANTA ELENA

This is my favorite hotel in the town of Santa Elena, and it's an excellent value to boot. The rooms are spread out in a variety of separate buildings. All have wood or tile floors and plenty of wood accents. I recommend one of the individual cabins, which come with a private balcony. Santa Elena center. ☎ 2645-5067. www.arcoirislodge.com. 19 units. $60–$120 double. AE, MC, V.

Hotel El Sapo Dorado MONTEVERDE

The individual and duplex cabins here are set on a high hill amidst lush gardens and surrounded by thick forests. The best cabins have a fabulous view of the sunset over the Gulf of Nicoya. All are built of hardwoods and have simple, yet attractive appointments. On the road btw. Santa Elena and the Monteverde Cloud Forest Biological Reserve. ☎ 2645-5010. www.sapodorado.com. 30 units. $122 double. Rate includes breakfast. MC, V.

★ Hotel Fonda Vela MONTEVERDE

One of the closest hotels to the Monteverde Cloud Forest Biological Reserve, this is also one of the best. Rooms are housed in a series of separate buildings scattered among the forests and pastures of this former farm, and most have views of the Gulf of Nicoya. Throughout the hotel, you'll see paintings by co-owner Paul Smith, who also handcrafts violins and cellos and is a musician himself. On the road btw. Santa Elena and the Monteverde Cloud Forest Biological Reserve. ☎ 2257-1413 for reservations or 2645-5125 to reach the lodge. www.fondavela.com. 40 units. $110–$130 double. AE, MC, V.

kids Hotel Poco a Poco SANTA ELENA

Close to the town of Santa Elena, this cute little hotel offers well-equipped rooms with a fair share of amenities at a good price. There's a heated pool and a children's pool, and every room comes with a DVD system and access to a huge DVD library. Just outside Santa Elena center. ☎ 2645-6000. www.hotelpocoapoco.com. 30 units. $92 double. MC, V.

★★ Monteverde Lodge & Gardens SANTA ELENA

Rooms are large and cozy at this pioneer ecolodge. The gardens and secondary forest surrounding the lodge have some gentle groomed trails and are home to quite a few species of birds. The guides and overall level of service are excellent. Just outside Santa Elena center. ☎ 2257-0766 for reservations or 2645-5057 to reach the lodge. www.monteverdelodge.com. 28 units. $88–$148 double. AE, MC, V.

Tree House Hotel SANTA ELENA

Taking up the third—and highest—floor of Santa Elena's first—and only—high-rise building, this hotel offers clean and spacious rooms in the center of town. The best rooms come with small balconies overlooking the town, although these are also susceptible to street noise, particularly early in the morning and on weekend nights. Santa Elena center. ☎ 2645-7475. 7 units. $56 double. MC, V.

Where to Dine

★★ **Café Caburé** MONTEVERDE *CHOCOLATES/ ARGENTINE* Specializing in homemade artisanal truffles and other organic chocolate creations, this cozy spot is perfect for breakfast, lunch, dinner, or a sinfully sweet coffee break. The menu includes curries and chicken mole alongside Argentine-style breaded steak and fresh empanadas. The large, simple space is located on the second-floor of the Bat Jungle (p. 235, ❷). Be sure to save room for some chocolates for dessert, or the chocolate-walnut soufflé. On the road btw. Santa Elena and Monteverde Cloud Forest Biological Reserve. ☎ 2645-5020. www.cabure.net. Entrees $6-$14. AE, MC, V. Breakfast, lunch, and dinner Mon–Sat.

★★ **Chimera** MONTEVERDE *FUSION/TAPAS* The tapas menu here features everything from soups and salads to main dishes, sides, and desserts. Culinary influences range from Asia to Latin America to the Old World. Standout

> The cuisine and the setting are sophisticated at Chimera.

dishes include slow-cooked pork with white beans and caramelized onions, and coconut shrimp "lollipops" with mango-ginger dipping sauce. Cerro Plano, on the road btw. Santa Elena and the Monteverde Cloud Forest Biological Reserve. ☎ 2645-6081. Entrees $2.50-$8.50. AE, DC, MC, V. Lunch and dinner daily.

★★ **Morpho's Café** SANTA ELENA *COSTA RICAN/INTERNATIONAL* This simple second-floor affair serves hearty, economical meals. There are soups, sandwiches, and *casados* (plates of the day) for lunch and dinner, and fresh-fruit juices, ice-cream shakes, and home-baked desserts throughout the day. The tables and chairs are made from rough-hewn branches and tree trunks. Morpho's is a very popular hangout for backpackers. In Santa Elena center, across from the supermarket. ☎ 2645-5607. Main courses $4.50-$16. MC, V. Lunch and dinner daily.

★★★**Sofia** SANTA ELENA *COSTA RICAN/FUSION* In a pretty setting, with picture windows looking out onto gardens, this restaurant serves excellent, contemporary takes on Costa Rican and Latin American classics. A mango-ginger mojito will get things going, and the seafood chimichangas are excellent. Cerro Plano, on the road btw. Santa Elena and Monteverde Cloud Forest Biological Reserve. ☎ 2645-7017. Entrees $12-$16. AE, DC, MC, V. Lunch and dinner daily.

Monteverde after Dark

In general, Monteverde is a quiet little mountain town. Most visitors are up very early and heading out for a day of hiking, tours, and adventures. Perhaps the most popular after-dark activities in Monteverde are night hikes. However, if you want a taste of the local party scene, head to ★ **La Taberna** (☎ 2645-5157), which is just outside of Santa Elena center, before the Serpentario Monteverde. This place attracts a mix of locals and tourists, cranks its music loud, and often gets people dancing.

Alternatively, ★ **Bromelias** (☎ 2645-6272; www.bromelias-cafe.com), located up a steep driveway from Stella's Bakery, sometimes features live music, theater, or open-mike jam sessions. These folks also run the neighboring **Monteverde Amphitheater** (☎ 2645-6272), a beautiful open-air performance space, up a steep driveway across from CASEM (p. 256, ❺). **Hotel El Sapo Dorado** (p. 258) has been hosting live dance bands from San José most Monday evenings.

La Fortuna

Lying at the eastern base of the Arenal Volcano is the tiny farming community of La Fortuna. This town has become a magnet for volcano watchers, adventure tourists, and other assorted travelers from around the world. In addition to volcano viewing, the area around La Fortuna is a prime spot for hiking and bird-watching and for indulging in adventures as varied as canyoning, white-water rafting, windsurfing, and kiteboarding. After all that activity, the volcanically heated hot springs here sure come in handy. Plan to spend 2 days here.

> *Arenal Volcano looms over La Fortuna's church.*

START La Fortuna is 140km (87 miles) north of San José.

1 ★★ **kids Arenal National Park.** ☺ Minimum 2 hr. See p. 230, **5**.

2 ★★★ **Sky Tram.** Take the gondola-style tram up the mountain, and the adrenaline-pumping zip-line tour back down. See p. 245.

3 ★★★ **Tabacón Hot Springs.** See p. 224, **10**.

4 ★★ **Canyoning tour.** A canyoning tour with either Pure Trek Canyoning or Desafío Adventure Company will take you through a narrow canyon set in the lush rain forest on the slope of Arenal Volcano. ☺ 3–4 hr. See p. 245.

5 ★ **Catarata Río Fortuna.** This beautiful jungle waterfall plunges some 70m (230 ft.) into a perfectly round pool. The hike down to the pool takes around 15 to 20 minutes; the hike back up will take slightly longer. You can swim, but stay away from the turbulent water at the base of the falls—several people have drowned here. Instead, check out and enjoy the calm pool just around the bend, or join the locals at the popular swimming hole under the bridge on the paved road, just after the turnoff for the road up to the falls. ☺ 2 hr. round-trip. 5.5km (3½ miles) south of La Fortuna on CR142 (toward La Tigre/San Ramón). ☎ 2479-8360. Admission $6. Daily 8am–4pm.

6 **Downtown La Fortuna.** La Fortuna retains some of its rural agricultural feel; start off in the central park area, which features a few gar-

Kaboom!

In July 1968, the Arenal Volcano, which had lain dormant for centuries, surprised everybody by erupting with sudden violence. The nearby village of Tabacón was destroyed, and some 80 or more of its inhabitants were killed. Since that eruption, Arenal has been Costa Rica's most active volcano. Frequent powerful explosions send cascades of red-hot lava rocks down the volcano's steep slopes. During the day these lava flows smoke and rumble. However, at night the volcano puts on its most mesmerizing show. If you are lucky enough to be here on a clear and active night—not necessarily a guaranteed occurrence—you'll see the night sky turned red by lava spewing from Arenal's crater.

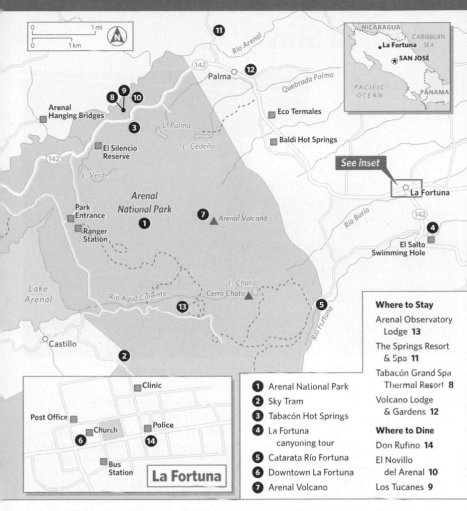

Where to Stay

Arenal Observatory Lodge **13**

The Springs Resort & Spa **11**

Tabacón Grand Spa Thermal Resort **8**

Volcano Lodge & Gardens **12**

Where to Dine

Don Rufino **14**

El Novillo del Arenal **10**

Los Tucanes **9**

1. Arenal National Park
2. Sky Tram
3. Tabacón Hot Springs
4. La Fortuna canyoning tour
5. Catarata Río Fortuna
6. Downtown La Fortuna
7. Arenal Volcano

dens. On the western side you'll find the town's Catholic church, which makes a good backdrop for photos, with the outline of the volcano in the background.

Most of the souvenir shops in La Fortuna are pretty basic, but it's worth the long walk or short drive to the ★★ **Original Grand Gallery** (no phone), west of town on the main road to Tabacón. This unique family-run shop specializes in carved local hardwoods. The owners produce works in a variety of styles and sizes. They specialize in faces, many of them larger than a typical home's front door. You can also find animal figures ranging in style from purely representational to rather avant-garde and abstract. ⏱ Minimum 2 hr.

7 ★★★ 🧒 **Night viewing of Arenal Volcano.** Night time is the right time for volcano viewing, as the molten lava that often flows or shoots from the cone glows in the dark. See "Volcano Viewing," p. 238, and "Kaboom!," p. 260.

Quick Getaway

Throughout the La Fortuna and Arenal Volcano region, most hotels, restaurants, shops, and attractions request that you park your vehicle facing out, so that you can make a quick getaway in the event of any major volcanic activity. Don't let that spook you. It's a wise, but as yet unnecessary, precaution.

Where to Stay

> *Arenal Observatory Lodge has spectacular views of the active cone, day and night.*

★★ **Arenal Observatory Lodge** ARENAL VOLCANO This place is built on a high ridge very close to the volcano and has a spectacular view of the cone. Rooms vary widely, from former bunks for volcano researchers to luxurious suites and villas. The lodge borders Arenal National Park, so there's great hiking all around. On the flank of Arenal Volcano, beyond the entrance to Arenal National Park. ☎ 2290-7011 for reservations or 2479-1070 to reach the lodge. www.arenalobservatorylodge.com. 42 units. $77–$155 double. Rates include breakfast buffet. AE, MC, V.

★★ **The Springs Resort & Spa** WEST OF LA FORTUNA Set on a high hillside with great volcano views, this new resort is opulent and luxurious. Rooms and bathrooms are large and beautifully appointed. The hotel has extensive pools, hot springs, and facilities. Off the road btw. La Fortuna and the volcano, about 8km (5 miles) northwest of La Fortuna. ☎ 954/727-8333 in U.S., or 2461-1700 in Costa Rica. www.thespringscostarica.com. 20 units. $375–$440 double. AE, DC, MC, V.

★★★ **Tabacón Grand Spa Thermal Resort** WEST OF LA FORTUNA The top resort in the Arenal area, this place has it all: plush rooms, a perfect location for volcano views, a luxurious spa, and the best hot springs (p. 224, **10**) in the country. Some of the rooms do not have views of the volcano, so be sure to specify that you want one when you make your reservation. On the road btw. La Fortuna and the volcano, 12km (7½ miles) northwest of La Fortuna. ☎ 877/277-8291 in U.S. and Canada, or 2519-1900 in Costa Rica for reservations; ☎ 2460-2020 to reach the resort. www.tabacon.com. 114 units. $230–$450 double. AE, DC, MC, V.

kids **Volcano Lodge & Gardens** WEST OF LA FORTUNA This place is large and sprawling. Still, rooms are cozy and tastefully decorated. The hotel has extensive facilities, including a couple of pools and a children's playground. On the road btw. La Fortuna and the volcano, about 5km (3 miles) west of La Fortuna. ☎ 866/208-9819 in U.S. and Canada, or 2460-6080 in Costa Rica. www.volcanolodge.com. 70 units. $125 double. AE, MC, V.

Where to Dine

> *Streetside tables at Don Rufino are the perfect place to watch the world (or at least La Fortuna) go by.*

★ **Don Rufino** LA FORTUNA *COSTA RICAN*
Set on a corner in the heart of town, this restaurant is the busiest option in downtown La Fortuna. The front wall and bar area open to the street and are often filled with a mix of local tour guides and tourists. Try the *pollo al estilo de la abuela* (Grandma's chicken), which is baked and served wrapped in banana leaves, or one of the excellent meat entrees. Downtown La Fortuna. ☎ 2479-9997. Entrees $6–$34. AE, DC, MC, V. Lunch and dinner daily.

★★ kids **El Novillo del Arenal** WEST OF LA FORTUNA *COSTA RICAN/STEAKHOUSE* Don't be put off by the simple lawn furniture set on the concrete slab under the high zinc roof. This place serves up excellent steaks and local fare. When it's clear, you get a view of the volcano to boot. On the road btw. La Fortuna and the volcano, 12km (7½ miles) northwest of La Fortuna. ☎ 2479-1910. Entrees $5–$14. MC, V. Lunch and dinner daily.

★★ **Los Tucanes** WEST OF LA FORTUNA *COSTA RICAN* The most formal restaurant at the Tabacón Grand Spa Thermal Resort, this open-air restaurant is also the most elegant and creative option in the area. The menu is long and varied, with everything from an Indonesian soft-shell crab tempura to a rib-eye steak served with Yorkshire pudding. At the Tabacón Grand Spa Thermal Resort. ☎ 2460-2020. Entrees $10–$35. AE, DC, MC, V. Breakfast, lunch, and dinner daily.

La Fortuna after Dark

La Fortuna's biggest after-dark attraction is the volcano, but the **Volcano Look Disco** (☎ 2479-9616), on the road to Tabacón, does its best to provide some competition. If you get bored of the eruptions and seismic rumbling, head here for heavy dance beats and mirrored disco balls. In downtown La Fortuna, the folks at **Luigi's Hotel** (☎ 2479-9636) have a midsize **casino** next door to their hotel and restaurant. Personally, I enjoy the open-to-the-street bar at **Don Rufino** (above) as a spot for a drink and some conversation.

Puerto Viejo de Sarapiquí

This tiny agricultural town, named for the Río Sarapiquí and its surrounding area, is a study in contradictions. It is home to some of Costa Rica's greatest, and best-protected, reserves and parks. You'll find some of the largest tracts of rain forest left in Central America here. But nearly every acre of land outside of these parks has been clear-cut and converted into massive banana, palm, and pineapple plantations. Bird-watching and rain-forest hikes are the area's primary attractions, but more adventure-oriented travelers will find plenty of other activities, including canopy tours and boating and rafting trips along the Sarapiquí. Plan to spend a day or two here.

> La Selva Biological Station has an extensive trail system through flora- and fauna-rich forest.

START Puerto Viejo de Sarapiquí is 82km (51 miles) north of San José.

❶ ★ Parque Archeologico Alma Ata. This modest archaeological site 17km (11 miles) west of Puerto Viejo de Sarapiquí features a series of excavated pre-Columbian gravesites, a few petroglyphs, and a small interpretive museum. During your visit here, tour the Chester Field Biological Gardens. ⏱ 1½ hr. See p. 230, **❸**.

❷ Colin Street Bakery's pineapple tour. I recommend taking this tour to get a sense of

the history and methods of pineapple production. These folks have more than 1,200 hectares (3,000 acres) of cultivated conventional, organic, and ornamental fields. The tour includes a trip through the plantation, explanations and demonstrations, and a pineapple sampling. ⏱ 2 hr. Finca Corsicana plantation, btw. Puerto Viejo de Sarapiquí and La Virgen, near La Quinta de Sarapiquí Country Inn. ☎ 8820-6489. Admission $24; discounts available for students and children. Tours Mon–Fri 8am, 10am, and 2pm; Sat and Sun by prior reservation.

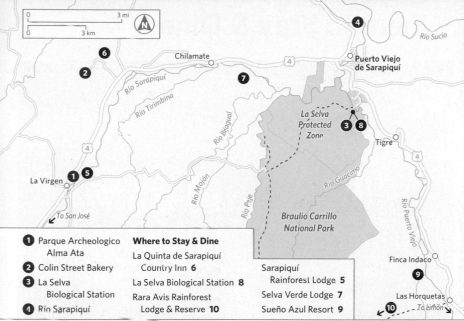

1 Parque Archeologico Alma Ata

2 Colin Street Bakery

3 La Selva Biological Station

4 Río Sarapiquí

Where to Stay & Dine

La Quinta de Sarapiquí Country Inn **6**

La Selva Biological Station **8**

Rara Avis Rainforest Lodge & Reserve **10**

Sarapiquí Rainforest Lodge **5**

Selva Verde Lodge **7**

Sueño Azul Resort **9**

Traveler's Tip

If you want to spend more time in the Puerto Viejo de Sarapiquí area, sign on for organized adventure or sightseeing tours. Options include hiking, white-water rafting, mountain biking, horseback riding, and a zip-line canopy tour. For more information on these types of activities see "Northern Zone Adventures on Land" (p. 242), "Northern Zone Adventures in & on the Water" (p. 240), and "The Northern Zone's Best Hikes" (p. 248).

> *A crested guan, one of La Selva's residents.*

3 ★★★ **La Selva Biological Station.** Don't leave the region without hiking the trails (p. 251) at this internationally renowned reserve and research station. The trails are well maintained and easy for all ages, and the on-site guides (you must take a guided hike unless you're a guest here) are extremely knowledgeable. ⏱ 4 hr. 3km (1¾ miles) south of Puerto Viejo de Sarapiquí on CR4. For staying at La Selva, see p. 266.

4 ★★ **Río Sarapiquí.** Get a different view of the local wildlife and forests on a boat ride along the Sarapiquí River. The ride is gentle

and dry—most of the boats have roofs and glass side enclosures to keep the rain out. In addition to numerous bird species, you may see a river otter or a crocodile or two. All of the hotel tour desks in the area can set this up for you. Or you can simply go down to the docks in the center of town and hire one of the boat captains. ⏱ 2–3 hr. See p. 228, **2**.

Where to Stay & Dine

> *Covered walkways at Selva Verde Lodge let you stay dry when the surrounding rain forest lives up to its name.*

La Quinta de Sarapiquí Country Inn

CHILAMATE Set on the banks of the Río Sardinal, this family-run operation makes a good base for exploring the region. The grounds are lush and flowering, and the various buildings are connected by covered walkways. Chilamate, 11km (6¾ miles) west of Puerto Viejo de Sarapiquí. ☎ 2761-1300. www.laquintasarapiqui.com. 31 units. $80–$125 per person, double occupancy. Rates include 3 meals. AE, MC, V.

La Selva Biological Station PUERTO VIEJO DE SARAPIQUÍ This is primarily a research institu-

All-in-One Service

All the hotels listed in this area are remote, self-contained ecolodges—I've named the small towns they're closest to. Virtually all visitors spend their time taking in-house tours and eat all of their meals at their lodge. There are no restaurants in the tiny town of Puerto Viejo de Sarapiquí that are worth seeking out.

tion catering to students and scientists, although it does offer rooms. Most of these have bunk beds and shared bathrooms. Although there's no price difference, try to nab one of the rooms with a queen bed and private bath. Either way, the rooms are pretty Spartan, and the whole place has the feel of a scientific research center.

Rates are pretty high for what you get, but take solace in the fact that you're helping to support valuable and valiant research and conservation efforts. 3km (1¾ miles) south of Puerto Viejo de Sarapiquí. ☎ 2524-0607 for reservations or 2766-6565 to reach the lodge. www.threepaths.co.cr. 24 units. $84 per person. Rate includes 3 meals, ½-day tour, and taxes. MC, V. For more on La Selva, see p. 251.

★★ Rara Avis Rainforest Lodge & Reserve

LAS HORQUETAS Rara Avis is one of the most responsible, biologically rich, and isolated ecolodge operations in Costa Rica. Of the several options here, choose the Waterfall Lodge, with rustic but comfortable rooms, near the main lodge and namesake waterfall. For those

> *A cozy common area in La Quinta de Sarapiquí Country Inn.*

who want closer communion with nature, there are a two-room cabin set deep in the forest beside a river, about a 10-minute hike from the main lodge; and three more rustic two-bedroom cabins with a shared bathroom, located in a small clearing about a 5-minute walk from the lodge. More than 362 species of birds have been sighted here, and the lodge consistently has excellent guides and naturalists. 15km (9⅓ miles) from Las Horquetas. ☎ 2764-1111 for reservations or 2710-8032 to reach the lodge. www.rara-avis.com. 16 units. $100–$170 per person, double occupancy. Rates include transportation from Las Horquetas, guided hikes, all meals, and taxes. AE, MC, V.

★★ **Sarapiquí Rainforest Lodge** LA VIRGEN
Located on a high bluff fronting the Sarapiquí River, this complex is the most unique project in the Sarapiquí region. Rooms are housed in three large, round buildings, or *palenques,* based on the traditional pre-Columbian constructions of the area. Each *palenque* has a towering thatch roof. All rooms are of good size, although a little dark. The Parque Archeologico Alma Ata is on the grounds here, and just across the river lies the 300-hectare (741-acre) Tirimbina Rainforest Center, with a small network of trails and several impressive suspension bridges, both over the river and through the forest canopy. La Virgen de Sarapiquí. ☎ 2761-1004. www.sarapiquis.org. 36 units. $104 per person, double occupancy. Rate includes 3 meals. V.

★★ **Selva Verde Lodge** CHILAMATE
One of Costa Rica's pioneer ecotourist lodges, this place offers simple yet cozy rooms in a thick forest setting on the banks of the Río Sarapiquí. The main lodge hotel comprises a series of buildings connected by covered walkways that keep you dry, even though this area receives more than 380cm (150 in.) of rain each year. The hotel has a network of trails, botanical gardens, a butterfly garden, and its own zip-line canopy tour. There are also a pretty, free-form pool and separate children's pool, as well as a natural swimming hole right on the river. Chilamate, 5km (3 miles) west of Puerto Viejo de Sarapiquí. ☎ 800/451-7111 in U.S. and Canada, or 2766-6800 in Costa Rica. www.selvaverde.com. 45 units. $187–$216 per person, double occupancy. Rates include 3 meals and taxes. AE, DC, MC, V.

★★★ kids **Sueño Azul Resort** LAS HORQUETAS
This lodge and wellness retreat offers some of the best accommodations in the area. Set at the juncture of two rivers and backed by forested mountains, its location is pretty sweet, as well. All rooms are spacious, with high ceilings, a large bathroom, and a private porch overlooking one of the rivers or a small lake. A wide range of spa treatments, tours, and activities is offered, including rain-forest hikes, horseback riding, mountain biking, and fly-fishing. Las Horquetas de Sarapiquí. ☎ 2253-2020 for reservations or 2764-1048 to reach the lodge. www.suenoazul resort.com. 65 units. $125–$180 per person, double occupancy. Rates include 3 meals. MC, V.

Northern Zone Fast Facts

> *Mobile ATMs are not uncommon in Costa Rica.*

Accommodations Booking Services
In just about all instances, you are best off booking direct with the hotels and resorts listed in this guide.

ATMs
You'll find banks with a cash machine (*cajero automatico*) in Monteverde, La Fortuna, and at many of the major tourist attractions.

Dentists & Doctors
The only major hospital in the Northern Zone, and the closest option for people staying in La

Fortuna and the Arenal Volcano area, is Ciudad Quesada Hospital (☎ 2460-1176), in Ciudad Quesada, 43km (27 miles) southwest of La Fortuna. There is also the small local Clinica La Fortuna (☎ 2479-9142).

From Monteverde, the closest major hospital is in Liberia (☎ 2666-0011). For minor conditions, try the local Clinica Santa Elena (☎ 2645-5076).

If you have a mild medical issue or dental problem while traveling in the Northern Zone, most hotels will be able to refer you to a local doctor (*medico*) or dentist (*dentista*) who speaks English.

Emergencies
In case of emergency, call ☎ 911 (there should be an English-speaking operator); if 911 doesn't work, contact the police at ☎ 2222-1365 or 2221-5337, and ask them to find someone who speaks English to translate. For an ambulance, call ☎ 128; to report a fire, call ☎ 118.

For a medical emergency that doesn't require an ambulance, see "Dentists & Doctors," above. To report lost or stolen items, see "Police," p. 269.

Getting There & Getting Around
BY PLANE Whether you fly into San José's **Juan Santamaría International Airport** or Liberia's **Daniel Oduber International Airport,** you'll have several options for onward travel into the Northern Zone. **Nature Air** (☎ 800/235-9272 in U.S. and Canada, or 2299-6000 in Costa Rica; www.natureair.com) and **Sansa** (☎ 877/767-2672 in U.S. and Canada, or 2290-4100 in Costa Rica; www.flysansa.com) both have daily commuter air service to La Fortuna, as well as connecting service to most major destinations in the country. Fares run between $70 and $130, one way. BY BUS OR SHUTTLE Though a rental car gives you more freedom and flexibility, the main towns and destinations here can also be toured by local buses and private shuttles. In fact, one of the best ways to travel between Monteverde and the Arenal Volcano is via an organized service; see "Going by Boat & Taxi," p. 225.

If you don't want to drive yourself, it's easy to get around the Northern Zone by bus, private shuttle, and taxi. **Gray Line** (☎ 2220-2126;

www.graylinecostarica.com) and **Interbus**
(☎ 2283-5573; www.interbusonline.com) are
two private shuttle companies with daily scheduled departures to all the major tourist destinations in the Northern Zone and around the
country. Local buses are extremely economical,
but you are at the mercy of their schedules and
time-consuming stops along the way.

BY CAR Driving yourself or taking a bus or private
shuttle is the best way to reach the towns and
destinations in the Northern Zone. A car comes
in handy when traveling around the region—just
be sure it's a four-wheel-drive vehicle. You're
probably best off renting a car upon arrival in the
country, either in San José or Liberia. See p. 478
for car rental information in these cities.

If you do need to rent a car once in the
Northern Zone (or if you're taking the jeep-
boat-jeep transfer, p. 225), **Alamo** (☎ 2479-
9090; www.alamocostarica.com) and **Poás**
(☎ 2479-8027; www.carentals.com) both have
offices in La Fortuna.

Roads vary widely, from rough dirt and gravel
tracks to recently paved two-lane thoroughfares. In general, most roads in Costa Rica are
very poorly marked. In many cases, your best
signage and directions will come from hotel and
attraction advertisements and billboards. If
you're traveling around the Northern Zone, it's a
good idea to know the names of a few hotels in
your target destination.

Internet Access
More and more hotels, resorts, and retailers
around Costa Rica are offering high-speed Wi-Fi
access, either free or for a small fee. Moreover,
you'll readily find Internet cafes in all major
towns and tourist destinations around the
Northern Zone. Rates run between 50¢ and $3
per hour, and connection speeds are generally
pretty good.

Pharmacies
You'll find pharmacies (*farmacias*) in downtown
Santa Elena and La Fortuna.

Police
To report a lost or stolen article, such as a wallet
or passport, visit the local police. Depending
upon your location, that may be either the OIJ

(judicial police), *guardia rural* (rural guard), or
policía metropolitana (metro police). The number
for the *policía de tránsito* (transit police) is
☎ 800/8726-7486, toll-free nationwide, or
☎ 2222-9330. See also "Emergencies," p. 268.

Post Offices
You'll find post offices in downtown Santa Elena
and La Fortuna.

Safety
Most of the towns and tourist destinations of
the Northern Zone are relatively safe. That said,
never leave items of value unattended in rental
cars, hotel rooms (unless locked in a safe), or on
the trailside. Moreover, single women, couples,
and small groups of tourists should probably
avoid walking in desolate parts of towns, cities,
or back roads after dark.

Toilets
These are known as *sanitarios* or *servicios sanitarios*. You might also hear them called *baños*.
They are marked *damas* (women) and *hombres*
or *caballeros* (men). Public restrooms are rare to
nonexistent, but most hotels, restaurants, and
tour attractions catering to tourists will let you
use their restrooms.

Visitor Information
There are no official information offices or bureaus in the Northern Zone. Your best source of
information—beyond this guide book—will be
your hotel front desk and any of the local tour
agencies.

Water
This is a very remote area, and most hotels advise you drink bottled water. Most restaurants
that cater to tourists use bottled or treated water.
Nonetheless, some travelers experience stomach discomfort during their first few days in
Costa Rica. If you want to be cautious, drink
only bottled water or *frescos* made with milk
instead of water. *Sin hielo* means "no ice," and
this is what you'll want to say if you're nervous
about the water—even when frozen it's still
water.

8
The Central Pacific Coast

My Favorite Central Pacific Coast Moments

The central Pacific coast, which stretches some 175km (110 miles) from the mouth of the Río Tárcoles to Dominical and the southern beach towns, is home to spectacular national parks, quiet beaches, and an outrageous variety of birds and wildlife. Whether you base yourself in the surfer and snowbird hangouts of Jacó and Playa Herradura, the ecotourist mecca of Manuel Antonio, or the isolated jungle environs of Dominical, you won't be disappointed.

> **PREVIOUS PAGE** *On the Mount Chirippó trail.*
THIS PAGE *Crocodile, Río Tárcoles.*

① **Seeing scarlet macaws in Carara National Park.** The national park itself is fabulous, but the real draw is the endangered scarlet macaw. Carara is a primary nesting ground for these vibrant and surprisingly raucous birds. Arrive in the morning or late afternoon, and you're almost guaranteed to see at least a few in flight. See p. 280, **⑤**.

② **Watching the sunset at Villa Caletas.** The Greek-style amphitheater of this luxury hotel near Jacó is built into a steep hillside and ide- ally oriented for prime sunset-viewing. Stop in for a sundowner and watch one of the region's loveliest natural displays: the sun sinking slowly into the Pacific. Most evenings at twilight the background music is a well-timed "Also Sprach Zarathustra." See p. 276, **④**.

③ **Rafting on the Río Savegre.** Although not nearly as popular, or quite as rough, as the Río Pacuare (see p. 73), the Río Savegre beats its more famous sister in terms of beauty. It snakes through a valley so thickly forested that you'll feel like you're a million miles from civilization. But it's not all about the stellar scenery—excellent class II and III rapids provide plenty of white water. See p. 301.

④ **Hiking the Punta Catedral loop.** The short rain-forest trail to Cathedral Point inside Manuel Antonio National Park offers up good wildlife-viewing opportunities (keep watch for three-toed sloths and endangered squirrel monkeys) in addition to panoramic views. See p. 292, **②**.

⑤ **Touring the Damas Island estuary by boat.** The mangroves and canals of the Damas Island estuary are fabulous spots for bird and wildlife viewing, especially in the late afternoon, when thousands of herons and ibises come to roost. The odds are also good that you'll be treated to a close encounter with a white-faced monkey or two. See p. 276, **⑥**.

1 Carara National Park
2 Villa Caletas
3 Río Savegre
4 Punta Catedral
5 Damas Island estuary
6 Río Tárcoles bridge
7 Dominical
8 Mount Chirripó
9 Cataratas Nauyaca

6 Counting crocs from the Río Tárcoles bridge. Just below the bridge over the Río Tárcoles lives a sizable collection of American crocodiles. At any time, you are likely to see 20 or more crocs down there. The thrill of seeing these fearsome reptiles is sometimes matched by the thrill (and danger) of standing on the bridge's narrow walkway, as cars and trucks speed by just inches away. See "Nice Crocs!," p. 313.

7 Going to surf camp in Dominical. Dominical is the quintessential surfer town, and it's the ideal place for you to join the club. Miles of beach break at Dominical and its surrounding beaches provide the waves, while the **Green Iguana Surf Camp** provides the room, grub, gear, and instruction. See p. 299.

8 Climbing Mount Chirripó. At 3,819m (12,530 ft.) elevation, Mount Chirripó is the tallest mountain in Costa Rica. The trails are challenging, but the views are well worth the effort made. And the experience of spending the night at the summit lodge is one you won't soon forget. See p. 294.

9 Visiting Cataratas Nauyaca. These jungle waterfalls are stunning, but the full-day tour required to see them is the real reason they make my list of favorite moments. Getting there necessitates a mix of hiking and horseback riding, but once you've arrived you'll be treated to a picnic lunch and a cooling dip in the large pool at the foot of the falls. See p. 283, **18**.

The Best of the Central Pacific Coast in 3 Days

It goes without saying that you won't get to see everything in just 3 days, and some may choose to simply spend their time at a beach resort. After all, this region is most famous for its sand and sea. But for the more adventurous, the central Pacific coast offers plenty of distractions. Just be forewarned that temperatures here can soar, and you're going to want to get an early start, even if you're just lounging on the beach. This tour will bring you both beach time and wildlife viewing—the highlights of this region. You will spend your first night in Jacó and the next 2 nights around Manuel Antonio. You'll need a car for your first day in the area, but after that you'll be taking guided tours.

> *Villa Caletas has a column-lined amphitheater for taking in its spectacular sunsets.*

START **Jacó.** To reach Jacó take CR27 west from San José to CR34 south; the drive is 117km (73 miles) and will take about 2 hours. TOUR LENGTH 153km (95 miles).

1 Jacó. Spend the morning exploring this bustling little town. You'll likely want to spend some time on the beach here, too. ⏱ 1 hr. to explore the town. See p. 310.

Take the Costanera Hwy. (CR34) 19km (12 miles) north and turn off at the sign for Hotel Villa Lapas; the entrance to the garden is 5.5km (3½ miles) farther.

More Information

For stops **1**–**4** of this tour we recommend a base in Jacó (p. 310); and for stops **5**–**8**, the Manuel Antonio area (p. 318).

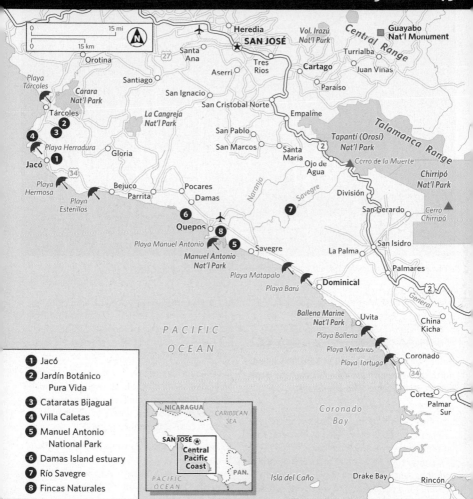

1 Jacó

2 Jardín Botánico
Pura Vida

3 Cataratas Bijagual

4 Villa Caletas

5 Manuel Antonio
National Park

6 Damas Island estuary

7 Río Savegre

8 Fincas Naturales

2 ★ **Jardín Botánico Pura Vida.** With paved trails and informative signage, this is an excellent botanical garden to explore on your own. The flora collection here is a mix of native and imported species, and the bird-watching is excellent, with toucan sightings common. The gardens are set on a high hilltop, with expansive ocean and coastal views, and there is a lookout over the Cataratas Bijagual (Bijagual Waterfalls; **3**). The restaurant here takes full advantage of the views. ⏱ 1–3 hr. 5.5km (3½ miles) uphill from the entrance to Hotel Villa Lapas. ☎ 2645-1001. puravidagarden.com. Admission $20. Daily 8am–5pm.

The Complejo Ecológico la Catarata is a quick drive downhill from Pura Vida.

3 ★★ **Horseback ride to Cataratas Bijagual.** The impressive Bijagual Waterfalls, fed by the Río Tarcolitos, is actually a series of some five stepped waterfalls, the tallest of which is 180m (590 ft.). The horseback tour is run by the Complejo Ecológico la Catarata, an "ecological

Crocodile Alert!

On your way to the central Pacific coast, be sure to stop at the bridge over the Río Tárcoles to see the crocodiles. See "Nice Crocs!," (p. 313) for more information.

> *Manuel Antonio National Park has both spectacular beaches and beautiful forest trails.*

complex" with an on-site campground and a very basic restaurant. You'll be led through beautiful virgin forests with wonderful views along the way. ⏱ Minimum 2 hr. See p. 312, **❷**.

Return to Jacó and take CR34 9km (5½ miles) north to the turnoff for Villa Caletas; the hotel entrance is another 2km (1¼miles).

❹ ★★ Sunset at Villa Caletas. Perched on a high hillside overlooking the Pacific Ocean, Villa Caletas is a perfect place to enjoy sunsets. The hotel's Greek-style amphitheater is set facing the nightly solar *sayonara*. Guests of the hotel and nonguests alike come around dusk each evening for a cocktail and to watch the sun sink into the sea. Unfortunately, the word has gotten

out, and during the high season quite a few fellow travelers come to share the pleasure. When it's crowded, getting a good seat can be difficult and service can be a little slow. See p. 315 for details on Villa Caletas.

On the morning of Day 2, get an early start and drive south on CR34 to Quepos (67km/42 miles). Check into your hotel in the Quepos–Manuel Antonio area, where you'll be picked up for a tour of the national park.

❺ ★★★ kids Manuel Antonio National Park. Since your time in this area is limited, a guided tour of the park is the best way to go. Book in advance through your hotel. ⏱ Minimum 3 hr. See p. 290.

You'll be dropped off at your hotel in time to be picked up for an afternoon tour. Again, be sure to book this in advance.

❻ ★★ kids Iguana Tours boat tour of Damas Island estuary. The mangrove forests and canals of the Damas Island estuary are friendly habitats for loads of birds and beasts. Watch for white-faced monkeys, boa constrictors coiled in mangrove branches, and crocodiles lounging on sandbanks. These boat trips generally include a stop on Damas Island for a short walk, as well as food and cold drinks. Of the many operators who run this sort of trip, several habitually feed the white-faced monkeys along the way. While that may be exciting for tourists,

What's in a Name?

You may find all the references to Manuel Antonio, its namesake national park, and its gateway city of Quepos a bit confusing. Don't worry—you're not alone. Here's the deal: The small port city of Quepos is the closest town to Manuel Antonio National Park. The road that runs the 6km (3¾ miles) from Quepos to the park entrance is lined with access points to hotels, shops, and restaurants. This area is called Manuel Antonio, though there isn't a town in the traditional sense.

> *Jacó's lively downtown.*

it is devastating for the monkeys, who suffer health problems as a result. That's why I highly recommend Iguana Tours, which respects the park and its denizens. ☉ Minimum 3 hr. Iguana Tours. ☎ 2777-1262. www.iguanatours.com. Rate $60; children 4 and under free. Daily; departures determined by the tides.

Begin Day 3 with a ride down the Río Savegre. You'll be picked up from your hotel in Manuel Antonio.

7 ★★★ **Río Savegre rafting trip.** The forest scenery is stunning along this river, which has predominantly class II and III rapids. The full-day trip includes both breakfast and lunch. ☉ 6 hr. See p. 301.

Once you've been returned to your hotel, you'll be picked up once more, this time for a night tour at Fincas Naturales, on the road to Quepos across from the Hotel Sí Como Nó.

8 ★★ kids **Night tour at Fincas Naturales.** Wrap up your time on the central Pacific coast with a look at the local nightlife. Be here in time for the 5:30pm tour of the Nature Farm Reserve—most rain-forest dwellers are nocturnal, and this expedition will put you into close contact with them and their habitat. You'll hear the pings, croaks, and varied calls of frogs, and you'll see a wide range of wildlife that might include anything from a golden orbweaver spider to a vine snake to a kinkajou. ☉ 2 hr. See p. 320, **2**.

Oil in Costa Rica?

As you travel around this region, particularly between Jacó and Quepos, you'll notice row after row of palm trees, stretching for miles on end. These are plantations, and the main crop is African oil palms, which were introduced to the area by the American-owned United Fruit Company in the 1940s and 1950s. The palms were an attempt to diversify after blight nearly wiped out the company's banana crop. These trees produce large clumps of oil-rich bright red and orange fruit. Once the oil is extracted—you'll see, and likely smell, processing plants scattered amid the rows—it has a variety of uses, from cooking to soap production.

These plantations are a major source of employment in the area—note the small, orderly "company towns" built for workers—but their presence is controversial. The palm trees aren't native, and the farming practices are thought by some to threaten Costa Rica's biodiversity.

The Best of the Central Pacific Coast in 1 Week

A full week will give you enough time to visit all of the central Pacific coast's main tourist towns and three of its principal national parks. In the process, you'll get in some beach time, do plenty of hiking and wildlife viewing, and maybe catch a few waves on a surfboard or body board. As an added bonus, you'll get to enjoy some fine wining and dining along the way. You'll need a rental car to get around.

> The gentle curve of Manuel Antonio's Playa Espadilla Sur ends at forested Cathedral Point.

START Jacó. To reach Jacó take CR27 west from San José to CR34 south; the drive is 117km (73 miles) and will take about 2 hours. **TOUR LENGTH** 166km (103 miles).

1 Jacó. Spend your first morning on the beach in Jacó. Unless you're really committed to lazing in the sun without a break, take a surf lesson at the **Jacó Surf School** (p. 298). Afterward, if you're not too exhausted, enjoy a stroll along the busy main strip of Jacó and do some shopping at ★ **La Galería Heliconia** (p. 313, **6**). ⊕ Minimum 3 hr. for shopping and the surfing lesson.

2 ☕ ★ **Caliche's Wishbone.** Since you'll be walking the main strip in Jacó, stop in for lunch at this relaxed spot. Grab a seat on the sidewalk patio, where you can watch the parade of passersby while enjoying a salad topped with some fresh seared tuna. On the main road in Jacó, near the center of town. ☎ 2643-3406. $$–$$$. See p. 316.

1. Jacó
2. Caliche's Wishbone
3. Chiclets Tree Tour
4. Villa Caletas
5. Carara National Park
6. Jardín Botánico Pura Vida
7. Cataratas Bijagual
8. Manuel Antonio National Park
9. Damas Island estuary
10. Agua Azul
11. Río Savegre
12. Sunset sail off Manuel Antonio National Park
13. El Patio Bistro Latino
14. Santa Juana Mountain Tour
15. Fincas Naturales
16. Ballena Marine National Park
17. Parque Reptilandia
18. Cataratas Nauyaca
19. Exotica

In early afternoon, head back to your hotel in time to be picked up for the 1pm Chiclets tour.

3 ★★ **Chiclets Tree Tour.** This zip-line canopy tour features 13 treetop platforms, one long suspension bridge that dangles above the treetops, and wonderful views of the Pacific Ocean. You'll want to take the 1pm tour to ensure that you have enough time to make it to

More Information

For stops **1**–**7** in this tour we recommend a base in Jacó (p. 310); for **8**–**15** in Manuel Antonio (p. 318); and for **16**–**19** in or around Dominical (p. 326).

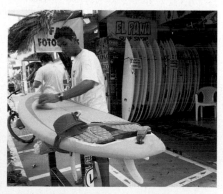

> Jacó is all about the surf.

> *Set on a bluff above Jacó, Villa Caletas is the place to go for the sunset.*

Villa Caletas for the sunset show. ⊕ 2 hr. Playa Hermosa (Jacó). ☎ 2643-1880. Rate $60 per person; includes round-trip transport from your hotel. Daily 7am, 9am, 1pm, and 3:30pm.

You'll be dropped off at your hotel after your afternoon at Chiclets—don't linger too long, as you'll want to get to Villa Caletas in time for sunset. It is 9km (5½ miles) north of Jacó on CR34, and another 2km (1¼ miles) to the hotel from the turnoff.

❹ ★★ **Sunset at Villa Caletas.** Come early to get a good seat and watch the day fade away into the glowing sunset. See p. 276, ❹.

Be sure to get a very early start on Day 2; take the Costanera Hwy. (CR34) 22km (14 miles) north from Jacó.

SITE GUIDE PAGE 282

❺ ★★★ **Carara National Park.** Carara National Park is a world-renowned nesting ground for the endangered scarlet macaw. The macaws migrate daily, spend-ing their days in the park and their nights among the coastal mangroves. The best time to see the birds is either early in the morning, when they arrive, or around sunset, when they head back to the coast for the evening. If that doesn't work with your schedule, local guides can usually find them for you during the day. Whether or not you see them, you are certain to hear their loud squawks.

The park's lush transitional forests are load-ed with wildlife—while you're here, you may run into caimans, coatimundis, armadillos, pacas, peccaries, river otters, and kinkajous. And, in addition to the macaws, the park is home to more than 400 species of birds.

You can hike the trails of Carara National Park independently, but my advice is to take a guided tour; you'll learn a lot more about your surroundings. Several companies offer tours to the park for around $30 to $60. Check at your hotel, or contact **Gray Line Tours** (☎ 2643-3231; www.graylinecostarica.com) or **Jagua Riders** (☎ 2643-0180; www.jaguariders.com). If you're the adventurous sort, or you'd like to explore in addition to the abovementioned guided tours, use this site guide as a reference. 22km (14 miles) north of Jacó on CR34. ☎ 2637-1054. Admission $10. Daily 7am–4pm.

Take CR34 south 4.3km (2⅔ miles) from Car-ara National Park to the turnoff for the Hotel Villa Lapas and Pura Vida Botanical Gardens.

❻ ★ **Jardín Botánico Pura Vida.** After visiting the national park, take a tour of these well-planned and extensive botanical gardens. The gentle trails lead through thousands of species of tropical plants, including a lovely assortment of orchids. This is also a great spot for lunch. ⊕ 2 hr. See p. 275, ❷.

Backtrack down the road from Pura Vida Bo-tanical Gardens to the entrance to Complejo Ecológico la Catarata.

❼ ★★ **Horseback ride to Cataratas Bijagual.** After lunch, rent horses at the family-run Complejo Ecológico la Catarata for a ride to these falls. ⊕ 2–3 hr. See p. 312, ❷.

On the morning of Day 3, take CR34 south to Quepos. The drive of 67km (42 miles) will take an hour. Manuel Antonio National Park is at the end of a winding road, 6km (3¾ miles) from downtown Quepos.

8 ★★★ kids **Manuel Antonio National Park.** ⏱ Minimum 3 hr. See p. 290.

Check into your hotel in time to be picked up for the following tour (booked in advance).

9 ★★ **Damas Island estuary.** ⏱ 3 hr. See p. 276, **6**.

Retrace your steps to Manuel Antonio in time for the sunset.

10 🍽 ★ **Agua Azul.** The setting at Agua Azul is not as theatrical or opulent as that at Villa Caletas (**4**), but the sunset views are no less stunning. Stick around for dinner, as the food's quite good, too. Manuel Antonio, near Villas del Parque. ☎ 2777-5082. $$$–$$$$. See p. 324.

Day 4 features a white-water rafting trip on the Río Savegre—you'll be picked up at your hotel.

11 ★★★ **Río Savegre rafting trip.** This is one of the country's most beautiful white-water rafting spots. ⏱ 6 hr. See p. 301.

You'll be dropped off at your hotel after your rafting adventure and picked up in time for an evening on the water.

12 kids **Sunset sail off Manuel Antonio National Park.** Board a boat for a sunset cruise in the waters fronting Manuel Antonio National Park. My favorite operator is **Planet Dolphin** (☎ 2777-1647; www.planetdolphin.com), which includes a snorkeling stop as well as the chance to see dolphins en route. Plan to spend $75 per person. ⏱ 3½ hr.

13 🍽 ★★★ **El Patio Bistro Latino.** This cozy little place in downtown Quepos is a must for anyone serious about Latin dining—actually, it's a must for anyone who enjoys great food. The menu features Latin American cuisine made with local ingredients and a contemporary flare. On the main road into Quepos, on the left just past the bridge. ☎ 2777-4982. $$$–$$$$. See p. 324.

> *Fincas Naturales nature reserve has both daytime and nighttime forest tours.*

> *A rafting trip on the Río Savegre is not to be missed.*

Begin Day 5 with a visit to the farming village of Santa Juana; you'll be picked up and dropped off at your hotel.

14 ★★ kids **Santa Juana Mountain Tour.** Based in a tiny rural community in the hills outside Quepos and Manuel Antonio, this extensive 1-day tour will give you a feel for typical Tico culture. As an added bonus, the operation is carbon-neutral, generating a zero carbon footprint. ⏱ 7½ hr. See p. 285, **3**.

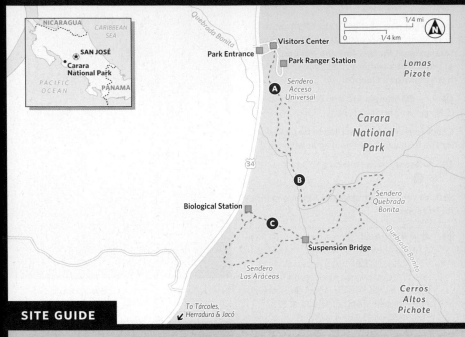

5 Carara National Park

The **A** ★ **Sendero Acceso Universal** (Universal Access Trail), which heads out from the park office, is broad, flat, and wheelchair-accessible. The first half of this 1km (.6-mile) stretch leads into the forest and features various informative plaques, in both English and Spanish, pointing out prominent flora. About 10 or 15 minutes into your hike, you'll see that the trail splits, forming a loop (you can go in either direction). The entire trail should take 30 to 45 minutes.

Next, make your way to **B** ★★ **Sendero Quebrada Bonita** (Beautiful Creek Trail). Leading off from the far end of the Universal Access Trail, this is the main hike within the park. As you venture along, you'll begin a 45-minute climb into the nearby foothills; the climb is pretty mild, and there are several benches for resting weary feet, as well as a few pretty lookout points. At a relaxed pace, you should be able to hike this 2.2km (1.4-mile) trail in about an hour. If you are here in the morning or evening, watch for scarlet macaws (right).

Heading off the far end of the Beautiful Creek Trail loop is the **C** ★ **Sendero Las Araceas** (Araceas Trail). Named after the Araceae fam-

ily of plants, which includes the philodendron, this relatively flat, 1.3km (.8-mile) trail runs through thick primary forest with plenty of tall, old-growth trees. It shouldn't take more than 40 minutes or so to walk the entire trail. ⏱ 1–4 hr.

You'll be picked up at your hotel for the tour to Fincas Naturales, on the road to Quepos across from the Hotel Sí Como No.

15 ★★ kids **Night tour at Fincas Naturales.** This reserve is run by the same people behind the Santa Juana Mountain Tour, so be sure to book both at the same time. ⏱ 2 hr. See p. 320, **2**.

On Day 6, take the Costanera Hwy. (CR34) 42km (26 miles) south from Manuel Antonio to Dominical. The marine park is another 16km (10 miles) south.

16 ★★★ **Ballena Marine National Park.** This national park was created to protect a coral reef and offshore waters that stretch from Playa Uvita south to Playa Piñuela. In addition to several beautiful beaches, the park also includes the little Isla Ballena, just offshore. The beach near the park entrance, Playa Uvita, is well protected and excellent for swimming. At low tide an exposed sandbar allows you to walk about and explore another tiny island. The park is named for the humpback whales (*ballena* is Spanish for "whale") that come here each year to calve and rear their young before heading back to colder feeding grounds; these massive mammals are sometimes sighted close to shore. If you ever fly over the area, you'll notice that this little island and the spit of land that's formed at low tide compose the perfect outline of a whale's tail—a wonderful and whimsical coincidence. There's also a small turtle-hatching shelter and program located near the ranger station. ⏱ Minimum 2 hr. 16km (10 miles) south of Dominical. ☎ 2743-8236. www.marino ballena.org. Admission $10. Daily 8am–4pm.

In the afternoon, head 7km (4⅓ miles) north-east on CR243, following signs to San Isidro de El General. The entrance to Parque Reptilandia is on your left.

17 ★★ kids **Parque Reptilandia.** You may encounter a snake or a poison-dart frog while simply hiking along a trail in Costa Rica, but for a guaranteed glimpse, you'll want to visit this reptile park, which I consider to be the best of its type in Costa Rica. ⏱ 2 hr. See p. 287, **9**.

Spend your final day on a tour to the Cataratas Nauyaca. You'll be picked up and dropped off at your hotel.

18 ★★★ **Cataratas Nauyaca.** Located just outside of Dominical, this two-tiered beauty,

> *Ballena National Park protects both the beach area and the underwater features offshore.*

also known as Santo Cristo Falls, features a rain-forest setting and an excellent swimming hole. These waterfalls are best visited as part of the full-day tour offered by local resident Don Lulo and his family, who own the surrounding land.

The tour takes you to and from the falls via horseback and a short hike. The horseback riding is through deep rain forest, and the horses are gentle, well cared for, and well trained. You'll stop at Don Lulo's house en route and back for a hearty local breakfast and lunch, and his humble abode features a small collection of local fauna, a sort of minizoo. But the highlights of the trip are the impressive sight and sound of the waterfalls and the time you get to play in and around them. Come prepared to get wet. Adventurous souls can use a fixed rope line to scramble up through the falls to a spot where they can jump off into the pool below. ⏱ 1 day. 5km (3 miles) northeast of Dominical. ☎ 2787-8013. www.cataratasnauyaca. com. Rate $50 per person; includes round-trip transportation from Dominical. Mon–Sat 8am–2pm.

19 🍽 ★★ **Exotica.** For your last meal on the central Pacific coast, drive south of Dominical to this intimate little open-air place. Despite the rustic furniture and setting, the food and service are quite refined. 1km (⅔ mile) inland from the turnoff for Ojochal, 31km (19 miles) south of Dominical. ☎ 2786-5050. $$$–$$$$. See p. 329.

The Central Pacific Coast with Kids

If your kids have an interest in animals, Costa Rica's central
Pacific coast is a great destination—the jungles teem with wildlife. And even if
your kids aren't so interested in critters, you're in luck: The surf is gentle, and
there are plenty of easy, age-appropriate hikes and horseback rides. Rent a villa or
condo near Manuel Antonio to use as a base (see "Renting a Home, Not a Room,"
p. 289). Most such places have a swimming pool, which will come in handy for
the inevitable periods of down, or recovery, time. You'll need a car to get around.

> *White-faced capuchins like to monkey around in Manuel Antonio National Park.*

START Manuel Antonio National Park. From
San José take the Costanera Hwy. (CR34)
140km (87 miles) southwest to Quepos. The
park is at the end of a 6km (3¾-mile) winding
road going south from Quepos. **TOUR LENGTH**
5 days; 300km (186 miles).

1 ★★★ **Manuel Antonio National Park.** This is
an outstanding spot to introduce kids to the joys
of biodiversity. Even those who seem to prefer
staying permanently glued to their iPods will
be wowed by what they see here, from brightly
colored birds to always-charming coatimundis.

If the seas are calm, bring snorkeling gear and
check out the rocky outcroppings at either end
of Playa Manuel Antonio. I suggest taking a
guided tour, which will include transport to and
from the park. ☺ Minimum 3 hr. See p. 290.

**You can either be picked up at your lodgings or
dropped off by your previous tour provider for
the following.**

2 ★★ **Iguana Tours boat tour of Damas Island
estuary.** In addition to seeing hundreds of birds,
odds are good that you'll have a close encounter

1 Manuel Antonio National Park

2 Damas Island estuary

3 Santa Juana Mountain Tour

4 Fincas Naturales

5 Rain Forest Aerial Tram Pacific

6 Rioasis

7 Jungle Crocodile Safari

8 Hacienda Barú

9 Parque Reptilandia

10 Playa Espadilla

11 El Avión

12 Planet Dolphin

with white-faced monkeys on this slow-paced boat tour. If monkeys aren't enough to get your kids excited (and who doesn't love monkeys?), have no fear. You're also likely to see a crocodile or two lurking amid the mangroves. If not, don't worry—you'll get your fill of crocodiles soon enough. ⏲ Minimum 3 hr. See p. 276, **6**.

For Day 2, arrange for the following tour to include pickup and drop-off from your lodgings.

3 ★★ **Santa Juana Mountain Tour.** I promise, this multifaceted tour of a working farm is as much fun as it is educational. You will learn about both coffee and citrus growing, and how sugarcane is milled. You'll also get a glimpse of

what life was once like on a traditional Costa Rican farm. Definitely try your hand at the tilapia fishing pond.

If your kids are adventurous enough (and, I suggest, at least 8 years old), sign up for the horseback-riding option, which allows about 2 hours of riding time through a mix of farmland and rain forest. Whether you choose the hiking or horseback-riding tour, bring a bathing suit for a dip in a cool rain-forest pool, fed by the Río Rodeo. ⏲ 7½ hr. Santa Juana. ☎ 2777-0850. Rates $65–$95 adults, $50 children 11 and under.

You'll be dropped off at your lodgings in time to make it to the night tour at Fincas Naturales, which is about halfway along the road

between Quepos and Manuel Antonio National Park, across from Hotel Sí Como No.

➍ ★★ Night tour at Fincas Naturales. Kids will get a thrill from spotting the creepy, crawly critters (think spiders, snakes, and frogs) that are among the many things you'll see on this night tour of the private Nature Farm Reserve. If you're lucky, you may even encounter an owl, kinkajou, or wildcat. ⏱ 2 hr. See p. 320, ➋.

On the morning of Day 3, take CR34 north; the entrance to the Aerial Tram is just north of Jacó.

➎ ★ Rain Forest Aerial Tram Pacific. The gondola-lift ride here is an easy, safe way to get little ones up into the rain-forest canopy. Everyone will enjoy taking in the views and hiking the gentle trails, and kids 12 and older can try the zip-line canopy tour. There is a specialized tour for families with children 11 and under. We're just stopping by for a few hours, but a full-day here ($78 per adult; $82 per child) includes a specialized guided tour, a ride on the tram, visits to the snake exhibit and botanical gardens, as well as interactive arts and crafts projects using natural dyes obtained from the gardens; other options are also offered. ⏱ 2–3 hr. See p. 310, ➊.

Drive into Jacó for lunch.

➏ 🍴 Rioasis. This loud and lively place is perfect for families. The pizzas, pastas, and Mexican fare go over well with even the pickiest eaters. But perhaps more important, parents can linger over their meals while the kids play at one of the pool or foosball tables. On the main road in Jacó, near the center of town. ☎ 2643-3354. $$–$$$. See p. 317.

Take CR34 north 19km (12 miles) to the turn-off for Jungle Crocodile Safari, across from the entrance to Hotel Villa Lapas; it's another 2km (1¼ miles) to their office.

➐ ★★ Jungle Crocodile Safari. Although I'm sure you've already stopped to see the crocodiles from the bridge above the Río Tárcoles, your kids will almost certainly enjoy getting up close and personal with these reptiles on a boat tour. The proximity a trip like this affords is thrilling. But full disclosure: Almost all of the boats use food to lure the crocs in close, and that has all sorts of negative environmental implications. That's why I'm specifically recommending Jungle Crocodile Safari—they're respectful of the wildlife. For more information, see "Nice Crocs!" (p. 313). ⏱ 2 hr.

On Day 4, head south on the road from Quepos to Dominical. You'll see the well-marked entrance to Hacienda Barú on your right at about 40km (25 miles).

> The green iguana is one of the charming residents of Parque Reptilandia.

8 ★★ **Hacienda Barú.** You'll find several miles of self-guided trails as well as a bird-watching tree platform, orchid garden, and butterfly garden at this private reserve. You can also sign up for any number of guided tours, ranging from mangrove and rain-forest hikes to tree-climbing and zip-line canopy adventures. In other words, there is a little something for everyone, regardless of age. For families, I recommend the tree-climbing adventure or a visit to the canopy observation platform. You and your kids will have to be in good shape to tackle the tree climbing, as it involves a 35m (115-ft.) ascent on climbing ropes (don't worry—it involves a harness and ascenders). However, anyone can visit the platform, which is located 34m (112 ft.) up a massive rain-forest tree: You strap on a climbing harness and are winched up to the top. ⏱ 2–3 hr. 1.5km (1 mile) north of Dominical on the road to Quepos. ☎ 2787-0003. www.haciendabaru.com. Rates $20–$60.

Take CR34 1.5km (1 mile) south; at the intersection before the bridge over Río Barú, turn left onto CR243. You'll see the entrance to this next stop on your left in 7km (4⅓ miles).

9 ★★ **Parque Reptilandia.** Kids love lizards, snakes, and crocodiles, and this reptile park has them in spades. In my opinion, this is the best reptile attraction in Costa Rica. The collection includes a wide range of snakes, frogs, turtles, and lizards, as well as crocodiles and caimans, in more than 55 well-designed and spacious terrariums and other enclosed areas. Some of my favorite residents here are the brilliant eyelash pit viper and the sleek golden vine snake. Both native and imported species are on display, including the only Komodo dragon in Central America. For those looking to spice up their visit, Fridays are feeding days. ⏱ 2 hr. 7km (4⅓ miles) northeast of Dominical on CR243. ☎ 2787-8007. www.crreptiles.com. Admission $10 adults, $5 children 13 and under. Daily 9am–4:30pm.

For your final day, hit the beach at the end of the road from Quepos to Manuel Antonio National Park.

10 ★ **Playa Espadilla.** You've earned a relaxing beach day. Rent a few plastic chaise longues and a large umbrella and set up camp. When the tide is on its way out, there is plenty of

> *Gondolas take visitors up into the rain forest at Rain Forest Aerial Tram Pacific.*

damp sand, making this a prime location for building sand castles. The gentle beach break here is also a great learning wave for aspiring surfers. **Manuel Antonio Surf School** (p. 298) specializes in small group lessons perfect for the whole family. ⏱ Minimum 2 hr. for surf lesson.

> *Kids will enjoy a Planet Dolphin sailing trip, especially if they get to see some leaping dolphins.*

> *Playa Espadilla is a great spot for a surfing lesson.*

Take the road back toward Quepos for a lunch stop.

⑪ 🍽 ★ **El Avión.** The view here is stunning, and while you wait for your lunch, you can let the kids check out the fuselage and wings of the cargo plane that forms part of the structure. (Shot down over Nicaragua during the Contra War, the plane was brought to Manuel Antonio on flatbed trucks). The menu ranges far and wide, offering seafood and fusion fare. **Manuel Antonio,** about midway along the road btw. Quepos and the national park. ☎ 2777-3378. $$$$. See p. 324.

Cap off your day with a sunset cruise off the national park, which will include round-trip transportation.

⑫ **Planet Dolphin sunset sail.** There's no need to worry that kids will get bored with simply gazing at the horizon. The trip—which I think is the best of its kind in the area—includes a snorkeling stop, and there is always the possibility that you will get to see a pod of dolphins frolicking in the sea or riding the boat's wake. **Quepos.** ⏱ 3½ hr. See p. 281, ⑫.

Renting a Home, Not a Room

The jungle-clad hills overlooking Manuel Antonio and Dominical are dotted with private villas and condo units available for rent. Quite of few of these are truly spectacular, with stunning views, private swimming pools, large recreation areas, and daily maid service. A vacation rental allows you to settle in, unpack, and get a feel for the area. Villas can also be economical. You can drastically reduce your expenses by cooking in—even if it's just breakfasts and lunches. Most villas and condo units come with a washing machine, DVD player, and satellite TV; many also have a Wi-Fi connection. Villas and condos are available in a range of sizes; some are big enough for 2 to 3 families or a large group of friends. A rental car comes in really handy when you rent a villa, but you can certainly get by with taxis and booked tours.

Rates run between $350 and $500 nightly for one- and two-bedroom units, and to $1,000 and up for some of the larger and more luxurious units.

In Manuel Antonio, ★★ **Escape Villas** (☎ 800/408-4990 in U.S. and Canada, or 2588-1590 in Costa Rica; www.villascostarica. com) is the go-to place, offering a broad selection of luxurious private villas with all the amenities and some of the best views in town. For a villa or condo rental in Dominical, check in with **Paradise Costa Rica** (☎ 800/708-4552 in U.S. and Canada, or 2787-8250 in Costa Rica; www. paradisecostarica.com) or with the folks at **Cabinas San Clemente** (p. 329) or the **Roca Verde** (p. 331). In the Jacó and Playa Herradura area, **Costa Rica Luxury Rentals** (☎ 866/525-2188 in U.S. and Canada, or 2637-7105 in Costa Rica; www.crluxury.com), specializing in the various condominium developments attached to Los Sueños Marriott Ocean & Golf Resort complex, is the place to go.

Manuel Antonio National Park

With just under 2,000 hectares (4,950 acres) of terra firma, Manuel Antonio is Costa Rica's smallest national park (55,000 hectares/136,000 acres of offshore marine area and some small islands are also part of the park). Most visitors come primarily for the picturesque beaches and to check out the white-faced capuchin monkeys, which sometimes seem as numerous as the tourists. But intrepid naturalists will be well rewarded here—the park is home to more than 350 bird and 100 mammal species. This is one of Costa Rica's few remaining habitats for the endangered Central American squirrel monkey, or *mono tití*. In fact, all four of Costa Rica's monkey species can be found here.

> *Playa Espadilla Sur is on one side of the tree-topped peninsula called Punta Catedral (Cathedral Point), Playa Manuel Antonio is on the other.*

START **The park is 6km (3¾ miles) south of Quepos.**

Entering the park. The principal park entrance is at **Playa Espadilla** (p. 287, ⑩), the beach at the end of the road from Quepos. To reach the ranger station there, you must cross a small stream. The stream is little more than ankle-deep at low tide, but it can be knee- or even waist-deep at high tide; it's even reputed to be home to a crocodile or two. For years there has been talk of building a bridge over this stream; in the meantime, you'll have to either wade it or pay a boatman a small tip for the quick crossing. Just across the stream and over a small rise, you'll find a small ranger station.

And there's a catch. Another entrance is located inland, at the end of the side road that runs perpendicular to Playa Espadilla, just beyond Marlin Restaurant. MINAE, the national ministry that oversees the park, has been inconsistent, to the point of frustration, about which entrance it wants visitors to use. As this book goes to press, admission tickets are being sold only at the inland entrance. In other words, you'll have to go to the inland entrance to buy your ticket, and then head back to the principal entrance at Playa Espadilla to begin your explorations. If all of this seems daunting (welcome to Costa Rica!), consider coming to the park as part of an organized tour. ☎ 2777-5155. Admission $10. Tues–Sun 7am–4pm.

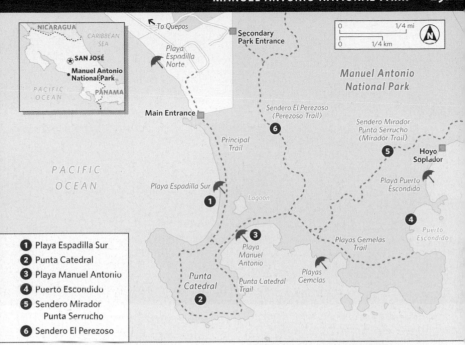

NICARAGUA
CARIBBEAN SEA
SAN JOSÉ
Manuel Antonio National Park
PACIFIC OCEAN
PANAMA

To Quepos

Secondary Park Entrance

Playa Espadilla Norte

Manuel Antonio National Park

Main Entrance

Sendero El Perezoso (Perezoso Trail)

Sendero Mirador Punta Serrucho (Mirador Trail)

Hoyo Soplador

Principal Trail

PACIFIC OCEAN

Playa Espadilla Sur

Lagoon

Playa Puerto Escondido

Playa Manuel Antonio

Playas Gemelas Trail

Puerto Escondido

Punta Catedral

Punta Catedral Trail

Playas Gemelas

1 Playa Espadilla Sur
2 Punta Catedral
3 Playa Manuel Antonio
4 Puerto Escondido
5 Sendero Mirador Punta Serrucho
6 Sendero El Perezoso

---

1 ★ Playa Espadilla Sur. This beach, not to be confused with Playa Espadilla, is the first beach you will reach within park boundaries coming from the principal entrance. It's also usually the least crowded beach in the park and one of the best places to find a quiet shade tree under which to spread your towel or beach mat. Just know that if you have swimming in mind, this may not be the place to do it: This beach has the roughest surf in the park.

I suggest you walk the length of Playa Espadilla Sur toward Punta Catedral. There is a flat, well-groomed trail that runs parallel to the beach just a few feet inland, with various access paths to the beach along its entire length. At the end of this .8km (.5-mile) stretch—about

Park Tips

The parks service allows only 600 visitors at a time to enter Manuel Antonio National Park on weekdays and a maximum of 800 visitors at a time on Saturdays and Sundays. If you arrive at midday or later during the high season, you might not be allowed in. The park is closed on Mondays. For information on where to stay in the area, see p. 321.

> With its prehensile tail, the spider monkey essentially has five limbs.

> *Playa Manuel Antonio has an offshore pit that served as a turtle trap in pre-Columbian times.*

a 15-minute walk—you'll come to a junction, with one trail leading to Punta Catedral and the other to Playa Manuel Antonio. This junction is a common place to spot white-faced capuchins.

2 ★★ **Punta Catedral.** Standing prominently at the southern end of Playa Espadilla Sur,

To Guide or Not to Guide

A guide is not essential here, although you'll see and learn a lot more with a guide than you would on your own. In addition to pointing out the more obvious wildlife sightings, a naturalist guide will be able to identify a vast amount of the local flora and fauna and explain the intricate symbiotic workings of the park's tropical lowland rain forest. Almost any of the hotels in town can help you set up a tour of the park. A 2- or 3-hour guided hike led by a naturalist should cost between $25 and $45 per person. Bird-watchers will want to book a tour with **Ave Natura** (☎ 2777-0973; www.avenatura. com), a local tour agency that specializes in bird-watching. Their 2½-hour tour includes the park entrance fee and a snack and costs $44 per person (40% discount for children 6 to 12; children 5 and under free).

Cathedral Point is an impressive-looking rain forest–covered hill. Once an island, it is now connected to the mainland by a narrow strip of land, a geological feature known as a "tombolo." The simple, 1.4km (.9-mile) loop trail leading up and around the point is the most popular hike inside the park and has wonderful ocean views from its highest point. Punta Catedral is comprised of a mix of primary and secondary rain forest; it's a good place to spot monkeys, although you're more likely to see a white-faced capuchin than a rare Central American squirrel monkey. The trail is slightly steep in places, but anybody in average shape can do it. I've done it in sturdy sandals, but you may want to wear sneakers or hiking shoes, especially if it has been raining. The entire loop should take you about 30 minutes.

3 ★★ **Playa Manuel Antonio.** A short, deep crescent of golden sand backed by lush rain forest, this is the park's most popular beach. The water here is usually fairly calm and sometimes clear enough to afford good snorkeling along the rocks at either end. Low tide at this beach reveals a very interesting relic: a circular stone turtle trap, known locally as **La Trampa** (The Trap), that was once used by the area's pre-Columbian residents. You'll find picnic tables spread out under the shade trees that back this beach all along its entire length. Get here early if you want to snag one, and you'd better keep an eye on your food and belongings, as the white-faced monkeys, iguanas, and coatimundis have gotten quite comfortable with the presence of humans and can be brazen thieves.

4 ★★ **Puerto Escondido.** From the eastern end of Playa Manuel Antonio, a mostly flat 1.4km (.9-mile) trail leads through the rain forest to Puerto Escondido (Hidden Cove). You'll find excellent wildlife viewing all along this trail. Between mid and low tide, you can hike to **El Hoyo Soplador** (The Blow Hole), a natural rock formation that funnels incoming swells into a geyserlike spout. *Warning:* Be careful when hiking beyond Puerto Escondido, as what seems like an easy beach hike when the tide is out becomes treacherous, if not impassable, as the tide comes back in. Trust me, I found this out the hard way. I very highly recommend asking about the tides at the guard station before attempting this. If you get stuck, wait for the tide to go back out—and make sure you bring lots of water, just in case.

5 ★★ **Sendero Mirador Punta Serrucho.** This trail, which begins just inland from the eastern end of Playa Manuel Antonio, leads to a beautiful high lookout point, or *mirador*. The trail gives you a good chance to experience a primary rain forest and is an excellent place to spot spider, howler, and sometimes Central American squirrel monkeys. Since it is largely uphill, it's also a good bit of exercise as a preamble to some relaxing beach time on Playa Manuel Antonio or Playa Espadilla Sur. About midway along the 1km (.6-mile) trail, you'll see a sign for a quick detour to the diminutive Playa Gemelas (Twins Beach). This small pocket cove is a perfect place to linger, especially if you are the only visitors.

6 **Sendero El Perezoso.** Sendero El Perezoso ("Sloth Trail" or "Lazy Trail") is in fact a rugged 1.4km (.9-mile) dirt road, used by park service utility vehicles, that leads through the forest from the inland park ranger station to Playa Manuel Antonio. During the rainy season this trail can get quite muddy. However, because it is wider than a traditional walking trail, there's often good bird and wildlife viewing.

> Hikers on Manuel Antonio's trails might spot four kinds of monkeys, kinkajous, toucans and their relatives the aracaris, roseate spoonbills, and purple-crowned fairy hummingbirds.

Chirripó National Park

At 3,819m (12,530 ft.), Mount Chirripó is the tallest mountain in Costa Rica. On a clear day, you can see both the Pacific Ocean and the Caribbean Sea from the summit. Although it's possible to hike from the park entrance to the summit and back down in 2 days (in fact, some daredevils even do it in 1 day), it's best to allow 3 to 4 days, in order to give yourself time to enjoy your hike fully and spend some time on top.

> Mount Chirripó is part of the Talamanca Range, which extends southward from San José.

START San Gerardo de Rivas, about 50km (30 miles) northeast of Dominical. Take the Pan-American Hwy. (CR2) southeast from San José 120km (75 miles) or drive northeast from Dominical 29km (18 miles) to the turnoff for San Gerardo at San Isidro de El General.

Entering the park. By far the best and most popular route to the top of Mount Chirripó begins in the tiny village of San Gerardo de Rivas. Here you'll find the national park office, as well as a small collection of rustic little hotels. You will need to get a very early start, so I strongly suggest you arrive the day before you want to begin your hike. See "Spending the Night in San Gerardo de Rivas," p. 296.

Note: It's possible to have guides carry your gear to the summit. The guides hang out at the park entrance in San Gerardo de Rivas. During the dry season (December to April) they travel to the summit on horseback; in the rainy season they take packs up on foot. The guides like to leave well before dawn, so arrangements are best made the day before. They charge between $20 and $30 per pack, depending on size and weight; you'll need to carry enough food and gear to spend at least 1 night on the summit, so the cost can be well worth it. **National park office in San Gerardo de Rivas. ☎ 2742-5083; fax 2742-5085. Admission $15 per day. Office hours 6:30am–4:30pm daily.**

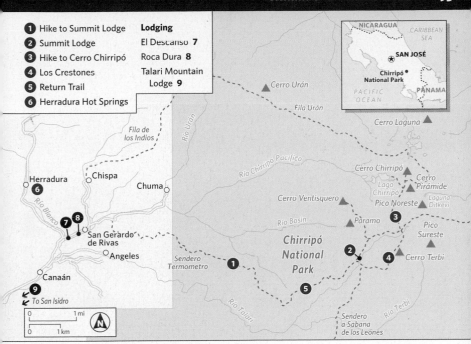

1 Hike to Summit Lodge
2 Summit Lodge
3 Hike to Cerro Chirripó
4 Los Crestones
5 Return Trail
6 Herradura Hot Springs

Lodging
El Descanso **7**
Roca Dura **8**
Talari Mountain Lodge **9**

The trailhead to the top of Mount Chirripó leaves from the outskirts of the village, about 2km (1¼ miles) beyond the national park office.

1 ★★★ **Hike to the summit lodge.** The 14.5km (9-mile) trail to the summit lodge is well marked and well maintained. The early parts of the trail are pretty steep and will take you through thick rain and cloud forests. After about 7.5km (4.7 miles), you will reach the "Water Ridge," a flat ridge that features a small shelter and water spigot. This is roughly the midway point to the lodge and a great place to take a break.

From Water Ridge, three steep uphill sections remain: Cuesta de Agua (Water Hill), Monte Sin Fe (Mountain without Hope), and La Cuesta de los Arrepentidos (The Hill of Regret). As you continue to climb, you will notice the flora changing. The entire elevation gain for this hike is 2,200m (7,220 ft.). Above 3,000m (9,840 ft.) you'll enter an ecosystem known as "paramo," a barren grassland with stunted trees and shrubs. La Cuesta de los Arrepentidos, your final ascent, brings you to a broad flat valley, where you'll find the summit lodge. This hike can take anywhere from 6 to 10 hours, depending on how long you linger along the way.

2 **Summit lodge.** The lodge, perched at an elevation of 3,393m (11,132 ft.), holds only 60 people and often fills up quickly. You must reserve well in advance, particularly during the dry season (see "Be Prepared," below). Inside, you'll find rooms with bunk beds, several bathrooms and showers, and a common kitchen area. The lodge provides good drinking water, but be forewarned—blankets, lanterns, and cook stoves are no longer for rent here. You must bring all your own food and gear, in addition to water for

Be Prepared

Before climbing Mount Chirripó, you *must* make a reservation and check in with the national park office in San Gerardo de Rivas. The office is open from 6:30am to 4:30pm daily (☎ 2742-5083; fax 2742-5085). If you plan to stay at the summit lodge, you must also make reservations in advance. Many of the local tour agencies prebook the lodge beds, which can make it difficult to impossible to do so on your own. If you can't book a bed by yourself, contact **Costa Rica Trekking Adventures** (☎ 2771-4582; www.chirripo.com) for help.

> *While hiking among the peaks in Chirripó National Park, be sure to stop and take in the spectacular glacier-carved landscape and its many lakes.*

the hike up (you can refill at the lodge). ***Note:*** Nights up here can be freezing, and the lodge seems to have been designed to be as cold, dark, and cavernous as possible. No consideration was made to take advantage of the ample passive-solar potential. The showers are freezing. Rate $10 per person per night.

Begin the hike to the summit from the summit lodge.

Spending the Night in San Gerardo de Rivas

If you want to stay close to the park so you can get an early start, there are several basic *cabinas* right in town. Prices run between $5 and $15 per person; the two best are **El Descanso** (☎ 2742-5061) and **Roca Dura** (☎ 8363-7318; luisrocadura@hotmail.com). For a bit more comfort (if not luxury), you might consider the nearby **Talari Mountain Lodge** (☎/fax 2771-0341; www.talari.co.cr), which charges $62 for a double, including breakfast.

❸ ★★ **Hike to Cerro Chirripó.** After spending a night at the summit lodge, it's time to actually summit the mountain. Follow the signs for Cerro Chirripó; the well-marked 2.3km (1.4-mile) trail leads first through the Valle de los Conejos (Valley of the Rabbits), which is home to an endemic breed of (what else?) rabbits. If you're lucky and keep quiet on the trail, you may spot a few. You'll then pass through the Valle de los Lagos (Valley of Lakes)—no luck needed to see plenty of (again, what else?) lakes here. This trail starts off relatively flat, but does involve some climbing and scrambling as you reach the summit, at just under 3,819m (12,530 ft.).

One piece of advice: in their rush to make it to the summit, many hikers fail to take the time to enjoy their surroundings. Don't be one of them. The peaks were carved by glaciers, and the lakes, the largest of which is Lago Chirripó, are their legacy. The terrain is beautiful, and unlike anything else you'll see in Costa Rica. Even with time allotted for taking in the views, the hike from the lodge to the summit should take about an hour.

Begin the following hike from the summit lodge.

④ ★★ Los Crestones. If you have an extra day to explore, you'll want to visit this impressive rock formation. Translating literally as "The Crests," Los Crestones features a series of steep exposed cliffs. At 3,760m (12,335 ft.), the highest point here is called Cerro Terbi. The 2.3km (1.4-mile) trail to Los Crestones is relatively short, although, again, it does include some climbing and scrambling. It should take about 1½ hours each way. The view from the top rivals that from the summit of Mount Chirripó, since you'll have the pleasure of seeing said summit in the foreground. Experienced rock climbers can find a variety of pitches to climb, even without ropes.

Begin the hike down the mountain from the summit lodge.

⑤ Return hike. The hike down (14.5km/9 miles) is fairly straightforward, and you should be able to cut an easy hour, if not two, off the time it took you going up (in other words, plan on anywhere from 4 to 9 hours). But be careful: Hiking down is often more difficult and treacherous, especially for knees and ankles, so don't rush. And keep an eye out for tapirs—the park is home to the country's biggest population.

The entrance to the springs is 1km (⅔ mile) beyond San Gerardo de Rivas.

⑥ Herradura Hot Springs. After so much strenuous hiking, you'll definitely savor a soak in these natural hot springs. Just northwest of San Gerardo de Rivas, you'll find one mid-size pool built into a natural rock formation. The water

> *Mount Chirripó's summit, or cerro, is the highest point in Costa Rica.*

is not steaming hot, but it is warm enough to soothe any sore and aching muscles or joints you may have. Just remember to keep yourself well hydrated. Admission $3. Daily 8am–6pm.

Watch Out for Falling Temperatures

I know you're on vacation in the tropics, but come prepared for chilly weather. In fact, come prepared for all sorts of weather: Because of the elevation, temperatures at the top of the mountain can quickly dip below freezing, particularly when the sun goes down. During the day, on the other hand, temperatures can soar—remember, no matter what the elevation, you're still only 9 degrees from the Equator. Layers are a must, as is rain gear. If you get wet on the way up, you're going to spend an awfully uncomfortable night in the summit lodge.

Race to the Top

If simply climbing the tallest peak in Costa Rica is a too mundane for you, why not join the annual **Carrera Ecológica Cultural Internacional Campo Traviesa al Cerro Chirripó** (☎ 2771-8731; www.carrerachirripo.com). Held the third Saturday of February, this is a grueling 34km (21-mile) footrace from the base to the summit of Mount Chirripó and back. The record time, to date: 3 hours, 15 minutes, 3 seconds.

Central Pacific Coast Adventures in & on the Water

Costa Rica's central Pacific coast is long and varied. It boasts the country's largest marina, some of its most coveted sportfishing waters, and several world-class surf breaks.

> Playa Hermosa, near Jacó, frequently hosts international surfing competitions.

Body Boarding & Surfing

There's some seriously good board surfing to be had all along the central Pacific coast, a major surf mecca and the gateway to a host of famous breaks. See "Surfing Costa Rica's Pacific Coast," p. 302.

Just south of Jacó, ★★ **Playa Hermosa** (p. 304) is a real board-breaker. This steep and hollow beach break is regularly the site of international surf competitions. Visitors to the Jacó area can also try the beach break at **Playa Tulín.**

If you want to learn how to surf while in Jacó, try the **Jacó Surf School** (☎ 8829-4697; www. jacosurfschool.com), which sets up shop on the sand each day, right near the center of Playa

Hermosa (Jacó). This is a great place for drop-in lessons and surf rentals—it will cost you $50 per person for a 2-hour lesson and you'll get to keep the board for an additional 24 hours.

While not nearly as well known, the surfing at Manuel Antonio is also pretty decent, especially toward the northern end of ★ **Playa Espadilla Sur** (p. 304), beyond the large rock outcropping. In fact, the lack of huge waves makes Manuel Antonio a prime spot for learning how to surf. If you're interested in taking lessons (and I can't recommend doing so enough), check in with the ★ **Manuel Antonio Surf School** (☎ 2777-4842; www.masurfschool. com). The school charges $65 for a 3-hour

Body Boarding & Surfing

Green Iguana Surf Camp 4

Jacó Surf School 2

Manuel Antonio Surf School 3

Kayaking

Kayak Jacó 2

Scuba Diving & Snorkeling

Mystic Dive Center 5

Oceans Unlimited 3

Sportsfishing

Costa Rica Dreams 1

Cuervo Sport Fishing 1

High Tec Sportfishing 3

Maverick Sportfishing Yachts 1

White-Water Rafting

Iguana Tours 3

Ríos Tropicales 3

---

group lesson (maximum 3 students per instructor), including equipment and transportation to and from your hotel.

★ **Dominical** (p. 304) has a long and powerful beach break that can churn out major tubes when the wind and swells are aligned. The ★★ **Green Iguana Surf Camp** (☎ 2787-0157 or 8825-1381; www.greeniguanasurfcamp.com) offers lessons and comprehensive surf camps here. They specialize in weeklong programs aimed at giving raw beginners a solid footing in the sport. Rates run between $1,345 and $1,415 (per person, double occupancy) for a full week and include daily lessons, two meals a day, un-

limited board use, and such perks as a 1-hour Spanish class and separate 1-hour massage.

Bodysurfing

The surf breaks along this section of Costa Rica's Pacific coast tend to be thick and unforgiving. Bodysurfers should probably steer clear of Playa Hermosa (Jacó), Playa Tulín, and Dominical, as the surf tends to be particularly rough there. But the inner section of ★ **Playa Espadilla Sur** (p. 304) is often excellent for bodysurfing, as is the southern end of **Playa Jacó.** Down in Dominical, I recommend heading south to ★ **Playa Hermosa** (Dominical, p. 304).

> *You can try both sea and river kayaking in the Jacó area.*

> *The Pacific coast is prime sportfishing territory.*

Kayaking

Whether you want to go sea kayaking, take a gentle float on the Río Tulín, or even try kayak surfing (yes, that's a sport), head to ★ **Kayak Jacó** (☎ 2643-1233; www.kayakjaco.com). This outfit also offers white-water paddling trips in easy-to-use inflatable kayaks and ocean-worthy eight-person outrigger canoes. Most of their tour options run around 4 hours and include transportation to and from the put-in, as well as fresh fruit and soft drinks during the trip. Expect to pay $55 to $70 per person.

Scuba Diving & Snorkeling

The central Pacific coast is not famous for its snorkeling or scuba diving, but that doesn't mean you give it a miss. Quite the contrary—when the seas are calm, there are often good snorkeling opportunities along the rocky out-croppings at either end of ★★ **Playa Manuel Antonio** (p. 305). You can rent gear at several open-air kiosks and stands lining the road that leads to the national park entrance. Rates run around $10 for a half-day, including mask, fins, and snorkel.

For really good snorkeling and scuba diving, you will want to head out to ★★★ **Isla del Caño,** which is technically in the Southern Zone, just off Drake Bay (see Chapter 9, p. 343, ⑫). But it's easy to book a trip by fast boat from Manuel Antonio (the ride will take 1½ hours), or Dominical (an hour-long ride).

In Manuel Antonio, ★ **Oceans Unlimited** (☎ 2777-3171; www.oceansunlimitedcr.com) offers scuba diving and snorkeling outings, including trips out to Isla del Caño, as well as certification and resort courses. If you're in the

A Fish Tale

All of the sportfishing operators that I've list-ed here have modern, well-equipped boats, professional crews, and top-notch tackle and gear. A half-day fishing trip for four people can run from $600 to $1,200, and a full day costs between $850 and $1,600, depending on the size of the boat, distance traveled, and how much food and drink and what amenities are provided. Still, you'll find a lot of competi-tion all up and down the coast, so it pays to shop around and investigate.

> The white water on the Río Savegre will keep you plenty busy, but be sure to cast your eyes around you occasionally—the scenery is gorgeous.

Dominical area and want to take a scuba diving trip out to the rocky sites off Ballena Marine National Park or all the way out to Isla del Caño, call ★ **Mystic Dive Center** (☎ 2786-5217; www.mysticdivecenter.com), which has its main office in a small roadside strip mall down toward Playa Tortuga and Ojochal. They only run trips between December 1 and April 15.

Rates for local diving or snorkeling excursions run around $90 per person for a two-tank dive and $55 to $65 for a snorkeling trip, including all equipment, transportation, lunch, and soft drinks. For trips out to Isla del Caño, Oceans Unlimited charges $220 for scuba divers and $149 for snorkelers. Mystic Dive Center, which is closer, charges $145 for scuba divers and $90 for snorkelers.

Sportfishing

The central Pacific coast is one of Costa Rica's sportfishing hot spots. Sailfish, marlin, dorado (mahimahi), roosterfish, wahoo, and tuna are all common game fish in the offshore waters here. There's a major marina at the Los Sueños Marriott Ocean & Golf Resort in Playa Herradura (p. 315), and another is under construction in Quepos, just outside of Manuel Antonio. See also "A Fish Tale," opposite

In the Jacó and Playa Herradura area, you should check in with ★ **Maverick Sportfishing Yachts** (☎ 866/888-6426 in U.S. and Canada, or 2637-8824 in Costa Rica; www.maverickyachtscostarica.com), ★ **Costa Rica Dreams** (☎ 732/901-8625 in U.S., or 2637-8942 in Costa Rica; www.costaricadreams.com), or ★ **Cuervo Sport Fishing** (☎ 800/656-1859 in U.S. and Canada, no Costa Rican number; www.costarica-fishingcharters.com).

If you're in the Quepos and Manuel Antonio area, try hooking up with ★★ **High Tec Sportfishing** (☎ 2777-3465; www.hightecsportfishing.com). If you catch some tuna or dorado (mahimahi), many local restaurants, including El Gran Escape (p. 324), will cook your fresh catch for you.

White-Water Rafting

The Savegre and Naranjo Rivers start in the rain-forested mountains above Quepos. They provide class II to IV white-water river rafting adventures, depending upon which section you run and how much it has been raining of late. Several rafting companies ply both these rivers. The best of these are ★★ **Iguana Tours** (☎ 2777-1262; www.iguanatours.com) and ★ **Ríos Tropicales** (☎ 2777-4092; www.h2ocr.com). Both offer full-day rafting trips for around $85 to $110 and also offer half-day rafting and sea-kayaking trips. Depending on rainfall and demand, they will run either the **Río Naranjo** or the ★★★ **Río Savegre.** I very much prefer the Savegre for its stunning scenery.

SURFING COSTA RICA'S PACIFIC COAST

Living the 'Pura Vida' **BY ELIOT GREENSPAN AND DAN TUCKER**

WHEN SURFING EXPLODED on to the world scene in the 1950s and 60s, thanks to *Gidget* (1959), Elvis (*Blue Hawaii*, 1961), and the Beach Boys, Costa Rica was ready and waiting with ample reward for adventurous wave-seekers. And board riders have been coming in increasing numbers ever since. Warm waters, clear weather, an easygoing beach culture, and consistent, exceptional surf year-round all contribute to making Costa Rica a surfer's paradise.

Surfers in Costa Rica generally subscribe to the Tico philosophy of *pura vida*—literally, "pure life." For visitors, the phrase is applicable to almost anything positive. To Costa Ricans, *pura vida* describes the experience of living life slowly and well—preferably on the crest of a wave.

Top Surf Breaks

The 1,000km (620-mile) Pacific Coast encompasses no fewer than eight of the finest breaks in the Western Hemisphere. Here's an overview.

DOMINICAL
Location: Central Pacific Coast
Type: Beach break
Good to know: The series of well-formed peaks on this long beach are good for beginners when the swell is small, but big, fast barrels form when the swell picks up.

PLAYA HERMOSA
Location: Central Pacific Coast
Type: Beach break
Good to know: This is a powerful and fast wave that is often used for local and international surf competitions.

MALPAÍS
Location: Nicoya Peninsula **Type:** Beach break **Good to know:** For all intents and purposes, Malpaís and neighboring Santa Teresa are one very long beach, with many, many peaks breaking both right and left.

PAVONES
Location: Southern Zone **Type:** Point break **Good to know:** This is often cited as the longest left in the world. Rides here can last several minutes. The wave works best with a south swell and needs some size to

form. When the swell isn't just right, there's not much happening here.

PLAYA GRANDE
Location: Guanacaste
Type: Beach break
Good to know: This long beach break has numerous peaks breaking both right and left. Playa Grande is especially good at holding a large swell, although the wave is well shaped no matter the size and works well at all but the lowest tides.

PLAYA GUIONES
Location: Nicoya Peninsula **Type:** Beach break **Good to know:** This long, white

sand beach is gorgeous, with plenty of peaks—both right and left—spread along its length. This is often a good spot to get away from the crowds.

PLAYA NEGRA
Location: Guanacaste
Type: Point break
Good to know: One

of the few points in Guanacaste, this right-breaking wave is perfectly formed, but relatively short. When it's working well, it can get very crowded here.

WITCH'S ROCK
Location: Guanacaste
Type: Beach break
Good to know: This very isolated spot is best reached by boat. You'll find both right

and left waves to ride. The namesake offshore rock formation gives this wave one of the most stunning backdrops in all of surfdom.

Central Pacific Coast Beaches A to Z

★ **Playa Dominical.** A dark-sand beach with a gentle gradual slope, this is a major surf destination. When the swell is big and the wind right, the waves become big barreling tubes suitable only for experienced surfers. The town behind this beach is a small, funky tourist outpost geared in large part to the surfers who come to ride the waves here. Dominical.

★ **Playa Espadilla Sur.** This is the first beach you'll encounter after entering Manuel Antonio National Park. The long span of golden sand is backed by sea grapes, coconut palms, and rain forest. It is my favorite beach to settle down on for sunbathing, swimming (though it can be rough), or a shady midafternoon siesta. A gentle national park trail runs parallel to the beach just inland, and toward the southern end of the

beach looms the impressive natural formation of Punta Catedral (Cathedral Point). Inside Manuel Antonio National Park.

★ **Playa Hermosa (Dominical).** Backed by coconut palms and close to the Costanera Highway, this beach is best accessed near its northern end, where you'll find several makeshift parking areas. The far, far southern end joins up with the "whale's tail" sandbar formation inside Ballena Marine National Park. 13km (8 miles) south of Dominical.

★★ **Playa Hermosa (Jacó).** This black-sand beach is a major surf destination. When the surf's up, the steep, fast, and powerful beach break here is packed with surfers. The main surf spot, along with a handful of small hotels and restaurants, is located near the northern end of the beach. From there, the sand stretches on for miles to the south with virtually no development. 7km (4⅓ miles) south of Jacó.

> *Playa Espadilla Sur, in Manuel Antonio National Park, is one of the coast's most beautiful beaches.*

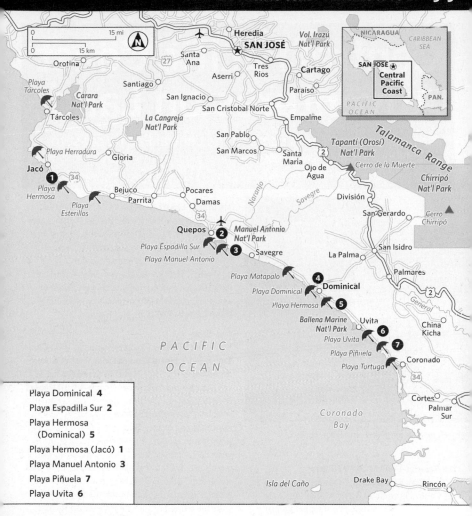

Playa Dominical **4**

Playa Espadilla Sur **2**

Playa Hermosa
  (Dominical) **5**

Playa Hermosa (Jacó) **1**

Playa Manuel Antonio **3**

Playa Piñuela **7**

Playa Uvita **6**

★★ **Playa Manuel Antonio.** Often called the "second beach," this is the most popular beach inside Manuel Antonio National Park. It's relatively small, with a deep crescent shape, and is tucked behind the famous Punta Catedral. It is often calm and good for swimming. A few picnic tables are set in the shade of sea grape trees, and there are even public restrooms and showers here. Inside Manuel Antonio National Park.

★ **Playa Piñuela.** Picturesque and often deserted, this small beach lies at the far southern end of Ballena Marine National Park. The beach itself almost disappears at high tide,

leaving only a narrow rocky band. Still, the water here is often calm and good for swimming. Local fishermen use the southern end as a makeshift port. Playa Piñuela is 26km (16 miles) south of Dominical.

★★ **Playa Uvita.** This is the first and most popular beach inside Ballena Marine National Park. The fine, dark gold sand stretches on for miles, and at low tide an exposed sandbar connects the northern end with a rocky outcropping. From the air, the entire formation looks strikingly like a whale's tail. 8km (5 miles) south of Dominical.

Central Pacific Coast Adventures on Land

Although most visitors come to the central Pacific coast to enjoy the beaches and ocean-based adventures available here, there's plenty to do on solid land. Take full advantage.

> La Iguana, the course at Los Sueños Resort.

All-Terrain-Vehicle (ATV) Tours

★ **Fourtrax Adventure.** These folks offer guided ATV tours in both Jacó and Manuel Antonio. Their signature tour heads out from Quepos through African palm plantations (see "Oil in Costa Rica?," p. 277), rural towns, and secondary forest to a jungle waterfall, where you stop for a dip. ☉ 3 hr. Quepos. ☎ 2777-1829. www.fourtraxadventure.com. Rates $95 per person, $115 for 2 people on the same ATV; includes breakfast or lunch and round-trip transport from your hotel. Daily 7:30am, 11am, and 2:30pm.

Canopy Tours

★★ **Chiclets Tree Tour.** Located south of Jacó, this is a canopy tour that will get your adrenaline pumping. It features 13 platforms and one treetop suspension bridge set in transitional forest, all with sweeping views of the Pacific. See p. 279, ❸.

★ **Canopy Safari.** This is the boldest and most exciting canopy tour in the Manuel Antonio area, with 10 zip lines, 18 platforms, and a hanging suspension bridge. The attraction also has a small butterfly garden and serpentarium. ☉ 3–4 hr. Quepos. ☎ 2777-0100. www.canopysafari.com. Rate $70 per person; includes full breakfast or lunch and round-trip transport from your hotel. Daily 7:30am, 10:30am, and 1:30pm.

Day Spas

You'll find excellent in-house spas at **Villa Caletas** (p. 315), **Hotel Club del Mar Resort & Condominiums** (p. 314), **Hotel Sí Como No** (p. 322), and **Los Sueños Marriott Ocean & Golf Resort** (p. 315). Down in Manuel Antonio, you can also check out **Raindrop Spa** (☎ 2777-2880; www.raindropspa.com) or **Spa Uno** (☎ 2777-2607; www.spauno.com), two excellent day spas. A wide range of massage treatments, wraps, and facials are available at all of these places. Rates run around $70 to $110 per hour, depending on which treatments you opt for. Most of these spas have one or more treatment rooms that open onto an ocean or jungle view; I recommend you ask for and reserve one of these whenever possible.

Golf

★ **La Iguana.** This excellent 18-hole golf course is at the Los Sueños Marriott Ocean & Golf Resort (p. 315). Designed by Ted Robinson, La Iguana is a gentle resort course, with some excellent forest views and the occasional ocean vista. It's easily accessible to folks staying in the Jacó and Playa Herradura area, and about an hour drive each way for those staying near Manuel Antonio. At Los Sueños Marriott Ocean & Golf Resort, Playa Herradura. ☎ 2630-9000. www.golflaiguana.com. Greens fees: $130 full

ATV Tours

Fourtrax Adventure Jacó **3**

Fourtrax Adventure
Manuel Antonio **6**

Canopy Tours

Canopy Safari **7**

Chiclets Tree Tour **4**

Day Spas

Hotel Club del Mar
Condominiums & Resort **3**

Hotel Sí Como No **6**

Los Sueños Marriott Ocean
& Golf Resort **2**

Raindrop Spa **6**

Spa Uno **6**

Villa Caletas **1**

Golf

La Iguana **2**

Horseback Riding

Brisas del Nara **5**

Finca Valmy Tours **5**

round for hotel guests, $160 for nonguests. Prices drop to $110 and $130, respectively, if you tee off after noon. Club and shoe rentals available.

Horseback Riding

There are lots of locals who rent horses on the beaches of both Jacó and Playa Espadilla, but I would discourage going this route, as there are just too many crowds (and frankly, horse droppings are a problem, as they draw flies). Instead, down in Manuel Antonio, ★★ **Finca Valmy Tours** (☎ 2779-1118; www.valmytours.com) and ★★ **Brisas del Nara** (☎ 2779-1235; www.horsebacktour.com) offer equally excellent horseback excursions that pass through primary

and secondary forest and feature a swimming stop at a jungle pool and waterfall. Both claim that children as young as 4 years old can ride their own, very gentle, very small horses. Personally, I think small children should ride along with their parents rather than climbing aboard a horse of their own, but that's for parents to decide. Both operations charge $70 for a full-day tour, including breakfast and lunch, and $55 for a half-day tour. Brisas del Nara charges $55 for children 4 to 12 for a full-day tour, $40 for a half-day tour; Finca Valmy offers a discounted rate of $35 for children riding on the same horse as a parent. Both companies include round-trip transport from your hotel.

Best Bird-Watching on the Central Pacific Coast

Thanks to its national parks, miles of coastline, mangroves, and wide range of elevations and ecosystems, the central Pacific coast is heaven both for birds and for serious bird-watchers (it's pretty great for novices, too). You'll find a jaw-dropping variety of feathered friends here, including the endangered scarlet macaw. Just remember to pack your binoculars.

> The blue-throated toucanet is found only from Costa Rica to Panama.

National Parks

One of the first and most popular stops for bird-watchers is ★★★ **Carara National Park** (p. 280, **5**), where well over 400 species of birds have been recorded. The transitional forests and riverside ecosystems are home to the endangered scarlet macaw, antbirds, manakins, hummingbirds, parrots, woodpeckers, and the black-throated trogon, among many others. In the dense forests, keep a lookout for owls, the black guan, and the great curassow. Along the river, you will most likely spot a variety of herons, egrets, and kingfishers.

A little farther south, ★★★ **Manuel Antonio National Park** (p. 290) is also a hit with bird-

watchers. From the hillsides overlooking the forest, one commonly sees euphonias, honeycreepers, toucans, aracaris, and parrots, as well as mixed flocks of scarlet-rumped, blue-gray, golden-hooded, and palm tanagers. The forest teems with antshrikes, antwrens, manakins, warblers, chachalacas, and other species. Meanwhile, high overhead, you might spot a laughing falcon or black-collared hawk. Along the beaches, you are almost certain to see brown pelicans and magnificent frigatebirds.

With a range of ecosystems and radical changes in elevation, ★★ **Chirripó National Park** (p. 294) and its namesake Mount Chirripó (3,819m/12,530 ft. elevation) offer a unique and abundant bounty for bird-watchers. Few visitors see the resplendent quetzal, although it is a resident of the lower elevations of the park. But the dense rain forests and cloud forests of the lower elevations often yield sightings of the black guan, elegant trogon, emerald toucanet, and a variety of antbirds and wrens. As you climb, keep an eye out for a volcano hummingbird or red-tailed hawk. Bird-watchers looking to explore the avifauna of Chirripó National Park might consider staying at **Talari Mountain Lodge** (see "Spending the Night in San Gerardo de Rivas," p. 296), which provides a comfortable base for trips around the park and neighboring regions.

If you're looking to rack up a number of shorebird and seabird sightings, the broad, uncrowded beaches of **Ballena Marine National Park** (p. 283, **16**) should be a prime destination. Here

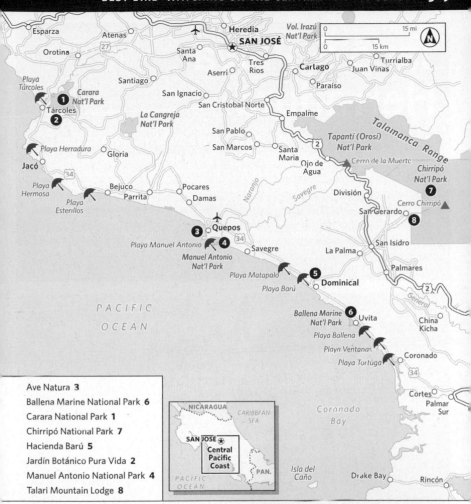

Ave Natura **3**

Ballena Marine National Park **6**

Carara National Park **1**

Chirripó National Park **7**

Hacienda Barú **5**

Jardín Botánico Pura Vida **2**

Manuel Antonio National Park **4**

Talari Mountain Lodge **8**

you'll spot gulls, terns, pelicans, petrels, and sandpipers.

Private Reserves

Near Carara National Park, the flowering plants at ★ **Jardín Botánico Pura Vida** (p. 275, **2**) draw a host of hummingbirds. This is also a good place to spot toucans.

★★ **Hacienda Barú** (p. 287, **8**) is another spectacular spot for bird-watchers. This private reserve encompasses a wide range of ecosystems, including coast, river, mangrove, and lowland rain forest. Not surprisingly, this yields an incredible variety of birds. There are experienced guides on hand to help you see as much as possible, and there is even a bird-watching tower.

Going with a Guide

Even if you're an experienced bird-watcher, hiring a guide can be a rewarding investment. Not only can guides help you spot even the more elusive birds on your must-see list, they provide a wealth of information about everything from habits to habitats. I highly recommend the bird-watching guides booked through **Ave Natura** (see "To Guide or Not to Guide," p. 292), a specialized tour agency based in Quepos. One of their customized 3-hour bird-watching tours will run you $55 per person, including transportation, park entrance fees, and a snack.

Jacó & Playa Herradura

Jacó and the neighboring Playa Herradura are two of the
closest beaches (and beach towns—the names are interchangeable) to San José.
Given that proximity, both are very popular with both Ticos and foreign visitors.
Playa Herradura is a rather unattractive brown-sand beach that is home to the
grand Los Sueños Marriott Ocean & Golf Resort, but Playa de Jacó and its southern neighbor Playa Hermosa are major surf destinations. These beaches have a
real tropical feel—the humidity is palpable, and you can see the lushness on the
forested hillsides that surround the towns. Ideally, you'll want to spend at least 3
days exploring this area.

> The Rain Forest Aerial Tram Pacific offers a great introduction to the forests of the central coast.

START Jacó is 117km (73 miles) west of
San José. For the first stop here, exit the
Costanera Hwy. (CR34) just north of Jacó at
the well-marked turnoff onto a dirt road, then
follow the signs.

1 ★ kids **Rain Forest Aerial Tram Pacific.** This
is a sister project to the original Rain Forest

Aerial Tram Atlantic (p. 69). Its main attraction
is a gondola that takes you through and above
forests similar to those in nearby Carara National Park. In addition to the guided tram tour
and a hike, your entrance allows you to wander
the trails at your leisure for as long as you like.
You'll also find botanical gardens specializing in
medicinal plants and various species of

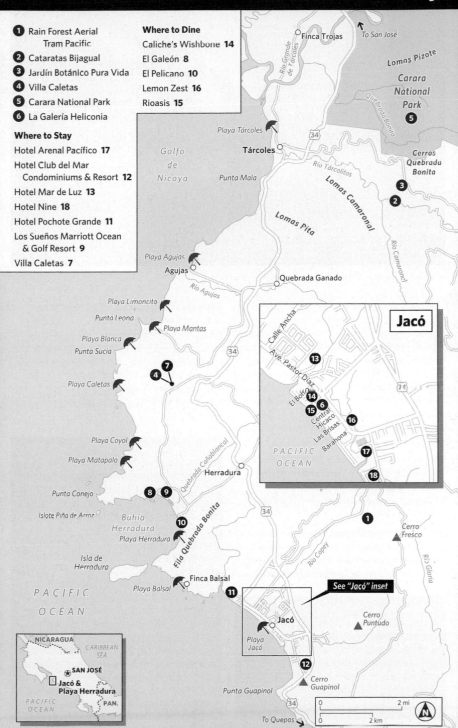

1. Rain Forest Aerial Tram Pacific
2. Cataratas Bijagual
3. Jardín Botánico Pura Vida
4. Villa Caletas
5. Carara National Park
6. La Galería Heliconia

Where to Stay

Hotel Arenal Pacífico **17**
Hotel Club del Mar Condominiums & Resort **12**
Hotel Mar de Luz **13**
Hotel Nine **18**
Hotel Pochote Grande **11**
Los Sueños Marriott Ocean & Golf Resort **9**
Villa Caletas **7**

Where to Dine

Caliche's Wishbone **14**
El Galeón **8**
El Pelicano **10**
Lemon Zest **16**
Rioasis **15**

> *Sunset cocktails at Villa Caletas are a Jacó-area tradition.*

heliconia, and a small serpentarium, with around 20 different snake species on display in glass enclosures. There is even a zip-line canopy tour. You can pick and choose what you'd like to do, or sign up for a tour, which will include transportation from San José or any area hotel. ⏱ Minimum 2 hr. North of Jacó. ☎ 2257-5961. www.rfat.com. Rates $55 adults, $28 students with valid ID and children 2–11; children under 2 free; includes guided 40-min. tram ride and guided 45-min. hike. Daily 7am–4pm.

The entrance to Bijagual is 19km (12 miles) north of Jacó, on CR34; exit at the sign for Hotel Villa Lapas and drive about 5km (3 miles) to lower entrance, 8km (5 miles) to top entrance.

❷ ★★ **Cataratas Bijagual.** Near the tiny remote village of Bijagual, you'll find a series of stepped jungle waterfalls. Just above the falls, a local family runs the **Complejo Ecológico la**

Catarata (no phone), which features a basic restaurant and a campground—and access to Bijagual. They offer horseback tours down to the falls, or you can hike up from a separate entrance below the falls. The hike takes about 45 minutes each way. Whether you walk or ride, you'll get to see quite a bit. ⏱ 2–4 hr. Admission $45 including horseback ride; $20 for hikers. Daily 8am–4pm.

Exercise Your Options

In addition to the tours and attractions mentioned here, a whole range of adventure tours and activities can be arranged from either Jacó or Playa Herradura. Options include sportfishing, sea kayaking, several canopy tours, ATV explorations, surfing, sailing, and white-water rafting. For information on these, check out "Adventures on Land" (p. 306) and "Adventures in & on the Water" (p. 298). You can also play golf at La Iguana course at the Los Sueños Marriott Ocean & Golf Resort (p. 306). In addition, tours to Manuel Antonio and any of the activities listed in the Manuel Antonio section can also be arranged. If your hotel desk can't arrange any of these for you, check in with the folks at **Gray Line Tours** (☎ 2643-3231; www.graylinecostarica.com) or **JaguaRiders** (☎ 2643-0180; www.jaguariders.com).

Bugging Out

Mosquitoes and other biting insects can be a serious problem in these parts. Be sure to bring along repellent or, better yet, wear lightweight cotton pants and shirts with long sleeves. I was once foolish enough to attempt a quick hike in beach clothes and flip-flops around sunset—not a good idea.

> *A blue and gold macaw at the Pura Vida gardens.*

Pura Vida Botanical Gardens are located just uphill from Complejo Ecológico la Catarata.

3 ★ **Jardín Botánico Pura Vida.** See p. 275, **2**.

The turnoff for Villa Caletas is 9km (5½ miles) north of Jacó on CR34.

4 ★★ **Sunset at Villa Caletas.** Make it to the bar at this boutique hotel in time to watch the sunset. See p. 276, **4**.

Carara National Park is 22km (14 miles) north of Jacó on CR34.

5 ★★★ **Carara National Park.** Make a visit to see the scarlet macaws. See p. 280, **5**.

6 ★ **La Galería Heliconia.** The main strip in Jacó, which runs parallel to the ocean, is an overcrowded and congested collection of restaurants, stores, and small strip malls. Most of the stores here are either surf shops or glorified souvenir stands hawking cut-rate craft works, T-shirts, and trinkets. La Galería Heliconia is the exception, with a broad selection of contemporary Costa Rican art, both functional and decorative, in a range of media. You'll find paintings, ceramic wares, and wood carvings by prominent artists such as Pefi Figueres, Barry Biesanz, and Lil Mena. ☺ 45 min. The main road in downtown Jacó, next to Rioasis restaurant. ☎ 2643-3613. Daily 9am–7pm.

Nice Crocs!

En route to Jacó and Playa Herradura, the Costanera Highway (CR34) passes over the Río Tárcoles just outside the entrance to ★★★ **Carara National Park** (p. 280, **5**). The river below this bridge is home to a hearty population of **American crocodiles.** This is a popular spot to pull over and take a gander at these gargantuan reptiles, some of which are up to 4.5m (15 ft.) in length. At any moment, as many as 20 crocs are usually visible, either swimming in the water or sunning on the banks.

You'll have to be careful on two counts. First, you'll be walking on a narrow sidewalk along the side of the bridge with cars and trucks speeding by. Second, car break-ins are common here, although an on-site police post has somewhat reduced the risk. Still, don't leave your car or valuables unguarded for long, or better yet, leave someone at the car and take turns watching the crocs.

If you're staying in any of the nearby beach towns, you might consider taking a boat tour of the river and mangroves here. Several companies offer such a tour, and every hotel and tour agency in the area can arrange it for you. Nearly all the operators bring along plenty of freshly killed chickens to attract the crocodiles and pump up the adrenaline—this is a practice I cannot endorse. That's why I suggest going with ★★ kids **Jungle Crocodile Safari** (☎ 2637-0338; www.junglecrocodilesafari.com). The cost of the 2-hour tour is $35 for adults and $25 for children ages 4 to 12 (children 3 and under free). Transportation from Jacó, Playa Herradura, Manuel Antonio, or San José is available. Jungle Crocodile Safari's trips depart daily at 8:30am, 10:30am, 1:30pm, and 3:30pm.

Where to Stay

> *The pool at Los Sueños Resort, with its canals and grottoes, is undeniably spectacular.*

★ **Hotel Arenal Pacífico** JACÓ

This is a good midrange option, and it's right on the beach, to boot. The rooms are nothing special—and very few offer ocean views—but they are clean and cool, and most are pretty spacious. I recommend the second-floor rooms, which have a private balcony. The superior rooms are larger and come with a coffeemaker and minifridge. There are two outdoor pools— one with a little waterfall filling it, another with a round children's pool. **On the beach, southern end of Jacó.** ☎ 2643-3419. www.arenalpacifico. com. 22 units. $99 double; $129–$137 superior double; $240 junior suite. Rates include breakfast. AE, MC, V.

★★ **Hotel Club del Mar Resort & Condominiums**

JACÓ With a fabulous location, friendly manage-ment, and plush rooms, Club del Mar has long been a top choice in Jacó. Set at the far south-ern end of the beach, where the rocky hills meet the sand, and where the swimming is the safest in town, this is a great place for families. Most of the rooms are one- or two-bedroom condo

units, with a full kitchen. All units come with an ocean view, although some are more open and expansive than others. The grounds are lush and chock-full of flowering heliconia and ginger. **On the beach, southern end of Jacó.** ☎ 866/978-5669 in U.S. and Canada, or 2643-3194 in Costa Rica. www.clubdelmarcostarica.com. 32 units. $153 double; $224–$320 condo; $383 penthouse. AE, DC, MC, V.

★ **Hotel Mar de Luz** JACÓ

This is one of Jacó's better deals. All the rooms are immaculate and comfortable. Some feature stone walls, a small sitting area, and one or two double beds on a raised sleeping nook. My only complaint is that in most rooms the windows are too small and mostly sealed, forcing you to use air-conditioning. In the gardens just off the pools are a couple of grills for guest use. **One block inland, central Jacó.** ☎ 2643-3259. www. mardeluz.com. 29 units. $91 double. Rate includes breakfast. V.

★ **Hotel Nine** JACÓ

This small hotel has contemporary architectural

design touches that would be right at home on Miami's South Beach. Rooms are decorated in a tropical style, with wood and rattan furnishings and bold colors. The premium suites have two separate rooms and a small kitchenette with microwave oven. The excellent restaurant here bills itself primarily as a steakhouse, but fresh fish and seafood options are also available. On the beach, southern end of Jacó. ☎ 2643-5335. www.hotelnine.com. 9 units. $130–$170 double; $220 suite. Rates include breakfast. AE, DC, MC, V.

Hotel Pochote Grande JACÓ

This well-kept hotel is located just off the beach toward the far northern end of Jacó. All the rooms are fairly large, although sparsely furnished, with white-tile floors, one queen-size and one single bed, a small fridge, and a balcony or patio. I prefer the second-floor rooms, which feature high ceilings. The grounds here were once shady and lush, but encroaching construction all around has left this place feeling a bit exposed, and ongoing construction can be a nuisance and source of noise. On the beach, northern end of Jacó. ☎ 2643-3236. www.hotelpochotegrande.net. 24 units. $80–$85 double. AE, MC, V.

★★ Los Sueños Marriott Ocean & Golf Resort

PLAYA HERRADURA This large resort is done in a Spanish colonial style, with stucco walls, heavy wooden doors, and red-clay roof tiles. Rooms facing the ocean are clearly superior, and a few of these have a large balcony with chaise longues and garden furniture. The pool is a vast, intricate maze built to imitate the canals of Venice, with private nooks and grottoes; kids love exploring it. The beach here is calm and good for swimming, although it's one of the least attractive beaches on this coast, with a mix of rocks and hard-packed, dark-brown sand. Playa Herradura. ☎ 888/236-2427 in U.S. and Canada, or 2298-0844 or 2630-9000 in Costa Rica. www.marriott.com. 201 units. $300–$350 double; $400–$700 suite; $1,300–$1,700 presidential suite. AE, MC, V.

★★★ Villa Caletas PLAYA CALETAS

Perched above the sea, Villa Caletas enjoys commanding views of the Pacific over forested hillsides. The rooms are all elegantly appointed,

> *A beautifully decorated room at Villa Caletas.*

but you'll want to stay in a villa or suite. All feature ornate neoclassical decor and a private terrace for soaking up the views. The larger junior suites come with their own outdoor Jacuzzi. The suites and master suites are larger still—and have their own swimming pool. The **Zephyr Palace** is a seven-suite addition, located a little bit apart from the main hotel and villas. Rooms here are immense and thematically designed—you can choose an African suite, an Arabian suite, an Oriental suite, and more. All have beautiful ocean views, a home theater system, Jacuzzi, private balcony, and personal concierge service. Playa Caletas, 11km (6¾ miles) north of Jacó. ☎ 2630-3003. www.hotelvillacaletas.com. 42 units. $178–$198 double; $230 villa; $300–$470 suite; $450–$600 Zephyr Palace suite. AE, MC, V.

Where to Dine

> *The chef at Lemon Zest is renowned for his sauces and creative menu.*

★ **Caliche's Wishbone** JACÓ *SEAFOOD/ MEXICAN* This casual spot is popular with surfers and specializes in Tex-Mex standards and homemade pizzas. However, you can also get excellent fresh fish and perfectly prepared seafood dishes, as well as a variety of sandwich fillings served in homemade pita bread. The portions are huge, so come with an appetite. There is almost always fresh tuna lightly seared and served with a soy-wasabi dressing. The nicest tables are streetside on a covered veranda. **On the main road in Jacó, near the center of town.** ☎ 2643-3406. **Entrees $5.50–$27. V. Lunch and dinner Thurs–Tues.**

★★ **El Galeón** PLAYA HERRADURA *FUSION* The setting here is elegant, the service refined, and the menu wide-ranging, creative, and eclectic. Appetizers range from an inventive plate of scallop sliders to crisp Asian-spiced soft-shell crabs and sea bass ceviche served with avocado and a local salsa. For a main course, I recommend the pumpkin-, ricotta-, and basil-filled ravioli served with grilled Creole jumbo shrimp. **At the marina of Los Sueños Marriott Ocean & Golf Resort.** ☎ 2630-4555 or 2637-8331. **Entrees $19–$43. AE, MC, V. Dinner daily.**

El Pelicano PLAYA HERRADURA *SEAFOOD/ COSTA RICAN* Heavy wooden tables and chairs are spread around a large, open-air dining room facing the beach and boats bobbing at anchor off Playa Herradura. The menu features a range of ceviches, salads, and main courses, with a heavy—and logical—emphasis on fresh seafood. The *corvina al ajillo* (sea bass in garlic sauce) is excellent, as is the *arroz con mariscos* (rice with seafood). **On the beach in Playa Herradura.** ☎ 2637-8910. **Entrees $7–$45. MC, V. Lunch and dinner daily.**

★★ **Lemon Zest** JACÓ *SEAFOOD/FUSION* Chef Richard Lemon has set up shop in a second-floor space right along Jacó's main strip. The decor is refined, with subdued lighting and cloth-covered tables. I recommend starting things off with the lobster and Manchego quesadilla, or the Korean BBQ satay skewers

> *Fish croquettes are among the specialties that keep locals and visitors returning to El Pelicano.*

served with homemade banana ketchup. Seafood main courses include macadamia-crusted mahimahi and seared fresh tuna. There are also daily specials and some outrageously decadent desserts. The wine list here is well priced, and includes several good selections offered by the glass. On the main road in Jacó, toward the southern end of downtown. ☎ 2643-2591. www.lemonzestjaco.com. Entrees $13–$20. AE, MC, V. Dinner Mon–Sat.

kids Rioasis JACÓ *PIZZA/MEXICAN*
Raucous and almost always brimming with diners, Rioasis serves hearty burritos, simple pasta dishes, and a wide array of pizzas freshly baked in a wood oven. My favorite item is probably the Greek pizza, topped with olives, feta cheese, and anchovies; the barbecued chicken pizza is also delicious. There is both indoor and terrace seating, as well as a bar area complete with a pool table, dartboards, and a couple of TVs for sports events and surf videos. On the main road in Jacó, near the center of town. ☎ 2643-3354. Entrees $6–$17. V. Lunch and dinner daily.

Jacó & Playa Herradura after Dark

Jacó is the central Pacific's party town, with tons of bars and several discos. **Disco La Central** (☎ 2643-3076), right on the beach near the center of town, is the largest, loudest, and most popular. For a more refined dance scene, try ★ **Congas** (☎ 2643-1200), located toward the southern end of town, which often has a live salsa band. Both of these spots charge a nominal cover fee. My favorite bar in Jacó is the new beachfront ★★ **Ganesha Lounge** (☎ 2643-3916), which has a laid-back Ibiza-like club vibe. Also new, ★ **Le Loft** (☎ 2643-5846) aims to attract a more sophisticated and chic clubbing crowd. For a more casual scene, head to **Los Amigos** (☎ 2643-2961), **Jacó Taco** (☎ 2643-1313), or ★ **Tabacón** (☎ 2643-3097), all located along the main strip through town. Sports fans can catch games at **Clarita's Beach Bar & Grill** (☎ 2643-2615), right on the beach toward the north end of town, or **Hotel Poseidon** (☎ 2643-1642), on a side street near the center of town. If you're into gaming, head to the large and swank ★★ **Stellaris Casino** at Los Sueños Marriott Ocean & Golf Resort (☎ 2630-9000) in Playa Herradura.

Manuel Antonio

The views from the hills overlooking Manuel Antonio are spectacular, the beaches—especially those inside the area's namesake national park—are idyllic, and the rain forests are crawling with howler, white-faced, and squirrel monkeys, among other forms of exotic wildlife. Offshore, rocky islands dot the vast expanse of blue, and all around, the rich, deep green of the rain forest sweeps down to the water. Manuel Antonio is really more of an area than a town per se, though it does encompass the small port city of Quepos. You'll want to spend at least 3 days exploring the area, which will give you time to visit Manuel Antonio National Park (p. 290).

> The area from Quepos to the southern tip of Manuel Antonio National Park is a favorite destination for surfers and nature lovers.

START **Manuel Antonio is 140km (91 miles) southwest of San José; and 73km (45 miles) south of Jacó.**

❶ ★ kids **Playa Espadilla.** This gray-sand beach is a great place to enjoy sun, sand, sea, and local scenery. Because it's outside the national park and no entrance fee is charged, this is the most popular beach with locals and visiting Ticos. This beach is often perfect for board surfing and bodysurfing, but at times it can be a bit rough for casual swimming. A series of makeshift shops and kiosks across from the water rent body boards, surfboards, beach chairs, and umbrellas. Rates run around $5 to $10 per hour and $20 to $40 per day for a surfboard or body

board. A full-day rental of a beach umbrella and two chaise longues costs around $10. End of the road to Manuel Antonio National Park.

Fincas Naturales is located about halfway along the road between Quepos and the national park, across from Hotel Sí Como No.

Traveler's Tip

As you walk north toward the far end of Playa Espadilla, away from the national park entrance and beyond a rock outcropping, you'll come to a section of the beach that is "clothing optional" and very popular with local and visiting gay and lesbian populations.

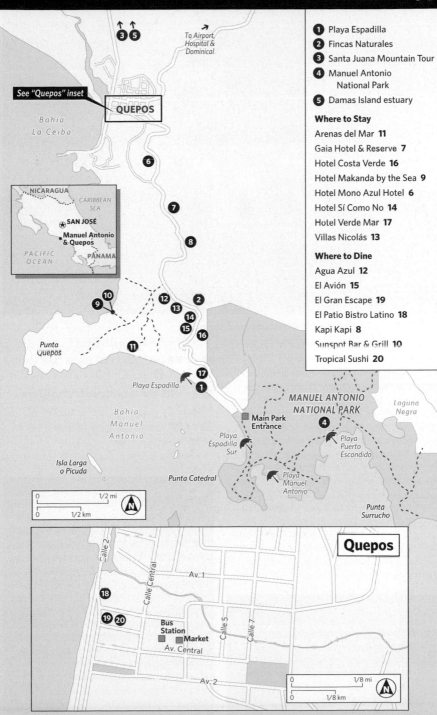

1 Playa Espadilla
2 Fincas Naturales
3 Santa Juana Mountain Tour
4 Manuel Antonio
   National Park
5 Damas Island estuary

Where to Stay
Arenas del Mar 11
Gaia Hotel & Reserve 7
Hotel Costa Verde 16
Hotel Makanda by the Sea 9
Hotel Mono Azul Hotel 6
Hotel Sí Como No 14
Hotel Verde Mar 17
Villas Nicolás 13

Where to Dine
Agua Azul 12
El Avión 15
El Gran Escape 19
El Patio Bistro Latino 18
Kapi Kapi 8
Sunspot Bar & Grill 10
Tropical Sushi 20

To Airport,
Hospital &
Dominical

See "Quepos" inset

QUEPOS

Bahía
La Ceiba

NICARAGUA

CARIBBEAN
SEA

★ SAN JOSÉ

Manuel Antonio
& Quepos

PACIFIC
OCEAN

PANAMA

Punta
Quepos

Playa Espadilla

Bahía
Manuel
Antonio

Isla Larga
o Picuda

Punta Catedral

MANUEL ANTONIO
NATIONAL PARK

Laguna
Negra

Main Park
Entrance

Playa
Espadilla
Sur

Playa
Puerto
Escondido

Playa
Manuel
Antonio

Punta
Surrucho

0   1/2 mi
0   1/2 km

Quepos

Calle 2

Calle Central

Av. 1

Calle 5

Calle 7

Bus
Station

Market

Av. Central

Av. 2

0   1/8 mi
0   1/8 km

> *Manuel Antonio's trails traverse both shoreline and forest.*

② ★★ kids **Fincas Naturales.** A lovely bi-level butterfly garden is the centerpiece attraction at the Nature Farm Reserve. Other exhibits include amphibian ponds, reptile terrariums, and a private reserve with a small network of well-groomed trails through the forest. Several guided tour options are offered, including a night tour, which allows you to see, hear, and get close to a host of rain-forest critters that are active only after dark. ⏱ Minimum 1 hr. On the road btw. Quepos and Manuel Antonio National Park. ☎ 2777-1043. www.wildliferefugecr.com. Rates: 1-hr. guided tour of butterfly garden $15 adults, $8 children 12 and under; butterfly tour and 1-hr. guided hike through forest $35 adults, $25 children 12 and under; 2-hr. night tour $35 adults, $25 children 12 and under. Daily 8am–4pm; night tour 5:30pm.

③ ★★ kids **Santa Juana Mountain Tour.** ⏱ 1 day. See p. 285, **③**.

④ ★★★ kids **Manuel Antonio National Park.** See p. 290.

⑤ ★★ kids **Iguana Tours trip to Damas Island estuary.** See p. 276, **⑥**.

More to Do

All of the hotel desks and tour agencies in town can arrange additional tours and activities, including sportfishing, snorkeling, and scuba trips, visits to Carara National Park (p. 280, **⑤**), sunset sails, white-water river rafting, and horseback-riding outings. See also p. 298 and p. 306.

Big Changes

Manuel Antonio was one of Costa Rica's first major ecotourism destinations and it remains one of its most popular. However, what was once a smattering of small hotels tucked into the forested hillside has become a long string of hotels, restaurants, and shops stretching the entire length of the road between Quepos and the national park entrance. Roofs now regularly break the tree line. A jumble of snack shacks, souvenir stands, and makeshift parking lots chokes the beach road just outside the park, making the entrance road look more like a shantytown than a national park. That said, this remains a beautiful, vibrant, and rewarding destination, with a wide range of attractions and activities.

Where to Stay

> *Arenas del Mar has a splendid beachside location to go with its lavishly appointed accommodations.*

★★★Arenas del Mar

This place has it all—direct beach access, a rain forest setting, fabulous views, and luxurious accommodations. Designed and built by the folks behind Finca Rosa Blanca Coffee Plantation & Inn (p. 89), Arenas del Mar is deeply committed to sustainability. Not all rooms have an ocean view, so be sure to specify if you want one. All are spacious, with stylish decorative accents, and most have an outdoor Jacuzzi on a private balcony. *Note:* The beautiful patch of beach right in front of Arenas has for decades been the town's de facto nude beach. Those who might find this objectionable can walk farther down the beach or stick to the pools. Manuel Antonio, on the beach, about midway between Quepos and the national park entrance. ☎ 2777-2777. www.arenasdelmar.com. 38 units. $260 double; $430 suite; $690 2-bedroom apt. Rates include breakfast. AE, MC, V.

★★ Gaia Hotel & Reserve

This upscale hotel, featuring chic postmodern design and decor, is set on a hilly patch of land and has its own private reserve. The rooms all have wood floors, contemporary furnishings, and a plasma-screen television with complete home-theater system. Each guest is assigned a personal concierge. The spa is extensive

and well run, with a wide range of treatment options and free daily yoga classes. Just outside of Quepos, on the road to the national park entrance. ☎ 800/226-2515 in U.S. and Canada, or 2777-9797 in Costa Rica. www.gaiahr.com. 17 units. $260–$330 double; $350–$495 suite; $840 Gaia suite. Rates include breakfast. AE, MC, V. No children under 16 allowed.

★ Hotel Costa Verde

The Costa Verde offers rooms in a wide range of sizes and prices—some are quite a hike from the hotel's reception area and restaurants, so be forewarned. The best rooms have an ocean view, kitchenette, private balcony, and loads of space. Three small pools are set into the hillside, with views out to the ocean, and the hotel has a

Great View vs. Beach Access

The signature views here do have some drawbacks. If you want a great view, you probably aren't going to be staying on the beach; in fact, you probably won't be able to walk to the beach. This means that you'll be driving back and forth, taking taxis, or riding the public bus—something to keep in mind when you're booking your room.

> *A suite at the sophisticated Gaia Hotel & Reserve.*

couple of miles of private trails through the rain forest. Manuel Antonio, on the road btw. Quepos and the national park entrance. ☎ 866/854-7958 in U.S. and Canada, or 2777-0584 in Costa Rica. www.costaverde.com. 63 units. $115–$350 double. AE, MC, V.

★★ Hotel Makanda by the Sea

Makanda is a gorgeous collection of studio apartments and villas. Every unit comes with a full kitchenette, cable television, and terrace or balcony. The well-tended grounds blend tropical exuberance with a Japanese garden aesthetic. The hotel's pool and Jacuzzi feature a view of the jungle-covered hillsides. The only potential downside? Makanda is set in thick forest, and, despite its name, is a hefty hike—or short drive—from the beach. Manuel Antonio, on a dirt road heading toward the beach about midway along the road btw. Quepos and the national park entrance. ☎ 888/625-2632 in U.S. and Canada, or 2777-0442 in Costa Rica. www.makanda.com. 11 units. $265 double; $400 villa. Rates include breakfast. AE, MC, V.

Hotel Mono Azul

The "Blue Monkey" offers clean and comfortable rooms at a good price. The more expensive rooms have air-conditioning and cable television. The villas have a separate sitting room and kitchenette. While all the rooms are rather Spartan, the place has a lively, hostel-like vibe. The owners are active in a children's arts program aimed at helping preserve the local rain forest and the endangered Central American squirrel monkey. Manuel Antonio, on the road btw. Quepos and the national park entrance, closer to Quepos. ☎ 800/381-3578 in U.S. and Canada, or 2777-2572 in Costa Rica. www.monoazul.com. 29 units. $60–$85 double; $95–$160 villa. AE, DC, MC, V.

★★★ Hotel Sí Como No

This long-standing favorite is a lively, upscale resort that blends in with, and respects, the rain forests and other natural wonders of Manuel Antonio. It is a place equally suited to families traveling with children and to couples looking for a romantic getaway. It's worth the splurge for a superior or deluxe room or a suite, as these are guaranteed to feature stunning views over the forest and onto the Pacific. Manuel Antonio, about midway along the road btw. Quepos and the national park entrance. ☎ 2777-0777. www.sicomono.com. 60 units. $210–$265 double; $305–$340 suite. Rates include breakfast buffet. AE, MC, V.

★ Hotel Verde Mar

This hotel is a great choice for those who want proximity to the national park and the beach. All the rooms have plenty of space, a wrought-iron queen-size bed, tile floors, and a small porch. All but two come with a basic kitchenette, making

> *Accommodations at Hotel Makanda by the Sea range from studio apartments to full villas.*

> *The ship's-prow-shaped balcony at Hotel Sí Como.*

it a good choice for families or those on a budget. The hotel has no restaurant, but plenty are within walking distance. There's also a small pool, for when the surf is too rough. Manuel Antonio, on the beach .75km (½ mile) before the national park entrance. ☎ 877/872-0459 in U.S.

and Canada, or 2777-1805 in Costa Rica. www.verdemar.com. 24 units. $100–$110 double. AE, MC, V.

★★ Villas Nicolás

Built as terraced units on a steep hill in thick forest, these large villas will have you feeling like you're deep in the jungle. Most are large and well appointed and have a separate living room and good-size balcony; some have a kitchenette. During the high season, the hotel opens a restaurant and bar near the pool that serves breakfast and sometimes lunch and dinner, depending on demand. The beach isn't all that close, but you probably won't mind. Manuel Antonio, about midway along the road btw. Quepos and the national park entrance. ☎ 2777-0481. www.villasnicolas.com. 20 units. $168 double; $192 suite. Weekly, monthly, and off-season rates available. AE, MC, V.

A Language School with a View

Escuela D'Amore (☎ 2777-1143; www.escueladamore.com) runs language-immersion programs out of a former hotel with a fabulous view, on the road to Manuel Antonio. A 2-week conversational Spanish course, including a home stay and two meals daily, costs $995.

Where to Dine

> *El Gran Escape, which needs no translation, is one of the best and most popular restaurants in Quepos.*

★ **Agua Azul** *INTERNATIONAL*

With a fabulous perch and panoramic view, this open-air restaurant serves fresh fish and seafood and what I'd call upscale bar food. Tables by the railing fill up fast, so get here well before sunset if you want to snag one. Start things off with a "tuna margarita," an inventive version of ceviche with a lime-and-tequila marinade. Main dishes include coconut-crusted mahimahi and panko-crusted tuna. Manuel Antonio, near Villas del Parque. ☎ 2777-5082. Entrees $9–$18. V. Lunch and dinner Thurs–Tues.

★ kids **El Avión** *SEAFOOD/INTERNATIONAL*

Set on the edge of Manuel Antonio's hillside, with a great view of the ocean and surrounding forests, this place sits under some permanent tents and the starboard wing of a retired military transport plane. You can get great seafood here—usually. Both food quality and service can be inconsistent, and I've had both excellent and extremely disappointing meals here. Manuel Antonio, about midway along the road btw. Quepos and the national park. ☎ 2777-3378. Entrees $8.50–$35. MC, V. Lunch and dinner daily.

★★ **El Gran Escape** *SEAFOOD*

This Quepos landmark is consistently one of the top restaurants in the area. The fish is fresh and expertly prepared, portions are generous, and the prices are reasonable. There is a wide assortment of delicious appetizers, including fresh tuna sashimi. For those who care to venture away from the fish, the menu features hearty steaks and giant burgers. On the main road into Quepos, on the left just past the bridge. ☎ 2777-0395. Entrees $5–$20. Breakfast, lunch, and dinner Wed–Mon.

★★★ **El Patio Bistro Latino** *NUEVO LATINO/FUSION*

By day, this bistro-style cafe serves up a wide range of coffee drinks, as well as full breakfasts, fresh-baked sweets, and salads, sandwiches, wraps, and light lunch dishes. By night, things get more interesting. Fresh mahimahi comes steamed in a banana leaf with a spicy *mojo*, and the tenderloin features a tamarind glaze and is served over roasted local yucca puree. There are nightly specials; you may even find some of their home-roasted coffee used as an ingredient in a glaze, sauce, or dessert. On the main road into Quepos, on the left just past the bridge. ☎ 2777-4982. Entrees $8–$22. AE, MC, V. Breakfast, lunch, and dinner daily.

★★ **Kapi Kapi** *ASIAN FUSION/NUEVO COSTA RICAN*

This open-air restaurant features elegant, understated Asian-influenced decor. Start things off with the Asian-spice-glazed baby

> *El Patio Bistro Latino serves all day, from morning coffee and breakfast to sophisticated nighttime meals.*

back ribs or some seared fresh yellowfin tuna. Or, have the main course seared tuna, which comes encrusted in peppercorns and served with a green papaya salad. For a sample of local flavors order up the grilled shrimp, which are served on sugarcane skewers, with a glaze made from local rum, tamarind, and coconut. On the road btw. Quepos and Manuel Antonio. ☎ 2777-5049. www.restaurantekapikapi.com. Entrees $14–$21. AE, MC, V. Dinner daily.

★★ Sunspot Bar & Grill INTERNATIONAL

Dining by candlelight under a purple canvas tent at one of the few poolside tables here is one of the most romantic dining experiences to be had in Manuel Antonio. The food is some of the best in town as well. The menu changes regularly but features prime meats, poultry, and fresh fish, all excellently prepared. There are nightly specials and a good selection of salads, appetizers, and desserts. At Hotel Makanda by the Sea (p. 322). ☎ 2777-0442. Entrees $10–$30. V. Lunch and dinner daily.

Tropical Sushi SUSHI/JAPANESE

While the ambience here is decidedly tropical, this is an excellent sushi joint. The maki, sushi, and sashimi are made with tuna and grouper brought in daily by local fishermen, as well as with Chilean salmon, smoked eel, and deep-fried soft-shell crabs. The sushi bar itself is tiny, and the main dining room is similarly small. The biggest problem here is that the service can be excruciatingly slow when the place is busy. On a side street next to El Gran Escape, Quepos. ☎ 2777-1710. Maki rolls $5–$10; entrees $6–$12. V. Dinner daily.

Manuel Antonio after Dark

The bars at **Barba Roja** (☎ 2777-0331) restaurant and **Hotel Sí Como No** (p. 322) are good places to hang out and meet people in the evening. For shooting pool, I head to the ★ **Billfish Sportbar & Grill** at the Byblos Resort (☎ 2777-0411). For drinks and tapas, try **Salsipuedes** (☎ 2777-5019), which translates as "get out if you can." All of the above are located along the road between Quepos and Manuel Antonio National Park. In downtown Quepos, **Sargento Garcia's** (☎ 2777-2960), **Wacky Wanda's** (☎ 2777-2245), and **Fish Head Bar** (☎ 2777-0395) at El Gran Escape are all popular hangouts. If you want live music, **Bambu Jam** (☎ 2777-3369), located along the road between Quepos and the national park entrance, and **Dos Locos** (☎ 2777-1526), in the heart of downtown Quepos, are your best bets. If you enjoy gaming tables, the **Hotel Kamuk** (☎ 2777-0811) in Quepos and the **Byblos Resort** (☎ 2777-0411) on the road to Manuel Antonio both have small **casinos** and will even foot your cab bill if you try your luck and lay down your money.

Dominical & the Coastline Southward

With miles of often-deserted beaches backed by rain forest–covered mountains, Dominical and the coastline southward are as isolated as you'll get in this part of Costa Rica. The tiny town of Dominical and its beach are one of Costa Rica's prime surf destinations. Continuing south, you'll find the remote beaches of Dominicalito and Playa Hermosa; Ballena Marine National Park, a protected area encompassing offshore reefs and whale feeding grounds; and a seemingly endless expanse of sea and sand. You'll want to spend a few days here, including some time to explore the nearby bird-watcher's paradise Carara National Park.

> Nauyaca is one of the most spectacular waterfalls in Costa Rica—and in this land of flowing water, that's saying something.

START **Dominical is 42km (26 miles) south of Quepos–Manuel Antonio; 160km (99 miles) south of San José.**

❶ ★★★ **Cataratas Nauyaca.** This full-day tour takes you to one of the most beautiful jungle waterfalls in Costa Rica. Run by a local farmer who owns the land, the tour includes both breakfast and lunch at the family farmstead, as well as a horseback ride to the falls. ⏱ 1 day. See p. 283, ⓲.

Parque Reptilandia is 7km (4⅓ miles) northeast of Dominical on CR243.

❷ ★★ kids **Parque Reptilandia.** This is the best reptile park in Costa Rica—which is really saying something. See p. 287, ❾.

Skyline Ultralight Flights is 16km (10 miles) south of Dominical on the Costanera Hwy.

❸ **Skyline Ultralight Flights.** Located near the beach in Uvita, this operation offers guided ultralight flights ranging from a short 20-minute introductory flight to an hour-long exploration of Ballena Marine National Park and its neighboring mangrove forests. This is a great way to get an aerial view of the "whale's tail" formation of sand, rock, and coral at Ballena.

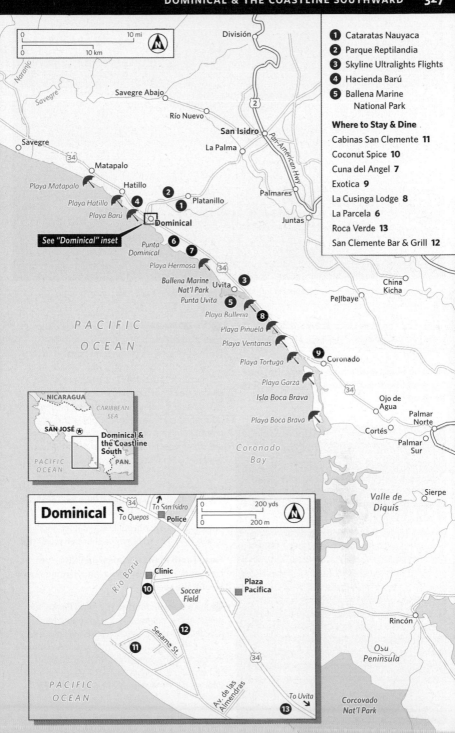

> *Sandbars in Ballena National Park make a formation in the shape of a whale's tail.*

🕐 20 min.–1 hr. Playa Uvita. ☎ 2743-8037. www.flyultralight.com. Rates $65–$160. Daily 8am–5pm.

Hacienda Barú is just north of Dominical on the road to Quepos, 1.5km (1 mile) north of the Río Barú bridge.

Additional Adventures

Like most Costa Rican beach towns, Dominical offers a host of adventure activities, including kayak tours of the mangroves, river floats in inner tubes, day tours by boat to Isla del Caño (p. 343, ⑫) and Corcovado National Park (p. 348), and sportfishing excursions. Humpback whales migrate southward each year and can be spotted from boats off Ballena Marine National Park between late July and November and mid-December through March. If you're lucky, your day tour to Isla del Caño or Corcovado National Park might include a whale sighting. To arrange any of these activities, check in with ★ **Dominical Adventures** (☎ 2787-0191; at the San Clemente Bar & Grill) or ★ **Southern Expeditions** (☎ 2787-0100; www.southernexpeditionscr.com). And if you're interested in scuba diving or snorkeling, contact the folks at ★ **Mystic Dive Center** (p. 301).

④ ★★ kids **Hacienda Barú.** This place offers several hikes and tours, including a good bird-watching walk through mangroves and along the riverbank; a rain-forest hike through 80 hectares (200 acres) of virgin jungle; an all-day trek from beach to mangrove forest to jungle, which includes a visit to see ancient petroglyphs; an overnight camping trip; and a combination horseback-and-hiking tour. There are even tree-climbing tours and a small canopy platform 30m (100 ft.) above the ground, as well as one of the more common zip-line canopy tours. Truly adventurous travelers might want to sign up for the night tour, which begins with an afternoon hike to a rustic rain-forest jungle camp, where you'll have dinner and spend the night. 🕐 Minimum 1 hr. See p. 287, ⑧.

Head south from Dominical on CR34, turn right at the village of Bahía, and continue until you hit the ocean.

⑤ ★★★ **Ballena Marine National Park.** The beach at this national park is arguably the prettiest along this whole section of coast—especially at low tide, when an exposed sandbar connects with some offshore rocks and reefs, forming what appears, from the air, to be a whale's tail. 🕐 Minimum 2 hr. See p. 283, ⑯.

Where to Stay & Dine

> *The second-floor rooms at Cuna del Angel have private balconies.*

Cabinas San Clemente DOMINICAL
The owners of this hotel also own the town's most popular restaurant, San Clemente Bar & Grill (p. 331). Rooms are in three separate buildings, all of them right on the beach. There are a variety of accommodations to suit most budgets; the best are second-floor rooms with wood floors and a wraparound veranda. On the beach, Dominical. ☎ 2787-0026 or 2787-0055. 19 units, 16 with private bathroom. $10 per person with shared bathroom; $30–$40 double with private bathroom. AE, MC, V.

★ **Coconut Spice** DOMINICAL *THAI/INDIAN*
This simple open-air place serves up excellent and reasonably authentic Thai, Malaysian, Indonesian, and Indian cuisine. The lemon-grass soup and Pad Thai are both excellent. Chicken, pork, and shrimp are all offered in a selection of red, green, yellow, and Panang curry sauces. Dominical, in the Pueblo del Río shopping complex. ☎ 2787-0073 or 8834-8103. Entrees $7–$13.50. V. Lunch and dinner daily.

★★ **Cuna del Angel** DOMINICALITO
The English translation is Angel's Cradle, and the owners take that seriously. Angel motifs are abundant, as are stained-glass windows and lampshades, carved wood details, tile mosaics, and other artistic touches. The hotel is a bit far from the beach, but there are ocean views from many of the rooms and from the common areas. Rooms come with either an open patio fronting the pool or a private balcony. I prefer the second-floor rooms with a balcony. 9km (5½ miles) south of Dominical, just off the Costanera Hwy. (CR34). ☎ 2787-8436. www.cunadelangel. com. 16 units. $97–$178 double. Rates include breakfast. AE, MC, V.

★★ **Exotica** OJOCHAL *FRENCH/INTERNATIONAL*
Tucked back along a dirt road in Ojochal, with polished concrete floors, roll-up bamboo screens for walls, and only a few tree-trunk slab tables and plastic lawn chairs for furniture, it's worth the 25-minute drive to seek out this local

> *San Clemente Bar & Grill is both a popular eatery and a happening nightspot.*

fave. The chalkboard menu changes regularly but might feature such dishes as shrimp in a coconut curry sauce or chicken exotica, which is stuffed with bacon, prunes, and cheese and topped with a red-pepper coulis. 31km (19 miles) south of Dominical, then 1km (⅔ mile) inland from the turnoff for Ojochal. ☎ 2786-5050. Entrees $5–$27. MC, V. Breakfast, lunch, and dinner Mon–Sat.

La Cusinga Lodge BALLENA

This should be a top choice for bird-watchers or anyone looking for a cozy lodge that feels entirely in touch with its natural surroundings. The cabins feature lots of varnished woodwork; large screened windows on all sides provide cross ventilation. Most have interesting stone and tile work in the bathroom. The lodge is set on a hill overlooking Ballena Marine National Park and Playa Uvita. Bahía Ballena. ☎ 2770-2549. www.lacusingalodge.com. 7 units. $135–$160 double. Rates include breakfast. MC, V.

La Parcela DOMINICALITO SEAFOOD/

INTERNATIONAL This open-air restaurant has a perfect setting on a rocky bluff overlooking the ocean. The menu features fresh seafood, meat, and poultry dishes, as well as a selection of pastas. Start things off with a tuna tartare tower, and then try either the fresh mahimahi with a mango relish or the filet mignon in a porcini mushroom sauce. At Punta Dominical, Dominicalito (5km/3 miles south of Dominical).

Honing Your Language & Surf Skills

If you're looking to learn or bone up on your Spanish, **Adventure Education Center** (☎ 2787-0023; www.adventurespanishschool.com), located right in the heart of Dominical, offers a variety of immersion-style language programs. One of their more interesting options is a combined language and surf school program. In addition to 4 hours a day of Spanish language classes, this week-long program includes a surfboard rental for the entire week and two 2-hour surf lessons. You have the option of staying in a hotel-like room on the campus, or living with a local family. The whole thing runs $490 per person.

> With its beachside location, Tortilla Flats is a great place to hang out after dark.

☎ 2787-0016. Entrees $8–$31. V. Breakfast, lunch, and dinner daily.

★ Roca Verde DOMINICAL

Located just south of town on a protected little cove with rocks and tide pools, this place has the best beachfront accommodations in Dominical. The rooms are located in a two-story building beside the swimming pool. Each comes with one queen-size and one twin bed and a small patio or balcony. The rooms are a bit close to the bar, and during high season, if the bar is raging, it can sometimes be hard to get to sleep early. 1km (⅔ mile) south of the Río Barú bridge in Dominical, just off the Costanera Hwy. (CR34). ☎ 2787-0036. www.rocaverde.net. 10 units. $65–$75 double. MC, V.

★ San Clemente Bar & Grill DOMINICAL

MEXICAN/AMERICAN The menu at this popular surfer hangout features a large selection of Mexican and American fare ranging from tacos and burritos to sandwiches, all of which you can get with fresh fish. There are also several more substantial plates and nightly specials. Just off the restaurant is a large bar that has pool and foosball tables; this is one of the town's livelier nightspots, particularly on Fridays. Next to the soccer field, Dominical. ☎ 2787-0055. Entrees $3.50–$8. MC, V. Breakfast, lunch, and dinner daily.

Dominical after Dark

The local party scene moves around town from night to night. **Maracutú** (☎ 2787-0091) hosts an open jam session every Tuesday and a reggae night every Thursday. A loud and late-night dancing scene usually takes place Fridays at **San Clemente Bar & Grill** (right), next to the soccer field, and Saturdays at **Roca Verde** (above), off the Costanera Highway just south of town. In addition, **Thrusters** (☎ 2787-0127), on the main road in Dominical, is a popular bar with pool tables and dartboards. If you want to hang within earshot of the waves, **Tortilla Flats** (☎ 2787-0168), located on the beach, is your best bet.

Central Pacific Coast Fast Facts

> A snow-cone vendor helps visitors beat the heat on Playa Espadilla.

Accommodations Booking Services
In just about all instances, you are best off booking direct with the hotels and resorts listed here. If you're looking for a longer-term stay or condo rental, see "Renting a Home, Not a Room," p. 289.

ATMs
You'll find at least one bank with a cash machine (cajero automatico) in all of the towns and villages listed in this chapter.

Dentists & Doctors
The only major hospital along the central Pacific coast is the Quepos Hospital (☎ 2777-0922) in Quepos. If you have a mild medical issue or dental problem while traveling around the central Pacific coast, most hotels will be able to refer you to a local doctor (medico) or dentist (dentista) who speaks English.

Emergencies
In case of emergency, call ☎ 911 (there should be an English-speaking operator); if 911 doesn't work, contact the police at ☎ 2222-1365 or 2221-5337, and ask them to find someone who speaks English to translate. For an ambulance, call ☎ 128; to report a fire, call ☎ 118.

For a medical emergency that doesn't require an ambulance, see "Dentists & Doctors," above. To report lost or stolen items, see "Police," p. 333.

Getting There & Getting Around
BY PLANE Whether you fly into San José's **Juan Santamaría International Airport** or Liberia's **Daniel Oduber International Airport,** you'll have several options for onward travel to the central Pacific coast.

Both local commuter airlines **Sansa** (☎ 877/767-2672 in U.S. and Canada, or 2290-4100 in Costa Rica; www.flysansa.com) and **Nature Air** (☎ 800/235-9272 in U.S. and Canada, or 2299-6000 in Costa Rica; www.natureair.com) have a host of daily flights from San José to the small airstrip in Quepos. Fares run between $75 and $80 each way. BY CAR A car comes in handy when traveling around the central Pacific coast. In general, the main roads along this stretch of coast are in pretty good shape. Off the main highway (the Costanera, CR34), road conditions vary widely, from rough dirt and gravel tracks to recently paved two-lane thoroughfares. Definitely rent a four-wheel-drive vehicle.

Like everywhere else in Costa Rica, roads here are poorly marked. In many cases, your best signage and directions will come from hotel and resort advertisements and billboards. If you're heading from one central Pacific beach town to another, it's always a good idea to know the names of a few major hotels in your target destination.

To get to the coast by car from San José, you'll take a narrow and winding two-lane road, the "old highway," known locally as La Cuesta del Aguacate (Avocado Hill), over and through mountains. The old highway meets the coastal highway, the Costanera (CR34), a few kilometers west of Orotina. From there it's a straight shot down the coast to Jacó, and on to Quepos/Manuel Antonio and Dominical. **Note:** By the time this book goes to press, the drive time should be substantially reduced with the opening of the new CR27 highway connecting San José (via the western suburbs of Escazú, Santa Ana, and Ciudad Colón) with Orotina and the Costanera Hwy. The tolls should total around $5, spread over several toll stations along the route.

BY BUS OR SHUTTLE Though a rental car gives you more freedom and flexibility, the main towns and beaches can be toured by local buses and private shuttles. **Gray Line** (☎ 2220-2126; www.graylinecostarica.com) and **Interbus** (☎ 2283-5573; www.interbusonline.com) are two private shuttle companies with daily scheduled departures to Jacó and Manuel Antonio, and connections elsewhere.

Internet Access

More and more hotels, resorts, and retailers around Costa Rica are offering high-speed Wi-Fi access, either free or for a small fee. Moreover, you'll readily find Internet cafes in all major towns and tourist destinations around the central Pacific coast. Rates run between 50¢ and $3 per hour, and connection speeds are generally pretty good.

Pharmacies

You'll find pharmacies (*farmacias*) on the main streets in Quepos, Manuel Antonio, Jacó, and

Dominical. If you have trouble finding one, ask at your hotel.

Police

To report a lost or stolen article, such as a wallet or passport, visit the local police. Depending upon your location, that may be either the OIJ (judicial police), *guardia rural* (rural guard), or *policía metropolitana* (metro police). The number for the *policía de tránsito* (transit police) is ☎ 800/8726-7486, toll-free nationwide, or ☎ 2222-9330. See also "Emergencies," p. 332.

Post Offices

Post offices are easy to find in all of the towns mentioned here—just ask at your hotel.

Safety

Most of the beach towns and tourist destinations of the central Pacific coast are relatively safe. That said, never leave items of value unattended in rental cars, in hotel rooms (unless locked in a safe), or on the beach. Moreover, single women, couples, and small groups of tourists should probably avoid walking on desolate stretches of beach or back roads after dark.

Toilets

These are known as *sanitarios* or *servicios sanitarios*. You might also hear them called *baños*. They are marked *damas* (women) and *hombres* or *caballeros* (men). Public restrooms are rare to nonexistent, but most hotels, restaurants, and attractions catering to tourists will let you use their restrooms if you ask.

Visitor Information

There are no official information offices or bureaus on the central Pacific coast. Your best source of information—beyond this guide book—will be your hotel front desk and any of the local tour agencies.

Water

Although most of this area has potable water, most hotels still advise you to drink bottled water, and I second that recommendation. *Sin hielo* means "no ice," and this is what you'll want to say if you're nervous about the water—even when frozen it's still water.

My Favorite Southern Zone Moments

Costa Rica's Southern Zone is a remote region of awe-inspiring beauty, where lushly forested mountains tumble into the sea, scarlet macaws squawk raucously overhead, and dolphins and whales frolic in the waters offshore. But seeing this area, which runs south of the Río Terraba to the Panamanian border, requires patience. It's remote and hard to reach. If you invest the time, the payoff is tremendous. The Southern Zone's most popular destination is the Osa Peninsula, home to massive Corcovado National Park and flanked to the east by the lovely Golfo Dulce (Sweet Gulf). Scattered around the park and the Golfo Dulce are some of the country's finest ecolodges.

> *PREVIOUS PAGE Pavones surf break.*
> *THIS PAGE Wilson Botanical Gardens.*

❶ Diving or snorkeling off Isla del Caño. The rock and coral formations off this uninhabited island provide some of the best scuba diving and snorkeling opportunities in the whole country. Even when the visibility is low, you'll still enjoy the trip, and you might see dolphins and whales en route. See p. 343, ⓬.

❷ Whale-watching out of Drake Bay. Humpback whales migrate to the waters just off Drake Bay each year between late July and November, and again from mid-December through March. See p. 355.

❸ Taking the "Bug Lady's" rain-forest night tour. There are scores of night tours around Costa Rica, but the informative hike offered by Tracie Stice is my favorite. In addition to the many invertebrates you will see, there's a chance you'll spot owls, snakes, and even, if you're lucky, a kinkajou. Just be warned, this is not for the arachnophobic. See p. 358, ❷.

❹ Kayaking on the Golfo Dulce. Kayaking the Sweet Gulf is an experience you won't soon forget. Whether you're poking around its coastal mangroves, paddling amongst a pod of dolphins, or bobbing lazily as the sun sets, it's—as they say—*pura vida* (pure life). See p. 354.

❺ Taking the Psycho Tours rain-forest adventure tour. This full-day tour begins with a hike up and through a rain-forest river and its rapids. You'll then climb a tree, take a flying leap into thin air (don't worry, you're in a harness), and finish up by rappelling down the face of a jungle waterfall. Even better, you're in the midst of deep, lush, and beautiful primary lowland

1. Dive or snorkel off Isla del Caño
2. Whale-watching trip from Drake Bay
3. The Bug Lady's night tour
4. Kayaking on the Golfo Dulce
5. Psycho Tours rain-forest adventure
6. Ecolodges
7. Corcovado National Park
8. Wilson Botanical Gardens
9. Drinking rainwater

tropical rain forest the entire time. See p. 341, **7**.

6 Basking in jungle luxury at a top ecolodge.
When everything around you is rough and rugged, it's nice to know you can count on a little pampering at the end of the day. This region is home to several of the country's top ecolodges. Whether you choose Bosque del Cabo Rainforest Lodge (p. 364), La Paloma Lodge (p. 361), Lapa Ríos (p. 365), or Playa Nicuesa Rainforest Lodge (p. 369), you'll be pleased. Trust me, they are all spectacular.

7 Hiking in Corcovado National Park.
Protecting Costa Rica's largest single expanse of lowland tropical rain forest, Corcovado

National Park is a hotbed of biodiversity and beauty. See p. 348.

8 Visiting Wilson Botanical Gardens. Part of a research facility, these amazingly well tended gardens feature more than 7,000 species of tropical flora from around the world. The trails are wide, well marked, and fascinating, and the bird-watching is also fabulous. See p. 367, **4**.

9 Drinking pure rainwater you've collected yourself. Don't let the rains here get you down—they put the "rain" in rain forest, after all. Instead, find a large leaf and fashion a jungle funnel into a glass or cup, and within minutes you'll be sipping delicious, unfiltered, pure water.

The Best of the Southern Zone in 1 Week

Because this region is so remote and spread out, and getting around is such a challenge, you'll definitely need a week to properly explore it. This trip takes in the country's biggest and most diverse botanical gardens and brings you into the heart of its most impressive national park. You'll start in the surf mecca of Pavones, and then head across the Golfo Dulce to the Osa Peninsula, where you'll explore Corcovado National Park before finishing your adventure in Drake Bay. You'll enjoy your fair share of intense adventure, traveling by small plane, boat, four-wheel-drive taxi, and foot. There are very few roads here, so don't worry about renting a car.

> Surfers flock to Pavones, which offers one of the longest continuous rides in the world.

START Pavones. Fly from San José to Golfito (flight time: 1 hour) and take a taxi or boat to Pavones, which is 40km (25 miles) south of Golfito by road, 32km (20 miles) by boat, and then a taxi on to Tiskita Jungle Lodge. **TOUR LENGTH** 274km (170 miles).

❶ ★★ Tiskita Jungle Lodge. This ecolodge, located just a bit south of Pavones, has an excellent network of trails through its private reserve. Even if you're not staying here (p. 373), sign up for the half-day hike, which will take you through a variety of ecosystems and includes a stop at a beautiful jungle waterfall. You'll also get to sample a wealth of fresh fruit from the resort's extensive collection of tropical fruit trees. ⊕ 4 hr. 6km (3¾ miles) south of Pavones. ☎ 2296-8125. www.tiskita-lodge.co.cr. Rate $20 half-day hike. See p. 372, ❺.

Key (map legend):

1. Tiskita Jungle Lodge
2. Café de la Suerte
3. Pavones
4. Sol y Mar
5. Wilson Botanical Gardens
6. Puerto Jiménez
7. Psycho Tours
8. Juanita's Mexican Bar & Grille
9. Pavo-Guanacaste-La Sirena loop trail
10. Claro Trail
11. Hike from La Sirena to San Pedrillo
12. Isla del Caño
13. Río Agujitas kayaking trip

Return to Pavones by taxi.

(2) ☕ ★ **Café de la Suerte.** Enjoy lunch at this lively little open-air joint, which specializes in vegetarian fare, fresh-baked goods, and fresh fruit smoothies. The falafel is excellent. Pavones center, across from Esquina del Mar, beside the soccer field. ☎ 8879-0302 or 2776-2388. www.cafedelasuerte.com. $.

(3) ★★★ **Pavones.** Rather confusingly, Pavones refers to a town, a beach, and a beach break. Perhaps that's because surfing is the main focus here—this is one of the most famous and

More Information

For stops 1–5 of this tour, you'll base yourself in the Playa Zancudo–Pavones area (p. 370); for stops 6–8 you'll be based in Puerto Jiménez (p. 362); and for 9–11 you'll stay at La Sirena ranger station in Corcovado National Park (p. 348). For stops 12 and 13, you'll want to pick an ecolodge in Drake Bay (p. 359).

For information on getting around this area by boat, see "Getting Around, Made Easy," p. 341.

> *Tiskita Jungle Lodge opens its beautiful grounds, including trails in a private nature reserve, to nonguests.*

sought-after waves on the planet. Either hit the water and catch a few waves, or grab a seat at **Esquina del Mar** (no phone), a funky bar and simple restaurant on the water's edge, and watch the steady stream of adventurous surfers take the ride of their lives. See p. 354.

Take a 30-minute boat ride from Pavones to Playa Zancudo.

❹ ★★ **Sol y Mar.** You'll want to get to Playa Zancudo in time for the sunset, because this beachfront hotel has the best bar and restaurant in town. Have them fix up your beverage of choice, and then hit the sand to watch the sun set over the Golfo Dulce. Once the light show is over, head back inside and have dinner. The fresh seafood is tops, but if you're here on a Monday or Friday, don't pass on the barbecue. At Cabinas Sol y Mar. ☎ 2776-0014. See p. 373.

On Day 2, you'll be picked up at your hotel for the following tour.

❺ ★★★ **Boat tour to Wilson Botanical Gardens.** These are the most extensive and impressive botanical gardens in the country, which is really saying something. The trails are wide, impeccably manicured, and well marked, making the gardens suitable for self-guided explorations. However, the best way to visit is as part

of a tour with the folks at **Zancudo Boat Tours** (p. 370, ❶). They make getting here easy, and you'll learn a lot about what you are seeing. ⏲ 4–6 hr. See p. 367, ❹.

On the morning of Day 3, you'll be picked up at your hotel for the 20-minute boat ride across the Golfo Dulce to Puerto Jiménez, 18km (11 miles) west of Playa Zancudo.

A Hard Rain

The Southern Zone is one of the wettest regions in Costa Rica, and you'll want to plan your visit here accordingly. From mid-September through October—the height of the rainy season—some of the Southern Zone's best hikes are impassable and closed to visitors. Additionally, many hotels and small lodges in the area close for all or parts of the period. But whether or not the hotel or lodge you choose is open, I strongly advise travelers to think twice about visiting this region during these months, which are the worst of the season. Not only will you get drenched, you'll miss out on seeing some truly fabulous sights.

6 Puerto Jiménez. Puerto Jiménez is a rustic jungle town and the principal gateway to Corcovado National Park. You'll need advance reservations for a park visit, and you'll spend the morning here making final arrangements for your excursion the next day (**9**–**11**). Upon arriving, you must check in with the **ACOSA** (Area de Conservación de Osa; see "Entering the park," p. 348), which manages access to the park. Now is also the time to stock up on any supplies you may need for your trip. Be sure to bring lots of water. See p. 362.

Spend the rest of Day 3 on the following adventure tour; make arrangements to be picked up in the late morning.

Getting Around, Made Easy

The Southern Zone is a remote and rugged region, and it's far less traveled than some other parts of Costa Rica. Your biggest logistical challenge likely won't be where to stay or what to do—it'll be how to get around. Not to worry—it's actually quite easy if you let others do the flying, driving, and captaining for you. Throughout the region, local lodges and tour operators generally provide transportation or facilitate the logistics. I'd recommend flying into Golfito and using **Zancudo Boat Tours** (☎ 2776-0012; www.loscocos. com) for your travels to, from, and between Playa Zancudo, Pavones, Puerto Jiménez, and Golfito. You can also easily hire a four-wheel-drive taxi in all of the tourist towns in this region. In Pavones, for example, four-wheel-drive taxi is the best way to and from Tiskita Jungle Lodge. For local flights in the region, contact **Alfa Romeo Air Charters** (☎ 2735-5353 or 2735-5112; www.alfaromeoair.com). Your hotel can help you make any needed arrangements, and prices will vary based on where you're going and when.

> The bar at Sol y Mar in Zancudo offers a great vantage for the sunset.

7 ★★★ **kids** **Rain-forest adventure tour with Psycho Tours.** You can choose from a veritable menu of adventure tours here, but I recommend their signature combo trip, which features a free-climb (with a safety rope attached) up the roots and trunks of a 60m-tall (200-ft.) strangler fig. You can climb as high as your ability allows, but most try to reach a natural platform at around 18m (60 ft.), where you take a leap of faith into space and let your guide belay you down. The climb is preceded by an informative hike through primary rain forest, often involving some wading through a small river, and followed by a couple of rappels down jungle waterfalls, the highest of which is around 30m (100 ft.). Alternatively, you can opt to stick with just a hike, the tree climb, or the waterfall rappelling. ◷ 3–6 hrs. Matapalo. ☎ 8353-8619. www.psychotours.com. Rates $45–$85 for individual tours, $120 6-hr. combination tour. Daily 8am–4pm.

⑧ 🍺 ★ **Juanita's Mexican Bar & Grille.** The night before you head off to the jungle, have a full meal and some good times at this lively downtown spot. Puerto Jiménez. ☎ 2735-5056. $$. See p. 365.

Day 4 begins with a quick flight from Puerto Jiménez to La Sirena, 33km (21 miles) across the Osa Peninsula (see "Flying to La Sirena," below, for more information). If you leave early enough you should have time to do two hikes in the park on Day 4.

⑨ ★★ **Pavo-Guanacaste–La Sirena loop trail, Corcovado National Park.** This trail takes you through the heart of the rain forest surrounding La Sirena ranger station and to the mouth of Río Sirena. I recommend starting on the Pavo Trail, which heads west from the ranger station, and is relatively flat and gentle. The Pavo, via the Guanacaste Trail, hooks up with La Sirena Trail, which will take you down along the river toward the river mouth and beach. This is a relatively short and easy hike—the entire loop is 5km (3.1 miles)—which makes it a nice warm-up for your upcoming long hike out of the park.

If the tide is rising or high, you should be able to spot the fins of bull sharks feeding in the river mouth. Up along the banks large crocodiles are common. After enjoying the river mouth, take the little spur that leads directly to the beach before heading back to the ranger station for lunch. ⏱ Minimum 3 hr. See p. 350, ❹.

⑩ ★★ **Claro Trail, Corcovado National Park.** This trail heads out from the southeastern side of the ranger station and takes you down to and along the banks of the Río Claro. If you plan on doing any swimming, you'll want to find the popular, calm, and clear swimming hole relatively far up the river, about 2km (1.25 miles) from La Sirena ranger station. Ask at the station

for directions, and be sure to check well for crocodiles—they are found around here—before you swim. It's another 1.4km (.9 miles) to the mouth of the river. I recommend finishing your hike by returning along the 2km (1.25-mile) Naranjo Trail, which is more direct and quicker. ⏱ Minimum 3 hr. See p. 350, ❹.

Get an early start on Day 5 (before dawn), as you will be embarking on a long day's hike out of the park. For details and alternative arrangements, see "Packing Up," p. 343.

Flying to La Sirena

Corcovado is one of Costa Rica's most awe-inspiring national parks. Unfortunately, there are only two ways into the heart of Corcovado National Park from Puerto Jiménez—a full-day hike or a 20-minute flight. I vote that you save your strength for hiking the trails inside Corcovado National Park around La Sirena ranger station (p. 350, ❹) and for the long hike out. Instead, fly in to La Sirena with **Alfa Romeo Air Charters** (p. 341). The flight will cost $400 total for a plane that can carry five passengers. Once you arrive you should set up your tent, or choose your bunk, and get ready for your first hike inside this spectacular national park. See the tour starting on p. 348 for more information on making arrangements both to visit and to stay in the park. ⏱ 1 hr. Puerto Jiménez airstrip.

Alternative Route

If camping isn't your idea of fun, or if you don't feel up to tackling several major hikes, you'll want to skip stops ⑨–⑪. Instead, stay at your hotel in Puerto Jiménez and arrange a day trip to Corcovado National Park on Day 4. On Day 5, take a boat to Drake Bay and relax on the beach.

⑪ ★★★ Hike from La Sirena to San Pedrillo.
This is the signature hike inside Corcovado
National Park. The trailhead begins just a bit
down the landing strip at La Sirena. Much of
the 23km (14-mile) trek is along beach that is
backed by thick rain forest. The trail takes you
across three major rivers and various streams.
It is best to start off on this hike at night, at
least a few hours before dawn, as there's little
protection from the sun. It is safe—a ranger will
go over the entire route with you and then walk
with you until you cross the first major river. Be
sure to have prior arrangements with a lodge in
Drake Bay to pick you up at the ranger station at
San Pedrillo. ⏱ 8–9 hr. See p. 351, **⑤**.

**On Day 6, you'll be picked up at your hotel for
a Caño Island trip.**

⑫ ★★★ kids Isla del Caño. You'll spend Day 6
enjoying a full-day tour to this stunning offshore
island. Officially known as the Caño Island
Biological Reserve, it is a must for any visitor to
Drake Bay. The island, currently uninhabited, was
home to a pre-Columbian culture about which
little is known. Most visits here include a hike to
an ancient cemetery, where you'll be able to see
some of the stone spheres believed to have been
carved by this area's ancient inhabitants. Few animals or birds live on the island itself, but the coral
reefs and rocky outcroppings just offshore teem
with life and are the main reason most people
come here. This is one of Costa Rica's prime
scuba diving and snorkeling spots. Visibility is
often quite good, and even snorkelers have been
known to spot sea turtles, eagle rays, whitetip
reef sharks, and many other oceanic creatures.
⏱ 1 day. 19km (12 miles) offshore from Drake Bay.
Rates $75–$120 for a full-day tour, arranged through
any Drake Bay–area lodging.

**On Day 7, use your hotel's kayaks and hit the
water in the morning.**

⑬ ★★ Kayaking the Río Agujitas. All flights out
of Drake Bay (and there aren't many, so book
ahead) leave either in the early morning or in
the late afternoon. I suggest you plan to catch an
afternoon flight, because then you'll have time to
play around in a kayak on the Río Agujitas and its
namesake bay. If the tide is high, I definitely recommend paddling as far up the Agujitas as you
can before floating back down in time to catch
your flight. ⏱ Minimum 2 hr. See p. 360, **⑤**.

> Kayakers on the Río Agujitas near its mouth at
  Drake Bay.

Packing Up

You can fly out of Corcovado National Park
from La Sirena to Drake Bay or hike out to San
Pedrillo and arrange to be picked up by your
hotel in Drake Bay. In order to do the hike
from La Sirena to San Pedrillo (⑪), you will
need to either travel with a backpack that can
carry all of your belongings, or else arrange
with your lodge in Drake Bay to not only pick
up you in San Pedrillo, but also to pick up
your bags in La Sirena. This is not as hard as it
sounds, as most lodges in Drake Bay run day
trips to La Sirena or can send a boat.

The Southern Zone with Kids

Families with a love of the outdoors will fare very well in the Southern Zone. I recommend basing yourselves along the southern Osa Peninsula. There are a host of active adventures to enjoy and great opportunities to interact with the rain forest's flora and fauna. For the most part, you should forget about such modern conveniences as televisions, air-conditioning, and video games—unless you bring your own. But between the surf lessons, kayak trips, dolphin viewing, and tree climbing, I don't think the televisions and video games will be that sorely missed. You'll be taking lots of guided tours, so there's no need for a rental car.

> The Central American squirrel monkey is Costa Rica's most endangered primate.

START Puerto Jiménez. Fly from San José to Puerto Jiménez (flight time: 1 hour). Make arrangements with your lodging for transportation from there. **TOUR LENGTH** 4 days; 100km (62 miles).

❶ ★★★ Escondido Trex mangrove kayak tour. On this gentle guided tour, parents paddle young children in two-person kayaks; kids over 10 should be able to handle their own boat.

This trip offers great bird-watching opportunities, with scores of shorebirds and seabirds on display. You'll see ibises and various species of herons. Keep your fingers crossed that you get to see a caiman or crocodile. Several operators run this sort of tour, but I recommend going with Escondido Trex. ⏱ 3–4 hr. ☎ 2735-5210. www.escondidotrex.com. Rates $40 adults, $25 children 11 and under. Reservations required.

Map legend:

1. Escondido Trex mangrove kayak tour
2. Herrera Botanical Gardens
3. Psycho Tours
4. Playa Platanares
5. Pollo's Surf School
6. Escondido Trex dolphin-watching tour
7. Corcovado National Park

Take a 15-minute taxi ride to the next stop.

2 ★★ **Herrera Botanical Gardens.** Your kids might be turned off by the idea of visiting a botanical garden, regardless of how fabulous the flora is. Fill them in: This place has very cool (and kid-friendly) tree platforms they can climb up to; the views are well worth the effort. ⏱ 2–3 hr. Puerto Jiménez; entrance across from Crocodile Bay Resort. ☎ 2735-5210. Admission $5 self-guided tour, $20 2½-hr. guided tour. Daily 9am–4pm.

You'll be picked up at your hotel early on Day 2 by Psycho Tours.

> Kids and adults alike will enjoy a paddle through the mangroves.

> *One thing you'll get to do on a rain-forest excursion with Psycho Tours is climb a strangler fig.*

❸ ★★★ Rain-forest adventure tour with Psycho Tours. Most kids older than 10 can handle this wild adventure tour, which includes hiking, waterfall rappelling, and a thrilling free-climb up a strangler fig tree. In fact, a lot of kids consider this tour the highlight of their trip to Costa Rica. If you're traveling with younger children, you'll want to arrange to leave them with a babysitter, which will take some advance coordination with your hotel or lodge. ⏱ 6 hr. See p. 341, ❼.

Ask Psycho Tours to drop you off at this beach south of Puerto Jiménez.

❹ ★ Playa Platanares. Located just outside of town, this beach has gentle waves that are custom-made for small fry. 5km (3 miles) south of Puerto Jiménez.

On Day 3, you'll be picked up at your hotel for surfing lessons.

⑤ ★★ Surf lesson at Pollo's Surf School.
The long, perfectly formed waves of the Osa
Peninsula are ideal for beginning surfers of all
sizes. Pollo's offers instruction on forgiving soft
boards. Depending upon the swell and tides,
they use any of a number of well-suited family-
friendly surf spots, including an inside section
of Pan Dulce beach affectionately known as
"Disneyland." You'll need to reserve lessons in
advance. ⊕ 2 hr. ☎ 8366-6559, or email rhoades_
gretchen@hotmail.com. Rate $55 per person, per
class.

Be sure to get back to your hotel in time to be
picked up for a sunset tour.

**⑥ ★★ Escondido Trex sunset and dolphin-
watching tour.** You'll be back with these folks
(**①**) for this boat tour of the Golfo Dulce. You'll
head out onto the bay aboard a small, open
motorboat. Dolphin sightings are common, although not guaranteed; however, I do guarantee
a few swimming stops. ⊕ 2 hr. Escondido Trex.
☎ 2735-5210. www.escondidotrex.com. Rates $50
adults, $35 children 11 and under. Reservations
required. Daily 4:30pm.

You'll be picked up early on Day 4 for a national park excursion.

⑦ ★★★ Corcovado National Park. This is a
rugged spot—too rugged for a family trek unless
you are traveling with older teens. Instead, take
an organized tour here. See p. 348.

> Dolphins enjoy the sweet life in the Golfo Dulce.

Spending the Night in Puerto Jiménez

Most of the accommodations in this area are
isolated ecolodges located outside of Puerto
Jiménez proper, spread out along the dirt
road that heads some 25km (15 miles) toward
Carate. (For detailed information on hotels
and restaurants, see p. 364.) All of the tours
mentioned here are offered at all of the area
lodges, with transportation arranged either by
the tour operator or your lodge.

If you'd prefer to stay closer to downtown
Puerto Jiménez, check out **Cabinas Jiménez**
(☎ 2735-5090; www.cabinasjimenez.com;
$50–$80 double; see p. 364) or **Iguana
Lodge** (☎ 8829-5865; www.iguanalodge.com;
$135–$310 double).

Costa Rican Family Robinson

For a truly unique family vacation, think
about renting the ★★ **Lapa's Nest Tree
House,** an impressive concoction built up
and around a giant Guanacaste tree in the
midst of thick forest. This gorgeous home,
just 13km (8 miles) north of Puerto Jiménez,
is chock-full of creative design touches.
Spread over six levels, it features three bedrooms, two bathrooms, and a full kitchen
and is available for weekly rentals. The price
for all of this ranges from $1,800 to $2,600,
depending on the season. For more information, call ☎ 508/ 714-0622 in U.S., or 8378-
3013 in Costa Rica, or check out their website at www.treehouseincostarica.com. And
not to worry—area tours treat the Tree
House like a hotel, and will pick you up
and drop you off for tours, which the
management is happy to help arrange.

Corcovado National Park

Exploring Corcovado National Park is not something to be undertaken lightly, but neither is it the intimidating proposition that some fear. The park is one of the richest and most biologically diverse places on the planet. It covers an area of some 42,470 hectares (105,000 acres) of lowland tropical rain forest, rivers, and lagoons. It is a remarkable place, and those who are willing to give it a try will be rewarded mightily. That said, if you're planning to head to Corcovado for more than a guided day trip, make sure you're prepared to truly rough it.

> *Corcovado National Park is the refuge of several New World wildcats, including the jaguar.*

START Puerto Jiménez, 332km (206 miles) south of San José.

Entering the park. Because of its size and remoteness, Corcovado National Park is best explored over several days; however, it is possible to enter and hike a bit of it on day trips. The best way to do this is to book a tour with a tour company in Puerto Jiménez (p. 350, ❶), or through a lodge in the Drake Bay area (p. 358). If you're planning to do some serious hiking, you'll need to camp in the park for at least 1 night.

The park has four primary entrances, or ranger stations: La Leona, Los Patos, San Pedrillo, and La Sirena. Only La Sirena station is equipped with dormitory-style lodgings and a basic restaurant; the others have basic campsites and toilet facilities. All facilities must be reserved in advance by contacting **ACOSA,** or Area de Conservación de Osa (☎ 2735-5036; fax 2735-5276; pncorcovado@hotmail.com), located in Puerto Jiménez adjacent to the airstrip. Only a limited number of people are allowed to camp at each ranger station, so make your reservations

1 Puerto Jiménez
2 Los Patos ranger station
3 Hike to La Sirena
4 La Sirena ranger station
5 Hike from La Sirena to San Pedrillo

well in advance. Park admission is $10 per person per day. Camping, which is permitted at all of the ranger stations, costs $4 per person per night. A dorm room bed at La Sirena costs $8 per person, and a full-day meal plan runs $40.

There are two other ranger stations, Los Planes and El Tigre (or Dos Brazos). Each has a small trail system nearby, but neither is connected by trails to the other major ranger stations.

Warning: Danger Ahead

Remember, this is quite a wild area. Never hike alone, and take all the standard precautions for hiking in a rain forest. In addition, be especially careful about crossing or swimming in any isolated rivers or river mouths. Most rivers in Corcovado are home to **crocodiles**; moreover, at high tide, they are frequented by **bull sharks.** For this reason, river crossings must be coordinated with low tides—park rangers will help you plan your timing.

During the wet months (July to November, with September and October being the rainiest), parts of the park may be closed. One of the longest and most popular hikes, between San Pedrillo and La Sirena, can be undertaken only during the dry season.

> *If you don't have much wilderness experience, you can opt for a guided trek in Corcovado.*

> *Corcovado's beach trail.*

❶ **Puerto Jiménez.** The first leg of your journey is Puerto Jiménez (p. 362), the primary gateway to the park. Parts of this town are rough-and-tumble, but if you plan to spend a night or more in the park, you'll want to stock up on food, water, and other essentials here. You will also need to stop in at the ACOSA park office to check in, pick up a tide chart, and get current information and advice. If you want to take a guided trek (which I recommend, particularly for those who feel a little unsure of their hiking and camping acumen), Puerto Jiménez is the place to find a good guide or operator. I recommend **Osa Aventura** (☎ 2735-5758 or 8830-9832; www. osaaventura.com), run by naturalist guide Mike Boston.

❷ **Los Patos ranger station.** This ranger station is 8km (5 miles) southwest of the town of La Palma, which is 24km (15 miles) northwest of Puerto Jiménez. (If you are not taking a guided tour, hire a taxi to bring you here.) Plan to spend the night at the campsite at Los Patos ranger station so that you can get a really early start for your hike into the park the next morning. Alternatively, there are a handful of very rustic and basic hotels a few kilometers before the ranger station and at La Palma. 8km (5 miles) southwest of La Palma.

❸ ★★ **Hike to La Sirena.** From Los Patos, it's easy to start the 19km (12-mile) hike to La Sirena. The wide and well-marked trail between Los

Patos and La Sirena heads through the center of Corcovado National Park. The hike is beautiful and fascinating; it should take you 7 to 8 hours. There are rises and falls in elevation, although no serious ascents. You'll also have to cross various streams and rivers. In some cases, I recommend you take off your hiking boots in order to keep them dry. Other rivers and streams can be crossed via rocks and fallen tree trunks.

❹ **La Sirena ranger station.** The rustic lodging and research station at La Sirena is the heart and soul of Corcovado National Park. The station is located a little bit inland, at the end of the small airstrip here, which begins, more or less, at the beach. There's a network of trails here that can easily keep you busy for several days. Just north of the station lies the mouth of the Río Sirena. Most days at high tide, bull sharks swarm and feed in this river mouth. There are also large crocodiles, so swimming is seriously

Jungle Life

Given Corcovado's massive size, the park is one of the few places left in Costa Rica that sustain viable populations of jaguars and Baird's tapirs—two of the neotropics' largest mammals—and it is the last remaining local habitat of the endangered harpy eagle. All four of Costa Rica's monkey species can be found here, and the rivers and lagoons are home to healthy populations of American crocodiles and spectacled caimans. Apart from the jaguar, other cat species found here include the ocelot, margay, jaguarundi, and puma. So keep a close lookout as you make your way through the park, and you may be in for a happy surprise.

> *Rivers and streams run through the park.*

discouraged. Still, it's quite a spectacle. A separate trail will bring you to the mouth of the Río Claro. A little bit smaller, this river also houses a healthy crocodile population, although allegedly fewer bull sharks. However, if you follow the Claro Trail upstream a bit, you can find several safe and appropriate swimming spots.

5 ★★★ **Hike from La Sirena to San Pedrillo.** This relatively easy 23km (14-mile) hike is predominantly on the beach and will take you about 8 to 9 hours. It is best to leave La Sirena about 1 to 2 hours after high tide, having arranged with the park guards for a boat ride across the Río Sirena river mouth. This will get you to the Río Corcovado when the tide is still low enough for an easy crossing. Depending upon tides, weather, and the moon, I like to do the early part of this hike, all along the beach, by moonlight, enjoying the dawn along the way. This also saves you from hiking so much in the brutal heat of day. San Pedrillo is still 20km (12.4 miles) from Drake Bay. It is best to have prior arrangements with a lodge in Drake Bay to pick you up at the San Pedrillo ranger station. Most have day trips here, so this is commonly done and easy to arrange. For more information on transport options, see "Packing Up," p. 343.

Alternative Routes

The route outlined here is the most popular one, and with good reason: In my opinion, it's the best way to truly experience the park in just a few days. However, you do have options. You could also enter or exit via La Leona station, which is reached by road from Puerto Jiménez to the tiny village of Carate, and then a 3km (1.9-mile) hike. Or you could enter at San Pedrillo or La Sirena via boat from Drake Bay.

You can also charter a plane in Puerto Jiménez to take you to or from Carate or La Sirena. A five-passenger plane costs between $200 and $400 one-way, depending on your destination. Contact **Alfa Romeo Air Charters** (☎ 2735-5353 or 2735-5112; www.alfaromeoair.com).

For a great overview of the park and its logistics, check out www.corcovado.org.

TRAIL DISTANCES IN THE PARK

LA LEONA TO LA SIRENA	**14KM** (8.7 MILES)
LA LEONA TO CARATE	**3KM** (1.9 MILES)
LOS PATOS TO LA SIRENA	**19KM** (12 MILES)
LA SIRENA TO SAN PEDRILLO	**23KM** (14 MILES)
SAN PEDRILLO TO DRAKE BAY	**20KM** (12.4 MILES)

WHITE-FACED CAPUCHIN MONKEY

Friendly, charming, and super-smart, this is the monkey you're most likely to see on your trip. And when you do, it may look familiar—because they're easily trained, capuchins are used for everything from movies to helping the disabled. In the wild, they hang out in virtually every type of forest, in troops of up to 16, and they tend to stick to the lower part of the forest canopy. But that's not the only reason they're easy to spot: They are curious, and they consider everything from bananas to cameras fair game. Keep a firm grip on your stuff if you have a close encounter with these charmers.

YES, COSTA RICA has amazing birds, world-class surfing, and awe-inspiring active volcanoes, but one of the coolest things about a visit here is getting to see monkeys in the wild. Costa Rica is home to four species of New World (meaning Central and South American) monkeys. Despite the fact that all of these very cute critters are considered at-risk in terms of conservation, odds are good that you'll see at least a few—they're found throughout the country. Here's what you need to know.

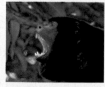

MANTLED HOWLER MONKEY

Whether or not you see a mantled howler monkey (and it's likely that you will—they're all over the place), you will almost certainly hear one. This is a *very* loud primate, thanks to a hollow bone near the vocal cords that lets these guys, well, howl. And just why are they howling? Although they eat leaves, howl-ers can weigh in at a whopping 10kg (22 lb.), making them the biggest monkeys in Central America. But since leaves are as tough to digest as you might think and don't provide much of an energy boost, howlers spend virtually all of their non-eating time either lounging or sleeping. Howling lets them locate the other monkeys in their family troop, usually numbering around 20, without using pre-cious energy.

CENTRAL AMERICAN SPIDER MONKEY

Named for their long,

MEET THE MONKEYS!
Costa Rica's Precious Primates
BY LINDA BARTH

thin legs and tail, spider monkeys are the swingingest simians you'll encounter here. A spider's tail is so strong and agile, it's essentially an extra limb, and can be used in moving from tree to tree. The tail even has a palm-like pad at the end—perfect for grabbing hold of branches

and fruit. Despite the ease with which spider monkeys, which live in groups of up to 40, cruise around the high rain-forest and mangrove canopies they inhabit, they do make it down to the ground more than the other Costa Rican species. If you're lucky, you'll get to see them scurrying around on all fours—but keep an eye on your gear, because these guys are intelligent (a recent study ranked them third, behind orangutans and chimpanzees, on a list

of the smartest nonhuman primates), and they've been known to engage in larceny.

CENTRAL AMERICAN SQUIRREL MONKEY
Squirrel monkeys may be a little harder to see—their territory is much smaller than that of the other monkeys listed here—but you've

got a good shot if you visit Manuel Antonio National Park (p. 290) or Corcovado National Park (p. 348). Standing just 23 to 36cm (9-14 in.) tall, with a tail up to 45cm (18 in.) long, these are the smallest of the Costa Rican species, but their troops are the largest, with up to 75 members. They spend most of their time in the forest canopy, feasting on insects and berries. Listen for the distinctive *chuck-chuck* call they use to keep in touch.

Southern Zone Adventures in & on the Water

At times it seems like there is water everywhere you turn in the Southern Zone: There's the Pacific Ocean, the Golfo Dulce, rain-forest rivers, jungle waterfalls, and plenty of rain. All this H_2O provides the platform for a wide range of adventure tours and activities—enjoy.

> Surfing the Golfo Dulce's western shore.

Bodysurfing, Body Boarding & Surfing

Hailed as the longest rideable left in the world, the surf break at ★★★ **Pavones** (p. 370, ❸) is Costa Rica's most famous wave. The Pavones break needs a south swell, and a fairly good-size swell at that, to really work. But when it is working, it provides rides that last as long as 3 minutes. If you need to rent, buy, or fix a board in Pavones, head to ★ **Sea Kings Surf Shop** (p. 371), and they'll take good care of you.

While not nearly as famous, the series of long, clean, and often crowd-free point breaks across the Golfo Dulce on the **Osa Peninsula** are a good bet for most surfers. ★★ **Pan Dulce,** ★★ **Backwash,** and ★ **Matapalo** are all major surf spots with consistently well-formed right point breaks. These three neighboring beaches and their accompanying waves are located south of Puerto Jiménez, in an area generally referred to as Matapalo. When the waves aren't too big, these are excellent places to take surfing lessons. If you want to rent a board or learn to surf in the Puerto Jiménez and Matapalo area, contact ★★ kids **Pollo's Surf School** (☎ 8366-6559; rhoades_gretchen@hotmail.com; see also p. 347, ❺), which is located near some excellent learning waves on Pan Dulce beach. A 2-hour lesson will cost $55 per person.

Body-boarders are welcome and common on all the waves mentioned above; however, most of these waves are not suitable for bodysurfing. The best place for bodysurfing down here is **Playa Zancudo** (p. 370).

Kayaking

The **Golfo Dulce** and **Pacific Ocean** both provide excellent kayaking opportunities. Most hotels and ecolodges located on the water have their own small fleet of kayaks for guests. If you're staying in or near Puerto Jiménez, you'll want to check in with ★★ kids **Escondido Trex** (p. 362, ❸), an all-purpose adventure tour operator with a very extensive selection of kayak outings.

Scuba Diving & Snorkeling

★★★ kids **Isla del Caño** (p. 343, ⓬) offers some of Costa Rica's best scuba diving and snorkeling. Sea life is abundant; whitetip reef sharks,

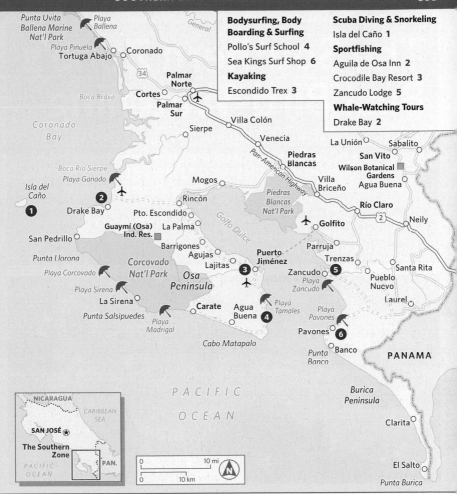

Bodysurfing, Body Boarding & Surfing

Pollo's Surf School **4**

Sea Kings Surf Shop **6**

Kayaking

Escondido Trex **3**

Scuba Diving & Snorkeling

Isla del Caño **1**

Sportfishing

Aguila de Osa Inn **2**

Crocodile Bay Resort **3**

Zancudo Lodge **5**

Whale-Watching Tours

Drake Bay **2**

eagle rays, moray eels, and sea turtles are common, and manta rays and whale sharks are sometimes spotted as well. All of the hotels and lodges in Drake Bay offer diving and snorkeling outings to Isla del Caño.

Sportfishing

The waters off the coast of southern Costa Rica are prime sportfishing grounds, and I recommend that any serious fishing enthusiast book a package deal at one of the region's dedicated fishing lodges. The top fishing lodges in these parts include ★★ **Aguila de Osa Inn** (p. 361), ★ **Crocodile Bay Resort** (☎ 800/733-1115 in U.S. and Canada, or 2735-5631 in Costa Rica; www.crocodilebay.com), and ★★★ **Zancudo Lodge** (p. 373).

While the places mentioned above are the best of the best, all hotels and tour operators in the area can arrange fishing outings. Rates range from $200 to $500 for a half-day trip, or $600 to $1,600 for a full day. These rates are for one to four people and vary according to boat size and accoutrements.

Whale-Watching Tours

The namesake waters off ★★★ **Drake Bay** (p. 358) are one of the best places to go whale-watching in Costa Rica; humpback whales can generally be spotted in the area between late July and November, and mid-December through March. There are no dedicated whale-watching operators in the area, but all of the hotels arrange whale-watching, as well as dolphin-spotting, trips.

The Southern Zone's Best Bird-Watching

Serious bird-watchers will definitely want to visit the Southern Zone. The lowland tropical rain forests of Corcovado National Park, innumerable private reserves and just plain wild patches of forest are all teeming with avian life. And that's not all—the coastal areas, beaches, mangroves, and Golfo Dulce are chock-full of seabirds and shorebirds. Some of the most sought-after species in the Southern Zone include the scarlet macaw, fiery-billed aracari, crested guan, great tinamou, chestnut-mandibled toucan, shining honeycreeper, lance-tailed manakin, sunbittern, and harpy eagle.

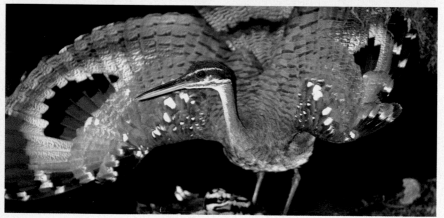

> *A sunbittern spreading its wings and revealing its vivid eyespot pattern.*

Osa Peninsula

★★★ **Corcovado National Park** (p. 348) is the prime draw here. It is huge. More than 390 species of birds have been recorded inside the park. Scarlet macaws are commonly sighted here, as well as in and around the outlying towns of Drake Bay and Puerto Jiménez. Other common species include any number of antbirds, manakins, toucans, tanagers, hummingbirds, and puffbirds. Once thought extinct in Costa Rica, the harpy eagle has recently been spotted here as well.

If you're staying in or around **Drake Bay** (p. 358), your best bird-watching will be had on a day tour to the San Pedrillo section of Corcovado National Park, although there's plenty of activity right on the grounds and surrounding forests of most of the ecolodges here.

Golfo Dulce–Golfito Area

If you're staying in or around Puerto Jiménez, Golfito, or Playa Zancudo, you'll definitely want to take a kayak or boat tour of ★★ **Golfo Dulce** (p. 354) and its various estuaries and mangrove systems. In addition to the numerous terns, gulls, sandpipers, and herons, you'll also be able to spot the white ibis and roseate spoonbill in this habitat. Of the herons, the bare-throated and fasciated tiger-herons are both impressive. This is also a good area to look for the mangrove black-hawk and osprey.

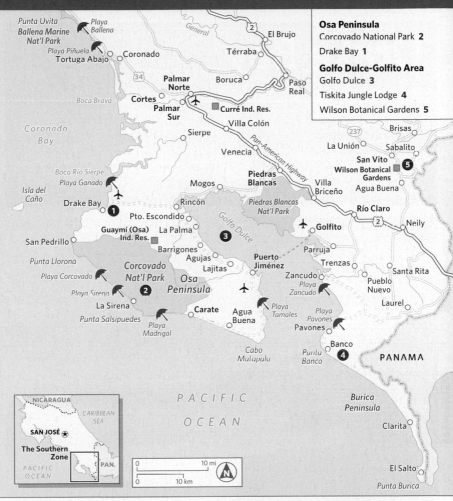

Punta Uvita
Ballena Marine
Nat'l Park Playa
Ballena
Playa Piñuela Coronado
Tortuga Abajo
El Brujo 2
Térraba
General
Palmar
Norte Boruca
Cortes 34 Boca Brava
Palmar
Sur Curré Ind. Res.
Boca Río Sierpe Villa Colón
Sierpe Venecia
Isla del
Caño Coronado
Bay Playa Ganado
Drake Bay 1 Rincón
Pto. Escondido
Guaymí (Osa)
Ind. Res. La Palma
San Pedrillo Barrigones
Punta Llorona Agujas
Playa Corcovado Corcovado
Nat'l Park Lajitas
La Sirena 2 Carate
Punta Salsipuedes Osa
Peninsula Agua
Buena
Playa Sirena Playa
Madrigal
Playa
Tamales
Cabo
Matapalo

Paso
Real
Pan-American Highway
Mogos Piedras
Blancas
Piedras Blancas
Nat'l Park Villa
Briceño
Golfo Dulce 3
Puerto
Jiménez Golfito
Parruja
Trenzas
Zancudo Playa
Zancudo
Pavones Playa
Pavones
Banco 4
Punta
Banco

Brisas
237
La Unión Sabalito
San Vito
Wilson Botanical 5
Gardens
Agua Buena
Río Claro
2 Neily
Santa Rita
Pueblo
Nuevo
Laurel

PANAMA

Osa Peninsula	
Corcovado National Park	**2**
Drake Bay	**1**
Golfo Dulce-Golfito Area	
Golfo Dulce	**3**
Tiskita Jungle Lodge	**4**
Wilson Botanical Gardens	**5**

PACIFIC

OCEAN

Burica
Peninsula

Clarita

El Salto
Punta Burica

NICARAGUA
CARIBBEAN
SEA
SAN JOSÉ
The Southern
Zone
PACIFIC
OCEAN PAN.

0   10 mi
0   10 km
N

Farther down the Golfo Dulce, near the Panamanian border, ★★ **Tiskita Jungle Lodge** (p. 372, **5**) offers a chance to see any number of more than 270 recorded species. The knowledgeable guides and varied habitats make this a very rewarding bird-watching destination.

Be sure to pay a visit inland, to the ★★★ **Wilson Botanical Gardens** (p. 367, **4**). More than 360 bird species have been recorded visiting these stunning gardens. The many flowering orchids, gingers, and heliconias here make this a top-notch place to spot a range of nectar-feeding hummingbird species, as well as tanagers, honeycreepers, euphonias, and manakins.

You Can Help Out

If you want to help with local efforts to protect the fragile rain forests and wild areas of the Osa Peninsula, contact the **Corcovado Foundation** (☎ 2297-3013; www.corcovadofoundation.org) or the **Friends of the Osa** (☎ 2735-5756; www.osaconservation.org). If you're looking to really lend a hand, both of the aforementioned groups have volunteer programs ranging from working on trail maintenance to teaching environmental and English-language classes to helping with bird-tagging and sea-turtle protection programs.

Drake Bay

Drake Bay is named after Sir Francis Drake, the famed British privateer, captain, and pirate, who is said to have anchored here in 1579. A tiny village at the mouth of the Río Agujitas (the town shares its name with the bay formed by the river's mouth), Drake Bay is one of the most isolated places in Costa Rica. It pretty much anchors the northern end of the Osa Peninsula, which makes it a great base for explorations of this natural treasure. Plan to spend 3 to 5 days here.

> San Josecito, reached by boat, is one of the best beaches in the Drake Bay area.

START Drake Bay is 145km (90 miles) south of San José.

1 ★★★ kids **Isla del Caño.** This beautiful, uninhabited island sits some 19km (12 miles) offshore from Drake Bay. A trip here takes up most of the day; it includes the opportunity to snorkel or scuba dive, a visit to a pre-Columbian gravesite, and a picnic lunch on the beach. ⊙ 1 day. See p. 343, **12**.

2 ★★★ kids **Night tour with the Bug Lady.** Affectionately known as the Bug Lady, Tracie Stice offers one of the most fascinating and informa-

tive night tours of the rain forest that I have ever taken. Equipped with flashlights, participants get a bug's-eye view of the forest at night. You might see your flashlight reflected in the eyes of some larger forest dwellers, but most of the tour is an in-depth exploration of the nocturnal insect and arachnid world. Consider yourself lucky if Tracie finds a tarantula or the burrow of a trap-door spider. Unless, of course, you're an arachnophobe, in which case this tour is not for you. Virtually every hotel in and around Drake Bay can get you a reservation for this tour, but the travel involved makes it impossible for those

1. Isla del Caño
2. The Bug Lady's night tour
3. Corcovado National Park
4. Horseback ride along Drake Bay
5. Kayaking on the Río Agujitas
6. Playa Cocolito

Where to Stay

Aguila de Osa Inn **10**

Casa Corcovado Jungle Lodge **7**

Drake Bay Wilderness Resort **9**

Hotel Jinetes de Osa **11**

La Paloma Lodge **8**

staying at hotels not within walking distance of town. ⏱ 2 hr. ☎ 8382-1619. www.thenighttour.com. Rate $35 per person. Daily 7:30pm.

Arrange for a guided tour of Corcovado National Park, or take a taxi to San Pedrillo.

③ ★★★ Kids **Corcovado National Park.** A visit to this sprawling gem of a park is a highlight of any stay in Drake Bay. The closest entrance is at San Pedrillo, where you'll find a basic ranger station and a small trail system. The trails wander through thick, primary rain forest that teems with life. You're almost guaranteed to spot one or more monkey species and to see dozens of bird species. Listen for the call of scarlet macaws overhead, and watch for the colorful flash of a trogon as you hike. The principal trail here passes by a beautiful jungle waterfall, with a broad, deep swimming hole at its base. Bring a bathing suit, and be sure to take a dip. ⏱ 4–6 hrs. See p. 348.

④ ★★ **Horseback riding along Drake Bay.** This is a wild and remote area, and for decades it was accessible to outsiders only by boat or small aircraft. For locals, horses were the cutting edge of rapid transit. All of the hotels in town can arrange for a horseback ride with one of the local villagers. You'll ride through a mix

> Corcovado National Park is south of Drake Bay.

> *Drake Bay Wilderness Resort, with the bay on one side and the river on the other, offers a real getaway.*

of rugged rural roads and rain-forest trails, and you'll certainly ford a river or two. Try to time the tour so that you finish on the beach at Drake Bay village right around sunset. ⊕ 2–3 hr. Rates $30–$50 per person.

⑤ ★★ Kayaking on the Río Agujitas. The protected waters of Drake Bay are a great place to get your feet (and butt) wet in a kayak—they're so calm that even beginners will feel comfortable. When the tide is high, I recommend you begin your outing by paddling up the mouth of the small Río Agujitas, where you might see scarlet macaws, basilisks, kingfishers, and perhaps even some monkeys. If the tide is low, you should head out into the bay and look for crocodiles and sea turtles. All hotels and ecolodges in the area maintain a small fleet of sea kayaks. ⊕ Minimum 2 hr. Leave from the dock area on the Río Agujitas.

Seeing the Sights

You will be picked up and dropped off at your hotel for all of the tours listed here. Your hotel desk can help you book them. Virtually every hotel in the area offers a host of tours and activities, including hikes in **Corcovado National Park** (p. 348), trips to **Isla del Caño** (p. 343, ⑫), horseback riding, scuba diving, snorkeling, and whale-watching (in season). Other options include mountain biking and sea kayaking. In some cases, tours are included in your room rate or package; in others, you must purchase them a la carte. Most of these tours run between $60 and $120 per person, depending on the activity; scuba diving ($90–$125 for a two-tank dive) and sportfishing ($450–$1,500, depending on boat size) cost a bit more.

⑥ ★★ Playa Cocolito. This small beach is reached in just a few minutes of easy hiking from La Paloma Lodge (p. 361). Along the way, keep an eye (and ear) out for troops of white-faced capuchins—look for them in the canopy. At low tide, some cool tide pools and swimming holes form at the northern end of the beach. 400m (¼ mile) southwest of La Paloma Lodge.

Where's the Beach?

While the dark-sand beach fronting the village of Drake Bay is calm enough for swimming, it's far from spectacular to look at. The most popular nearby beach is an attractive little stretch of sand, Playa Cocolito (⑥), about a 7-minute hike down from La Paloma. However, the best beaches around require taking a day trip to either Isla del Caño, San Josecito, San Pedrillo, or La Sirena. The latter two are inside Corcovado National Park, while **San Josecito** is located in a pretty, little protected cove about 20km (12 miles) south of Drake Bay by boat.

Where to Stay

★★ Aguila de Osa Inn DRAKE BAY

This plush hillside lodge is a great choice for serious sportfishers and scuba divers. Situated high on a hill overlooking Drake Bay and the Pacific Ocean, the Aguila de Osa Inn offers large rooms with hardwood or tile floors, ceiling fan, large bathroom, and excellent views. Varnished wood and bamboo abound. The biggest drawback, however, is the lack of a swimming pool, which most of the other high-end places have. On the south bank of the mouth of the Río Agujitas, Drake Bay. ☎ 866/924-8452 in U.S. and Canada, or 2296-2190 in Costa Rica. www.aguila deosainn.com. 13 units. $524–$648 for 3 days/2 nights; $789–$975 for 4 days/3 nights. Rates are per person based on double occupancy and include all meals and taxes. AE, MC, V. Closed Oct.

★ Casa Corcovado Jungle Lodge SAN PEDRILLO

This remote lodge borders Corcovado National Park. The rooms are all private bungalows built on the grounds of a former cacao plantation on the jungle's edge. When the sea is calm, the beach here is great for swimming; when it is rough, it's a great place to grab a hammock in the shade and read a book. The lodge has two swimming pools, both surrounded by thick rain forest. Just north of the San Pedrillo entrance to Corcovado National Park. ☎ 888/896-6097 in U.S. and Canada, or 2256-3181 in Costa Rica. www.casacorcovado.com. 14 units. $855 for 3 days/2 nights with 1 tour; $1,015–$1,165 for 4 days/3 nights with 2 tours. Rates are per person based on double occupancy and include round-trip transportation from San José, all meals, park fees, and taxes. AE, MC, V. Closed Sept–Oct.

★ Drake Bay Wilderness Resort DRAKE BAY

Backing onto the Río Agujitas and fronting the Pacific, this is one of the best-situated lodges in Drake Bay. The nicest room is the deluxe honeymoon suite, set on a little hill toward the rear of the property, which boasts a great view of the bay. At the other end of the budget spectrum, there are five rustic cabins that share bathroom and shower facilities. There's a saltwater pool in front of the bay, and, depending on the tide, you can bathe in a beautiful small tide pool formed by the rocks. On the north bank of the mouth of

the Río Agujitas, Drake Bay. ☎ 561/762-1763 in U.S., or 2770-8012 in Costa Rica. www.drakebay. com. 25 units. $90 per day with shared bathroom; $130–$165 per day standard and deluxe; $770 for 4 days/3 nights, with 2 tours. Rates are per person based on double occupancy and include all meals and taxes. AE, MC, V.

★ Hotel Jinetes de Osa DRAKE BAY

Although no longer a true budget lodging, this is a good alternative to the more upscale options in the area. The best rooms here are spacious and well appointed, and they even have a view of the bay. A wide range of tours and activities is available, as are dive packages, weekly adventure packages, and scuba certification courses. North of Drake Bay village, 350m (¼ mile) from the Río Agujitas river mouth. ☎ 866/553-7073 in U.S. and Canada, or 2231-5806 in Costa Rica. www.drakebayhotel.com. 9 units. $132–$176 double. Rates are per person based on double occupancy and include all meals. MC, V.

★★★ La Paloma Lodge DRAKE BAY

On a steep hill overlooking the Pacific, with Isla del Caño in the distance, the luxurious bungalows at La Paloma offer expansive ocean views that make this my top choice in Drake Bay. All the bungalows feature a private veranda and are set among lush foliage facing the Pacific. The large two-story Sunset Ranchos are the choice rooms here, with fabulous panoramic views. The beach is about a 7-minute hike down a winding jungle path. Drake Bay. ☎ 2293-7502 or 2239-0954. www.lapalomalodge.com. 11 units. $1,115–$1,470 for 4 days/3 nights, with 2 tours; $1,310–$1,700 for 5 days/4 nights, with 2 tours. Rates are per person based on double occupancy and include round-trip transportation from San José, all meals, park fees, indicated tours, and taxes. AE, MC, V. Closed Sept 15–Oct 31.

Dining in Drake Bay

While you're staying in Drake Bay, much of your time will revolve around your lodge, which will provide all the services you'll need. You'll eat all of your meals there— hence, there is no "Where to Dine" section.

Puerto Jiménez & the Southern Osa Peninsula

Puerto Jiménez is a bustling little burg where rough jungle gold-panners mix with upscale ecotourists, budget backpackers, serious surfers, and a smattering of celebrities seeking a dose of anonymity. It is truly an escape. Corcovado National Park has its headquarters here, and this town makes an ideal base for exploring its vast wilderness. The town of Puerto Jiménez itself is of little interest to most visitors, but it is the gateway to the national park, as well as to several of Costa Rica's finest ecolodges, located farther out on the Osa Peninsula. You'll want to spend 3 or 4 days here.

> Bird-watchers shouldn't miss out on a paddle into the mangroves with Escondido Trex.

START Puerto Jiménez is 332km (206 miles) south of San José; and 35km (22 miles) west of Golfito by boat or 90km (56 miles) by road.

1 ★★ **kids** **Herrera Botanical Gardens.** This place features more than 105 hectares (260 acres) of botanical gardens, working permaculture gardens, and secondary forest. There are even a few platforms built high in the trees here—they're accessed by ladders, so be prepared to do some climbing. The trails are easy to tour on your own (a map and explanations are provided), but you will learn a lot more and see more wildlife on the guided hike. ⏱ Minimum 1 hr. See p. 345, **2**.

2 ★★★ **kids** **Rain-forest adventure tour with Psycho Tours.** ⏱ 3–6 hrs. See p. 341, **7**.

3 ★★ **kids** **Escondido Trex.** These folks offer kayaking trips around the Puerto Jiménez estuary, into the mangroves, and out into the Golfo Dulce. The trips into the mangroves provide the best bird-watching opportunities and the easiest paddling. However, you might want to consider a sunset paddle out into

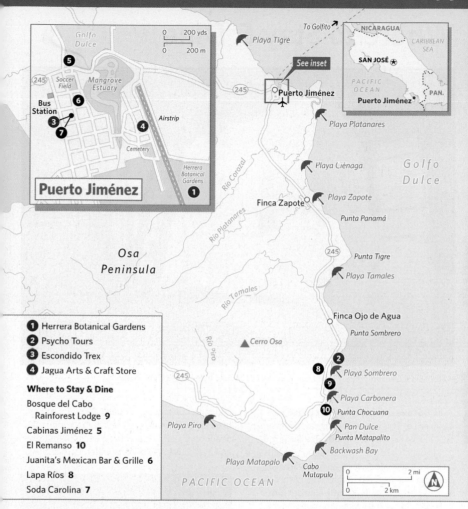

Puerto Jiménez

1 Herrera Botanical Gardens
2 Psycho Tours
3 Escondido Trex
4 Jagua Arts & Craft Store

Where to Stay & Dine

Bosque del Cabo
   Rainforest Lodge 9
Cabinas Jiménez 5
El Remanso 10
Juanita's Mexican Bar & Grille 6
Lapa Ríos 8
Soda Carolina 7

the gulf, which includes the possibility of a dolphin sighting. Both of these trips are fine for beginners, and more adventurous multiday kayaking and camping trips are also available. ⊕ 2 hr. to several days. Office inside Soda Carolina (p. 365), on the main street, Puerto Jiménez. ☎ 2735-5210. www.escondidotrex.com. Rates $40–$75 for half- and full-day tours; $110–$160 per day for multiday tours. Daily 7am–5pm.

4 ★★ **Jagua Arts & Craft Store.** This gift shop is definitely worth a visit. Owner Karen Herrera has found excellent local and regional arts and crafts works, including some excellent jewelry and blown glass. **Tip:** Many folks head to this store while waiting for their departing flight out of Puerto Jiménez. Be sure to give yourself enough time, as the store has a fairly extensive collection. Just across from the airstrip. ☎ 2735-5267. Daily 9am–4pm.

Travel Tip

You will be picked up and dropped off at your hotel for all of the tours covered here. Your hotel desk can help you book them. And in addition to the specific tours listed here, there are plenty of others available, including trips to Corcovado National Park.

Where to Stay & Dine

> *Bosque del Cabo Rainforest Lodge has individual cabins set in the Osa's wilderness.*

★★★ Bosque del Cabo Rainforest Lodge

MATAPALO This secluded lodge is my favorite spot in this neck of the woods. The large individual cabins are set amid beautiful gardens and have a wooden deck or veranda for catching the ocean views. The Congo cabin is my choice for its spectacular view of the sunrise from your bed. All have an indoor bathroom with toilet and sink. The artistically tiled showers are set outdoors amid flowering heliconia and ginger; about half the cabins also have outdoor bathtubs. Trails wind through rain forest in the lodge's 260-hectare (650-acre) private reserve. If you're too lazy to hike down to the beach, there's a beautiful pool by the main lodge. Matapalo, Osa Peninsula. ☎ 2735-5206 or 8389-2846. www.bosquedelcabo.com. 10 units. $350–$390 cabins. Rates based on double occupancy and include all meals and taxes. Round-trip transportation from Puerto Jiménez $25. MC, V.

★ kids Cabinas Jiménez PUERTO JIMÉNEZ

If you're looking for a good hotel in Puerto Jiménez, check out this spot at the northern end of the town's soccer field. All of the rooms have air-conditioning, tile floors, hand-carved headboards, and Guatemalan bedspreads. Several even have views of the water, from either

Roughing It

This listing includes some of the best ecolodges Costa Rica has to offer, and they are, accordingly, pricier than those in other parts of the country. All prices are based on double occupancy, and they include extras, like meals, as noted. But keep in mind that despite paying top dollar, you won't have access to TVs, in-room telephones, air-conditioning, nightclubs, or even paved roads. On the plus side, there are also no crowds and very few modern distractions. Note also that all of the lodgings listed here except Cabinas Jiménez are located out along the Osa Peninsula, anywhere from 30 to 45 minutes by four-wheel-drive vehicle from Puerto Jiménez.

a shared or private veranda. **On the waterfront, Puerto Jiménez.** ☎ 2735-5090. www.cabinas jimenez.com. 10 units. $50–$80 double. MC, V.

★★ El Remanso MATAPALO

This collection of cabins is set in a deep patch of primary forest. The best view of the ocean, over and through thick forest, can be had from the two-story deluxe La Vanilla unit, which can be rented whole or split into two separate one-bedroom affairs. If you want an individual cabin, Azul de Mar has the best view. A host of adventure activities is available, and there's a large, open-air yoga platform. For chilling out, there's a small oval pool set in a stone deck area with great views to the ocean. As an added bonus, the owners are deeply committed to environmental protection. In fact, Joel and Belen Stewart met aboard the Greenpeace vessel *Rainbow Warrior,* which Joel captained for a number of years. **Matapalo, Osa Peninsula.** ☎ 2735-5569. www.elremanso.com. 14 units. $320–$370 rooms and cabins. Rates are based on double occupancy and include all meals and taxes. MC, V.

★ Juanita's Mexican Bar & Grille PUERTO

JIMÉNEZ *MEXICAN* This place serves hearty California-style Mexican food and seafood. You can get fajitas with chicken, beef, fish, or grilled vegetables. Juanita's also has pizza by the slice or pie, and there are nightly specials and a popular happy hour. **Just off the main street.** ☎ 2735-5056. Entrees $5–$15. V. Lunch and dinner daily.

★★ Lapa Ríos MATAPALO

Surrounded by its own 400-hectare (988-acre) private rain-forest reserve, this is one of Costa Rica's pioneering ecolodges. Each room is oriented toward the view, with open screen walls and a high-peaked thatched roof. A large deck and small tropical garden, complete with a hammock and outdoor shower, more than double the living space. Just off the main lodge is a pretty little pool with great views. The beach, however, is a good 15-minute hike away, and it's even a bit of a hike back and forth between the main lodge and the farthest rooms. **Matapalo, Osa Peninsula.** ☎ 2735-5130. www.laparios.com. 16 units. $710 double. Rate based on double occupancy and includes all meals, round-trip trans-

> At Lapa Ríos ecolodge you'll have the best of both worlds—a rain-forest perch and an ocean view.

portation btw. the lodge and Puerto Jiménez, and taxes. AE, MC, V.

Soda Carolina PUERTO JIMÉNEZ *COSTA RICAN* This is the town's main travelers' hangout and also serves as an unofficial information center. The walls are painted with colorful jungle and wildlife scenes. As for the fare, seafood is the way to go. There's good fried fish, as well as a variety of ceviches. The black-bean soup is usually tasty, and the *casados* (plates of the day) are filling and cost around $4. **On the main street.** ☎ 2735-5185. Entrees $3.50–$14. V. Breakfast, lunch, and dinner daily.

Puerto Jiménez after Dark

If you're looking for any after-tours action in Puerto Jiménez, I recommend you start off at either **Juanita's Mexican Bar & Grille** or the **Soda Carolina** (above). You might also try the new **Sarpe's** (☎ 2753-5373), located next to the Bosque del Mar hotel, in the center of town. *Sarpe* translates roughly as "last call," and this is often a good place to end the evening.

Golfito & the Golfo Dulce

Golfito, in and of itself, is not a major tourist destination. Once the center of operations for United Fruit, it was a principal banana port. Today, Golfito is a mostly rundown port city that serves as a base for itinerant sailors and some sportfishing enthusiasts. So why is it getting a mention? Because it's the gateway to some of the country's most gorgeous and isolated hotels and lodges, all of which rest along the shores of the Golfo Dulce, or "Sweet Gulf." Plan to spend 2 or 3 days here.

> *The port of Golfito is the gateway to southwestern Costa Rica's gardens and reserves.*

START Golfito is 337km (209 miles) south of San José.

❶ ★ Cataratas y Senderos Avellán. A visit to the Avellán Waterfalls and Trails includes a 2-hour guided hike through the forests and to a beautiful waterfall with several refreshing pools perfect for swimming. It is also possible to get to the falls via horseback or a zip-line canopy tour. ⏱ Minimum 2 hr. 6km (3¾ miles) north of downtown Golfito along a gravel road that heads out from behind the airstrip. ☎ 8397-8318. Admission $5 for guided hike.

❷ Golfito National Wildlife Reserve. With a trailhead located just on the outskirts of town, this is the closest place to Golfito for a hike in one of the typical local lowland rain forests. This reserve is home to much of the same wildlife and flora you'll find in other, more famous national parks. A well-marked trail begins near the ranger station—you can hike it yourself or go as part of an organized tour. ⏱ Minimum 2 hr. West of downtown Golfito, just past the airstrip. No phone. Admission $10. Daily 8am–4pm.

Taking a Tour

The best way to see most of the attractions listed in this section is as part of a tour. I recommend either booking through your hotel or using the always-reliable **Land Sea Tours** (☎ 2775-1614).

① Cataratas y Senderos Avellán	**Where to Stay & Dine**	Hotel Sierra
② Golfito National	Bilge Bar, Restaurant	Resort & Casino **7**
Wildlife Reserve	& Grill **10**	Playa Nicuesa
③ Casa Orquídeas	Casa Roland Marina Resort **8**	Rainforest Lodge **5**
④ Wilson Botanical Gardens	Golfo Dulce Lodge **6**	Samoa del Sur **9**

③ ★★ **Casa Orquídeas.** Casa Orquídeas is a private botanical garden on an isolated cove about 30 minutes by boat from Golfito. You'll find a broad array of tropical flowers, and during the tour you'll sample fresh fruits picked right off the trees. You'll need to come as part of a tour. ⏱ 3 hr., including travel by boat from Golfito. Admission $5; transportation extra. Sat–Thurs 8:30am.

④ ★★★ **Wilson Botanical Gardens.** Owned and maintained by the Organization for Tropical Studies as part of their Las Cruces Biological Station, this place is a must-see for anyone with a serious interest in flora (or in bird-watching). The gardens feature more than 7,000 species of tropical plants from around the world, many of them endangered. There are so many beautiful and unusual flowers around the manicured grounds that even a botanist would be astounded. And all of this lush flora has attracted at least 360 species of birds.

A range of tours is available with advance reservations; I highly recommend you stick with a guide for at least part of your time here. Self-guided explorations of the gardens are also possible, and if you book a half-day guided tour, you should allow yourself some time to wander around on your own. ⏱ Minimum 4–6 hr. 65km

> The tropical plants at Wilson Botanical Gardens attract a stunning array of wildlife.

(40 miles) northeast of Golfito, just outside the town of San Vito. ☎ 2524-0607 for the office in San José, or 2773 4004 for the gardens. www.threepaths.co.cr. Admission $8 adults; children 11 and under free. Guided hikes: half-day $22 adults, $10 children 11 and under; full-day (lunch included) $41 adults, $28 children 11 and under. Daily 7:30am–5pm.

Where to Stay & Dine

★★ Bilge Bar, Restaurant & Grill GOLFITO

INTERNATIONAL/SEAFOOD The open-air restaurant attached to the Banana Bay Marina is the best restaurant in Golfito. The seafood is fresh and excellently prepared, but you can also get hearty steaks and great burgers. I personally recommend the fresh fish burger. Breakfasts are also hearty and well prepared. Grab a table toward the water and watch the boats bob up and down while you enjoy your meal. **At the Banana Bay Marina, on the waterfront downtown. ☎ 2775-0838. Entrees $6–$18. AE, MC, V.** Breakfast, lunch, and dinner daily.

Casa Roland Marina Resort GOLFITO

Located near the airstrip and duty-free zone, this place is several blocks from the water, so I find the name a bit misleading. Still, the rooms are large and well equipped, with interesting artwork and comfortable, heavy wood furnishings. Geared equally toward Tico shoppers, tourists, and sportfishers, the corporate rooms, which I would call "standards," come with only a ceiling fan, a real handicap in this climate, so be sure to upgrade to a luxury room or suite, which has air-conditioning. **Old American zone, near the duty-free zone. ☎ 2775-0180. www.fishingmarinaresort.com. 53 units. $125–$165 double; $215–$260 suite. Rates include continental breakfast. AE, MC, V.**

★★ Golfo Dulce Lodge GOLFO DULCE

This Swiss-run lodge is about a 30-minute boat ride from Golfito. The cabins and main lodge buildings are all set back away from the beach into the forest. Cabins are spacious and airy and feature a solar hot-water shower, small sitting area, and porch with a hammock. The rooms are all cozy and well appointed; they also have private verandas but are not nearly as nice as the cabins. **Golfo Dulce. ☎ 8821-5398. www.golfodulcelodge.com. 8 units. $190 double; $230 cabin. Rates based on double occupancy and include all meals and taxes. Transportation to and from Golfito $30 per person. A 3-night minimum stay is required. No credit cards. Closed May–June, Oct.**

Hotel Sierra Resort & Casino GOLFITO

Set right beside the airstrip, the Sierra was originally built as a business-class hotel geared toward middle-class Ticos in town to shop. It's currently trying to sell itself as a sportfishing and ecotourism lodge, although it's not particularly well suited for either. However, the swimming pool is the largest and most appealing in town. **Beside the airstrip. ☎ 2775-0666. www.hotelsierra.com. 72 units. $80 double. AE, MC, V.**

> *The cabins at Playa Nicuesa Lodge blend in seamlessly with their rain-forest surroundings.*

★★★ Playa Nicuesa Rainforest Lodge GOLFO DULCE

Set on its own private bay with a large stretch of black-sand beach, this is the most impressive lodge along the shores of the Golfo Dulce. You'll definitely want to snag one of the private cabins, which are set amid dense forest, with a large open-air shower, a private veranda, and a true sense of being in touch with nature. There's an excellent network of trails on the lodge's 66 hectares (163 acres), and a whole host of tours and activities is offered. Golfo Dulce. ☎ 866/504-8116 in U.S. and Canada, or 2258-8250 in Costa Rica. www.nicuesalodge.com. 8 units. $380 double; $420–$630 cabin. Rates based on double occupancy and include all meals, taxes, and transfers to and from either Golfito or Puerto Jiménez. A 2-night minimum stay is required. Closed Oct 1–Nov 15. AE, MC, V.

Golfito after Dark

Golfito is a rough-and-tumble port town, and it pays to be careful here after dark. Right in town, about 1½ blocks inland and uphill from the *muellecito* (the spot where the ferry docks), **Latitude 8** (☎ 2775-1295) is the most popular spot. Another popular, if somewhat unlikely, spot is **La Pista** bar (☎ 2775-9015), located near the airstrip. Most folks stick pretty close to their hotel bar and restaurant. If you're feeling lucky, you can head to the **casino** at the **Hotel Sierra** (p. 368).

★ Samoa del Sur GOLFITO *INTERNATIONAL*

This open-air restaurant features an extensive menu of Continental and French dishes (the owners are French), including such specialties as onion soup, *salade Niçoise*, filet of fish *meunière*, and, in a nod to their southern neighbor, paella. There are also pizzas and spaghetti. In addition to the food, the giant *rancho* houses a pool table, several high-quality dartboards, and two big-screen TVs. The bar sometimes stays open all night, so stop in for a drink if you're staying nearby. One block north of the public dock. ☎ 2775-0233. Entrees $6–$28. AE, MC, V. Breakfast, lunch, and dinner daily.

Playa Zancudo & Pavones

Playa Zancudo and Pavones are two of Costa Rica's most remote and isolated beach towns. Surfers flock to Pavones to ride what has been described as the longest left point break in the world while others come to Playa Zancudo for the sportfishing and to get away from it all. This is just about as far south as you can go along Costa Rica's Pacific coast without hitting Panama. You'll want to spend at least 2 days here.

> *The two favorite pastimes at Pavones beach are surfing and watching surfing.*

START **Playa Zancudo** is 35km (22 miles) south of Golfito by road, 15km (9 miles) by boat; Pavones is 40km (25 miles) south of Golfito by road, 32km (20 miles) by boat.

❶ ★ Zancudo Boat Tours. These folks offer a wide range of tours around the area, including bird-watching trips through the mangroves, tours to Casa Orquídeas (p. 367, **❸**), and outings to the Río Coto to observe wildlife and swim in a clear jungle river. They also offer transport between Golfito, Playa Zancudo, Pavones, and Puerto Jiménez. ⏱ 2–6 hr. At Cabinas Los Cocos, Playa Zancudo. ☎ 2776-0012. www.loscocos.com. Rates $50–$75 per person.

❷ ★★★ Sportfishing with Zancudo Lodge. The Pacific waters just off Playa Zancudo are prime sportfishing grounds for two types of marlin, sailfish, and a host of other big game fish. Zancudo Lodge (p. 373) is the biggest and best-equipped operator in the area, and serious fishermen will want to stay there. If you're not staying at the Lodge, **Zancudo Boat Tours** (**❶**) can set you up for a day of fishing. ⏱ Minimum 6 hr. Playa Zancudo. Rates: $600–$1,600 per boat.

❸ ★★★ Surfing Pavones. The wave breaks right in front of the center of the tiny town of Pavones, and it's considered the longest rideable left point break on the planet. The put-

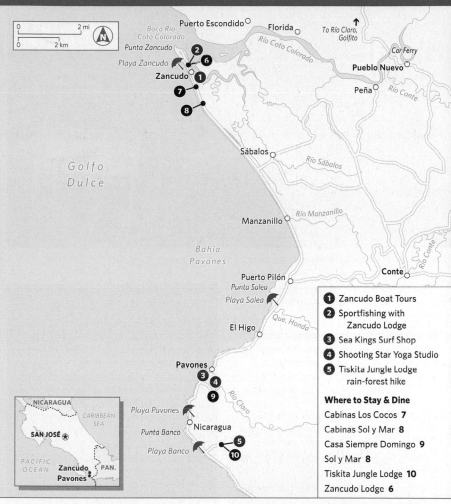

0 —— 2 mi
0 —— 2 km

Boca Río
Coto Colorado
Punta Zancudo
Playa Zancudo
Zancudo
Puerto Escondido
Florida
Río Coto Colorado
To Río Claro,
Golfito
Car Ferry
Pueblo Nuevo
Peña
Río Conte

*Golfo
Dulce*

Sábalos
Río Sábalos

Manzanillo
Río Manzanillo

*Bahía
Pavones*

Puerto Pilón
Punta Salea
Playa Salea
Conte
Río Conte

El Higo
Que. Honda

Pavones
Río Claro

Playa Pavones
Punta Banco
Nicaragua
Playa Banco

NICARAGUA
CARIBBEAN
SEA
SAN JOSÉ
PACIFIC
OCEAN
Zancudo
Pavones
PAN.

1 Zancudo Boat Tours
2 Sportfishing with
   Zancudo Lodge
3 Sea Kings Surf Shop
4 Shooting Star Yoga Studio
5 Tiskita Jungle Lodge
   rain-forest hike

Where to Stay & Dine
Cabinas Los Cocos **7**
Cabinas Sol y Mar **8**
Casa Siempre Domingo **9**
Sol y Mar **8**
Tiskita Jungle Lodge **10**
Zancudo Lodge **6**

in is a bit rocky, and some surfers wear booties here. If you need to rent, buy, or fix a board, head to **Sea Kings Surf Shop** (☎ 2776-2015; www.surfpavones.com), located right in the center of town, just off the soccer field. Even if you don't surf, it's worth heading to the shore

Travel Tip

Your hotel desk can help you book all of the tours listed here, including transportation to and from the hotel. And your hotel can also arrange day tours to Golfito and Puerto Jiménez, and any of the tour activities listed in those sections.

> *There is great sportfishing out of Zancudo.*

> *Tiskita Jungle Lodge has wonderful trails through primary rain forest.*

here to watch who is shredding this world-class break. Pavones, just offshore from the town center.

④ ★ Shooting Star Yoga Studio. When there are no waves pumping, or if you just want a change of pace, this place offers regular drop-in yoga and karate classes, as well as private instruction. Many of the classes are geared toward surfers, with Strength Yoga and Ashtanga the two most popular styles taught. ⏱ 1–2 hr. Pavones center, just off the soccer field. ☎ 8393-6982. www.yogapavones.com. Rates $10 group class, $20 private 1-hr. class. Mon–Fri 9am–4:30pm.

From Pavones, take a 10-minute taxi ride to Tiskita.

⑤ ★★ Tiskita Jungle Lodge rain-forest hike. My favorite hike in the Pavones area is a half-day outing through the on-site trail system of this ecolodge (see p. 373). Most of the land here is primary rain forest; the rest is a mix of secondary forest, reforestation projects, orchards, and pastures. You can visit jungle rivers and waterfalls and sample a wide range of tropical fruits. More than 270 species of birds have been spotted here. Guests at the lodge get one guided hike per day included with their room rate. Guided hikes for nonguests are available with prior notice. ⏱ 4–6 hr. 6km (3¾ miles) south from Pavones. ☎ 2296-8125. Rate $20 guided half-day hike. See also p. 338, ❶.

What a Wild Ride

Surfers first discovered the amazing wave off Pavones in the late 1970s. When conditions are right, this wave peels off in one continuous ribbon for more than 2km (1¼ miles). Your skills better be up to snuff, and your legs better be in good shape, if you want to ride this wave. Pavones got some good press in Allan Weisbecker's 2001 memoir *In Search of Captain Zero: A Surfer's Road Trip Beyond the End of the Road* (Tarcher, 2001). The word was out and surfers began flocking to Pavones from all over the world. On any given day—when the wave is working—you are likely to find surfers from the United States, Brazil, Argentina, Israel, Australia, Peru, and any number of other countries.

Unfortunately, the town and wave are not without controversy. Aside from the typical territorial squabbles that erupt over the most popular surfing spots, Pavones has been the site of a series of prominent land disputes, drug busts, fist fights, and even murders. For a unique and in-depth account of the town, its wave, and some of these scandals, check out Weisbecker's *Can't You Get Along with Anyone?: A Writer's Memoir and a Tale of a Lost Surfer's Paradise* (Bandito Books, 2007).

Where to Stay & Dine

> One of the cabins at Cabinas Los Cocos.

★★ **Cabinas Los Cocos** PLAYA ZANCUDO
The four rustic cabins here are set beneath palm trees just steps from the beach. Two of them served as banana-plantation housing in a former era. All offer plenty of space, a small kitchenette, and a private veranda. Playa Zancudo. ☎ 2776-0012. www.loscocos.com. 4 units. $60 double. No credit cards.

★★ **Cabinas Sol y Mar** PLAYA ZANCUDO
This friendly owner-run establishment has a mix of individual and duplex cabins. I recommend the individual cabins for their privacy. You can even camp here for a few bucks per night. Everything is just steps away from the beach. The hotel's open-air restaurant (see **Sol y Mar**) is one of the best and most popular places to eat in town. Playa Zancudo. ☎ 2776-0014. www. zancudo.com. 6 units. $25–$45 double. MC, V.

★ **Casa Siempre Domingo** PAVONES
This hillside hotel offers up the best rooms in Pavones. All feature towering ceilings and tile floors. The beds are custom-made and high off the ground. The best feature here is the huge deck, with its ocean view. Pavones. ☎ 8820-4709. www.casa-domingo.com. 4 units. $100 double. Rate includes breakfast and taxes. No credit cards.

★★ **Sol y Mar** PLAYA ZANCUDO *INTERNATIONAL/ SEAFOOD* The menu here is heavy on seafood, but it also features dishes you won't find elsewhere in town, including thick-cut pork chops in a teriyaki sauce. The fresh seared tuna is always excellent, as are the barbecues on Monday and Friday. Horseshoe tournaments are held on Sundays throughout the high season, and there's free Wi-Fi. At Cabinas Sol y Mar. ☎ 2776-0014. Entrees $3.50–$15. MC, V. Daily 7am–9pm.

★★★ **Tiskita Jungle Lodge** PAVONES
This ecolodge is set on a forested hill a few hundred meters from the beach and commands a superb view of the ocean. There are a dark-sand beach, tide pools, jungle waterfalls, a farm, and forest to explore, and great bird-watching. Accommodations are in cozy rustic cabins with screen walls and verandas. Most of the bathrooms are actually outdoors, although they are private and protected, allowing you to take in the sights and sounds as you shower and shave. My favorite cabin is number 6, which has a great view and ample deck space. Some cabins have two or three rooms; these are perfect for families but less private for couples. 6km (3¾ miles) down the road from Pavones. ☎ 2296-8125. www.tiskitalodge.co.cr. 17 units. $272 double. Rate based on double occupancy and includes all meals and taxes, and 1 guided walk daily. Packages including transportation to and from Golfito or Puerto Jiménez available. AE, MC, V.

★★ **Zancudo Lodge** PLAYA ZANCUDO
Primarily a fishing lodge, this place is located at the far northern end of Zancudo, and it is easily the plushest option in the vicinity. All of the well-equipped rooms look out onto a bright green lawn of soft grass and the small swimming pool and Jacuzzi; the beach is just a few steps beyond that. Fishing is the focus, and the boats, captains, and fishing gear are all top-notch. Playa Zancudo. ☎ 800/854-8791 in U.S. and Canada, or 2776-0008 in Costa Rica. www.thezancudolodge.com. 26 units. $185 nonfishing; $400–$500 including full-day fishing. Rates are per person based on double occupancy and include all meals, drinks (alcoholic and carbonated), and taxes. MC, V.

Southern Zone Fast Facts

> *Wi-Fi pops up in the unlikeliest places in Costa Rica, such as this Osa Peninsula beach.*

Accommodations Booking Services
In just about all instances, you are best off booking direct with the hotels and resorts listed in this guide.

ATMs
This is a very remote region. You will find banks with a cash machine (*cajero automatico*) only in Golfito and Puerto Jiménez. At press time, there are no banks or ATMs in Drake Bay, Zancudo, or Pavones, and I don't expect that to change anytime soon.

Dentists & Doctors
The principal hospital in the Southern Zone is Hospital Golfito (☎ 2775-7900), although there are several doctors and a local clinic (☎ 2735-5029) in Puerto Jiménez.

If you have a mild medical issue or dental problem while traveling around the Southern Zone, most hotels will be able to refer you to a local doctor (*medico*) or dentist (*dentista*) who speaks English.

Emergencies
In case of emergency, call ☎ 911 (there should be an English-speaking operator); if 911 doesn't work, contact the police at ☎ 2222-1365 or 2221-5337, and hopefully they can find someone who speaks English to translate. For an ambulance, call ☎ 128; to report a fire, call ☎ 118. For a medical emergency that doesn't require an ambulance, see "Dentists & Doctors," above. To report lost or stolen items, see "Police," p. 375.

Getting There & Getting around
BY PLANE San José's Juan Santamaría International Airport is the closest gateway to the Southern Zone. From San José, you have several options for onward travel to the Southern Zone.

Two local commuter airlines—**Sansa** (☎ 877/767-2672 in U.S. and Canada, or 2290-4100 in Costa Rica; www.flysansa.com) and **Nature Air** (☎ 800/235-9272 in U.S. and Canada, or 2299-6000 in Costa Rica; www.natureair.com)—have daily flights from San José to the airstrips in Drake Bay, Golfito, Palmar Sur, and Puerto Jiménez. These airlines also have connecting flights to the Southern Zone from most other tourist destinations around the country. Fares run $105 to $130 each way.

For smaller destinations and specific lodges,

try **Alfa Romeo Air Charters** (☎ 2735-5353 or 2735-5112; www.alfaromeoair.com), which runs airline charters to most of the nearby destinations, including Carate, Drake Bay, Sirena, and Golfito. A five-passenger plane costs between $200 and $400 one way, depending on your destination.

BY CAR This is an extremely isolated area, and I don't recommend that you drive here. You won't need a car to get around, and indeed, you won't be able to drive to some of the places on your itinerary. But if you decide to go by car, you can get to some of the beach towns and destinations in the Southern Zone (though again, not all of them). Take the Pan-American Hwy. (CR2) south from San José; the turnoff for Golfito, Playa Zancudo, and Pavones is in Río Claro, just before the border with Panama. The turnoff for Puerto Jiménez and Drake Bay is farther north, in the tiny town of Chacarita.

BY BUS, BOAT, OR TAXI The main bus company serving this region is **Tracopa** (☎ 2221-4214 or 2258-8939; Calle 5 between Avenidas 18 and 20, San José).

Taxis, often four-wheel-drive vehicles, are available in Golfito, Playa Zancudo, Pavones, and Puerto Jiménez.

Several speedboats work as boat taxis between Puerto Jiménez and Golfito. The fare is $5, and the ride takes a little less than 30 minutes. These boats leave five or six times throughout the day, or whenever they fill up, beginning at around 5am and finishing up at around 5pm. Ask around town or at the docks for current schedules.

There is a daily passenger launch service from Puerto Jiménez to Golfito from the public dock at 6am. Much slower, this trip takes 1½ hours; the fare is $3. The launch departs Golfito's municipal dock at 11:30 am.

You can also charter a water taxi for the trip across the Golfo Dulce to Golfito. You'll have to pay between $40 and $80 for an entire launch, which can carry as many as 12 people.

Internet Access

More and more hotels, resorts, cafes, and retailers around Costa Rica are offering high-speed Wi-Fi access, either free or for a small fee. More-over, you'll readily find Internet cafes in all major towns and tourist destinations, even in the Southern Zone. Rates run between 50¢ and $3 per hour, and connection speeds are generally pretty good.

Police

To report a lost or stolen article, such as a wallet or passport, visit the local police. Depending upon your location, that may be either the OIJ (judicial police), *guardia rural* (rural guard), or *policía metropolitana* (metro police). The number for the *policía de tránsito* (transit police) is ☎ 800/8726-7486, toll-free nationwide, or ☎ 2222-9330. See also "Emergencies," p. 374.

Post Offices

Your best bet is to go to the post office in Puerto Jiménez. Note that stamps (*estampillas*) can be purchased only at a post office. Similarly, you can mail your postcards and letters only from a post office—you won't find any public mail-boxes or drops around Costa Rica. However, most hotels will gladly offer to post your letters and postcards for you.

Safety

Most of the towns and tourist destinations of the Southern Zone are very isolated and relatively safe. That said, never leave items of value unattended in rental cars, hotel rooms (unless locked in a safe), or on the beach. Moreover, single women, couples, and small groups should probably avoid walking on desolate stretches of beach or back roads after dark.

Visitor Information

There are no official information offices or bureaus in the Southern Zone. Your best source of information—beyond this guide book—will be your hotel front desk and any of the local tour agencies.

Water

This is a very remote area, and most hotels advise you drink bottled water. Some have their own clean wells, or collect and purify rain water. In these cases, they will tell you so. Most restaurants that cater to tourists use bottled or treated water. Order it "*sin hielo*," which means "no ice"—even when frozen it's still water.

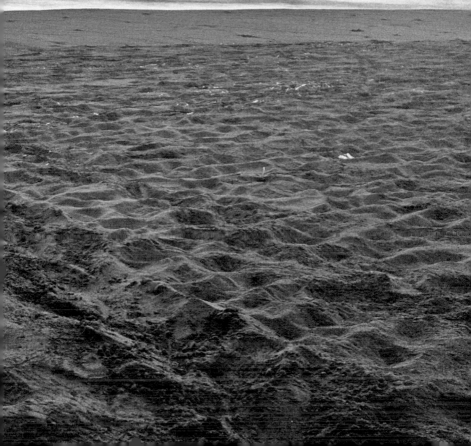

My Favorite Caribbean Coast Moments

Costa Rica's Caribbean coast is a world apart from the rest of the country. The pace is slower, the food is spicier, the tropical heat more palpable, and the rhythmic lilt of the local English-based patois fills the air. This is, for the most part, a region unexplored by visitors—indeed, more than half of the coastline is accessible only by boat or small plane. As a result of the coast's isolation, large tracts of virgin rain forest have been preserved, and the area boasts sprawling national parks and pristine beaches. It's not easy to get here, but it's well worth the effort.

> PREVIOUS PAGE *Sea turtle tracks in the sand, Tortuguero.* THIS PAGE *A resident of Aviarios Sloth Sanctuary of Costa Rica.*

❶ Hiking Cahuita National Park. This stunning national park offers fabulous scenery and great wildlife-viewing opportunities. Start off on the rain-forest trail, looking for birds and monkeys, and finish with a walk back along the soft white sands of the park's beach, with the Caribbean Sea lapping at your feet. See p. 381, ❷.

❷ Floating along the jungle canals of Tortuguero. Sometimes called the Venice of Costa Rica, the tiny town of Tortuguero and its namesake national park are connected to the rest of the country by a maze of rivers and canals. This aquatic highway is lined with dense tropical rain forests that are home to howler monkeys, three-toed sloths, and great green macaws, to name a few. See p. 417 ❹.

❸ Watching sea turtles lay eggs in Tortuguero. Despite crossing thousands of miles during their seaborne migrations, female sea turtles typically return to their birth beach to lay their clutches of eggs. This is one of the best places in Costa Rica to catch a glimpse. See p. 417, ❻.

❹ Enjoying Punta Uva. Arguably Costa Rica's nicest beach, this stretch of white sand is backed by thick rain forest and fronted by the crystal blue waters of the Caribbean Sea. Best of all, this lovely spot is crowd-free. See p. 399.

❺ Watching surfers take on Salsa Brava. Often called "Little Pipeline," because of its similarity to Hawaii's classic surf spot, Salsa Brava throws up a thick and fast barrel that breaks over shallow coral. Only serious surfers need apply. Still, the reef is close to shore, and you don't have to be a pro to enjoy watching

NICARAGUA

1 Cahuita National Park
2 Tortuguero canals
3 Tortuguero turtle-nesting tour
4 Punta Uva
5 Salsa Brava
6 Aviarios Sloth Sanctuary
7 Manzanillo
8 Soda Tamara
9 Maxi's

Punta Castilla
San Juan
Boca del Río Colorado
Isla Calero
Barra del Colorado
Barra del Colorado Wildlife Refuge
La Zapota
3 **Tortuguero**
Tortuguero Nat'l Park
Cariari
Río Jiménez
2
Parismina
Guapiles
Guacimo
Braulio Carrillo Nat'l Park
Carmen
San Rafael
Reventazón
Pacuare
Vol. Turrialba Nat'l Park
Siquirres
Barbilla
Boca Río Matina
Matina
32
Central Range
Turrialba Volcano
Estrada
Moín
Playa Bonita
Limón
Guayabo Nat'l Monument
Westfalia
Vol. Irazú Nat'l Park
Turrialba
Bomba
Beverly
Juan Vinas
Barbilla Nat'l Park
San Andrés
Playa Vizcaya
Moravia
Chirripó
Atlántico
6
Penshurst
Playa Negra
Cahuita Nat'l Park
Estrella
Tapantí (Orosi) Nat'l Park
Hitoy-Cerere Biological Res.
Cahuita
1
Uatsi
Puerto Viejo
5
7
Ojo de Agua
Cerro de la Muerte
Chirripó Nat'l Park
Telire
8 **4**
Manzanillo
2
Cabécar Ind. Res.
Bratsi
9
La Amistad Int'l Park
Talamanca Ind. Res.
Sixaola
36
PANAMA
Talamanca Range
Cerro Chirripó

CARIBBEAN SEA

NICARAGUA
SAN JOSÉ
The Caribbean Coast
PACIFIC OCEAN
PANAMA

0   15 mi
0   15 km

the thrills and spills on this world-class wave. See p. 394.

6 Touring Aviarios Sloth Sanctuary of Costa Rica. Sloths are among the more fascinating residents of Costa Rica's rain forests—they eat, sleep, and even give birth while hanging upside down. At this private reserve, you'll get the chance to see them up close. See p. 381, **3**.

7 Snorkeling on the reefs off Manzanillo. Some of Costa Rica's finest snorkeling is just 100 yards or so offshore from the tiny village of Manzanillo. You can sign up for a boat tour to these shallow reefs, or better yet, simply rent equipment and swim out on your own. See p. 387, **7**.

8 Eating rice 'n' beans cooked with coconut milk. You'll find *arroz y frijoles* (rice and beans) all across Costa Rica—it's practically the national dish. But along the Caribbean coast, "rice 'n' beans," as it's known here, is cooked with coconut milk, imparting a distinctive and delicious flavor. **Soda Tamara** (p. 411) in Puerto Viejo is an excellent spot to try some.

9 Savoring the lobster at Maxi's. On the beach in Manzanillo, Maxi's is little more than a glorified wooden shack serving up rice 'n' beans accompanied by fresh lobster, fish, or stewed chicken. And yet it's one of my favorite restaurants in the country. See p. 411.

The Best of the Caribbean Coast in 3 Days

Frankly, 3 days are just not enough to fully explore the Caribbean coast, given how time-consuming it can be to get here. But 3 days are better than nothing, and this itinerary will give you a good taste of what Costa Rica's Caribbean coast has to offer. You'll be able to visit both Cahuita and Puerto Viejo and take excursions into the rain forests and out to the coral reefs. Just make sure you've made all of your arrangements well in advance of your arrival—you'll be dependent on your lodge and on tour operators to get you around.

> The coastal forest that lines the beaches in Cahuita National Park is home to monkeys, sloths, birds, and other wildlife.

START Cahuita, 200km (124 miles) east of San José. Fly from San José to Limón (flight time: 45 minutes) the day before your tour begins, then take a taxi the 42km (26 miles) to Cahuita. **TOUR LENGTH** 52km (32 miles).

❶ ★★ Snorkeling over Cahuita Reef. All of the hotel desks and local tour operators offer snorkel excursions to the reefs just off Cahuita National Park. Silt and pesticides washing down from nearby banana plantations have taken a

heavy toll on the coral reefs, so don't expect the snorkeling to be world-class. But on a calm day, it can be pretty good. It can rain almost any time of year here; the most dependably dry and calm months are September and October. A 2- to 3-hour snorkel trip costs between $15 and $30 per person and includes equipment. You can arrange one with any of the hotel desks or local tour companies in town. I recommend **Cahuita Tours** (p. 396). *Note:* These trips are best

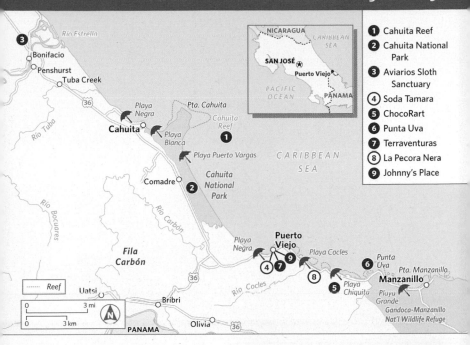

1 Cahuita Reef
2 Cahuita National Park
3 Aviarios Sloth Sanctuary
4 Soda Tamara
5 ChocoRart
6 Punta Uva
7 Terraventuras
8 La Pecora Nera
9 Johnny's Place

taken when the seas are calm, for safety's sake, visibility, and comfort. ☉ Minimum 2 hr. On the reefs just offshore; most tours depart from hotels in and around town. Rates $15–$30.

Arrange to be dropped off by your snorkel tour at the park entrance.

SITE GUIDE
PAGE 382

2 ★★ **Cahuita National Park.** With roughly 1,000 hectares (2,470 acres) of land and more than 22,400 hectares (55,350 acres) of marine territory, Cahuita National Park is a multifaceted gem. The principal trail here runs through dense lowland tropical coastal forests, which are great places to spot monkeys and sloths. Just offshore, the coral reefs contain 35 species of coral and provide a haven for hundreds of brightly colored tropical fish. This is one of Costa Rica's most popular spots for snorkeling (**1**).

You won't find a lunch place out here, so pack a picnic—you'll find several small general stores where you can stock up on provisions on the main road through town.

If you get tired of basking in the sun, take a walk on the beach itself or follow the trail that runs through the rain-forest just behind the

More Information

For stops **1**–**3**, plan to stay in Cahuita (p. 412); for stops **4**–**9**, plan to stay in Puerto Viejo (p. 404). For the most part, you'll be taking guided tours—ask your hotel to book these for you in advance.

beach. This trail (p. 382, **A**), goes all the way from the town of Cahuita and the Playa Blanca ranger station to the Puerto Vargas ranger station, for a total of 9km (5.6 miles). **The main, or Playa Blanca, entrance is at the southern edge of Cahuita town.** ☎ 2775-0268. Admission: voluntary donation at Playa Blanca entrance; $10 at Puerto Vargas entrance. Daily 8am–4pm.

On Day 2, get an early start, taking a taxi to the next stop.

3 ★★★ **kids Aviarios Sloth Sanctuary of Costa Rica.** It's virtually impossible not to fall for the strange, and strangely charming, sloth. It spends most of its life upside down, clinging to tree branches with its specially adapted (and especially sharp) claws. These slow-moving critters are found all over Costa Rica, but they can be hard to spot, as they

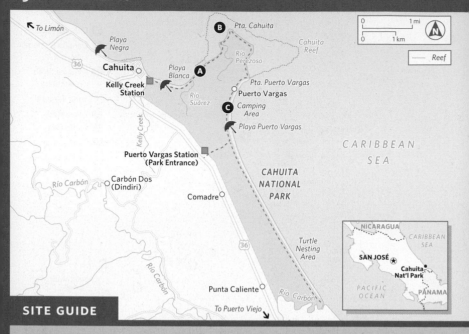

SITE GUIDE

② Cahuita National Park

As soon as you enter the park, you'll feel the siren-like lure of the scimitar of beach that stretches southward from the edge of town. Resist. Instead, take the ④ **main trail,** a wide, flat, and well-maintained path, which leaves from behind the ranger station and runs through thick forest, parallel to the beach, all the way to the Puerto Vargas ranger station. Make Punta Cahuita, a pretty finger of land jutting into the sea, your stopping point.

This 3.8km (2.4-mile) hike should take about an hour, but bear in mind that you're likely to stop along the way to take a refreshing dip (or two) and to check out the wildlife. Those grunts you hear are howler monkeys—they can be heard up to a kilometer away. Nearer at hand, you're likely to hear the rustling of coatimundis (pictured at left) and the scuttling of crabs amid the leaves on the forest floor. Look especially for the bright orange-and-purple Pacific land crabs. A little before the halfway point, the trail meets the beach near the **Río Perezoso** (Lazy River), a great spot to swim and to look for shorebirds such as herons and ibises.

Once you reach ⑧ ★★ **Punta Cahuita,** settle in for a stay on the little white-sand beach. You've spent the morning snorkeling, but if you're still in the mood, there are some good reefs just offshore. Enjoy a picnic lunch here before you move on.

On the way back, spend as much time as possible on the soft, golden sand by taking advantage of the ⑨ **beach trail** (which is basically just the beach itself). There are a few places where the forest comes right to the sea and the beach disappears. In these spots, you'll simply duck back onto the main trail.
⏱ Minimum 4 hr.

Travel Tip

Most roads in this region aren't named or numbered. They also aren't marked. Addresses are often based on location, and nothing more.

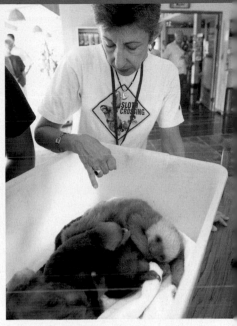

blend in with their surroundings so beautifully. Thankfully, the Aviarios Sloth Sanctuary offers visitors the chance to get an up-close look. The site houses a number of two and three-toed sloths, all recuperating from injuries. In addition to a tour of the rehabilitation center, Aviarios offers a canoe trip through the narrow rivers and estuaries just behind the property. I recommend you take both. ⏱ 3½ hrs. 9km (5½ miles) north of Cahuita, off CR36. ☎ 2750-0775. www.slothrescue.org. Admission $25 adults, $15 children 5–11; children 4 and under free. Daily 6am–4pm.

Take a taxi down to Puerto Viejo and check into your hotel.

④ 🍴 ★★ **Soda Tamara.** Stop for lunch at this typically Tico restaurant. The local rice 'n' beans with fresh fish or lobster is the way to go. On the main road in downtown Puerto Viejo. ☎ 2750-0148. $$–$$$. See p. 411.

In the afternoon, you'll be picked up in town for the day's last tour.

⑤ ★ **ChocoRart.** The best part of this tour of an organic cacao plantation and chocolate-maker is the end, when you get to taste the goods. But before you get to indulge in a sugar rush, you'll get a fascinating look into the process of growing, harvesting, and making chocolate. ⏱ 2 hr. Playa Chiquita, 5km (3 miles) south of Puerto Viejo. ☎ 2750-0075. Admission $15. By prior reservation only; 4-person minimum.

On the morning of Day 3, take a 15-minute taxi ride south to this beach.

⑥ ★★★ **Punta Uva.** Plan to spend some quality time on what I, and many others, consider to be the most beautiful beach on Costa Rica's Caribbean coast. Be sure to bring water and snacks, and maybe even a picnic lunch, as there's nothing for you right on the beach. See p. 399.

Head back to Puerto Viejo in time to be picked up at your hotel for the 12:30pm canopy tour.

> Napping sloths at Aviarios Sloth Sanctuary of Costa Rica, Cahuita.

⑦ ★ 🧒 **Terraventuras canopy tour.** With 23 platforms, a large harnessed swing, and a rappel, this tour will end your day with an adrenaline rush. ⏱ 4 hr. On the outskirts of Puerto Viejo. ☎ 2750-0750. www.terraventuras.com. Rates $55 adults, 10% discount for students with valid ID, $27.50 children 7–11; children 6 and under free; includes transportation. Daily 8am and 12:30pm.

You'll be returned to your hotel in time for dinner.

⑧ 🍴 ★★★ **La Pecora Nera.** On your final night on this coast, treat yourself to a meal at this standout Italian restaurant just south of Puerto Viejo. Playa Cocles, 50m (165 ft.) inland on a well-marked turn-off from the main road heading south past the soccer field. ☎ 2750-0490. $$$–$$$$. See p. 411.

⑨ ★★ **Johnny's Place.** Finish off the night dancing at this down-home joint set right on the sand. The open-air dance floor gets hot and sweaty, while the plastic tables and chairs set in the sand are a great place to cool off, sip a cold drink, and watch the stars as the waves lap against the shore just steps away. See p. 411.

The Best of the Caribbean Coast in 1 Week

A full week will allow you to experience the many charms of Costa Rica's Caribbean coast at a relaxed pace. In addition to the beach towns, reefs, beaches, and rain forests covered in the 3-day tour, you'll be able to explore the jungle canals of Tortuguero and spend a night in a remote mountain ecolodge. Once again, you'll be relying on taxis and organized tours, and since Tortuguero is accessible only by boat or small plane, it's imperative that you make your plans well in advance. You won't want to waste time trying to coordinate your transportation once you're here.

> A week on the Caribbean coast gives you plenty of time to take in laid-back beach towns such as Cahuita, shown here.

START Tortuguero, 250km (155 miles) northeast of San José. If your hotel does not provide transportation (many do), fly from San José to Tortuguero (flight time: 45 minutes). There is only one flight per day, so book early.

① ★★ kids **Tortuguero.** Spend a leisurely morning taking in the charms of the tiny village that shares its name with the surrounding national park and canals. Most of the buildings here are on stilts, thanks to frequent flooding, and the main street is a dirt path that leads to a beach.

There's a little church to check out, and you can pay a visit to the Caribbean Conservation Corporation's visitor center and museum.

Most of the rest of your time here will be spent on organized tours either provided by or booked through your hotel. You'll definitely want to take a boat trip on the canals that make up part of the park—you might get to see jaguars, anteaters, and collared peccaries, among other forest dwellers. I suggest you take this tour in the morning, as that's the best time for wildlife and bird viewing.

1. Tortuguero
2. Cahuita
3. Selva Bananito Lodge
4. Punta Uva
5. Finca La Isla Botanical Gardens
6. Luluberlu
7. Manzanillo

In the evening, arrange to see a turtle nesting. These magnificent creatures have been coming here to lay their eggs since at least 1592, when records were first kept. Despite problems with poaching, which peaked in the 1950s (the area is now protected), green, leatherback, and loggerhead turtles return every year.

One word of caution: as lovely as the beaches of Tortuguero National Park may look, they're not appropriate for swimming, as the surf is often very rough and the waters are prime shark territory. The turtle hatchlings make a tasty snack for these predators, so they tend to linger just offshore. ☺ 2 days. See p. 416.

> The forest-backed beach at Punta Uva.

> A waterfall at Selva Bananito, an inland ecolodge.

> Craftwork at Puerto Viejo's Luluberlu.

On the morning of Day 3, you'll be dropped off in Cahuita.

2 ★★ **Cahuita.** For Day 3 and the morning of Day 4, follow stops **1**–**3** in the 3-day tour (p. 380).

For lunch on Day 4, pay a visit to ★ **Sobre Las Olas** (p. 415). Pick a table close to the window and watch the waves break over the coral as you enjoy some fresh seafood. After your meal, slide into one of the hammocks hung between the coconut palms.

In the afternoon, sign up for a horseback ride with ★★ **Brigitte's Horses** (p. 413, **6**). I suggest a guided ride on the beach—Brigitte's will help you time it so you can watch the sun sink into the sea. ☺ 2 days.

Make arrangements with Selva Bananito Lodge to be picked up early on Day 5 for the 1-hour transfer from your hotel to their rainforest setting.

3 ★★ **Selva Bananito Lodge.** Most people come to the Caribbean coast to enjoy the beaches and the jungle canals of Tortuguero and never leave the coast. That's a shame, because there's great wildlife viewing and a host of adventure activities offered at this excellent ecolodge, just inland from Cahuita. Try the hike to a beautiful jungle waterfall, which has a rope set up that allows you to gently rappel down through the cascade. ☺ 1½ days. See "A Remote Ecolodge," p. 403.

More Information

For stop **1** you will stay in Tortuguero (p. 416). Many of the hotels there will arrange for your travel to Tortuguero, and to have you dropped you off in Cahuita (p. 412) for stop **2**. For stop **3**, Selva Bananito Lodge (p. 403) will make arrangements for you to be picked up in Cahuita, and then dropped off in Puerto Viejo (p. 404) for stops **4**–**7**. You must make these plans in advance—leaving them until the last minute may lead to major hassles.

> This tree-topped outcrop is part of the scenery in Gandoca-Manzanillo Wildlife Refuge, which extends south to the Panama border.

Have the lodge drop you off at your hotel in Puerto Viejo at midday on Day 6. Take a taxi to the beach.

④ ★★★ Punta Uva. Punta Uva is perhaps the prettiest beach on the Caribbean coast. Find a shady spot under a sea grape tree toward the far southern end of the beach and be sure to check out the short loop trail around the forested point. ⏱ 1 hr. for the loop trail. See p. 399.

Take a taxi for the 20-minute ride to these gardens.

⑤ ★★ Finca La Isla Botanical Gardens. The Kring family has poured a lot of time and love into the creation of this meandering collection of native and imported tropical flora. You'll see medicinal, commercial, and just plain wild flowering plants, fruits, herbs, trees, and bushes. Visitors get to gorge on whatever fruit is ripe at the moment. There's also a rigorous rain-forest loop trail. Hour-long guided tours leave on demand, with a 3-person minimum, and you are encouraged to linger and explore on your own after the tour. ⏱ Minimum 2 hr. Puerto Viejo, a couple of blocks inland from Playa Negra, north of El Pizote Lodge. ☎ 2750-0046 or 8886-8530. Email crgarden@mac.com. Admission: self-guided tour $5; guided tour $10; children 11 and under $2.50. Fri–Mon 10am–4pm; tours on other days can be arranged. Reservations recommended.

Before heading back to your hotel, make a stop in town.

⑥ ★ Luluberlu. You'll find loads of souvenir stands selling handmade jewelry and Indonesian imports in makeshift kiosks and storefronts all over town, but this small shop offers the most creative arts and crafts creations to be found in Puerto Viejo. **Downtown Puerto Viejo.** ☎ 2750-0394. Daily 10am-5pm.

On the morning of Day 7, take a taxi for the 25-minute ride south to Manzanillo.

⑦ ★★ kids Manzanillo. This is literally the end of the road: There's nothing beyond Manzanillo but sand, sea, and jungle. Enjoy the pristine beach—the water here is protected by a coral reef just offshore, making it almost always calm enough for swimming and good snorkeling (p. 396). If you want a break from the beach, hike the trail that leaves from downtown and takes you into the ★★ **Gandoca-Manzanillo Wildlife Refuge** (p. 407, **⑦**).

In the evening, before grabbing a taxi back to your hotel, stop for dinner at ★★★ **Maxi's** (p. 411) and try the ridiculously tasty fried fresh red snapper with rice 'n' beans. ⏱ 1 day.

Turtle Tour Tips

On turtle-nesting tours, flashlights, flash cameras, and lighted video cameras are prohibited, as is smoking. Wear dark clothes, and sneakers or sturdy shoes rather than sandals, as you may need to walk quite a way to encounter a nesting turtle. The beach is very dark at night, and it's easy to trip or step on driftwood or other detritus.

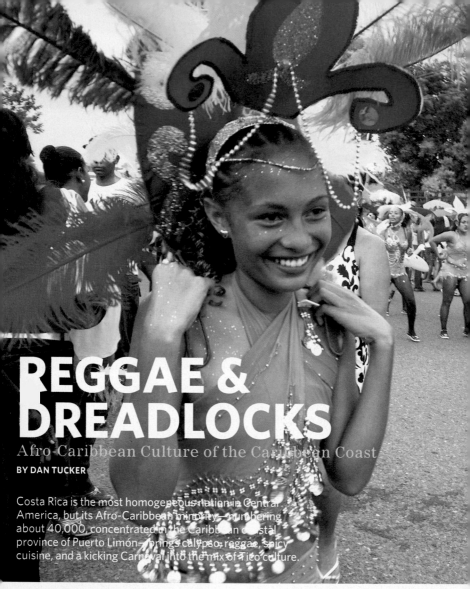

REGGAE &
DREADLOCKS
Afro-Caribbean Culture of the Caribbean Coast

BY DAN TUCKER

Costa Rica is the most homogeneous nation in Central America, but its Afro-Caribbean minority—numbering about 40,000, concentrated in the Caribbean coastal province of Puerto Limón—brings calypso, reggae, spicy cuisine, and a kicking Carnaval into the mix of Tico culture.

The Banana's Legacy

Small numbers of enslaved Africans were brought into the country in the 16th century by large estate owners to cultivate cacao; it wasn't until the 19th

century that freed Jamaican slaves were imported in significant numbers by Minor Keith to build the Atlantic Railroad, harvest coffee, and almost as an afterthought, grow bananas for what was to become the United Fruit Company. (Bananas were initially grown to feed the workers. The enormous surpluses became an exotic and luxurious hit when exported to the United States, Europe, and elsewhere.)

Due to their geographical isolation in Puerto Limón, and the fact that they are generally English-speaking Protestants, Afro–Costa Ricans have retained their unique cultural identity to this day, adding a distinct reggae lilt to an otherwise Latin culture.

Dancing in the Street

Today, music and dance of the Limón region blend elements of calypso, reggae, and hip-hop. Unlike Latin music, calypso and reggae emphasize the offbeat or "skank" beat (the 2nd and 4th beats in a 4-beat measure), offering a different, but no less descriptive take on the phrase "island time." Drums and the bass often take primacy over guitars and other instruments, and the banjo—an African instrument in its DNA—is frequently seen here.

CARNAVAL

There is no better place to immerse yourself in Afro-Costa Rican music and culture than Limón during Carnaval, a fantastical, riotous, cacophony of parades, concerts, street food, and carnival rides. Celebrated annually for several days around the weekend closest to October 12, Limón's Carnaval parades feature floats and *comparsas*, community-organized marching bands with teams of dancers in elaborate costumes. Performing precisely choreographed routines, the wildly costumed *comparsas* compete for prizes.

Carnival in Costa Rica, a 1947 musical confection starring Cesar Romero and Celeste Holm, offers a predictably cheesy and hilarious take on the festival.

Cool Characters, Hot Food

If Costa Rican cuisine is fresh and tasty but relatively undistinguished, Afro-Costa Rican food is the remedy for those craving stronger flavors. Many dishes are composed of yam, cassava, plantain, sweet potatoes, cocoyam, coconut, lentils, rice,

fish, meat, and other readily available ingredients. Salted codfish and akee (a lychee-like fruit, only part of which is edible), jerk chicken,

stewed goat, fried breadfruit, and rice and beans cooked in coconut milk or spiked with scotch bonnet or habanero peppers—a far cry from the usual *gallo pinto*—are West Indian specialties that are widely enjoyed in Puerto Limón. All are readily available on the streets of Limón during Carnaval.

The Caribbean Coast with Kids

The Caribbean coast is not your typical family destination:
There are no resorts with dedicated children's programs. In fact, hotels with air-conditioning and swimming pools are at a premium. Still, the area is a good choice for hearty, inquisitive, and adventurous families looking to experience the unique bounty offered up by the distinct cultures and ecosystems found along this coast. You will be picked up and dropped off at your hotel for most of these stops—they're organized tours—and for the rest, you can rely on cheap and easy-to-find taxis. No need for a rental car here.

> *It's impossible to resist the charms of the two- and three-toed sloths in residence at the Aviarios Sloth Sanctuary.*

START Puerto Viejo, 200km (124 miles) east of San José; 55km (34 miles) south of Limón. Fly from San José to Limón (flight time: 45 minutes) and take a 30-minute taxi ride to your hotel in Puerto Viejo. Plan to arrive the day before, as you'll be picked up at your hotel for your first tour. **TOUR LENGTH** 5 days.

① ★★ **Crocodive Caribe snorkeling trip to Manzanillo Reef.** Crocodive Caribe has a daily 9am trip to the coral reefs off Manzanillo—book in advance to ensure that you're on it. By going early in the day, when the seas are calmest and the skies are clearest, you'll have a good shot at seeing a seemingly endless parade of colorful

fish, and maybe even a barracuda or two. Crocodive provides all the equipment you'll need, as well as soft drinks, fruit, and snacks. Flotation devices are provided for nonswimmers. ⊕ 3½ hr. See p. 396.

In the afternoon, take a taxi for the 10-minute drive to Cacao Trails.

More Information

For stops **①**–**⑦**, you'll be based in Puerto Viejo (p. 404); for stop **⑧**, you'll stay at Tortuga Lodge (p. 419). Make your arrangements well in advance.

1 Snorkeling trip to Manzanillo Reef
2 Cacao Trails
3 Mariposarlo Cahuila
4 Aviarios Sloth Sanctuary
5 Surf lesson with Aventuras Bravas
6 Bread & Chocolate
7 Terraventuras canopy tour
8 Tortuga Lodge tour of Tortuguero

2 ★★ Cacao Trails. This comprehensive one-stop attraction features botanical gardens, a serpentarium, an open-air museum demonstrating the tools and techniques of cacao cultivation and processing, another section dedicated to the archaeology and history of local indigenous tribes, and a series of trails. You can also take canoe rides on the Río Carbón and even, during the nesting season, watch sea turtles lay their eggs. As if this weren't enough, there's a large open-air restaurant and a swimming pool for cooling off. ⏱ Minimum 2 hr. On CR36, 7.5km (4⅔ miles) north of Puerto Viejo; 10km (6¼ miles) south of Cahuita. ☎ 2756-8186. www.cacaotrails.com. Admission $25 including

> *A young crocodilian in the hands of a guide at Cacao Trails.*

> *There is no road access to tiny Tortuguero village, and people locomote by bike, boat, cart, horse, and foot.*

2-hr. guided tour; $47 including guided tour, canoe ride, and lunch; children 15 and under half-price. Daily 8am–5pm.

On the morning of Day 2, take a 15-minute taxi ride to Cahuita.

③ ★★ Mariposario Cahuita. The residents of the Cahuita Butterfly Garden are most active in the morning, before it gets too hot. And they are quite active—you and your kids will marvel at the bursts of color fluttering around you. You'll also learn quite a bit about the life cycle and natural history of butterflies. Don't worry—your kids won't get bored. This place is as mesmerizing as it is educational. ⏱ 1½ hr. On CR36, just north of the main entrance to Cahuita. ☎ 2755-0361. Admission $8. Sun–Fri 8:30am–3:30pm; Sat 8:30am–2pm.

Grab another taxi for the next stop, a 20-minute drive.

④ ★★★ Aviarios Sloth Sanctuary of Costa Rica. Watching super-slow sloths make their way around (or, as often is the case, not make their way anywhere) may remind you of watch-ing your kids get ready for school. Either way, both you and your brood are likely to fall hard for the charms of these critters, which are here to be rehabilitated in the wake of injuries. Take the combination tour, as it includes plenty of sloth face time and a kid-friendly canoe ride through the sanctuary's jungle canals and estuaries, where bird and wildlife viewing is spectacular. ⏱ 3½ hours. See p. 381, ③.

On the morning of Day 3, walk or take a taxi to the beach.

⑤ ★★ Surf lesson with Aventuras Bravas. Take a group lesson, together as a family, with this outfitter, which will provide an instructor, boards, and even rash guards (the lycra shirts worn by competitive surfers). Whether or not your kids get hooked on the sport, they'll likely enjoy watching you take a spill or two as you learn. Be sure to reserve in advance; depending upon the size of your clan, you may want to book more than one instructor. ⏱ 2 hr. Puerto Viejo. ☎ 8849-7600. www.aventurasbravas.com. Rates $30 per person for groups of 4–6 (with 1 instructor); $40 per person for groups of 2–3.

> *A thorough tour of the Tortuguero area includes a bird-watching boat trip along the canals.*

⑥   🍽 ★ **Bread & Chocolate.** Come for a lunch of peanut butter, jelly, and chocolate sandwiches, made with all fresh and homemade ingredients—just like home, only better. Downtown Puerto Viejo. ☎ 2750-0723. $–$$. See p. 410.

In the afternoon, return to your hotel in time to be picked up for a canopy tour.

❼ ★ **Terraventuras canopy tour.** Your kids will love the thrills and chills of the Terraventuras zip-line canopy tour. Not to fear—it's gentle enough even for younger ones. See p. 383, ❼.

On the morning of Day 4, you'll be picked up at your hotel and dropped off at Tortuga Lodge in Tortuguero.

❽ ★★★ **Tortuga Lodge tour of Tortuguero.** Finish up your time on the Caribbean coast with Tortuga Lodge's organized 2-day tour of the village, the national park, and the canals. You'll explore the canals by boat, visit some isolated beaches, go wildlife-watching—it's an ideal family package. There are a swimming pool and gentle rain-forest trails right on the site. ⏲ 2 days. See p. 419.

> *At the Cahuita Butterfly Garden you might see how the shimmering Blue Morpho looks with its wings folded.*

Caribbean Coast Adventures in & on the Water

While it's easy to slip into a reggae- and heat-induced stupor here, the Caribbean Sea, which runs all along this coastline, provides plenty of opportunities for waterborne activities and adventures. Some of the area's most popular options include sportfishing, surfing, and snorkeling.

> The wave breaks over coral at Salsa Brava, and is for experienced surfers only.

Body Boarding & Surfing

Board surfing on the Caribbean coast is very specialized. You won't find nearly as many breaks here as you will in Guanacaste, on the Nicoya Peninsula, or all along the central Pacific coast. Moreover, the waves here are dependent upon transient storms and wind swell, as opposed to ground swell, and thus are much less dependable and consistent than those found on the Pacific side. The best months for surfing the Caribbean coast are between December and March, although waves can be found here most of the year.

That said, Puerto Viejo's ★★★ **Salsa Brava** (p. 406, ❹) is one of the most coveted breaks in the country. A fast, steep, hollow tube that breaks over a shallow coral reef, this wave is for serious surfers only. The paddle out is through a tricky, short maze of a channel cut in the coral. And once you catch the wave, if you don't know where to bail, it can deposit you right on top of sharp coral. Despite its ferocity, when this wave is working, it can get crowded. Be polite and defer to locals.

South of Salsa Brava, ★★ **Playa Cocles** (p. 398) is a thick and powerful beach break

Body Boarding & Surfing

Aventuras Bravas **4**

Cahuita Tours **3**

Playa Blanca **3**

Playa Bonita **2**

Playa Cocles **5**

Playa Negra (Cahuita) **3**

Playa Negra (Puerto Viejo) **4**

Salsa Brava **4**

Turística Cahuita Information Center **3**

Bodysurfing

Playa Bonita **2**

Playa Cocles **5**

Playa Negra (Cahuita) **3**

Scuba Diving & Snorkeling

Cahuita Tours and Adventure Center **3**

Turística Cahuita Information Center **3**

Reef Runners Dive Shop **4**

Crocodive Caribe **4**

Sportfishing

Bacalao Tours **6**

Río Colorado Lodge **1**

Silver King Lodge **1**

White Water Rafting

Exploradores Outdoors **4**

with several different peaks. With more room to spread out, this break doesn't feel as crowded as Salsa Brava, and it's a better bet for most visitors. However, don't be lulled into complacency: This wave regularly breaks boards.

When the swell is really big, you can sometimes find a very gentle wave, perfect for beginners, at the far southern edge of ★ **Playa Negra** (p. 399) near the entrance to Puerto Viejo. It's a beautiful spot, with the wave's takeoff beginning just off a sunken, rusting barge that ran aground here.

Those staying in Cahuita can try to catch waves right at the very start of **Playa Blanca** (p. 398), just inside Cahuita National Park, or a few kilometers north of town on the other

Playa Negra (p. 399). Finally, surfers staying in Limón will want to head north of the city, to **Playa Bonita** (p. 398).

At all beach towns in the area, locals rent surf and body boards out of makeshift kiosks. For lessons and board rentals in Puerto Viejo, try ★★ kids **Aventuras Bravas** (p. 392, **5**), which has an office just across the road from Salsa Brava. In Cahuita, try ★ **Cahuita Tours** or ★ **Turística Cahuita Information Center** (see "Scuba Diving & Snorkeling," p. 396, for information on both operations). Rates are pretty standard and run around $10 for a half-day board rental and $15 for a full-day rental. Surf lessons run around $30 to $40 per person for group lessons, $50 for a 1-hour private lesson.

> *Shooting the rapids on the Río Pacuare, which runs from the central mountains down to the Caribbean Sea.*

Bodysurfing

This coastline is best known for its several thick and furious surf breaks, most of which are better suited to surfers using boards. The best breaks for bodysurfing are **Playa Bonita** (p. 398) in Limón, **Playa Cocles** (p. 398) just south of Puerto Viejo, and **Playa Negra** (p. 399) in Cahuita.

Scuba Diving & Snorkeling

The reefs off **Cahuita National Park** and fronting the tiny village of **Manzanillo** offer some excellent snorkeling and scuba diving opportunities. All of the hotel desks in Cahuita offer snorkeling outings to the nearby reefs. If your hotel desk doesn't, check in with ★ **Cahuita**

Tours (☎ 2755-0000; www.cahuitatours.com) or ★ **Turística Cahuita Information Center** (☎ 2755-0071), both located on the village's main street. Snorkeling trips should run between $25 and $40 per person, including equipment, depending upon group size and how long you will be out. There are no dedicated scuba operators in Cahuita.

Down in Puerto Viejo, ★ **Reef Runners Dive Shop** (☎ 2750-0480) and ★★ **kids Crocodive Caribe** (☎ 2750-2136; www.crocodivecaribe.com) are the best operators. Both frequent a variety of dive sites between Punta Uva and Manzanillo. If you're lucky, the seas will be calm and visibility good—although throughout most of the year it can be a bit rough and murky here. Snorkel tours generally run around $35 to $45 per person. Longer outings in search of dolphins are also offered. Scuba diving outings can be done from the beach or a boat. Individual tanks run around $35 for a beach dive and $60 for a boat dive, with equipment rental an extra $15 to $20. Multiple dive packages are available.

Bring Your Own Beach Gear

If you plan to spend time at the beach, it's often a good idea to pack your own beach towel or mat. Quite a few of the midrange and budget hotels along the Caribbean coast do not provide them.

Sportfishing

Fishing on the Caribbean coast is liveliest near river mouths, in estuaries, and along the inland canals and rivers. Following current trends in sportfishing, more and more anglers have been using fly rods, so pack accordingly.

Sportfishermen come here primarily in the hopes of landing a tarpon, known locally as the "silver king." Tarpon can grow to impressive sizes, maxing out at about 2m (6½ ft.) in length and weighing as much as 160kg (350 lbs). In addition to their prodigious size, tarpon are prized for the fight they put up, with numerous full-body leaps out of the water. Tarpon can be caught year-round, both in the river mouths and, to a lesser extent, in the canals; however, they are much harder to land in July and August—the two rainiest months—probably because the rivers run so high and are so full of runoff and debris.

Snook are aggressive river fish that peak in April, May, October, and November; fat snook, or *calba*, run heavy November through January. In the rivers and canals, fishermen regularly bring in *mojarra, machaca,* and *guapote* (rainbow bass). Depending on how far out to sea you venture, you might hook up with barracuda, jack, mackerel (Spanish and king), wahoo, tuna, dorado (mahimahi), marlin, or sailfish.

Barra del Colorado is the prime fishing destination on the Caribbean coast, with several dedicated fishing lodges. The best of these are **Silver King Lodge** (☎ 877/335-0755 in U.S. and Canada [no Costa Rica number]; www. silverkinglodge.net) and **Río Colorado Lodge** (☎ 800/243-9777 in U.S. and Canada, or 2232-4063 in Costa Rica; www.riocolorado lodge.com). Both of these lodges offer full package tours, with serious amounts of fishing and top-notch gear. Rates run between $2,200 and $3,000 per person, double occupancy, for

> *A scuba diver encounters a ray in Costa Rican waters.*

a weeklong, all-inclusive package that includes about 4 full days of fishing, all meals, drinks, tackle, taxes, and in-country transportation.

In the Puerto Viejo area, check in with the folks at **Bacalao Tours** (☎ 2759-9116; email bacalaomanzanillo@yahoo.com), down in Manzanillo. In Tortuguero or Cahuita, your best bet is to ask your hotel to help you set something up. A half-day fishing outing with gear, tackle, drinks, and snacks should run from $200 to $400, while a full day will cost between $500 and $800, with lunch thrown in to boot.

White-Water Rafting

Costa Rica's principal white-water rivers, the **Pacuare** and **Reventazón,** both empty out on the Caribbean side of the country. The main put-in point, near Turrialba, is just a couple of hours away from Cahuita and Puerto Viejo by car. ★ **Exploradores Outdoors** (☎ 2222-6262 in San José or 2750-2020 in Puerto Viejo; www.exploradoresoutdoors.com) runs daily white-water rafting trips on both of these rivers from all of the tourist towns along the Caribbean coast except Tortuguero. A full-day trip, including breakfast and lunch, costs $99.

If you want to combine white-water rafting with your transportation along the Caribbean coast, Exploradores will pick you up at your hotel in San José with all your luggage, take you for a day of white-water rafting, and drop you off at day's end at your hotel anywhere on the Caribbean coast from Limón to Manzanillo. I personally think this beats the heck out of driving yourself or riding in a tourist van or public bus.

Timing Your Dive Trip Right

This area gets plenty of rain. Still, September and October are oddly some of your best bets for sun—although sunny days are not guaranteed even in those months. Coinciding with this mini dry season, the winds and seas are calm all along the Caribbean coast. This is typically the best time of year for snorkeling and scuba diving.

Caribbean Coast Beaches A to Z

★★ **kids Manzanillo.** Located literally at the end of the road—it's just forests, the sea, and footpaths from here all the way to the Panamanian border—this is a straight stretch of white sand. There are several picnic tables spread out under tall coconut palms along the final section of road, just before it ends. The reef is located just offshore, and there is generally very good snorkeling here. **13km (8 miles) south of Puerto Viejo.**

★★★ **Playa Blanca.** This is the principal beach inside Cahuita National Park, and it's a stunning sweep of gently curving white sand backed by thick lush forest. It's quite common to hear howler monkeys calling as you sunbathe or swim here. **Inside Cahuita National Park (p. 381, ②).**

Playa Bonita. The closest beach to Limón, it is a short, deep, scallop-shaped section of white sand. It is also a favorite surf spot for local board and bodysurfers; it's sometimes a bit rough for casual swimming. **2km (1¼ miles) north of Limón.**

★ **Playa Chiquita.** The English translation of Playa Chiquita is "little beach." That's misleading, because the beach itself is actually a fairly lengthy stretch running between Playa Cocles and Punta Uva, though it is broken up into smaller sections by rocks and exposed reef. There's a daily pick-up volleyball game here, right in front of Playa Chiquita Lodge (p. 409). **5km (3 miles) south of Puerto Viejo.**

★ **Playa Cocles.** The first beach south of the town of Puerto Viejo, this is also known as "surf beach." The steady beach break here is a lot easier and more dependable than Salsa Brava (p. 394). The beach itself is a long, straight stretch of white sand. Riptides can be strong here; swimmers are probably best off heading toward the far southern end of the beach. **2km (1¼ miles) south of Puerto Viejo.**

> *Costa Rica has several beaches named Playa Negra, but the one at Puerto Viejo is distinguished by a beached barge sporting a sea-grape tree.*

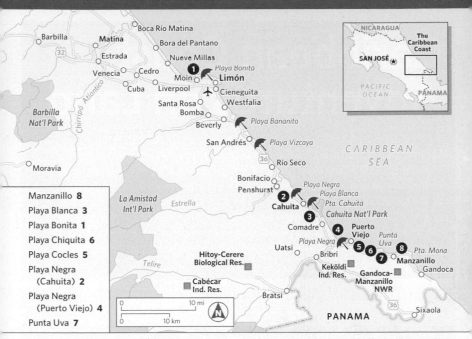

Manzanillo **8**
Playa Blanca **3**
Playa Bonita **1**
Playa Chiquita **6**
Playa Cocles **5**
Playa Negra
  (Cahuita) **2**
Playa Negra
  (Puerto Viejo) **4**
Punta Uva **7**

★ **Playa Negra (Cahuita).** Located north of Cahuita, this is an isolated and picturesque stretch of black volcanic sand. Local kids like to surf and bodysurf here, while tourists tend to stick to Playa Blanca (p. 398), inside Cahuita National Park (p. 381, ②). 2km (1¼ miles) north of Cahuita village.

★★ **Playa Negra (Puerto Viejo).** Not to be confused with its northern neighbor (see above), this is a wide black volcanic sand beach. The surf can get a bit rough here—your best bet for swimming is the section closest to town. However, if you want to take a long walk on a desolate beach backed by virgin rain forest, simply head north. The beach stretches on, uninterrupted, all the way to Cahuita National Park. **Northern end of Puerto Viejo.**

★★★ **Punta Uva.** Punta Uva translates as "Grape Point," and the rain-forest-covered promontory that gives this beach its name does look like a bunch of grapes from a distance. A long, gently curving stretch of white sand, backed by thick forests and fronted by the Caribbean Sea, this is one of the top beaches in the country. 8.4km (5¼ miles) south of Puerto Viejo.

> *The long stretch of white-sand beach that stretches north and south from Manzanillo.*

Caribbean Coast Adventures on Land

There are numerous active tourism and adventure opportunities up and down the Caribbean coast and in the rain-forest-covered mountains just inland. In most cases, your hotel desk will be your best bet for arranging land-based tours and adventures. This is especially true in Tortuguero, where almost all visitors come as part of an organized tour. Alternatively, in the towns of Cahuita and Puerto Viejo, there are several all-purpose operators who can arrange any number of tour and activity options, including guided hikes, bird-watching excursions, ATV tours, zip-line canopy adventures, and visits to nearby indigenous communities.

> *Egg-laying completed, a green turtle heads back out to sea.*

All-Purpose Tour Operators

Most people book their tours through their hotels, but if you'd rather do your own thing, there's no reason not to. In Cahuita, check in with ★ **Cahuita Tours** (p. 396), ★ **Turística Cahuita Information Center** (p. 396), or **Roberto Tours** (☎ 2755-0117). All are located within a 3-block area on the main road through town. In the Puerto Viejo, Punta Uva, and Manzanillo area, I recommend ★★ **Aventuras Bravas** (p. 392, **5**), ★ **Exploradores Outdoors** (p. 397), or ★ **Terraventuras** (☎ 2750-0750; www.terraventuras.com; see also p. 383, **7**).

For an alternative experience, try the ★★ **Asociación Talamanqueña de Ecoturismo y Conservación** (ATEC; Talamancan Association of Ecotourism and Conservation; ☎ 2750-0398 or ☎/fax 2750-0191; www. ateccr.org), located in Puerto Viejo across

NICARAGUA

Punta Castilla

Isla Calero

San Juan

Boca del Río Colorado

Barra del Colorado Wildlife Refuge

Barra del Colorado

La Zapota

Boca del Río Tortuguero

Tortuguero **8**

Tortuguero Nat'l Park 7

Tortuguero

Cariari

Parismina

Río Jiménez

Guapiles

Guacimo

Carmen

San Rafael

Boca Río Matina

Siquirres

Vol. Turrialba Nat'l Park

Turrialba Volcáno

Barbilla

Matina

Estrada

Liverpool

Guayabo Nat'l Monument

Turrialba

Juan Vinas

Barbilla Nat'l Park

Moravia

Moin

Limón

Playa Bonita

Bomba

Westfalia

6

Beverly

San Andrés

Playa Vizcaya

CARIBBEAN SEA

Tapantí (Orosi) Nat'l Park

Chirripó

Atlántico

5

Penshurst

4

Playa Negra

Cahuita

3

Cahuita Nat'l Park

Estrella

NICARAGUA

SAN JOSÉ

The Caribbean Coast

PACIFIC OCEAN

PANAMA

Hitoy-Cerere Biological Res.

Uatsi

Telire

Cabécar Ind. Res.

Bratsi

2

Puerto Viejo

Manzanillo

Gandoca-Manzanillo NWR 1

Talamanca Range

La Amistad Int'l Park

Talamanca Ind. Res.

Sixaola

PANAMA

0   15 mi
0   15 km

Tour Operators

Asociación Talamanqueña de Ecoturismo y Conservación **2**

Aventuras Bravas **2**

Cahuita Tours **3**

Exploradores Outdoors **2**

Roberto Tours **3**

Terraventuras **2**

Turística Cahuita Information Center **3**

ATV Tours

Terraventuras **2**

Bird-Watching

Aviarios Sloth Sanctuary **4**

Tortuguero canals **7**

Canopy Tours

Terraventuras **2**

Veragua Rainforest Park **6**

Hiking

Asociación Talamanqueña de Ecoturismo y Conservación **2**

Cahuita National Park **3**

Selva Bananito Lodge **5**

Horseback Riding

Brigitte's Horses **3**

Seahorse Stables **2**

Turtle-Watching

Gandoca-Manzanillo National Wildlife Refuge **1**

Tortuguero National Park **8**

---

the street from Soda Tamara (p. 411). ATEC is actively involved in preserving the environment and the cultural heritage of this area and promoting ecologically sound development. It offers quite a few tours, including half-day walks that focus on nature and either the local Afro-Caribbean culture or the indigenous Bribri culture. These walks pass through farms and forests, and along the way you'll learn about local history, customs, medicinal plants, and Central American Indian mythology, and do some bird and wildlife viewing.

You can also sign up for walks through the Bribri's nearby Kéköldi Reserve, as well as hikes through the primary rain forest. The local guides have a wealth of information and make

> *The multicolored keel-billed toucan can be seen all along the Caribbean coast.*

> *The beach trail, Cahuita National Park.*

the hikes truly educational experiences. Half-day walks (and night walks) are $20 to $35, and a full-day tour costs between $30 and $65. If you plan to stay in Puerto Viejo for an extended period of time and would like to contribute to the community, ask at ATEC about volunteer opportunities.

All of the tour operators along the Caribbean coast can also arrange day tours and overnight trips to **Tortuguero** (p. 416).

All-Terrain-Vehicle (ATV) Tours
The back roads and forest trails here are well suited to ATV exploration. The only dedicated operator currently offering ATV tours and excursions is ★ kids **Terraventuras,** in Puerto Viejo (see "All-Purpose Tour Operators," p. 400). Plan to spend 4 to 5 hours and $80 on your ride. The cost for two riders sharing an ATV is $110; children 11 and under can ride on a parent's vehicle for an additional $10.

Bird-Watching
There's spectacular bird-watching all along the Caribbean coast. In fact, more than 400 species have been recorded here. In Tortuguero, you can sometimes see the rare great green macaw. All along the coast you might spot a keel-billed toucan, rufescent tiger-heron, and any number of parrot, tanager, and kingfisher species. Some of the best bird-watching in this region takes

place on boat tours through the ★★★ canals of **Tortuguero** (p. 417, ❹) and at ★★★ **Aviarios Sloth Sanctuary of Costa Rica** (p. 381, ❸). In Tortuguero, you'll find that all of the hotels and lodges have specialized bird-watching guides and tours. Similarly, the canal tours at Aviarios del Caribe are led by experienced and specialized birding guides.

Canopy Tours
★ kids **Terraventuras.** This Puerto Viejo–based operator runs one of the only zip-line canopy tours down along the coast. See p. 383, ❼.

★ kids **Veragua Rainforest Park.** The canopy tour here features nine treetop platforms. In addition, these folks have several other attractions, including a serpentarium, a butterfly garden and breeding exhibit, a hummingbird garden, an extensive insect exhibit, and a network of rainforest trails. See p. 420, ❸.

Hiking
The forests of the Caribbean coast are dense, lowland coastal forests, in many areas mixing with or replaced by mangrove forests. The best hiking in the area is in ★★ **Cahuita National Park** (p. 381, ❷) or on the trails at ★★ **Selva Bananito Lodge** (see "A Remote Ecolodge," p. 403). In the Puerto Viejo area, the folks at ★★ **Asociación Talamanqueña de Ecoturismo y Conservación** (see "All-Purpose Tour Operators," p. 400) offer a range of guided hikes through the surrounding forests.

Horseback Riding
Not an especially hot spot for equestrian activities, the Caribbean coast tends to offer rather basic and rugged horseback-riding opportunities. You'll find no shortage of locals offering up simple rides on poorly tended horses.

But that doesn't mean you'll miss out—there are two exceptions. In the Cahuita area, go with ★★ **Brigitte's Horses** (☎ 2755-0053; www.brigittecahuita.com), which offers both guided and self-guided outings on well-cared-for and gentle horses. The signature half-day tour takes you to a remote jungle waterfall. In the Puerto Viejo area, check in with ★ **Seahorse Stables** (☎ 2750-0468; www.horsebackridingincostarica.com). Rates run around $20 to $35 per person for a 1-hour guided tour and from $10 to $20 per person for an hour of unguided riding.

Turtle-Nesting Tours

By far the most popular spot for partaking in turtle tours is Tortuguero. All of the lodges here specialize in turtle-nesting tours, in season.

Four species of sea turtles nest on beaches up and down the Caribbean coast. Green turtles are probably the most common species found here. You're more likely to see one of these than any other species if you visit during their prime nesting season, from July to mid-October (August and September are peak months). Loggerhead and hawksbill turtles are very rare here, so don't be disappointed if you don't see one. The giant leatherback is perhaps the most spectacular to watch. The largest of all turtle species, the leatherback can grow to 2m (6½ ft.) long and weigh well over 455kg (1,000 lbs.). It nests from early March to mid-April, predominantly on the southern beaches of ★★★ **Tortuguero National Park** (p. 417, ❻), and inside the ★★ **Gandoca-Manzanillo Wildlife Refuge** (p. 407, ❼).

A Remote Ecolodge

Located deep in the rain forest of the Talamanca mountain range, ★★ **Selva Bananito Lodge** provides excellent active adventure opportunities. Staying here is a great way to combine beach time on the Caribbean coast and an inland ecolodge experience into one compact itinerary. A wide range of tours and activities is offered, including rain-forest hikes and horseback rides in the jungle, tree climbing, self-guided trail hikes, and rappels down the face of a jungle waterfall. The bird-watching here is also superb. The owners are involved in conservation efforts and sustainable tourism practices, and approximately two-thirds of their 840 hectares (2,075 acres) are primary forest managed as a private reserve.

The large, individual stilt-raised cabins here feature an abundance of varnished woodwork, large private bathrooms, and a wraparound veranda with a hammock and some chairs. Half the cabins have views of the Río Bananito and a small valley, the other half views of the Matama mountains (part of the Talamanca range). There are no electric lights at Selva Bananito, but each evening as you dine by candlelight, your cabin's oil lamps are lit for you. Hot water is provided by solar panels. *Note:* You'll need a four-wheel-drive vehicle to reach the lodge itself, although most folks leave their rental cars in Bananito and let the lodge drive them the final bit. You can also arrange to be picked up in San José. Bananito. ☎ 2253-8118. www.selvabananito.com. 11 units. $260-$280 cabins. Rates are based on double occupancy and include all meals and taxes. No credit cards.

Puerto Viejo & Southward

Puerto Viejo is the hottest spot on Costa Rica's Caribbean coast. And I'm not just talking about the often stifling heat. Much of the town's popularity and lively vibe is owed to the scores of surfers who come here to ride the famous and fearsome Salsa Brava wave. To the south of Puerto Viejo are some of the most beautiful beaches on this coast, with white sand and turquoise seas. Whether you surf or not, you will appreciate the abundance of active adventure options, nearby rain-forest trails, and great local and international cuisine. Plan to spend 3 or 4 days here.

> *Wild and unspoiled coastline in Gandoca-Manzanillo Wildlife Refuge.*

START **Puerto Viejo is 200km (124 miles) east of San José; 55km (34 miles) south of Limón.**

① ★★ Finca La Isla Botanical Gardens.
Spend the afternoon walking the trails of these impressive botanical gardens. In addition to the informative tour and samples of fresh fruit and fresh fruit juices, you will almost certainly see one or more species of poison dart frog. See p. 387, **⑤**.

② ★ Luluberlu. Amidst an abundance of cheap souvenir stores and streetside stands selling Indonesian imports and standard T-shirts, this place really stands out. Artistically crafted functional and decorative arts make use of

local materials, like sea shells and bamboo. I particularly like some of the lampshades and mirror frames. ⏱ 45 min. See p. 387, **⑥**.

You'll be picked up at your hotel for the following tour.

③ ★★ kids Cacao Trails. This multifaceted attraction has plenty for the whole family. After you've toured the botanical garden trails, seen the snakes in the serpentarium, and learned all about cacao cultivation and production at the open-air chocolate museum, you can have lunch here, and then spend as much of the afternoon as you like playing in their pool. ⏱ Minimum 2 hr. See p. 391, **②**.

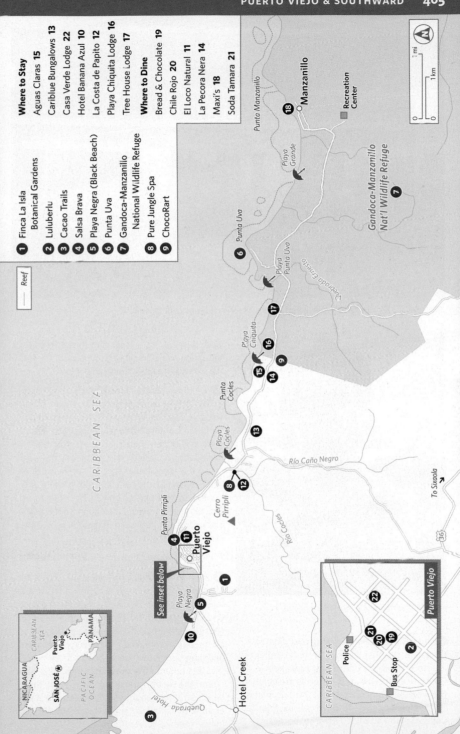

Where to Stay
Aguas Claras **15**
Cariblue Bungalows **13**
Casa Verde Lodge **22**
Hotel Banana Azul **10**
La Costa de Papito **12**
Playa Chiquita Lodge **16**
Tree House Lodge **17**

Where to Dine
Bread & Chocolate **19**
Chile Rojo **20**
El Loco Natural **11**
La Pecora Nera **14**
Maxi's **18**
Soda Tamara **21**

1. Finca La Isla Botanical Gardens
2. Luluberlu
3. Cacao Trails
4. Salsa Brava
5. Playa Negra (Black Beach)
6. Punta Uva
7. Gandoca-Manzanillo National Wildlife Refuge
8. Pure Jungle Spa
9. ChocoRart

Reef

CARIBBEAN SEA

NICARAGUA
CARIBBEAN SEA
Puerto Viejo
SAN JOSÉ
PACIFIC OCEAN
PANAMA

Punta Pirripli
Cerro Pirripli
Puerto Viejo
See inset below
Playa Negra
Hotel Creek
Quebrada Hotel

Río Caño Negro
Río Cocles
To Sixaola
36

Playa Cocles
Punta Cocles
Playa Chiquito
Playa Punta Uva
Punta Uva
Quebrado Ernesto
Playa Grande
Playa Manzanillo
Manzanillo
Recreation Center
Gandoca-Manzanillo Nat'l Wildlife Refuge

Puerto Viejo
Police
Bus Stop
CARIBBEAN SEA

1 mi
1 km

> *Luluberlu, a shop in Puerto Viejo, offers works of local artists and craftspeople.*

> *Visitors learn about chocolate at Cacao Trails.*

4 ★★★ **Salsa Brava.** Breaking over a patch of shallow reef just offshore from the center of Puerto Viejo, this is one of best surf spots in Costa Rica. When offshore storms are pumping, the wave here can reach 6m (20 ft.). Dubbed "Little Pipeline," this is a wave only experienced surfers should attempt. However, because it's so close to shore, it's a great spot to simply watch the action, which is fast and furious whenever the wave is breaking. **South end of town.**

5 ★★ **Playa Negra (Black Beach).** Beginning at the northern limit of town, this broad, black volcanic sand beach runs all the way to Punta Vargas in Cahuita National Park (p. 381, **2**). Right at the start there's a rusted, grounded barge with a cute little sea-grape tree growing on it—this is a popular spot for surf lessons. As you head north, the beach becomes more and more deserted, backed only by thick rain forest. One word of warning: Don't go barefoot, as the black sand can get hot in the midday sun. **North of downtown.**

Take a taxi south of town to reach this beach.

6 ★★★ **Punta Uva.** Don't leave this area without spending at least a few hours on this beautiful beach. Take some time to walk the short loop trail that runs around the area's namesake point. Most days there are folks renting out kayaks on the beach here, and you have your choice of paddling out on the ocean, or up a small river that lets out into the sea. While most folks hang out on the section just north of the point, the beach stretches southward for miles and is just as spectacular all along the way. **8.4km (5¼ miles) south of Puerto Viejo.**

Take a taxi south of town to reach this refuge.

7 ★★ **Gandoca-Manzanillo Wildlife Refuge.**
The Gandoca-Manzanillo Wildlife Refuge encompasses the small village of Manzanillo and
extends all the way to the Panamanian border.
Manatees, crocodiles, and more than 350 species of birds live within the boundaries of the
reserve. The reserve also includes the coral
reef offshore—when the seas are calm, this
is the best snorkeling and diving spot on this
entire coast. Four species of sea turtles nest
on one 9km (5½-mile) stretch of beach within
the reserve between March and July, and three
species of dolphins frolic in the waters just off
Manzanillo. Many local tour guides and operators offer boat trips out to spot them.

    If you want to explore the refuge, you can
easily find the single, well-maintained trail by
walking along the beach just south of town
until you have to wade across a small river.
On the other side, you'll pick up the trailhead.
Otherwise, check around the village for local
guides. Several beachfront kiosks rent kayaks
($6 an hour) and snorkel gear. Depending on
tides and sea conditions, this can be a relaxing
way to explore the mangroves and estuaries,
visit nearby beaches, and even snorkel at the
nearby coral reef. Guided tours and snorkel
excursions will run anywhere from $15 to $65
per person. ◷ Minimum 1 hr. 13km (8 miles)
south of Puerto Viejo. Free admission.

8 ★★ **Pure Jungle Spa.** This small spa has a
couple of open-air, bamboo treatment rooms in
a lush forest setting. A wide range of massages,
wraps, manicures, and pedicures is offered. Try
the Total Body Chocolate Decadence, which
uses locally grown organic cacao as a exfoliant,

> *Massage at Pure Jungle Spa.*

and cocoa butter as a lubricant. ◷ Minimum 45
min. At La Costa de Papito, Playa Cocles. ☎ 2750-
0536. www.purejunglespa.com. Rates $40–$95.

You'll be picked up at your hotel for a tour with
ChocoRart.

9 ★ **ChocoRart.** If you want to learn about
the harvesting, handling, and production of
cacao, I recommend this informative tour. This
humble organic cacao plantation and chocolate
production operation is owned and run by a
friendly Swiss couple, and the tour takes you
through the entire process. Happily, it ends with
a wonderful tasting. ◷ 2 hr. See p. 383, **5**.

Local Folklore

Many residents of the Caribbean coast trace
their heritage to Afro-Caribbean fishermen
and laborers who settled in this region in the
mid-1800s. Today, the area's population is
still composed largely of English-speaking
blacks whose culture and language set them
apart from other Costa Ricans. If you're
interested in the history and culture of the
region, pick up a copy of Paula Palmer's
What Happen: A Folk-History of Costa Rica's
Talamanca Coast (Zona Tropical, 2005). The
book is an oral history of Costa Rica's Caribbean coast based on interviews with many
of the area's oldest residents. Much of it is
sprinkled with and punctuated by the traditional patuis (which the locals call Creole),
from which the title is taken. It makes fun
and interesting reading—and on your visit
you just might meet someone mentioned in
the book.

Where to Stay

> *Common areas are friendly and welcoming at Case Verde Lodge.*

★★ Aguas Claras PLAYA CHIQUITA

These brightly painted individual bungalows are raised on stilts and feature fancy gingerbread trim. They all come with a private veranda and kitchen—although some have just a two-burner cooktop, while others feature a full stove and oven. They are an excellent option for families looking for an extended stay or to do some of their own cooking. The bungalows are just a few steps away from a lovely section of Playa Chiquita. Maid service is provided every other day. Playa Chiquita, 5km (3 miles) south of Puerto Viejo. ☎ 2750-0131. www.aguasclaras-cr.com. 5 units. $70–$220 bungalow. AE, DC, MC, V.

★★ Cariblue Bungalows PLAYA COCLES

Rooms here are housed in bungalows spread around well-tended and lush grounds, at the center of which is a large pool with swim-up bar. Deluxe rooms and bungalows have television and air-conditioning. 90m (300 ft.) or so inland from the southern end of Playa Cocles, 2km (1¼ miles) south of Puerto Viejo. ☎ 2750-0035 or 2750-0057. www.cariblue.com. 16 units, 1 house. $95–$120 double; $220 house. Rates include breakfast. AE, MC, V.

★★ kids Casa Verde Lodge PUERTO VIEJO

A distinct air of tropical tranquility pervades this place. Most rooms here are large, with high ceilings, tile floors, and a private veranda. Everything is very well maintained, and even the shared bathrooms are immaculate. The hotel has lush gardens, a small but well-stocked gift shop, and a good-size outdoor pool with a waterfall. Downtown Puerto Viejo. ☎ 2750-0015. www.cabinascasaverde.com. 17 units, 9 with private bathroom. $38–$50 double with shared bathroom; $70 double with private bathroom. AE, MC, V.

★ Hotel Banana Azul PLAYA NEGRA

Rooms here abound in varnished hardwood. Most are on the second floor of the main lodge building and open onto a broad veranda with ocean views. The end-unit Howler Monkey suite

> The Beach Suite, at Tree House Lodge, just might have the most exuberantly decorated bathroom in Costa Rica.

is my favorite room here. An almost private section of beach just in front of the hotel stretches on for miles northward, all the way to Cahuita National Park. **Northern end of Playa Negra, Puerto Viejo. ☎ 2750-2035 or 8351-4582. www.bananaazul.com. 12 units. $69–$84 double; $139 suite. Rates include breakfast. MC, V. No children under 16 allowed.**

★★ La Costa de Papito PLAYA COCLES
This small collection of individual and duplex cabins is just across from Playa Cocles. The wooden bungalows come with an artfully tiled bathroom and an inviting private porch with a table and chairs and either a hammock or swing chair. There's an excellent restaurant, and the Pure Jungle Spa (p. 407, **❽**) is located on the grounds as well. **Playa Cocles, 2km (1¼ miles) south of Puerto Viejo. ☎/fax 2750-0080 or ☎ 2750-0704. www.lacostadepapito.com. 13 units. $54–$78 double. AE, DISC, MC, V.**

★ kids Playa Chiquita Lodge PLAYA CHIQUITA
This lodge has several wooden buildings set on stilts and connected by a garden walkway. Wide verandas offer built-in seating and rocking chairs. The spacious rooms are painted in bright colors. A short trail leads down to a semiprivate little swimming beach with tide pools and beautiful turquoise water. **Playa Chiquita, 5km (3 miles) south of Puerto Viejo. ☎ 2750-0062 or 2750-0408. www.playachiquitalodge.com. 12 units. $60 double. Rate includes breakfast. AE, MC, V.**

★★★ Tree House Lodge PUNTA UVA
The unique individual houses here are the most stylish options on this coast. All are distinctive, with fluid and fanciful architectural details and tons of brightly varnished woodwork. The crowning achievement is the three-bedroom, two-bathroom Beach Suite, with its spectacular domed bathroom, which during the day is lit by sunlight streaming through scores of colored-glass skylights. **Punta Uva, 5km (3 miles) south of Puerto Viejo. ☎ 2750-0706. www.costaricatreehouse.com. 4 units. $250–$390 double. No credit cards.**

Where to Dine

> *Soda Tamara is a favorite of local Puerto Viejans, and you won't go wrong by following their lead.*

★ kids **Bread & Chocolate** PUERTO VIEJO *AMERICAN* Breakfasts feature waffles, French toast, and pancakes served with the restaurant's fresh chocolate sauce, or egg dishes served with home-baked biscuits, bagels, or whole wheat bread. For lunch, you can opt for a BLT, grilled cheese, or jerk chicken sandwich. Those with kids or a child within will want to sample the PB&J or PB & chocolate, with all-homemade ingredients. Don't leave without trying or buying some brownies and truffles. Downtown Puerto Viejo. ☎ 2750-0723. Entrees $3.75–$6. MC, V. Breakfast and lunch Wed–Sun.

The Local Specialty

While on the Caribbean coast, be sure to try some *rondon* soup or stew. The word comes from "run down," but it's not road-kill—it's a spicy coconut-milk stew made with anything the cook can run down. Ingredients usually include some fresh seafood, as well as a mix of local tubers, roots, and vegetables.

★★ **Chile Rojo** PUERTO VIEJO *PAN-ASIAN/ MEDITERRANEAN* This long-standing restaurant serves up excellent Pan-Asian, Mediterranean, and vegetarian fare at very reasonable prices. Bright tablecloths, a lively bar scene, and an open kitchen make this place inviting. If you want to people-watch, grab one of the stools that line the street-facing, open-air half wall that runs along one side of the restaurant. 2nd floor of new downtown shopping center. ☎ 2750-0025 or 8994-7636. Entrees $3.50–$11. No credit cards. Lunch and dinner Thurs–Tues.

★★ **El Loco Natural** PUERTO VIEJO *INTERNATIONAL* A friendly, hippie vibe pervades this open-air joint. The short menu features several vegetarian items, as well as fresh fish and some chicken and meat dishes, prepared in curry, Thai, and Mexican sauces. There's often live music here, ranging from reggae to jazz to Latin American folk. On the main road just south of downtown ☎ 2750-0530. Entrees $4–$15. No credit cards. Dinner Thurs–Mon.

★★★ La Pecora Nera PLAYA COCLES *ITALIAN*

This is the finest Italian restaurant in the region, if not the country. The menu has a broad selection of pizzas and pastas, but your best bet is to just ask what's fresh and special for that day and trust the chef's instincts and inventions. Playa Cocles, 50m (165 ft.) inland on a well-marked turnoff from the main road heading south past the soccer field. ☎ 2750-0490. Entrees $10–$22. AE, MC, V. Dinner Tues–Sun.

★★★ Maxi's. MANZANILLO *COSTA RICAN/ SEAFOOD*

This second-floor restaurant is always packed, especially at lunch time. The kitchen specializes in locally caught seafood that is simply prepared and served alongside the local rice 'n' beans, fried plantain chips, and some cabbage salad. The best seats are those next to large open windows that overlook the beach and the sea. On the beach, Manzanillo. ☎ 2759-9086. Entrees $5–$35. MC, V. Lunch and dinner daily.

★★ Soda Tamara PUERTO VIEJO *COSTA RICAN*

This little restaurant is a local institution. The menu features standard fish, chicken, and meat entrees, served with a hefty helping of Caribbean-style rice 'n' beans. You can also get *patacones* (fried plantain chips) and a wide selection of fresh fruit juices. On the main road in downtown Puerto Viejo. ☎ 2750-0148. Entrees $3.50–$30. AE, MC, V. Lunch and dinner daily.

> Fresh seafood and generous proportions at Maxi's.

Puerto Viejo after Dark

There are two main discos/bars in town: ★★ **Johnny's Place** (☎ 2750-0623), next to the Rural Guard station, and **Stanford's** (☎ 2750-0016), near Salsa Brava just as the main road heads south of town. Both have small dance floors with ground-shaking reggae, dub, and rap rhythms blaring, and tables, chairs, and candles set out on the sand near the water's edge. For a more sophisticated ambience, try the downtown **Baba Yaga** (☎ 8388-4359). Another downtown place I like, **E-Z Times** (☎ 2750-0663), has a more relaxed vibe, with live music performances and an oceanfront setting. One of the more popular places in town is the **Tex Mex** (☎ 2750-0525) restaurant and bar, located right where the main road hits the water. The open-air bar on the second floor of **Soda Tamara** (above) is a casual and quiet place to gather after dark. Finally, for a more local scene, check out **Bar Maritza's** (☎ 2750-0003), a long-standing local joint, which really seems to go off on Sunday nights. You'll find Maritza's across from the basketball court on the main oceanfront street downtown.

Just south out of town, the backpacker hangout **Rocking J's** (☎ 2750-0657) often features live music. Even farther south, at the start of Playa Cocles, **Café Mango** (☎ 2750-0128), at Cabinas El Tesoro, shows large-screen movies or has live music just about every night.

Cahuita

Cahuita is one of the most laid-back towns in Costa Rica.
The few dirt and gravel streets here are host to a languid parade of pedestrian traffic, parted occasionally by a bicycle, car, or bus. Most folks come to Cahuita for its miles of pristine beaches, which stretch both northward and southward from town. The beaches south of town, the forest behind them, and the coral reef offshore are all part of Cahuita National Park. Plan to spend at least 3 days here.

> The beach and the forest along it seem to go on forever in Cahuita.

START Cahuita is 200km (124 miles) east of San José; 42km (26 miles) south of Limón.

❶ ★★ kids **Mariposario Cahuita.** This is a large, informative butterfly farm where you'll see a wide range of butterfly species and learn all about their life cycles. It's best to come in the early morning on a sunny day, when the butterflies are most active. ⏲ 1½ hr. See p. 392, ❸.

Take a taxi for the 20-minute ride to the sloth sanctuary.

❷ ★★★ kids **Aviarios Sloth Sanctuary of Costa Rica.** The folks here run a sloth rehabilitation project and also take you on a guided canoe tour through the surrounding estuary and river system. More than 330 species of birds have been spotted here. The tour includes a visit to the sloth center, a canoe trip, and a little bit of hiking on some rain-forest trails. ⏲ 3 hr. See p. 381, ❸.

You'll be picked up at your hotel for a snorkeling excursion.

❸ ★★ **Snorkeling over Cahuita Reef.** ⏲ Minimum 2 hr. See p. 380, ❶.

Cahuita's Calypso Legend

Ninety-year-old Walter "Gavitt" Ferguson is a living legend. For decades, Ferguson labored and sang in obscurity. Occasionally he would record a personalized cassette tape of original tunes for an interested tourist willing to part with $5. Finally, in 2002, Ferguson was recorded by the local label Papaya Music (www.papayamusic.com). Today, he has two CDs of original songs, *Babylon* and *Dr. Bombodee*. Ask around town and you should be able to find a copy. If you're lucky, you might even bump into Gavitt himself.

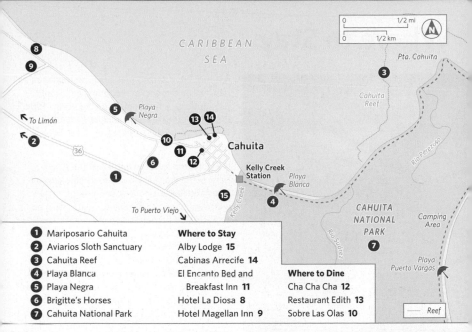

		Where to Stay	Where to Dine

1 Mariposario Cahuita

2 Aviarios Sloth Sanctuary

3 Cahuita Reef

4 Playa Blanca

5 Playa Negra

6 Brigitte's Horses

7 Cahuita National Park

Where to Stay

Alby Lodge **15**

Cabinas Arrecife **14**

El Encanto Bed and
  Breakfast Inn **11**

Hotel La Diosa **8**

Hotel Magellan Inn **9**

Where to Dine

Cha Cha Cha **12**

Restaurant Edith **13**

Sobre Las Olas **10**

4 ★★★ **Playa Blanca.** Playa Blanca (White Beach) begins right where the town ends and the national park takes over. The beach is backed by thick forest, palm trees, and sea grapes that come right up to the sand and provide numerous shady spots for those looking to avoid direct sunlight. The sea and swimming get calmer the farther along you walk.

5 ★ **Playa Negra.** Although nowhere near as picture-perfect as Playa Blanca inside the national park, Cahuita's Playa Negra (Black Beach) has its charms. This long stretch of black volcanic sand is backed for most of its length by

> *Playa Blanca, Cahuita National Park.*

tall coconut palms that provide good shade, and you'll almost always find it nearly deserted. It is also a prime spot for bodysurfing, body boarding, and surfing. North of downtown.

6 ★★ **Horseback ride with Brigitte's Horses.** Whether you want to take a short ride on the beach or a half-day tour on horseback to a jungle waterfall, I recommend you check in with Brigitte's Horses. The horses are gentle and well-cared-for, and you can take them out with or without a guide. On a side road north of downtown. ☎ 2755-0053. www.brigittecahuita.com. Rates: $20 per hr. (you must have experience riding); guided tours $35–$55 per person.

7 ★★ **Cahuita National Park.** ⏱ Minimum 2 hr. See p. 381, **2**.

See p. 381, **2**.

Where to Stay

> Rooms at El Encanto are comfortable and tastefully decorated.

★ Alby Lodge NEAR PARK ENTRANCE

With the feel of a village, Alby Lodge features four small cabins surrounded by a broad lawn and gardens. Each simple cabin has a thatched roof, mosquito nets, hardwood floors, big shuttered windows, a tiled bathroom, and a hammock slung on the front porch. There's no restaurant, but you may cook your own meals in a communal kitchen if you wish. 150m (500 ft.) down a narrow, winding lane from the national park entrance. ☎ 2755-0031. www.albylodge.com. 4 units. $40 double. No credit cards.

★★ Cabinas Arrecife CAHUITA

Located near the water, this is an excellent budget choice. A shared veranda has some chairs, where you can catch a glimpse of the sea through a dense stand of coconut palms hung with hammocks. The rooms are simple but spotless. A tiny pool fronts the ocean. 100m (330 ft.) east of the post office. ☎ 2755-0081. www.cabinasarrecife.com. 12 units. $30 double. AE, MC, V.

★ El Encanto Bed and Breakfast Inn PLAYA NEGRA

The individual bungalows here are spacious and feature wooden bed frames, arched windows, Mexican-tile floors, Guatemalan bedspreads, and framed Panamanian *molas* (wall hangings). The hotel has a small kidney-shaped pool, a wood-floored meditation and yoga hall, a covered garden gazebo, and an open-air massage room. Just outside of town, on the road to Playa Negra. ☎ 2755-0113. www.elencantobedandbreakfast.com. 7 units. $70–$185 double. Rates include breakfast. MC, V.

Hotel La Diosa PLAYA NEGRA

Close to the sea north of Playa Negra, this hotel has cozy rooms, great grounds, and friendly hosts. The best rooms have air-conditioning and a private Jacuzzi. All have cool tile floors, rattan furnishings, and plenty of ventilation. There's a midsize pool, as well as a yoga and meditation room. North of town, toward the end of the Playa Negra road. ☎ 877/632-3198 in U.S. and Canada, or 2755-0055 in Costa Rica. www.hotelladiosa.net. 18 units. $70–$105 double. Rates include breakfast. MC, V.

★★ Hotel Magellan Inn PLAYA NEGRA

This small bed-and-breakfast exudes an understated air of tropical sophistication. Each room comes complete with its own tiled veranda with a Persian rug and bamboo sitting chairs. As nice as the rooms are, the best things here are the hotel's sunken pool and lush gardens, both of which are built into a crevice in the ancient coral reef that underlies this entire region. North of town, toward the end of the Playa Negra road. ☎ 2755-0035. www.magellaninn.com. 6 units. $79–$99 double. Rates include continental breakfast. AE, MC, V.

Where to Dine

> Cha Cha Cha, one of the coast's best restaurants, is a tiny place with a small menu of dishes from around the globe.

★★ Cha Cha Cha CAHUITA SEAFOOD/ INTERNATIONAL In addition to the fresh catch of the day and filet mignon, the eclectic menu here includes everything from jerk chicken and Thai shrimp salad to pasta primavera and fajitas. The grilled squid salad with a citrus dressing is one of the house specialties and a great light bite. Be prepared to wait: The restaurant has only a half-dozen or so tables, and they fill up fast. On the main road in town, 3 blocks north of Coco's Bar. ☎ 8368-1725. Entrees $6–$22. MC, V. Lunch and dinner Tues–Sun.

Restaurant Edith CAHUITA CREOLE/SEAFOOD The menu at this local institution is long, with lots of local seafood dishes, as well as Creole concoctions such as yucca in coconut milk with meat or vegetables. The sauces have spice and zest. This restaurant is often crowded, so don't be bashful about sitting down with total strangers at any of the big tables. Hours can be erratic; it sometimes closes without warning, and service can be slow and gruff at times. By the police station. ☎ 2755-0248. Entrees $3.50–$25. No credit cards. Lunch and dinner Mon–Sat.

★ Sobre Las Olas PLAYA NEGRA SEAFOOD/ ITALIAN Perched on a slight rise above a coral cove and breaking waves, this place serves a mix of local and Italian fare. You can get excellent fresh squid or shrimp in a tangy sauce made with coconut milk that's a local specialty, as well as a host of pasta dishes. The views are as good as the service Just north of town, on the road to Playa Negra. ☎ 2755-0109. Entrees $5–$30. MC, V. Lunch and dinner Wed–Mon.

Cahuita after Dark

With cold beer and loud reggae music, and located right on the main crossroads in town, **★ Coco's Bar** (no phone) is a classic Caribbean watering hole that has traditionally been the most popular place in town to spend your nights (or days, for that matter). Toward the Playa Blanca park entrance, the **National Park Restaurant** (☎ 2755-0244) has a popular bar and disco on most nights during the high season and on weekends during the off-season.

Tortuguero

Tortuguero translates roughly as "place of the turtles," or "turtle town." The name is used to denote the tiny village here and the area around it—much of which makes up Tortuguero National Park. Tortuguero is connected to the rest of mainland Costa Rica by a series of rivers and canals. This aquatic highway is lined and surrounded almost entirely by a dense tropical rain forest that is home to howler and spider monkeys, three-toed sloths, toucans, and great green macaws. A trip through the canals is similar to touring the rain forests of the Amazon basin—on a much smaller scale. You'll want to spend at least 2 days, and ideally 4, exploring this area, and you'll need to arrive by plane or boat.

> Tortuguero is surrounded by water and, with no road access, must be reached by boat or plane.

START Tortuguero is 250km (155 miles) northeast of San José; and 79km (49 miles) north of Limón.

❶ ★ Tortuguero village. Set on a narrow strip of land between the Caribbean Sea and the Tortuguero Canal, this tiny village has no roads or cars. It is predominantly a laid-back collection of simple wooden houses built on stilts, connected by dirt footpaths. Modern touches include a few concrete buildings, and a small section of paved "sidewalk." You'll find a few basic souvenir stores sprinkled around town. ⏱ 30 min.

❷ ★ kids Caribbean Conservation Corporation visitor center and museum. The primary focus of the small museum here is the life and natural history of sea turtles. Most visits to the museum include a short, informative video on the turtles. The museum also features information and exhibits on a whole range of native flora and fauna. ⏱ 1 hr. Tortuguero village. ☎ 2709-8091. www.cccturtle.org. Admission $1. Mon-Sat 10am–noon and 2pm–5:30pm; Sun 2–5pm.

3 Dorling's Bakery, Coffee Shop & Restaurant. This is a great spot to stop in for a coffee break, fresh fruit drink, or light meal. The best tables are in a lush garden bordering the town's main canal. Next to Casa Marbella. ☎ 2709-8132.

4 ★★★ kids Boat tour of Tortuguero canals. The principal activity in these parts is touring the canals, lagoons, and rivers of this region in a small boat with a naturalist guide. The bird and wildlife viewing is spectacular. In addition to seemingly countless bird species, you're likely to see caimans in the water and monkeys in the trees. The better hotels here conduct their tours in boats that feature quiet electric motors, which won't scare the wildlife. ◷ Minimum 2 hr.

5 ★ Cerro de Tortuguero. At 119m (390 ft.), this lone peak—Turtle Hill—towers over the lowland coast. The hike to the top is relatively easy and offers some good views of the Tortuguero canals and village, as well as the Caribbean Sea. ◷ 2-3 hr. At the far northern end of the main canal.

6 ★★★ kids Turtle-nesting tour. The town (and park) name "Tortuguero" comes from the Spanish name for the giant sea turtles (*tortugas*) that come ashore at night to nest on the beaches of this region. The turtles arrive every year from early March to mid-October; the prime season for seeing them is July to October, and peak months are August and September. If you want to come watch the turtles, you must book an organized tour led by a licensed guide into **Tortuguero National Park.** All of the hotels and tour operators in town can arrange this adventure for you—happily, the official guides are all well informed. ◷ Minimum 2 hr. All along the beach. Rates for night-time guides $10–$20.

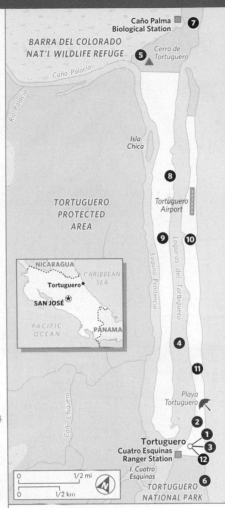

1 Tortuguero village
2 Caribbean Conservation Corporation's visitor center and museum
3 Dorling's Bakery, Coffee Shop & Restaurant
4 Tortuguero canals
5 Cerro de Tortuguero
6 Turtle-nesting tour

Where to Stay
Casa Marbella **12**
Laguna Lodge **10**
Manatus Hotel **9**
Mawamba Lodge **11**
Tortuga Lodge **8**
Turtle Beach Lodge **7**

Traveler's Tip

Independent travel is not the norm in Tortuguero. Most travelers rely on their lodge for transportation to and from the area, as well as for all tours and activities. In fact, almost everything is done in groups. Depending upon your hotel or lodge, this group feeling can be intimate and rewarding, or overwhelming and impersonal.

Where to Stay

> *The Manatus Hotel is a bastion of comfort, luxury, and fine dining in remote Tortuguero.*

★ Casa Marbella TORTUGUERO

Right in the village of Tortuguero, this is an excellent option for budget travelers looking for a bit more comfort and care than that offered at the other inexpensive in-town options. It's also a good alternative for those wishing to avoid the large groups and cattle car–like operations of most big lodges here. Owner Daryl Loth is a longtime resident and well-respected naturalist guide. Tortuguero, ☎/fax 2709-8011 or ☎ 8833-0827. http://casamarbella.tripod.com. 8 units. $40 double; $50–$60 superior double. Rates include breakfast. No credit cards.

★★ Laguna Lodge TORTUGUERO

Most of the spacious rooms here have wood walls, hardwood floors, and a tiled bathroom with screened walls to let in air and light. The large dining area is on a free-form deck that extends out over the main Tortuguero Canal. Another covered deck, also over the water, is strung with hammocks for lazing away the afternoons. There's a large pool, as well as a butterfly garden and botanical garden. Tortuguero. ☎ 2272-4943 (reservations) or 2709-8082 (lodge). www.lagunatortuguero.com. 80 units. $263 per person for 2 days/1 night; $330 per person for 3 days/2 nights. Rates are based on double occupancy and include round-trip transportation from San José, tours, all meals, and taxes. AE, DC, MC, V.

★★★ Manatus Hotel TORTUGUERO

This hotel offers the most luxurious accommodations in Tortuguero. The large rooms are plush and well equipped, with high ceilings, wood floors, and a host of amenities you won't find anywhere else in the area. The amoeba-shaped pool is set just off the dark waters of the main canal with a broad deck and plenty of inviting chaise longues surrounding it. *Note:* Only children over 10 years of age are allowed. Tortuguero. ☎ 2239-4854 (reservations in San José) or 2709-8197 (hotel). www.manatushotel. com. 12 units. $390 per person for 2 days/1 night; $495 per person for 3 days/2 nights. Rates are based on double occupancy and include round-trip transportation from San José, daily tours, all meals, and taxes. AE, MC, V.

★★ Mawamba Lodge TORTUGUERO

This lodge is located just north of Tortuguero village on the ocean side of the main canal. Rooms are painted in bright Caribbean colors. The gardens are lush and overgrown with flowering ginger, heliconia, and hibiscus. There are plenty of hammocks around for anyone who wants to kick back and a beach volleyball court for those who don't. Tortuguero. ☎ 2293-8181 or 2709-8100. www.grupomawamba.com. 54 units. $263 per person for 2 days/1 night; $330 per person for 3 days/2 nights. Rates are double occupancy, and include round-trip transportation from San José, some tours, all meals, and taxes. AE, MC, V.

★★ kids Tortuga Lodge TORTUGUERO

All the rooms here feature contemporary furniture, Caribbean-influenced decor, and loads of freshly varnished hardwood. If possible, opt for a second-floor room, which comes with a small, covered veranda. My favorite feature here is the long multilevel deck, where you can have your meals, sip a cool drink, or just take in the view as the water laps against the docks at your feet. There are several acres of forest behind

the lodge, and a few kilometers of trails wind their way through the trees—look for howler monkeys and poison-dart frogs. If you're traveling with kids, they won't get bored. Tortuguero. ☎ 800/886-2609 in U.S. and Canada; 2257-0766 for reservations in San José; or 2709-8034 for the lodge. www.costaricaexpeditions.com. 27 units. $338 per person for 2 days/1 night; $438 per person for 3 days/2 nights. Rates are based on double occupancy and include round-trip transportation from San José, tours, all meals, and taxes. AE, MC, V.

Turtle Beach Lodge CAÑO PALMA

This isolated lodge is located 8km (5 miles) north of the village of Tortuguero, about 20 minutes by boat. Set on a narrow strip of land between the Caribbean Sea and the Caño Palma Canal, the rooms are somewhat more Spartan than those at the lodges listed above, but they are clean and comfortable. There's a small, turtle-shaped pool in the center of the grounds, and a stable of horses is available for riding tours. If you're looking to truly get away from it all, this is the place to do it. Caño Palma, Tortuguero. ☎ 2248-0707 (San José) or 8837-6969 (lodge). www.turtlebeachlodge.com. 47 units. $210 per person for 2 days/1 night; $288 per person for 3 days/2 nights. Rates are based on double occupancy and include round-trip transportation from San José, tours, all meals, and taxes. AE, MC, V.

Where to Dine?

Given the difficulties of getting around Tortuguero, you will likely eat all of your meals at your lodge or while you're out on a tour. For that reason, I don't make any restaurant recommendations. Cuisine isn't the draw here anyway.

Package rates listed here are for the least expensive travel option, which is a bus and boat combination both in and out. All of the lodges also offer packages with the option of a plane flight either one or both ways.

Limón

The rough-and-tumble port city of Limón is a major stop for cruise ships, and few beyond cruise ship passengers take the time to explore it. That's a shame, as it has a distinctly Caribbean charm. While I don't recommend staying here, except during Carnaval (see "A Fall Festival," p. 474), it's worth a visit if you're interested in Costa Rica's Afro-Caribbean culture. You won't need more than a day here.

> *The port city of Limón has been a center of banana exporting since 1870; cruise ships regularly stop here today.*

START Limón is 160km (99 miles) east of San José.

❶ Mercado Municipal and pedestrian mall. The city's main market is a tight warren of stalls selling everything from fresh fruits and meats to housewares, tools, toys, and clothing. If you

A Word of Warning

Street crime and violence are problems in Limón. Tourists should stick to the area around the cruise ship dock, the compact city center, and the spots mentioned. I don't recommend walking anywhere at night—take a taxi instead.

exit the market at Avenida 2, you'll find yourself in a car-free zone lined with simple restaurants, shops, and street vendors. Both spots give a good sense of daily life in Limón. ⏱ 1 hr. Btw. Avenidas 2 and 3 and Calles 3 and 4. Daily 6am–6pm.

❷ ★ Parque Vargas. Occupying one city block on the waterfront, this is a lush oasis in the heart of downtown. Look for the resident two-toed sloths in the trees. ⏱ 20 min. On the waterfront, on the eastern end of downtown.

Take a taxi for the 45-minute drive to this park.

❸ ★ kids Veragua Rainforest Park. Built primarily as a destination for cruise ship excursions, this extensive complex is a worthy stop. At-

tractions here include a serpentarium, butterfly garden, hummingbird garden, extensive insect exhibit, free-range rain-forest frog room, zip-line canopy tour, and a rain-forest trail system. ⊙ Minimum 3½ hrs. ☎ 2296-5056; www.veraguarainforest.com. Admission $65 adults, $45 children. Price includes half-day tour and lunch. Both half- and full-day tour packages, with transportation included, are available from all of the beach towns on the Caribbean coast. Tues–Sun 8am–4pm.

Where to Stay & Dine

Beach Hotel Cocori PLAYA BONITA

Set right on Playa Bonita, this hotel commands a fine view of the cove, a small beach, and crashing surf. A pair of two-story buildings house the rooms, most of which are small and basic. Those on the second floor have better sea breezes and views. A long veranda runs along both floors. Playa Bonita, 2km (1¼ miles) north of Limón. ☎ 2795-1670. 25 units. $40–$55 double. Rate includes breakfast. AE, MC, V.

Brisas del Caribe LIMÓN SEAFOOD/COSTA RICAN

The increase in cruise ship traffic to Limón has been a shot in the arm for this local landmark. When the weather permits, grab a table on the sidewalk, under a big umbrella. The local cuisine served up here is dependable, if not particularly special or memorable. North side of Parque Vargas, Limón. ☎ 2758-0138. Entrees $4–$15. AE, DC, MC, V. Breakfast, lunch, and dinner daily.

Park Hotel LIMÓN

This hotel has an excellent location fronting the ocean. Unlike much of Limón, which seems to be in a state of prolonged and steady decay, the Park Hotel receives regular and fairly competent upkeep year in and year out. Ask for a room on the ocean side of the hotel because these are brighter, quieter, and cooler than those that face the fire station. Avenida 3 btw. Calles 1 and 3, Limón. ☎ 2758-3476 or 2798-0555. 32 units. $54–$65 double. AE, MC, V.

Eat on the Street

I highly recommend sampling some *pati* while you're here. This fried dough concoction is stuffed with a slightly spicy ground meat filling, and it's a local staple. You'll find *pati* vendors all over downtown Limón.

Caribbean Coast Fast Facts

> *Sign for an Internet cafe in Tortuguero.*

Accommodations Booking Services

In just about all instances, you are best off booking direct with the hotels and resorts listed in this guide.

ATMs

With the exception of Tortuguero, all of the towns and tourist destinations on the Caribbean coast have at least one bank with a cash machine (*cajero automatico*). To find a bank, look for signs saying *banco*. At press time, there is no bank or ATM in Tortuguero, but rumor has it that may change.

Dentists & Doctors

The only major hospital on the Caribbean coast is the Tony Facio Hospital (☎ 2758-2222) in Limón. There are small local clinics in Cahuita, Hone Creek, and Puerto Viejo.

If you have a mild medical issue or dental problem while traveling on the Caribbean coast, most hotels will be able to refer you to a local doctor (*medico*) or dentist (*dentista*) who speaks English.

Emergencies

In case of emergency, call ☎ 911 (there should be an English-speaking operator); if 911 doesn't work, contact the police at ☎ 2222-1365 or 2221-5337, and ask them to find someone who speaks English to translate. For an ambulance, call ☎ 128; to report a fire, call ☎ 118.

For a medical emergency that doesn't require an ambulance, see "Dentists & Doctors," above. To report lost or stolen items, see "Police," p. 423.

Getting There & Getting Around

San José's **Juan Santamaría International Airport** is the closest gateway to the Caribbean Coast. From San José, you have several options for onward travel to the coast. For the purposes of this trip, you won't need to rent a car. In the case of Tortuguero, accessible only by boat or commuter airline, your best bet is to arrange transportation with your hotel or lodge, or go as part of an organized tour. Many hotels in the other towns will arrange for you to get to them from San José—if yours does not, you'll want to fly or take a private shuttle.

Gray Line (☎ 2220-2126; www.grayline costarica.com) and **Interbus** (☎ 2283-5573; www.interbusonline.com) are two private shuttle companies with daily scheduled departures to Limón, Cahuita, and Puerto Viejo. Local buses are extremely economical, but you are at the mercy of their schedules and time-consuming stops along the way.

Nature Air (☎ 800/235-9272 in U.S. and Canada, or 2299-6000 in Costa Rica; www.natureair.com) and **Sansa** (☎ 877/767-2672 in U.S. and Canada, or 2290-4100 in Costa Rica; www.flysansa.com) both have daily commuter air service to Tortuguero. Nature Air also has service to Limón four times weekly. Fares run between $98 and $110 one way.

Internet Access

More and more hotels, resorts, and retailers around Costa Rica are offering high-speed Wi-Fi access, either free or for a small fee. Moreover, you'll readily find Internet cafes in all major towns and tourist destinations around the Caribbean coast. Rates run between 50¢ and $3 per hour, and connection speeds are generally pretty good.

Pharmacies

There is a pharmacy (*farmacia*) on the main road in all of the beach towns, with the exception of Tortuguero.

Police

To report a lost or stolen article, such as a wallet or passport, visit the local police. Depending upon your location, that may be either the OIJ (judicial police), *guardia rural* (rural guard), or *policía metropolitana* (metro police). The number for the *policía de tránsito* (transit police) is ☎ 800/8726-7486, toll-free nationwide, or ☎ 2222-9330. See also "Emergencies," p. 422.

Post Offices

You'll find post offices on the main streets in Cahuita, Puerto Viejo, and Limón.

Safety

The Caribbean coast has garnered a reputation as being a dangerous, drug-infested zone, rife with crime and danger. While the city of Limón is particularly dangerous, most tourist towns and destinations are relatively safe. There have been several high-profile crimes in the area over the years, but overall this reputation is exaggerated. The same crime and drug problems found here exist in San José and most of the more popular beach destinations on the Pacific coast. Use common sense and take normal precautions, and you should have no problems on the Caribbean coast. Never leave items of value unattended in rental cars, hotel rooms (unless locked in a safe), or on the beach. Moreover, single women, couples, and small groups of tourists should probably avoid walking on desolate parts of towns, cities, beaches, and back roads after dark.

Toilets

These are known as *sanitarios* or *servicios sanitarios*. You might also hear them called *baños*. They are marked *damas* (women) and *hombres* or *caballeros* (men). Public restrooms are rare to nonexistent, but most hotels, restaurants, and tour attractions catering to tourists will let you use their restrooms.

Visitor Information

There are no official information offices or bureaus around the Caribbean coast. Your best source of information—beyond this guide book—will be your hotel front desk and any of the local tour agencies.

Water

This is a remote area, and most hotels advise you drink bottled water. Most restaurants that cater to tourists use bottled or treated water. *Sin hielo* means "no ice," and this is what you'll want to say if you're nervous about the water—even when frozen it's still water.

11
Costa Rican History & Culture

The History of Costa Rica

> PREVIOUS PAGE *A banana farm in Puerto Viejo.* THIS PAGE *Costa Rican coffee bagged for shipping.*

Costa Rica enjoyed thousands of years of human occupation before it was "discovered" by Christopher Columbus in 1502. Its history includes the introduction of coffee as a cash crop, a civil war, the abolition of its standing army, and the building of a banana exporting empire. The country's political and economic stability, adherence to the democratic process, and staunch position of neutrality are a source of great pride to Costa Ricans, who like to think of their country as the "Switzerland of Central America."

The Early Years: 13,000 B.C. to A.D. 1502

Little is known of Costa Rica's history before its colonization by Spanish settlers. The pre-Columbian native peoples who made their home in this region of Central America lived primarily in small communities and nomadic tribes, never developing the large cities or advanced cultures that flourished to the north and south. Ancient artifacts excavated around the country, primarily in the northwest, demonstrate a high level of artistic achievement. Many of these artifacts are thought to have been influenced by sporadic contact with and immigration of Olmec, Aztec, and Mayan peoples from the north. Beautiful gold and jade jewelry, intricately carved grinding stones, and artistically painted terra-cotta objects point to a small but highly skilled population. Estimates of the total indigenous population at the time of the Spanish arrival range from 30,000 to 500,000.

Colonization

On his fourth and final voyage to the New World, in 1502, Christopher Columbus anchored just offshore present-day Limón. Whether he actually gave the country its name is open to discussion, but it was around this time that the moniker took hold. However, Costa Rica, or the "Rich Coast," failed to live up to its name, instead providing the Spanish crown with very few riches and more than a few challenges.

The early Spanish settlers learned the hard way that the native inhabitants of Costa Rica would fight valiantly for their land, despite their small numbers, scattered villages, and tribal differences. Ultimately, the natives were overcome by superior firepower and European diseases, such as smallpox. In a strange bit of irony, the fighting proved so costly in terms of lives lost that few natives were left for the settlers to force into servitude. The few settlers who braved this outpost were often left to till their own lands, a situation unheard of in other such colonies. Costa Rica was nearly forgotten, as the Spanish crown looked elsewhere for riches to plunder and souls to convert.

It didn't take long for Costa Rica's few Spanish settlers to head for the hills, where they found rich volcanic soil and a climate that was less oppressive than that of the lowlands. Cartago, the colony's first capital, was founded in 1563. It was not until the 1700s that additional cities were established in the agriculturally rich Central Valley. These cities included San José, Heredia, and Alajuela. In the late 18th century, the first coffee plants were introduced; they thrived in the highlands, giving Costa Rica its first and foremost cash crop.

Staking Out Independence

In 1821, Spain granted independence to its colonies in Central America. Costa Rica joined with its neighbors to form the Federal Republic of Central America, but by 1838, this experiment at a united Central America had devolved, and Costa Rica withdrew and declared independence.

By the mid-1800s, coffee had become the country's main export. Free land was given to those willing to plant coffee on it, and plantation owners soon grew wealthy and powerful, creating Costa Rica's first elite class. Coffee plantation owners were powerful enough to elect their own representatives to the presidency.

This was a stormy period in Costa Rican history. In 1856, the country was invaded by William Walker (see "William Walker's War," p. 125), an ambitious mercenary from Tennessee who, with the backing of prominent U.S. businessmen and industrialists, was attempting to fulfill his grandiose dream of presiding over a slave state in Central America. Walker began his conquest in Nicaragua with a band of just 56 paid mercenaries. He was actually successful enough to have himself declared president of Nicaragua before heading south. However, the people of Costa Rica, led by their own president, Juan Rafael Mora, rose up against Walker and chased him back to Nicaragua. In 1860, Walker was defeated and captured for the last time in Honduras, where he was promptly executed.

The Era of Big Plantations

Until 1890, coffee growers had to transport their coffee either by oxcart to the Pacific port of Puntarenas or by boat down the Río Sarapiquí to the Caribbean. In the 1870s, President Tomás Guardia Gutiérrez proposed a railway from San José to the Caribbean coast to facilitate the transport of coffee to European markets. It took nearly 20 years for this plan to reach fruition, and more than 4,000 workers lost their lives constructing the railway, which passed through dense jungles and rugged mountains on its journey from the Central Valley to the coast. Partway through the project, as funds were dwindling, the second chief engineer, Minor Keith, proposed an idea that not only enhanced his fortunes but also changed the course of Central American history.

Keith's idea was to develop banana plantations along the railway right of way on either side of the tracks. The export of this crop would help finance the railway, and, in exchange, Keith would get a 99-year lease on the land, with a 20-year tax deferment. The Costa Rican government gave its consent, and in 1878 the first bananas were shipped from the country. In 1899, Keith and a partner formed the United Fruit Company, a business that

The Little Drummer Boy

Costa Rica's national hero is Juan Santamaría. The legend goes that young Juan enlisted as a drummer boy in the campaign against the American invader William Walker (p. 125). On April 11, 1865, when Costa Rican troops had a band of Walker's men cornered in a downtown hostel in Rivas, Nicaragua, Santamaría volunteered for a nearly certain suicide mission to set the building on fire. Although mortally wounded, Santamaría was successful in torching the building and driving Walker's men out, where they were swiftly routed. Today, April 11 is a national holiday.

> *This 1910s image shows banana crops planted along Costa Rica's railway, which was built to transport the ever-growing coffee yield to Caribbean ports.*

Presidential Welcome

President John F. Kennedy visited Costa Rica in March 1963. Upon his arrival, the Irazú Volcano (p. 64, **❶**) woke up and erupted, after more than two decades of dormancy. Soot and ash reached as far as San José, where the soon-to-be-assassinated leader was addressing students and political figures.

In 1994, history seemed to repeat itself—peacefully this time—when José María Figueres, the son of José "Pepe" Figueres, took the reins of government from the son of his father's adversary, Rafael Angel Calderón.

In 2004, major corruption scandals landed two former presidents, Miguel Angel Rodríguez and Rafael Angel Calderón, in jail; another, José María Figueres, remains abroad, avoiding calls for his return to face corruption allegations. These former presidents, as well as a long list of other high-level government employees and deputies, are implicated in various financial scandals and bribery cases.

In 2006, former president Oscar Arias Sánchez, who won the Nobel Peace Prize for brokering a Central American peace accord in the mid-1980s, was reelected. The election was historic on two fronts. First, Arias needed to amend national law prohibiting reelection (consecutive terms are still prohibited). Second, and perhaps more important, runner-up Ottón Solís's upstart PAC (Citizen's Action Party, in English) placed second by an extremely slim margin, ending the dominance of a seemingly entrenched bi-party system,

eventually became the largest landholder in Central America and was the cause of political disputes, social unrest, and wars throughout the region.

Growing Democracy in Central America

In 1889, Costa Rica held what is considered the first free election in Central American history: The opposition candidate won the election, and the control of the government passed from the hands of one political party to those of another without bloodshed or hostilities. This pattern of peaceful democracy continued for the next 60 years.

In 1948, things got heated in Costa Rican politics. Former president and repeat candidate Rafael Angel Calderón refused to concede to the rightfully elected new president, Otilio Ulate. Calderón contested the results and was backed by a legislature controlled by his party. Civil war ensued. Calderón was defeated by forces led by José "Pepe" Figueres Ferrer. Following the civil war, a new constitution was drafted; among other changes, it abolished Costa Rica's army, so that such a revolution could never happen again.

The Last Costa Rican Warrior

"Military victories, by themselves, are not worth much. It's what are built from them that matters."
—José "Pepe" Figueres Ferrer

> *John F. Kennedy in Costa Rica, March 1963.*

Mysterious Spheres

For many travelers, Costa Rica's ancient stone spheres, precisely round and smooth, are a striking introduction to its pre-Columbian culture—you may even see a ball serving as a lawn ornament at someone's private home. Ranging in size from a few centimeters to more than 2m (6 ft.) in circumference, and dating from about 200 B.C. to A.D. 800, these balls once numbered in the hundreds, concentrated mainly in the Diquís delta near Palmar Sur and Palmar Norte. Sadly, many have been destroyed, looted, or taken from their original sites, and today they are scattered about the country.

which had shared governance of Costa Rica for decades.

Costa Rica Today

For the last decade or so, tourism has been the nation's principal source of income, surpassing cattle ranching, textiles, and exports of coffee, pineapples, bananas, and Intel microchips. More than two million tourists visit Costa Rica each year, and more than half of Costa Rica's working population is employed in the tourism and service industries. Ticos whose fathers and grandfathers were farmers and ranchers find themselves hotel owners, tour guides, and waiters. Although most have adapted gracefully and regard the industry as a source of new jobs and opportunities for economic advancement, some are resentful. And, unfortunately, an increase in the number of visitors has led to an increase in crime, prostitution, and drug trafficking.

The 2009 global economic crisis was slow to hit Costa Rica. Because credit here has historically been tight, there was no major mortgage or banking crisis in the country. Still, early anecdotal reports show tourism down substantially in 2009, and it's unclear how profound an impact on the economy this and other global factors will have.

The Peace President

"Peace is the most honorable form of exhaustion, and the most exhausting form of honor."
—Oscar Arias Sánchez

Where There Is a Tico, There Is Freedom

In 1989, on a visit to Costa Rica, Uruguayan president Julio María Sanguinetti famously declared: *"Donde hay un costarricense, esté donde esté, hay libertad,"* which roughly translates to the title above. Personally, I get a kick out of the version co-opted by a local condiment company in their advertising campaign, which states, "Where there is a Tico, there is Salsa Lizano." I find it to be equally true.

A Timeline of Costa Rican History

PRE-COLUMBIAN

50,000 B.C. What is now Costa Rica is submerged beneath the ocean—it will gradually become land.

13,000 B.C. Earliest evidence of human inhabitants in Costa Rica.

1000 B.C. Olmec people from Mexico arrive in Costa Rica searching for rare blue jade.

1500–800 B.C. Indigenous peoples of the Diquis Valley carve perfect granite spheres (pictured at left), some more than 2m (6½ ft.) in diameter and weighing up to 15 tons.

COLONIAL ERA

1502 Columbus lands in Costa Rica in September, at what is now Limón (pictured at left).

1561 Spanish military officer Juan de Cavallón leads first group of settlers to successfully establish themselves in the Central Valley, although they face resistance and sabotage from the local indigenous peoples.

1563 City of Cartago is founded in the Central Valley.

1723 Irazú Volcano erupts and destroys much of Cartago.

1737 San José is founded.

LATE 1700S Coffee is introduced as a cash crop.

INDEPENDENCE

1821 On September 15, Central America, including Costa Rica, gains independence from Spain.

1823 San José is named Costa Rica's capital, although the decision is disputed and not officially settled until 1835.

1838 Costa Rica is proclaimed an independent republic.

1856 Battle of Santa Rosa: Costa Ricans defeat the forces of proslavery advocate and regional troublemaker William Walker.

1859 Juan Rafel Mora, who led the fight against Walker, is forced from power in a bloodless coup.

1869 Costa Rica claims ownership of Isla del Coco.

1870S First banana plantations (pictured at left) are established.

1888 Costa Rica's population is just over 240,000.

1889 First truly free and fair elections held, establishing democratic process in Costa Rica.

1899 The United Fruit Company is founded by railroad builder Minor Keith.

20TH CENTURY

1910 Earthquake devastates Cartago (pictured at left).

1917 General José Federico Tinoco and his brother José Joaquin Tinoco lead a coup against democratically elected President Alfredo González. José Joaquin is assassinated in 1919, and José Federico flees into exile.

1941 Costa Rica's social security and health system is instituted by President Rafael Angel Calderón, founder of the United Christian Socialist Party (PUSC).

1948 After an aborted revolution and short civil war, a new constitution is drafted that abolishes the Costa Rican army, which is replaced by a civil guard.

1949 Women and blacks are given the right to vote, banks are nationalized, and a new social security system is introduced.

1963 Cabo Blanco Nature Reserve becomes Costa Rica's first protected area, in a crucial first step in the development of the country's national park system.

1968 Arenal Volcano erupts.

1974 After more than a decade and a half of conservative rule, socialist Daniel Oduber is elected president.

1978 Amid an economic decline, conservatives regain power.

1986 Oscar Arias Sánchez is elected president, a year affter U.S.–trained Costa Rican forces clash with Sandanistas.

1987 President Oscar Arias Sánchez is awarded the Nobel Peace Prize for orchestrating the Central American Peace Plan.

1991 A major earthquake rocks the Caribbean coast.

1994 President Rafael Angel Calderón hands over the reins of government to José María Figueres in a peaceful replay of their fathers' less amenable and less democratic transfer of power in 1948.

MODERN TIMES

2002 For the first time in history, the presidential elections are forced into a second-round runoff. Abel Pacheco of the Social Christian Unity Party (PUSC) emerges as the winner.

2004 An aggressive public prosecutor and national press expose massive governmental scandals, landing two former presidents in jail and leaving another on the lam.

2006 In an intensely close election, Oscar Arias Sánchez (pictured at left) is elected president. However, the upstart Citizen's Action Party has profoundly changed the face of the country's long-standing bi-party system.

A GLITTERING PAST

The Pre-Columbians

BY MEGAN MCFARLAND

A THOUSAND YEARS BEFORE ecolodges and surfing beaches turned Costa Rica into a tourist mecca, the country was a destination of another sort: a bustling pre-Columbian crossroads where trade in gold, jade, and pottery flourished among indigenous tribes, the Maya and Aztec civilizations to the north, the Chiriquí in Panama, and the vast Inca empire to the south.

Who Were Costa Rica's Pre-Columbians?

The pre-Columbian Ticos—the people of Costa Rica before Christopher Columbus reached the "new world"—left modest traces compared to their more famous trading partners. Instead of massive stone pyramids, they built wood-and-thatch structures that eventually disappeared; and their exquisite but diminutive gold and jade artifacts made easy plunder for centuries of tomb robbers.

When Columbus arrived in 1502, the indigenous population was about 400,000. By 1529 diseases brought by the newcomers had reduced the population to about 120,000. Within 100 years it numbered in the few thousands. At Guayabo National Monument, located about 100km (60 miles) east of San José, you can see stone foundations, roads, tombs, remains of an aqueduct system, and petroglyphs dating as far back as 3,000 years left by these early inhabitants.

A Golden Touch

Much to the disappointment of the Spanish explorers, gold was relatively scarce in Costa Rica. Most of the country's pre-Columbian metal artifacts are no more than a few inches high and made out of *tumbaga*, a gold-copper alloy. Despite their size, the medallions, pendants, and figurines are rich in detail and represent a fascinating array of animals and deities. Gold ornaments often accompanied the dead to their tombs and were frequently broken before burial to release the object's "spirit," enabling it to travel into the afterlife.

Frogs These frequently appear with flat, horizontal bars below or behind the figure that represent the

frog's feet spread in mid-jump. Some have spirals at the mouth, indicating foam or bubbles produced by the animals. Frogs are thought to symbolize life and fertility.

Birds Another common figure is a front-facing

bird with a head, neck, talons, and rounded

body in three-dimensional form. Sometimes multiple snakes emerge from the side of the head, and a double-headed bat motif is also prevalent.

Medallions Most gold objects were made using the lost-wax technique, which produced a mold into which smelted gold was poured. These rounded medallions were made instead

by hammering small fragments of gold, then decorating

them using a *repoussé* method—pressing on the back with a tool to create reliefs.

Going Green

Costa Rica was one of the principal sites of pre-Columbian jade carving, though the stone itself came from Guatemala. The classic Costa Rican jade works are "ax-god" pendants, shaped like an ax with a bird head and protruding curved beak, which were worn on a cord around the neck. The earliest known of these was found at La Regla, on the Nicoya Peninsula, and dates to about 500 B.C.

While reflective gold objects symbolized the sun and celestial activity, the subtle greens and translucent quality of pre-Columbian jade likely represented agriculture and the earth, the "basic vital force" responsible for sustenance and survival.

The Lay of the Land

> *Plant life, Monteverde Cloud Forest Biological Reserve.*

> *Chirripó National Park, in Costa Rica's volcanic spine.*

Costa Rica occupies a central spot in the isthmus that joins North and South America. For millennia, this land bridge served as a migratory thoroughfare and mating ground for species native to the once-separate continents. It was also where the Mesoamerican and Andean pre-Columbian indigenous cultures met.

The country comprises only .01% of the earth's landmass, yet it is home to 5% of the planet's biodiversity. More than 10,000 identified species of plants, 880 species of birds, 9,000 species of butterflies and moths, and 500 species of mammals, reptiles, and amphibians are found here. The key to Costa Rica's biological richness lies in its many distinct life zones and ecosystems. The country might seem like one big mass of green to the untrained eye, but its diversity is profound.

For more information and details on Costa Rican flora and fauna, see the "Guide to Costa Rica's Flora & Fauna" (p. 452).

Costa Rica's Ecosystems
Costa Rica's **lowland rain forests** are quintessential tropical jungles. Some are deluged with more than 500cm (200 in.) of rainfall per year and have a hot, humid climate. Trees grow tall and fast, fighting for sunlight in the forests' upper reaches. In fact, life and foliage on the forest floor are surprisingly sparse: The action is typically 30m (100 ft.) up, in the canopy, where long vines stream down, lianas climb up, and bromeliads grow on the branches and trunks of towering hardwood trees. You can find these lowland rain forests along the southern Pacific coast, on the Osa Peninsula, and along the Caribbean coast. **Corcovado** (p. 348), **Cahuita** (p. 381, ②), and **Manuel Antonio** (p. 290) **National Parks,** as well as the **Gandoca-Manzanillo Wildlife Refuge** (p. 407, ⑦), support fine examples of lowland rain forest.

At higher elevations you'll find Costa Rica's famed **cloud forests.** Here the steady flow of moist air meets the mountains and creates a nearly constant mist. Epiphytes—resourceful plants that live cooperatively on the branches and trunks of host trees—grow abundantly in the cloud forests, extracting moisture and nutrients from the air. Because cloud forests are found in generally steep, mountainous terrain, the canopy here is lower and less uniform than in lowland rain forests, providing better chances for viewing elusive fauna. Costa Rica's most spectacular cloud forest is protected within **Monteverde Cloud Forest Biological Reserve** (p. 218, ①).

At the highest reaches, the cloud forests give way to **elfin forests** and **paramos.** More commonly associated with the South American Andes, a paramo is characterized by a variety of tundralike shrubs and grasses, with a scattering

> *Palo Verde National Park, at the confluence of river and sea, is largely wetlands.*

of twisted, windblown trees. Reptiles, rodents, and raptors are the most common residents here. **Chirripó National Park** (p. 294) is where you'll find Costa Rica's principal paramo.

In a few protected areas of Guanacaste, you will still find examples of the otherwise vanishing **tropical dry forest.** During Guanacaste's long and pronounced dry season (late November to late April), when no rain relieves the unabated heat, the trees drop their leaves in order to conserve much-needed water. But they bloom in a riot of color: Purple jacaranda, scarlet *poró,* and brilliant orange flame-of-the-forest are just a few of the colorful species that bloom at this time. During the rainy season, these deciduous forests are transformed into a lush and verdant landscape. Because the foliage is not so dense, dry forests are excellent places to view a variety of wildlife species, especially howler monkeys and *pizotes* (coati-

mundis). Dry forests are found in **Santa Rosa** (p. 125, ❺) and **Rincón de la Vieja** (p. 111, ❽) **National Parks.**

Along Costa Rica's coasts, primarily where river mouths meet the ocean, you will find extensive **mangrove forests** and **swamps.** Around these seemingly monotonous tangles of roots exists one of the most diverse and rich ecosystems in the country. All sorts of fish and crustaceans live in the brackish tidal waters. Caimans and crocodiles cruise the maze of rivers and unmarked canals, and hundreds of herons, ibises, egrets, and other marsh birds nest and feed along the silted banks. Mangrove swamps are often havens for waterbirds, including cormorants, frigatebirds, pelicans, and herons. The larger birds tend to nest high in the canopy, while the smaller ones nestle in the underbrush. You'll find fabulous mangrove forests in **Palo Verde National Park** (p. 128), just outside

Manuel Antonio National Park (p. 290), and all along the **Golfo Dulce** (p. 366).

Conservation and Threats
Over the last 15 or so years, Costa Rica has taken great strides toward protecting its rich biodiversity. Thirty years ago it was difficult to find a protected area anywhere, but now more than 11% of the country is protected within the national park system. Another 10% to 15% of the land enjoys moderately effective preservation as part of private and public reserves, Indian reserves, and wildlife refuges and biological corridors. Still, Costa Rica's precious tropical hardwoods continue to be harvested at an alarming rate, often illegally, while other primary forests are clear-cut for short-term agricultural gain. Many experts predict that Costa Rica's unprotected forests will be gone within the early part of this century.

Costa Rica in High & Popular Culture

> *The Ridley Scott movie* 1492: Conquest of Paradise, *starring Gerard Depardieu as Christopher Columbus, was shot in Costa Rica.*

Several of the books mentioned in this section may be difficult to track down in U.S. bookstores and online, but you should be able find most of them in Costa Rica. If you're in San José, a good place to peruse is **Seventh Street Books** (p. 75).

Fiction

Costa Rica is a small Central American nation with a limited literary tradition, very little of which has been translated into English. A good book to start with is **Costa Rica: A Traveler's Literary Companion,** edited by Barbara Ras and with a foreword by Oscar Arias (Whereabouts Press, San Francisco,

CA: 1993), a collection of short stories by Costa Rican writers, organized by region.

If you're lucky, you may find and pick up a copy of **The Stories of Tata Mundo,** by Fabián Dobles (University of Costa Rica Press, San José, Costa Rica: 1998); this collection of short stories is based on the character Tata Mundo, a rural peasant, who has come to embody and represent much of Costa Rica's national identity, or at least the idealized version of that identity— simple, kind, open, joyful, and wise.

Pachanga Kids (www.pachangakids.com) has published several illustrated bilingual children's books with

delightful illustrations by Ruth Angulo. Another bilingual children's book worth checking out is **Zari & Marinita: Adventures in a Costa Rican Rainforest,** by Melina Valdelomar (Zona Tropical, San José, Costa Rica: 2008).

Nonfiction

For an enjoyable, in-depth look into the makeup, myths, and quirks of Costa Rican politics and society, check out **The Ticos: Culture and Social Change,** by Mavis Hiltunen Biesanz, Richard Biesanz, and Karen Zubris Biesanz (Lynne Rienner Publishers, Boulder, CO: 1998), the authors of the out-of-print The Costa Ricans. Another good choice is **The**

> A Pachanga Kids book.

Costa Rica Reader: History, Culture, Politics, a broad selection of stories, essays, and excerpts edited by Steven Palmer and Iván Molina (Duke University Press, Durham, NC: 2004).

To learn more about the life and culture of Costa Rica's Talamanca coast, an area populated by Afro-Caribbean people whose forebears emigrated from Caribbean islands in the early 19th century, look for **What Happen: A Folk-History of Costa Rica's Talamanca Coast,** by Paula Palmer (Zona Tropical, San José, Costa Rica: 2005). This book is a collection of oral histories taken from a wide range of local characters.

Natural History
I personally think that everyone coming to Costa Rica should read **Tropical Nature: Life and Death in the Rain Forests of Central and South America,** by Adrian Forsyth and Ken Miyata, with a foreword by Dr. Thomas Lovejoy (Simon & Schuster, New York: 1987). My all-time favorite book on tropical biology, this

is a wonderfully written and lively collection of tales and adventures by two neotropical biologists who spent quite some time in the forests of Costa Rica.

Mario A. Boza's beautiful **Costa Rica National Parks** (INCAFO, San José, Costa Rica: 2005) has been reissued in an elegant coffee-table edition. Other worthwhile coffee-table books include **Nature of the Rainforest: Costa Rica and Beyond,** by Adrian Forsyth, with photographs by Michael and Patricia Fogden and a foreword by E. O. Wilson (Cornell University Press, Ithaca, NY: 2008), and **Costa Rica: A Journey Through Nature,** by Adrian Hepworth (Firefly Books, Ontario, Canada: 2008).

There is a host of field guides for wildlife enthusiasts. Perhaps the best all-around option is **Travellers' Wildlife Guides: Costa Rica,** by Les Beletsky (Interlink Books, Northampton, MA: 2004). For a more complete list of field guides and further recommendations, see "Guide to Costa Rica's Flora & Fauna" (p. 452).

Film
Costa Rica has a budding yet promising young film industry. Local feature films such as Percy Angress and Livia Linden's **Tropix** (2002) and Esteban Ramírez's **Caribe** (2004) are available on subtitled DVDs. In 2008, **El Camino** (The Path), by Costa Rican filmmaker Ishtar Yasin Gutiérrez, was screened at the Berlin Film Festival.

Several other feature films by Costa Rican directors are expected to be released in 2010, including Hilda Hidalgo's **Del Amor y Otros Demonios,** based on a novel by Columbian author Gabriel García Márquez.

Major films that use Costa Rica as a backdrop include **1492: Conquest of Paradise,** directed by Ridley Scott and starring Gérard Depardieu and Sigourney Weaver; **Congo,** starring Laura Linney and Ernie Hudson; and **The Blue Butterfly,** starring William Hurt. All feature sets and scenery from around the country. Interestingly, even though Michael Crichton's novel Jurassic Park is set in Costa Rica, the movie was not filmed here.

The **Costa Rica International Film Festival** (www.montezumafilmfestival.com) is held in Montezuma in November.

Music
Several musical traditions and styles meet and mingle in Costa Rica. The northern Guanacaste region is a hotbed of folk music that is strongly influenced by the marimba (wooden xylophone) traditions of Guatemala and Nicaragua, while also featuring guitars, maracas, and the occasional harp. On the Caribbean coast you can hear traditional calypso sung by descendants of the original black workers brought over to build the railroads and tend the banana plantations. Roving bands play a mix of guitar, banjo, washtub bass, and percussion in the bars and restaurants of Cahuita (p. 412) and

> *These Tamarindo musicians carry on a strong tradition of folk music in the Guanacaste region.*

Puerto Viejo (p. 410).

Costa Rica also has a healthy contemporary music scene. The jazz-fusion trio **Editus** has won two Grammy awards for its work with Panamanian salsa giant (and movie star and tourism minister) **Rubén Blades.** Meanwhile, **Malpaís,** the closest thing Costa Rica has to a supergroup, is a pop-rock outfit that is tearing it up in Costa Rica and around Central America.

You should also seek out discs by **Cantoamérica,** which plays upbeat dance music ranging from salsa to calypso to merengue. Jazz pianist **Manuel Obregón** (a member of Malpaís) has several excellent solo albums out, including **Simbiosis,** on which he improvises along with the sounds of Costa Rica's wildlife, waterfalls, and weather; he has also worked with the Papaya Orchestra, a collaboration and gathering of musicians from around Central America.

Local label **Papaya Music** (www.papayamusic.com) has done an excellent job promoting and producing albums by Costa Rican musicians in a range of styles and genres. Their offerings range from the Guanacasteca folk songs of **Max Goldemberg,** to the boleros of **Ray Tico,** to the original calypso of **Walter "Gavitt" Ferguson** (see "Cahuita's Calypso Legend," p. 412). You can find their discs at gift shops and record stores around the country, as well as at airport souvenir stores.

Art

Unlike Guatemala, Mexico, or even Nicaragua, Costa Rica does not have a strong tradition of local or indigenous arts and crafts. The strong suit of Costa Rican art is European and Western influenced, although these influences are expressed in a range of styles from neoclassical realism to abstract expressionism.

Pura Vida

Pura Vida! (Pure Life!) is Costa Rica's unofficial national slogan, and in many ways it defines the country. You'll hear it exclaimed, proclaimed, and simply stated by Ticos from all walks of life, from children to octogenarians. It can be used as a cheer after your favorite soccer team scores a goal, or as a descriptive response when someone asks, "How are you?" ("*¿Cómo estás?*"). It is symbolic of the easygoing nature of this country's people, politics, and personality.

Early painters to look out for include **Max Jiménez** (1900–1974), **Francisco Amighetti** (1907–1998), **Manuel de la Cruz** (1909–1986), and **Teodorico Quirós**(1897–1977). Other legends of the Costa Rican art world include **Rafa Fernández** (1935–), **Lola Fernández** (1926–), and **César Valverde** (1928–1998). Contemporary artists making waves and names for themselves include painters **Fernando Carballo, Rodolfo Stanley, Lionel Gonzalez,** and **Manuel Zumbado,** and photographer **Karla Solano.**

Sculpture is perhaps one of the strongest aspects of the Costa Rican art scene, with the large bronze works of **Francisco "Paco" Zúñiga** among the best of the genre. In addition, artists **José Sancho, Edgar Zúñiga,** and **Jorge Jiménez Deredia** are all producing internationally acclaimed pieces, many of monumental proportions. You can see examples by all of these sculptors at San José's downtown **Museo de Arte Costarricense** (p. 54, ❶) and at other museums around the country. I also enjoy the whimsical works of **Leda Astorga,** who sculpts and then paints plump and voluptuous figures in interesting, and at times compromising, poses.

You'll find several excellent art museums and galleries in San José (chapter 4), and you'll find good galleries in some of the larger and more popular tourist destinations.

Architecture

Costa Rica lacks the grand cities and distinctive Spanish-influenced architecture of many former Spanish colonies.

> *The Basílica de Nuestra Señora de los Angeles in Cartago.*

Still, the original capital of Cartago has some old ruins (p. 65, ❷), and a few colonial-era buildings, as well as the country's grandest church, **Basílica de Nuestra Señora de los Angeles** (Basilica of Our Lady of the Angels; p. 65, ❸), which was built in honor of the country's patron saint, La Negrita, the Black Virgin.

In downtown San José, Barrio Amón and Barrio Otoya are two side-by-side upscale neighborhoods full of a stately mix of architectural styles, with everything from colonial-era residential mansions to Art Deco apartment buildings and modern high-rise skyscrapers. One of the standout buildings here is the **Escuela Metalica** (Metal School), which dates

to the 1880s and was shipped over piece by piece from France and erected in place.

On much of the Caribbean coast, you will find wooden houses raised on stilts above occasional flooding. Some of these houses feature ornate gingerbread trim. Much of the rest of the country's architecture features simple concrete-block houses with zinc roofs.

A few modern architects are creating names for themselves. **Ronald Zurcher,** who designed the Four Seasons Resort Costa Rica on the Papagayo Peninsula (p. 158), as well as several other large hotel projects, is one of the shining lights of contemporary Costa Rican architecture.

Colonial-Era Remnant or Crime Deterrent?

Most Costa Rican homes feature steel or iron grating over the doors and windows. I've heard more than one tour guide say this can be traced back to colonial-era architecture and design. However, I'm fairly convinced it is a relatively modern adaptation to the local crime scene.

Eating & Drinking in Costa Rica

> *Soda Tamara in Puerto Viejo; a* soda *is a diner-style restaurant.*

> Gallo pinto *for breakfast.*

Costa Rican food is not especially memorable. Simply grilled or roasted meat or poultry accompanied by rice and beans is the national staple. Vegetables are served sparingly. Perhaps this is why there's so much international food available here. In San José and most of the major tourist destinations, you will find excellent French, Italian, and contemporary fusion restaurants, as well as the occasional joint serving Peruvian, Japanese, or Spanish fare.

Outside the capital and major tourist destinations, your options get very limited, very fast. In fact, many of Costa Rica's popular destinations are so remote that you have no choice but to eat in your hotel's dining room. At isolated jungle lodges, the food is usually served buffet- or family-style and can range from bland to inspired, depending on who's doing the cooking.

Food is relatively inexpensive in Costa Rica. At the more high-end restaurants, it's hard to spend more than $50 per person unless you really splurge on drinks and wine. However, if you really want to save money, Costa Rican, or *típico,* food is always the cheapest nourishment available. It's primarily served in *sodas,* Costa Rica's equivalent of diners.

Keep in mind that there is an additional 13% sales tax added on to all bills and a 10% service charge tacked on to most as well. Ticos rarely tip, but that doesn't mean you shouldn't. If the service was particularly good and attentive, you should probably leave a little extra.

Meals & Dining Customs

Rice and beans are the basis of Costa Rican meals—all three of them. At breakfast, they're called *gallo pinto* and are served with everything from

eggs to steak to seafood. At lunch or dinner, rice and beans are an integral part of a *casado* (which translates as "married" and is the name for the local version of a blue-plate special). A *casado* usually consists of cabbage-and-tomato salad, fried plantains (a starchy, banana-like fruit), and a chicken, fish, or meat dish of some sort. On the Caribbean coast, rice and beans are called "rice 'n' beans" (rather than *arroz y frijoles*) and are cooked in coconut milk.

Dining hours in Costa Rica are flexible but generally follow North American customs. Some downtown restaurants in San José are open 24 hours; however, expensive restaurants tend to be open for lunch between 11am and 3pm and for dinner between 6 and 11pm.

See "Useful Phrases & Menu Terms" (p. 484) for help on how and what to order while in Costa Rica.

> On both coasts, seafood is frequently the centerpiece of the evening meal.

> Ceviche (marinated fish).

Appetizers

Known as *bocas* in Costa Rica, appetizers are served with drinks in most bars. Sometimes the *bocas* are free, but even if they aren't, they're very inexpensive. Popular *bocas* include *gallos* (tortillas piled with meat, chicken, cheese, or beans), *ceviche* (a marinated seafood salad), tamales (stuffed cornmeal patties wrapped and steamed inside banana leaves), *patacones* (fried green plantain chips), and fried yucca.

Meat

Costa Rica is beef country, having converted much of its rain-forest land to pastures for raising cattle. Consequently, beef is cheap and plentiful, although it might be a bit tougher—and cut thinner—than it is back home. One typical local dish is called *olla de carne,* a bowl of beef broth with large chunks of meat, local tubers, and corn. Spit-roasted chicken

is also very popular, and surprisingly tender, here.

Seafood

Costa Rica has two coasts, and, as you'd expect, plenty of seafood is available everywhere in the country. *Corvina* (sea bass) is the most commonly served fish and is prepared innumerable ways, including as ceviche. (**Be aware:** In many cheaper restaurants, particularly in San José, shark meat is often sold as *corvina*.) You should also come across *pargo* (red snapper), dorado (mahimahi), and tuna on some menus, especially along the coasts.

Vegetables

On the whole, you'll find vegetables surprisingly scarce in the meals you're served in Costa Rica—usually nothing more than a little pile of shredded cabbage topped with a slice or two of tomato. For a much more satisfying and filling salad, order *palmito*

(hearts of palm salad). The heart (actually the stalk or trunk of these small palms) is first boiled and then chopped into rings and served with other fresh vegetables, with a salad dressing on top. If you want something more than this, you'll have to order a side dish such as *picadillo,* a stew or purée of vegetables with a bit of meat in it.

Though they are giant relatives of bananas and are technically considered a fruit, *plátanos* (plantains) are really more like a vegetable; they require cooking before they can be eaten. Green plantains have a very starchy flavor and consistency, but they become as sweet as candy as they ripen. Fried *plátanos* are one of my favorite dishes. *Yuca* (manioc root or cassava in English) is another starchy staple root vegetable in Costa Rica.

One more local delicacy worth mentioning is the

> Mango, star fruit, and papaya are just a few of the fruits commonly encountered in Costa Rica.

> A chocolate dessert.

pejibaye, a form of palm fruit that looks like a miniature orange coconut. Boiled *pejibayes* are frequently sold from carts on the streets of San José. When cut in half, a *pejibaye* reveals a large seed surrounded by soft, fibrous flesh—it's starchy and tastes more like a vegetable than a fruit. You can eat it plain, but it's usually topped with a dollop of mayonnaise.

Fruits

Costa Rica is blessed with a wealth of delicious tropical fruits. The most common are mangoes (the season begins in May), papayas, pineapples, melons, and bananas. Other fruits include *marañón,* which is the fruit of the cashew tree and has orange or yellow glossy skin; *granadilla,* or *maracuyá* (passion fruit); *mamón chino,* which Asian travelers will immediately recognize as rambutan; and *carambola* (star fruit).

Desserts

Queque seco, literally "dry cake," is similar to pound cake. *Tres leches* cake, on the other hand, is so moist that you almost need to eat it with a spoon. *Flan* is a typical custard dessert, often served as either *flan de caramelo* (with caramel) or *flan de coco* (with coconut). There are numerous other sweets, many made with condensed milk and raw sugar. *Cajetas* are popular handmade candies made from sugar and various mixes of evaporated, condensed, and powdered milk. They are sold in different-size bits and chunks at most *pulperías* (general stores) and streetside food stands. Cacao was one of the country's major crops before coffee gained prominence, and it is still grown, and chocolate produced, especially on the Caribbean slope.

Beverages

Frescos, refrescos, and *jugos naturales* are my favorite drinks in Costa Rica. They are usually made with fresh fruit and milk or water. Among the more common fruits used are mangoes, papayas, blackberries *(moras),* and pineapples *(piñas).* You'll also come across passion fruit *(maracuyá)* and star fruit *(carambola)* drinks. Some of the more unusual frescos are *horchata,* made with rice flour and a lot of cinnamon; and *chan,* made with the seed of a plant found mostly in Guanacaste. The former is wonderful; the latter is an acquired taste (it's reputed to be good for the digestive system). Order *un fresco con leche sin hielo* (a *fresco* with milk but without ice) if you're avoiding untreated water.

If you're a coffee drinker, you might be disappointed here. Most of the best coffee has traditionally been targeted

> *Costa Rica has been a major coffee producer for over a century.*

for export, and Ticos tend to prefer theirs weak and sugary. Better hotels and restaurants are starting to cater to gringo and European tastes and are serving up superior blends. If you want black coffee, ask for *café negro;* if you want it with milk, order *café con leche.*

For something different for your morning beverage, ask for *agua dulce,* a warm drink made from melted sugarcane and served either with milk or lemon, or straight up.

Beer, Wine & Liquor

The German presence in Costa Rica over the years has resulted in the production of several fine beers, which are fairly inexpensive. Most Costa Rican beers are light pilsners. The most popular brands are

Bavaria, Imperial, and Pilsen. I personally can't tell much of a difference between any of them. Licensed local versions of Heineken and Rock Ice are also available.

You can find imported wines at reasonable prices in the better restaurants throughout the country. You can usually save money by ordering a Chilean wine over a Californian or European bottle.

Costa Rica distills a wide variety of liquors, and you'll save money by ordering these over imported brands. The national liquor is *guaro,* a crude cane liquor that's often combined with a soft drink or tonic. If you want to try *guaro,* stick to the Cacique brand. The Café Britt and Salicsa brands

> *A coffee cocktail is a Costa Rica–style pick-me-up.*

produce a couple of types of coffee-based liqueurs. Salicsa's Café Rica is similar to Kahlúa and is quite good.

12
The Best
Special
Interest
Trips

Organized Adventure Tours

Organized ecotourism or adventure-travel packages are a good option for those with limited time and resources looking to combine several activities. In the best packages, group size is kept small (10 to 20 people), and tours are escorted by knowledgeable guides who are either naturalists or biologists. If you're booking a tour that includes outdoor activities such as hiking and surfing, be sure to ask about the level of difficulty involved. Most companies offer "soft adventure" packages that those in moderately good, but not phenomenal, shape can handle; others focus on more hard-core activities geared toward only seasoned athletes or adventure travelers.

In addition to the companies listed below, many established U.S.–based environmental organizations, including the **Sierra Club** (☎ 415/977-5500 in U.S.; www.sierraclub.org) and the **Smithsonian Institution** (☎ 877/338-8687 in U.S. and Canada; www.smithsonian-journeys.org), regularly offer organized trips to Costa Rica.

Costa Rica–Based Tour Operators

Many U.S. tour companies subcontract portions of their tours to established Costa Rican companies. Some travelers like to cut out the middle-man and set up their tours directly with these local companies, as the packages are often less expensive than those offered through U.S. companies. However, that doesn't mean they are cheap: You're still paying for the convenience of having your arrangements handled for you.

Coast to Coast Adventures (☎ 2280-8054; www.ctocadventures.com) has a unique excursion that doesn't involve motor vehicles. The company's namesake 2-week trip spans the country, with participants traveling on horses and rafts, by mountain bike, and on foot. Custom-designed trips (with a minimum of motorized transport) of shorter duration are also available.

Costa Rica Expeditions (☎ 2257-0766; www.costaricaexpeditions.com) offers everything from 10-day tours covering the entire country to 3-day/2-night and 2-day/1-night tours of Monteverde Cloud Forest Biological Reserve and Tortuguero National Park, where the company runs its own lodges. Its tours are some of the most expensive in the country, but this is the most consistently reliable outfitter, and its customer service is excellent.

Costa Rica Sun Tours (☎ 2296-7757; www.crsuntours.com) offers a wide range of tours and adventures; it specializes in multiday tours that include stays at small country lodges for travelers interested in experiencing nature.

While not specifically an adventure-oriented operator, **Horizontes** (☎ 2222-2022; www.horizontes.com) offers a number of individual and group package tours geared toward active and adventure travelers. The company generally hires responsible and knowledgeable guides, and it employs sustainable practices at every turn.

Serendipity Adventures (☎ 877/507-1358 in U.S. and Canada, or 2558-1000 in Costa Rica; www.serendipityadventures.com) offers everything from ballooning to mountain biking, and sea kayaking to canyoning, as well as most of the popular white-water rafting trips.

Other Adventure-Tour Operators

Abercrombie & Kent (☎ 800/554-7016 in U.S. and Canada; www.abercrombiekent.com) is a luxury tour company that offers upscale trips around the globe, and it has several tours of Costa Rica on its menu. It specializes in a 9-day Highlights Tour, which takes in the Monteverde, Arenal, and Tortuguero regions. Service is personalized, and the guides are top-notch.

Butterfield & Robinson (☎ 866/551-9090 in U.S. and Canada; www.butterfield.com) is another company specializing in the very high-end market. One of its most interesting options is a trip designed for families with children over 8 years old. The trip provides a wealth of activities and adventures for parents and children to enjoy both together and apart.

Costa Rica Experts (☎ 800/827-9046 or 773/935-1009 in U.S. and Canada; www.costaricaexperts.com) offers a large menu of a la carte options and package deals, as well as day trips and adventure tours.

For those looking for something a little different, **Overseas Adventure Travel** (☎ 800/493-6824 in U.S. and Canada; www.oattravel.com) has good-value natural history and "soft adventure" itineraries with optional add-on excursions. Tours are limited to 16 people and are guided by naturalists. All accommodations are

> *PAGE 444 An excursion with Costa Rica Rainforest Outward Bound School. THIS PAGE The area around Lake Arenal and Arenal Volcano is great for bicycling, and the scenery never disappoints.*

in small hotels, lodges, or tent camps.

If you'd like a trip that focuses more on the beauty and history of Costa Rica, and less on adventure, try **Nature Expeditions International** (☎ 800/869-0639 in U.S. and Canada; www.naturexp.com), which specializes in educational "low intensity adventure" trips tailored to independent travelers and small groups. These folks have a steady stream of programmed departures, or they can customize a trip to your needs.

Outdoor Activities A to Z

Biking

The area around **Lake Arenal** (p. 240) and **Arenal Volcano** (p. 230, ❺) wins my vote as the best place for mountain biking in Costa Rica. The scenery's great, taking in primary forests and waterfalls, and there are plenty of trails. **Bike Arenal** (☎ 866/465-4114 in U.S. and Canada, or 2479-7150 in Costa Rica; www.bikearenal.com) is based in La Fortuna and specializes in 1-day and multiday trips around the Arenal area.

For longer tours, **ExperiencePlus!** (☎ 800/685-4565 or 970/484-8489 in U.S. and Canada; www.experienceplus.com) offers group and individual guided bike tours around

the country. This is the only company I know of that uses touring bikes. It also offers guided group hiking and multisport tours.

Coast to Coast Adventures (☎ 2280-8054; www.ctocadventures.com) and **Serendipity Adventures** (☎ 877/507-1358 in U.S. and Canada, or 2558-1030 in Costa Rica; www.serendipity-adventures.com) offer mountain-biking itineraries among their many tour options.

Bird-Watching

In addition to the operators listed below, you might want to check in with the **Birding Club of Costa Rica** (costaricabirding@hotmail.com), which runs monthly outings and provides you with the opportunity to connect with local bird-watchers. These are also the folks to contact if you want to participate in the annual Christmas Bird Count. This event is part of a worldwide network of bird counts loosely coordinated by the National Audubon Society.

Field Guides (☎ 800/728-4953 or 512/263-7295 in U.S. and Canada; www.fieldguides.com) offers bird-watching tours that range from a 9-day stay at one well-located lodge to a 16-day tour that touches down at almost all of the country's main bird-watching regions.

Victor Emanuel Nature Tours (☎ 800/328-8368 or 512/328-5221 in U.S. and Canada;

> Visitors to Costa Rica, with its wide variety of eco-systems and incredible biodiversity, will find many opportunities to commune with nature.

www.ventbird.com) is a pioneering operator that offers several different bird-watching tours to Costa Rica each year.

WINGS (☎ 888/293-6443 or 520/320-9868 in U.S. and Canada; www.wingsbirds.com) is a major bird-watching operator with more than 30 years of experience in the field. In addition to their exclusive bird-watching itineraries, these folks also offer wildlife-viewing tours that focus on some of Costa Rica's other interesting types of fauna, such as butterflies and sea turtles.

Canyoning & Canopy Tours

Canopy tours are all the rage in Costa Rica, largely because they are such an exciting and unique way to experience a tropical rain forest. Most involve strapping yourself into a climbing harness and either being winched up to a plat-form some 30m (100 ft.) above the forest floor or doing the work yourself. Many of these op-erations have a series of treetop platforms con-nected by taut cables known as zip-lines. Once up on the first platform, you click your harness into a pulley and glide across the cable to the next (slightly lower) platform, using your hand (protected by a thick leather glove) as a brake. When you reach the last platform, you usually rappel down to the ground.

Canyoning tours are even more adventurous. Although hardly standardized, most involve hik-ing along a mountain stream, river, or canyon, with periodic breaks to rappel down the face of a waterfall or swim in a jungle pool.

Although this can be a lot of fun, do **be careful;** these tours are popping up all over the place, and there is precious little regulation of the activity. Some of the tours are set up by fly-by-night op-erators (obviously, I haven't listed any of these). See the "Adventures on Land" section in each chapter for my recommendations. Be especially sure that you feel comfortable and confident with the safety standards, guides, and equipment before embarking. Before you sign on to any tour, ask whether you have to hoist yourself to the top under your own steam, and then make your deci-sion accordingly.

Golfing

Costa Rica is not one of the world's great golfing destinations—at least not yet, anyway. Golfers who want the most up-to-date information, or those who are interested in a package deal that includes play on a variety of courses, should con-tact **Costa Rica Golf Adventures** (☎ 877/258-2688 in U.S. and Canada; www.golfcr.com).

Horseback Riding

Costa Rica's rural roots are evident in the con-tinued use of horses for real work and transportation throughout the country. Most travelers simply saddle up for a couple of hours, but those looking for a more specifically equestrian-based visit should check in with these two operations.

Nature Lodge Finca Los Caballos (☎ 2642-0124; www.naturelodge.net) specializes in horse tours and has the healthiest horses in the Montezuma area.

Serendipity Adventures (☎ 877/507-1358 in U.S. and Canada, or 2558-1030 in Costa Rica; www.serendipityadventures.com), based near La Fortuna, offers multiday horseback treks and tours countrywide.

Scuba Diving & Snorkeling

Many islands, reefs, caves, and rocks lie off the coast of Costa Rica, providing excellent spots for underwater exploration. Visibility varies with season and location. Generally, heavy rainfall tends to swell the rivers and muddy the waters, even well offshore. Runoff from banana plantations has destroyed most of the reefs around Costa Rica's Caribbean coast, although there's still good diving at **Isla Uvita,** just off the coast of Limón, and in **Manzanillo** (p. 398), down near the Panamanian border. Most divers choose Pacific dive spots such as **Isla del Caño** (p. 343, ⑫), the **Bat Islands** (p. 160), and the **Catalina Islands** (p. 160), where you're likely to spot manta rays, moray eels, whitetip sharks, and plenty of smaller fish and coral species.

Snorkeling is not incredibly common or rewarding in Costa Rica. The rain, runoff, and wave conditions that drive scuba divers well off-shore tend to make coastal and shallow-water conditions less than optimal. The best snorkel-ing experience to be had in Costa Rica is on the reefs off **Manzanillo** (p. 396) on the southern Caribbean coast, particularly during the calm months of September and October.

Sportfishing

Anglers in Costa Rican waters have landed more than 100 world-record catches, including of blue marlin, Pacific sailfish, yellowfin tuna, and snook. You can raise a marlin anywhere along the Pacific coast. Many of the Pacific port and beach towns—Quepos, Puntarenas, Playa del Coco, Tamarindo, Playa Flamingo, Golfito, Drake Bay, Playa Zancudo—support large charter fleets.

Costa Rica Outdoors (☎ 800/308-3394 in U.S. and Canada, or 2231-0306 in Costa Rica;

www.costaricaoutdoors.com) is a well-estab-lished operation, founded by local fishing legend and outdoor writer Jerry Ruhlow, specializing in booking fishing trips around the country.

If you're looking for a dedicated fishing lodge, you might check out **Aguila de Osa Inn** (☎ 866/924-8452 in U.S. and Canada, or 2296-2190 in Costa Rica; www.aguiladeosainn.com) in Drake Bay, or the **Zancudo Lodge** (☎ 800/854-8791 in U.S. and Canada, or 2776-0008 in Costa Rica; www.thezancudolodge.com) in the remote southern Pacific town of Playa Zancudo. Both of these specialize in large, offshore sailfish and other game fish.

On the Caribbean coast, **Silver King Lodge** (☎ 877/335-0755 in U.S. and Canada [no Costa Rica number]; www.silverkinglodge.net) and **Río Colorado Lodge** (☎ 800/243-9777 in U.S. and Canada, or 2232-4063 in Costa Rica; www.riocoloradolodge.com), both located in Barra del Colorado, specialize in tarpon.

Surfing

When *Endless Summer II,* the sequel to the all-time surf classic, was filmed, the production crew brought its boards and cameras to Costa Rica. **Playas Hermosa, Jacó,** and **Dominical,** on the central Pacific coast, and **Tamarindo** in Gua-nacaste and **Playa Gulones** on the Nicoya Pen-insula, are becoming mini surf meccas. **Salsa Brava** in Puerto Viejo on the Caribbean coast is a steep and fast wave that peels off both right and left over shallow coral. It has a habit of breaking boards, but the daredevils keep coming back for more.

Beginners and folks looking to learn should stick to the mellower sections of **Jacó** (p. 298) and **Tamarindo** (p. 130). Crowds are starting to gather at the more popular breaks, but you can still stumble onto secret spots on the **Osa** (p. 354) and **Nicoya** (p. 186) **Peninsulas** and along the northern Guanacaste coast. Costa Rica's signature wave is found at **Pavones** (p. 354) in the Southern Zone, which is reputed to have one of the longest lefts in the world. The cognoscenti also swear by places such as **Playa Grande** and **Witch's Rock** (p. 130) along the Guanacaste coast; **Matapalo** (p. 354) on the Osa Peninsula; and **Malpaís** (p. 174) on the Nicoya Peninsula. An avid surfer's best bet is to rent a dependable four-wheel-drive vehicle with a rack and take a surfin' safari around the breaks of Guanacaste.

> *Costa Rica offers many volunteer and educational opportunities.*

If you're looking for an organized surf vacation, contact **Tico Travel** (☎ 800/493-8426 in U.S. and Canada; www.ticotravel.com), or check out **www.crsurf.com**. For swell reports, general surf information, live wave-cams, and great links pages, set your browser to **www.surfline.com**.

White-Water Rafting, Kayaking & Canoeing
Whether you're a first-time rafter or a world-class kayaker, Costa Rica's got some white water for you. Rivers rise and fall with the rainfall, but you can get wet and wild here even in the dry season. The best white-water rafting ride is the scenic **Río Pacuare** (p. 73). If you're just experimenting with river rafting, stick to class II and III rivers, such as the **Reventazón** (p. 397), **Sarapiquí** (p. 241), **Peñas Blancas** (p. 241), and **Savegre** (p. 301). If you already know which end of the paddle goes in the water, there are plenty of class IV and V sections to run.

Die-hard river rats should get *Chasing Jaguars: The Complete Guide to Costa Rican Whitewater,* by Lee Eudy (Earthbound Sports, Inc., Chapel Hill, NC: 2003), a book loaded with photos, technical data, and route tips on almost every rideable river in the country.

Nature Adventures (☎ 800/321-8410 in U.S. and Canada, or 2225-3939 in Costa Rica; www.toenjoynature.com) and **Ríos Tropicales** (☎ 866/722-8273 in U.S. and Canada, or 2233-6455 in Costa Rica; www.riostropicales. com) are the two largest rafting operators in the country, running a variety of rivers, with daily departures. Both have wonderful riverside lodges on the Pacuare River, making their 2-day Pacuare trips exciting and luxurious at the same time.

Exploradores Outdoors (☎ 2222-6262; www.exploradoresoutdoors.com) is another good operation run by a longtime and well-respected river guide. They run the Pacuare, Reventazón, and Sarapiquí Rivers, and even combine their river trips with onward transportation to or from the Caribbean coast or the Arenal Volcano area for no extra cost.

Canoe Costa Rica (☎/fax 732/736-6586 in U.S., or 2282-3579 in Costa Rica; www. canoecostarica.com) is the only outfit I know of that specializes in canoe trips; it works primarily with custom-designed tours and itineraries, although it does have several set departure trips each year.

Learning Trips & Language Classes

Most Spanish schools can arrange for home stays with a middle-class Tico family for a total-immersion experience. Classes are often small, or even one-on-one, and last anywhere from 2 to 8 hours a day. Rates average between $350 and $500 per week, depending upon a variety of factors and options. Contact the schools for current pricing.

Adventure Education Center (AEC) Spanish Institute (☎ 800/237-2730 in U.S. and Canada, or 2258-5111 in Costa Rica; www.adventure spanishschool.com) has branches in La Fortuna, Dominical, and Turrialba, and specializes in combining language learning with adventure activities.

In San José, **Costa Rican Language Academy** (☎ 866/230-6361 in U.S. and Canada, or 2280-1685 in Costa Rica; www.spanishandmore.com) has intensive programs that integrate Latin dance and Costa Rican cooking classes with its language classes. Classes are held Monday to Thursday to give students a chance for longer weekend excursions.

International House Costa Rica (☎ 2234-9054; www.institutobritanico.co.cr), formerly the Instituto Británico, is a venerable institution with installations in the Los Yoses neighborhood of San José. A bit more attention seems to be paid to teacher training and selection here than at other institutions around town.

Nature

Costa Rica's diverse climate and geography offer lots of opportunities for nature lovers. Britain-based **Naturetrek** (☎ 1962-733-051; www.naturetrek.co.uk) offers excellent and varied nature tours, such as a 15-day Costa Rica bird-watching tour.

Volunteer & Educational Trips

APREFLOFAS (Association for the Preservation of the Wild Flora and Fauna) (☎ 2574-6816; www.preserveplanet.org) is a pioneering local conservation organization that accepts volunteers and runs environmentally sound educational tours around the country.

Asociación de Voluntarios para el Servicio en Areas Protegidas (ASVO; ☎ 2258-4430; www.asvocr.org) organizes volunteers to work in Costa Rican national parks. A 2-week minimum commitment is required, as is a basic ability to converse in Spanish. Housing is provided at a basic ranger station, and there is a $17 daily fee to cover food, which is basic Tico fare.

Caribbean Conservation Corporation (☎ 800/676-2018 in U.S. and Canada, or 2278-6058 in Costa Rica; www.cccturtle.org) is a nonprofit organization dedicated to sea turtle research, protection, and advocacy. Their main operation in Costa Rica is headquartered in Tortuguero, where volunteers can aid in various scientific studies, as well as participate in nightly patrols of the beach during nesting seasons to prevent poaching.

Costa Rica Rainforest Outward Bound School (☎ 800/676-2018 in U.S. and Canada, or 2278-6058 in Costa Rica; www.crrobs.org) is the local branch of this well-respected international adventure-based outdoor-education organization. Courses range from 2 weeks to a full semester, and offerings include surfing, kayaking, tree climbing, and learning Spanish.

Earthwatch Institute (☎ 800/776-0188 in U.S. and Canada; www.earthwatch.org) organizes volunteers to go on research trips to help scientists collect data and conduct field experiments in a number of scientific fields and a wide range of settings. Expeditions to Costa Rica range from studies of the nesting habits of leatherback sea turtles to research into sustainable coffee-growing methods. Fees for food and lodging average around $2,650 for a 2-week expedition, excluding airfare.

Eco Teach (☎ 800/626-8992 in U.S. and Canada; www.ecoteach.com) works primarily in facilitating educational trips for high school and college student groups. Trips focus on Costa Rican ecology and culture. Costs run around $1,495 to $1,675 per person for a 10-day trip, including lodging, meals, classes, and travel within the country. Airfare to Costa Rica is extra.

Global Volunteers (☎ 800/487-1074 in U.S. and Canada; www.globalvolunteers.org) is a U.S.–based organization that offers a unique opportunity to travelers who've always wanted a Peace Corps–like experience but can't make a 2-year commitment. For 2 to 3 weeks, you can join one of its working vacations in Costa Rica. A certain set of skills, such as engineering or agricultural knowledge, is helpful but by no means necessary. Each trip is undertaken at a particular community's request, to complete a specific project. However, be warned: These "volunteer" experiences do not come cheap. You must pay for your transportation as well as a hefty program fee, around $2,395 for a 2-week program.

Habitat for Humanity International (☎ 2296-3436; www.habitatcostarica.org) has several chapters in Costa Rica and sometimes runs organized Global Village programs here.

The **Institute for Central American Development Studies** (☎ 2225-0508; www.icads.org) offers internship and research opportunities in the areas of environment, agriculture, human rights, and women's studies. An intensive Spanish-language program can be combined with work-study or volunteer opportunities.

Vida (☎ 2221-8367; www.vida.org) is a local nongovernmental organization working on sustainable development and conservation issues; it often places volunteers. However, its website is entirely in Spanish, and some reasonable Spanish language skills are recommended for working with this group.

Guide to Costa Rica's Flora & Fauna

> *OPPOSITE PAGE A wildlife-viewing platform on the Río Pacuare. THIS PAGE A pair of three-toed sloths.*

For such a small country, Costa Rica is incredibly rich in biodiversity: It comprises just .01% of the earth's landmass but is home to some 5% of its biodiversity. Whether you come to Costa Rica to check 100 or so species off your lifetime bird list, or just to check out of the rat race for a week or so, you'll be surrounded by a rich and varied collection of flora and fauna. The information below is meant to be a selective introduction to some of what you might see. The prime viewing recommendations should be understood within the reality of actual wildlife viewing. Most casual visitors and even many dedicated naturalists will never see a wildcat or kinkajou. However, anyone working with a good guide should be able to see a broad selection of Costa Rica's impressive flora and fauna.

Searching for Wildlife

Unless you have lots of experience in the tropics, your best hope for getting the most out of a walk through the jungle lies in employing a trained and knowledgeable guide. Most animals of the forest are **nocturnal** (active at night), and those that are **diurnal** (active by day) are usually elusive and on the watch for predators. Birds are easier to spot in clearings or secondary forests than they are in primary forests, since primary forests are darker, with denser foliage and a higher canopy.

Helpful Hints for Finding Wildlife

Listen. Pay attention to rustling in the leaves; whether it's a monkey up above or a coatimundi on the ground, you're most likely to hear an animal before seeing it.

Keep quiet. Noise will scare off animals and prevent you from hearing their movements and calls.

Don't try too hard. Soften your focus and allow your peripheral vision to take over. This way you can catch glimpses of motion and then focus in on the area.

Bring binoculars. It's also a good idea to practice a little first to get the hang of them. It would be a shame to be fiddling around and staring at empty sky while everyone else in your group *oohs* and *aahs* over a resplendent quetzal.

Dress appropriately. You'll have a hard time focusing your binoculars if you're busy swatting mosquitoes. Light-colored long pants and long-sleeved shirts are your best bet. Comfortable hiking boots are a real boon, except where heavy rubber boots are necessary. Avoid loud colors; the better you blend in with your surroundings, the better your chances of spotting wildlife.

Be patient. The jungle isn't on a schedule.

Timing is everything. Your best shots at seeing forest fauna are during the very early morning and late afternoon.

Fauna
Mammals

Costa Rica has more than 230 species of mammals. Roughly half of these are bats. While it is very unlikely that you will spot a wildcat, you have good odds of catching a glimpse of a monkey, coatimundi, peccary, or sloth, or more likely, any number of bats. For more on Costa Rica's monkeys, see "Meet the Monkeys," p. 352.

Mantled Howler Monkey

SCIENTIFIC NAME *Alouatta palliata*

WORTH NOTING Known locally as *mono congo,* the mantled howler monkey grows to 56cm (22 in.) in length. A highly social species, this diurnal primate often travels in groups of 10 to 30. The loud roar of the male can be heard from as far as a mile away.

PRIME VIEWING Wet and dry forests throughout Costa Rica. Almost entirely arboreal, tending to favor higher reaches of the canopy.

White-Faced Capuchin

SCIENTIFIC NAME *Cebus capucinus*

WORTH NOTING Known as *mono carablanca* or *mono capuchin* in Costa Rica, the white-faced capuchin is a midsize, diurnal monkey, 46cm (18 in.) in length, with distinctive white fur around its face, head, and forearms. It can be found in forests all around the country and travels in large troops or family groups.

PRIME VIEWING
Wet and dry forests throughout Costa Rica.

Central American Squirrel Monkey

SCIENTIFIC NAME *Saimiri oerstedii*

WORTH NOTING The smallest and friskiest of Costa Rica's monkeys, the Central American, or red-backed, squirrel monkey, is also its most endangered. Active in the daytime, this monkey—known locally as *mono titi*—travels in small to midsize groups. Squirrel monkeys do not have a prehensile (grasping) tail.

PRIME VIEWING Manuel Antonio National Park (p. 290) and Corcovado National Park (p. 348).

Central American Spider Monkey

SCIENTIFIC NAME *Ateles geoffroyi*

WORTH NOTING The Central American spider monkey, one of Costa Rica's more acrobatic monkeys, is known as *mono araña* or *mono colorado* in Costa Rica. Large (64cm/25 in.), with brown or silvery fur, it has long, thin limbs and a long, prehensile tail. It is active both day and night, traveling in small to midsize bands or family groups.

PRIME VIEWING Wet and dry forests throughout Costa Rica.

Northern Tamandua

SCIENTIFIC NAME *Tamandua mexicana*

WORTH NOTING Also known as the collared anteater (*oso hormiguero* in Spanish), the northern tamandua grows up to 77cm (30 in.) long, not counting its thick tail, which can be as long its body. It is active both day and night.

PRIME VIEWING Low- and middle-elevation forests over most of Costa Rica.

Three-Toed Sloth

SCIENTIFIC NAME *Bradypus variegatus*

WORTH NOTING The larger and more commonly sighted of Costa Rica's two sloth species, the three-toed has long, coarse, brown-to-gray fur and a distinctive eye-band. There are three long, sharp claws on each foreleg. Except for brief periods to defecate, these slow-moving creatures are entirely arboreal.

PRIME VIEWING Low- and middle-elevation forests over most of Costa Rica, in a wide variety of trees; most commonly spotted in the relatively sparsely leaved cecropia tree (p. 470).

Nine-Banded Armadillo

SCIENTIFIC NAME *Dasypus novemcinctus*

WORTH NOTING *Armadillo* is Spanish for "little armored one," and that's an accurate description of this carapace-carrying mammal. It can reach 65cm (26 in.) in length and weigh up to 4.5kg (10 lb.). The female gives birth to identical quadruplets from a single egg.

PRIME VIEWING Low- and middle-elevation forests and farmlands over most of Costa Rica.

Paca

SCIENTIFIC NAME *Agouti paca*

WORTH NOTING The paca, known as *tepezquintle* in Costa Rica, is a nocturnal rodent that feeds on fallen fruit, leaves, and tubers. Its dark brown to black back fur has rows of white spots. You may also see its diurnal cousin, the agouti, which is lighter brown with no spots.

PRIME VIEWING Near water in many habitats throughout Costa Rica, from river valleys to swamps to dense tropical forests.

Kinkajou

SCIENTIFIC NAME *Potos flavus*

WORTH NOTING The nocturnal, tree-dwelling kinkajou is some-times mistaken for a monkey, but is actually related to the raccoon and coatimundi (p. 456). With large eyes and a fluffy brown coat, the kinkajou has an average body length of some 50cm (20 in); its prehensile tail is about the same length

PRIME VIEWING Strictly nocturnal, the kinkajou is found in rain and cloud forests throughout Costa Rica. The reflection of its large eyes is sometimes seen on night tours.

Coatimundi

SCIENTIFIC NAME *Nasua narica*

WORTH NOTING Known as *pizote* in Costa Rica, the raccoonlike co-atimundi can adapt to disturbed habitats and is often spotted near hotels and nature lodges. It is active both day and night and equally comfortable on the ground and in trees. This social animal is often found in groups of 10 to 20.

PRIME VIEWING A variety of habitats, from dry scrub to dense forests, throughout Costa Rica, including its coastal islands.

Tayra

SCIENTIFIC NAME *Eira barbara*

WORTH NOTING This midsize animal of the weasel family is known in Costa Rica as *tolumuco* or *gato de monte*. Long and low to the ground, it is dark brown to black, with a brown to tan head and neck and a long, bushy tail. Tayras are active both day and night, and travel both individually and in small groups.

PRIME VIEWING In trees and on the ground in forests, as well as open areas throughout Costa Rica.

Jaguar

SCIENTIFIC NAME *Panthera onca*

WORTH NOTING This cat measures 1 to 1.8m (3½–6 ft.), not includ-ing its long tail, and is distinguished by its tan-yellow, black-spotted fur. It is often called simply *tigre* (tiger) in Costa Rica. Jaguars are considered nocturnal, although some say it would be more accurate to describe them as crepuscular, most active in the periods around dawn and dusk. They are endangered and hard to see in the wild.

PRIME VIEWING Major tracts of primary and secondary forest in Costa Rica, as well as some open savannas; greatest concentration in Corcovado National Park (p. 348) on the Osa Peninsula.

Ocelot

SCIENTIFIC NAME *Leopardus pardalis*

WORTH NOTING The ocelot is known as *manigordo*, or "fat paws," in Costa Rica. The tail of this small cat is longer than its rear leg, which makes for easy identification. The ocelot is mostly nocturnal; it sleeps in trees by day.

PRIME VIEWING Forests throughout Costa Rica; greatest concen-tration on the Osa Peninsula.

Jaguarundi

SCIENTIFIC NAME *Herpailurus yaguarondi*

WORTH NOTING This small to midsize cat has a solid black, brown, or reddish coat and an oval-shaped face often compared to that of a weasel or otter, giving it a unique look. The jaguarundi is a diurnal hunter; it can occasionally be spotted in a clearing or climbing a tree.

PRIME VIEWING Often spotted in middle-elevation moist forests.

Baird's Tapir

SCIENTIFIC NAME *Tapirus bairdii*

WORTH NOTING Known as *danta* or *macho de monte,* the endangered Baird's tapir is the largest land mammal in Costa Rica. Average adults are some 2m (6½ ft) in length, stand over 1m (3 ft.) tall, and can weigh as much as 400kg (880 lbs). It is active both day and night, foraging along riverbanks, streams, and forest clearings.

PRIME VIEWING Wet forested areas, particularly on the Caribbean and southern Pacific slopes.

Collared Peccary

SCIENTIFIC NAME *Tayassu tajacu*

WORTH NOTING Called *saino* or *chancho de monte* in Costa Rica, the collared peccary is a black or brown, piglike animal that is active in the daytime. Collared peccaries travel in groups and have a strong musk odor.

PRIME VIEWING Low- and middle-elevation forests over most of Costa Rica.

Hairy-Legged Bat

SCIENTIFIC NAME *Myotis keaysi*

WORTH NOTING The hairy-legged bat grows to just 5cm (2 in.) long, not including the length of its tail. This bat has brown woolly fur on its back and body, and darker fur on its legs. An insect-eating bat, it begins feeding around sunset and finishes roughly an hour before dawn.

PRIME VIEWING Low- to mid-level elevations throughout Costa Rica; roosts in caves, rock crevices, under bridges, and in buildings.

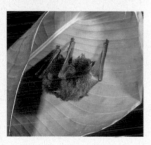

Sucker-Footed Bat

SCIENTIFIC NAME *Thyroptera tricolor*

WORTH NOTING This small, reddish-brown bat averages 3.2cm (1¼ in.) long and weighs only 4.5g (⅜ oz.). Tiny suction cups on its ankles allow this bat to cling to the undersides of large, broad leaves. The sucker-footed bat is a night-feeding insectivore.

PRIME VIEWING Lowland rain forests and gardens on both coasts. Roosts in small groups in the young, rolled-up leaves of banana and heliconia plants.

Birds

Costa Rica has more than 880 identified species of resident and migrant birds. The variety of habitats and compact nature of the country make it a major bird-watching destination.

Magnificent Frigatebird

SCIENTIFIC NAME *Fregata magnificens*

WORTH NOTING The magnificent frigatebird is a naturally agile flier. It swoops (it doesn't dive into the water or swim as other seabirds do) to pluck food from the water's surface or, more commonly, to steal prey from the mouths of other birds.

PRIME VIEWING Year-round on shores and coastal islands of both coasts; often seen soaring high overhead.

Cattle Egret

SCIENTIFIC NAME *Bubulcus ibis*

WORTH NOTING Part of the year the cattle egret is a snow-white bird with a yellow bill and black legs. It changes color for the breeding season (April to October): A yellowish-buff color appears on the head, chest, and back, and a reddish hue emerges on the bill and legs.

PRIME VIEWING Seen year-round near cattle, or following tractors, throughout Costa Rica.

Boat-billed Heron

SCIENTIFIC NAME *Cochlearius cochlearius*

WORTH NOTING The midsize boat-billed heron (about 51cm/20 in. long) has a large black head, a large broad bill, and rusty brown plumage.

PRIME VIEWING Resident year-round in marshes, swamps, rivers, and mangroves throughout Costa Rica.

Roseate Spoonbill

SCIENTIFIC NAME *Platalea ajaja*

WORTH NOTING The roseate spoonbill, also known as *garza rosada* (pink heron), is a large waterbird with pink or light red plumage and a large, spoon-shaped bill. The species almost became extinct in the United States because its pink wing feathers were used to make fans.

PRIME VIEWING Year-round resident found in low-lying freshwater and saltwater wetlands nationwide, although rare along the Caribbean coast and plains. Common on the Pacific coast, north-central lowlands, and in the Golfo de Nicoya and Golfo Dulce areas.

Jabiru

SCIENTIFIC NAME *Jabiru mycteria*

WORTH NOTING One of the largest birds in the world, this stork stands 1.5m (5 ft.) tall and has a wingspan of 2.4m (8 ft.) and a 30cm-long (1-ft.) bill. The Jabiru is an endangered species, and there are only a dozen or so nesting pairs in Costa Rica. Jabirus arrive in Costa Rica from Mexico in November and return north with the rains in May or June.

PRIME VIEWING From November to June, in the wetlands of Palo Verde National Park (p. 128) and Caño Negro Wildlife Refuge (p. 231).

Osprey

SCIENTIFIC NAME *Pandion haliaetus*

WORTH NOTING This large (.6m/2-ft. tall, with a 1.8m/6-ft. wing-span) raptor, which has a distinctive white head, is also known as *gavilan pescador,* or "fishing eagle." In flight, the osprey's wings angle backward.

PRIME VIEWING A small population is resident year-round, although most are winter migrants, arriving September to October and de-parting April and May. Found in lowland coastal areas and wetlands throughout Costa Rica; seen flying or perched in trees near water.

Laughing Falcon

SCIENTIFIC NAME *Herpetotheres cachinnans*

WORTH NOTING The laughing falcon, also known as *guaco* in Costa Rica, gets its name from its loud, piercing call. This bird of prey is large (56cm/22 in. long), with a wingspan that reaches an impres-sive 94cm (37 in.). It specializes in eating both venomous and non-venomous snakes but will also hunt lizards and small rodents.

PRIME VIEWING Year-round resident, most common in lowland ar-eas, forest edges, grasslands, and farmlands throughout Costa Rica.

Ferruginous Pygmy-Owl

SCIENTIFIC NAME *Glaucidium brasilianum*

WORTH NOTING Unlike most owls, this small (about 38cm/15 in.), grayish brown or reddish brown owl is most active during the day.

PRIME VIEWING Year-round, forest edges and farmlands of low and middle elevations along the northern Pacific slope.

Mealy Parrot

SCIENTIFIC NAME *Amazona farinosa*

WORTH NOTING This large, vocal parrot is almost entirely green, with a touch of blue on the top of its head and small red and blue ac-cents on its wings. It is called *loro verde* (green parrot), and you and locals alike might confuse it with any number of other local species.

PRIME VIEWING Year-round resident, lowland tropical rain forests on both coasts.

Scarlet Macaw

SCIENTIFIC NAME *Ara macao*

WORTH NOTING Known as *guacamaya* or *lapa* in Costa Rica, the scarlet macaw is a long-tailed member of the parrot family. It can reach 89cm (35 in.) in length, including its long, pointed tail. The bird is endangered over most of its range, mainly because it is coveted as a pet. Its loud squawk and rainbow-colored feathers are quite distinctive.

PRIME VIEWING Year-round resident, Carara National Park, Osa Peninsula, and in the forests around the Golfo Dulce.

Violet Sabrewing

SCIENTIFIC NAME *Campylopterus hemileucurus*

WORTH NOTING The largest hummingbird found in Costa Rica, the violet sabrewing shines a deep purple when the sun strikes it right. It can reach a length of 15cm (6 in.), and has a long, thick, and gently curving beak.

PRIME VIEWING Year-round in middle- and higher-elevation rain and cloud forests throughout Costa Rica.

Resplendent Quetzal

SCIENTIFIC NAME *Pharomachrus mocinno*

WORTH NOTING Perhaps the most distinctive and spectacular bird in Central America, the resplendent quetzal, of the trogon family, can grow to 37cm (15 in.) long. The males are distinctive, with iridescent blue-green plumage, a bright red chest, a yellow bill, and tail feathers that can reach 64cm (24 in.) in length. The females lack the long tail feathers and have a duller beak and less pronounced red chest. See also "The Resplendent Quetzal: Mesoamerica's Holiest Bird," p. 10.

PRIME VIEWING Year-round resident in high-elevation wet and cloud forests, particularly Monteverde Cloud Forest Biological Reserve (p. 218, **1**) and along the Cerro de la Muerte.

Chestnut-mandibled Toucan

SCIENTIFIC NAME *Ramphastos swainsonii*

WORTH NOTING The large, canoe-shaped bill of this toucan is divided by a distinct diagonal line, bright yellow above and dark chestnut below. The chestnut-mandibled toucan's striking coloration includes a yellow face and breast, red body below the breast, and blue legs. This bird is slightly larger than the keel-billled toucan, reaching a length of 56cm (22 in).

PRIME VIEWING Year-round resident of lowland and mid-elevation forests on the Caribbean slope and coast, up to 1,200m (4,000 ft).

Keel-Billed Toucan

SCIENTIFIC NAME *Ramphastos sulfuratus*

WORTH NOTING Its large rainbow-colored, canoe-shaped bill makes the keel-billed toucan a favorite on bird-watching tours. This toucan can grow to about 51cm (20 in.) long, and aside from its bill coloration, it is similar in shape and coloring to the chestnut-mandibled toucan. Costa Rica is also home to several smaller toucanet and aracari species.

PRIME VIEWING Year-round resident of lowland forests on the Caribbean and north Pacific slopes, up to 1,200m (4,000 ft.).

Clay-Colored Robin

SCIENTIFIC NAME *Turdus grayi*

WORTH NOTING In a country with such a rich variety of spectacularly plumaged bird species, this plain brown robin (also called the clay-colored thrush) is an unlikely choice to be Costa Rica's national bird. However, it is extremely widespread and common, especially in urban areas of the Central Valley, and it has a wide range of pleasant calls and songs. Known locally as the *yigüirro,* it has uniform brown plumage, with a lighter brown belly and yellow bill.

PRIME VIEWING Resident year-round in clearings, secondary forests, and around human settlements in low and middle elevations throughout Costa Rica.

Scarlet-Rumped Tanager

SCIENTIFIC NAME *Ramphocelus costaricensis*

WORTH NOTING With a striking scarlet red patch on its rump, this is one of the most commonly sighted tanagers in Costa Rica. It is known locally as *sargento* or *sangre de toro.* A recent scientific reclassification has divided the Costa Rican scarlet-rumped tanager into two distinct species: Passerini's tanager and Cherrie's tanager.

PRIME VIEWING Year-round, in lowlands and middle-elevation areas throughout Costa Rica; Passerini's tanager on the Caribbean slope and lowlands, Cherrie's tanager on the Pacific slope and lowlands. Prefers secondary forests, forest edges, clearings, and gardens.

Montezuma Oropendola

SCIENTIFIC NAME *Psarocolius montezuma*

WORTH NOTING The Montezuma oropendola has a black head; brown body; yellow-edged tail; large, black, orange-tipped bill; and a blue patch under the eye. This bird builds long, teardrop-shaped hanging nests that are often found in large groups. It has several distinct, loud calls, including one it makes while briefly hanging upside down.

PRIME VIEWING Year-round in low and middle elevation forests along the Caribbean slope and some sections of eastern Guanacaste.

Amphibians

Frogs, toads, and salamanders are actually some of the most beguiling, beautiful, and easy-to-spot residents of tropical forests.

Ring-Tailed Salamander

SCIENTIFIC NAME *Bolitoglossa robusta*

WORTH NOTING This midsize black salamander can grow to 13cm (5 in.) long; it is distinguished by the namesake yellow to orange ring near the upper portion of its tail.

PRIME VIEWING Middle- and higher-elevation wet forests throughout Costa Rica.

Mexican Burrowing Toad

SCIENTIFIC NAME *Rhinophrynus dorsalis*

WORTH NOTING The bloblike, 7.6cm (3-in.) Mexican burrowing toad will inflate like a blowfish when frightened. There is often a single red, orange, or yellow line down the center of its back.

PRIME VIEWING Lower-elevation forests, moist grasslands, and farmlands of the Pacific coast.

Marine Toad

SCIENTIFIC NAME *Bufo marinus*

WORTH NOTING The largest toad in the Americas, the 20cm (8-in.), wart-covered marine toad (or cane or giant toad) eats small mammals, other toads, lizards, and insects. Females are mottled in color, males are brown. Glands near the eyes secrete a milky-white toxin when the toad feels threatened—do not touch.

PRIME VIEWING Forests and open areas throughout Costa Rica.

Red-Eyed Tree Frog

SCIENTIFIC NAME *Agalychnis callidryas*

WORTH NOTING The colorful 7.6cm (3-in.) red-eyed tree frog usually has a pale or dark green back, sometimes with white or yellow spots; blue-purple patches and vertical bars on the body; orange hands and feet; and deep red eyes.

PRIME VIEWING Found on the undersides of broad leaves, in low- and middle-elevation wet forests throughout Costa Rica.

Green-and-Black Poison-Arrow Frog

SCIENTIFIC NAME *Dendrobates auratus*

WORTH NOTING The small green-and-black poison-arrow frog ranges from 2.5 to 4cm (1–1½ in.) in length. It has distinctive markings of iridescent green mixed with deep black.

PRIME VIEWING On the ground, around tree roots, and under fallen logs in low- and middle-elevation wet forests of the Caribbean and southern Pacific slopes.

Reptiles

Costa Rica's reptile species range from the frightening and justly feared fer-de-lance pit viper and massive American crocodile to a wide variety of turtles and lizards. *Note:* Sea turtles are included in the "Sea Life" section (p. 465).

American Crocodile

SCIENTIFIC NAME *Crocodylus acutus*

WORTH NOTING Although still an endangered species, the massive American crocodile has made an impressive comeback in recent years, thanks to environmental awareness and protection policies. This reptile can reach lengths of 6.4m (21 ft.), but most individuals are much smaller, usually less than 4m (13 ft.).

PRIME VIEWING Near swamps, mangrove swamps, estuaries, large rivers, and coastal lowlands throughout Costa Rica. Guaranteed viewing from the bridge over the Tárcoles River (p. 313), on the Costanera Highway (CR34) just north of Carara National Park.

Leaf-Toed Gecko

SCIENTIFIC NAME *Phyllodactylus xanti*

WORTH NOTING Spotting the 6.8cm (2½-in.) leaf-toed gecko is easy—it loves to be around buildings and other areas of human activity.

PRIME VIEWING Common on the ground and in leaf litter of low- and middle-elevation forests throughout Costa Rica.

Smooth Gecko

SCIENTIFIC NAME *Thecadactylus rapicauda*

WORTH NOTING The smooth gecko's autonomous tail detaches from its body, creating a diversion to a potential predator; it grows back later in a lighter shade.

PRIME VIEWING Low-elevation wet forests on the Caribbean and southern Pacific slopes; also urban and rural residential areas.

Slender Anole

SCIENTIFIC NAME *Anolis (Norops) limifrons*

WORTH NOTING This thin, olive-colored lizard can reach 5cm (2 in.) in length. There are some 25 related species of *Anolis (Norops)* lizards.

PRIME VIEWING Lowland rain forests throughout Costa Rica.

Green Iguana

SCIENTIFIC NAME *Iguana iguana*

WORTH NOTING Despite the name, green iguanas vary in shade, from neon bright to a dull grayish green, with quite a bit of red and orange mixed in. Predominantly arboreal, this lizard often perches on a branch overhanging a river and will plunge into the water when threatened.

PRIME VIEWING Lowland regions near rivers and streams along both coasts.

Basilisk

SCIENTIFIC NAME *Basiliscus vittatus*

WORTH NOTING The basilisk can run across the water's surface for short distances on its hind legs, holding its body almost upright; thus its alternate name, "Jesus Christ lizard."

PRIME VIEWING In trees and on rocks near water in wet forests throughout Costa Rica.

Boa Constrictor

SCIENTIFIC NAME *Boa constrictor*

WORTH NOTING An adult boa constrictor (*bécquer* in Costa Rica) averages about 1.8 to 3m (6–10 ft.) in length and weighs more than 27kg (60 lb.). Its coloration camouflages it: Look for patterns of cream, brown, gray, and black ovals and diamonds.

PRIME VIEWING Low- and middle-elevation wet and dry forests throughout Costa Rica. Often found living in rafters and eaves of homes in rural areas.

Mussurana

SCIENTIFIC NAME *Clelia clelia*

WORTH NOTING This bluish black, brown, or grayish snake grows to 2.4m (8 ft.) in length. While slightly venomous, it has rear fangs and is of little danger to humans. In fact, the mussurana is prized and protected by locals, since its primary prey happens to be venomous pit vipers like the fer-de-lance.

PRIME VIEWING Open forests, pastures, and farmlands throughout Costa Rica.

Fer-de-Lance

SCIENTIFIC NAME *Bothrops atrox*

WORTH NOTING Known as *terciopelo* in Costa Rica, the aggressive fer-de-lance can grow to 2.4m (8 ft.) in length. Beige, brown, or black triangles flank either side of the head; the area under the head is yellowish. These snakes begin life as arboreal creatures but become increasingly terrestrial as they grow older and larger.

PRIME VIEWING Predominantly lower-elevation forests, but has spread to almost all regions up to 1,300m (4,265 ft), including towns and cities in agricultural areas.

Tropical Rattlesnake

SCIENTIFIC NAME *Crotalus durissus*

WORTH NOTING The tropical rattlesnake, known as *cascabel* in Costa Rica, is a pit viper with a triangular head, a pronounced ridge running along the middle of its back, and (of course) a rattling tail. It can reach 1.8m (6 ft.) in length.

PRIME VIEWING Mostly low-elevation dry forests and open areas of Guanacaste.

Sea Life

With more than 1,290km (800 miles) of shoreline on both the Pacific and Caribbean coasts, Costa Rica has a rich diversity of underwater flora and fauna.

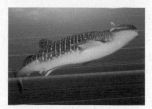

Brain Coral

SCIENTIFIC NAME *Diploria strigosa*

WORTH NOTING The distinctive brain coral is named for its striking physical similarity to a human brain.

PRIME VIEWING Reefs off both coasts.

Whale Shark

SCIENTIFIC NAME *Rhincodon typus*

WORTH NOTING Although the whale shark is large, growing to a length of 14m (45 ft.) or more, its gentle nature makes swimming with it a special treat for divers and snorkelers.

PRIME VIEWING Occasionally spotted off Isla del Caño, more frequently off Isla del Coco.

Bull Shark

SCIENTIFIC NAME *Carcharhinus leucas*

WORTH NOTING These dangerous sharks can be found in shallow waters, and because they can tolerate fresh water, they are able to swim upstream in rivers. Females, which are much larger than males, can reach up to 4m (13 ft.) in length and 318 kg (700 lbs) in weight. They are aggressive (one of the shark species most likely to attack humans) and should be treated with caution.

PRIME VIEWING Bat Island, off Guanacaste, and Río Sirena inlet in Corcovado National Park.

Manta

SCIENTIFIC NAME *Manta birostris*

WORTH NOTING The manta is the largest species of ray, with a wingspan that can reach 6m (20 ft.) and a body weight known to exceed 1,360kg (3,000 lb.). Despite its daunting appearance, the manta is quite gentle. If you are snorkeling or diving, watch for one of these extraordinary and graceful creatures.

PRIME VIEWING All along the Pacific coast.

Moray

SCIENTIFIC NAME *Gymnothorax mordax*

WORTH NOTING Distinguished by a swaying, serpentlike head and a tooth-filled jaw that continually opens and closes, the moray is most commonly seen only as a head appearing from behind rocks. At night, however, it leaves its home along the reef to hunt for small fish, crustaceans, shrimp, and octopi. Morays can range in color from light or dark brown to green, usually mottled.

PRIME VIEWING Rocky areas and reefs off both coasts.

Olive Ridley

SCIENTIFIC NAME *Lepidochelys olivacea*

WORTH NOTING Also known as *tortuga lora,* the olive ridley is the most popular of Costa Rica's sea turtles, famous for its massive group nestings, or *arribadas.* A small sea turtle species with a large, heart-shaped head, the olive ridley averages 46kg (101 lbs.), with a carapace length of just 76cm (30 in).

PRIME VIEWING Playa Nancite in Santa Rosa National Park (p. 125) and Playa Ostional (p. 209, **4**) are the prime nesting sites. Large *arribadas* occur from July through December, and smaller ones from January through June.

Leatherback

SCIENTIFIC NAME *Dermochelys coriacea*

WORTH NOTING The world's largest sea turtle (reaching nearly 2.4m/8 ft. in length and weights of more than 544kg/1,200 lb.), the leatherback is now an endangered species. Unlike most other turtle species, the leatherback's carapace is not a hard shell, but rather a thick, leathery skin. Distinct ridges run lengthwise along the turtle's back, which is black, with white spots.

PRIME VIEWING Playa Grande (p. 120, **7**), near Tamarindo, is a prime nesting site from early October through mid-February; also nests off Tortuguero in much smaller numbers from February through June, peaking during the months of March and April.

Green Turtle

SCIENTIFIC NAME *Chelonia mydas*

WORTH NOTING A large sea turtle, the green turtle has a teardrop-shaped carapace that can range in color from dull green to dark brown. Adults reach some 1.5m (5 ft.) long and weigh an average of 200kg (440 lbs).

PRIME VIEWING Caribbean coast around Tortuguero National Park, from July through mid-October, with August through September the peak period.

Hawksbill

SCIENTIFIC NAME *Eretmochelys imbricata*

WORTH NOTING The hawksbill turtle is a shy tropical-reef-dwelling species that feeds primarily on sponges. Adults can reach up to a meter in length, and weigh some 80kg (175 lbs.). The hawksbill's most distinguishing feature is a sharp, distinctly beaklike mouth that gives this turtle its name. Commercial exploitation exacerbates the species' continued decline; it is on the endangered species list.

PRIME VIEWING On the Caribbean coast, March through October, with a peak in September.

Loggerhead

SCIENTIFIC NAME *Caretta caretta*

WORTH NOTING Called *carey* in Costa Rica, this sea turtle has a reddish brown carapace. It can grow to a length of 1.1m (3½ ft.), and weighs in at some 350kg (770 lbs.). The loggerhead uses its powerful jaws to feed on a range of shellfish.

PRIME VIEWING On the Caribbean coast, May through August, with a peak in July.

Bottle-Nosed Dolphin

SCIENTIFIC NAME *Tursiops truncates*

WORTH NOTING A wide tail fin, dark gray back, and light gray sides identify the bottle-nosed dolphin. These dolphins grow to 13.7m (12 ft.) long and weigh up to 635kg (1,400 lb.).

PRIME VIEWING Along both coasts and inside the Golfo Dulce.

Humpback Whale

SCIENTIFIC NAME *Megaptera novaeangliae*

WORTH NOTING The humpback whale has a black back and whitish chest. This migratory species winters in warm southern waters. It has increasingly been spotted close to the shores of Costa Rica's southern Pacific coast, where females have been known to calve.

PRIME VIEWING Most common in the waters off Drake Bay and Isla del Caño from December through April.

Get a Good Guide

There are scores of good field guides out there; two of the best general guides are *Field Guide to the Wildlife of Costa Rica* (University of Texas Press, Austin, TX: 2002), by Carrol Henderson, and *Travellers' Wildlife Guides: Costa Rica* (Interlink Books, Northampton, MA: 2004), by Les Beletsky. Bird-watchers will want to pick up one or both of the following two books: *A Guide to the Birds of Costa Rica* (Cornell University Press, Ithaca, NY: 1990), by F. Gary Stiles and Alexander Skutch, and *Birds of Costa Rica* (Cornell University Press, Ithaca, NY: 2007), by Richard Garrigues and Robert Dean. Specialized guides to mammals, reptiles, insects, flora, and more are also available. In Costa Rica, **Seventh Street Books** (p. 75) in San José always has a great selection, including many specialized guides they produce under their own imprint, Zona Tropical Publications (www.zonatropical.net).

Invertebrates

Creepy-crawlies, biting bugs, spiders, and the like give most folks chills. But this group, which includes moths, butterflies, ants, beetles, bees, and even crabs, includes some of the most abundant, fascinating, and easily viewed fauna in Costa Rica. In fact, there are nearly 500,000 recorded species of invertebrates here.

Blue Morpho

SCIENTIFIC NAME *Morpho peleides*

WORTH NOTING The large blue morpho butterfly, with a wingspan of up to 15cm (6 in.), is a brilliant iridescent blue on the upperside of its wings. It is a fast and erratic flier, and you can often catch only glimpses of it as it flits across your peripheral vision.

PRIME VIEWING Throughout Costa Rica, in dense, humid forests.

Leafcutter Ant

SCIENTIFIC NAME *Atta cephalotes*

WORTH NOTING You can't miss the miniature rain-forest highways formed by industrious little red leafcutter ants carrying their freshly cut payload. The ants do not actually eat the leaves, but instead feed off a fungus that grows on the decomposing leaves stored in their massive underground nests.

PRIME VIEWING Most forests throughout Costa Rica.

Golden Silk Spider

SCIENTIFIC NAME *Nephila clavipes*

WORTH NOTING The golden silk spider weaves a meticulous web that can be up to 46cm (1½ ft.) across. Adult females can reach 7.6cm (3 in.) in length, including the legs; males are tiny. The extremely strong silk is being studied for industrial purposes.

PRIME VIEWING Lowland forests on both coasts.

Mouthless Crab

SCIENTIFIC NAME *Gecarcinus quadratus*

WORTH NOTING The nocturnal mouthless crab is a distinctively colored land crab: bright orange legs, purple claws, and a deep black shell, or carapace.

PRIME VIEWING All along the Pacific coast.

Sally Lightfoot Crab

SCIENTIFIC NAME *Grapsus grapsus*

WORTH NOTING Known simply as *cangrego* ("crab"), this is the crab most commonly spotted in Costa Rica. It is midsize and has a colorful carapace that can range from dark brown to deep red to bright yellow, with a wide variation in striations and spotting.

PRIME VIEWING Rocky outcroppings near the water's edge along both coasts.

Flora

Trees

Despite the cliché to the contrary, it's often a good thing to be able to identify specific trees within a forest. I've included some of Costa Rica's most prominent species to get you started.

Ceiba

SCIENTIFIC NAME *Ceiba pentandra*

WORTH NOTING Also known as the kapok tree, the ceiba tree is typically emergent (its large umbrella-shape crown emerges above the forest canopy), reaching as high as 60m (197 ft.); it is among the tallest trees of Costa Rica's tropical forest. The ceiba tree has a thick, columnar trunk, often with large buttresses. The ceiba's seedpod produces a light, airy fiber that is resilient, buoyant, and insulating (the tree is sometimes called the silk cotton tree in English). Throughout history this fiber has been used for bedding and as stuffing for pillows, clothing, and even life jackets. The ceiba flowers infrequently, sometimes only once every 5 years, especially in wetter forests.

PRIME VIEWING Tropical forests throughout Costa Rica.

Guanacaste

SCIENTIFIC NAME *Enterolobium cyclocarpum*

WORTH NOTING The guanacaste gives its name to Costa Rica's northwesternmost province, and is the country's national tree. With a broad and pronounced crown, the guanacaste can reach heights of over 39m (130 ft.), with a trunk measuring more than 1.8m (6 ft.) in diameter. The guanacaste is prized as a shade tree, and is often planted on pasturelands to provide relief to cattle from the hot tropical sun.

PRIME VIEWING Low-elevation forests and plains throughout Costa Rica. Most commonly viewed in the open plains and savannas of Guanacaste.

Strangler Fig

SCIENTIFIC NAME *Ficus aurea*

WORTH NOTING This parasitic tree gets its name from the fact that it envelops and eventually strangles its host tree. Also known as *matapalo,* the strangler fig begins as an *epiphyte* (from the Greek for "air plant"), its seeds deposited high in a host tree's canopy by bats, birds, or monkeys. The young strangler then sends long roots down to the ground. The sap of this tree is used to relieve burns.

PRIME VIEWING Primary and secondary forests throughout Costa Rica.

Cecropia

SCIENTIFIC NAME *Cecropia obtusifolia*

WORTH NOTING Several *Cecropia* (trumpet tree) species grow in Costa Rica. Most are characterized by large clusters of broad leaves, and a hollow, bamboolike trunk. They are "gap specialists," fast-growing opportunists that can fill in a gap caused by a tree fall or landslide. Their trunks are usually home to Aztec ants.

PRIME VIEWING Primary and secondary forests, rivers, and road-sides throughout Costa Rica.

Gumbo Limbo

SCIENTIFIC NAME *Bursera simaruba*

WORTH NOTING The bark of the gumbo limbo is its most distinguishing feature: A paper-thin layer of peeling red bark that reveals a bright green inner bark. In Costa Rica the tree is called *indio desnudo* (naked Indian); in other tropical countries it is known as "tourist tree"—the flaking outer bark said to resemble the peeling skin of a sunburnt tourist. A remarkable property of this tree is its ability to root from a cut branch; when planted right end up, the branch develops roots and leaves, forming a new tree within a few years. The bark of the gumbo limbo is used as a remedy for gum disease; it is also used to make a tea that allegedly alleviates hypertension.

PRIME VIEWING Primary and secondary forests throughout Costa Rica.

Sea Grape

SCIENTIFIC NAME *Coccoloba uvifera*

WORTH NOTING Commonly found lining beaches, this tree, with its broad, round leaves and sprawling crown, provides great shade for overexposed sunbathers. Some specimens can reach 8m (26 ft.) in height, but most average less than half that. The tree bears an inedible fruit that grows in small clusters somewhat resembling grapes.

PRIME VIEWING Coastal areas bordering beaches throughout Costa Rica.

Flowers & Other Plants

Costa Rica has an amazing wealth of tropical plants, including some 1,200 orchid species and more than 2,000 bromeliad species.

Guaria Morada

SCIENTIFIC NAME *Cattleya skinneri*

WORTH NOTING The purple and white guaria morada (or Easter orchid) is the national flower of Costa Rica. While usually epiphytic, this orchid is also found as a terrestrial plant.

PRIME VIEWING Blooms in March and April in humid forests from sea level to 1,220m (4,000 ft.) throughout Costa Rica.

Heliconia

SCIENTIFIC NAME *Heliconia collinsiana*

WORTH NOTING More than 40 species of heliconia are found in Costa Rica. The flowers are darkish pink in color, and the undersides of the large leaves are coated in white wax.

PRIME VIEWING Blooms year-round in low to middle elevations in moist forests and gardens throughout Costa Rica.

Hotlips

SCIENTIFIC NAME *Psychotria poeppigiana*

WORTH NOTING Related to the coffee plant, hotlips is a forest plant that boasts thick red "lips." The small white flowers (found inside the red lips) attract a variety of butterflies and hummingbirds.

PRIME VIEWING Blooms year-round in undergrowth of dense forests throughout Costa Rica.

Red Torch Ginger

SCIENTIFIC NAME *Nicolaia elatior*

WORTH NOTING Called *bastón del emperador* (the emperor's cane) in Costa Rica, the tall red torch ginger has impressive bulbous red bracts, which are often mistaken for the flower. Numerous, small white flowers actually emerge out of these bracts. Native to Indonesia, it is now very common in Costa Rica.

PRIME VIEWING Blooms year-round in moist environments and gardens throughout Costa Rica.

Poor Man's Umbrella

SCIENTIFIC NAME *Gunnera insignis*

WORTH NOTING The poor man's umbrella, a broad-leaved rain-forest ground plant, is a member of the rhubarb family. The massive leaves are often used, as its name suggests, for protection during rainstorms.

PRIME VIEWING Seen year-round in low- to middle-elevation moist forests and cloud forests throughout Costa Rica. Common in Poás and Braulio Carrillo National Parks.

14
The Savvy Traveler

Before You Go

Government Tourist Offices

The Costa Rican government doesn't maintain official tourist information offices abroad. You can get basic information on Costa Rica by contacting the **Costa Rican Tourist Board** (ICT, Instituto Costarricense de Turismo) at ☎ 2223-1733 or www.visitcostarica.com. Travelers from the United Kingdom, Australia, and New Zealand will have to rely primarily on ICT's website, as there is no toll-free access in these countries. There's an ICT desk at both international airports in Costa Rica, where you can pick up maps and browse brochures; they might even lend you a phone to make or confirm a reservation. The main ICT visitor information center (☎ 2222-1090) is located in San José, below the Plaza de la Cultura at the entrance to the Gold Museum, on Calle 5 between Avenidas Central and 2. The people here are helpful, although the information they have to offer is rather limited. This office is open Monday through Saturday from 9am to 5pm.

Best Times to Go

Costa Rica's high season for tourism runs from late November to late April, which coincides almost perfectly with the chill of winter in the United States, Canada, and Great Britain, and includes Christmas, New Year's Day, Easter, and most school spring breaks. The high season is also the dry season. If you want some unadulterated time on a tropical beach and a little less rain during your rain-forest experience, this is the time to come. During this period (and especially around the Christmas holiday), the tourism industry operates at full tilt—prices are higher, attractions are more crowded, and reservations need to be made in advance.

Local tourism operators call the tropical rainy season (May through mid-November) the "green season." The adjective is appropriate. At this time of year, even brown and barren Guanacaste province becomes lush and verdant. I personally love traveling around Costa Rica during the rainy season (but then again, I'm not trying to flee cold snaps in Canada). It's easy to find or at least negotiate reduced rates, there are far fewer fellow travelers, and the rain is often limited to a few hours each afternoon (although you can occasionally get socked in for a week at a time). **A drawback:** Some of the country's rugged roads become downright impassable without a four-wheel-drive vehicle during the rainy season.

Festivals & Special Events

Some of the events mentioned here might be considered more of a *happening* than an event—there's not, for instance, a Virgin of Los Angeles PR committee that readily dispenses information. If I haven't listed a contact number, your best bet is to call the **Costa Rican Tourist Board** (ICT) at ☎ 2223-1733 in Costa Rica, or visit www.visitcostarica.com.

JANUARY

Each year during the first week of January, San José's Costa Rica Country Club (☎ 2228-9333) is the site of the **Copa del Café** (Coffee Cup), an international event on the junior tennis tour.

Meanwhile, a little farther north in the city of Palmares, the Fiesta of Palmares is the largest and best organized of these traditional celebrations. Held each year in mid-January, and lasting nearly 2 weeks, this massive party includes bullfights, a horseback parade (*tope*), and many concerts, carnival rides, and food booths.

MARCH

On the second Sunday of March, the hills above Escazú are filled with colorfully painted oxcarts, as the town of San Antonio de Escazú celebrates **Día del Boyero (Oxcart Drivers' Day).** On this day, the town's streets are filled with a procession of brightly painted traditional ox-drawn carts. There are street stands selling food and drink, and a general sense of merriment pervades the whole affair.

In mid-March, flower lovers gather in San

A Fall Festival

The biggest event of the year in Limón, and one of the liveliest festivals in Costa Rica, is the annual **Carnaval,** which is held around Columbus Day (October 12). For a week, languid Limón shifts into high gear for a nonstop bacchanal orchestrated to the beat of reggae, soca, and calypso music. During the revelries, residents don costumes and take to the streets in a dazzling parade of color. See "Dancing in the Street," p. 389.

José for the **National Orchid Show.** Orchid growers from around the world gather to show their wares, trade tales and secrets, and admire the hundreds of species on display. Contact the Costa Rican Tourist Board (ICT) for location and dates.

APRIL

Holy Week, the week before Easter, is celebrated with religious processions—often with actors reenacting Christ's march to the crucifixion—and gatherings in cities and towns throughout the country. Many banks and businesses shut down during the period from Ash Wednesday through Easter Sunday. A national dry law also goes into effect, and public transportation is reduced in some places.

April 11 is **Juan Santamaría Day** (see "The Little Drummer Boy," p. 427), and in Alajuela Costa Rica's national hero is honored with parades, concerts, and dances.

JULY

On the Saturday closest to July 16, a regatta of colorfully decorated boats carrying a statue of Puntarenas's patron saint is the highlight of the celebrations for the **Fiesta of the Virgin of the Sea.** On land, the city is the site of street fairs, concerts, and parades.

Up in Liberia, on July 25, **Annexation of Guanacaste Day** is celebrated with Tico-style bullfights, folk dancing, horseback parades, rodeos, and concerts. This national holiday commemorates the country's 1824 annexation of Guanacaste province.

AUGUST

Costa Rica's patron saint is honored each year on August 2, with the **Fiesta of the Virgin of Los Angeles.** Tens of thousands of Costa Ricans make the pilgrimage each year to the saint's namesake basilica (p. 65, ❸) in Cartago.

SEPTEMBER

Costa Rica's **Independence Day,** September 15, is celebrated all over the country in a variety of ways. The most distinctive is the tradition of having nighttime parades of children in their school uniforms playing the national anthem on steel xylophones.

OCTOBER

On the Caribbean coast, especially in the city of Limón, the week around October 12 is celebrated as **Carnaval** (see "A Fall Festival," p. 474). A smaller version of Mardi Gras, complete with floats and dancing in the streets, these celebrations were originally coordinated with the commemoration of Columbus's stumbling upon the Americas; they are now locally referred to as the Día de la Raza (Day of the Race).

NOVEMBER

Although their observances are not as elaborate or ritualized as those in Mexico, most Costa Ricans take some time on November 2, **Día de los Muertos** (All Souls' Day), to remember the dead with flowers and trips to cemeteries.

DECEMBER

Beginning on December 15, children and carolers nationwide go door-to-door seeking lodging, in a reenactment of Joseph and Mary's search for a place to stay, a tradition known locally as **Las Posadas.**

Just after Christmas, San José's downtown streets are taken over by two parades: **El Tope** on December 26, a horse parade in proud recognition of the country's important agricultural heritage; and **Carnaval** on December 27, with carnival floats, marching bands, and street dancers.

Throughout the final week of December, the city of San José holds its **Festejos Populares** (Popular Party). Bullfights and a pretty respectable bunch of carnival rides, games of chance, and fast-food stands are set up at the fairgrounds in Zapote.

Weather

Temperatures in Costa Rica vary primarily with elevation, not season: On the coasts it's always hot; in the mountains it can be cool at night any time of year. Frost is common at the highest elevations (3,000m/9,840 ft. and above).

Costa Rica is a tropical country and has distinct wet and dry seasons. Generally, the **rainy season** (or "green season") is from May to mid-November. Costa Ricans call this wet time of year their winter. The **dry season,** considered summer by Costa Ricans, is from mid-November to April. In Guanacaste, Costa Rica's northwestern province, the dry season lasts several weeks longer than in other places. Even in the rainy season, you'll get some sun—mornings are clear, with rain arriving in the afternoon. The Southern Zone, on the other hand, is decidedly damp year-round, and particularly so during the rainy season. On the Caribbean coast, especially south of Limón, you can also count on rain year-round, although,

AVERAGE DAYTIME HIGH TEMPERATURES & RAINFALL IN SAN JOSÉ

	JAN	FEB	MAR	APR	MAY	JUNE	JULY	AUG	SEPT	OCT	NOV	DEC
Temp. (°F)	75	76	79	79	80	79	77	78	79	77	77	75
Temp. (°C)	24	24	26	26	27	26	25	26	26	25	25	24
Days of Rain	1.3	1.5	2.2	4.2	11.5	14.5	13.7	14.5	18.1	17.9	8.6	2.3

oddly, this area tends to stay drier than the rest of the country during September and October.

In general, the best time of year to visit, weather-wise, is in December and January, when everything is still green from the rains, but the sky is clear.

Cell Phones (Mobiles)

Costa Rica primarily uses GSM networks. If your cellphone is on a GSM system, and you have a world-capable multiband phone such as many Sony Ericsson, LG, Motorola, or Samsung models, you can make and receive calls around much of the globe. Just call your wireless operator and ask for "international roaming" to be activated on your account. Per-minute charges can be high, though—up to $5 in Costa Rica, depending upon your plan.

Unfortunately, those with unlocked tri- and quad-band GSM phones still cannot simply buy a local SIM card in Costa Rica. However, a free-trade agreement with the United States and other Central American nations is expected to open up the state monopoly on telecommunications during 2010, and this should change.

Useful Websites

Tico Times (www.ticotimes.net): The English-language *Tico Times* makes it easy for *norteamericanos* (and other English speakers) to find out what's happening in Costa Rica. It features the top story from its weekly print edition, as well as a daily update of news briefs, a business article, regional news, a fishing column, and travel reviews. There's also a link to current currency-exchange rates.

Latin American Network Information Center (http://lanic.utexas.edu/la/ca/cr): This site houses a vast collection of information about Costa Rica and is hands-down the best one-stop shop for browsing.

Costa Rica Maps (www.maptak.com): In addition to offering, for sale, a wonderful waterproof map of the country, this site features several excellent downloadable nationwide,

Ecotourism: The Heart of Costa Rica

Costa Rica is one of the planet's prime ecotourism destinations. Many of the isolated nature lodges and tour operators around the country are pioneers and dedicated professionals in the ecotourism and sustainable tourism field. Many other hotels, lodges, and tour operators are simply "greenwashing," using the terms "eco" and "sustainable" in their promo materials, but doing little real good in their daily operations. The government-run Costa Rican Tourist Board (ICT; p. 474) provides a sustainability rating of a host of hotels, called the Certification for Sustainable Tourism program (CST). You can look up hotel ratings at the website, www.turismo-sostenible.co.cr; however, the list is far from comprehensive, and die-hard ecologists find some of these listings somewhat suspect.

You can find ecofriendly travel tips, statistics, and touring companies and associations—listed by destination under "Your Travel Choice"—at The International Ecotourism Society (TIES) website, www.ecotourism.org. Ecotravel.com is part online magazine and part eco-directory that lets you search for touring companies in several categories (water-based, land-based, spiritually oriented, and so on).

Many airlines now let you offset your carbon emissions for a small surcharge; ask when booking. For more information on how carbon offsetting works, see the Climate Care website, www.climatecare.org.

For information about the ethics of swimming with dolphins and other outdoor activities, visit the Whale and Dolphin Conservation Society (WDCS; www.wdcs.org) and Tread Lightly (www.treadlightly.org).

regional, and city maps and a host of other useful information.

CostaRicaLiving E-Board (www.crl-eboard. info): This is an information clearinghouse site put together by the folks at Costa Rica Living newsgroup. This site is chock-full of useful information, suggestions, reviews, and tips.

Getting There

By Plane

It takes anywhere from 3 to 7 hours to fly to Costa Rica from most U.S. cities. Most international flights still land in San José's **Juan Santamaría International Airport** (☎ 2437-2626 for 24-hr. airport information; airport code SJO). San José is a convenient gateway if you are planning to head to Manuel Antonio or elsewhere on the central Pacific coast, the Caribbean coast, or the Southern Zone.

However, more and more direct international flights are touching down in Liberia's **Daniel Oduber International Airport** (☎ 2668-1010 or 2688-1117; airport code LIR). Liberia is the gateway to the beaches of the Guanacaste region and the Nicoya Peninsula, and a direct flight here eliminates the need for a separate commuter flight in a small aircraft or roughly 5 hours in a car or bus. If you are planning to spend all, or most, of your vacation time in the Guanacaste region, you'll want to fly in and out of Liberia.

FROM NORTH AMERICA

Air Canada (☎ 888/247-2262; www.aircanada. ca) flies from Toronto to San José.

American Airlines (☎ 800/433-7300; www. aa.com) flies direct to San José from Fort Lauderdale, Miami, and Dallas–Fort Worth, and direct to Liberia from Miami and Dallas–Fort Worth. **Continental Airlines** (☎ 800/231-0856; www.continental.com) has direct flights from Houston and Newark to both San José and Liberia. **Delta Air Lines** (☎ 800/221-1212; www. delta.com) flies from Atlanta to both San José and Liberia. **Frontier Airlines** (☎ 800/432-1359; www.frontierairlines.com) flies daily direct from Denver to San José. **JetBlue Airways** (☎ 800/538-2583; www.jetblue.com) flies once daily direct to Orlando to San José. **Spirit Airlines** (☎ 800/772-7117; www.spiritair.com) flies once daily direct between Fort Lauderdale and San José. **U.S. Airways** (☎ 800/622-1015; www.

usairways.com) has direct flights between both Phoenix and Charlotte, North Carolina, and San José, and one weekly flight between Charlotte and Liberia. **United Airlines** (☎ 800/538-2929; www.united.com) flies direct from Los Angeles, Miami, and New York's JFK Airport to San José, and once weekly direct from Chicago to Liberia.

FROM EUROPE

Iberia (☎ 800/772-4642 in U.S. and Canada; ☎ 0870/609-0500 in the U.K.; www.iberia. com) is the only European carrier with routes to San José. Alternatively, you can fly to any major U.S. hub city and make connections to one of the airlines mentioned above.

Getting Around

By Plane

Flying is a great way to get around Costa Rica. Because the country is quite small, flights are short and not too expensive. One-way fares run between $70 and $130.

Sansa (☎ 877/767-2672 in U.S. and Canada, or 2290-4100 in Costa Rica; www.flysansa. com) operates from a separate terminal at San José's **Juan Santamaría International Airport,** while **Nature Air** (☎ 800/235-9272 in U.S. and Canada, or 2299-6000 in Costa Rica; www. natureair.com) operates from **Tobías Bolaños International Airport** (SYQ) in Pavas, 6.4km (4 miles) from San José. Both service most major tourist destinations in the country. In the high season (late November to late April), be sure to book reservations well in advance.

By Car

Driving a car in Costa Rica is no idle undertaking. The roads are riddled with potholes, most rural intersections are unmarked, and, for some reason, sitting behind the wheel of a car seems to turn peaceful Ticos into homicidal maniacs. But unless you want to see the country from the window of a bus or pay exorbitant amounts for private transfers, renting a car might be your best option for independent exploring. That said, if you don't want to put up with any stress on your vacation, it might be worthwhile springing for a driver.

Be forewarned, however: Although rental cars no longer bear special license plates, they are still readily identifiable to thieves and are frequently targeted. Nothing is ever safe in a car in Costa

Rica (although parking in guarded parking lots helps). Transit police also seem to target tourists; never pay money directly to a police officer who stops you for a traffic violation.

Before driving off with a rental car, be sure to inspect its exterior and point out to the rental company representative every scratch, dent, tear, or other damage, no matter how tiny. It's a common practice with many Costa Rican car-rental companies to claim that you owe payment for minor dings and dents that the company finds when you return the car. Also, if you get into an accident, be sure that the rental company doesn't try to bill you for a higher amount than the deductible on your rental contract.

These caveats aren't meant to scare you off from driving in Costa Rica. Thousands of tourists rent cars here every year, and the large majority of them encounter no problems.

Note: Double-check your credit card's policy on picking up the insurance on rental cars. Almost none of the American-issued cards—including gold cards—cover the collision damage waiver (CDW) on car rentals in Costa Rica anymore. In addition, most will not cover four-wheel-drive vehicles and any travel considered off-road.

RENTALS

Try to make car-rental arrangements before traveling to Costa Rica. In most cases you will get a better deal. In addition, during the high season, the local rental fleet often cannot meet the demand.

Keep in mind that four-wheel-drive vehicles are particularly useful in the rainy season (May to mid-November) and for navigating the bumpy, poorly paved roads year-round.

The following rental-car agencies have offices at both major airports in Costa Rica: **Adobe** (☎ 800/769-8422; www.adobecar.com), **Alamo** (☎ 877/222-9075; www.alamo.com), **Avis** (☎ 800/331-1212; www.avis.com), **Budget** (☎ 800/472-3325; www.budget.com), **Dollar** (☎ 800/800-3665; www.dollar.com), **Hertz** (☎ 800/654-3001; www.hertz.com), **National** (☎ 800/227-9058; www.nationalcar.com), **Payless** (☎ 800/729-5377; www.paylesscarrental.com), and **Thrifty** (☎ 800/847-4389; www.thrifty.com).

GASOLINE

Gasoline is sold as "regular" and "super." Both are unleaded; super is just higher octane. Diesel is available at almost every gas station as well. When going off to a remote place, try to leave with a full tank of gas, because gas stations can be hard to find. If you need to gas up in a small town, you can sometimes get gasoline from enterprising families who sell it by the liter from their houses. Look for hand-lettered signs that say GASOLINA.

PARKING

Parking in Costa Rica isn't much of a challenge—but that doesn't mean you won't need to be careful. Try to avoid parking on public streets, especially in San José; there are plenty of public parking lots around the city. Elsewhere, look for public lots or secure lots run by the establishments you're visiting. If neither of these is available, just be sure not to leave anything of value in the car—not even in the trunk.

ROAD MAPS & ATLASES

You can pick up a map when you arrive at the ICT information desk at the airport, or at its downtown San José offices (although the map included with this book is generally better). Most rental-car agencies will also provide you with a workable map of the country. Other sources in San José for detailed maps include **Seventh Street Books,** Calle 7 between Avenidas Central and 1 (☎ 2256-8251); **Librería Lehmann,** Avenida Central between Calles 1 and 3 (☎ 2223-1212); and **Librería Universal,** Avenida Central between Calles Central and 1 (☎ 2222-2222).

Perhaps the best map to have is the waterproof country map of Costa Rica put out by **Toucan Maps** (www.mapcr.com), which can be ordered directly from their website or from any major online bookseller, such as Amazon.com.

DRIVING RULES

A current foreign driver's license is valid for the first 3 months you are in Costa Rica. Seat belts are required for the driver and front-seat passengers. Motorcyclists must wear helmets. Highway police use radar, so keep to the speed limit (usually 60–90kmph/37–56 mph) if you don't want to get pulled over. Speeding tickets can be charged to your credit card for up to a year after you leave the country if they are not paid before departure.

BREAKDOWNS & ACCIDENTS

Be warned that emergency services, both vehicular and medical, are extremely limited outside San José; the availability of such services is directly related to the remoteness of your location. You'll find service stations spread over the entire length of the Pan-American Highway (CR1/CR2), and most of these have tow trucks and mechanics. The major towns of Puntarenas, Liberia, Quepos, San Isidro, Palmar, and Golfito all have hospitals, and most other moderate-size cities and tourist destinations have some sort of clinic or health-services provider.

If you're involved in an accident, contact the *policía de tránsito* or **transit police** (☎ 2222-9330 or 2222-9245 or toll-free nationwide at 800/8726-7486); if they have a unit close by, they'll send one, and an official transit police report will greatly facilitate any insurance claim. You should also call the **National Insurance Institute** (INS; ☎ 800/800-8000). These folks will also send an agent to the scene if you are in a populated area. If you can't get help from either the transit police or INS, try to get written statements from witnesses. Finally, you can also call ☎ 911, and the operator there should be able to redirect your call to the appropriate agency.

If you don't speak Spanish, expect added difficulty in any emergency or stressful situation. Don't assume that police officers, hospital personnel, service-station personnel, or mechanics will speak English.

Warning: Although not common, there have been reports of folks being robbed by seemingly friendly Ticos who stop and offer roadside assistance. To add insult to injury, there have even been reports of organized gangs who puncture tires of rental cars at rest stops or busy intersections, only to follow them, offer assistance, and make off with belongings and valuables. If you find yourself with a flat tire, try to ride it to the nearest gas station. If that's not possible, try to pull over into a well-lit public spot. Keep the doors of the car locked and an eye on your belongings while changing the tire by yourself.

By Bus

This is by far the most economical way to get around Costa Rica. Buses are inexpensive and relatively well maintained, and they go nearly everywhere. There are two types: **Local buses** are the cheapest and slowest; they stop frequently and are generally a bit dilapidated. **Express buses** run between San José and most beach towns and major cities; these tend to be newer units and more comfortable, although very few are so new or modern as to have bathroom facilities, and they sometimes operate only on weekends and holidays.

Two companies run regular, fixed-schedule departures in passenger vans and small buses to most of the major tourist destinations in the country. **Gray Line** (☎ 2220-2126; www.graylinecostarica.com), run by Fantasy Tours, has about 10 departures leaving San José each morning and heading or connecting to Jacó, Manuel Antonio, Liberia, Playa Hermosa, La Fortuna, Tamarindo, and Playas Conchal and Flamingo. There are return trips to San José every day from these destinations and a variety of interconnecting routes. A similar service, **Interbus** (☎ 2283-5573; www.interbusonline.com), has a slightly more extensive route map and more connections. Fares run between $27 and $45, depending upon the destination. *Beware:* Both of these companies offer pickup and drop-off at a wide range of hotels. This means that if you are the first picked up or last dropped off, you might have to sit through a long period of subsequent stops before finally hitting the road or reaching your destination. Moreover, I've heard some horror stories about both lines, concerning missed or severely delayed connections and rude drivers.

Tips on Accommodations

The Basics

There are hotels to suit every budget and travel style in Costa Rica. The country's strong suit is its **moderately priced hotels.** In the $80 to $125 price range you'll find comfortable and sometimes outstanding accommodations almost anywhere in the country. However, room size and quality vary quite a bit within this price range; don't expect the kind of uniformity that you may find at home.

If you're even more budget- or bohemian-minded, you can find quite a few good deals for less than $50 for a double. *But beware:* Budget-oriented lodgings often feature a shared bathroom and either a cold-water shower or one heated by electrical heat-coil units mounted at the shower head, affectionately known as a "suicide shower." If your hotel has one, do not adjust it while the water is running.

Those looking for luxury will not be disappointed in Costa Rica. In addition to the Four Seasons Costa Rica (p. 158) and JW Marriott Guanacaste Resort & Spa (p. 149), there is a host of amazing boutique hotels all around the country that will satisfy high-end and luxury travelers.

Air-conditioning is not necessarily a given in many midrange hotels and even some upscale joints. In general, this is not a problem. Cooler nights and a well-placed ceiling fan are often more than enough to keep things pleasant, unless I mention otherwise in the hotel's review.

Types of Accommodations

Costa Rica is still riding the ecotourism wave (see "Ecotourism: The Heart of Costa Rica," p. 476), and you'll find small nature-oriented ecolodges throughout the country. These lodges offer opportunities to see wildlife (including sloths, monkeys, and hundreds of species of birds) and learn about tropical forests. They range from Spartan facilities catering primarily to scientific researchers to luxury accommodations that are among the finest in the country. Many are quite remote and isolated. Be sure to find out how you get to and from the ecolodge and what tours and services are included in your stay.

An *apartotel* is just what it sounds like: an apartment-hotel, with a full kitchen, one or two bedrooms, and daily maid service. *Cabinas* are Costa Rica's version of cheap vacation lodging. They're very inexpensive and very basic—often just cinder-block buildings divided into small rooms. Occasionally, you'll find a *cabina* in which the units are actually cabins, but these are a rarity. *Cabinas* often have a clothes-washing sink (*pila*), and some come with a kitchenette; they cater primarily to Tico families on vacation.

The best way to book lodging in Costa Rica is to negotiate directly with the hotels themselves,

especially the smaller ones. Almost every hotel in Costa Rica has e-mail, if not its own website; you'll find the contact information in this book. However, be aware that response times might be slower than you'd like, and many of the smaller hotels might have some trouble communicating in English.

Fast Facts

ATM Networks

Costa Rica has a modern and widespread network of ATMs. You should find ATM machines in all but the most remote tourist destinations and isolated nature lodges.

In 2009, in response to a rash of "express kidnappings" in San José, in which folks were taken at gunpoint to an ATM to clean out their bank accounts, both Banco Nacional and Banco de Costa Rica stopped ATM service between the hours of 10pm and 5am. Other networks still dispense money 24 hours a day.

It's probably a good idea to have a four-digit PIN for your trip. While many ATMs in Costa Rica will accept five- and six-digit PINs, some will accept only four-digit PINs. It's a good idea to speak to someone about this at your bank at home before you leave.

Business Hours

Banks are usually open Monday through Friday from 9am to 4pm, although many have begun to offer extended hours. Post offices are generally open Monday through Friday from 8am to 5:30pm, and Saturday from 7:30am to noon. (In small towns, post offices often close on Saturday.) Stores are generally open Monday through Saturday from 9am to 6pm (many close for an hour at lunch); stores in modern malls generally stay open until 8 or 9pm and don't close for lunch. Most bars are open until 1 or 2am, although some go later.

Car Rentals

See "Getting Around," p. 477.

Customs

Visitors entering Costa Rica are legally entitled to bring in 500g (1 lb.) of tobacco, 5L (1.3 gal.) of liquor, and $500 in merchandise. Cameras, computers, and electronic equipment for personal use are permitted duty-free. Customs officials in Costa Rica seldom check tourists' luggage.

Warning: Skip the Motel

You'll want to avoid motels in Costa Rica. To a fault, these are cut-rate affairs geared toward lovers consummating their (usually illicit) affairs. Most rent out rooms by the hour, and most have private garages with roll-down doors outside each room, so that snoopy spouses or ex-lovers can't check for cars or license plates.

Electricity

The standard in Costa Rica is the same as in the United States: 110 volts AC (60 cycles). However, three-pronged outlets can be scarce, so it's helpful to bring along an adapter.

Embassies & Consulates

The following are all located in San José: **United States Embassy,** in front of Centro Commercial, on the road to Pavas (☎ 2519-2000, or 2220-3127 after-hours in case of emergency); **Canadian Consulate,** Oficentro Ejecutivo La Sabana, Edificio 5 (☎ 2242-4400); **British Embassy,** Paseo Colón between Calles 38 and 40 (☎ 2258-2025). There are no Australian or New Zealand embassies in San José.

Emergencies

In case of emergency, call ☎ 911 (there should be an English-speaking operator); if 911 doesn't work, contact the police at ☎ 2222-1365 or 2221-5337, and hopefully they can find someone who speaks English to translate. For an ambulance, call ☎ 128; to report a fire, call ☎ 118.

Gay & Lesbian Travelers

Costa Rica is a Catholic, conservative, and macho country where public displays of same-sex affection are rare and considered somewhat shocking. Public figures, politicians, and religious leaders periodically denounce homosexuality. That said, gay and lesbian tourism to Costa Rica is quite robust, and gay and lesbian travelers are generally treated with respect. For a general overview of the current situation, news of any special events or meetings, and up-to-date information, **Gay Costa Rica** (www.gaycostarica.com) is your best bet.

Health

Staying healthy on a trip to Costa Rica is predominantly a matter of being a little cautious about what you eat and drink and using common sense. Know your physical limits. Don't overexert yourself in the ocean, on hikes, or in athletic activities. Respect the tropical sun and protect yourself from it. Limit your exposure to the sun, especially during the first few days of your trip, during the period from 11am to 2pm. Use sunscreen with a high protection factor, and apply it liberally. Remember that children need more protection than adults.

The water in San José and in most of the heavily visited spots is safe to drink, although some travelers will experience stomach discomfort during the first few days of their visit. In more remote areas of Costa Rica, such as the Caribbean coast, it is advisable to drink only bottled water. I recommend you err on the side of caution and drink bottled water, soft drinks, or *frescos* made with milk instead of water. *Sin hielo* means "no ice"—just because it's frozen doesn't mean it's not water.

If there is an emergency and you need a doctor, ask at your hotel, or consult the Fast Facts listings in individual chapters.

Holidays

Official holidays in Costa Rica include **January 1** (New Year's Day), **March 19** (St. Joseph's Day), Thursday and Friday of Holy Week, **April 11** (Juan Santamaría Day), **May 1** (Labor Day), **June 29** (St. Peter and St. Paul Day), **July 25** (annexation of the province of Guanacaste), **August 2** (Virgin of Los Angeles Day), **August 15** (Mother's Day), **September 15** (Independence Day), **October 12** (Discovery of America/Día de la Raza), **December 8** (Immaculate Conception of the Virgin Mary), **December 24** and **25** (Christmas), and **December 31** (New Year's Eve).

Insurance

For information on traveler's insurance, trip cancellation, and medical insurance while traveling, go to www.frommers.com/planning.

Internet Access

Cybercafes can be found all over Costa Rica, and many hotels, restaurants, cafes, and retailers around the country are offering high-speed Wi-Fi access, either free or for a small fee.

Language

Spanish is the official language of Costa Rica. However, in most tourist areas, you'll be surprised by how well Costa Ricans speak English. Even attempting a little Spanish will go a long way with the locals—consult "Useful Phrases & Menu Terms," p. 484. *Frommer's Spanish Phrase-Finder & Dictionary* (Wiley Publishing, 2006) is probably the best phrase book to bring with you.

Legal Aid

If you need legal help, your best bet is to contact your local embassy or consulate. See "Embassies & Consulates," above, for contact details.

Lost Property

If your passport is lost or stolen, contact your

country's embassy immediately. Be sure to tell all your credit card companies the minute you discover that your wallet has been lost or stolen, and file a report at the nearest police precinct. To report a lost or stolen American Express card from inside Costa Rica, call ☎ 800/012-3211; for MasterCard, ☎ 800/011-0184; for Visa, ☎ 800/011-0030; for Discover, ☎ 801/902-3100; and for Diners Club, call Credomatic, ☎ 2295-9898.

Mail & Postage

The Spanish word for post office is *correo*. At press time, it cost 170 colones (30¢) to mail a letter to the United States, and 190 colones (34¢) to Europe. You can get stamps (*estampillas*) at a post office and at some gift shops in large hotels. Given the Costa Rican postal service track record, I recommend paying an extra 500 colones (89¢) to have anything of value certified. Better yet, use an international courier service or wait until you get home to post it. Letters take about 10 to 14 days to arrive at their destination.

Money

The unit of currency in Costa Rica is the **colón.** At press time there were approximately 521 *colones* to the American dollar, but that is likely to change as the economy shifts. The colón is divided into 100 *céntimos.* Currently, two types of coins are in circulation. The older and larger nickel-alloy coins come in denominations of 10, 25, and 50 *céntimos* and 1, 2, 5, 10, and 20 colones; however, because of their evaporating value, you will probably never see or have to handle *céntimos,* or anything lower than a 5-*colón* coin. In 1997 the government introduced gold-hued 5-, 10-, 25-, 50-, 100-, and 500-*colón* coins. They are smaller and heavier than the older coins, and while the plan was to have them eventually phase out the other currency, this hasn't happened.

There are paper notes in denominations of 1,000, 2,000, 5,000, and 10,000 colones. **Forged bills** are not entirely uncommon. When receiving change in colones, it's a good idea to check the larger-denomination bills, which should have protective bands or hidden images that appear when held up to the light.

You can change money at all banks in Costa Rica. The principal state banks are Banco Nacional and Banco de Costa Rica. However, be forewarned that service at state banks can be slow and tedious. You're almost always better off finding a private bank. Luckily, there are hosts of private banks around San José and in most major tourist destinations.

The best way to get cash in Costa Rica is at ATMs (see "ATM Networks," p. 480). While credit cards are accepted at almost all shops, restaurants, and hotels, some places won't take them (and banks often levy a 2% to 3% conversion fee above the 1% the credit card company takes in order to convert purchases made in a foreign currency). Always have some cash on hand for incidentals and sightseeing admissions.

Passports

Always keep a photocopy of your passport with you while you're traveling. If your passport is lost or stolen, having a copy will significantly facilitate the reissuing process. And always keep your passport in a secure place, such as your hotel safe.

Pharmacies

A drugstore or pharmacy is called *farmacia* in Costa Rica. You will find them in just about every town and city around the country. Major cities have scores of them.

Safety

Although Costa Rica is relatively safe, petty crime and robberies are common. Tourists are targeted for robbery across the country. San José is known for its pickpockets, so never carry a wallet in your back pocket. A woman should maintain a tight grip on her purse and keep it tucked under an arm. Thieves also target gold chains, cameras, video cameras, prominent jewelry, and nice sunglasses. Be sure not to leave valuables unlocked in your hotel room. Rental cars generally stick out and are easily spotted by thieves. Don't leave anything of value in a car parked on the street or out of your sight, unless it is in a secure parking lot.

Public intercity buses are frequented by stealthy thieves. Never check your bags into the hold of a bus if you can avoid it. If you have to check your bags, keep an eye on what leaves the hold. If you put your bags in an overhead rack, be sure you can see them at all times. Try not to fall asleep.

Finally, don't leave anything of value unattended on beaches or park benches or while dining or touring.

Senior Travelers

Although it's not common policy in Costa Rica to offer senior discounts, don't be shy about asking for one. You never know. Always carry some kind of identification, such as a driver's license, that shows your date of birth, especially if you've kept your youthful glow.

Smoking

A large number of Costa Ricans smoke, and public smoking regulations and smoke-free zones have yet to take hold. Restaurants are required by law to have nonsmoking areas, but enforcement is often lax, air-circulation poor, and the "separation" almost nonexistent. Bars, as a whole, are often very smoke-filled in Costa Rica.

Most higher-end hotels have at least some nonsmoking rooms. However, many midrange hotels and most budget options are pretty laissez-faire when it comes to smoking.

Taxes

All hotels charge 16.3% tax. Restaurants charge 13% tax and also add on a 10% service charge, for a total of 23% more on your bill.

There is a $26 departure tax for all visitors leaving Costa Rica by air. This tax must be purchased prior to check-in. There are desks at the main terminal of all international airports where you can pay this tax. Some local travel agencies and hotels offer to purchase the departure tax in advance, as a convenience for tourists. You must give them authorization, your passport number, and a small service fee.

Telephones

To call Costa Rica from home:
1. **Dial the international access code:** 011 from the U.S., 00 from the U.K., 0011 from Australia, or 0170 from New Zealand.
2. **Dial the country code:** 506.
3. **Dial the local 8-digit number.**
   To make international calls from Costa Rica: First dial 00 and then the country code (U.S. or Canada 1, U.K. 44, Australia 61, New Zealand 64). Next dial the area code and local number. For example, to call U.S. number 212/000-0000, you'll dial ☎ 00-1-212/000-0000. The toll-free international access code for AT&T is ☎ 0800/114-114; for MCI, ☎ 0800/122-222; for Sprint, ☎ 0800/130-123; and for Canada Direct, ☎ 0800/151-161.
   To make local calls within Costa Rica: There are no area codes in Costa Rica. To make a local

call, simply dial the 8-digit number.
   For directory assistance: Dial 113 to find a number inside Costa Rica; dial 124 to find a number in all other countries.
   For operator assistance: Dial 116 if you're trying to make an international call and 0 if you want to call a number inside Costa Rica.
   To call toll-free numbers: Numbers beginning with 0800 or 800 within Costa Rica are toll-free, but calling a 1-800 number in the U.S. from Costa Rica is not toll-free. In fact, it costs the same as an overseas call.

Time Zone

Costa Rica is on Central Standard Time (same as Chicago and St. Louis), 6 hours behind Greenwich Mean Time. Costa Rica does not use daylight savings time, so the time difference from the U.S. is an additional hour April through October.

Tipping

Tipping is not necessary in restaurants, where a 10% service charge is always added to your bill (along with a 13% tax). If service was particularly good, you can leave a little at your own discretion, but it's not mandatory. Porters and bellhops get around 75¢ per bag. You don't need to tip a taxi driver unless the service has been superior; a tip is not usually expected. (Note that it's also not uncommon for passengers to sit in the front seat of a taxi.)

Travelers with Disabilities

Although Costa Rica does have a law mandating Equality of Opportunities for People with Disabilities, and facilities are beginning to be adapted, there are generally relatively few buildings for travelers with disabilities in the country. Sidewalks in San José are crowded and uneven; they are nonexistent in most of the rest of the country. Few hotels offer wheelchair-accessible accommodations, and there are no public buses so equipped.

One local agency specializes in tours for travelers with disabilities and restricted ability. **Vaya Con Silla de Ruedas** (☎/fax 2454-2810; www.gowithwheelchairs.com) has a ramp- and elevator-equipped van and knowledgeable, bilingual guides. It charges very reasonable prices and can provide anything from simple airport transfers to complete multiday tours.

Useful Phrases & Menu Terms

Phrases

ENGLISH	SPANISH	PRONUNCIATION
hello	buenos días	*bweh*-nohss dee-ahss
How are you?	¿Cómo está usted?	*koh*-moh ehss-*tah* oo-*stehd*
very well	muy bien	mwee byehn
thank you	gracias	*grah*-syahss
goodbye	adiós	ad-*dyohss*
please	por favor	pohr fah-*vohr*
yes	sí	see
no	no	noh
excuse me (to get by someone)	perdóneme	pehr-*doh*-neh-meh
excuse me (to begin a question)	disculpe	dees-*kool*-peh
give me	deme	*deh*-meh
Where is . . . ?	¿Dónde está . . . ?	*dohn*-deh ehss-*tah*
the station	la estación	la ehss-tah-*syohn*
the bus stop	la parada	la pah-*rah*-dah
a hotel	un hotel	oon oh-*tehl*
a restaurant	un restaurante	oon res-tow-*rahn*-teh
the toilet	el servicio	el ser-*vee*-syoh
to the right	a la derecha	ah lah deh-*reh*-chah
to the left	a la izquierda	ah lah ees-*kyehr*-dah
straight ahead	adelante	ah-deh-*lahn*-teh
I would like . . .	Quiero . . .	*kyeh*-roh
to eat	comer	ko-*mehr*
a room	una habitación	oo-nah ah-bee-tah-*syohn*
How much is it?	¿Cuánto?	*kwahn*-toh
the check	la cuenta	la *kwen*-tah
When?	¿Cuándo?	*kwan*-doh
What?	¿Qué?	keh
yesterday	ayer	ah-*yehr*
today	hoy	oy
tomorrow	mañana	mah-*nyah*-nah
breakfast	desayuno	deh-sah-*yoo*-noh
lunch	almuerzo	ahl-*mwehr*-soh
dinner	cena	*seh*-nah
Do you speak English?	¿Habla usted inglés?	*ah*-blah oo-*stehd* een-*glehss*
I don't understand Spanish very well.	No entiendo muy bien el español.	noh ehn-*tyehn*-do mwee byehn el ehss-pah-*nyohl*

Numbers

ENGLISH	SPANISH	PRONUNCIATION
1	uno	*oo*-noh
2	dos	dohss
3	tres	trehss
4	cuatro	*kwah*-troh
5	cinco	*seen*-koh
6	seis	sayss
7	siete	*syeh*-teh
8	ocho	*oh*-choh
9	nueve	*nweh*-beh
10	diez	dyehss
11	once	*ohn*-seh
12	doce	*doh*-seh
13	trece	*treh*-seh
14	catorce	kah-*tohr*-seh
15	quince	*keen*-seh
16	dieciséis	dyeh-see-*sayss*
17	diecisiete	dyeh-see-*syeh*-teh
18	dieciocho	dyeh-see-*oh*-choh
19	diecinueve	dyeh-see-*nweh*-beh
20	veinte	*bayn*-teh
30	treinta	*trayn*-tah
40	cuarenta	kwah-*rehn*-tah
50	cincuenta	seen-*kwehn*-tah
60	sesenta	seh-*sehn*-tah
70	setenta	seh-*tehn*-tah
80	ochenta	oh-*chehn*-tah
90	noventa	noh-*behn*-tah
100	cien	syehn
1,000	mil	meel

Days of the Week

ENGLISH	SPANISH	PRONUNCIATION
Monday	Lunes	*loo*-nehss
Tuesday	Martes	*mahr*-tehss
Wednesday	Miércoles	*myehr*-koh-lehss
Thursday	Jueves	*wheh*-behss
Friday	Viernes	*byehr*-nehss
Saturday	Sábado	*sah*-bah-doh
Sunday	Domingo	doh-*meen*-goh

Restaurant & Menu Terms

Fish

ENGLISH	SPANISH	PRONUNCIATION
clam	almeja	ahl-*meh*-hah
cod	bacalao	bah-kah-*lah*-o
crab	cangrejo	kan-*grey*-ho
dolphin or mahimahi	dorado	doh-*rah*-doh
lobster	langosta	lan-*goh*-stah
seafood salad, marinated	ceviche	seh-*vee*-chay
mussel	mejillón	meh-hil-*yon*
oyster	ostra	*oh*-strah
octopus	pulpo	*pool*-poh
red snapper	pargo	*par*-go
sea bass	corvina	core-*vee*-nah
shrimp	camarón	ka-ma-*rohn*
sole	lenguado	len-*gwa*-doh
squid	calamár	cala-*mar*
trout	trucha	*tru*-cha
tuna	atún	ah-*toon*

Meats

ENGLISH	SPANISH	PRONUNCIATION
beefsteak	bistec	*bis*-teck
chicken	pollo	*poh*-yo
chop (usually pork)	chuleta	choo-*let*-tah
duck	pato	*pah*-to
fried pork rind	chicharrón	chee-chah-*rrohn*
ham	jamón	hah-*mohn*
hot dog, sausage	salchicha	sal-*chee*-cha
lamb	cordero	cor-*der*-o
meatball	albóndiga	al-*bohn*-dee-gah
pork	cerdo	*sehr*-doh
rib eye	delmonico	del-*mon*-neeh-ko
ribs	costillas	cos-*tee*-yahs
sausage	chorizo	koh-*ree*-zoh
sirloin	lomo	*loh*-moh
tenderloin	lomito	loh-*mee*-toh
tongue	lengua	len-goo-*ah*
turkey	pavo	*pah*-voh

Restaurant & Menu Terms

Vegetables

ENGLISH	SPANISH	PRONUNCIATION
artichoke	alcachofa	ahl-kah-*cho*-fa
avocado	aguacate	ah-wah-*kah*-teh
beans	frijoles	free-*hoh*-lehs
carrot	zanahoria	sah-nah-*oh*-ryah
corn	maíz	mah-*ees*
corn on the cob	elote	eh-*loh*-teh
cucumber	pepino	peh-*pee*-noh
eggplant	berenjena	beh-rehn-*heh*-nah
hearts of palm	palmito	pahl-*mee*-to
lettuce	lechuga	leh-*choo*-gah
olive	aceituna	ah-sehee-*too*-nah
onion	cebolla	seh-*boh*-yah
potato	papa	*pah*-pah
salad	ensalada	enh-sah-*lah*-dah
spinach	espinaca	ehs-pee-*nah*-kah
tomato	tomate	toh-*mah*-teh
yucca, cassava, or manioc	yuca	*yoo*-kah

Fruits

ENGLISH	SPANISH	PRONUNCIATION
apple	manzana	mahn-*zah*-nah
banana	banano	bah-*nah*-no
blackberry	mora	*moh*-ra
cherry	cereza	seh-*reh*-sah
coconut	coco	*koh*-koh
grapefruit	toronja	toh-*rohn*-hah
lemon or lime	limón	lee-*mohn*
mango	mango	*mahng*-goh
melon	melón	meh-*lohn*
orange	naranja	nah-*rahn*-hah
papaya	papaya	pah-*pah*-yah
passion fruit, sweet	granadilla	grah-nah-*dee*-jah
passion fruit, tart	maracuyá	mah-rah-coo-*jah*
peach	durazno	doo-*rahs*-noh
pineapple	piña	pee-*nyah*
plantain	plátano	*plah*-tah-noh
plum	ciruela	seer-*weh*-lah
raspberry	frambuesa	frahm-*bway*-sah
star fruit	carambola	car-amh-*boh*-la

Restaurant & Menu Terms

Basics

ENGLISH	SPANISH	PRONUNCIATION
bread	pan	*pahn*
butter	mantequilla	mahn-teh-*key*-yah
cheese	queso	*keh*-so
corn bread, flat	tortilla	tor-*tee*-yah
cornmeal pastry, filled	tamal	tah-*mahl*
corn tortilla with meat or chicken	gallo	*gah*-loh
green plantain chips	patacones	pah-tah-*koh*-nehs
garlic	ajo	*ah*-hoh
hash	picadillo	pee-cah-*dee*-yoh
honey	miel	*mee*-ehl
ice	hielo	*yeh*-loh
meat and vegetable soup	olla de carne	oh-yah-deh-*kar*-neh
mustard	mostaza	moh-*stah*-sah
oil	aceite	ah-*seh*-ee-teh
pepper	pimienta	peeh-*myehn*-tah
plate of the day	casado	cah-*sah*-doh
rice and beans	gallo pinto	*gah*-yoh *pin*-toh
salt	sal	*sahl*
sour cream	natilla	nah-*tee*-jah
sugar	azúcar	ah-*zuh*-kar

Beverages

ENGLISH	SPANISH	PRONUNCIATION
alcoholic drink	trago	*trah*-goh
beer	cerveza	ser-*vay*-sah
coffee	café	kah-*feh*
coffee with milk	café con leche	kah-*feh* kohn *leh*-cheh
drink	bebida	beh-*bee*-dah
fruit juice	natural	nah-*too*-rahl
hot chocolate	chocolate caliente	cho-koh-*lah*-teh kah-*lyehn*-teh
juice	jugo	*hoo*-go
milk	leche	*leh*-cheh
milkshake	natural con leche	nah-*too*-rahl kohn *leh*-cheh
rum	ron	*rohn*
soft drink	refresco	reh-*frehs*-koh
tea	té	*teh*
water, plain	agua sin gas	*ah*-gwah sin gahs
water, purified	agua purificada	*ah*-gwah pur-ee-fah-cah-dah
water, sparkling	agua con gas	*ah*-gwah kohn *gahs*

Other Restaurant Terms

ENGLISH	SPANISH	PRONUNCIATION
big or large	grande	*grahn*-day
cold	frío	*free*-oh
cooked	cocido	koh-*see*-doh
food	comida	koh-*mee*-dah
fried	frito	*free*-toh
frozen	congelado	kohn-*gel*-ah-doh
grilled	al grill	ahl-greel
hot	caliente	kahl-*yen*-tay
medium	medio	*meh*-dyoh
medium-rare	medio rojo	*meh*-dyoh *roh*-ho
medium-well-done	tres cuartos	tress koo-*ar*-tohs
oven-baked	al horno	al *hor*-no
rare	rojo	*roh*-hoh
raw	crudo	*kroo*-doh
roasted	asado	ah *sah*-doh
small	pequeño	peh-*kay*-nyoh
steamed	al vapor	ell-*vah*-poor
well-done	muy cocido	mwee-koh-*see*-doh

Hotel Terms

ENGLISH	SPANISH	PRONUNCIATION
air-conditioning	aire acondicionado	*aye*-reh ah-cohn-dee-syoh-*nah*-doh
bathroom	baño	*bah*-nyoh
bed	cama	*cah*-mah
blanket	cobija	koh-*bee*-hah
cable tv	telecable	teh-leh-*kah*-bleh
chair	silla	*sill*-ah
desk	escritorio	ehs-krih-*tore*-ee--oh
double room	habitación doble	ah-bee-tah-*syon doh*-bleh
fan	ventilador	ven-tee-lah-*door*
key	llave	*yah*-veh
mattress	colchón	kohl-*chohn*
mosquito net	mosquitero	mohs-*kweh*-teh-roh
pillow	almohada	ahl-*moh*-hah-dah
private bathroom	baño privado	*bah*-nyoh pree-*vah*-doh
room	habitación	ah-bee-tah-*syon*
safe	caja de seguridad	*cah*-hah deh seg-*yoo*-reh-dad
sheets	sábanas	*sah*-bah-nahs
single room	habitación simple	ah-bee-tah-*syon seem*-pleh
triple room	habitación triple	ah-bee-tah-*syon tree*-pleh

Travel Terms

ENGLISH	SPANISH	PRONUNCIATION
airplane	avión	ah-vee-*yohn*
airport	aeropuerto	ah-roh-*pwer*-toh
ATM	cajero	kah-*heh*-roh
avenue	avenida	ah-ve-*nee*-dah
boarding	embarque	em-*bar*-keh
boarding gate	puerta de salida	*pwer*-tah deh sah-*lee*-dah
boarding pass	tarjeta de embarque	tar-*heh*-tah de em-*bar*-keh
boat	lancha	*lahn*-cha
border	frontera	frohn-*tehr*-rah
bus	autobús	ow-toh-*boos*
customs	aduana	ah-*dwah*-nah
east	este	*ess*-teh
embassy	embajada	em-bah-*hah*-dah
entrance	entrada	en-*trah*-dah
exit	salida	sah-*lee*-dah
flight	vuelo	*vweh*-loh
luggage	equipaje	eh-kee-*pah*-heh
mail, post office	correo	koh-*reh*-ho
money	dinero	dee-*nehr*-oh
north	norte	*nor*-teh
passport	pasaporte	*pah*-sa-*por*-teh
street	calle	*cah*-yeh
warning	aviso	ah-*vee*-soh
west	oeste	oh-*ess*-teh

Emergency Terms

ENGLISH	SPANISH	PRONUNCIATION
ambulance	ambulancia	ahm-boo-*lahn*-see-yah
clinic or hospital	clínica	*kleen*-ee-kah
dangerous	peligroso	peh-lee-*groh*-soh
doctor	doctor or médico	*meh*-dee-koh
emergency	emergencia	eh-mer-*gen*-see-yah
fire	fuego	*fway*-goh
fire brigade	bomberos	bohm-*behr*-ohs
go away!	¡váyase!	*vy*-ah-seh
help!	¡auxilio!	ox-*ill*-yoh
hospital	hospital	*hoh*-pee-tal
nurse	enfermera	ehn-*fehr*-mehr-ah
pharmacy	farmacia	far-mah-*chee*-yah
police	policía	poh-lee-*see*-yah

Index

Photo Credits

Note: l= left; r= right; t= top; b= bottom; c= center